Library of Shakespearean Biography and Criticism

I. PRIMARY REFERENCE WORKS ON SHAKESPEARE

II. CRITICISM AND INTERPRETATION

    A. Textual Treatises, Commentaries
    B. Treatment of Specal Subjects
    C. Dramatic and Literary Art in Shakespeare

III. SHAKESPEARE AND HIS TIME

    A. General Treatises. Biography
    B. The Age of Shakespeare
    C. Authorship

Series III, Part C

THE BACONIAN HERESY

THE
BACONIAN HERESY

A CONFUTATION
BY
JOHN M. ROBERTSON M.P.

DO YOU THINK SO? ARE YOU IN
THAT GOOD HERESY, I MEAN OPINION?
Ben Jonson, The Sad Shepherd, Act i, Sc. ii

BOOKS FOR LIBRARIES PRESS

FREEPORT, NEW YORK

First Published 1913
Reprinted 1970

STANDARD BOOK NUMBER:
8369-5269-3

LIBRARY OF CONGRESS CATALOG CARD NUMBER:
74-109660

PRINTED IN THE UNITED STATES OF AMERICA

PREFACE

THIS treatise was in large part compiled some years ago, under the shock of the revelation that Mark Twain had died a " Bacon-Shakespearean." Laid aside under a misgiving that the drudgery it involved had not been worth while, it has been finished, by way of a holiday task, at the instance of a friend somewhat disturbed by Baconian solicitings. It is finally published with a hope not merely of checking in some degree the spread of the Baconian fantasy, but of stimulating to some small extent the revival of scientific Shakespearean criticism. Any close reader of the Baconian literature will recognise that its doctrine flourishes mainly on the unsunned sides of the Shakespeare problem. If only the specialists had done their proper work of discriminating between the genuine and the alien in the Shakespeare plays, much of the Baconian polemic would have been impossible, if indeed it could have proceeded at all. What we latterly get from the professed historians of English literature is mostly " cathedral " declamation, somewhat analogous to much of the Baconian asseveration.

It has been a question for me how far the confutation of Baconian fallacies may usefully be carried. The Baconian case constantly tends to new exorbitances of nonsense, as when Sir Edwin Durning-Lawrence intimates that Bacon did the authorised version of the Bible, and Mr. Parker Woodward, with calm confidence, intimates that Bacon also wrote Lilly's EUPHUES, Spenser's poems, Puttenham's ARTE OF ENGLISH POESY, all the works of Thomas Nashe, all the works and plays of Greene, Peele, Kyd, and Marlowe, Burton's ANATOMY OF MELANCHOLY, and I know not what else.   Many of these claims, indeed, were made years before ; but they seem to recur spontaneously.   When Mr. Woodward is at a loss for a pretext for any such attribution, he alleges a statement by Bacon in a " cipher."   I have drawn the line at ciphers, which are rejected even by leading Baconians such as Dr. Theobald and Lord Penzance ; and I have likewise put aside all the extra-Shakespearean attributions.   It seems sufficient to call the attention of the reader to them, and to point out to what the Baconian theory commonly carries its devotees.

It may be argued, on this, that they reason on their wildest propositions very much as they do on their primary doctrine ; and that Dr. R. M. Theobald, on whose " classical " and other fallacies I have spent some time, is quite as sure about what he calls " the Marlowe branch of our theory " as about the Shakespearean.   I can but answer that I have been astonished to see quite intelligent men, for lack of knowledge of Elizabethan literature, deluded by the Bacon-Shakespeare case, and by the misinformation supplied to them by orthodox Shakespeareans ; and I have been willing to take some trouble to prevent the spread of such error, which goes on without regard to the lengths of further extravagance attained by the Baconians.   But I am not concerned to spend time over people who can believe that Bacon wrote the entire Elizabethan drama, the English Bible, and Spenser, Montaigne, Nashe, and Burton to boot. *Non ragioniam di lor.*

But, once more, all this divagation has been made possible by the old fashion of contemplating Shakespeare *in vacuo*, and as a miracle at that.   As a good critic put it a generation ago : " Even he must be partly interpreted by his age.   We cannot duly appreciate his position without careful study of this whole chapter of literary history.   Unless we are acquainted with the soil from which he grew, and with the other products which that soil was capable of bearing, he remains, not marvellous merely, but prodigious. If he be regarded after the fashion of the last generation but one, as a *lusus naturæ*, out of relation to the ordinary laws of human development, he loses his interest for us as a human being; his actual bodily existence, which has little enough of the substance imparted by the biographer, becomes altogether shadowy and mythical : we fall an easy prey to some ' Baconian hypothesis ' about the authorship of his plays, and take a final leave, so far as he is concerned, of criticism and common sense."[1]

It may be, then, that a discussion which involves a constant application of the comparative method will be serviceable to genuine Shakespeare-study, whatever it may avail in the way of averting further lapses into Baconianism. I have been encouraged to complete my task—in so far as it can be said to be completed—by the declaration of Mr. Charles Crawford : " It seems to me that scholars are making a big mistake in allowing this question to assume such serious proportions."[2] Mr. Crawford has himself done so much to clear it up that I am moved respectfully to reproach him for not doing the whole of the work. Differing from him upon only one serious issue in matters Shakespearean—the authorship of TITUS ANDRONICUS—I realise none the less the fulness and exactness of his Elizabethan learning, by which I have here profited.

The task, indeed, is one that should have been undertaken by a small company of scholars. A few leisured and vigilant readers together could in a short time have compiled a much fuller refutation than the following ; and might incidentally have done a much greater service to Shakespeare scholarship than is possible to one who lacks due leisure even if he had scholarly qualifications.

[1] G. C. Macaulay, *Francis Beaumont : A Critical Study*, 1883, p.5.
[2] Preamble to essay on " The Bacon-Shakespeare Question " in *Collectanea*, Second Series, Stratford-on-Avon, 1907.

If a study which for me has necessarily been subsidiary could yield, with the help of such previous workers as Mr. Crawford and Judge Willis, and some recent editors of plays, what I think to be a fair sufficiency of refutation of the Baconian case on all its lines, much more efficiently might the work have been done by scholars who have been able to devote their lives to matters of philology and literary history.

Such scholars have not thought it worth while. I still hope, however, that some of them may be moved to carry out anew the scholarly annotation of Shakespeare's text. Nothing has ever made up for the turning away of Farmer from the task which he was so uniquely fitted to perform. His brief ESSAY ON THE LEARNING OF SHAKESPEARE remains an unmatched performance in its kind, after a century and a half. At its close he made a half-promise to extract more elucidatory matter from " the chaos of papers " from which he had compiled the essay ; but the unkind fates set him to other work ; and no man of quite equal scholarly opulence, perhaps, has put his hand to the task since. The multifarious erudition for which he half apologised is, as he said, " the reading necessary for a comment on Shakespeare " ; and much of his was buried with him. But half a dozen specialists of to-day, including some of the most competent of recent Shakespearean editors, if they would put their heads together, could give us such annotation as was never compassed by the old variorum men. And then, mayhap, they or another company might give us that annotated edition of Spenser, the lack of which is a standing scandal to English scholarship.

．　　　．　　　．　　　．

Since this book was put in the hands of the printers, there has appeared the posthumous work of the late Mr. Andrew Lang, SHAKESPEARE, BACON, AND THE GREAT UNKNOWN. Very naturally, a number of Mr. Lang's arguments coincide with mine, and I am heartily glad to have such support. To the general argument of my friend Mr. Greenwood, in my opinion the most consummate paralogism in the literature of biography, he seems to me to have supplied a very complete rebuttal, by simple analysis of its steps. Incidentally, by reproducing Dugdale's version of the Carew monument in Stratford Church and confronting it with a photograph of the actual monument, he has exploded the small mystery built up by Mr. Greenwood out of the difference between the actual Shakespeare monument and Dugdale's representation of it in 1656. In 1908 I urged upon my friend a solution of his mystery which can now, I think, be seen to be the true one. Dugdale, it is pretty evident, was in the habit of making slight and rude outline sketches of the monuments he saw, and these were afterwards elaborated for him by a professional draughtsman, who took a large licence. There was no support for either the Baconian or the " Great Unknown " hypothesis in the Dugdale mystery at best ; and even the mystery is now disposed of.

Mr. Lang, unfortunately, was " bluffed " by the asseverations of the lawyers as to the " law " in the plays. Had he applied comparative tests to that part of the problem he would have discovered what, I trust, is made clear in the following pages—that Shakespeare had no more law than half a dozen other Elizabethan dramatists who were not lawyers ; and would so have exploded that " mystery " also instead of facing it with tentative hypotheses.

Somewhat unexpectedly, again, Mr. Lang has touched but lightly on a part of the problem upon which one would have expected him to enlarge—the thesis as to the " classical scholarship " in the plays—contenting himself with commenting on the self-contradictions of the late Mr. Churton Collins, and generally denying that the thesis squares with the facts. In this connection, how-

ever, he has fallen into supererogatory error, which I
am constrained to point out, as it partly concerns myself.

So arbitrary is taste in these matters [he writes] that Mr. Collins,
like Mr. Grant White, but independently, finds Shakespeare
putting a thought from the ALCIBIADES I of Plato into the mouth
of Achilles in TROILUS AND CRESSIDA, while Mr. J. M. Robertson
suggests that the borrowing is from Seneca—where Mr. Collins
does not find "the smallest parallel." Mr. Collins is certainly
right : the author of TROILUS *makes Ulysses quote Plato as "the
author of" a remark, and makes Achilles take up the quotation,
which Ulysses goes on to criticise.* [1]

As Mr. Lang did not live to revise his proofs, it must
suffice to state the facts, without protest.

If he had read with attention the second edition of my
MONTAIGNE AND SHAKESPEARE, which he reviewed on
its appearance, he would have noted my exposure of
Mr. Collins's blunder.[2] I had *not* referred the lines of
Achilles to Seneca : my reference was to the lines of
Ulysses. Mr. Collins, professing to cite the entire passage,
elided the relevant lines of Ulysses, and made Ulysses
mention of "a strange fellow's" writing apply to the
speech which Achilles makes in reply. *That* I never
referred to Seneca. I did incidentally point out that
the whole reference to Plato is gratuitous, seeing that
the argument about the inability of the eye to see itself,
which is the gist of the passage, had appeared already in
JULIUS CÆSAR, in which connection the commentators
long ago traced it to the NOSCE TEIPSUM of Sir John
Davies, where, as I had further pointed out, there is
found also the phrase, "spirit of sense," used in the
passage in TROILUS. At the same time, I had shown
that the "eye" passage might also be traced to *Cicero*,
who had given the idea common currency. The primary
speech of Ulysses, which I had shown to be traceable to
both Seneca and Cicero, has nothing to do with the item
about the eye not seeing itself, put by the dramatist in

---

[1] Work cited, p. 74.   [2] Work cited, p. 97 sq.

the mouth of Achilles. Mr. Collins had hopelessly blundered over the matter he argued; and Mr. Lang, unwatchfully following him, has given a gratuitous advantage to the very Baconian thesis he was countering. The alleged reproduction of Plato in TROILUS, claimed by two strong " Stratfordians," is one of the stock themes of the " anti-Stratfordians." The reader will find it fully dealt with in my book above cited, and hereinafter.

The final words quoted above from Mr. Lang are so completely astray that they should have been deleted by those who edited his MS. The author of TROILUS assuredly does not " make Ulysses quote Plato as ' the author ' of a remark " ; neither does he make " Achilles take up the quotation." Plato is never once mentioned in the Shakespeare plays. Achilles in the play meets the philosopheme " quoted " by Ulysses with another and a different philosopheme, which Mr. Collins and Mr. Grant White insisted upon ascribing to Plato, without accounting for its previous appearance in JULIUS CÆSAR.

These critical misadventures on the part of three strong " Stratfordians " are " chastening," as the phrase goes. The academics err on classical matters even as the lawyers err about the law in the plays : evidently we are all apt to trip. One can but say, with Frederick, that " the best general is he who makes *fewest* mistakes " ; adding that mistakes differ in degree of fatality. It is the object of this treatise to show that the mistakes alike of the Baconians and of the mainly negative " anti-Strat- fordians " are irredeemable. My friend Mr. Greenwood, who is so Draconic towards every over-strong inference, every " doubtless " and every " certainly " of the " Strat- fordians," has built his own case [1] mainly on current propositions concerning the " law " and " scholarship " of the plays to which he had never applied the slightest comparative criticism, taking them without question from writers whose Stratfordian orthodoxy should have

[1] See *The Shakespeare Problem Re-stated*, 1908.

vetoed his faith in these as in their other theories. And, inexorable towards all defects of biographical evidence for the main tradition, he maintains for his own part a hypothesis which is not only unsupported by a grain of evidence but is in constant and deadly conflict with the very arguments by which he seeks to disallow the claims of the Stratford actor. So much has been shown by Mr. Lang ; and will, I think, be shown independently in the following pages. If they, in turn, should be found to evolve any equipollent fallacy, let it be shown. If not, the candid reader will presumably rate at their true weight the mistakes of detail from which such a treatise cannot conceivably be free.

The deficiency which I recognise in it is the incompleteness of its survey of the literary field that should be covered. For lack of leisure, I have had to leave uncollated at least a score of books that I had noted for re-perusal in this connection. One cannot remember all the allusions and the vocabulary of old books that one had read without any special note-taking : they must be re-read for an argument which turns largely on vocabulary and allusion. Still, I am fain to think that the confutation undertaken has been substantially made out ; and if its incompleteness at many points is noted by any more leisured reader, I trust he will make good the deficiency.[1]

Christmas Week, 1912.

[1] Since the above lines were written, I have read, in the enforced leisure of a brief illness, Canon Beeching's little book, *William Shakespeare : Player, Playmaker, and Poet : a Reply to Mr. George Greenwood* (1908), in which, as in Mr. Lang's volume, I find some of my " points " already made, with many others to boot. All this consensus of argument among independent writers will, I think, impress the open-minded reader, as it has done me.

CONTENTS

CONTENTS

CHAPTER VII

THE ALLEGED CLASSICAL SCHOLARSHIP OF THE PLAYS

§1. *Lord Penzance and Mr. Donnelly*

§2. *Mr. G. G. Greenwood*

CONTENTS

CHAPTER VIII

THE ARGUMENT FROM CLASSICAL SCHOLARSHIP :
ii. DR. R. M. THEOBALD'S LIST OF WORDS

CHAPTER IX

COINCIDENCES OF PHRASE IN SHAKESPEARE AND BACON

§1. *The Evidential Problem*

§2. *Lord Penzance and Mr. Donnelly*

CHAPTER X

THE ARGUMENT FROM COINCIDENCES OF PHRASE :
ii. DR. R. M. THEOBALD

CHAPTER XIV

EXTERNAL AND CIRCUMSTANTIAL EVIDENCE : LIVES AND PERSONALITIES

CHAPTER XV

CONCLUSION

THE BACONIAN HERESY

THE BACONIAN HERESY

CHAPTER I

THE CONDITIONS OF THE PROBLEM

IT is to be hoped that the term " heresy " will not be resented by those to whom it may here apply. The present writer, being himself open to indictment for serious heresy in more than one field of doctrine, is not likely to employ it as an aspersion. A heresy is but a mode of opinion, the word having originally meant a sect ; and it serves conveniently to specify a dissent from an opinion or belief normally held. It is a heresy, for instance, to hold that the " Rokeby Venus " is not the work of Velasquez ; and that heresy the present writer inclines to share, being indeed prone to give a hearing to heresy of all kinds. But a heresy, to start with, is an opinion like another, as likely to be wrong as right ; and the belief that the " plays of Shakespeare " were written by Bacon is to be termed a heresy until it can establish itself.

That it has never done so for careful students is put by many of these as a reason for ignoring it ; and some will doubtless pronounce the present examination a waste of time. But there is, I find, a surprisingly large sprinkling of intelligent people who, without any studious examination, have either accepted the Baconian theory or taken up a non-committal " anti-Stratfordian " position on the score of difficulties which they find in the " orthodox " case, as put by both sides. Such readers I take to be victims of misinformation ; and I think that

their perplexity can, in many instances, be removed.
But their trouble is caused, to begin with, by the reiteration of " orthodox " errors, to which the doubters give
harbourage, and of which the Baconians make their
capital. If one side were wholly scientific, and the other
wholly the reverse, the conscious " expert " might do
well perhaps merely to shrug his shoulders. But opinion
is not so distributed. It is very doubtful whether the
Baconian theory would ever have been framed had not
the idolatrous Shakespeareans set up a visionary figure
of the Master. Broadly speaking, all error is consan-
guineous. Baconians have not invented a new way of
being mistaken.

Some there are, certainly, who are not open to correction. I have small hope of converting a believer in any
of the hundred-and-one ciphers by which Bacon is alleged
to have inserted in the plays and in the prefatory verses
to the folio a multitude of grotesque " revelations " of
what, if he had any occasion to, he could have sanely
established by sealed documents, to be opened at any
specified time. The cipher-mongers as a rule destroy
their case in advance by arguing that Bacon's " secret "
was known not only to Ben Jonson and other friends,
but to Shakespeare's partners—as indeed it must have
been if such secret there were. It is this open secret that
Bacon is declared to have embedded in a series of ciphers
the concoction of any one of which would have been a
task outside of rational contemplation on the part of
any poet or dramatist. The man who took incalculable
pains to get at the minds of his contemporaries and
posterity in his avowed works is represented as spending
an immensity of time and trouble in fantastically contriving ciphers which were never to be suspected by
any reader till Mr. Ignatius Donnelly professed to
discover one of them. The Baconians, I believe, have
now abandoned Mr. Donnelly's egregious cryptogram
as lightly as many of them adopted it ; but new

ciphers are forthcoming from their camp every few years.

The latest is that set forth by Sir Edwin Durning-Lawrence in his munificently produced volume entitled BACON IS SHAKESPEARE (1910). One of the clues which he presents with the utmost confidence is the anagram he evolves from the monster-word " Honorificabilitudinitatibus " in LOVE'S LABOUR'S LOST (v, 1). This he knows to be an old byword among grammarians ; but, finding he can anagrammatise it into *Hi ludi F. Baconis nati tuiti orbi :* " These plays F. Bacon's offspring are preserved to the world "—a portent of Latin that vies with the original prodigy, and an unspeakable " hexameter " like that, to boot—he goes about to show that Bacon inserted it in the original play for the conveyance of his secret to posterity, and expressly arranged the paging of the folio and the place of the word in the page so as to give by the numbers a clue to the coming interpreter. That is to say, the allusion to *Hi ludi,* " these plays," (1) was put in one play before there were any other plays to claim ; (2) was duly printed in the quarto of 1598 with the same intention ; and (3) was circumspectly reproduced in the folio with a Pythagorean machinery of cross-numbering of lines and pages which must have cost inconceivable trouble to arrange, supposing it to have been possible. And Bacon, who always latinized his name *Baconus*, is here made to put it as *Baco*.

All the while the mystery-making author is to be regarded as having left uncorrected the grossest errors of the press found in the quarto on the very page in question. To the first long speech of the Pedagogue on that page the Curate answers, " *Laus deo, bene intelligo* " ; and the Pedagogue rejoins, " *Bome boon for boon prescian*; a little scratched, 'twill serve." This verbal mess, which reappears in the folio, has been reduced to meaning in two ways. The earlier editors, in their enterprising fashion, made the Curate say " *bone* " instead of *bene.*

and made the Pedagogue reply, " Hum, *bone* for *bene ;* Priscian, a little scratched," which would pass very well. But there is the less adventurous solution of the reading latterly adopted, " *Bon, Bon, fort bon :* Priscian, a little scratched," which takes fewer liberties with the text, while doing nothing to explain the closing phrase. Which- ever emendation be right, the original " *Bome boon for boon* " is unintelligible gibberish, which no critical reader can believe to have been written by the dramatist, who- ever he was. But this gibberish was left unremedied by " Baco," on the Baconian view, when he was taking incredible pains to arrange the folio page in an arith- metical puzzle ; and Sir Edwin, undisturbed by the gibberish, but agreeing to read " Priscian " for " prescian," actually proceeds to explain that the grammarian's name is introduced for the purpose of expressing a humorous disregard of his dictum that the letter *f* is a mute ! In Sir Edwin's incomparable anagram-hexameter " F " is to be sounded " eff " : hence the alleged avowal by the anagrammatist of an intention to strain the grammarian's code. In point of fact, be it observed, the anagram- word has not at this point of the action been uttered : it occurs eleven lines later, after the entrance of the Braggart and the Boy ; and it is then uttered by the Clown, who was not present when the Pedagogue alluded to Priscian.

It is impossible to guess how many or what order of readers will either assent to this " revelation " or keep their countenances over it ; but I am quite sure that Sir Edwin will never give it up. And when I point out to him that " Honorificabilitudinitatibus " occurs in Nashe's LENTEN STUFF (1599), on line seven of Signature D, and is to be found on the thirty-third line of page 176 of the third volume of Mr. McKerrow's edition of Nashe's works (1904), he will, I expect, at once proceed to prove that Bacon had somehow arranged these things also for the revelation of the fact that he wrote THE PRAISE OF THE

RED HERRING.[1] For Sir Edwin is satisfied that Bacon " caused to be issued " the PALLADIS TAMIA : WIT'S TREASURY which is " attributed to Francis Meres " ; and further, as he once informed me, believes Bacon to have written Montaigne's Essays in the original French— here improving on Mr. Donnelly, who regarded Florio's translation as the original, and ascribed that to Bacon. Latterly, he has proclaimed to a staring world that Bacon is the translator of the Authorised version of the Bible ; and I make no doubt that he has embraced Dr. R. M. Theobald's demonstration that Bacon wrote Marlowe—not to mention the rest of the Elizabethan playwrights.

Now, Sir Edwin, like Dr. Theobald, is a learned man, which Mr. Donnelly was not, and the fact that the Baconian theory can lead both learned and unlearned men to such weird conclusions might be held sufficient to warn off ordinary folk from taking the first step. If, however, I can forecast the future with any safety from my know-ledge of the Baconian movement, the common run of Baconians will go on as before, some believing that Bacon wrote most of the Elizabethan drama, Spenser, Nashe, Montaigne and Burton ; and some drawing the line at Shakespeare ; while the anti-Stratfordians will continue simply to disparage the " Stratford actor " or " rustic," denying responsibility for Baconian doings. All that one can hope to do is to arrest a minority on their path of mounting credence, by confronting them with some evidence at least as valid as that on which they decided

[1] This, I find, is actually claimed by Mr. Parker Woodward, who sees decisive proof in the fact that Nashe, like Bacon, girds at Ramus. (*Have with you to Saffron Walden : Works*, ed. McKerrow, iii, 136.) To this I may add, for Sir Edwin's edifica-tion, that Nashe, like Bacon, rejects the doctrine of Copernicus (*Id.* p. 94), and uses the " Baconian " phrase, *Veritas temporis filia* (*Id.* p. 29). For a Baconian nothing more can be needed to prove that Bacon wrote Nashe. The trouble is that Shake-speare does none of the things in question.

to take the Baconian turning. It was by garbled and erroneous information that they were first set agoing ; fuller and more accurate information may turn them.

From the point of view of an ordinary Shakespearean scholar, the Baconian opinion is an extravagant hallucination. But he will perhaps admit, on reflection, that all of us are likely to be under some hallucinations on points of past history. If, as most of us frequently discover, we can be seriously misled by accepting current statements about contemporary matters, it is broadly inconceivable that we are not at times much misled by remote evidence about matters on which we are of necessity scantily informed. And the Baconian opinion— the wilder extravagances apart—is in my opinion a hallucination actually derivable and derived from opinions promulgated by some good Shakespearean scholars who scout the other. If this judgment should be made good in the course of our inquiry, the gain may even extend beyond the plucking of some brands from the Baconian bonfire. For the true humanist, all divagations of belief should as such possess some interest ; and the variety of grounds on which my " anti-Stratfordian " friends of all shades have reached their negation have seemed to me quite noteworthy. One of the most entertaining cases is that of my friend X, an acutely intelligent barrister of foreign parentage, who learned English as a foreigner, and mastered it with an enviable perfection. Coming into our literature as an observant tourist, so to speak, he met with the mountainous work of Mr. Donnelly, and, studying it with the impartiality of an entire stranger, decided that Mr. Donnelly had made out his case. Later he chanced to meet with Bacon's Essays, which he read with the same cheerful detachment, reaching the quite unexpected conclusion that the man who wrote " such commonplace stuff " as the Essays could never have written the plays ; though, on the other hand, the explorer still found it incredible that the plays could have been written by " the Stratford actor." If he should follow the present inquiry, his pronouncement upon it will not be among the least interesting to the author.

Whatever may be the utility of the discussion, it is in any case inevitable, and it may as well be gone about systematically. Issue has already been joined with the Baconians by defenders of the ordinary belief ; and some have done it with a competence to which I gladly bear testimony. To say nothing of the many essays which have appeared in the reviews, such a study as that of Mr. Charles Crawford on " The Bacon-Shakespeare Question," originally published in NOTES AND QUERIES, and reprinted in his COLLECTANEA,[1] needs only, I believe, a wider circulation to make it a fountain of healing to many distracted inquirers. If the present treatise should do much less for the elucidation of other points at issue than Mr. Crawford has done for those with which he specially deals, it may still be well worth producing. The wider field that has to be traversed cannot well be here explored with such fulness of relevant learning as his ; but the extension of the survey may still be usefully attempted.

And indeed, if the question is to be discussed at all, it had better be dealt with concretely, in detail, and comprehensively, by the methods of argument which establish or overthrow theories in other provinces of inquiry. Individual students may quite fitly dismiss the Baconian theory on the strength of their *literary* perception that the works of Bacon and the plays of Shakespeare are the production of two utterly different personalities, whose ways of handling language—to mention nothing else—are about as different as the ways, say, of Herbert Spencer and Charles Lamb. To those of us who have lived long in the society of the Plays and

[1] Stratford-on-Avon, 1906–7, 2 vols.

the Works separately, the failure to recognise this profound difference is always perplexing. But since it lies on the face of the debate that such perception is incommunicable, there is nothing to be gained by asseverating the difference. For here again, if we stake our case on our literary sense, we shall find the claim to be two-edged. I at least am conscious of no great aid from the support, on that issue, of a Shakespearean who has no misgivings about the real authorship of certain of the plays and portions of others. If I diverge from my allies there, the "literary" sense is a precarious guide ; and indeed, I find critics whose confidence in their literary sense is of the most complacent and aggressive kind, passing what seem to me very ill-founded opinions on these matters.

The literary sense, then, cannot well be arbitrator in our dispute ; and while each may fitly rely upon his own, there is nothing to be settled by citing it as a decisive witness in this trial, though it will be found cited as an "expert" on both sides. We must proceed rather to operate on the general sense of evidence ; and it is perhaps possible to present the case a little more judicially than it has sometimes been put in the past. Thus far, it has been often debated on both sides with heat enough to set up an ample suggestion of *odium theologicum*, though on both sides it has been at times handled with amenity. For a time, the "orthodox" were apt to be the more provocative in their language,[1] resenting as they often did the lack of scholarly and critical preparation on the part of the heretics. It is the fact, I think, that no expert in Elizabethan literature, indeed no good scholar in English literature, has ever held the heresy. Many

[1] The first explicit Bacon-Shakespeare treatise, the *Bacon and Shakespeare* of William Henry Smith (1856), was promptly replied to in a book entitled *William Shakespeare not an Impostor*, "By an English Critic" (1857), in which the appearance of Smith's booklet was declared to be "to the eternal disgrace of English literature."

" Baconians " know little even about Bacon ; those who have gone at all fully into his work or that of his contemporaries seem always to have read *ad hoc* ; and few have even done much in that way. Those who do, seem unable to stop short of attributing to Bacon the authorship of every book in which they find a phrase or idea used in common with Bacon. But whatever inadequacy of survey or fallacy of reasoning may be noted among the Baconians is to be partly matched in the writings of " orthodox " persons who have expressly discussed either the Baconian heresy or some other important problem of Shakespearean criticism. To me, at least, some of the most accomplished of " orthodox " Shakespearean scholars seem to be very far astray in their conclusions at highly important points. I am therefore not disposed to cast at the Baconians in general, or at any one in particular, epithets which might in my opinion be fairly retorted on some of my allies in the present dispute. Rather I would deprecate the use of the *argumentum ad hominem* on both sides in a debate where, in any case, it can advantage neither. Both sides have resorted to it freely. Baconians, with every reason to conciliate the normal Shakespearean, hardly ever contrive, latterly, to abstain long from hard flings at the " Stratford actor," the blackening of whose character they seem to think part of the disproof of his authorship of the plays published in his name ; and the orthodox Shakespeareans, in turn, seem unable to forego retaliations on the assailants, whether or not they abstain from countervailing attacks on the variously vulnerable reputation of Bacon. Even the mere " anti-Stratfordians," so ably represented by my friend Mr. G. G. Greenwood; apparently cannot conduct their case without a manifold impeachment of a man of whom, they confess, we know but little. A constant cross-fire of personalities between the two—or three—camps is thus generated, and the most competent antagonists of the Baconian theory do not disguise their contempt for its exponents in general, though even expressly justified contempt is notoriously provocative rather than persuasive.

In view of it all, a professed partisan of the " orthodox " cause can hardly hope to escape giving at times the usual kind of offence. But at least he may try—try, that is, to bring his criticism to bear, whether or not severely; on positions and arguments, and to treat antagonists as producers of arguments, good or bad. Realising the logical nullity of Mark Twain's happiest shots at the Stratford bust, and at the tombstone verses, he may abstain, not only from responsive shots at the verses and the effigies and the character of Bacon, but from extra-judicial comment on the personal demerits of those whose arguments he rebuts. And he had better so refrain. For there has been, as aforesaid, much untenable argument on the " orthodox " side, both positive and negative, whatever may be the quality of the reasoning on the other ; and, indeed, it will be strange if there be not some logical or material imperfections in the present treatise.

CHAPTER II

THE POSITIONS OF MARK TWAIN

ENGLISHMEN are wont, with small justification, to lay Bacon-Shakespearism at the door of "America." It was in point of fact first clearly propounded in England,[1] and has been nourished from the start on the dicta of "orthodox" English

[1] In Hawthorne's laboured and clouded preface to Delia Bacon's *Philosophy of the Plays of Shakespeare Unfolded* (1857), where the Baconian theory is only vaguely to be inferred from the mass of declamation which constitutes the book, the novelist states that "A single article from her pen, purporting to be the first of a series, appeared in an American magazine," naïvely adding that "An English writer (in a 'Letter to the Earl of Ellesmere' published within a few months past) has thought it not inconsistent with the fair-play on which his country prides itself, to take to himself this lady's theory, and favour the public with it as his own original conception, without allusion to the author's private claim." This appears to assert that Miss Bacon had definitely stated the Bacon-Shakespeare theory before 1857 ; since the angry allusion is to William Henry Smith's *Bacon and Shakespeare : an Inquiry touching Players, Playhouses, and Play-Writers in the Days of Elizabeth* (1856). Smith, however, at once wrote to Hawthorne protesting that he had known nothing whatever of Miss Bacon's magazine article, and that on reading it over, he thought it preposterous to suggest that he had thence derived his theory of Bacon's authorship of the plays, which he could prove he had held for upwards of twenty years. Hawthorne thereupon wrote a letter of retractation and apology, and both are printed by Smith in his second edition (1857). Smith had in fact propounded the Baconian theory with an explicitness and circumstantiality of which there is no trace in Delia Bacon's bulky book. It was after he had started the battle that Judge Nathaniel Holmes built up an "American School" on the same lines. But even before Smith's book, as Holmes has noted, there appeared in *Chambers's Edinburgh Journal*, Aug. 5, 1852, an article entitled "Who Wrote

devotees who had either never heard of the Baconian heresy or regarded it as beneath contempt ; and the avowed heretics have latterly seemed to swarm, or at least to hive, as actively in England as in the States. But since the publication of Mark Twain's Is SHAKE-SPEARE DEAD ? the cult bids fair to become predominantly an American movement, like " Christian Science."

To a Briton, however, who knows it to be all a woeful mistake, there is no comfort in this.   Error is as inevitable in its reactions as depression in trade ; and the brother-hood of culture can no more than that of science recognise tribal divisions.   We claim to cherish Mark Twain " on this side " with a special regard, and it is the possession of a full share in that bias that proximately moves the present writer to lift up a systematic testimony " on the other side " in what Mark Twain has called the " Bacon-Shakespeare scuffle."   The thing has become serious since he entered the fray.

Mark Twain's championship of the Baconian theory, or at least of the " anti-Stratford " thesis, gives to the antis a dangerous advantage.[1]   He is apt to win the laughers—a thing not before to be apprehended from Baconian propaganda ; and his influence in that way is probably even mere potent since his death.   And no man is likely to seek to meet him with his special weapons. The fun of Is SHAKESPEARE DEAD ? is nearly as good as it had need be.   But, as usual, the serious purpose or purport of its author is perfectly clear ; and he is likely, as usual, to have fortified or induced a serious belief by his fun where he so wished.   It is accordingly justifiable to take his statement of the case as specially important; if not typical, and, by controverting it, to supply an up-to-date introduction to the whole dispute.   If the process involves some serious strictures on a beloved author's

Shakespeare ? " in which it was argued that the actor could not have written the plays. (Nathaniel Holmes, *The Authorship of Shakespeare*, 3rd ed. 1875, App. p. 605.)

wilful way of handling a complex problem, it cannot be helped : the master of thirty legions in the order of humour must just take his chances in a literary war in which he was the challenger. Against one form of hostility he is secure : against Mark Twain on no score can any man bear malice.

Mark Twain's anti-Shakespearean case condenses into these two main theses :

1. Shakespeare was of no account in Stratford-on-Avon in his lifetime ; was utterly forgotten there from the moment of his death ; and was therefore as a personality wholly incommensurate with the vast achievement of the plays.

2. " The " plays are saturated with an exact, technical knowledge of law, which the Stratford actor cannot conceivably have possessed. On this thesis Mark Twain is willing to stake the whole question : for him it is a " crucial instance."

Other contentions arise in the course of the exposition, but these are the main fighting points. And as the first is Mark Twain's special contribution to the debate, and may be much more briefly dealt with than the second, it may be well to give it primary attention. A clearing-up of this issue may indeed promote a better understanding of others.

Both theses are formulated, as it happens, without even a glance at the contrary case, and the first with an almost burlesque extravagance. While making hard play against the biographers because they have tried to fill in by more or less reasonable conjecture the outlines given them by the few precise data we possess concerning Shakespeare, the Baconian thus sets out on his own course :

When Shakespeare died, in 1616, great literary productions attributed to him as author had been before the London world and in high favour for twenty-four years. Yet his death was not an event. It made no stir, *it attracted no attention. Apparently his eminent literary contemporaries did not realize that a celebrated poet had passed from their midst.* Perhaps they knew a play-actor of minor rank had disappeared, but did not regard him as the author of his works. " We are justified in assuming " this.

His death was not even an event in the little town of Stratford, . . . He had spent the last five or six years of his life there, *diligently trading in every big and little thing that had money in it ;* so we are compelled to assume that many of the folks there in those said latter days knew him personally, and the rest by sight and hearsay. But not as a *celebrity ?* Apparently not. For everybody soon forgot to remember any contact with him or any incident connected with him.

If the biographers of Shakespeare had done their conjecturing in this fashion they would indeed have given scope for jest. We have here a series not of rational conjectures, but of wild positive assertions, for none of which, save where a known fact is grossly exaggerated for the sake of the argument, is there the slightest ground; and which singly and collectively do not even approximate to decent plausibility. Supposing Shakespeare to have been the merest actor, or the " illiterate clown " of Sir Edwin Durning-Lawrence's amiable fancy, the chances are that he would be remembered by his neighbours as most ordinary people are. Nobody has the slightest right to say that they soon " forgot to remember any contact with him or incident connected with him," or that he was not known to any one of them as a celebrity. How could the epitaph in the parish church remain unknown to everybody in the place ? On the other hand, supposing the literary world and the neighbours to have known *and appreciated* the plays, and yet to have regarded Shakespeare as a man of no account (and this appears to be the point of the argument before us), we are to infer that it was in Shakespeare's day a matter of *common notoriety* that the plays were the work of some one else, presumptively the Lord Chancellor, Viscount of St. Albans. Over such a proposition it is difficult to be serious ; and yet this or nothing is the argument in hand.

And this impossible hypothesis, as it happens, Mark Twain has taken over from my friend Mr. Greenwood;

with the sole difference that while Mark makes Bacon the author, Mr. Greenwood names nobody, stipulating only for a lawyer. In a case which trades so constantly on the alleged difficulties of the orthodox view, it is important to realise at the outset the absolutely mortal difficulties of the objectors. Mr. Greenwood knows, though Mark Twain did not, the more or less continuous series of testimonies to the literary repute of William Shakespeare, from Meres onwards. When, then, and to whom, did the alleged spuriousness of the actor's claim become known ?   Mr. Greenwood,[1] greatly daring, selects Spenser as a poet about whose life we are much better informed than we are concerning Shakespeare's. It is a sufficiently untenable position, as will be shown a little later ; but it is clear that for Mr. Greenwood the strongest point in it is Camden's statement that when Spenser died, " contemporary poets thronged to his funeral and cast their elegies and the pens that wrote them into the tomb " ; whereas nothing of the sort happened at Shakespeare's [or " Shakspere's "] death. " Look upon this picture," writes Mr. Greenwood "— " and on *that*. What a contrast ! " Mr. Greenwood maintains a politic silence as to the dispute over Ben Jonson's two conflicting statements that Spenser " died for lack of bread," and that he refused Essex's gift of twenty pieces, saying he had no time to spend them. But let that pass.   The question is as to Mr. Greenwood's implication concerning " Shakspere."

In the concluding part of his chapter on " The Later Life and Death of Shakespeare," Mr. Greenwood develops his case. He takes it for granted that the epitaph on the tomb was really written by " Shakspere," the actor, and cannot have been the work of Shakespeare, the dramatist.   The argument is in parts so incoherent that I cannot be sure of its drift. " Another extraordinary fact in this amazing life," writes Mr. Greenwood (p. 199),

---

[1] *The Shakespeare Problem Restated,* p. 53.

" is that *with the exception of* the Plays, and VENUS AND ADONIS, and the LUCRECE and the SONNETS, and that puzzle-poem, THE PHŒNIX AND THE TURTLE, *Shakespeare appears to have written nothing, unless we are to accept the above-mentioned doggerels* as his indeed ! If ' Shakespeare ' was but a *nom de plume* this need not excite surprise. . . ." " With the exception of . . . ! " Mr. Greenwood seems to mean that the man who wrote the Plays and Poems *must* (for some occult reason) have written many other things ; [1] and that these other things are presumably extant over another man's signature. Yet he makes no attempt whatever to identify the man.

Of such reasoning I can make nothing ; and I must therefore confine myself to the portion of the argument that is intelligible. It develops the innuendo put in the previous contrast of Shakespeare's and Spenser's funerals. " Surely," he writes (p. 200), " when this great poet died there was a great burst of lamentation, a great concert of praise ! Surely all his brother minstrels who survived him vied with each other to write his elegy. Alas ! Again silence—the silence that can be felt. . . . It was not till seven years after the death of Shakspere that ' Shakespeare's ' elegy was written by . . . Ben Jonson."

I hesitate to press upon my friend's notice the simple fact that whereas Spenser died tragically in London, after being tragically driven out of Ireland, and thus *could* have a distinguished funeral, " Shakspere " died, apparently after a short illness, in comfortable circumstances; at Stratford-on-Avon ; and that in the then state of means of communication his literary friends could not very well attend his funeral. These facts, which seem to me to collapse his dramatic contrast, must have been present to his mind. His argument seems to be that the non-publication of elegies by friends proves that " Shak-

[1] Does Mr. Greenwood deny the hall-mark of the sonnet to Florio, prefixed to the *First Frutes* ? And is he quite sure about the *Lover's Complaint* ?

spere " was held at his death to be of no literary account—
though he has omitted to say what became of the elegies
said to have been written on Spenser.[1]   What then does
he make of the poems that *were* written for the Folio in
1623 ?   And of Ben Jonson's mention of Shakespeare
in 1619 to Drummond ?   In another chapter he professes
to find it inexplicable that in talk with Drummond Ben
should say that " ' Shakespeare wanted art,' when he was
to give him such praise later " ; but as regards the problem
of testimonies that is mere trifling.   The fact stands out
that Ben spoke of " Shakespeare " to Drummond as a
faulty poet, but still a poet.   Mr. Greenwood is arguing
that " Shakspere " was no poet at all ; and that *at the
time of his death this was generally known to literary men*.
Now, in his later panegyrical poem and in his DISCOVERIES
Ben Jonson identifies " Shakspere," the Stratford actor,
with " Shakespeare," the dramatist—a writer with faults
of art, but a great genius.   Does Mr. Greenwood then
mean to suggest that Ben at the actor's death—and this
in common with all his literary contemporaries—thought
the actor a literary fraud, and later reverted to the other
view ?   If so, what explanation of his nightmare does
Mr. Greenwood offer ?   If not, what point is there in the
argument from Ben's silence at " Shakspere's " death ?
And what about all the other men, first " silent " and
later panegyrical ?   Was it a universal conspiracy, or
a twice enacted mystification ?

I decline at this point to go into the side issues as to
Jonson's diverging criticisms of Shakespeare.   Knowing
that many men of letters—*e.g.* Carlyle on Emerson;
Tennyson, Dickens, and Browning—have talked and
written in diverging strains of their literary friends—I

---

[1] If buried without being copied, they were probably well
interred. It is not quite inconceivable that such a poet as
Shakespeare, after reading Spenser's *Astrophel* and the other
dirges over Sidney, might say to his friends, with regard to his
own latter end, " No elegies, by request ! "

B

am not in the least puzzled by the moods of so moody
a man as Jonson. On the other hand, I claim that anybody putting forward such an amazing argument as Mr.
Greenwood's, above summarised, is bound to bring it
into some appearance of rationality if he desires it to be
seriously considered ; and I confess I cannot see how
he is ever to do so. The thesis he has propounded by
implication is the most hopeless of literary chimeras
—a riddle beside which all the anomalies he discovers
in the " Shakespeare Problem " are trifles. And this
chimera it is that Mark Twain complacently adopts, and
embodies in *his* " anti-Stratfordian " argument.

Leaving it standing in its naked insanity, we can but
turn to the remainder of the exposition, and criticise that
on its merits. It is sufficiently fantastic with the chimera
left out. Mark Twain's statements are those of a man of
letters who ostensibly knew substantially nothing of the
conditions of literary life in Elizabethan England, and
who yet assumed that he knew it in virtue of his knowledge
of the modern United States. This is the kind of trouble
that faces us all through the Baconian controversy. The
Baconians are often studious, and, in some matters,
well-informed people : unfortunately they do not acquire
the information that is relevant to this discussion. Mark
writes that " For seven years after Shakespeare's death
nobody seems to have been interested in him." What
is here meant by " seems " ? That there was no biography published ? That was not the usage of the time.
And there were positively no newspapers to deal with
such matters. But who wrote the lines of the epitaph
commemorating the Shakespeare " with whom quick
nature died ? " Certainly a man of culture, improbably
a Stratfordian. When they were written we know not ;
but it was inferribly before 1623, when we know the bust
to have been in place.

" Then," writes Mark, " the *quarto* was published."
Such a blunder could not have been made by a properly

informed student. " Ben Jonson," he goes on, " *awoke out of his long indifference.*" In no other controversy, surely, could such an assertion have been so advanced. No man has the faintest right to say, on the bare ground of his not having published an elegy, that Jonson had shown indifference to the death of the man whom he tells us he had loved. " Then," continues our investigator, " silence fell *again. For sixty years.* Then inquiries into Shakespeare's life began to be made of Stratfordians."

It is difficult to be sure as to what is here meant. Mark Twain explicitly asserts an absolute " silence " in the way of printed allusions to Shakespeare over a period of sixty years. But he was following Mr. Greenwood, who is of course aware of the many literary allusions to Shakespeare in the period in question. Mr. Greenwood's case is [1] that allusions to the work of Shakespeare have no evidential force inasmuch as they do not say " who " he was—a kind of test which would reduce to nullity most of the literary allusions in all literature. One can but note the self-stultifying character of the argument, for the purposes either of Mark Twain or of Mr. Greenwood. If in a long series of allusions to Shakespeare there is no specification or designation of the man, the only inference rationally to be drawn so far is that nobody had ever hinted a doubt of the genuineness of his claims. Had any such doubt been current, we might look for either a qualifying " whosoever he was " or a positive claim for the " swan of Avon." The complete absence of any questioning is obviously a very strong proof that no questioning ever took place. Simple references to Shakespeare have exactly the force of simple references to Chaucer or Spenser : they signify that only one poet so named was known ; and that no outside claimant to the honours of the name had ever been heard of.

But, as it happens, the post-Shakespearean allusions do often point to an unlearned poet, and exclude a

[1] *Shakespeare Problem Re-stated*, 1908, ch. xi.

learned one. Let us follow the series. Ben Jonson, as aforesaid, was discussing Shakespeare with Drummond in or about 1619. In 1620 John Taylor wrote [1] that " Spencer and Shakespeare did in art excel " ; and it is a scholarly and not an ignorant " conjecture " that the anonymous lines " On the Time-Poets " reprinted in the CHOYCE DROLLERY in 1656, naming " *Ben* . . . fluent *Flétcher, Beaumont* rich in sense, . . . ingenious *Shakespeare . . . Massinger . . . Chapman*," were written between 1620 and 1626. To the Folio of 1623 there are prefixed not only the noble eulogy by Jonson, but others as high pitched, by Hugh Holland, Leonard Digges, and I.M. ; and the fine epitaph by William Basse, referred to in Jonson's memorial, is assigned to 1622. It was in 1627, again, that Drayton published his lines :

> Shakespeare, thou hadst as smooth a comic vein,
> Fitting the sock, and in thy natural brain
> As strong conception and as clear a rage
> As any one that traffick'd with the stage ;

Cowley's passing allusion to Shakespeare's plays was made between 1628 and 1631 ; and Ben Jonson's paragraph with the phrase, " I loved the man, and do honour his memory, on this side Idolatry, as much as any," published in his TIMBER : OR DISCOVERIES in 1641, is to be dated between 1630 and 1637. Milton's eulogium, prefixed to the second Folio, 1632, appeared again in 1640 and in 1645, and in the edition of his poems of the latter year it is dated 1630. In the last-named year appeared A BANQUET OF JESTS, in which (No. 259) there is an allusion to " Stratford upon *Avon*, a Towne most remarkable for the birth of famous William Shakespeare " ; and Milton's lines on " sweetest Shakespeare, Fancy's child," in L'ALLEGRO, are to be dated between 1632 and 1638. To the second Folio, of which, evidently, Mark Twain knew nothing, are further prefixed the glowing panegyric verses of I.M.S. and the anonymous lines " upon the

[1] *The Praise of Hemp-Seed*, 1620, p. 26.

effigies of my worthy friend the Author, Master William Shakespeare and his Workes "; and in the same year Shakespeare is named with Spenser, Jonson, Beaumont, and Fletcher in the commendatory verses of Sir Aston Cokaine prefixed to Massinger's EMPEROR OF THE EAST. In William Habington's CASTARA, 1634, appear the lines " To a Friend," praising a wine of which

should Prynne

Drink but a plenteous glass, he would begin
A health to Shakespeare's ghost ;

and the famous eulogium passed on Shakespeare by Hales of Eton, though only traditionally preserved, is reasonably to be dated before 1633. That testimony, to be sure, is ill-documented ; but in 1635 we have Heywood's mention of " mellifluous Shakespeare " in THE HIERARCHIE OF THE BLESSED ANGELLS ; and the three allusions to Shakespeare by Suckling in his posthumous FRAGMENTA AUREA, published in 1646, that in his comedy THE GOBLINS, in the same volume, and those in his letters, are to be dated between 1636 and 1641.

In JONSONUS VIRBIUS, published in 1638, there are praises of Shakespeare by Jasper Mayne, Owen Feltham, Richard West, H. Ramsay, and T. Terrent ; and in the same year appeared Sir William Davenant's MADAGASCAR, WITH OTHER POEMS, containing his Ode " In Remembrance of Master William Shakespeare." Then in 1640 comes the edition of the POEMS, to which are prefixed the preface of John Benson, the laudatory poem on " lofty Shakespeare " by John Warren, and the well-known lines of Leonard Digges on " never-dying Shakespeare," whereto is appended the anonymous " Elegy on the death of that famous Writer and Actor, Mr. William Shakespeare," which is to be dated 1637 or earlier, since it speaks of Ben Jonson as living. To 1638 belong the lines of James Mervyn, naming " Beaumont, Fletcher, Shakespeare, and a train of glorious poets " ; and to 1639 the eulogy of Thomas Bancroft in his TWO BOOKES OF EPIGRAMMES

and that of the anonymous quatrain in WITTS RESERVA-
TIONS.

And so the stream of testimony goes on through the
century—all this independently of mere references to and
imitations of the plays.   There is no difficulty in ascertaining these testimonies : they are all duly collected for the
students of Shakespeare by Dr. Ingleby in his Shakespeare's CENTURIE OF PRAYSE, of 1874, which has been
repeatedly reprinted since ;   and again in Mr. C. E.
Hughes' compilation, THE PRAISE OF SHAKESPEARE (1904).
Yet of all this commemoration Mark Twain ostensibly
knew nothing : he writes confidently of a " silence " of
" sixty " years after the printing of the Folio, which he
calls a quarto.   It is a distressing spectacle.   For, if he
merely meant that the literary allusions to Shakespeare
during sixty years after his death convey no specification
of the man, but are simply praises of the work, he still
betrays an entire inacquaintance with the record.   The
allusions do repeatedly indicate Shakespeare the actor ;
some profess personal acquaintance with him ;   yet others
are applicable only to an unlearned poet.   Jonson,
Drayton, and Milton, to say nothing of Digges, all
indicate the knowledge that the poet was not a scholar.
Heywood, who must have known much of Shakespeare the
man, calls him " mellifluous," even as Milton had
spoken of his " native wood-notes wild," and as Webster,
in his lifetime, had praised his " right happy and copious
industry."   All these testimonies significantly exclude
any hint of ·' learning," and cannot sanely be supposed to
hint at any " concealed author " whatever.

It is thus mere wilful myth-mongering to pretend that
any one of the references under notice leaves the slightest
opening for the notion that Shakespeare was for a moment
suspected to be but the mask of another man.   All the
later testimonies plainly proceed upon a universal acceptance.   The Shakespeare of the later eulogies is just
Ben Jonson's Shakespeare, the actor, the man of Stratford-

on-Avon.   If it be still complained that they convey no
" gossip," no stories or reminiscences of the man, one can
but ask how much personal reminiscence we find of
Heywood, Dekker, Greene, Peele, Marlowe, Kyd, Nashe ;
of Spenser, the laurelled poet ; nay, even of Ben Jonson,
the foremost and most personally remembered man of
letters in that age ; and of Bacon himself, who lived in the
eye of the court and the nation as well as of the men of
letters ?   Save for the published observations of Rawley,
his chaplain, how much should we have known of *him* in
his simple capacity of man of letters ?   How much did
Fulke Greville tell of the private life of Sidney ?   When
will the " antis " realise that in Bacon's day the age of
modern biography had not begun ?

Sparing comment, we turn to Mark Twain's handling of
his theorem that *after* sixty years " inquiries into Shakespeare's Stratford life began to be made by Stratfordians."
He asks : " Has it ever happened before—or since—that
a celebrated person who had spent exactly half of a fairly
long life in the village where he was born and reared, was
able to slip out of this world and leave that village *voiceless
and gossipless behind him—utterly voiceless, utterly gossipless* ?   And permanently so ? "   This is really as bad as
what went before.   To assume that there was no gossip
in Stratford about Shakespeare after his death, because
none of it has been preserved, is to bring into the Baconian
propaganda a new exorbitance of absurdity.   When
Mark Twain goes on to tell how his own name and fame
have been preserved to his own knowledge, in the village
of Hannibal, Missouri, in an age and a land of newspapers
and newspaper readers, of cheap books and universal
literary comment, in a country where every one is taught
to read and books are printed by the billion, he does but
show that he has never even tried to realise what Elizabethan life in England was like.   Yet he knew, for he
has said as much, that the people of Stratford in Shakespeare's day were mostly illiterates.   The more reason,

surely, to expect that they would not publish reminiscences of a man of letters.

If such a wit as Mark Twain's could so divagate, there must be many who wander after him ; and perhaps the best way to call up for them some idea of the relevant facts is to note briefly how little has been preserved of biographical detail concerning the general run of the English poets and dramatists of Shakespeare's age. After noting such matters they may begin to realise how entirely beside the case is Mark Twain's argument.

1. John Lilly was one of the most famous English men-of-letters of his day, yet we know not the place or the date of his birth. We have extant letters of his writing, and know him to have been a university man and a member of Parliament ; but fifty years ago an editor could say that beyond his writings " we know three facts only, that he was a little man, was married, and was fond of tobacco." [1] The date and place of his death are gathered only from entries which may refer to another man ; and we cannot clearly tell how he subsisted.

2. Thomas Dekker was one of the most popular of the Elizabethan dramatists, but " the outline of his life is indeed singularly blank. We do not know exactly when he was born, or where ; there is scarcely any clue to the important period of his youth, and his early struggles as a poet and playwright : we do not even know when he died." [2]

3. Thomas Heywood, by his own account, had either " an entire hand or at least a main finger " in two hundred and twenty dramas ; and he published twenty-four ; yet we know not his birthplace. He " was a Lincolnshire man, presumably of good family," says Mr. Symonds,

[1] Memoir by Fairholt, prefixed to Lilly's *Works* in " Library of Old Authors."

[2] Memoir by E. Rhys, prefixed to the " Mermaid " edition of Dekker's Plays. Dekker tells, however, that he was born in London.

" though I cannot find that the Visitations of that county record any pedigree of his name." He was a Cambridge University man ; he began to write for the stage in 1596, and in 1598 he was an actor and sharer in Henslowe's company. " Little else is known about his life; and though it is certain that he lived to a ripe age, we are ignorant of the date of his death." [1]

4. Thomas Kyd was the author of some of the best-known plays of his age : in at least four contemporary plays mention is made of his JERONYMO. By a rare chance, the entry of his baptism has lately been discovered, and his parentage has thus been traced : we know too, from recent research, not from contemporary mention, that he was sent to the Merchant Taylors' School. " But between 1565 and 1589 history is entirely silent about him." We know from official documents, never published till our own time, that he was involved in the " atheistic academy " associated with the name of Raleigh ; but " henceforth we lose all trace of Kyd's person. It is as a rule supposed that he died in 1594 or 1595 " ; all that is certain is that he died before 1601. [2]

5. Of the life of Ben Jonson we know more than of that of any dramatist or poet of the Shakespearean age ; but we have not the exact date or the place of his birth, though we know it was in Westminster ; and we lack the dates of his matriculation at Cambridge, of the length of his stay, and of the time of his soldiering in Flanders. All the biographical details we have of him will go into small space.

6. But in the case of Spenser, the most illustrious poet of his age, the lack of biography is most signal. Mr. Greenwood's account contrasts pleasantly with that of the biographers. " The life of Spenser is wrapt in a

[1] Symonds' Essay, prefixed to the " Mermaid " edition of Heywood's Plays.

[2] Professor J. Shick's preface to the " Temple " edition of *The Spanish Tragedy*.

similar obscurity to that which hides from us his great predecessor Chaucer, and his still greater contemporary Shakespeare. As in the case of Chaucer, our principal external authorities are a few meagre entries in certain official documents, and such facts as may be gathered from his works. The birth-year of each poet is determined by inference. The circumstances in which each died are a matter of controversy." [1] " Of his parents, the only fact secured is that his mother's name was Elizabeth ; this appears from sonnet 74 " ; there is no other trace, though he was highly connected on his father's side. We infer that he was born in 1552 ; we have it on his own testimony that he was born in London, but we know not in what part. Quite recently it has been discovered that he went to the Merchant Taylors' School ; and we trace him at Cambridge in 1569 ; but of the rest of his life up to that year we know nothing whatever.

Here is a fair analogy to the case of Shakespeare. But for the school and college entries we should know nothing of Spenser till he had reached manhood ; and we know Shakespeare's parentage and place of schooling with certainty. We also know the name of his wife : we do not certainly know the surname of Spenser's, nor the names of his children.

7. Finally, let us take the case of Drake, one of the most famous Englishmen of Shakespeare's day. He was a national hero, and his ship, *The Golden Hind*, was treasured as long as she held together. Yet the research of Professor Laughton has failed to establish either his parentage or the place of his birth.[2] The ascertaining of such data, in fact, when there was any obscurity about

---

[1] Prof. Hales' Memoir, prefixed to the " Globe " edition of Spenser's Works.

[2] More recent research is understood to have established the birthplace. But the fact of the long blank in English knowledge on the subject bears out our case.

them, never preoccupied the Elizabethans even in the case of their greatest celebrities.

Nevertheless it is not rationally to be supposed that there was not current, in the age of Shakespeare and Jonson, abundant gossip concerning all of these men; alike in London and in the country places with which they had been at all intimately connected. The contrary is inconceivable : gossip is universal and irrepressible. Of what else does the bulk of human conversation ever consist ? The residual literary fact is simply this, that in the England of that time even the most famous poets and men of action and the most popular dramatists were, for lack of literacy and periodicals, not commemorated as much less distinguished people are to-day. They could not be. There were no journals in which to do it, and the custom of writing biographies of writers or even of heroes had hardly begun.

But as regards the poets and the dramatists in particular there came into play a process of partial disrepute, which could account only too easily for that absence of a *cult* of Shakespeare at Stratford-on-Avon which is the sole residual fact in Mark Twain's argument under the head of non-commemoration. When the antiquaries did begin to seek for reminiscences of Shakespeare at his native town two or more generations after his death they found little to record. But why ? Mark Twain all along absurdly subsumes the extreme Baconian explanation— that Shakespeare's contemporaries *knew* that he was not really a man of genius ; and that, by consequence, there was a general inkling that the plays, recognised to be works of genius, were the works of another man. This theorem, which puts the Baconian theory in its most entirely incredible form, has literally not a shred of evidence to support it. There is abundant testimony to the belief of the bookish and literary men that William Shakespeare was a man of genius. This recognition is prominent in Ben Jonson's talk even when he is carping ; it suffuses with fire his panegyric. But every explicit testimony in his own day and among the next generation of readers recognises the dramatist-actor as a man of rare powers ; there is never the shadow of a hint to the contrary.

On the other hand, there is not the slightest reason to suppose that the average inhabitants of Stratford did or could *appreciate the plays as literature*, all questions of authorship apart. If for most of them Shakespeare was not " a celebrity " it was because, first, many could not read ; and, secondly, because they tended to be puritanical, and did not dream that stage plays could be great or serious matter. Many of them, in fact, would regard everything connected with the " harlotry players " as savouring of sin. As Halliwell-Phillipps summed up :

> When the monument was first erected, there can, indeed, be little doubt that most of the inhabitants of Stratford-on-Avon, including the puritanical vicar, regarded it as the memorial of one whose literary career had, to say the least, been painfully useless to society. A like fanaticism no doubt pervaded no insignificant section of Londoners ; but it was not sufficiently dominant in the metropolis to restrain the continued popularity of the works of the great dramatist.[1]

This is not a matter of mere " conjecture," legitimate or other. There is solid evidence of the growth of Puritanism in Stratford-on-Avon as elsewhere in Shakespeare's latter years. A rigorous bylaw against theatrical performances was passed by the town in 1612 ; and when it was found that this could not well be enforced against players under Court protection, resort was had to other devices ; for instance, that of the year 1622, when six shillings were " pay'd to the Kinges players for not playing in the hall." We know further that Shakespeare's daughter, Mrs. Hall, entertained a Puritan preacher at New Place, the town paying for his drink—a very tolerable deal of sack—while she presumably provided his food. Yet when her epitaph came to be written, after her death

[1] *Outlines of the Life of Shakespeare*, 5th ed. p. 241.

in 1649, even the pious hand that composed it testified that among the more cultured folk of Stratford the memory and the fame of her father were still green :

> Witty above her sexe, but that's not all :
> Wise to salvation was good Mistress Hall :
> Something of Shakespeare was in that, but this
> Wholly of him with whom she's now in blisse.

This epitaph, apparently, was as unknown to Mark Twain as all the rest of the evidence which confutes him.

To sum up, a playwright and actor was the last man to be made a local hero in Stratford-on-Avon in the days of deepening Puritanism. The not wholly undeserved disrepute of the theatre affected all connected with it; as we can already see in the Sonnets.[1] A population at once unlettered and fanatical could not conceivably cherish the literary memory of the author of ROMEO AND JULIET and ANTONY AND CLEOPATRA, VENUS AND ADONIS and THE RAPE OF LUCRECE ; though they must have gossiped somewhat about his memory while his generation lasted. But in the special circles outside, where literary genius could be and was appreciated, while Puritanism was doing its best and worst against free art, the name of Shakespeare never ceased to be a word to conjure with ; and the English avowals are more abundant than the testimonies to the differing fame of Bacon himself, no one ever indicating a suspicion that the Stratford actor was not the great poet he was reputed to be. And even in Stratford itself, as we have seen, three and thirty years after Shakespeare's death, the quasi-Puritan composer of the epitaph of his Puritan daughter takes for granted the knowledge of all educated people that Shakespeare was a man of intellectual distinction, whose daughter a

[1] Even in France, long afterwards, it was told that two kinswomen of Molière in the religious life—it may have been his sister and his cousin—" blushed to recognise as a relative the author of *Tartuffe*, and fasted on a fixed day every year to expiate the misfortune of such a connection." Fournier, *Études sur la vie et les œuvres de Molière*, 1885, pp. 9–10.

Puritan woman might be proud to be, though his sole fame was as a writer of poems and plays, and mayhap, in some little degree, as an actor.

Thus the documentary identification of " the Stratford actor " as the author of the plays, though not copious, is perfectly valid, especially in view of the scantiness of biographical record all round for the period. Those who make much of the sparsity of exact traces of Shakespeare might be led to pause in their propaganda if they realised that for the birth, upbringing, and life of Cervantes, the most famous writer of Spain, the record is just as scanty. The enthusiastic devotion of Cervantes' countrymen has failed to ascertain his parentage or his place of birth ; and what we know of him has been preserved not by biographical research among his contemporaries but by the chance of his own statements and of non-biographical documents. It is sometimes urged as a strange circumstance that there survives no known manuscript of Shakespeare. But there survives no known manuscript of Molière ; and concerning even that dramatist, who lived so much nearer the age of biography, it is uncertain whether he was or was not called to the Bar. The latter-day biography of Molière, indeed, has been built up only by a " miracle of investigation " [1] which has left openings for endless disputes.[2] The argument from lack of early biographical commemoration or research, in short, has no weight whatever for the earlier part of the seventeenth century.

The ground being thus cleared of the first section of Mark Twain's unhappy mystification, we may proceed to the somewhat lengthier task of disposing of the second, which, however, is a mere repetition of an elaborate mystification evolved by others and taken by him on trust.

[1] The *Recherches sur Molière* of Eudore Soulié, 1863.

[2] Cp. the *Etudes sur la vie et les œuvres de Molière* of Edouard Fournier, *passim;* the préface to that work by Auguste Vitu ; and the *Autour de Molière* of Auguste Baluffe, 1889, *passim.*

CHAPTER III

THE ARGUMENT FROM LEGAL ALLUSIONS IN SHAKESPEARE : LORD CAMPBELL'S CASE

§ 1

TAKING Mark Twain as the protagonist of the Baconian case, we have found him rejecting the normal view of the authorship of the Shakespearean plays on the strength of a series of gross errors as to the documentary evidence, and an all-pervading misconception as to the conditions of Elizabethan life. Protesting against the acceptance of "conjecture" as biographical material, he founded his own case upon mere wild misstatement in matters of notorious fact, followed up by an argument which on a little scrutiny is found to be wholly irrelevant. When, however, the whole case thus far is disposed of, the unabashed Baconians are found confidently justifying their unexampled "conjecture" by a proposition or propositions in regard to which they can claim the support of Shakespearean scholars of good standing,—the general theorem, to wit, that the author of the plays in question was demonstrably possessed of a deep and technically expert knowledge of English law.

On the strength of this affirmation, confidently accepted by him from others, Mark Twain embraced the "conjecture" that Bacon wrote VENUS AND ADONIS, THE MERCHANT OF VENICE, ROMEO AND JULIET, OTHELLO, LEAR, and all the rest of the plays. In his view " we are entitled to assume " (even as Stratfordian biographers might put it) that where lawyers profess to find legal *expertise* in the plays they cannot be mistaken ; that only a lawyer

therefore can have written them ; and that the lawyer
must have been Bacon. The foe of conjectures died
ostensibly in full reconcilement to the conjecture that
HAMLET was written by Bacon for a company of actor-
partners, all in the secret, after the trial of Essex and
while Bacon was scheming for the favour of King James ;
and that THE TEMPEST, THE WINTER'S TALE, CYMBELINE,
and HENRY VIII were written under similar conditions
of open secrecy by King James' Solicitor-General—the
last-named play just before his elevation to the Attorney-
Generalship. And it is expressly insisted on that while
thus carrying on a kind of authorship which he was deeply
concerned to keep secret, Sir Francis, either deliberately
or through inability to refrain from " talking shop," went
on garnishing the plays with a multitude of legal expressions which to any trained ear must have betrayed their
emanation from a legal source, and which, be it observed,
he never introduces in his Essays.

To this extremity of conjecture we are exhorted to
come on the bare authority, cited at third hand, of certain
pronouncements by lawyers of high and other status,
not one of whom had a fair knowledge of the Elizabethan
and Jacobean drama in general. In a dispute in which
the principle of mere authority is expressly sought to
be overthrown, we are asked to let an inference from the
dicta of one or two purely legal authorities reverse at a
stroke the whole structure of Shakespearean and Baconian
biography. The authority of the great mass of Shakespearean students is to go for nothing, whether as to
biography or as to comparison of styles ; but the authority
of certain lawyers, and these of the " idolatrous " school,
is to settle once for all the question whether the author
of the plays had a professional knowledge of law. Thus,
it may be said, is idolatry pursued by its Nemesis : the
Shakespeare-worshippers' habit of ascribing to the author
of the plays every accomplishment in a superlative degree
is made a ground for taking away the Stratford actor's

kingdom and giving it to another.   And the same sequence occurs in respect of the ascription to the playwright of a wide knowledge of the classics.   The idolaters are in effect slain by their own lintel-stones.   But for the non-idolater all this concludes nothing.   As simple student; he asks :

1. What expressions, in which plays, prove the playwright to have had an incomparably exact knowledge of law, possible only to a trained lawyer ?

2. Is it averred that the dramatic use of these expressions has the effect of making personages speak out of character, in respect of their being endowed with a legal knowledge which they could not reasonably be supposed to possess ?   If so, is this admitted to be a detraction from the dramatist's own artistic credit ?   If, on the other hand, his characterisation is not on this score called in question, with what fitness can he be credited with abnormal legal knowledge on the score of expressions which can dramatically pass muster as " in character " ?

3. Is it claimed that such legal expressions do not occur in the works of other Elizabethan and Jacobean dramatists in similar quantity and quality ?   Have the lawyers ever faced this problem ?

4. How is it to be *proved* that the mere habit of haunting law courts, common to multitudes in Shakespeare's day as in ours, *could not* yield to a quick mind precisely the amount of familiarity with legal terminology seen in the plays ?

5. Is it *true*, as asserted by Lord Campbell and others, that the Shakespearean handling of law terms and phrases is constantly and impeccably correct ?

6. *Does Bacon*, in his non-legal works, make any such play with legal terms and phrases ?

Every one of these six questions, to raise no others; is vital to the issue which Mark Twain declares to be vital to the problem of the authorship of the plays.   And he does not raise one of them ; does not even indicate that

C

it has occurred to him that any one of them might be raised. He simply cites on the legal question nine pages of Mr. George Greenwood's able but *ex parte* treatise, THE SHAKESPEARE PROBLEM RESTATED, ascribing to *that* a conclusiveness which is denied to any argumentation on the " Stratfordian " side, and there makes an end of discussion on that issue, declared to be central.

Now, Mr. Greenwood, setting out to challenge the whole " Stratford " tradition, and all the dogmatism thereon accruing, has made out his own negative case largely by means of the uncritical deliverances of men who adhered uncritically to the tradition in question. He has done this as regards the vital problem of the classical learning said to be exhibited in the plays. Rejecting absolutely the late Mr. Churton Collins's verdict on the main issue, he accepts without scrutiny Mr. Collins's judgment on the primary point of the dramatist's learning. Yet it can be demonstrated that at every important point Mr. Collins's judgment breaks down on analysis.[1] The author of the plays exhibits, on exact scrutiny, no such learning as he ascribes to him. Ben Jonson's ascription to Shakespeare of " small Latin and less Greek," which Mr. Collins arbitrarily and illicitly sets aside, turns out on close examination to be in perfect accord with the internal evidence of the plays, after these have been carefully considered with a view to the whole problem of authenticity. If, then, evidence which, with his own scholarly investigations, satisfies Mr. Greenwood as to the playwright's learning, is found to be quite inadequate, evidence which satisfies him as to the playwright's mastery of English law may turn out to be no less inadequate, albeit he is himself a lawyer.

The thesis of the juristic knowledge of the dramatist, long ago set up by Steevens and Malone, on the basis of the " attorney's clerk " tradition, is specially insisted

---

[1] *See* the present writer's *Montaigne and Shakespeare, and other Essays on Cognate Questions,* 1909, per index.

on by Mr. Churton Collins as part of his proof that TITUS
ANDRONICUS is a genuine Shakespearean work.   Now
this, of all of " the " plays, has moved the largest number
of critics to reject it, on general grounds, as alien work ;
and an all-round survey of the problem is found to bear
out their conclusion.   As to this, Mr. Greenwood is of
my opinion.   So far as demonstration in such matters
can be said to be attainable, TITUS is demonstrably the
work, in the main, of Peele and Greene, with portions
possibly by Kyd or Lodge or Marlowe.[1]   Its legal allusions, then, tell of no legal knowledge on the part of the
author of OTHELLO, CORIOLANUS, AS YOU LIKE IT, and
the unquestioned plays.   Nor is this all.   The legal
knowledge exhibited in the plays is found to be assigned
by the lawyers mainly on the score of phrases which will
not in the least bear out their assertion.   Mr. Greenwood
cites (from Lord Penzance) the astounding judgments
of Lord Chief Justice Campbell (afterwards Lord Chancellor) without quoting, save in subsequent discussion
and in other connections, one specimen of the grounds
given by his lordship for them ; and Mark Twain thereupon adopts without inquiry a verdict which, had he had
the grounds before him, he would, I believe, have regarded
as much better matter for jest than any of the themes he
has jested on—unless, indeed, he recognised in the Lord
Chancellor a fellow humorist.   It is important to keep
in view from the outset the evolution of the argument ;
because Mr. Greenwood will be found ere long putting a
thesis which is only in appearance Campbell's, while
citing Campbell's pronouncements in support of it.
Campbell goes about to prove his general proposition by
a series of items of evidence, consisting substantially of
legal phrases used in the plays.   By that series of items
his general pronouncement must stand or fall.   But
Mr. Greenwood at a certain stage of the debate in effect

[1] *See* the present writer's *Did Shakespeare Write " Titus
Andronicus "?* 1905.

repudiates the very grounds of Campbell's judgment while asking us to accept that judgment as decisive.

§ 2

Let us first examine Lord Campbell's entire case, put in the form of a letter to J. Payne Collier under the title SHAKESPEARE'S LEGAL ACQUIREMENTS CONSIDERED (1859).[1] This case, which Mark Twain had never seen, and the tenuity of which no one could imagine from a mere reading of Mr. Greenwood's extracts, made through Lord Penzance, is framed, bad as it is, merely to support the theory that Shakespeare *may* have been a clerk in a country attorney's office.

[?] Great as is the knowledge of law which Shakespeare's writings display, and familiar as he appears to have been with *all its forms and proceedings*, the whole of this would easily be accounted for if for some years he had occupied a desk in the office of a country attorney in good business—attending sessions and assizes—keeping leets and law days—and *perhaps* being sent up to the metropolis in term time to conduct suits before the Lord Chancellor or the superior courts of common law at Westminster, according to the ancient practice of country attorneys who would not employ a London agent to divide their fees.[2]

And here, at the very outset, we have radical conflict between the champions of the lawyer theory. " We quite agree with Mr. Castle," [3] writes Mr. Greenwood, " that Shakespeare's legal knowledge is *not* what could have been picked up in an attorney's office, but could only have been learned by an actual attendance at the

[1] A year before, W. L. Rushton, then a law student, had published *Shakespeare a Lawyer* (Liverpool, 1858) ; and Mr. Jaggard writes, in his *Shakespeare Bibliography* (p. 271), that " Lord Campbell coolly plundered and plagiarised it a year later, in his imitation work, entitled *Shakespeare's Legal Acquirements*, without the least acknowledgment." But Rushton also followed Malone. Cp. Rushton's own Appendices to his brochure, *Shakespeare's Testamentary Language*, 1869.

[2] Work cited, pp. 22–23.

[3] E. J. Castle, *Shakespeare, Bacon, Jonson, and Greene : A Study*, 1897, pp. 8, 26.

Courts, at a Pleader's in Chambers, and on circuit, or by associating intimately with members of the Bench and Bar."[1] Mr. Greenwood is thus in conflict with his chief witness, upon whose testimony have apparently been built the opinions of nearly all the other witnesses whom he cites. Further, Mr. Castle finds plenty of law in plays in which Lord Campbell finds none ; no law at all in plays in which Lord Campbell finds some ; and "laughable mistakes" where Lord Campbell declares there is no deviation from strict legal accuracy. With Mr. Castle we shall deal later : for the present we have to follow the variegated reasoning of the Chief Justice.

It is significant of the texture of Campbell's argument that after the explicit statement last cited from him he finds in the plays a "wonderful" and "profound"[2] knowledge of law—implying that profundity in that knowledge may be attained by a village attorney's clerk in a few years. But still more staggering is the circumstance that after putting his whole case he writes : "*Still I must warn you* (Collier) *that I myself remain rather sceptical. All that I can admit to you is that you may be right, and that while there is weighty evidence for you there is nothing conclusive against you.*"[3] And he further points out to Collier : "You must likewise remember that you require us implicitly to believe a fact which, were it true, positive and irrefragable evidence in Shakespeare's own handwriting might have been forthcoming to establish. Not having been actually enrolled as an attorney, neither the records of the local court at Stratford; nor of the superior courts at Westminster, would present his name as being concerned in any suits as an attorney ; but it might have been reasonably expected that there would have been deeds or wills witnessed by him still extant ;—and after a very diligent search none such can be discovered."

[1] *The Shakespeare Problem Restated*, p. 31.
[2] P. 113.   [3] Pp. 110–11.

Upon this caveat Mr. Greenwood expressly insists ;
and whereas Campbell's argument went solely to prove
possible clerkship, Mr. Greenwood turns his evidence to
the support of the thesis that the playwright must have
been a lawyer trained on a higher plane. He in turn
refuses to accept the Baconian theory ; whereas the
Baconians turn his and Campbell's arguments alike to
the support of that. Mr. Greenwood must have a lawyer,
but cannot accept Bacon, and can name no other. And
the whole theorem rests on the forensic if not insincere
reasoning of a judge who would have laughed the Baconian theory to scorn. Campbell's argumentation, as he
himself observed, is " worthy of Serjeant Eitherside " ;
and still it is the sole or main foundation of his summing-
up or judgment, which constitutes Mr. Greenwood's case.
Lord Campbell had in fact been indulging in a forensic
exercise, using the language of exaggerated conviction
in the forensic manner, as a barrister would in a defence
of a clouded client before an ignorant jury. To make
clear the truth of this, it is necessary only to summarise
his argument.

It sets out by taking for granted (*a*) that Nashe's allusion, in the epistle prefixed to Greene's MENAPHON (1589),
to " shifting companions that . . . leave the trade of
noverint, whereto they were born," must have referred
to Shakespeare, in respect of the further allusion to
HAMLET ; and (*b*) that Greene, in respect of his later
" Shake-scene " fling, must be held to have been party
to the description of Shakespeare as a lawyer by trade.
Now, it has long been established to the satisfaction, I
think, of absolutely all Shakespearean scholars, that
Nashe's allusion is to Kyd, whose father was a law scrivener,
and who was in all probability the author of the old
HAMLET, upon which, by common consent (Campbell's
included), Shakespeare's play is founded. Lord Campbell's preliminary case thus goes by the board at once :
the testimony of " two contemporaries . . . . who must

have known him [Shakespeare] well," with which he presents Collier at the outset, is a myth of mistaken inference. In passing, it may be noted that he is equally astray (p. 25) in taking Spenser's " pleasant Willy " to be the dramatist. No scholar, at least, now agrees with him.

The adherents of the lawyer theory should further note, what Mr. Greenwood omits to mention, that Campbell " entered " the following caveat :

In THE TWO GENTLEMEN OF VERONA, TWELFTH NIGHT, JULIUS CAESAR, CYMBELINE, TIMON OF ATHENS, THE TEMPEST, KING RICHARD II, KING HENRY V, KING HENRY VI, Part I ; KING HENRY VI, Part II ; KING RICHARD III, KING HENRY VIII, PERICLES OF TYRE, and TITUS ANDRONICUS—fourteen of the thirty-seven dramas generally attributed to Shakespeare,— I find nothing that fairly bears upon this controversy. Of course I had only to look for expressions and allusions that must be supposed to come from one who has been a professional lawyer. Amidst the seducing beauties of sentiment and language through which I had to pick my way, I may have overlooked various specimens of the article of which I was in quest, which would have been accidentally valuable, although intrinsically worthless.

In this connection it should be noted (a) that the late Professor Churton Collins found a long series of " unquestionable " legal allusions in TITUS ANDRONICUS— where it can hardly have been " seducing beauties of sentiment " that prevented Campbell from seeing them ; (b) that Mr. Greenwood in turn finds these allusions to be " very ordinary expressions," which it is " ridiculous " to ascribe to a trained lawyer, though they are just such expressions as Campbell cites from other plays ; and (c) that while the Lord Chancellor finds only one passage " with the juridical mark " upon it in MACBETH, Mr. Castle, K.C., goes further, and denies that there is any sign of legal knowledge in that play at all. Thus in both early and late plays, in genuine and ungenuine alike, the experts themselves confess to lack of evidence over nearly forty per cent of the area involved.

Let us now take Lord Campbell's evidential passages in detail. The mere presentment will probably suffice to dispose of them for most readers, so utterly void are they of justification for the thesis built upon them. Comment is often entirely needless ; the one constant difficulty is to believe that the judge is serious.

1. In THE MERRY WIVES (ii, 2) Ford says his love was

Like a fair house built upon another man's ground ; so that I have lost my edifice by mistaking the place where I erected it.

Upon which Lord Campbell pronounces that " this shows in Shakespeare a knowledge of the law of real property, *not generally possessed*." It might suffice to answer that such knowledge is to-day possessed by millions of laymen : and that in the litigious days of Elizabeth it must have been at least as common. But let the lawyer be answered in legal form. In Dekker's SHOEMAKER'S HOLIDAY, published in 1597, Hodge says (v, 2) : " The law's on our side ; he that sows on another man's ground forfeits his harvest." Hodge is a foreman shoemaker. Was Dekker an attorney's clerk, or was Hodge talking in character and saying what any shoemaker might ? Or was it a lawyer who penned in Heywood's ENGLISH TRAVELLER (iv, 1) the lines :

> Was not the money
> Due to the usurer, took upon good ground
> That proved well built upon ? We are no fools
> That knew not what we did——?

Or is Chapman to be credited with a legal training because he cites the legal maxim, *Aedificium cedit solo* in MAY-DAY (iii, 3) ? According to Mr. Rushton, *this* [1] is the legal maxim underlying the words of Ford, and not the formula, *Cujus est solum, ejus est usque ad cœlum*,[2] cited by Campbell.

2. In Act IV of the same play, says Campbell, " Shakespeare's head was so full of the recondite terms of the law

---

[1] More strictly, *Aedificatum solo solo cedit*.
[2] *Shakespeare's Legal Maxims*, 1907, pp. 24–25.

that he makes a lady . . . pour them out in a confidential
tête-à-tête conversation with another lady. . . ." The
passages thus characterised are :

> May we, with the *warrant* of womanhood and the *witness* of
> a good conscience pursue him ? . . . If the devil have him
> not *in fee simple, with fine and recovery,* he will never, &c.

On Lord Campbell's principles, then, what inference
shall we draw from this piece of dialogue between wooer
and lady in one of Greene's stories ?—

> Yet Madame (quoth he) when the debt is confest there re-
> maineth some hope of recovery. . . . The debt being due, he
> shall by constraint of law and his own confession (maugre his
> face) be forced to make restitution.
>
> Truth, Garydonius (quoth she), if he commence his action in
> a right case, and the plea he puts in prove not imperfect.   But yet
> take this by the way, it is hard for that plaintiff to recover his
> costs where the defendant, being judge, sets down the sentence.
>   *The Card of Fancy,* 1587 : Works, ed. Grosart, iv, 108.

The " debt " in question is one of unrequited love.
Shall we then pronounce that Greene wrote as he did
because " his head was full of the recondite terms of the
law " ?

And what, again, shall we say of the passage in Dekker's
HONEST WHORE (Pt. I, iv, 1) in which Hippolito points
to the portrait of Infelice as

> The copy of that obligation
> Where my soul's bound in heavy penalties ;

and Bellafront replies :

> She's dead, you told me : she'll let fall her suit.

Must Dekker too be a lawyer ?   The reader has already
begun, perhaps, to realise that lawyership is out of the
question.   Greene was no lawyer.   He wrote legalisms
as he wrote Euphuism, because it was a fashion of the
time ; and he did it, as we shall see later, to a far greater
extent, in the way of elaboration, than Shakespeare ever
did.   Dekker and the other dramatists in general did the
same thing as Shakespeare.

Lord Campbell is here imputing lawyership on the score of terms far less technical than many which occur in a multitude of non-Shakespearean plays of the period. When such expressions as " warrant " and " witness " and " fee simple " are seriously asserted to come from a head " full of recondite terms," it seems necessary to explain that " warrant " was long before Shakespeare's day a term in constant non-legal use (as in the colloquial phrase, " I'll warrant you ") ; that the word occurs many hundreds of times, alike in the literal and in the metaphorical sense, in non-Shakespearean plays ; and that " witness " was in the same case, being habitually used in theological speech and in the common phrase " God is my witness," to say nothing of plays. If the use of such terms is proof of legal knowledge on the play-wright's part, then such knowledge is clearly possessed by Webster, who in APPIUS AND VIRGINIA has :

Show'd him his hand a witness 'gainst himself. (iii, 1.)

By what command ?
By warrant of these men. (ib.)

By warrant of our favour. (iii, 2.)

Clown. . . . Though she have borrow'd no money, yet she is enter'd into bonds ; and though you may think her a woman not sufficient, yet 'tis very like her bond will be taken.

First Servant. . . . What witness have they ?

Clown. Witness these fountains. . . . The Lord Appius hath committed her to ward. His warrant is out for her. (iv, 1.)

Here's witness, most sufficient witness. (iv, 2.)

So we must infer a legal training on the playwright's part when, in Dekker's SHOEMAKER'S HOLIDAY (iv, 4), Rose says to her lover :

Rose is thine own. To witness I speak truth,
Where thou appoint'st the place I'll meet with thee ;

as also when her father uses the same phrase in the next scene ; again in Heywood's WOMAN KILLED WITH KIND-NESS (iv, 3) when Mistress Frankford says to her lover,

" You plead custom " ; again in THE WITCH OF EDMON-
TON (by Dekker, Rowley, and Ford) when Winnifred (i, 2)
speaks of her lover's promise

> That never any change of love should cancel
> The bonds in which we are to either bound
> Of lasting truth ;

and yet again when Massinger, in THE FATAL DOWRY,
makes Beaumelle (iii, 1) speak of " sufficient warrant "
in love-making, and Romont (*ib.*) deliver the line " Will
warrant and give privilege to his counsels " ; to say
nothing of a judge's " You had not warrant for it " (v,
end). In the same play, as it happens, Romont says
" Bear witness " (iii, *near end*) ; Beaumelle says " To
witness my repentance " (iv, 3) ; and Charalois, " I ask
him for a witness " (iv, 2). All three are non-legal characters, one a woman. Again in A NEW WAY TO PAY
OLD DEBTS (iv, 2) we have Margaret's lines :

> My vows, in that high office register'd,
> Are faithful witnesses.

So, on Lord Campbell's principle, Massinger must have
been giving reckless rein to his legal knowledge.

Ben Jonson is similarly certificated, for in EVERY
MAN IN HIS HUMOUR (i, 1) we have :

> You are his elder brother, and that title
> Both gives and warrants your authority.

And though Justice Clement there talks of warrants by
professional right, the lay folk in the play say " I warrant
you " without scruple ; while Bobadill pleads that he had
a " warrant of the peace served " on him ; and Matthew
intimates that " we determine to make our amends by
law," and asks " the favour to procure a warrant."
" Warrants," in fact, swarm through the play. Which
clearly proves that Jonson must have been an attorney's
clerk ! And between " warrant " and " witness " every
other Elizabethan dramatist would be in the same list.

As to the " fee simple " passage, we have first to put

the queries : (1) Was Shakespeare, or was he not, aiming at a realistic effect in the play before us ? (2) Is it not one of the most realistic of all he has written ? (3) Would he then be likely to put in the mouth of one of his " merry wives " language which to his audience would seem utterly out of character, and fit only for an attorney ? To answer in the affirmative is at once to accuse the playwright of utterly bad art, and to ignore the testimony of the great mass of Elizabethan literature, summed up in Mr. Hubert Hall's generalization that " every man in these days was up to a certain point his own lawyer ; that is, he was well versed in all the technical forms and procedure." [1] But let us waive authority, here as elsewhere, and note decisive data. Out of a score of parallels to such phrases as " fee simple " and " fine and recovery " in other dramatists and writers, it may here suffice to note (1) in Lilly's MOTHER BOMBIE (i, 2) :

A good evidence to prove the fee simple of your daughter's folly ;

(2) in the old dialogue or quasi-interlude, Roye's REDE ME AND BE NOT WROTHE (1528), one speaker's description of the friars as

> Fre coppy holders of hell
> And fe fermers of purgatory,
>   Whittingham's rep. p. 72 ;

and (3) Thomas Nashe's second prefatory epistle to his STRANGE NEWS OF THE INTERCEPTING CERTAIN LETTERS (1592), where Gabriel Harvey is told that he is " here indited for an encroacher upon the fee simple of the Latin." Are we to pronounce all three writers lawyers ?

3. In MEASURE FOR MEASURE (i, 2) when Mrs. Overdone laments that places such as hers are to be put down, Pompey says : " Fear not you, good counsellors lack no clients." [2] Whereupon Lord Chancellor Campbell writes :

---

[1] *Society in the Elizabethan Age*, by Hubert Hall, of H.M. Public Record Office, 2nd ed. 1887, p. 141.

[2] It may be worth noting that the word " client " occurs only

" This comparison is not very flattering to the bar, *but it seems to show a familiarity with both the professions alluded to.*" Upon these principles, what would his lordship not have made of the remark of Justiniano in WESTWARD HO (ii, 1) : " Like country attorneys, we are to shuffle up many matters in a forenoon " ? Dekker and Webster, surely, *must* have been country attorneys ! And what depths of legal experience must he not have divined behind the suggestion of Webster and Rowley, in A CURE FOR A CUCKOLD (iv, 3), that " long vacations may make lawyers hungry "! Or behind Jonson's lines :

> Or if thou hadst rather to the Strand down to fall,
> 'Gainst the lawyers dabbled from Westminster hall,
> And mark how they cling with their clients together,
> Like ivy to oak, so velvet to leather.
>
> *The Devil is an Ass,* i, 1.

Or in Dekker's passage about

> the shaving of poor clients, especially by the attorneys' clerks of your courts, and that's done by writing their bills of costs upon cheverel.
>
> *Seven Deadly Sins of London,* ed. Arber, c. 6, p. 40.

Or in the page on lawyers in Stubbes' ANATOMIE OF ABUSES.[1] But we waste illustration over a contention which belongs to the plane of farce.

The only other items offered from MEASURE FOR MEASURE are (1) Elbow's clownism, " I'll have mine action of battery on thee " (ii, 1) ; (2) the ironical reply of Escalus suggesting an action for slander for a box on the ear ; and (3) Escalus' phrases : " my brother Angelo," " my brother," " my brother justice " (iii, 2). This, says the Lord Chancellor, " is so like the manner in which one English judge designates and talks of another that it *countenances the supposition* that Shakespeare *may* often, as an attorney's clerk, have been in the presence

thrice in all Shakespeare's plays, an odd fact if he were so obsessed by lawyer-reminiscences as the legalists allege.

[1] Collier's Rep. p. 116.

of English judges "—as ten thousand laymen had been. After this, there is an air of great self-restraint about the suggestion that there is a " tinge " of legal terminology in Isabella's speech to Angelo on the theme that

All the souls that were, were forfeit once.

4. " Fine and recovery " occurs again in the COMEDY OF ERRORS (ii, 2) ; and this time we are told that the puns extracted from the terms " *show the author to be very familiar with some of the most abstruse proceedings in English jurisprudence.*" The same deep knowledge is doubtless to be credited to Nashe, who writes of " suing the least action of recovery " and " a writ of *Ejectione firma.*" [1] And as " fine and recovery " is not ostensibly a more abstruse conception than " livery and seisin," which is mentioned by both Jonson and Webster, we are once more led to extend to them the diploma of attorney-ship so liberally bestowed on Shakespeare. " Fine," as it happens, is a common figure in the drama of Shakespeare's day. Bellafront in Dekker's HONEST WHORE (Part II, iv, 1) speaks of

an easy fine,
For which, me thought, I leased away my soul.

From Mall, in Porter's TWO ANGRY WOMEN OF ABINGTON (iii, 2), we have :

Francis, my love's lease I do let to thee
Date of my life and time : what say'st thou to me ?
The ent'ring, fine, or income thou must pay.

There is nothing more technical in the COMEDY OF ERRORS.

5. In the last-named play (iv, 2) we have the line :

One that before the judgment carries poor souls to hell,

and the phrase, " 'rested on the case," upon which the Lord Chancellor declares that " there we have a most circumstantial and graphic account of an English arrest on *mesne process* " (" before the judgment ") " in an action *on the case.*" It seems necessary to explain that

[1] *The Praise of the Red Herring*, Works, iii, 157.

Dromio's " before the judgment " has reference to the theological " last day " ; and to suggest that the whole effect of the latter part of the passage quoted turns upon the naturalness of a serving-man's fumbling with two legal tags, as serving-men and others constantly do throughout the bulk of Elizabethan drama.   What would Lord Campbell have made, once more, of Mistress Honeysuckle's speech in WESTWARD HO (ii, 1) :

> You have few citizens speak well of their wives behind their backs ; but to their faces they'll cog worse and be more suppliant than clients that sue *in forma paper.*

Dyce, who could not have dreamt of what a Lord Chief Justice could attain to by the light of a comprehensive ignorance of Elizabethan drama outside Shakespeare, has upon this the note : " Our early dramatists have a pleasure in making their characters miscall terms of law," citing a similar instance from Rowley's WHEN YOU SEE ME YOU KNOW ME.   Perhaps we may leave the point at that.

6. Rosalind's gibe in As YOU LIKE IT (i, 2) : " Be it known unto all men by these presents," is cited for the purpose of suggesting that it was " introduced in order to show contempt for Nashe's criticism."   To this theorem is devoted a page of space.   If we reply that Nashe's criticism, as aforesaid, applies to Kyd, Lord Campbell's successors will probably rejoin that on that view the phrase under notice must be held to stand for the dramatist's tendency to talk law under any circumstances.   It may therefore be worth while to ask whether the same theory is required to explain the passage in CYNTHIA'S REVELS in which Jonson makes Amorphus read the " bill " beginning, " Be it known to all that profess courtship, by these presents " : and again, whether it is further required to explain the citation of

> *Sciant praesentes et futuri*
> Witeth and Witnesseth
> That wonieth upon this erthe,

in THE VISION OF PIERS PLOWMAN (ed. Wright, 1030–32) ;
or the phrase *Noverint universi* in Chapman's MAY-DAY
(ii, 1) ?

7. It is considerately admitted that the words " testament " and " bankrupt," in Jaques' speech (ii, 1);
" might be used by any man of observation " ; but it
is claimed that in Act iii, 1, " a deep technical knowledge
of law is displayed." The sole proof is the single phrase :

> Make an extent [1] upon his house and lands.

To this demonstration is added the assurance that in
HENRY VIII (III, ii, 340) " we have an *equally accurate
statement* of the omnivorous nature of a writ of *Præmunire.*" As usual, there is nothing in the matter special to
Shakespeare, who, as it happens, uses the word *Præmunire* only once in all his plays. " Extent " occurs in the
pre-Shakespearean play SELIMUS, ascribed to Greene
(Sc. 1, l. 21) :

> Though on all the world we make extent ;

and in Greene's tract THE DEFENCE OF CONEY-CATCHING :

> They have you in suit, and I doubt not will ere long have some
> extent against your lands.[2]

Greene, as we shall see, has many legal phrases not found
in Shakespeare, and though no lawyer, uses them in a
more lawyerlike fashion.

The meaning of a *Præmunire*, again, was presumably
quite well known to Philip Stubbes, who in his ANATOMIE
OF ABUSES warns all men that he who supports stage-
plays "must needs incur the damage of *premunire* " ; [3]
as it was to Foxe the martyrologist,[4] and to Thomas
Nashe, who in PIERCE PENNILESSE'S SUPPLICATION TO

---

[1] This word occurs in *Titus Andronicus*, where Lord Campbell
had not noticed it.

[2] Greene's *Works*, ed. Grosart, xi, 56.

[3] *i.e.* of damnation. *Anatomie of Abuses*, 1583, Collier's Rep.
p. 140.

[4] *Acts and Monuments*, Cattley's ed. 1841, i, 25.

THE DIVELL [1] suggests to that potentate that he might
" *make extent* upon the souls of a number of uncharitable
cormorants " who have " incurred the danger of a
Præmunire with meddling with matters that properly
concern your own person." Again, in CHRIST'S TEARES
OVER JERUSALEM [2] there is the phrase, " O pride, of all
heaven-relapsing præmunires the most fearful " ; and
yet again in THE UNFORTUNATE TRAVELLER :

lamenting my Jewish Præmunire that body and goods I
should light into the hands of such a cursed generation. [3]

In the same tale we again have " to extend upon,"
meaning " to make extent upon " ; and in Massinger's
plays the phrase occurs repeatedly :

There lives a foolish creature
Called an under-sheriff, who, being well paid, will serve
An extent on lords or lowns' lands.
The City Madam, v, 2.

When
This manor is extended to my use :
You'll speak in a humbler key.
A New Way to Pay Old Debts. v, near middle.

The meaning of " extent " and the nature of a writ of
Præmunire were in fact matters of common knowledge
in Elizabethan days, and had been so long before her
reign. In the BEGGAR'S PETITION AGAINST POPERY,
presented to Henry VIII in 1538, it is remarked that
" Had not Richard Hunne commenced an action of
præmunire against a priest, he had yet been alive, and
no heretick at all, but an honest man." [4] The procedure
of " extent " was at least equally familiar, and both
terms were certainly understood by the writers who so
often allude to them. If Lord Campbell had found in
Shakespeare the lines :

If I were a justice, besides the trouble,
I might, or out of wilfulness or error,

---

[1] Nashe's *Works*, ed. McKerrow, i, 165.
[2] Ed. cited, ii, 80.   [3] Ed. cited, ii, 305.
[4] Rep. in Harl. Misc. ed. 1808, i, 222, also p. 224.

D

> Run myself finely into a præmunire,
> And so become a prey to the informer—

spoken by Sir Giles Overreach in Massinger's A New Way
to Pay Old Debts (ii, 1), or the phrase " That's a shrewd
premunire," in the same playwright's The Old Law
(v, near end) ; or Jonson's lines

> Lest what I have done to them, and against law,
> Be a præmunire,
>
> *(The Staple of News,* v, 2, end);

he would not have hesitated to pronounce that they
showed a practical knowledge of the operation of the kind
of writ in question. Yet no biographer has ever hinted
that either Massinger or Jonson was a lawyer.

8. The phrase of Rosalind in As You Like It (iii, 2)
about lawyers " sleeping between term and term " is
formally produced as showing that Shakespeare " *was
well acquainted with lawyers themselves and the vicissitudes
of their lives* " ! With what zest, then, would his lordship
have cited, if he could, the saying of Sanitonella in
Webster's The Devil's Law Case, that " no proctor
in the term-time be tolerated to go to the tavern above
six times i' the forenoon ! " Must not Webster have been
a lawyer ?

9. Concerning Rosalind's jest in As You Like It (iv, 1),
" die by attorney," we learn that Shakespeare gives us
the true legal meaning of the word ' attorney,' viz.
representative or *deputy."* It will perhaps be equally
edifying to mention that Ben Jonson exhibits the same
recondite learning in The Alchemist (ii, 1) :

> *Face.* You'll meet the captain's worship ?
> *Surly.* Sir, I will—But by attorney ;

and again in Cynthia's Revels (v, 3, Palinode), in the
phrase " making love by attorney." And Webster and
Dekker, once more, jointly lay themselves open to suspicion of deep legal knowledge when they make Mistress
Tenterhook say in Westward Ho (iii, 1) :

When they owe money in the city once, they *deal with their lawyers by attorney*, follow the court, though the court do them not the grace to allow them their diet.

10. Finally, it is explained that Shakespeare again evinces *his* love for legal phraseology and imagery " by making Rosalind say, ' Well, Time is the old Justice that examines all such offenders, and let Time try.' " By the same test, it must have been a writer steeped in legal experience who made Hammon in THE SHOEMAKER'S HOLIDAY (iv, 1) woo Jane with the demand :

> Say judge, what is they sentence, life or death ?
> Mercy or cruelty lies in thy breath.

So that Dekker must have been a lawyer, unless, indeed, he has unconsciously revealed his avocation in the phrase, " that lean tawny-faced tobacconist Death, that turns all into smoke " (OLD FORTUNATUS ? i, 1). If he were not a tobacconist, he must needs have been a lawyer, since he makes the Duke in THE HONEST WHORE (Part I, i, 1) tell Hippolito :

> For why, Death's hand hath sued a strict divorce
> 'Twixt her and thee.

Apparently the Lord Chief Justice would see a passion for legal phraseology in a modern allusion to " the bar of public opinion," to say nothing of the saw, " Time tries all," or " Time and truth try all," as Porter has it in THE TWO ANGRY WOMEN OF ABINGTON (iv, 3). In point of fact the learned judge sees legal preoccupation in

11. TROILUS AND CRESSIDA, (iv, 5) :

> That old common arbitrator, Time.

By parity of reasoning, Nashe was a lawyer, inasmuch as he wrote " Let Antiquity be Arbiter " ;[1] and again : " Judge the world, judge the highest courts of appeal from the miscarried world's judgment, Oxford and Cambridge, wherein I have trespassed . . . " ;[2] and yet again

---

[1] *Anatomie of Absurdity :* Works, ed. McKerrow, i, 16.
[2] *Four Letters Confuted*, vol. cited, p. 302.

when he tells his antagonist, " All is ink cast away : : you recover no costs and no charges." By the same reasoning, too, it was a lawyer who described the sun as " indifferent arbiter between the night and the day " in the first sentence of Sir Philip Sidney's ARCADIA ; and another who spoke of " Nature's Sergeant (that is Order) " in the FAERIE QUEENE (B. VII, c. vii, 4). And what shall we say of the Reverend Philip Stubbes, who writes of " the high justice-of-the-peace, Christ Jesus " ?[1]

12. Dealing with Dogberry and Verges in MUCH ADO ABOUT NOTHING, the Lord Chancellor concludes that " the dramatist seems himself to have been well acquainted with the terms and distinctions of our criminal code, or he could not have rendered the blunders of the parish officers so absurd and laughable "—absurd and laughable, that is, to an audience who in the terms of the argument *could not appreciate the absurdity*, being themselves devoid of the alleged " profound legal knowledge " of the dramatist. Thus can a judge reason. His further remark that in the line

Keep your fellows' counsel and your own,

" Dogberry uses the very words of the oath administered by the Judge's marshal to the grand jury at the present day," needs no comment. Does it require a lay mind to realise that the words must then have been known to myriads of laymen ?

13. On the speech of Don Adriano in LOVE'S LABOUR'S LOST (i, 1) beginning " Then for the place where," and ending " a man of good repute, carriage, bearing and estimation," we have this pronouncement : " The gifted Shakespeare might perhaps have been capable, by intuition, (!) of thus imitating the conveyancer's jargon ; but no ordinary man could have hit it off so exactly, without having *engrossed* in an attorney's office."

When therefore Puntarvole in Ben Jonson's EVERY

---

[1] *Anatomie of Abuses*, 1583, Collier's Rep. p. 171.

MAN OUT OF HIS HUMOUR (iv. 4) begs the notary to draw
the indentures, and gives directions, we know what to
think.   There are scores of lines such as these :

That, after the receipt of his money, he shall neither in his
own person nor any other, either by direct or indirect means,
as magic, witchcraft, or other exotic arts, attempt, practise or
complot anything to the prejudice of me, my dog or my cat ;
neither shall I use the help of any such sorceries or enchantments,
as unctions to make our skins impenetrable, or travel invisible
by virtue of a powder, or a ring, or to hang any three-forked
chains about my dog's neck, secretly conveyed into his collar ;
but that all be performed sincerely, without fraud or imposture.

Clearly, Ben must have " *engrossed* in an attorney's
office," unless, indeed, Bacon wrote Ben's plays as well
as Shakespeare's, as not a few Baconians aver.

14. This, be it observed, is the sole example cited
from that which passes for Shakespeare's earliest comedy;
in which, if ever, the proclivity of the " attorney's clerk "
to legal phraseology on his own account should have
asserted itself.   And from a comedy which is perhaps as
early, and in any case is among the three or four earliest,
Lord Campbell is again able to cite only one instance of
legal phraseology :

> According to our law
> *Immediately provided in that case.*
> *Midsummer Night's Dream*, 1, i.

On this Steevens had long ago observed, citing the
attorney-clerk's tradition, that " the line before us has
an undoubted smack of legal commonplace.   Poetry
disclaims it."   That is to say, the young poet was so
much of an attorney's clerk as to obtrude his office
reminiscences where poetry would have been more
appropriate.   As it happens, the whole speech of Egeus
in which the line occurs is prosaic ; and once more the
question arises whether the dramatist is or is not making
one of his characters speak out of character.   Lord
Campbell, never asking the question, naïvely confesses that
" the prosaic formula runs :   ' In such case made and

provided.' '' Then the attorney's clerk is not true to his office reminiscences. But his lordship explains that the precise formula " would not have stood in the verse "—as if Shakespeare could not have made one line end with " in such case " and the next begin, " Made and provided " ! And Mr. Grant White, carried away by Lord Campbell's simple prosodical argument, writes of Egeus' speech that " He pleads the statute ; and the words run off his tongue in heroic verse as if he were reading them from a paper." [1]

The process of self-confusion has here become curiously interesting. Lord Campbell admits the legal phrase to be laxly used, but pleads the trammels of the verse : Mr. White argues that the words run " in heroic verse, as if he were reading them from a paper "—when the whole speech of Egeus is in the same sort of verse, and any line might equally be said to run as if read from a paper. The simple fact is that the dramatist has put in the mouth of a lay citizen one of those more or less loosely used legal tags which are to be found in almost every play of the Elizabethan and Jacobean era. In an argument which undertakes to prove " profound legal knowledge," this rag of evidence is thus manipulated with a solemnity that transcends burlesque. If Shakespeare's legal knowledge is to be thus proved, what diploma can be refused to the authors of such lines as these :

> How ! strike a justice of peace ! 'tis petty treason
> *Edwardi quinto :* but that you are my friend,
> I would commit you without bail or mainprize.
> > Massinger, *A New Way to Pay Old Debts*, iii, 2.
>
> Nor bond, nor bill, nor bare acknowledgment.
> > *Id.* v, i.
>
> We may put off a commission : you shall find it
> *Henrici decimo quarto.* *Id.* i, 3.

Well, if you'll save me harmless, and put me under *covert barn* (⚊ *baron*), I am content to please you.
> Dekker, *The Honest Whore*, Part I, iii, 2.

---

[1] Memoir of Shakespeare in 1865 ed. of *Works*, i, p. xlvi.

Citizens' sons and heirs are free of the house by their father's copy.
            Dekker, *The Honest Whore*, v, 2.

Return your *habeas corpus* : here's a *certiorari* for your *precedendo*.
            Peele, *Edward I*, ed. Dyce, p. 382

They'll make a solemn deed of gift of themselves, you shall see.
            Jonson, *Cynthia's Revels*, i, 1.

15. In THE MERCHANT OF VENICE (i. 3 ; ii. 8), we are assured, " Antonio's bond to Shylock is prepared and talked about according to all the forms observed in an English attorney's office. The distinction between a ' single bill ' and a ' bond with a condition ' is clearly referred to ; *and punctual payment* is expressed in the technical phrase, ' Let good Antonio *keep his day*.' '' By which token Dekker and Webster were probably attorneys' clerks, because they make Monopoly in WESTWARD HO (i. 2), when told that he has forfeited his bond, reply " I'll pay him fore's day " ; and again, in Dekker's THE HONEST WHORE (1. 2) Fustigo protests : " By this hand, I'll discharge at my day."

Heywood's legal experience must be even greater, for he is thus technical at least four times—thrice in one play :

Like debtors, such as would not break their day.
            The English Traveller, iii, 1.

Broke our day.   *Ib.* iii, 2.

Break his day.   *Ib.*

I'll hold my day.
            A Woman Killed with Kindness, i, 1.

Yet again, Dekker in his tract THE SEVEN DEADLY SINS OF LONDON (1606), says of his first type-character, " the politic bankrupt," that " he will be sure to keep his days of payment more truly than lawyers keep their terms " ; and Jonson in THE ALCHEMIST (iii, 2) has : " take the start of bonds broke but one day." And, yet again, Nashe in PIERCE PENILESSE says of Gabriel Harvey's astrological brother that " his astronomy broke his day with his creditors." (*Works*, i, 196-97.)

Sooth to say, the phrase had been current among the
laity in the time of Langland, who (PIERS PLOWMAN,
2961 *sq.*) makes Coveteise tell how he seized the manor
of a borrower " if he his day breke." And it would
seem to have been no less familiar in the time of Caxton,
since in the MORTE DARTHUR we read " How that Sir
Palomides kept his day for to have foughten " (Title of
c. 88 of B. x). These trade secrets will out, somehow !
Sir John Fortescue avows, about 1475, that the King's
creditors " defame his highness off mysgovernance, and
defaute of kepynge of days " (GOVERNANCE OF ENGLAND,
ch. v). Even the preachers knew about it. Roger
Hutchinson in a sermon (*c.* 1550) mentions that " the
defendant's office is, when he is summoned or cited, to
appear at his day " (Second Sermon OF OPPRESSION, &c.;
Parker Soc. ed. of Works, p. 332).

In THE MERCHANT OF VENICE however, " it appears
further," by iii, 2, " that Antonio has been arrested on
mesne process." The action for a pound of flesh, then, is
dramatised by an English attorney's clerk (if not by
Bacon) in the light of his professional knowledge ; and
we are further told : " Antonio is made to confess that
Shylock is entitled to the pound of flesh according to the
plain meaning of the bond and condition, and the rigid
strictness of the common law of England :

> *Salarino.* I am sure the Duke
> Will never grant this forfeiture to hold.
> *Antonio.* The Duke cannot deny the course of law.

" All this has a strong odour of Westminster Hall."
Since the Duke, as represented by Portia, after putting
other " English " arguments *does* disallow the forfeiture
as a criminal device, two contradictory views are thus
alike homologated by the Lord Chief Justice as " strict
English law." And it would appear to follow that the
Italian novelists from whom the tale is derived had the
same " profound legal training " as shines forth in the
drama.

The trial, further, is "duly conducted according to the strict forms of legal procedure." That is to say, it was in the strict fashion of Westminster Hall (1) to let the Duke of Venice (who later announces that (2) he is going to "dismiss the court" failing the arrival of Bellario of Padua, "a learned doctor" whom he has "sent for to determine this"), begin (3) to abuse the plaintiff to the defendant before the case has been stated on either side. Portia is described (4) as "the Podestà or judge called in to act under the authority of the Doge" (which she is not), so that Bellario would on that theory take the same status. (5) Nevertheless the proceedings begin as aforesaid in Bellario's absence. The Podestà theory, by the way, is illuminated by the fact that at the close of the proceedings the Duke (6) exhorts Antonio to reward Portia, *i.e.* the judge.

The business having been started by the Duke as aforesaid, (7) Shylock delivers in reply a psychological essay, and (8) Bassanio intervenes with invective in the capacity of a friend of the defendant, who (9) in turn conveys his opinion of the plaintiff's character. After (10) this highly professional discussion has been further continued, (11) Nerissa, "dressed as a lawyer's clerk," in strict Westminster Hall style presents a letter to the Duke ; and (12) Bassanio, Shylock and Gratiano exchange amenities. (13) The letter is then read out by the Duke; with scrupulous attention to legal forms. It announces (14) that Bellario, the "Podestà," being ill, appoints a "young doctor" from Rome as his substitute, the Duke of Venice concurring as in duty bound ; though (15) he thoughtfully inquires whether the substitute knows anything about the case. (16) He is assured that the substitute knows all about it—before having heard anything from the parties. (17) Portia, dressed as "a doctor of laws," then discusses moral issues with Shylock in a fashion which illustrates *her* profound acquaintance with Westminster Hall usage, the plaintiff (18) alternately retorting and applauding, in Westminster Hall fashion. Portia's line is (19) to urge the plaintiff to accept thrice his debt, knowing all the while that it is because of his refusal to do so that the case is in court. On his refusal (20) she admits that he may " lawfully " have his pound of flesh, and (21) advises Antonio to prepare for the operation there and then, at the hands of the plaintiff, as was the wont at Westminster Hall. Incidentally (22) she intervenes in the conversation between Bassanio and Antonio with a jest—here, certainly, conforming to English legal usage—and Nerissa follows suit, ostensibly as clerk to the court ; whereupon the plaintiff (23) rebukes the court for wasting time. (24) The court then develops the interesting legal theory that flesh does not, according to the vulgar notion, contain or include blood, and warns the plaintiff accordingly. (25) In reply to him, the court courageously alleges that an Act to that effect is in existence ; proceeding further (26) to aver that the plaintiff must exact the whole penalty due under his bond, and will himself incur the capital penalty if he takes more or less. (27) Having thus already, in effect, non-suited the plaintiff, the court unexpectedly does it afresh, intimating that he has all along lain under the capital penalty, inasmuch as the laws of Venice—of which the Venetian authorities and public appear to have no knowledge—define his entire proceedings as homicidal ; and further (28) that the same occult code awards half of his property to the defendant, and the other half to " the privy coffer of the State," whose interests have been so indifferently represented by the Duke.

The plaintiff is now advised to throw himself on the mercy of the Crown, which he contumaciously fails to do ; but the Crown, now getting a word in, spontaneously remits the death penalty, and (having apparently some doubts as to the revelation just made concerning its fiscal privileges) suggests a substantial remission of the pecuniary

penalty so far as the State is concerned. (29) The
defendant, however, intervenes with a somewhat obscure
proposal that, he retaining his half of the plaintiff's
property, the plaintiff shall "let me have the other half
in use, to render it upon his death" to plaintiff's son-
in-law ; adding, "Two things provided more," to wit,
(*a*) that "for this favour" plaintiff shall turn Christian,
and (*b*) "record a *deed of gift*, here in the court, *of all he
dies possessed*," to his son-in-law and daughter.   Defendant has justifiably taken for granted the assent of the
court and Crown, which latter (30) accommodatingly
intimates that plaintiff's pardon will be "recanted" if
he does not do as he is told.   (31) With the same business-
like promptitude the plaintiff assents, and the court
directs the clerk to "draw up a deed of gift." (32) The
plaintiff is nevertheless allowed to withdraw, directing
that the deed be "sent after him" ; whereupon the
Crown invites the court to dinner ; adding, when the
learned judge pleads lack of time, its celebrated
suggestion to the defendant, to see that the judge
is well paid.   The courthouse then becomes the scene
of domestic amenities, according to Westminster Hall
practice.

And this "trial," we are told by a Lord Chief Justice,
later Lord Chancellor, "is duly conducted according to
the strict forms of legal procedure," whence arises a
highly strengthened presumption that the dramatist was
a practised attorney's clerk.   His lordship brilliantly
concludes with the reflection that Gratiano's speech :

> In christening thou shalt have two godfathers,
> Had I been judge, thou shouldst have had ten more,
> To bring thee to the gallows, not the font,

is "an ebullition which might be expected from an
English lawyer."

I should expect further ebullitions from any lawyer
who should chance to peruse Lord Campbell's pages.
It is not too much to say that, apart from downright

Baconism, the theorem before us is the worst nonsense
that has ever been penned in Shakespearean discussion,
which is saying a good deal. I leave it to the lawyers
to decide whether or not his lordship was writing with
his tongue in his cheek ; and I invite Mr. Greenwood to
say on what critical principles he makes use of such a
critic's declaration that " to Shakespeare's law, lavishly
as he expounds it, there can neither be demurrer, nor bill
of exceptions, nor writ of error." " There is nothing so
dangerous," wrote Lord Campbell, " as for one not of
the craft, to tamper with our freemasonry." It would
appear that there are still more dangerous undertakings
open to lawyers.

It may be worth noting in this connection that, as a
legal friend of mine has put it, whosoever wrote the
trial scene in THE MERCHANT OF VENICE, it cannot have
been Bacon, the equity lawyer. Mr. Devecmon and other
lawyers have been so struck by the disregard of equity
in Portia's rulings as to be unable to refrain from severe
censure of Shakespeare's conception of justice. They
in turn, in their revolt against the entire lack of true
legal feeling in the play, have perhaps grown blind, by
reaction, to the moral enormity of Shylock's position.
An equity lawyer, I suppose, would have set aside alike
Portia's " blood " argument and Shylock's " bond " argument, and given simple decree for payment of the debt.
We can imagine what Bacon would have thought of the
theorem that if A lends money on condition of being
allowed to cut off half a newly killed pig belonging to B,
he cannot be permitted to cut off less than half, and is
precluded from taking any blood. But whatever the
equity lawyer might decide on the final merits, the playwright has in view an audience who—to say nothing of
their primary prejudice against the Jew—were at least
justified in regarding Shylock as a miscreant in the matter
of the pound of flesh. And it is the utterly unlawyerlike punishment of the miscreant for his *intentions* that

finally makes the legalist theory so completely preposterous in regard to this particular play.

As regards Shakespeare's moral outlook in the matter, it may suffice to remind the reader of the existence of an older play, referred to by Stephen Gosson in his SCHOOL OF ABUSE (1579), on the subject of the caskets and the Jewish usurer's bond ; and to suggest that Shakespeare, who has done so much to humanise the figure of the hated Jew in other respects, probably stopped short of the vengeance meted out in the older drama.

16. Portia's phrase (V, i, 298),

> Charge us there upon inter'gatories,

is justly alleged to contain a " palpable allusion to English legal procedure." It does ; and so do the four other instances of the word in the plays.   And so does Ariosto's

> What should move you
> Put forth that harsh inter'gatory ?

in Webster's THE DEVIL'S LAW CASE (ii, 3).   And so does Gelaia's "Slight, he has me upon interrogatories," in Ben Jonson's CYNTHIA'S REVELS (iv, 1).   And so does Andelocia's phrase in Dekker's OLD FORTUNATUS (iv, *end*) : "Are you created constable ?   You stand so much upon interrogatories."   And so does Black Will's "You were best swear me on the inter'gat'ries," in ARDEN OF FEVERSHAM (III, vi, 6).   And so do Nashe's phrases : "Let me deal with him for it by interrogatories" (First Part of PASQUIL'S APOLOGIE : *Works*, i, 115), and "Pilate's interrogatory ministered unto him was, Art thou the King of the Jews ? " (*Ib.* p. 129.)

And so does the question, " What are you, sir, that deal thus with me by interrogatories, as if I were some runaway ? " in Greene's MENAPHON (Arber's rep. p. 57). What then ?   Were these writers all lawyers ?

17. The servant's phrase, " present her at the leet, because," &c.; in the Induction to THE TAMING OF

THE SHREW, is alleged to betray an " intimate knowledge of the matters which may be prosecuted as offences before the Court Leet, the lowest court of criminal judicature in England." It shows exactly such knowledge as was, in the terms of the case, necessarily possessed in every alehouse in England ; otherwise Sly is presented as a tinker impossibly learned in the law. An even wider range of legal knowledge of the same order, as it happens, is exhibited by Justice Overdo in Ben Jonson's BARTHOLO-MEW FAIR (ii, 1). What is the inference there ?

18. Because Tranio in the TAMING OF THE SHREW (i, 2) remarks that

> adversaries in law
> Strive mightily, but eat and drink as friends,

the Lord Chief Justice is moved to observe that the dramatist " had been accustomed to see the contending counsel, when the trial is over, or suspended, on very familiar and friendly terms with each other." 'Tis like ! Ten thousand laymen have noted as much ; and a hundred popular tales have been current from time immemorial which convey the fact from generation to generation. Similar lore, to a layman's thinking, presumptively underlay the remark put by Dekker and Webster in the mouth of Mistress Justiniano in WEST-WARD HO (i, 1), to the effect that she sleeps " as quietly as a client having great business with lawyers." But if that had been said in a Shakespearean play, what depth of legal experience would Lord Campbell not have found in it ! What would he not have made, again, of the lines :

> The man of law,
> Whose honeyed hopes the credulous clients draw,
> As bees by tinkling basins,

in the WITCH OF EDMONTON (iv, 1), by Dekker, Ford, and Rowley ; or of the phrase, " They'll hold no more than a lawyer's conscience " in Dekker's MATCH ME IN LONDON (Act i, *end*). If he had only read THE DEVIL'S LAW

CASE (v, 2), he would perhaps have been content to stake his whole thesis upon one sentence of Sanitonella :

You have lawyers take their clients' fees, and their backs are no sooner turned but they call them fools and laugh at them.

For Sanitonella is actually a lawyer's clerk ; and it clearly follows that the dramatist must have been one !

19. Whereas Katherine in the same play (ii, 1) says, "You crow too like a craven," we are seriously assured that the playwright " shows that he was acquainted with the law for regulating trials by battle " between champions; one of which had been fought in Tothill Fields before the judges of the Court of Common Pleas in the reign of Elizabeth, because " all lawyers " know that " craven " is " the word spoken by a champion who acknowledged that he was beaten, and declared that he would fight no more ; whereupon judgment was immediately given against the side which he supported,and he bore the infamous name of *craven* for the rest of his days." " We have like evidence in HAMLET (iv, 4)," adds his lordship, " of Shakespeare's acquaintance with the legal meaning of this word," inasmuch as Hamlet has the phrase, " some craven scruple."

I invite Mr. Greenwood's critical attention to the rubbish upon which he has been building his case. He is, I know, the last man that would attend a cockfight ; but he will perhaps admit that cockfighters called a timid cock a craven without possessing the lore of " all lawyers " as to the nomenclature of trial by battle—concerning which, more anon. He will also, I think, grant me that Shakespeare did *not* write THE TAMING OF THE SHREW, the " profound " legal learning of which play must accordingly be credited in some other quarter.

20. Lord Campbell gives three pages to the proposition that the bare plot of ALL'S WELL, as regards the legal position of Bertram, is proof " that Shakespeare had an *accurate knowledge* of the law of England respecting . . .

tenure in chivalry " and " wardship of minors." The wardship of Bertram, we are told, " Shakespeare drew from his own knowledge of the common law of England, which . . . was in full force in the reign of Elizabeth." That is to say, the alleged knowledge must have been common to the multitude, since there is not a word of technicalities in the play. And after all we learn, in a foot-note, that " according to Littleton it is doubtful whether Bertram . . . might not have refused to marry Helena on the ground that she was not of noble descent."

21. The profundity and accuracy of legal knowledge exhibited in the WINTER'S TALE is vouched for (a) by the fact that Hermione mentions, (i, 2), " a piece of English law procedure which . . . could hardly be known to any except lawyers, *or those who had themselves actually been in prison on a criminal charge*—that, whether guilty or innocent, the prisoner was liable to pay a fine on his liberation." Lord Campbell appears to have assumed that released prisoners would keep this strange circumstance to themselves as a dark secret. Mr. Greenwood will probably admit that it was likely to be known to Ben Jonson (who had been twice in prison, and may have revealed his occult knowledge to Shakespeare) ; to Marston and Dekker, who had also been in jail ; and to Greene and Nashe, to say nothing of certain thousands of other Elizabethans ! Lest, however, he or his Baconian friends should refuse to grant that anybody but a lawyer was likely to disclose the mystic secret in a play, it may be well to cite Heywood's A WOMAN KILLED WITH KIND-NESS, where it is thoughtlessly revealed thrice over :

Prison Keeper. Dischargey our fees and you are then at
   freedom.
Sir Charles. Here, Master Keeper, take the poor remainder
   Of all the wealth I have. . . .

(Act ii, 2).

Prison Keeper. . . . You are not left so much indebted to us
   As for your fees : all is discharged, all paid.

(Act iv, Scene 2).

In the same scene, when Sir Charles discovers that he is released by his enemy Acton, he cries, " Hale me back ! " and concludes :

> I am not free : I go but under bail ;

to which the keeper replies :

> My charge is done, Sir, now I have my fees
> As we get little, we will nothing leese [lose].

Yet again, in Part II of his KING EDWARD THE FOURTH (Pearson's ed. i, 139) Heywood proclaims the usage which Lord Campbell thinks could have been known only to lawyers or ex-prisoners. Jane Shore, securing the pardon of the prisoners for piracy, about to be hanged, says to the officer :

> You must discharge them, paying of their fees
> Which, for I fear their store is very small,
> I will defray.

And if this be not enough, we have yet another revelation in Dekker's THE WONDER OF A KINGDOM (iv, 1) :

> *Gentile.*   Go and release him
> Send him home presently, and pay his fees.

If Lord Campbell and Mr. Greenwood had but handled this case as they would have done a legal one, and taken a little trouble to discover precedents, they and their readers might have been saved the construction and demolition of a legal house of cards. That which Lord Campbell thinks could hardly have been known to any but lawyers and prisoners was known to every spectator, and is known to every reader, of Heywood's best play, to say nothing of ordinary means of knowledge.

22. With a supreme effort of candour, Lord Campbell admits that the indictment of Hermione (iii, 2) " is not altogether according to English legal form, *and might be held insufficient on a writ of error.*" But he comforts himself with the reflection (*b*) that " we lawyers cannot but wonder at seeing it so near perfection in charging the

E

treason; and alleging the overt act committed by her contrary to the faith and allegiance of a true subject."

With what wonder, then, must the lawyers read the indictment of Crispinus and Fannius in Jonson's POET-ASTER (v, i), where the technicalities are to Shakespeare's as three to one! The culprits there are " jointly and severally indicted and here presently to be arraigned " as having acted " contrary to the peace of our liege lord, Augustus Cæsar, his crown and dignity," and " mutually conspired and plotted at sundry times, as by several means, and in sundry places, for the better accomplishing your base and envious purpose. . . ." Mere clerkship in an attorney's office, surely, could not yield such profundity of legal learning! THE POETASTER, like the rest of the Elizabethan drama, must be by Bacon !

And only the same hand, surely, could have penned the " wonderful " indictment of Guildford and Lady Jane in the FAMOUS HISTORY OF SIR THOMAS WYAT, by Dekker and Webster, where the culprits are " here indicted by the names of Guilford Dudley, Lord Dudley; Jane Grey, Lady Jane Grey, of capital and high treason against our most sovereign lady the Queen's majesty," for having " sought to procure unto yourselves the royalty of the crown of England, to the disinheriting of our now sovereign lady the queen's majesty," and " manifestly adorned yourselves with the state's garland imperial," and so forth. And only a lawyer, clearly, could have made Norfolk order that the accused shall " directly plead unto the indictment."

Returning to Lord Campbell, we learn (c) that Cleomenes and Dion " are sworn to the genuineness of the document they produce *almost* in the very words now used by the Lord Chancellor when an officer presents at the bar of the House of Lords the copy of a record of a court of justice." Which completes the case for the WINTER'S TALE and the Comedies.

23. Coming to the Histories, our jurist notes that the

English history plays contain fewer "legalisms" than "might have been expected," and that there are more in the foreign plays. He recalls, however, that in the history plays Shakespeare was working upon foundations already laid by other men who had no "technical knowledge" of the recondite kind we have just been considering. And after all, we find that in King John's speech to Robert Faulconbridge, beginning :

> Sirrah, your brother is legitimate,

we have the "true doctrine, *Pater est quem nuptiæ demonstrant.*" Unhappily, the author or authors of the older play, THE TROUBLESOME RAIGNE OF KING JOHN (whom I take to be mainly Marlowe and Greene), though necessarily devoid of technical knowledge, had been inconsiderate enough to develop the argument more fully and with more use of technical terms than Shakespeare has done. When, accordingly, it is further argued that the line (ii, 1),

> As seal to this indenture of my love,

"might come naturally from an attorney's clerk," we can but remark that the metaphor in question seems to have come naturally to most of the poets and dramatists of Elizabethan England. Take fifteen instances out of a hundred :

> Be this day
> My last of bounty to a wretch ingrate ;
> But unto thee a *new indenture sealed*
> Of an affection fixed and permanent.
> > Heywood, *The English Traveller*, i, 2

> Not till my pardon's sealed.   *Ib.* iv, 6.

> *Mary.* Yes sir ; a bond fast sealed with solemn oaths,
> Subscribed unto, as I thought, with your soul ;
> Delivered as your deed in sight of Heaven :
> Is this bond cancelled : have you forgot me ?
> > Middleton, *The Roaring Girl*, i, 1.

> He and I
> Have sealed two bonds of friendship.
> > Dekker, *The Honest Whore*, Part I, i, 1.

Then with thy lips seal up this new-made match.
> *Arden of Feversham*, III, v, 150.

Francis. Bid her come seal the bargain with a kiss.
Mall. To make love's patent with my seal of arms.
> *The Two Angry Women of Abington*, iii, 2.

And have his lips seal'd up.
> Jonson, *Every Man out of his Humour*, Induction.

Seal it with thy blood. (*twice*)
> Dekker, *The Witch of Edmonton*, ii, 1.

the tragedy,
Though it be seal'd and honour'd with the blood
Both of the Portugal and barbarous Moor.
> Peele, *The Battle of Alcazar*, iv, 2.

Join you with me to seal this promise true
That she be mine, as I to her am true. . . .
First Four but say, next Four their saying seal
But you must pay the gage of promised weal.
> Sir Philip Sidney, *Arcadia*, b. iii.

I seal your charter-patent with my thumbs.
> Greene, Eclogue in *Menaphon*, end.

You all fixt
Your hands and seals to an indenture drawn
By such a day to kill me.
> Dekker, *Match Me in London*,
> Act iv.   Pearson's ed. iv, 200.

I'll bear him such a present,
Such an acquittance for the knight to seal,
As will amaze his senses.
> Heywood, *A Woman Killed with Kindness*, v, 1.

I seal you my dear brother, her my wife.   *Ib.*

Or seal our resolution with our lives.
> Heywood, *First Part of Edward IV*.
> Pearson's Heywood, i, 14.

I seal myself thine own with both my hands
In this true deed of gift.
> *Blurt, Master-Constable*, 1602, v, 3.

It is edifying to know, in the same connection, that
Bishop Wordsworth found in Shakespeare's metaphorical
use of " seal " a proof of his study of the Bible.[1]

[1] *On Shakespeare's Knowledge and Use of the Bible*, 2nd ed.
1864, p. 333.

As there is no more " law " in KING JOHN, our jurist fills a page by demonstrating that his author " spurned the ultramontane pretensions of the Pope." It is even so.

24. A brighter prospect opens for the Baconian when we reach KING HENRY IV, Part I, for there (iii, 1) " the partition of England and Wales " is carried out " in as clerk-like, attorney-like fashion as if it had been the partition of a manor between joint tenants, tenants in common, or coparceners." All this because Mortimer has the lines

> And our indentures tripartite are drawn,
> Which, being sealed interchangeably. . . .

" It may well be imagined," says the learned judge; " that . . . Shakespeare was recollecting how he had seen a deed of partition tripartite drawn and executed in his master's office at Stratford "—though in the critic's opinion he probably was never in any attorney's office ! And when Hotspur asks : " Are the indentures drawn ? " he shows that he " fully understood this conveyancing proceeding." By the same reasoning, Dekker knew as much when he wrote the lines last above cited from him ; and Greene and Lodge may well be imagined to be drawing on office reminiscences when they made the Usurer in A LOOKING GLASS FOR LONDON say to his victim : " Have you not a counterpane of your obligation ? " thus making their personage " fully understand " what only lawyers could know ! And, once again, we find that Ben Jonson's plays must have been written by a trained lawyer, inasmuch as he not only has :

> Here determines the indenture tripartite
> 'Twixt Subtle, Dol, and Face,

in THE ALCHEMIST (v, 2), but makes the scrivener in the Induction to BARTHOLOMEW FAIR present a full-drawn " indenture "—of which the Bookholder gets the " counterpane "—in strict quasi-legal form, between the spectators and the author. As the document runs to over a hundred

lines, the claims for Shakespeare's legal training would seem
to be at this point as dust in the balance. The only question
open on the juristic principles under notice is, whether
Jonson was an attorney's clerk or Bacon's amanuensis !

And the problem does not end with the dramatists.
Bishop Hooper, the martyr, in a long passage of legalist
theology quoted hereinafter (ch. vi), speaks of a contract
" confirmed with obligations sealed interchangeably."
Hooper is known to have been a monk before he became
a Protestant preacher. Is it to be inferred that he had
also been a lawyer's clerk ?

25. Our jurist adds : " Shakespeare *may* have been
taught that ' livery of seisin ' was not necessary to a deed
of partition, *or he would have probably directed this ceremony
to complete the title.*" Such modesty of statement should
be fitly acknowledged. But the judge is more assured
in noting that " so fond was Shakespeare of law terms "
that he makes Henry IV use (iii, 2) the " forced and harsh "
figure, " *Enfeoff'd* himself to popularity." Upon this
we have a copy of Malone's note on the passage, but not
of Steevens's mention that in the old comedy of WILY
BEGUILED there is the phrase : " I protested to enfeoffe
her in forty pounds a year." When Shakespeare uses
a legal term in a strained sense, such as probably would
never suggest itself to a lawyer, he is held to exhibit his
profound and accurate legal knowledge. When, then,
Serlsby in Greene's FRIAR BACON (sc. 10) says :

> I am the lands-lord, keeper, of thy holds ;
> By copy all thy living lies in me ;
> Laxfield did never see me raise my dues ;
> I will enfeoff fair Margaret in all,

it merely proves that Greene had " no technical knowledge." In point of fact, the " forced and harsh " use
of this very term occurs often in Nashe :

Might the name of the Church infeoffe them in the kingdom
of Christ. . . .
The Anatomie of Absurditie, 1589. Works, ed. McKerrow, i, 22.

A kind of verse it is he hath been enfeoft in from his minoritie.
Ep. Ded. to *Have with You to Saffron Waldon*, Works, iii, 7.

    I . . . enfeofe thee with indefinite blessedness—
        Christ's Teares over Jerusalem, ed. cited, ii, 32.

—in a fashion which indicates that it was a trick of speech
of the period, analogous to that of the phrase, " Shall I
contract myself to wisdom's love ? " in Dekker's OLD
FORTUNATUS (i, 1). The words " feoffee " and " feoff-
ment " occur again in the legal sense many times in
two acts of Jonson's play, THE DEVIL IS AN ASS. It is
thus abundantly evident that both the normal and the
abnormal use of such legal terms were common in Elizabethan phraseology. Yet because Hotspur in 1 HENRY IV
(iv, 3) simply tells how Henry on a historic occasion said
he came to " sue his livery " when he actually did so,
we are asked to believe that Shakespeare's language is
determined by his special legal training. What inference
then shall we draw when Ben Jonson in THE STAPLE OF
NEWS (i, 1) makes Pennyboy junior declare,

    I'll sue out no man's livery but mine own—?

Are we to be told here also that Jonson exhibits lack of
a technical knowledge which Shakespeare possessed ?

    26. Whereas some have argued that the conversation
between Falstaff and the Chief Justice does *not* exhibit
a close observation of the manner of speech of judges,
Lord Campbell demonstrates that Lord Chancellor
Jeffreys once actually *did* talk of laying a man " by the
heels." He further delivers the judgment that the
author who made Falstaff talk of " the wearing out of
six fashions, which is four terms, or two actions," " *must*
have been *early* initiated in the *mysteries* of terms and
actions." So, it appears, was Greene, who in JAMES IV
(iii, 3) makes Andrew say that " dead " is " a terrible
word at the latter end of a sessions," and further makes
the Divine (v, 4) complain that the lawyers " delay your
common pleas for years." And so must have been Dekker

and Webster, since they make Justiniano in WESTWARD
HO speak of "the motion in law that stays for a day
of hearing"; and Dekker in IF THIS BE NOT A GOOD
PLAY, THE DEVIL IS IN IT (ed. Pearson, iii, p. 274) makes
Octavio say :

> Yet term time all the year !
> A good strong lawsuit cannot now cost dear ;

and again in THE HONEST WHORE (Part I, iv, 2) makes
Fustigo reflect : " I could have mine action of battery
against him, but we may haps be both dead and rotten
before the lawyers would end it " ; and yet again makes
Doll in NORTHWARD HO (i, 3) protest : " I'm as melancholy now as Fleet Street in a long vacation ; . . . so
soon as ever term begins I'll change my lodging." As
for Heywood, he once more betrays his lawyership in THE
ENGLISH TRAVELLER (iii, 3) :

> Besides, 'tis term,
> And lawyers must be followed ; seldom at home,
> And scarcely then at leisure.

Lord Campbell, it would appear, had not mastered the
simple fact, which lies on the face of a hundred Elizabethan books dealing with contemporary life, that the
" terms " of the law-courts were then a normal way of
dividing time, as we now commonly divide it by the
seasons. The reader, however, can now understand that
when Nashe writes : " My clue is spun ; the term is at
an end ; wherefore I will end and make vacation " (HAVE
WITH YOU TO SAFFRON WALDEN ; *Works*, iii, 136) he
is really not giving any proof of legal experience ; but
is simply using the every-day language of the period ;
as he does when, at the close of the pamphlet, he says he
will " keep back till the next term " his further scolding.

27. Pistol's " *absque hoc* " (v, 5) is of course cited as
" remarkable," that being " an expression used, when the
record was in Latin, by special pleaders in introducing
a special traverse or negation of a positive material allegation on the other side, and so framing an issue of fact

for the determination of the jury." So that Shakespeare, whose genius is subsumed throughout the inquiry, was really incapable of drawing the character of the swaggerer Pistol without falsifying it by making him utter phrases which were within the ken only of trained lawyers, and which he could never have heard even as scraps and tags ! Similarly, when Heywood in THE FAIR MAID OF THE WEST (i, 5) makes a tavern drawer say : " It is the commonest thing that can be, for these captains to score and to score ; but when the scores are to be paid; *non est inventus*," he must be held to have bewildered his audience by putting in a tapster's mouth a Latin phrase possible only to lawyers. It really seems saner to suppose that tags of law Latin were common currency.

28. Our jurist reaches his high-water mark in the HENRY VI plays, where Dick's proposal (2 H. VI, iv, 2), " let's kill all the lawyers," and Jack Cade's allusions to parchment and beeswax, show " a *familiarity with the law and its proceedings* which strongly indicates that the author must have had *some professional practice or education as a lawyer*." And on the sentencing of the Clerk of Chatham, who could " make obligations and write court hand," and always signed his name instead of making his mark, the Lord Chancellor pens this reflection (italics his) : " Surely Shakespeare must have been employed to write *deeds* on *parchment* in *court hand*, and to apply the *wax* to them in the form of *seals :* one does not understand how he should, on any other theory of his bringing up, have been acquainted with these details." Over this nonsense one's only doubt is as to whether the writer can have penned it with any consciousness of its purport ; or whether he was deliberately farcing. It seems incredible that it should be necessary to mention that the parchment, beeswax, and seal, and the scene with the Clerk of Chatham, are all in the FIRST PART OF THE CONTENTION OF THE TWO FAMOUS HOUSES OF YORK AND LANCASTER, which was no more written by Shake-

speare than by Lord Campbell. But the argument before us is part of the case upon which Lord Campbell founds his deliverance as to the profound legal knowledge exhibited in Shakespeare's plays, upon which bare deliverance Mr. Greenwood in turn mainly rests *his* case, which convinced Mark Twain !

29. Of course we are next told that the indictment of Lord Say (iv, 7) was drawn by " no inexperienced hand," inasmuch as it contains the burlesque phrase " contrary to the king, his crown and dignity," and the further legal phrase, " such abominable words as no Christian ear can endure to hear," which are the equivalent of *"inter Christianos non nominand'."*

It is quite certain that the drawer of this indictment must have had some acquaintance with " The Crown Circuit Companion," and must have had a full and accurate knowledge of that rather obscure and intricate subject—" Felony and Benefit of Clergy."!

Cade's proclamation, which follows, we are as gravely told, " deals with still more recondite heads of jurisprudence." Thus it runs :

The proudest peer in the realm shall not wear a head on his shoulders unless he pay me tribute : there shall not a maid be married but she shall pay me her maidenhead ere they have it. Men shall hold of me *in capite ;* and we charge and command that their wives be as *free as heart can wish or tongue can tell.*

" Strange to say," writes the jurist, " this phrase, *or one almost identically the same,* 'as free as tongue can speak or heart can think,' is feudal, and was known to the ancient laws of England." *Ergo,* only a trained lawyer can have heard of it ! Nashe, as it happens, is inconsiderate enough to employ the phrase in his HAVE WITH YOU TO SAFFRON WALDEN (*Works*, ed. cited, iii, 33). But that is a trifle. Once more, it appears, we must point out that " against the king's crown and dignity," and the " abominable words as no Christian ear is able to endure to hear it," and the edifying lines on the " still more recondite heads of jurisprudence" which Lord Campbell describes as "legislation on the *mercheta mulierum*," are all in the FIRST PART OF THE CONTENTION, where, instead of "heart can wish," we have the professionally accurate "heart can think." What does Mr. Greenwood think of it all?

30. At a bound we pass from 1 HENRY VI to TROILUS AND CRESSIDA, where, as we might have expected, Pandarus' phrases (iii, 2) "a kiss in fee-farm" and "in witness the parties interchangeably" are solemnly cited, with the comment that the latter phrase is the "*exact* form of the *testatum* clause in an indenture"—"in witness whereof the parties interchangeably have hereto set their hands and seals"; whereas the word "whereof" has been left out. Then we are reminded of the "seals of love" in the song in MEASURE FOR MEASURE and the "sweet seals" in VENUS AND ADONIS, which are once more implicitly declared to be the lyrical expressions of an attorney's clerk. It would seem again necessary to vindicate the poethood of the poet against his legalist idolaters by pointing out that this too is a poetic commonplace of the time :

> Sweet lady, seal my pardon with a kiss.
>> Dekker, *The Wonder of a Kingdom*, iv, end.
> Seal me a pardon
> In a chaste turtle's kiss.
>> Randolph, *The Jealous Lovers*, i, 7.
> I had taught
> Our lips ere this, to seal the happy mixture
> Made of our souls.
>> Jonson, *The Devil is an Ass*, i, 1.
> Thus I seal it (*kisses her*).
>> Beaumont and Fletcher, *Monsieur Thomas*, v, 10.
> My lips . . . seal my duty.
>> Massinger, *The Picture*, iv, 1.
> Our bargain thus I seal. (*He kisses her.*)
>> Heywood, *The Brazen Age*. Pearson's Heywood, iii, 215.

31. In LEAR, naturally, the Fool's phrase (i, 4), "'tis like the breath of an unfee'd lawyer," is held "to show

that Shakespeare *had frequently been present at trials in courts of justice*, and now speaks from his recollection." Dekker and Webster, evidently, must have had the same recondite training, inasmuch as Mistress Birdlime in their WESTWARD HO (ii, 2) says, " I spake to her, as clients do to lawyers without money, to no purpose."

32. Gloucester's phrase (ii, 1), " I'll work the means to make thee capable," is characterised as " a remarkable example of Shakespeare's use of technical legal phraseology," inasmuch as " capable " is the technical formula for " capable of inheriting." " It is only a lawyer who would express the idea " so. So that, once more, Chapman must have been a lawyer, since he makes Almanzor in REVENGE FOR HONOUR (iv, 1) tell his son Abilqualit that he is " deprived of being capable of this empire " ; Heywood must have been a lawyer, since he puts this very term " capable " in the same special sense in the mouth of the vintner's apprentice, Clem, in THE FAIR MAID OF THE WEST (v, 2) :

Please your majesty, I see all men are not capable of honour : what he refuseth, may it please you to bestow on me ;

and Massinger must have been a lawyer, since he has the phrase in an edict (OLD LAW, v, 1), " no son and heir shall be held capable of his inheritance . . . unless. . . ." And Heywood, Chapman, Massinger, and Shakespeare stand alike convicted—if there be any validity whatever in the legalist argument—of at once putting their characters out of drawing and bewildering their audiences by making their non-legal personages use terms which none but lawyers could understand ! It may suffice to mention that the terms " capable " and " incapable " are used in More's HISTORY OF RICHARD III (Murray's rep. pp. 194, 195) with reference to the succession to the crown, that they occur in the chronicles, and that they must have been used in all men's common talk for many generations.

33. The words of Cornwall to Edmund, " Seek out where thy father is, that he may be ready for our apprehension," are cited without any explicit claim to find in them signs of profound legal knowledge ; but inasmuch as Edmund says, aside : " If I find him comforting the king, it will stuff his suspicion more fully," we are duly reminded that " comforting " is the term used in " the indictment against an accessory after the fact, *for treason*." The Lord Chancellor would appear to have been unaware that the word is used in indictments after the fact for lesser crimes than treason ! It must have been heard as so used in every Elizabethan court, and would be familiar in every village.[1] It may be mentioned incidentally that " back up " or " encourage " is the original meaning of " comfort," and that the word is used often by Wiclif in that sense.[2]

34. There being no other " law " in LEAR, we are finally assured that at least " In Act iii, Sc. 6, the imaginary trial of the two unnatural daughters (*by the mad Lear*) is conducted in a manner showing a perfect familiarity with criminal procedure." In this case I spare comment.

35. In HAMLET the simple phrase, " should it be sold in fee " (iv, 4) is alleged to be one of the various expressions " showing the substratum of law in the author's mind." We then learn that the mention of impressed shipwrights who work on Sunday " has been quoted; both by text writers and by judges on the bench, as an authority upon the legality of the *press-gang*, and upon the debated question whether shipwrights, as well as common seamen, are liable to be pressed into the service of the royal navy." That is to say, the passage tells of

[1] In a recent English case which excited much interest, the newspapers printed the phrase in question, some misreading it " comport." In Elizabeth's day, the mistake would have been impossible.

[2] Treatise *Against the Order of Friars*, chs. 20, 24, 31.

Elizabethan usage. There is no question of " legal knowledge " in the matter.

36. Hamlet's phrase, " As this fell sergeant Death is strict in his arrest," cannot be let pass without the remark that in this metaphor Death comes " *as it were* to take him into custody under a *capias ad satisfaciendum.*" His lordship would doubtless have said the same had he met in Shakespeare with Ben Jonson's " He'll watch this sen'night but he'll have you : he'll out-wait a sergeant for you " (Epicœne, iv, 2). Had Lord Campbell read Chapman's All Fools he would have known from a phrase about Dame Nature sending " her serjeant John Death to arrest his body " (i, 1), that the trope was in common use. Chapman's " executioner of justice, Death " (Revenge for Honour, iii, 1), and Massinger's " Summoned to appear in the court of Death " (The Duke of Milan, v, 2) are simply samples of a vein of metaphor which runs through all English speech of the period. We have it in Nashe's Christs Teares over Jerusalem (1593) :

The Judge [shall] deliver thee to Death, his Sarjant, the Sarjant to the divel.

Works, ed. McKerrow, ii, 32.

We have it again in Dekker :

They have broke Virtue's laws; Vice is her serjeant, Her jailer and her executioner.

Old Fortunatus, v, 2.

37. Over the grave-diggers' scene, naturally, we have special exultation : it is " the mine which produces the richest legal lore." Inasmuch as the talk of *felo de se* bears on the case of Sir James Hales, puisne Judge of the Common Pleas, who became insane and committed suicide soon after the accession of Queen Mary, we are assured that " Shakespeare had *read and studied* Plowden's Report of the celebrated case of Hales *v.* Petit, tried in the reign of Philip and Mary." The sole basis for this now familiar stress of asseveration is that in the lawsuit

over Hales' estate, in which one side argued that a man
" cannot be attainted of his own death " and " cannot
be *felo de se* till the death is fully consummate," whereas
" the death precedes the felony and the forfeiture," the
other side argued that " the act consists of three parts "
—imagining, resolving, and executing.   In the play, the
Clown says, with regard to the suicide of Ophelia, " an
act hath three branches, it is to act, to do, and to perform."   That is the whole case.

Now, it is obvious that such a notable argument as
that in the Hales case must have been reported, discussed, and commented on for two generations all over
England ; and it would be discussed among common
folk as among the educated.   Shakespeare could often
have heard just some such confabulation as he ascribes
to the grave-diggers.   If this be denied, we must decide
that he put in the mouths of common folk quasi-legal
talk which neither they nor the audience could even
loosely understand.   There is not the slightest reason to
suppose that he went to Plowden to study a case of
common notoriety for the sole purpose of framing a few
burlesque phrases for a comic dialogue—for that is the
sole use to which he puts the matter.   Once more the
legalist case, at its highest pretension, collapses on a
moment's scrutiny.

38. Over Hamlet's speech on the skull, however, we
have inevitably a further sweeping claim, inasmuch as
it " abounds with lawyer-like thoughts and words."
" These terms of art are all used seemingly with a full
knowledge of their import ; and it would puzzle some
practising barristers with whom I am acquainted to go
over the whole *seriatim* and to define each of them satis-
factorily."   So that Shakespeare, once more, is in-
artistic enough to put in the mouth of a prince a string
of law terms which a Victorian barrister would be hard
put to it to define !

But, as usual, other dramatists of the time do likewise.

In Ben Jonson's EPICŒNE (iv, 2) we have Morose's list of terms to match Hamlet's :

> There is such noise in the court that they have frighted me home with more violence than I went ! such speaking and counter-speaking, with their several voices of citations, appellations, allegations, certificates, attachments, interrogatories, references, convictions and afflictions, indeed, among the doctors and proctors, that the noise here is silence to't.

Then, in the scene (v, 1) in which Otter and Cutbeard play the parts of a divine and a canon lawyer, we have these legal terms :

> Divortium legitimum ; divinere contractum ; irritum reddere matrimonium, " as we say in the canon law, not to take away the bond, but cause a nullity therein " ; impedimentum erroris ; error personae ; error fortunae ; error qualitatis nec post nuptiarum benedictionem ; irrita reddere sponsalia ; conditio ; votum ; cognatio spiritualis ; crimen adulterii ; cultus disparitatis ; vis ; ordo ; ligamen ; publica honestas, which is inchoata quaedam affinitas ; affinitas orta ex sponsalibus ; leve impedimentum—and yet more.

Why should Ben Jonson be denied his diploma as canon lawyer ?

39. In MACBETH the only phrases cited as having " the juridical mark " upon them are Macbeth's " take a bond of fate " and " live the lease of nature " (iv, 1). Upon these citations there follow certain professional pleasantries which laymen may pass by. It is fitting, however, to note that Mr. Castle, K.C., [1] classes MACBETH among " the non-legal plays," and pronounces the " bond of fate " phrase " mere sound, not sense," as he does the " lease of nature " phrase to be " nonsense." [2] Above all, he is impressed by the legal ignorance displayed in the story of the traitor Cawdor, concerning whom Angus

---

[1] Work cited, p. 96 *sq.*
[2] If so, it was popular nonsense. In Webster's *White Devil*, Brachiana tells Flamineo : " I will not grant your pardon. . . . Only a lease of your life ; and that shall last But for one day " (iv, 5, *end*).

alleges " treasons capital, confessed and proved," without being able to tell the king what they were.   In particular, Mr. Castle insists that the passage :

> Is execution done on Cawdor ?
> Are not those in commission yet returned ?

" is an inaccurate and improper expression," inasmuch as Cawdor had not been tried.   I leave this crux to the Baconians and the other legalists, merely noting that Mr. Castle finds " this condemnation of Cawdor to death without trial . . . the most convincing proof that Shakespeare had no legal assistance in writing this play."   The poet, he thinks, personally leant to the view that the king could condemn any one to death without trial—as did James, to the scandal of the lawyers, in the case of a cutpurse, on his journey to London to be crowned. Perhaps James had read RICHARD III !

40. From OTHELLO Lord Campbell contrives to wring a larger harvest than from any other play.   As thus :

(a) *Nonsuits* my mediators (i, 1).

(b) *Lawful prize* (ii, 2)—the trope indicating that there would be a suit in the High Court of Admiralty to determine the validity of the capture.

(c) The trial of Othello (i, 3) before the Senate as if he had been indicted on Stat. 33 Hen. VII, c. 8, for practising conjuration, witchcraft, enchantment, and sorcery, to provoke to unlawful love.

(d) The lines of Desdemona (iii, 3) :
> I'll intermingle everything he does
> With Cassio's *suit :* Therefore be merry, Cassio :
> For thy *Solicitor* shall rather die
> *Than give thy cause away.*

(e) Iago's line (*ib.*) :
> *Keep leets and lawdays,* and *in session sit.*

In (d) Desdemona's appeal, we are told, " is made to assume the shape of a juridical proceeding " ; in (e) the language " shows that Shakespeare was *well acquainted with all courts, low as well as high.*"   Noting the utter futility of the two last cited pleas, we can best rebut the

F

whole five instances by citing a much longer series of
" legal " passages from one play of Ben Jonson—EPICŒNE,
OR THE SILENT WOMAN :

They say he has been upon divers treaties with the fishwives
and orange-women, and articles propounded to them. (i, 1.)

It gives thee the law of plaguing him. . . . Disinherit thee !
he cannot, man. Art not thou next of blood, and his sister's
son ? (*Ib*.)

He shall never have that plea against me. (*Ib*.)

Have I ever cozened any friends of yours of their land ?
bought their possessions ? taken forfeit of their mortgage ?
begged a reversion for them ? (*Ib*.)

Daw. Syntagma juris civilis ; Corpus juris civilis ; corpus
juris canonici. . . .
Daup. What was that Syntagma, sir ?
Daw. A civil lawyer, a Spaniard.
Daup. Sure, Corpus was a Dutchman. (ii, 2.)

He's better read in *jure civile* than . . . (*Ib*.)

I'll kiss you, notwithstanding the justice of my quarrel. (iii, 2.)

I have an execution to serve upon them, I warrant thee, shall
serve. (iv, 2.)

Batter ! If he dare, I'll have an action of battery against him. (*Ib*.)

In addition, we have all the other Jonsonian legalisms
noted above and hereinafter—in all fifty times as much
" law " as Lord Campbell finds in OTHELLO.   It is doubtless a work of supererogation to cite parallels to " nonsuits," " lawful prize," " leets," and " sessions," but here
they are.   In one speech in a play of Jonson we have :

Pennyboy jun. But Picklock, what wouldst thou be ?   Thou
canst cant too.
Picklock. In all the languages in Westminster Hall,
Pleas, Bench, or Chancery.   Fee-farm, fee-tail
Tenant in dower, at will, for term of life,
By copy of court-roll, knight's service, homage,
Fealty, escuage, soccage, or frank almoigne,
Grand serjeantry, or burgage.
The Staple of News, iv, 1.

Had Lord Campbell found such a catalogue in Shakespeare, with what superlatives would he have cited it !

" Lawful prize " is a standing Elizabethan term : witness—

> 'Tis a lawful prize
> That's ta'en from pirates.
>> Dekker, *Match Me in London*, Act iii.
>> Pearson's ed. of Work, siv, 187.

> 'Twas lawful prize when I put out to sea
> And warranted in my commission
>> Heywood, *Edward IV*, Part II.
>> Pearson's ed. of Works, i, 123.

Take further the following :

> But now the sessions of my power's broke up,
> And you exposed to actions, warrants, writs ;
> For all the hellish rabble are broke loose
> Of serjeants, sheriffs, bailiffs.
>> Heywood, *The English Traveller*, iv, 5.

> There's subject for you ; and, if I mistake not,
> A *supersedeas* of your melancholy.
>> Jonson, *The Poetaster*, i, 1.

Many are the yearly enormities of this fair, in whose Courts of Pie-poudres I have had the honour, during the three days, sometimes to sit as judge.   *Id. Bartholomew Fair*, ii, 1.

> Such a plea
> As nonsuits all your princely evidence.
>> Greene, *Orlando Furioso*, Sc. 1.
> Set a *supersedeas* of my wrath.   *Id. ib.*

As for " leets and lawdays," it was evidently a standing phrase. In the publisher's or editor's address " to the Reader," prefaced to Latimer's Second Sermon before King Edward VI, 1549, we have :

Why, but be not lawyers diligent, say ye ? Yea truly are they ; about their own profit there are no more diligent men, nor busier persons in all England. They trudge, in the term time, to and fro. They apply the world hard. They foreslow ! They follow *assizes and sessions, leets, law-days, and hundreds*. They should serve the king, but they serve themselves.
Sermons by Hugh Latimer, Ed. in " Everyman's Library," p. 94.

This surely is not a lawyer's outburst !

Add that in a dozen other plays by non-lawyer dramatists of Shakespeare's day there are far more elaborate and realistic trials—to be noted hereafter—than any in Shakespeare, and the case founded on OTHELLO is done with.

41. Avowing that he can find no instance in JULIUS CÆSAR " of a Roman being made to talk like an English lawyer," Lord Campbell proceeds to claim that in ANTONY AND CLEOPATRA (i, 4) Lepidus " uses the language of a conveyancer's chambers in Lincoln's Inn " when he says that the faults of Antony seem " hereditary rather than *purchased ;* " adding in a footnote a citation of the king's lines in 2 HENRY IV, iv, 4 :

> What in me was *purchas'd*
> Falls upon thee in a more fairer sort.

The point is that in legal terminology " whatsoever does not come through operation of law by descent is *purchased*, although it may be the free gift of a donor." As we shall have occasion to go fully into this point later in connection with a similar claim by Mr. Grant White, it may suffice here to say that, as usual, Lord Campbell puts it in entire ignorance of the common phraseology of other Elizabethan dramatists and writers, and that we shall find the word used in the same way by them in scores of instances. What he describes as a specifically legal use of the term " purchase " was in fact the primary and normal sense of the word in English, as may be seen by tracing it through ordinary literature down to Shakespeare's day.

42. Citing the speech of Menenius in CORIOLANUS (ii, 1), reproaching the tribunes Sicinius and Brutus with their fashion of wasting time over trifling causes, and embroiling issues " between party and party " by wanton displays of impatience and temper, Lord Campbell argues that here " Shakespeare shows that he *must have been present* before some tiresome, testy, choleric judges at Stratford, Warwick, or Westminster." He admittedly " mistakes the duties of the *tribune* for those of the *prætor* " (a likely thing on the part of a trained lawyer !) ; but " in truth he was recollecting with disgust what he

had himself witnessed in his own country." And if so, what then ? Is this any proof of profound legal knowledge ? Where the claim is so feeble, it is hardly worth while to offer parallel instances ; but as usual, they are easily found. The testy and choleric judge, a lamentably common figure in Tudor England, [1] appears in Webster's WHITE DEVIL ; in Chapman's ADMIRAL OF FRANCE ; in Massinger's THE FATAL DOWRY, and in Lodge and Greene's LOOKING GLASS FOR LONDON. In the DUCHESS OF MALFY (i, 1) Webster makes Antonio say of the Duke that he " will seem to sleep o' the bench, Only to trap offenders." Is *this* such a reminiscence as proves legal training ?

43. Concerning ROMEO AND JULIET, we are assured that the first scene may " be studied by a student of the Inns of Court to acquire a knowledge of the law of assault and battery." Without bringing a microscope to bear on the few *minutiæ* put forward in support of this characteristic assertion, we may note that so much knowledge of the law of assault and battery could probably be picked up by any inhabitant of Stratford, to say nothing of those who attended the inferior courts of London. Lord Campbell himself evidently feels the triviality of the detail that the elder Montagu and Capulet are bound over, in the English fashion, " to keep the peace," as is Bobadill in EVERY MAN IN HIS HUMOUR. But he strives to make a good finish by citing Mercutio's phrase, " buy the fee simple of my life for an hour and a quarter " (iii, 1), and adding in a footnote that Parolles in ALL'S WELL (iv, 3) " is made to talk like a conveyancer of Lincoln's Inn "

---

[1] *See* Latimer's Third Sermon before Edward VI. Bishop Bale, recounting the Examination of Anne Askewe, tells of " the judges, without all sober discretion, running to the rack, tugging, hauling, and pulling thereat, like tormentors in a play. Compare me here," he adds, " Pilate with Wrisley, the high chancellor of England, with Rich, and with other . . . and see how much the pagan judge excelled in virtue and wisdom the false christned judge." *Select Works*, Parker Soc. rep. p. 241.

when he says : " He will sell the fee-simple of his salvation . . . and cut the entail from all remainders."

As we have already seen, the phrase " fee simple " is shown by other men's plays to have been a household word; but it may be well to conclude with further analogies and parallels :

> You helped me to three manors in fee-farm.[1]
> > Heywood, *Edward IV*, Pt. II.
> > Pearson's ed. of Works, i, 150.

There is only in the amity of women an estate for will, and every person knows that is no certain inheritance.
> > Webster and Dekker, *Westward Ho*, i, 2.

> Runs it [the warrant]
> Both without bail and mainprize ? [2]
> > Heywood, *The English Traveller*, iv, 1.

I'll hire thee for a year by the Statute of Winchester.
> > *Id.   The Wise Woman of Hogsdon*, ii, 1.

> Now thou art mine
> For one and twenty years, or for three lives,
> Choose which thou wilt, I'll make thee a copyholder,
> And thy first bill unquestioned.
> > Jonson, *The Staple of News*, i, 1.

They stand committed without bail or mainprize:
> > *Id. ib.* v, 2.

> I told you such a passage would disperse them
> Although the house were their fee-simple in law.
> > *Id.   The Magnetic Lady*, ii, 1, *near end*.

This concludes Lord Campbell's case as regards the plays. It remains to note his citations from the poems. They are nearly all instances of metaphor such as we have already dealt with :

1. But when the *heart's attorney* once is mute,
   The client breaks as desperate in the suit.
   > *Venus and Adonis*, l. 335.

2. Which *purchase* if thou make for fear of slips,
   Set thy *seal-manual* on my *wax-red* lips.
   > *Id.*   515–16.

3. Her *pleading* hath deserved a *greater fee*.   *Id.* 609.

---

[1] *This* term occurs only once in Shakespeare.
[2] *This* term never occurs in Shakespeare.

4. Dim *register* and *notary* of shame.

                         Rape of Lucrece, 765.

5. Since that *my case is past the help of law.*   *Id.* 1022.

6. No rightful *plea* might plead for justice here.   *Id.* 1649.

7. Hath served a dumb *arrest* upon his tongue.   *Id.* 1780.

8. When to the *sessions of sweet silent thought*
   I *summon up* remembrance of things past.   *Sonnet* 30.

9. So should that beauty which you hold *in lease.*

                              Sonnet 13.

10. And summer's *lease* hath all too short a date.

                              Sonnet 18.

11. And 'gainst thyself a *lawful plea* commence.

                              Sonnet 35.

12.   When that fell arrest
   Without all bail shall carry me away.   *Sonnet* 74.

13. Of faults concealed, wherein I am *attainted.*

                              Sonnet 88.

14. Which works on *leases* of short numbered hours.

                            Sonnet 124.

15. *Lord of my love,* to whom in *vassalage.*

                              Sonnet 26.

16. And I myself am *mortgag'd* to thy will.

                              Sonnet 134.

17. Why so large cost, having so *short a lease ?*

                              Sonnet 146.

18. So should that beauty which you *hold in lease*
   Find no determination.   *Sonnet* 13.

Finally, Sonnet 46 is quoted entire, with the claim that it " smells as potently of the attorney's office as any of the stanzas penned by Lord Kenyon while an attorney's clerk in Wales."

Hitherto, the legalist case has proceeded on the implicit assumption that Shakespeare chronically vitiates his art by putting in the mouths of lay characters phraseology which only lawyers could understand.   Now the implication is that he similarly flavours his sonnets and poems in a way that only a lawyer would have done.   Again, all that is necessary is to cast a glance over that contemporary poetry which Lord Campbell never takes into account.   This has already been duly done by Sir

Sidney Lee ; and it will here suffice to quote a few of the sonnets to which he points as the patterns and precedents [1] of those in which Shakespeare plays the lawyer :

> Then to Parthenophe, with all post haste
> (As full assurèd of the *pawn fore-pledged*),
> I made ; and with these words disordered placed
> Smooth (though with fury's sharp outrages edged).
> Quoth I, " Fair Mistress ! did I set mine Heart
> At liberty, and for that, made him free ;
> That you should win him for another start,
> Whose certain *bail* you promised to be ! "
> " Tush ! " quoth Parthenophe, " before he go,
> I'll be his *bail* at last, and doubt it not ! "
> " Why then," said I, " that *Mortgage* must I show
> Of your true love, which at your hands I got.
> Ay me ! She was and is his *bail*, I wot,
> But when the *Mortgage* should have cured the sore
> She passed it off, by *Deed of Gift* before.

Barnabe Barnes, *Parthenophil and Parthenophe,*
Sonnets, &c., 1593. Sonnet 8. (In rep. of
Arber's *Elizabethan Sonnets,* 1904, i, 173.)

> , . . . Why then, inhuman, and my secret foe,
> Didst thou betray me ? yet would be a woman !
> From my chief wealth, outweaving me this woe,
> Leaving thy love in *pawn*, till time did come on
> When that thy trustless *bonds* were to be *tried* !
> And when, through thy *default*, I thee did *summon*
> Into the *Court* of Steadfast Love, then cried,
> " As it was promised, here stands his Heart's *bail* !
> And if in *bonds* to thee my love be tied,
> Then by those *bonds* take *Forfeit of the Sale* ! "

Id. ib. Sonnet 11, as cited, p. 174.

> Those Eyes (thy Beauty's *Tenants !*) pay due tears
> For occupation of mine Heart, thy *Freehold*,
> In *tenure* of Love's service ! If thou behold

---

[1] Before the fashion of sonnets broke out as it did in the 'nineties, George Gascoigne had produced his poem " The Arraignment of a Lover " (in *Posies,* 1575), wherein the lover is tried at " Beauty's Bar," accused by False Suspect, whereon " Craft, the Crier, called a Quest," and after sentence " Jealous, the Jailor, bound we fast, To hear the verdict of the Bill " ; the procedure ending with " Faith and Truth my Sureties," than which there is " no better warrantise." *See* the poem in Arber's *Spenser Anthology,* p. 132 ; Gascoigne's Works, ed. Cunliffe, i, 38.

With what *exaction* it is held through fears ;
And yet thy *Rents, extorted* daily, bears.
  Thou wouldst not thus consume my quiet's gold !
And yet, though covetous thou be, to make
  Thy beauty rich, with *renting* me so roughly
And at such *sums*, thou never thought dost take
But still consumes me !   Then, thou dost misguide all !
  Spending in sport, for which I wrought so toughly !
When I had felt all torture, and had tried all ;
  And spent my stock through 'strain of thy extortion ;
On that, I had but good hopes for my portion.
                                   Id. ib. Sonnet 20, p. 181.

Shall we be told, in the absence of all biographical evidence;
that Barnes *must* have been a lawyer ?   There is simply
no legal trace of him.   But what is quite clear is that
Shakespeare had read his poems, published in 1593.   It
is not merely that he writes " legal " sonnets in Barnes's
fashion, and distinctly echoes him at various points :

A quest of thoughts all *tenants* to the Heart.
                                   Sonnet 46.

That fell arrest without all *bail*.
                                   Sonnet 73 (Cp. 133).
            Your *charter* is so strong
That you yourself may privilege your time.
                                   Sonnet 58 (Cp. 87).

—the two last recalling Barnes's

                    that charter,
Sealed with the wax of stedfast continence
                                   Sonnet 10,

and

            Thy love's large *Charter*,
                                   Sonnet 15 ;

but that there are so many echoes of *tune* and theme that
in reading Barnes one seems half the time to be hearing
undertones of the more powerful song of Shakespeare.
And as Lord Southampton was one of Barnes's as well
as one of Shakespeare's proclaimed patrons, the two men
are very likely to have been acquaintances.[1]   Shake-

---

[1] Dr. Creighton, in his *Shakespeare's Story of his Life* (1904),
works out a wildly speculative tale of Shakespeare's use of Barnes

speare's sonnets are in any case notably in the manner
of Barnes's, and he was following him in legalism as in
other fashions. And the same holds of his relation to the
anonymous sonneteer who in 1594 published the volume
entitled ZEPHERIA. Here we have the same trick of
legal phraseology :

> Mine eyes (quick pursuivants !) the sight attached
> Of Thee . . .
> Mine heart, Zepheria ! then became thy fee.
>> Canzon 3. Vol. II of *Eliz. Sonnets*, as cited, p. 158,
>
> Care's Usher ! Tenant to his own Oppression.
>> Canzon 5, p. 159,
> Wherein have I on love committed trespass ?
> O, if in justice thou must needs acquit me,
> Reward me with thy love.
>> Canzon 16, p. 165,

and so forth. Two complete " canzons " show how far
the fashion went :

> How often hath my pen (mine heart's Solicitor !)
> Instructed thee in Breviat of my case !
> While Fancy-pleading eyes (thy beauty's Visitor !)
> Have patterned to my quill, an angel's face.
> How have my Sonnets (faithful Counsellors !)
> Thee, without ceasing, moved for Day of Hearing !
> While they, my plaintive Cause (my faith's Revealers !)
> Thy long delay, my patience, in thine ear ring.
> How have I stood at bar of thine own conscience ;
> When in Requesting Court my suit I brought !
> How have thy long adjournments slowed the sentence,
> Which I (through much expense of tears) besought !
> Through many difficulties have I run ;
> Ah, sooner wert thou lost, I wis, than won !
> When last mine eyes dislodgèd from thy beauty,
> Though served with process of a parent's Writ :
> A Supersedeas countermanding duty,
> Even then, I saw upon thy smiles to sit !
> Those smiles which we invited to a Party,
> Disperpling clouds of faint respecting fear,
> Against the Summons which was served on me
> A larger privilege of dispense did bear.

as " devil " after lampooning him as Parolles. All this is idle
myth-mongering ; but the two men must have met.

Thine eyes' edict, the statute of Repeal,
  Doth other duties wholly abrogate,
Save such as thee endear in hearty zeal,
  Then be it far from me, that I should derogate
From Nature's Law, enregistered in thee !
So might my love incur a *Præmunire.*

It will hardly be disputed that either Shakespeare had read in manuscript, or heard some one quote, ZEPHERIA, or the sonneteer had read VENUS AND ADONIS. That one poet should write of his " heart's solicitor," and another of the " heart's attorney," by sheer coincidence, is not plausibly to be argued. And even if it could be proved; which it cannot, that the more lawyerlike poet was a lawyer, it would be sufficiently idle to contend that the other must also have been so, in view of what we have seen of the habit of legalism among all the dramatists of the day. We are witnessing a fashion of the time, comparable with the vogue of Euphuism. The many echoes and parallels of earlier sonnets in those of Shakespeare are weighty hints of the slightness of our ground for taking his as direct records of his heart's experience. Even when he youthfully imitated other men's modes, he could not but give to his echoes the deeper vibration of his larger spirit, even as he avoided his models' grosser crudities. In ZEPHERIA, the canzon last above cited is followed by two in which we have the barbarisms " irrotulate " and " foyalty," " excordiate " and " exordiate "—outrages possible to a pedant, but not to our poet. But however his finer taste and deeper feeling might preserve him from such offences, he is none the less mannered by the " form and pressure " of the time, which in this matter of legalist vocabulary and imagery is nearly universal. The Elizabethan sonneteers, like the old troubadours, have their tunes and themes in common, and each man's collection is visibly suggested by or suggestive of others. Their very titles, PHILLIS, LICIA, DELIA, DIANA, COELIA, IDEA, ZEPHERIA, FIDESSA, CHLORIS, LAURA, tell of a reigning mode, setting in with Sidney's ASTROPHEL AND

STELLA, and drawing much on French originals. It was in full force in 1593, and culminated about 1597—the years between which we know Shakespeare to have written many of his " sugred sonnets." That he should copy a particular fashion as he copied the general was entirely natural. Drayton, who was no lawyer, but was a poet, could not so far resist the legalist craze as to abstain from working out in one Sonnet [1] the fancy that his mistress may be tried for murdering his heart :

> The verdict on the view
> Do quit the dead, and me not accessory.
> Well, well ! I fear it will be proved of you !
> The Evidence so great a proof doth carry.

Shakespeare had thus the example, in these matters, of a poet whom he could not but esteem, and whom in one of his later sonnets he has so closely imitated that there can be no question of the influence. In this case the parallel is so striking that once more we are led to doubt the primary character of the experience suggested in Shakespeare's sonnet :

DRAYTON

> An Evil Spirit (your Beauty) haunts me still,
>   Wherewith, alas, I have been long possest ;
> Which ceaseth not to attempt me to each ill,
>   Nor gives me once, but one poor minute's rest.
> In me it speaks, whether I sleep or wake ;
>   And when by means to drive it out I try,
> With greater torments then it me doth take,
>   And tortures me in most extremity.
> Before my face, it lays down my despairs,
>   And hastes me on unto a sudden death :
> Now tempting me to drown myself in tears ;
>   And then in sighing to give up my breath.
> Thus am I still provoked to every evil,
> By this good-wicked Spirit, sweet Angel-Devil.
>   No. 22 in 1599 ed. of *Idea* ; No. 20 in ed. cited, p. 191.

---

[1] No. 51 of ed. 1599 of *Idea ;* No. 2 in reprint in *Elizabethan Sonnets*, as cited, ii, 182.

SHAKESPEARE

Two loves I have, of comfort and despair
    Which like two spirits do suggest me still :
The better angel is a man right fair,
    The worser spirit a woman, colour'd ill.
To win me soon to hell, my female evil
    Tempteth my better angel from my side,
And would corrupt my saint to be a devil,
    Wooing his purity with her foul pride.
And whether that my angel be turned fiend,
    Suspect I may, yet not directly tell ;
But being both from me, both to each friend,
    I guess one angel in another's hell :
Yet this shall I ne'er know, but live in doubt,
Till my bad angel fire my good one out.

Sonnet 144.

Drayton has told in another sonnet (21) how :

A witless Gallant, a young wench that wooed. . . .
    Intreated me, as e'er I wished his good,
    To write him but one Sonnet to his Love ;

and how he did so, with the success desired. It is not
easy to believe that these sombre lines of Shakespeare's
were but such an exercise. Yet they may have been.
In any case, there is no excuse now left for imputing to
an overmastering devotion to law, the result of a deep legal
training, the legalisms in which he outwent Drayton.

So far from being " lawyerlike " in the sense of striking
the literary note natural to a trained lawyer, they struck
such a lawyer, to wit Sir John Davies, as rather ridiculous.
Davies, in one of his " gulling sonnets," avowedly parodies
the legalist sonnets of the poet of ZEPHERIA ; and he
seems to have had before him in manuscript Shakespeare's
Sonnet 26 when he penned his parody beginning :

To love, my lord, I do Knight's service owe.

" B. Griffin, Gent." who dedicated his FIDESSA (1596) to
the Gentlemen of the Inns of Court, and was presumably
one of them, makes only one slight excursion into legal
imagery in his sonnets. Yet the Baconians would have
us believe that Bacon, who in his non-legal works so

rarely resorts to legal phraseology, touched the sonnets
with it so abundantly by reason of a natural professional
propensity.

In this connection, however, it is hardly necessary
to consider the theorem which, on the strength of the
legalisms and of the fixed Baconian idea, would ascribe
to Francis Bacon, as a real expression of experience, all
the Sonnets. In no other aspect and over no other
issue is that theorem more staggering to judgment.   But
we shall recur to it in a later chapter.   For the present
it is enough to have shown how entirely nugatory is the
non-comparative process by which Lord Campbell has
unwittingly fooled the Baconians to the top of their bent.
Citing him, they have relieved themselves of the trouble
of outgoing his research.   The whole phenomenon is
a warning instance of the heedless pretence, and the more
heedless acceptance, of authority in criticism. " All law
critics admit," says Dr. R. Theobald,[1] that such language
as that of the 46th Sonnet " is not the writing of an
amateur but of an expert."   Lord Campbell alone is cited
for the " all " : Mr. Devecmon's counter-doctrine is unknown to the Baconian.   We have seen the value of Lord
Campbell's pronouncement, and we shall similarly
examine some others.

But critics like Dr. Theobald, themselves habitually
dogmatising on a basis of literary ignorance, are willingly
at the mercy of any false evidence that chimes with
their predilection.   " Lawyers say," writes Dr. Theobald,
" that one of the most difficult things to acquire in their
profession is the phraseology."   Dr. Theobald need only
have read in the Elizabethan drama a little further than
he went for material to prove that Bacon wrote Shakespeare and Marlowe, in order to learn that the lawyers
talked ignorantly.   When, however, he proceeds to help
them in their mystification by asserting that " the outsider is *sure*, sooner or later, to be found out.   He will

[1] *Shakespeare Studies in Baconian Light*, 1904, p. 19.

traverse what he approves (!),—or *empanel* a witness (!) instead of a jury—or in some way his legal chatter will degenerate into jargon." On this principle, Dr. Theobald's assent to the lawyer's claim is of no value ; he being no lawyer. Unable to illustrate his proposition save by imaginary enormities of blundering, he must by his own account be unable to detect any slighter deviations from legal accuracy. Then his endorsement of their *expertise* is admittedly worthless to start with.

Lawyers of literary competence will be the first to admit, on a study of the case, that Lord Campbell's handling of the literary problem before us partakes of the nature of literary charlatanism ; and that Lord Penzance's professed " summing-up " of the Bacon-Shakespeare problem, being a grossly *ex parte* statement, is entitled to neither lay nor professional respect. In this matter the sole authorities are critical reason and literary evidence. Unhappily we shall find some professed Shakespearean scholars as uncritical as the judges.

CHAPTER IV

THE ARGUMENT FROM LEGAL PHRASEOLOGY:
MR. GRANT WHITE'S CASE.

UNCRITICAL as are the arguments alike of Lord Campbell and the Baconians about the legal learning of Shakespeare, they are not more so than those put forth to the same effect by Mr. Grant White, a Shakespearean scholar and a hearty contemner of the entire Baconian theory. From him Mr. Greenwood is able to cite the allegation that

legal phrases flow from his (Shakespeare's) pen as part of his vocabulary, and parcel of his thought. Take the word "purchase," for instance, which in ordinary use means to acquire by giving value, but applies in law to all legal modes of obtaining property except by inheritance or descent, and in this peculiar sense the word occurs five times in Shakespeare's thirty-four plays, and only in one single instance in the fifty-four plays of Beaumont and Fletcher. ![1]

This passage, which follows Lord Campbell's lead, forms part of a longer one in which the infirmity of Mr. White's handling of the problem lies on the surface.

Malone [he writes], noticing the frequency with which Shakespeare uses law terms, conjectured that he had passed some of his adolescent years in an attorney's office. In support of his conjecture, Malone, himself a barrister, cited twenty-four passages distinguished by the presence of law phrases ; and to these he might have added many more. *But the use of such phrases is by no means peculiar to Shakespeare.* The writings of the poets and playwrights of his period, Spenser, Drayton, Greene, Beaumont and Fletcher, Middleton, Donne, and many

---

[1] *Memoirs of William Shakespeare* in 1866 ed. of *Shakespeare's Works*, I, pp. xlv. Repr. later.

others of less note, are *thickly sprinkled with them.*   In fact *the application of legal language to the ordinary affairs of life was more common two hundred and fifty years ago than it is now ; though even nowadays the usage is far from uncommon in the rural districts.   There law shares with agriculture the function of providing those phrases of common conversation which, used figuratively at first, and often with poetic feeling, pass into mere thought-saving formulas of speech.*

Having thus reached a point of view from which his own theory is manifestly open to suspicion, since the first purpose of drama must be to be " understanded of the people," Mr. White nevertheless proceeds to offer " reasons for believing that Shakespeare had more than a layman's knowledge of the law."   Yet the sole " reason " suggested is the merest begging of the question.   Needy young lawyers in the Elizabethan period, we are told, turned to play-writing as they now do to journalism ; " and of those who had been successful in their dramatic efforts how inevitable it was that many would give themselves up to play-writing, and that *thus* the language of the plays of that time should show a remarkable infusion of law phrases."   That is to say, we expect to find lawyer-dramatists filling their plays with law.   Then comes the logical somersault :

To what, then, must we attribute *the fact* that of all the plays that have survived of those written between 1580 and 1620 Shakespeare's are most noteworthy in this respect ?   For no dramatist of the time, not even Beaumont, who was a younger son of a Judge of the Common Pleas, and who, after studying in the Inns of Court, abandoned law for the drama, used legal phrases with Shakespeare's readiness and exactness.

Shakespeare; that is to say, is more given to legalisms than are the lawyer dramatists, and must therefore have been much more of a lawyer than they !   Shakespeare, accordingly, is likely to have had not the mere superficial training of a lawyer's clerk ;   the probability is that he

was allowed to commence his studies for a profession for which his cleverness fitted him—and that he continued those studies until his father's misfortunes, aided, perhaps, by some of those

G

acts of youthful indiscretion which clever lads as well as dull
ones will sometimes commit, threw him upon his own resources ;
and that then, law failing to supply his pressing need, he turned
to the stage, on which he had townsmen and friends.

Thus a new hypothesis, outgoing all tradition, and
resting on no shred of direct testimony, is superimposed
on a dubious tradition, by way of supporting an un-
proved assumption. For Mr. White does not make one
attempt to reach a true quantitative or qualitative
estimate of the legal element in Shakespeare and his
contemporaries by way of detailed comparison. He
makes the blank affirmation, and merely follows it up
with the before-cited passage about purchase, and by a
further non-comparative recital of legal terms from the
Shakespearean plays in rebuttal of the view that the
whole vocabulary may have been acquired by haunting
the law courts.

Those terms his use of which is *most remarkable* . . . are not
such as he would have heard at ordinary proceedings at *nisi
prius*, but such as refer to the tenure or transfer of real property—
" fine and recovery," " statutes marchant," " purchase," " indenture," " tenure," " double voucher," " fee simple," " fee
farm," " remainder," " reversion," " forfeiture," &c. This
conveyancer's jargon could not have been picked up by hanging
round the courts of law in London two hundred and fifty years
ago, *when suits as to the title to real property were comparatively
rare.* And besides, Shakespeare uses his law just as freely in
his early plays, written in his first London years, as in those
produced at a later period.

It is necessary to show in some detail that we have
here, once more, merely a forensic " bluff " ; and it is
hardly possible to begin the demonstration without a
word of protest against the hand-to-mouth fashion in
which a critic who was most unsparing in his denunciation
of other men's laxities and inadequacies went about a
task which obviously called for the most exact critical
procedure. He has been so heedless as to assign to
Shakespeare the common phrase " statutes marchant,"
which is not to be found in any of the plays or poems,

while he cites eight terms which are to be found by the hundred in Elizabethan drama. But his lack of caution becomes still more clear when we examine the first-cited illustration, upon which he most relies—that which turns upon the word " purchase." In point of fact the words " purchase," " purchased," " purchaseth," and " purchasing " occur in all some fifty times in Shakespeare's plays, and twice in LUCRECE, and they have their primary force—which Mr. White fallaciously reduces to a " legal " one—far oftener than five times, else Shakespeare would indeed have been peculiar among his contemporaries in giving the word its secondary and modern force. By the definition " *legal* modes of obtaining property " the critic merely obscures the fact that the term covered *all* modes of acquisition save inheritance. There was no more a " legal " sense of the *term* " purchase " than there was or is of the term " property " or " obtain " : the law simply discriminated, on legal lines, between right and wrong *modes of "purchase."* To pick out cases in the plays in which " purchase " means *lawful* acquisition is thus pure mystification : any lawyer, even, might say " lawful purchase " by way of expressly distinguishing between lawful and unlawful purchase, as he might say " stolen property " on occasion. As Mr. White does not specify his five cases, and Mr. Greenwood, quoting Mr. White as he quotes Lord Campbell, makes no scrutiny of the assertion, I will simply clear the matter up by citing many instances of the use of the quasi-" legal " use of the word in other writers and dramatists, noting that it is frequently applied in the sense of " booty " or plunder. To begin with, Mr. White is merely mystifying us in his assertion that the " legal " sense of " purchase " occurs only once in Beaumont and Fletcher's fifty-four dramas. In its original and general sense, which *is* the " legal," it occurs twice in one of their plays : '

> *Lovegood.*   I thought till now
> There had been no such living, no such purchase

> (For all the rest is labour), as a list
> Of mensurable friends.
> > *Wit without Money*, iii, 4.

> *Luce.*   Must every slight companion that can purchase
> A show of poverty, and beggarly planet [?],
> Fall under your compassion ?
> > *Ib*. iv, 4.

—these being the only instances of the word, in any application, in the play in question.   And it occurs repeatedly in others by the same authors :

> *Morecraft*. I purchased, wrung, and wire-drawed for my wealth, lost, and was cozened.
> > *The Scornful Lady*, v, 4.

(Here the meaning is " got by stratagems "—within the limits of the law.)

> *Dinant*. Yet, but consider how this wealth was purchased [= acquired] . . .
> > In brief,
> All you shall wear, or touch, or see, is *purchased*
> By *lawless force* [prize-taking at sea].
> > *The Little French Lawyer*, i, 1.

> Let us enjoy our purchase [= capture].
> > *Ib*. iv, 6.

Again, these two last are the only instances of the word " purchase " in the play cited.

A partial collation of Beaumont and Fletcher's large mass of work yields the following additional instances :

> You make me more a slave still to your goodness,
> And only live to purchase thanks to pay you.
> > *A King and No King*, iv, 1.

> [Can] his arms rust in ease
> That bears the charge, and sees the honoured purchase
> Ready to gild his valour ?
> > *Thierry and Theodoret*, iv, 1.

> I hear some noise : it may be new purchase [= booty].
> > *Ib*. v, 1.

> Here, you dull slaves : purchase, purchase ! the soul of the rock, diamonds, sparkling diamonds !
> > *Id. ib.*

Why, what remains but new nets for [= to effect] the purchase.
Valentinian, i, 1, end.

    Let not this body . . . now be purchase
    For slaves and base informers.
Id. i, 3, end.

Can any but a chastity serve Cæsar,
And such a one the gods would kneel to purchase.
Id. iv, 1.

I need no company to that, that children
Dare do alone, and slaves are proud to purchase.
Id. iv, 4.

    To purchase fair revenge.
Id. v, 2.

What have I got by this now ? what's the purchase ?
The Chances, i, 1.

My holy health . . . to purchase which . . .
Monsieur Thomas, v, 4.

I have purchased to myself, besides mine own undoing, the ill opinion of my friends.
Knight of the Burning Pestle, iv, 3.

This sessions, purchased at your suit, Don Henrique,
Hath brought us hither.
The Spanish Curate, iii, 3.

    Grant he purchase
Precedency in the country.
The Elder Brother, i, 1.

    Oh, Honour !
How greedily men seek thee, and, once purchased,
How many enemies to man's peace bringst thou !
The Prophetess, iii, 3.

The philological fact is that the sense of " acquisition," " a thing got," is the fundamental meaning of the word " purchase," of which the starting-point is the idea of the chase (Fr. *pourchasser*), the product of hunting or foraging. It is the idea of buying that is secondary, though that has now become the normal force of the word. That is to say, the so-called " legal " meaning of " acquisition of property by one's personal action as distinct from inheritance " is the original meaning, and is the likely sense of the word in the whole feudal period. The meaning of " buy " is merely an evolution from that, buying being a common way of obtaining, a *mode* of " purchase." The fact that " purchase " still means " hold "—as in " get a purchase on a rope "—shows the primary meaning subsisting on one line of extension while it has ceased on another.   But down to the age of Shakespeare the original and quasi-legal sense was normal.   To begin with, that use of the word in ordinary literature is established as early as Chaucer.   Professor Skeat there assigns to the verb the meanings " to procure or acquire, to win, to buy, to promote, to contrive, to provide ; " and to the noun the meanings " proceeds, gifts acquired, gain ; " with the further sense of " conveyancing " in the form " purchasing." [1]   In the Canterbury Tales we have :

> His purchas was wel better than his rente ;
> *Prologue,* 256.

and again :

> My purchas is the effect of al my rente.
> *Frere's Tale,* 1451.

Yet again, in another place, we have :

> My purchas is better than my rent.
> *Romaunt of the Rose,* 6837.

In Troilus and Criseyde also (iv, 557) we have :

> Sin wel I wot I may her not purcháce

—in the sense of " obtain."   And again in the Prologue we have a secondary use (318–20) :

> So greet a purchasour was nowher noon.
> Al was fee symple to him in effect,
> His purchasyng myghté not been infect.

That is, he (the Sergeant) was a great conveyancer, whose conveyancing could not be impugned.   In The Persone's Tale, in the phrase " for to purchasen many earthly things (sent. 742), and in the Tale of Melibeus (§ 55), in the phrase " they that loven and purchasen

---

[1] *Prol. to Cant. Tales,* l. 320.   Other scholars (*see* Glossary of Globe ed.) assign the meanings " prosecuting " and " prosecutor " in the case of the description of the Man of Lawe.   Skeat's seems the correct view.   In the *Frere's Tale,* 1449, however, purchasing means acquiring.

peace," the meaning is clearly the primary one. We have the word again in Langland :

> And purchased him a pardon
> *A pœna et a culpa*——
> Manye wepten for joie
> And preiseden Piers the Plowman
> That purchased this bulle.
>
> *Vision of Piers Ploughman,*
> ed. Wright, 4469–70, 4538–40.

—where the idea is not buying but obtaining. It has the same force in the phrase "favour craftily purchasing" in Roye's Rede me and be nott Wrothe (1528) and in Sir Thomas More's Dialogue of Comfort against Tribulation (1534) :

> If we might once purchase the grace to come to that point,
>
> Dent's rep. with *Utopia*, p. 187 ;

and again, in the editor's preface to Latimer's Second Sermon before Edward VI, the word is used in the alleged "legal" sense, though the writer is ostensibly a foe to lawyers :

> Thou that purchasest so fast, to the utter undoing of the poor.
>
> *Sermons of Latimer*, Dent's rep. p. 90.

Obviously this was the regular force of the term, and it is in that sense that Latimer himself uses it :

> A certain great man that had purchased much lands.
>
> *Last Sermon before King Edward*, ed. cited, p. 240.

So in Roger Hutchinson :

> Now they [who "were wont to . . . maintain schools and houses of alms "] be purchasers and sellers-away of the same.
>
> *Epistle to Archbishop Cranmer ;* Parker Soc. vol. of Works, p. 4.

In theology the term is often used metaphorically with the same force : *e.g.*

> The everlasting heritage which he [Christ] hath purchased for us.
>
> Trans. of *Calvin on Ephesians*, 15, fol. 146, *verso*.

A metaphorical use of the word, resting on the " legal " sense, was in fact normal throughout Tudor literature ; and a dozen instances of it may be found in the early version (from the Italian) of the Phœnissæ of Euripides by Gascoigne and others under the title of Jocasta (1566). It is common, again, in Spenser, in various senses which all turn upon the alleged " legal " one :

> For on his back a heavy load he bare
> Of nightly stelths and pillage severall
> Which he had got abroad by purchas criminall.
>> *Faerie Queene*, B. I, C. iii, St. 16.

> That [sword] shall I shortly purchase to your hand.
>> *Id.* B. II, C. iii, St. 18.

> Made answere that the mayd of whom they spake
> Was his owne purchase and his onely prize.
>> *Id.* B. VI, C. xi, St. 12.

> Sicker I hold him for a greater fon (fool)
> That loves the thing he cannot purchase.
>> *Shepheard's Calendar*, 158–9.

Again in the prose dedication of Muiopotmos he has :

> That honourable name which ye have by your brave deserts purchast to yourself.

In Puttenham's prose this sense of the term is explicit :

> No doubt the shepheard's . . . trade was the first act of lawful acquisition or purchase, for at these days robbery was a manner of purchase.
>> *Art of Poetrie*, Arber's rep., p. 53.

That the word was in normal Elizabethan use in the quasi-legal sense might be inferred from its occurring twice metaphorically with such a meaning in Nicholas Breton's Tom the Page's Song :

> Faith ! she will say, you wicked page !
> I'll purchase you an heritage.

> To purchase me an heritage.
>> *Joys of an Idle Head*, in *A Flourish uponFancy*, 1582.
>> Rep. in Arber's *Spenser Anthology*, 1899, p. 187.

In homiletic literature it has the same metaphorical force :

> Thereby purchase to himself . . . eternal damnation.
>> Stubbes, *Anatomie of Abuses*, Collier's Rep. p. 37.
>> Again, p. 68.

And unless we are to suppose that all the dramatists

alike made their personages talk out of character—as in effect the legalists imply that Shakespeare did—we must draw the same inference from their plays, for they all introduce the word in the broad primary sense, and this far more often than in the limited modern one :

> He that will purchase things of greatest prize
> Must conquer by his deeds, and not by words.
> > Lilly, *Woman in the Moon*, ii, 1.

> My valour everywhere shall purchase friends.
> > Kyd, *Soliman and Perseda*, IV, ii, 6.

> To purchase Godhead, as did Hercules.
> > *Id. ib.* l. 19.

> To purchase fame to our posterities.
> > *Id. Cornelia*, v, 5.

> His company hath purchased me ill friends.
> > *Arden of Feversham*, v, 1 [twice].

> *Jeron.* How like you Don Horatio's spirit ?
> What, doth it promise fair ?
> *K. of Spain.* Ay, and no doubt his merit will purchase more.
> > *First Part of Jeronimo* [1605] Sc. i, ll. 17–19.

> *Sadoc.* God save Lord Cusay.   And direct his zeal
> To purchase David's conquest 'gainst his son.
> > Peele, *David and Bethsabe*, iii, 2.

> To purchase hearing with my lord the King.
> > *Id. ib.*

> *Messenger.* How many friends I purchase everywhere.
> > *King Leir and his Three Daughters*, Sc. 17.

> That purchas'd kingdoms by your martial deeds.
> > Marlowe, I. *Tamb.* v, 2, end.

> To purchase towns by treachery.
> > *Id. Jew of Malta*, v, 4.

> He that will not when he may
> When he desires shall surely purchase nay.
> > Greene, *Alphonsus King of Arragon*, v, ed. Dyce, p. 245.

> Your pardon is already purchased.
> > *Id. ib.* p. 246.

Greene uses the word in the same way in his prose tales :

He thought no victuals to have their taste which were not purchased by his own sweat.
> *Id.* Tale of *Perimedes the Blacksmith* [1588],
> Works, ed. Grosart, vii, 12.

Thou may'st practise virtue if thou take heed, or purchase discredit if thou beest careless.

> *Id. Card of Fancy.* Works, iv, 20.

and in his play JAMES IV (v, 4) :

The crafty men have purchased great men's lands.

Jonson in his plays uses it many times :

> I glory
> More in the cunning purchase of my wealth
> Than in the glad possession.
>
> Jonson, *Volpone*, i, 1, near beginning.

A diamond, plate, chequines.   Good morning's purchase.
[In this case — acquisitions by gift].

> *Id. ib.* near end of Scene.

Do you two pack up all the goods and purchase.
[In this case = cheaters' booty].

> *Ib.* iv, 4.

I think I must be enforced to purchase me another page.

> *Id. Cynthia's Revels*, ii, 1.

I will not rob you of him, nor the purchase.

> *Id. The Magnetic Lady*, v, 6, end.

Wittipol.   I will share, Sir,
In your sports only, nothing in your purchase [in this case = gains].

> *The Devil is an Ass*, iii, 1.

> This second blessing of your eyes
> Which now I've purchased.
>
> *Ib.* i, 1.

Purchase to themselves rebuke and shame.

> *Sejanus*, iii, 1.

(Here the sense is " attained to."   Wittipol would not tell the lady that he has bought the sight of her.)

No less common is the word in Webster and his collaborators :

> I will not purchase by thee [Laverna] but to eat.
>
> Webster and Rowley, *A Cure for a Cuckold*, ii, 1.

And will redeem myself with purchase [= booty].

> *Id.* ii, 2.

> Of all my being, fortunes, and poor fame
> (If I have purchased any) . . .
> You have been the sole creatress.
>
> *Id.* iii, 3.

I made a purchase lately, and in that
I did estate the child—
Joint-purchaser in all the land I bought.

Id. iv, 1.

Ignorance, when it hath purchased honour,
It cannot wield it.

Webster, *Duchess of Malfi*, ii, 3.

Were all of his mind, to entertain no suits
But such they thought were honest, sure our lawyers
Would not purchase half so fast.

Id. The Devil's Law Case, iv, 1.

They do observe I grew to infinite purchase
The left-hand way.

Id, iii, 1.

That noblemen shall come with cap and knee
To purchase a night's lodging of their wives.

Id. iii, 2.

In the same sense we have it in Randolph :

Here is a conquest purchas'd without blood.

The Jealous Lovers, i, 10.

In Thomas Heywood the word is particularly frequent :

I'll gain her, or in her fair quest
Purchase my soul free and immortal rest.

Heywood, *A Woman Killed with Kindness*, iii, 1.

I have a trade,
And in myself a means to purchase wealth.

Id. The Foure Prentises of London, i, 1.

They are all on fire
To purchase [= win booty] from the Spaniard.

Id. The Fair Maid of the West, i, 1.

Now could your lady purchase
Their pardon from the king.
[Here the force is, " obtain by favour "].

Id. ib. v, 1.

I'll purchase 't with a danger.
Id. Part II, *Fair Maid of the West*. Pearson's
Heywood, ii, 349.

Purchased by this bold answer.

Id. ib. p. 350.

Show me the way
To gain this royal purchase.

Id. ib. p. 350.

Not to do it
May purchase his displeasure.

Id. ib. p. 351.

Here the word is used in the quasi-legal sense four times in three successive pages. But it constantly recurs in the same general sense, as distinct from that of buying.

To purchase to yourself a thrifty son.

Id. The English Traveller, iv, 6.

Could I have purchased houses at that rate,
I had meant to have bought all London.
[Here the sense is " acquired by fraud "].

Id. ib.

Your grace may purchase glory from above,
And entire love from all your people's hearts.

Id. If you know not me you know nobody. Pt. I
Pearson's Heywood, i, 225.

When my poor wife and children cry for bread,
They still must cry till these [hands and spade] have purchast it.

Id. ib. Part II, ed. cited, p. 304.

My love to her may purchase me his love.

Id. Pt. I of King Edward IV, ed. cited, i, 129.

Jupiter. Hadst thou asked love, gold, service, Empiry,
This sword had purchased for Callisto all.

Id. The Golden Age, ii, 1, ed. cited, iii, 26.

I'll wake her
Unto new life. This purchase I must win.

Id. ib. iv, 1, p. 68.

Saturn. Re-purchast and re-lost by Jupiter.

Id. ib. v, 1, p. 75.

I'll try conclusions,
And see if I can purchase it with blows.

Id. ib. p. 76.

Pluto. Ceres nor Jove, nor all the Gods above,
Shall rob me this rich purchase [Proserpine].

Id. The Silver Age, iii, vol. cited, p. 137.

Hercules. We take but what our valour purchast us.

Id. The Brazen Age, i, 1, p. 177.

Atreus. Without some honour purchast on this Boar.

Id. ib. p. 188.

Meleager. To have purchased honour in this hasty quest.

Id. ib. p. 189.

Thou hast purchast honour and renown enough.

Id. ib. p. 192.

> *Jason.*   Rename all Greece
> By the rich purchase of the Colchian fleece.
> > *Id. ib.* p. 203.
>
> *Hercules.*   Now is the rich and precious fleece
> By Jason's sword repurchast.
> > *Id. ib.* p. 218.
>
> *Medea.*   To redeem the fleece,
> And it repurchase with your tragic deaths.
> > *Id. ib.* p. 219.
>
> *Hercules.*   She is the warlike purchase of thy sword.
> > *Id. ib.* p. 225.
> And by our deeds repurchase our renown.
> > *Id. ib.* p. 246.

Here we have the word used nine times in one play, and *only* in the primary sense. For Heywood, in fact, " purchase " *normally* means acquisition otherwise than by inheritance or buying ; and there is no inference open save that this was a normal sense of the word in his day. But we have it also in Dekker :

> That would have purchased sin alone to himself.
> > Dekker.   *The Honest Whore*, Pt. I, ii, 1.
>
> The purchase [booty] is rich.
> > *Ib.* Pt. II, iv, 1.
> It shall concern thee and thy love's purchase.
> *The Witch of Edmonton*, by Rowley, Dekker, Ford, &c. iii, 1.

Of this as of other " legal " uses of terms we have frequent examples in the prose of Nashe :

> It may be that he meaneth about purchasing [acquiring property] as he hath done.
> > *First part of Pasquil's Apology.*   Works, ed.
> > McKerrow, i, 128.
>
> That recantation purchased his liberty.
> > *Four Letters Confuted.*   Vol. cited, p. 297.
>
> Their purchased [=granted by the King] prerogatives.
> > *Nashe's Lenten Stuff*, ed. cited, iii, 165.
>
> Voyages of Purchase of Refusals.
> > *Id.* p. 180.
>
> Men that have no means to purchase credit with their prince.
> > *Id.* p. 218.

In Massinger the usage abounds :

> Style not that courtship, madam, which is only
> Purchased on your part.
>
> *A New Way to Pay Old Debts*, i, 2.

> By that fair name I in the wars have purchased.
>
> *Id.* iii, 1.

> Purchased with his blood that did oppose me.
>
> *Id.* iii, 2.

> Honour
> By virtuous ways achieved, and bravely purchased.
>
> *Id.* iv, 1.

> I can do twenty [tricks] neater, if you please,
> To purchase and grow rich.
>
> *Id.* v, near end.

> the knowledge of
> A future sorrow, which, if I find out,
> My present ignorance were a cheap purchase.
>
> *The Picture*, i, 1.

> this bubble honour . . .
> With the loss of limbs or life is, in my judgment,
> Too dear a purchase.
>
> *Id.* i, 2.

There are other toys about you the same way purchased
[=received in gift].

> *Id.* iii, 6.

> I would not lose this purchase [=gain].
>
> *The City Madam*, v, 1.

> This felicity, not gained
> By vows to saints above, and much less purchased
> By thriving industry.
>
> *Id. ib.* v, 3.

> I shall break
> If at this rate [by marriage] I purchase you.
>
> *Id. The Guardian*, i, 1.

> Here purchase the reward that was propounded.
>
> *Id. The Virgin Martyr*, v, near end.

> The danger in the purchase of the prey.
>
> *Id. The Unnatural Combat*, ii, 1.

> You have purchased
> This honour at a high price [moral].
>
> *Id. ib.*

> My scrip, my tar-box, hook, and coat, will prove
> But a thin purchase [=booty].
>
> *Id. The Bashful Lover*, iii, 1.

> I would purchase
My husband by such benefits.

> *Id. ib.* iii, 2, near end.

> I will practise
All arts for your deliverance, and that purchased . . .

> *Id.   The Bondman,* v, 2.

And it is frequent in Chapman :

> Borrowing
With thee is purchase.

> *Byron's Conspiracy,* i, 1.

> My purchased honours.

> *The Admiral of France,* ii, 2.

> Consume
All he hath purchased.

> *All Fools,* i, 1.

> While we abroad fight for new Kingdoms' purchase.

> *Revenge for Honour,* ii, 1.

> So much I prize the sweetness
Of that unvalued purchase.

> *Id.* iv, 1.

> Then your purchase holds.

> *The Ball,* ii, 2.

We have it in the anonymous play NERO [1624] :

> That heady and adventurous crew
That go to lose their own to purchase but
The breath of others and the common voice.   i, 3.

and in Henry Porter's TWO ANGRY WOMEN OF ABINGTON :

> What shall I do purchase company ? (v, 1)

It seems unnecessary to carry the comparison further. The primary and quasi-" legal " sense of " purchase," so far from being peculiar to Shakespeare, is far more common than the other in the dramas of other writers in his and the next generation.   And so absolutely normal was this use of the word that it enters into the old rhymed version of the Psalms, authorised for use in the churches in 1645 :

> The swallow also for herself
Hath purchased a nest.   Ps. lxxxiv, 3.[1]

[1] Hopkins' sixteenth-century version of this Psalm, still retained in Scotland.   Tate and Brady (1696) give a changed rendering.

When therefore we find the word used by Bacon (ESSAY OF HONOUR AND REPUTATION) we are not reading a legalism imposed on *belles lettres* by a lawyer, but a current English word used in its current meaning.[1]   So widely was that meaning established that we find it as late as 1727 in a preface of Bishop Warburton's :

> For now the Invention of Printing hath made it [the usage of dedications] a Purchase for the Vulgar.
> *A Critical and Philosophical Enquiry into the Causes*
> *of Prodigies and Miracles*, 1727, ded. p. vii.

For the rest, Mr. Grant White's general case is obviously as void as that of Lord Campbell.   To say no more of his divagation over the term " purchase," it is astonishing that such a scholar, who must have had a general acquaintance with the Elizabethan and Stuart drama, should find evidence of special and technical knowledge of conveyancing in the bare use of such terms and phrases " fine and recovery," " indenture," " tenure," " double voucher," " fee simple," " remainder," " reversion," and " forfeiture."   A perusal of two plays of Massinger's might have led the critic to cancel his whole thesis.   In A NEW WAY TO PAY OLD DEBTS we have, in addition to the passages already cited, this swarm of legal terms :

> On forfeiture of their licences.
>
> Makes forfeiture of his breakfast.
>
> On the forfeit of your favour.
>
> Sue in *forma pauperis*.
>
> Put it to arbitrament.
>
> Come upon you for security.
>
> By mortgage or by statute.
>
> You had it in trust, which if you do discharge,
> Surrendering the possession, you shall ease
> Yourself and me of chargeable suits in law.

[1] Bacon uses the word in its *modern* sense thrice in the Essay *Of Usury*.

> If thou canst forswear
> Thy hand and seal, and make a forfeit of
> Thy ears to the pillory.
>
> Indented, I confess, and labels, too,
> But neither wax nor words !
>
> There is a statute for you.
>
> I know thou art
> A public notary, and such stand in law
> For a dozen witnesses : the deed being drawn too . . . and delivered
> When thou wert present, will make good my title.
>
> Your suit is granted
> And you loved for the motion.

In THE CITY MADAM, by the same playwright, we have these :

> I can make my wife a jointure of such lands too
> As are not encumbered : no annuity
> Or statute lying on them.
>
> His bond three times since forfeited.
>
> Ten thousand pounds apiece I'll make their portions,
> And after my decease it shall be double.
> Provided you assure them, for their jointures,
> Eight hundred pounds per annum, and entail
> A thousand more upon the heirs male
> Begotten on their bodies.
>
> The forfeiture of a bond.
>
> His whole estate
> In lands and leases, debts and present monies,
> With all the movables he stood possess'd of:
>
> Cancel all the forfeited bonds I sealed to.
>
> I will likewise take
> The extremity of your mortgage, and the forfeit
> Of your several bonds : the use and principal
> Shall not serve.

From almost no play of Shakespeare can there be cited so many " legalisms " as occur in either of these two of Massinger. But Massinger is not singular. We have already noted dozens of legalisms in Jonson, Dekker, Heywood, and Chapman.

H

In Lilly's MOTHER BOMBIE alone I find some thirty "legal" allusions :

A good evidence to prove the fee simple of your daughter's folly.

I convey a contract.

Impannelled in a jury.

Carrying the quest to consult.

A deed of gift.

Witnesses to their contract.

Let us join issue with them.

He arrests you at my suit for a horse.

Sergeant, wreak thine office on him.

Nay, let him be bailed.

I'll enter into a statute marchant to see it answered. But if thou wilt have bonds, then shalt have a bushelful.

Thou bound in a statute marchant ? A brown thread will bind thee fast enough. But if you will be content all four jointly to enter into a bond, I will withdraw the action.

A scrivener's shop hangs to a sergeant's mace like a bur to a frieze coat.

You must take a note of a bond.

The scrivener cannot keep his pen out of the pot : every goblet is an ink-horn.

I, such as they cry at the 'sizes, a work in issues.

Where did I consent ? When ? What witness ?

Our good wills being asked, which needed not, we gave them, which booted not.

Wast thou privy to this practice ?

Thou shalt be punished as principal.

Let the conveyance run as we agreed.

You convey cleanly indeed, if cozenage be clean dealing.

You shall presently be contracted.

Upon submission escape the punishment.

Thy fact is pardoned, though the law would see it punished.

I was content to take a bond jointly of them all.

Sealed me an obligation, nothing to the purpose.

By this bond you can demand nothing.

I have his acquittance : let him sue his bond
With such a *noverint* as Cheapside can show none such.

Every one of these phrases would have been certified by
Lord Campbell and Senator Davis as a proof of legal
knowledge had they found it in Shakespeare, and in
no Shakespearean play can they find half as many. Was
Lilly then a lawyer ? If Shakespeare's plays exhibit a
professional knowledge of conveyancing, what inference,
once more, are we to draw from this series of conveyancer's
phrases in a single play of Ben Jonson's ?—

> The thing is for recovery of drown'd land
> Whereof the crown's to have a moiety
> If it be owner ; else the crown and owners
> To share that moiety, and the recoverers
> To enjoy the t'other moiety for their charge.
>
> *The Devil is an Ass*, ii, 1.

> He keeps more stir
> For that same petty sum, than for your bond
> Of six, and statute of eight hundred.
>
> *Id.* ii, 3.

> Then we grant out our process, which is diverse
> Either by chartel, Sir, or *ore tenus*.
>
> *Id.* iii, 1.

> Have your deed drawn presently,
> And leave a blank to put in your feoffees
> One, two, or more, as you see cause.
>
> *Id.* iii, 2.

> Get the feoffment drawn, with a letter of attorney
> For livery and seisin.
>
> *Id.* iv, 2.

> But, sir, you mean not to make him feoffee.
>
> *Id. ib.*

> Sir Paul Eitherside willed me give you caution
> Whom you did make feoffee ; for 'tis the trust
> Of your whole state.
>
> *Id. ib.*

> He has a quarrel to carry, and has caused
> A deed of feoffment of his whole estate
> To be drawn yonder.
>
> *Id.* iv, 3.

> I am ready
> For process now, Sir ; this is publication.
>
> *Id. ib.*
>
> By which means you were
> Not *compos mentis* when you made your feoffment.
>
> *Id.* v, 3.
>
> Move in a court of equity.
>
> *Id. ib.*

In Jonson, as in Lilly, we have one of the law terms erroneously ascribed by Grant White to Shakespeare :

> I'll be his Statute staple, Statute-marchant
> Or what he please.
>
> *The Staple of News*, iii, 1.

We find it in Nashe :

> : . . The Divell used to lend money upon pawnes, or anything, and would let one for a need have a thousand pounds upon a Statute Marchant of his soul, or . . . would trust him upon a bill of his hand. . . .
> *Pierce Penilesse his Supplication to the Divell.* Works, i, 161.

It occurs also in at least two stories of Greene's :

> Lends him money and takes a fair statute-marchant of his lands before a judge.
> *Life and Death of Ned Browne.* Works, xi, 30.

> He must bind over his lands in a statute marchant or staple.
> *Quip for an Upstart Courtier.* Works, xi, 277.

And this particular law term occurs in one of the old morality plays :

> Bounde in statute marchante.
> *Impatient Poverty* (1560), Rep. 1909, l. 191,

—with other legalisms such as " surety," " bill of sale," " writ of privilege," and the maxim that " the law is indifferent to every person " (l. 6)—all going to show that legal phraseology and discussion pervaded Elizabethan drama from its earliest stages.

CHAPTER V

THE ARGUMENT FROM LEGAL PHRASEOLOGY :
MR. RUSHTON ; SENATOR DAVIS ; MR. CASTLE

§ I. *Rushton*

A DISTINCTION should be drawn between the argumentation of Mr. W. L. Rushton and that of the later advocates, Baconian or other, of the theory that the Shakespearean plays exhibit special knowledge of law. Mr. Rushton, as has been noted above, preceded and apparently primed Campbell ; and throughout his series of small books on Shakespearean questions he exhibits at once a wider literary learning and a somewhat sounder judgment than are to be seen in the other writers with whom we have to deal. His SHAKESPEARE'S EUPHUISM is a painstaking performance, the work of an industrious literary antiquary. Yet there is in all his work an element of laborious trifling, and he is always somewhat indiscriminate in his citation of parallels.

In so far as his case for Shakespeare's knowledge of law is appropriated and embodied in Campbell's, it has been disposed of in our examination of that. He himself, however, never committed Campbell's folly of claiming for the law of the plays an entire freedom from error. As he puts it in his laconic way, taking his revenge for plagiarism :

> We all know that Lord Campbell was a lawyer of great experience, yet in his book he has made several mistakes in law ; how then could any errors in law which I might show in Shakespeare's works afford conclusive evidence that Shakespeare was not a lawyer ? [1]

[1] Appendix B to *Shakespeare's Testamentary Language*, 1869, p. 53 ; *Shakespeare's Legal Maxims*, 1907, p. 12.

As a matter of fact, however, Rushton had undertaken in his SHAKESPEARE A LAWYER " to show that Shakespeare had acquired a general knowledge of the principles and practice of the Law of Real Property, of the Common Law and Criminal Law, that he was familiar with the exact letter of the Statute Law, and that he used law terms correctly." Of the value of that thesis we have been able to judge in our examination of Campbell ; and it need but be added that even a generally " correct " use of law terms by an Elizabethan dramatist has been seen to be no warrant for supposing him a lawyer, since it can be predicated more largely of Jonson and Webster, to name no others, than of Shakespeare. When, for instance, Rushton argues that Macbeth's

> But yet I'll make assurance double sure,
> And take a bond of fate,

" refers not to a single but to a conditional bond, under or by virtue of which the principal sum was recoverable," [1] he says nothing to the purpose. In his later work, SHAKESPEARE ILLUSTRATED BY THE LEX SCRIPTA (1870), the augmentation is equally nugatory, in so far as it is not a mere " illustration " of the text. The first item is that in Suffolk's " præmunire " speech in HENRY VIII (iii, 2) the phrase about forfeiting goods, lands, tenements, &c., and being " out of the king's protection," is " the exact letter of the statute law "—an assertion which carries us nowhere. [2]   The last item is the proposition that when Speed, in THE TWO GENTLEMEN OF VERONA (ii, 1) says first " do you not perceive her jest ? " and then " did you perceive her earnest? " he uses " perceive " first in its usual meaning, but the second time in the sense of a statute phrase, " take, perceive, and enjoy." If

[1] *Shakespeare a Lawyer*, 1858, p. 19.
[2] I do not here stress the fact that the speech in question belongs to the share assigned to Fletcher in *Henry VIII* by the critics.   It stands in any case for no special knowledge.

this be " illustration " of anything, it is not of the thesis that the plays are written by a lawyer.

Of more significance is Rushton's more recent thesis that Shakespeare's use of legal maxims tells of legal training. It is put with comparative circumspection, and partly in bar of the Baconian view. " Although Bacon's legal maxims are twenty-five in number," he writes, " I have not found any of them in Shakespeare's plays ; but a portion of one of them. . . .

> Sententia interlocutaria revocare potest, definitiva non potest,

expresses the law to which Shakespeare refers in the COMEDY OF ERRORS (i, 1) :

> And passed sentence cannot be recalled.

To impute legal knowledge on the strength of that commonplace, however, is but to continue the idle mystification which we have been occupied in clearing up. And the case is little better when Rushton puts his point that Shakespeare in his use of legal maxims translates correctly from the Latin :

> In the plays of Ben Jonson, George Chapman and other dramatists of their time, legal maxims are to be seen in Latin, Shakespeare never quotes legal maxims in Latin, but he gives correct translations of them which are so embodied in his verse and prose that they have not the appearance of quotations. . . . Shakespeare's correct translations of legal maxims are, I think, the only satisfactory evidence we have of his knowledge of Latin.[1]

Here the case for the dramatist's legal knowledge is in effect abandoned, and the question shifted to that of his scholarship, with the admission that the evidence usually cited on that head is not satisfactory. If Ben Jonson and George Chapman, who are not lawyers, admittedly cite legal maxims in Latin, what is to be proved from Shakespeare's citation of any in English, when the same thing is done by Heywood and Massinger, who also were

---

[1] *Shakespeare's Legal Maxims*, p. 9.

not lawyers ? Massinger (THE FATAL DOWRY, i, 2)
writes, quite " correctly " :

> though it be a maxim in our laws,
> All suits die with the person.

Is he then not to be credited with Shakespearean lawyership ?

The instances given from Shakespeare by Rushton are
sufficient to entitle us once more to dismiss the whole
case :

I now give one example of Shakespeare's correct translation
of the Latin maxims, and of the good verse (!) he makes of it :

> Dormiunt aliquando leges, moriuntur nunquam
> (The law hath not been dead, though it hath slept),

where the verbs *dormior* and *morior* in Latin are represented (!)
by the verbs sleep and die in English.[1]

It is not clear why we are not further informed that *leges*
is represented by " law." The whole point is a futility.
Shakespeare was citing a legal commonplace which must
have been familiar to thousands of laymen ; as he was
when he made Portia say :

> To offend and judge are distinct offices,
> > *Merchant of Venice*, ii, 9 ;

or Olivia say :

> both the plaintiff and the judge,
> > *Twelfth Night*, v, 1.

Rushton gravely cites these simple utterances, with
Cranmer's

> I shall both find your lordship judge and juror,
> > *Henry VIII*, v, 2,

as standing for knowledge of the legal maxims :

> Nemo debet esse judex in sua propria causa,

and

> Ad questionem facti non respondent judices ;
> Ad questionem legis non respondent juratores.

One can but patiently put the old questions. When

---

[1] Work cited, p. 10.

Massinger makes Alonso in THE BASHFUL LOVER (ii, 7) say :

> No man's a faithful judge in his own cause,[1]

was he drawing upon a professional knowledge of law ? When Greene in one of his stories wrote : " They both agreed I should be judge and juror in this controversy " (QUIP FOR AN UPSTART COURTIER : Works, xi, 229) did he prove himself a trained lawyer ? Or did Rowley and Dekker do so when they made characters say :

> You are in effect both judge and jury yourselves,
>> *A Cure for a Cuckold*, iv, 1 ;
> Thou my evidence art,
> Jury and judge——?
>> *The Witch of Edmonton*, iv, 2.

A good many thousand laymen have in their time remarked that " Possession is nine points of the law " without expecting to be reckoned experts for it ; but inasmuch as we have in KING JOHN (i, 1) the lines :

> *King J.* Our strong possession and our right for us.
> *Elinor.* Your strong possession much more than your right,

our antiquary would have us see in them a translation of the legal maxim :

> In aequali jure melior est conditio possidentis.

And when Hamlet says, unpretentiously enough,

> Man and wife is one flesh,

it is held to stand for the canonical knowledge that

> Vir et uxor sunt quasi unica persona, quia caro una, et sanguis unus.

So much for the last stages of the first attempt to prove " Shakespeare a lawyer."

§ 2. *Davis*

We need spend little time over the kindred performance of Senator Cushman Davis, who in his work THE LAW

---

[1] Cp. *The City Madam*, iii, 2.

IN SHAKESPEARE does but eke out the method and matter of Campbell and Rushton with a multitude of more trivial details. Like Campbell, he finds that Cade's talk of parchment, wax, seals, the killing of lawyers, and the charge against the clerk of Chatham, " are expressions such as a lawyer *would naturally put in the mouth of a brutal and ignorant insurgent* " ; and with Campbell he sees recondite legal knowledge in the alleged allusion to the *mercheta mulierum*, though he seems to ascribe it to the rebel and not to the dramatist : " Cade undoubtedly had this atrocious custom in his mind." [1]

Like the Lord Chancellor, the Senator does not ask whether the lawyer-dramatist could or could not expect the audience, devoid of legal training, to appreciate the allusions ; and he makes nothing of the fact that they are all in the pre-Shakespearean play. When, again, Cade speaks of being " seized for a stray for entering his fee-simple without leave," we are simply assured that he " uses technical language." [2] It should be suitably acknowledged that in the phrase :

I here entail the crown,

3 *Henry VI*, i, 1,

the learned Senator is scrupulous enough to confess that the expression is inaccurate, inasmuch as there is needed the use of the term " body " " to make it a fee-tail." [3] But as against this stand for technical exactitude, we have from him a multitude of claims for legal knowledge where even Campbell would have blenched at the suggestion. Thus in the first scene of CORIOLANUS the words *verdict, statutes, act,* and *repeal,* are all cited as displays of legal knowledge, the word *edicts* being unintelligibly ignored. Elsewhere he makes " legal " capital of such words as *arrest, arrested, abjure, appellant, avouch, addition* (of name), *bond, cases, depose, earnest,* " execution done

[1] *The Law in Shakespeare*, St. Paul, U.S.A., 1884, pp. 195–7.
[2] *Id.* p. 198.   [3] *Id.* p. 200.

on Cawdor," *matter,* " made good," *indenture, object; tenor,* &c. &c. It may suffice to say that on the Senator's principles every Elizabethan dramatist may be pronounced a lawyer without further research.

That some of the other dramatists do display similar legal knowledge he appears to be aware, herein transcending Campbell. But the knowledge only moves him to the assertion that Ben Jonson is " not so precise in his use of legal terms or in reports of legal proceedings " as is Shakespeare, and that in Beaumont and Fletcher, though both were lawyers, " we can find no such disposition or facility in the use of law terms or the procedure of the courts." [1] The last proposition may be left to work its effect on readers who have had in view the Baconian thesis that it was lawyership that inspired the alleged lawyerism of the plays. The first statement is simply false. As we have seen, Jonson uses a multitude of legal expressions of a more technical character than any used by Shakespeare ; and his treatment of legal procedure is realistic where Shakespeare's is merely romantic. On the trial scene in THE MERCHANT OF VENICE the Senator pronounces that " The whole of this exquisite scene is forensic. The author's mind, in its employment of legal terms, has, like the dyer's hand, been subdued to what it works in." [2] On that particular folly, the reader may be referred to what has been said in the previous chapter. But the Senator's words might with fair propriety be applied to the mimicry of legal procedure in Ben Jonson, as here :

> *Pru.* Nor murmur her pretences : master Lovel,
> For so your libel here, or bill of complaint
> Exhibited, in our high court of sovereignty,
> At this first hour of our reign, declares
> Against this noble lady, a disrespect
> You have conceived, if not received, from her.
>   *Host.* Received : so the charge lies in our bill.
>   *Pru.* We see it, his learned counsel, leave your plaining.

[1] *The Law in Shakespeare,* pp. 52–3.   [2] *Id.* p. 116.

We that do love our justice above all
Our other attributes . . . do here enjoin . .
   Host. Good !
   Pru. Charge, will, and command
Her ladyship, pain of our high displeasure,
And the committing an extreme contempt
Unto the court, our crown and dignity. . . .
To entertain you for a pair of hours. . . .
To give you all the titles, all the privileges
The freedoms, favours, rights, she can bestow. .
Or can be expected, from a lady of honour
Or quality, in discourse, access, address. . . .
           For each hour a kiss
To be ta'en freely, fully, and legally
Before us in our court here, and our presence.
                       The New Inn, ii, 2.

   Pru. Here set the hour ; but first produce the parties,
And clear the court : the time is now of price: . . .
   Ferret. Oyez, oyez, oyez.
   Trundle. Oyez, oyez, oyez.
   Ferret [*Trundle repeating each line*].
Whereas there hath been awarded—
By the queen regent of love—
In this high court of sovereignty—
Two special hours of address—
To Herbert Lovel, appellant—
Against the lady Frampul, defendant—
Herbert Lovel come into the court—
Make challenge to thy first hour—
And save thee and thy bail—

[*Enter Lady Frampul, and takes her place on the other side.*]

   Host. She makes a noble and a just appearance.
Set it down likewise, and how arm'd she comes.
   Pru. Usher of Love's court, give them both their oath
According to the form, upon Love's missal.
   Host. Arise, and lay your hands upon the book.

Herbert Lovel, appellant, and Lady Frances Frampul, defendant, you shall swear upon the liturgy of Love, Ovid *de
arte amandi*, that you neither have, nor will have, nor in any wise
bear about you, thing or things, pointed or blunt, within these
lists, other than what are natural and allowed by the court :
no inchanted arms or weapons, stones of virtue, herb of grace,
charm, character, spell, philtre, or other power than Love's
only, and the justness of your cause. So help you Love, his

mother, and the contents of this book. Kiss it. [Lovel *kisses the book*.] Return unto your seats.—Crier, bid silence.

> *Ferret* [*Trundle repeating*]
> In the name of the sovereign of Love—
> Notice is given by the court—
> To the appellant and defendant—
> That the first hour of address proceeds—
> And Love save the sovereign—
> Every man or woman keep silence, pain of imprisonment. . . .

> [*Conclusion*]
> *Lady F.* Prue, adjourn the court.
> *Pru.* Cry, Trundle.
> *Trund.* Oyez.
> Any man or woman that hath any personal attendance
> To give unto the court : keep the second hour,
> And Love save the sovereign !　　　　　　*Id.* iii, 2.

All this in two scenes of one play. For more matter of the same order of realistic parody, *see* CYNTHIA'S REVELS, v, 2 ; EVERY MAN OUT OF HIS HUMOUR, iii, 1 ; THE POETASTER, v, 1 ; THE SILENT WOMAN, v, 1 ; to say nothing of the Induction to BARTHOLOMEW FAIR and the trial scene in VOLPONE. Could they have found a fraction of it in Shakespeare, Lord Campbell and Senator Davis would have thankfully dropped half the rest of their case ; and the latter would have been more sure than ever that the dramatist knew more law than Beaumont and Fletcher. As it is, he is satisfied that Shakespeare must have had a hand in the play SIR JOHN OLDCASTLE, because " the scene where Harpool forces the Sumner to eat the citation he has come to serve, and the other legal phrases, taken together, *seem to* indicate this."[1] The Senator is unaware that just such a scene occurs in GEORGE A-GREENE, which some deny to Robert Greene, but none has yet assigned to Shakespeare ; and seeing that just such an escapade is narrated *of* Greene by his friend Nashe,[2] the legalist's simple solution of the authorship of the other play, it is to be feared, will not be found

---

[1] *The Law in Shakespeare*, pp. 51–52.
[2] *Four Letters Confuted.* Works, ed. McKerrow, i, 271.

decisive. And as SIR JOHN OLDCASTLE undoubtedly contains legal matter such as (i, 1) :

> The King's justices, perceiving what public mischief may ensue this private quarrel, in his majesty's name do straitly charge and command all persons, of what degree soever, to depart this city of Hereford, except such as are bound to give attendance at this assize, and that no man presume to wear any weapon, especially Welsh-hooks and forest-bills—and that the Lord Powis do presently disperse and discharge his retinue, and depart the city in the King's peace, he and his followers, on pain of imprisonment,

we are left to wonder whether Drayton, Hathway, Munday, and Wilson, to whom Fleay ascribes the play, were all lawyers like their dramatist brethren.

Characteristically, Senator Davis finds the best ground for ascribing Act I of THE TWO NOBLE KINSMEN to Shakespeare in the fact that it includes the phrases, " the tenor of thy speech," " prorogue," " fee," " moiety," and " seal the promise."[1] He can thus be thankful for small mercies ; but if he had found in any alleged or putative Shakespearean play such a trial-scene as that in Massinger's THE OLD LAW, of which he declares that " as a forensic representation " it " is crude, *lacks detail*, and displays none of that pomp of justice which all courts of any dignity exhibit,"[2] he would probably have seen it with other eyes. Massinger certainly yields many less scanty crops of quasi-legal terminology than that culled by the Senator from Act I of the TWO NOBLE KINSMEN.

His treatise, in fine, is a piece of indiscriminate and uncritical special pleading, serving only to prove how a fixed idea can hypnotise judgment. Without adopting the Baconian theory, the Senator has taken up a standpoint which equally excludes any rational conception of dramatic art. For him the author of the plays is a writer obsessed with legal knowledge, and constantly bent on embodying it in the plays, to the extent of grafting it all over his recast of the old HAMLET, " all with the

---

[1] *The Law in Shakespeare*, p. 52.   [2] *Id.* p. 54.

greatest painstaking to be full and accurate "[1]—as if the end of drama for Shakespeare were the communication of legal lore. As we have seen, the entire conception is a hallucination. Shakespeare, like his corrivals, made his characters talk law as they talked Euphuism, because it was the fashion of the age ; and we have only to compare his legal phraseology with theirs to see that he was no more a lawyer than were Jonson, Chapman, Heywood, Greene, Peele, and Dekker in his own day, and Massinger after him.

§ 3. *Castle*

Something of a diversion is created in our inquiry by the performance of Mr. E. J. Castle, K.C., entitled SHAKESPEARE, BACON, JONSON, AND GREENE. Mr. Castle, albeit something of a Baconian, is driven, as we have seen, to reject the hyperbolical panegyric of Shakespeare's law by Lord Campbell, and to formulate a theory of his own, to the effect that there are " non-legal " as well as " legal " plays ; that in the latter only did the dramatist " receive assistance " from a lawyer, probably Bacon ; and that in the former he makes so many mistakes as to prove that he " personally had not the education of a lawyer." We thus have one of the profession denying that all the plays exhibit a firm hold of its " freemasonry." Indeed he premises a doubt as to the force of the general argument from the use of legal terms.

I do not lay so much stress upon their presence in the plays, &c., as other persons have done, because I believe they are capable of being learned from books, and are therefore not so valuable a test, to my mind, as the familiarity with the habits and thoughts of counsel learned in the law, which I think is the peculiar characteristic of the legal plays.[2]

Further, he notes that Lord Campbell was " in many

[1] *The Law in Shakespeare*, p. 14.
[2] *Shakespeare, Jonson, Bacon, and Greene. A Study.* By Edward James Castle, One of Her Majesty's Counsel. (Late Lieutenant Royal Engineers.) London, 1897. P. 11.

cases only repeating what Malone had said before him. The consequence of confining his attention to legal expressions is that he has missed entirely the more subtle evidence which points to the life and habits of a lawyer, which may not happen to be clothed in legal language."

I am not concerned to found upon this conflict of authorities, or to dwell upon the chaos which the half-and-half theory makes of the Baconian case in general. It is more important to point out that Mr. Castle is as innocent as Lord Campbell of any general knowledge of Elizabethan literature, and frames his own theory *in vacuo*, finding " subtle evidence " of lawyerism in what any familiarity with Elizabethan drama would have shown him to be the ordinary run of lay conversation. As little need we curiously inquire whether in the " non-legal " plays Shakespeare commits the " laughable mistakes " which Mr. Castle discovers. Mr. Castle speaks modestly enough of his handling of his own legal case, avowing that " mistakes may have crept in."[1] What is much more serious in his total ignorance of the *similar* literature of the period. He discusses the sonnets in general, No. 134 in particular, and the lawyerlike lines in VENUS AND ADONIS, with no suspicion that other Elizabethan poets wrote so. The result is that when he proceeds to make his own contribution to the legal theory he wastes his labour as utterly as did Campbell.

Thus he finds " some of the most remarkable references to law " in LUCRECE ;[2] and he dwells especially on the use of the word " colour," which, he tells us, " as used in legal pleadings has a very specialized meaning." Knowing vaguely that the legal meaning has partly survived in ordinary language, he cites the definition that " colour in pleading is a feigned matter which the defendant or tenant uses in his bar," and so forth ; concluding that " colour sets out a title which, though probable, is really false." Then he undertakes to show that " in the plays

---

[1] *Shakespeare, Jonson, Bacon, and Greene*, p. 25.   [2] *Id.* p. 18.

we find ' colour ' used in the strict legal sense as I have
explained it, as well as in its more colloquial manner of
pretence or appearance."

The very first instance he offers is conclusive against
him. He cites :

> Cæsar's ambition . . . against all colour, here
> Did put the yoke upon us.
>
> *Cymbeline*, iii, i.

That is to say, on Mr. Castle's own interpretation,
Cæsar's ambition put a yoke on Britain *against a probable
but false title.* A layman could hardly be guilty of such
self-stultification. The lines simply mean that Cæsar
usurped sovereignty in defiance of legal forms : there is
no special or technical connotation whatever. Citing
Florizel's lines in the WINTER'S TALE (iv, 3) :

> What colour for my visitation shall I
> Hold up before him ?

Mr. Castle uneasily writes : " Here the technical use of
the word is perhaps not quite so certain, but I think a
stronger meaning is given to the language if we use it
in the legal sense of title or justification. However, in
the next example, the word is used in its strict legal sense."
The next example is the passage :

> For, of no right, or colour like to right,
> He doth fill fields with harness in the realm.
>
> 1 *Henry IV*, iii, 2.

Then we have Beaufort's

> But yet we want a colour for his death.
>
> 2 *Henry VI*, iii, 1,

—with the explanation that " the Cardinal does not
seek a pretext, but a justification or title for the act, as
he is to be condemned by law."

Any competent lay reader will at once see that the
whole theorem is a mare's nest. Shakespeare uses
" colour " just as a hundred other Elizabethans use
it, in a sense which includes both " pretext " and

I

"justification." Pretext is alleged justification ; and
pretended title is just alleged title—Mr. Castle's own
definition. In this broad sense the word was used constantly in Shakespeare's day. I find it four times in
ten pages of Fenton's translation of Guicciardini (1579) :

> They attempted, under *colour* to defend the liberty of the
> people of Milan, to make themselves lords of that State (P. 3).
>
> The original of the *colour* under the which [two kings were]
> . . . stirred up by the Popes to make many invasions . . . (P. 12).
>
> She brake that adoption under *colour* of ingratitude (*Ib.*).
>
> The *titles and colours of right* changing with the time (P. 13).

Again we have it twice on two successive pages (24, 25) :

> To give some *colour* of justice to so great an injustice.
>
> The better to strengthen their usurpation with a show of
> right, to strengthen first with *colours* lawful.

The translator of Gentillet's diatribe against Machiavelli
(1577) uses it as legally as may be :

> He hath a certain subtilty (such as it is) to give *colour* unto
> his most wicked and damnable doctrines.
>> *Discourse upon the Means of Well Governing, &c.,* . . .
>> *against Nicholas Machiavel,* trans. by Simon Patericke.
>> Ed. 1608, pref. A ii, *verso.*

The word was in fact of very old standing in common
English. In Wiclif's treatise AGAINST THE ORDERS OF
FRIARS we have the statement that the friars

> *colour* their own wicked laws under the name of these saints . . .
> and so . . . sin is maintained by *colour* of holiness ;

and again :

> Yet friars will *colour* these sins and undertake for these
> sinful men.
>> Treatise cited, ch. ii. (Rep. from ed. of 1608 in *Tracts
>> and Treatises of Wycliffe,* 1845, pp. 228, 253.)

In the sixteenth century it was in constant use. We
have it frequently in Elyot's GOVERNOUR :

> Inasmuch as liberality wholly resteth in the giving of money,
> it sometime coloureth a vice.   B. II, c. 10   (Dent's rep. p. 160).

Under the colour of holy Scripture, which they do violently wrest to their purpose. B. III, c. 3 (p. 205).

It seems to have been equally common in books and in sermons. Thus we have it in Latimer's sermons again and again :

Under a colour of religion they turned it [church property] to their own proper gain and lucre.

Third Sermon before Edward VI.

And so under this colour they set all their hearts and minds only upon this world.

Seventh Sermon on the Lord's Prayer.

It occurs repeatedly in Ralph Robinson's translation (1551) of More's UTOPIA :

Under the same colour and pretence.

Under this colour and pretence.

A shew and colour of justice.

B. I (Dent's rep. pp. 22, 37, 38).

It is used in the same way by Jewel (1565) :

By any sleight or colour of appeal.

Reply to M. Harding's Answer, Art. V, 21st Div. Works, Parker Soc. ed. i, 389.

and again :

Pighius granteth simply, without colour . . .

Sermon at Paul's Cross, 1560. Works, as cited, i, 8.

The translator (Tyndale ?) of the ENCHIRIDION MILITIS CHRISTIANI of Erasmus (1533) has :

With *false title and under a feigned colour* of honesty.

Methuen's rep. p. 75.

Lest under a colour of pastime he might entice . . .

Id. p. 101.

It was evidently a normal term for the clergy. Bale has it many times :

Sincerely and faithfully, without craft or colour.

The Image of Both Churches : Works, Parker Soc. ed. p. 265.

As the matter is without feigned colour in every point performed.

Examination of Oldcastle, vol. cited, p. 43.

Seekest . . . the blood of this innocent woman, under a colour of friendly handling.
Examination of Anne Askewe, vol. cited, p. 162.

The Protestant Roye, who attacked Wolsey in 1528, has

> By coloure of their faulce prayres,
> Defrauded are the ryght heyres
> From their true inheritance.
>
> *Rede Me and be nott Wrothe*, Whittingham's rep. p. 57.

Hooker uses it repeatedly :

Some judicial and definitive sentence, whereunto neither part that contendeth may under any pretence or colour refuse to stand.
Pref. to B. I of *Eccles. Polity* (1549), ch. vi, 1.

Under this fair and plausible colour whatsoever they utter passeth for good and current.
Id. B. I. ch. i, §1.

And in the CONSTITUTIONS AND CANONS ECCLESIASTICALL issued in 1604 we have :

Purely and sincerely, without any colour or dissimulation (P. 2.).

Spenser uses it in his VIEW OF THE PRESENT STATE OF IRELAND :

But what colour soever they allege, methinks it is not expedient that the execution of a law once ordained should be left to the discretion of the judge or officer.
Globe ed. of Works, p. 639.

and in the SHEPHEARD'S CALENDAR (February) he has :

His coloured crime with craft to cloak.

Among Shakespeare's known books, again, we find the word in North's Plutarch, as in these passages :

That it might appear they had just cause and colour to attempt that they did against him.

Cloak and colour the most cruel and unnatural fact.
Life of Julius Cæsar (Skeat's *Shakespeare's Plutarch*, pp. 13, 92);

and in many others, for which *see* Skeat's index. The legal metaphor had in fact entered into the body of the language, and is as common in the drama as elsewhere.

It is used at least five times, with more or less concrete application, in Lady Lumley's translation of IPHIGENIA AT AULIS, written about 1550, the English law term being imposed on the classic diction.

If there is anywhere a " technical " use of the word in ordinary literature it is in Greene and Lodge's LOOKING-GLASS FOR LONDON, where we have twice :

> It was your device that, to colour the statute.
> A device of him to colour the statute.
> > Dyce's ed. of Greene and Peele, pp. 121, 125.

Jonson uses it with the same " legal " bearing :

> How, how, knave, swear he killed thee, and by the law ?   What pretence, what colour hast thou for that ?
> > *Every Man in his Humour*, iii, 3.

Dekker and Webster are just as technical :

> Though your attempt, lord treasurer, be such
> That hath no colour in these troublous times
> But an apparent purpose of revolt.
> > *The Famous History of Sir Thomas Wyat*, Sc. 6.

Massinger uses the term as does Shakespeare :

> There is no colour of reason that makes for him.
> > *The Unnatural Combat*, i, 1.

Similarly Chapman :

> Passion, my lord, transports your bitterness
> Beyond all colour.
> > *Byron's Tragedy*, v, 1.
> His own black treason in suggesting Clermont's,
> Colour'd with nothing but being great with me.
> > *Revenge of Bussy D'Ambois*, iv, 1.

If there were not all this habitual use of the word in plays and books, the public were made familiar with it in the ordinary course of executive justice. An offender, we read, was pilloried with a paper on his breast stating that he was punished " For practising to colour the detestable facts of George Saunders' wife." [1] But the literary, dramatic, and theological usage, as we have

---

[1] *Brief Discourse of the Murther of George Saunders*, 1573, in Simpson's *School of Shakespeare*, ii, 228.

seen, was universal. Shakespeare was in fact simply using the word as every one else did.

Thus Mr. Castle's laboured argument from Shakespeare's use of " colour " comes to nothing, being but one more instance of the " method of ignorance " by which the Baconians and the simple legalists alike proceed. When he goes on to set forth his view of the " legal plays " he pursues the same method ; but in nearly every instance his argument destroys itself. Thus he contends that MEASURE FOR MEASURE is a truly legal play inasmuch as it shows knowledge of the law of precontract of marriage. He is aware that the play is founded upon Whetstone's PROMOS AND CASSANDRA ; and he avows that in refining upon the old plot by positing a precontract between Claudio and Julia the recast " takes all point out of the story," " so that in reality there is no motive left for the play." [1]   This is partly true : the case of Julia and Claudio is on all fours with the case of Mariana and Angelo, in which the Duke, after treating Claudio as liable for the same thing to capital punishment, plans the intercourse of the precontracted persons. And we are asked to believe that the dramatist who thus played fast and loose with his legal plot was " one thoroughly acquainted with legal proceedings " ! [2]

As if this were not fiasco enough, Mr. Castle adds a piece of elaborate nonsense in the shape of a theory that the name Escalus was coined from the " escue " in the name of Sir John Fortescue, the famous English judge and legalist. " Escalus " is the name of the Prince in ROMEO AND JULIET—the first name in the *dramatis personæ* of that play, produced long before MEASURE FOR MEASURE. Shakespeare got it from Brooke, and it was the kind of stage name that could do repeated duty. Over such a chimera one is disposed to ask what kind of minds we are dealing with in the debate over the " legal element " in the plays.

[1] *Id.* p. 37.   [2] *Id.* p. 41.

On the general question as to MEASURE FOR MEASURE it suffices to say that Mr. Castle's summing-up, to the effect that the play must have been " written either by one who has drawn the scene from the life or has been assisted by one well versed in the every-day life of English law courts," [1] is naught. Many Elizabethan dramatists were so " versed " ; and Shakespeare had the same opportunities as they. In reading Nashe's SUMMER'S LAST WILL AND TESTAMENT one can see that Nashe had attended courts. But who in his day had not ? Had Mr. Castle read Chapman and Shirley's play, THE ADMIRAL OF FRANCE, he would have found a much more elaborate parody of legal proceedings, perhaps based upon a reading of French law reports. He gravely tells us that Angelo, when exposed by the Duke, " acknowledges his guilt as a lawyer would." The wicked judge in Whetstone's PROMOS AND CASSANDRA and the corrupt Chancellor in THE ADMIRAL OF FRANCE do the same thing. Were Whetstone and Chapman and Shirley then lawyers ?

Proceeding in his vain task, Mr. Castle, after granting that TITUS ANDRONICUS is non-Shakespearean, insists upon treating the HENRY VI plays as Shakespeare's, representing that Malone pronounced 1 HENRY VI non-Shakespearean " principally because there were certain contradictions about Henry's age." This is an idle travesty : the ground on which Malone and the great majority of critics reject the play is substantially that of its plainly non-Shakespearean style. Mr. Castle accepts the argument in the case of TITUS, and rejects it in the case of the other play, mainly because that course suits his argument. But we need not try that issue here. The authors of the play were probably Marlowe, Peele, and Greene ; and that they were no more lawyers than Shakespeare might be gathered from Mr. Castle's own argument. Thus he notes that in the third scene the law style of the proclamation is correct, adding :

[1] *Id.* p. 50.

" but the occasion was not one, in my opinion, in which it would or should have been used." [1] To what end, then, is all the learned research to show that the author exhibited special knowledge of Temple life in making Plantagenet say, " Come, let us four to dinner " ? The recondite legal fact that " four makes a mess " was available to Shakespeare in Lilly's MOTHER BOMBIE (ii, 1).

Coming to 2 HENRY VI, we find Mr. Castle endorsing Lord Campbell's deliverance in regard to the legal language of Jack Cade. Contentedly ascribing both the CONTENTION and the later play to Shakespeare, he makes no difficulty over the discrepancy of " heart can wish " and " heart can think," and gravely concludes that " it requires a lawyer of some study to be able to quote from the Year Books, and we find the author of both Quarto and Folio doing this." [2] So that, once more, Thomas Nashe was a lawyer of some study, inasmuch as he tells how his PIERS PENNILESSE has been

maimedly translated into the French tongue, and in the English tongue as rascally printed and ill interpreted as heart can think or tongue can tell.

Have with You to Saffron Walden : Works, iii, 33.

Legal learning, as Hobbes would say, is capable of a more excellent foolishness than laymen could well attain to. If Mr. Castle had but read Udall's RALPH ROISTER DOISTER, which was written about 1553, he would have found Gawyn Goodlucke saying to Dame Christian Custance (v, 3) :

> Neither heart can thinke nor tongue tell
> How much I joy in your constant fidelity.

If he had read KING LEIR AND HIS THREE DAUGHTERS, he would have noted the line (sc. 24) :

> My toung doth faile to say what heart doth think.

And if he had further read a little in Elizabethan literature outside of drama and law he might have divined that

<hr>

[1] *Id.* p. 63.   [2] *Id.* p. 74.

ordinary folk in those days even read many "legal" documents for various reasons. When Nashe in his tirade against Harvey cries : "Letters do you term them ? they may be Letters patents well enough for their tediousness. . . . Why they are longer than the Statutes of clothing or the Charter of London,"[1] he is not addressing himself to lawyers. He knows that many lay folk had seen the Charter, and that many traders had read the Statute of Clothing ; and when he speaks of "calling a fellow knave that hath read the Book of Statutes, since by them all in general they were made,"[2] he really does not mean that lawyers are all, or are the only, knaves, or that only lawyers read the volume. Even when he writes of

> never reading to a period (which you shall scarce find in thirty sheets of a lawyer's declaration),
>
> *Lenten Stuff :* Works, iii, 214,

he is assuming that others than lawyers have perused lawyers' documents. That he was no lawyer may be held to be proved by his lines :

> Smooth-tonguèd Orators, the fourth in place,
> Lawyers our commonwealth entitles them ;
> Mere swash-bucklers and ruffianly mates
> That will for twelve pence make a doughty fray,
> Set men for strawes together by the ears.
> *Summer's Last Will and Testament :* Works, iii, 276.

When Mr. Castle goes on to quote Gloster's lines :

> Let these have a day appointed them
> For single combat in convenient place,

with the comment that "All this correctly states the appeal by combat, the essential point of which is, there must be a doubt,"[3] he does but show that, like Lord Campbell, he knew nothing of Webster, who exhibits a detailed and technical knowledge of the law of trial by combat, without being a lawyer. Ten thousand lay-

---

[1] *Have with You,* as cited, p. 34.
[2] *Id.* p. 119.   [3] Work cited, p. 75.

men could have said all that is implied in the lines cited ;
as they might have known and said that Gloster had
used torture beyond legal rule.[1] It is edifying to learn
that, on re-reading HENRY VI, Mr. Castle finds " something fresh " for his purpose in the story of Gloster's
cross-examination of the sham blind-man.   This, he
assures us, is a further " trace of the author being acquainted with a lawyer's training." [2]   As if any intelligent
layman who told the well-known tale would not have
brought out the points in the same fashion.

It is after this lamentable series of *non sequiturs* that
Mr. Castle claims to have indicated in Shakespeare's
works " not only the mere legal acquirements as collected
by Lord Campbell . . . but . . . pictures drawn of the
different members of the legal profession."   What then
are we to say of the " pictures " drawn by Jonson and
Chapman, Greene, Webster, and Massinger ?   Mr. Castle
modestly begins his preface with the avowal : " I have
some doubts whether I should publish this book.   The
world does not like to have its established beliefs questioned. . . ."   The world might fairly urge that those
who undertake such questioning should take a reasonable
amount of pains to prove their case.   Mr. Castle has not
done so.   He writes concerning " Shakespeare, Bacon,
Jonson, and Greene " without having read beyond Shakespeare and Bacon, save in so far as the commentators
tell him of the relations of Greene and Jonson to Shakespeare.   Of the plays of the two last-named, and of
Greene's prose writings, he appears to know nothing.
He is careful and laborious in matters of strictly legal
research : of the necessary literary research he has
apparently no idea.

The result is that when he approaches the strictly
literary question of the alleged coincidences of phrase in
Bacon and Shakespeare he is wholly at the mercy of such
an egregious guide as Mr. Ignatius Donnelly, from whom

[1] *Id*. p. 76.   [2] *Id*. p. 77.

he cites! instances of (1) identical expressions, (2) identical metaphors, (3) identical opinions, and (4) identical studies. Under the first head he gives only this egregious example :

> Custom ! an ape of nature.
> *Bacon.*
> Oh sleep, thou ape of death.
> *Shakespeare.*

In a later chapter we shall deal with that and many other of the alleged " identities " of expression in Bacon and Shakespeare. But it is impossible to part from Mr. Castle without a final protest against the sheer thoughtlessness of his handling of this aspect of his problem. From Mr. Donnelly, whose cipher he sees to be a farce, he accepts a few utterly inconclusive parallels as proof of Mr. Donnelly's conclusion, without even putting the question whether other Elizabethan writers do not exhibit the same kind of " identities " with Bacon. In the same way he ascribes to Bacon and Shakespeare " identical studies " on the sole strength of one allusion in each to gardens and one to the formation of knots in trees, never even inquiring how it comes that all the main lines of Bacon's studies and aims are wholly unrepresented in Shakespeare. Such incredible laxity in the handling of evidence would discredit any literary critic as such.

When it is exhibited by trained lawyers and judges, it is one more ground for disregarding their mere asseverations as to the presence of legal knowledge in the plays. If Mr. Castle's argument be regarded as an improvement upon Campbell's, the breakdown of the whole is complete, for his specially selected and presented instances of legal knowledge in the plays, as we have seen, are just as nugatory as the rest.

[1] *Id.* p. 196.

CHAPTER VI

LITIGATION AND LEGALISM IN ELIZABETHAN ENGLAND

FOR all who have cared to follow it, the process of confronting with parallel passages the evidence offered for the legal training of the author of the Shakespearean Plays must be decisive as to the fallacy involved. But even without that tedious process of confutation, any alert student of Elizabethan literature might be expected to reject a thesis which proceeds upon lack of familiarity with the life which that literature more or less clearly mirrors. Most of the champions of the " legal " theory—orthodox, Baconian, and anti-Stratfordian alike—simply ignore the evidence for the general currency of legal phrases in the Elizabethan and Jacobean period. Mr. Grant White, as we have seen, does avow the frequency of legal allusions in the drama in general, but goes on to posit the false proposition that in Shakespeare they are much more numerous than elsewhere. In reality, as we have already to some extent seen, they pervade all Elizabethan literature, and they tell of a general litigiousness which is at once the cause and the explanation. " Thou'lt go to law with the vicar for a tithe goose," says Hobson in Heywood's EDWARD IV.[1] As Nashe has it in PIERCE PENILESSE HIS SUPPLICATION TO THE DIVELL : " Lawyers cannot devise which way in the world to beg, they are so troubled with brabblements and suits every term, of yeomen and gentlemen that fall out for nothing. If John a Nokes his hen do but leap into Elizabeth de Yappe's close, she will never

[1] Part I. Pearson's Heywood, vol. i, p. 71.

leave to haunt her husband till he bring it to a *Nisi prius*. One while the parson sueth the parishioner for bringing home his tithes : another while the parishioner sueth the parson for not taking away his tithes in time." [1] All the while the burden of " the law's delays " was known to all men. Chapman makes a character declare that " cures are like causes in law, which may be lengthened or shortened at the discretion of the lawyer : he can either keep it green with replications or rejoinders, or sometimes skin it fair a' th' outside for fashion sake : but so he may be sure 'twill break out again by a writ of error, and then he has his suit new to begin." [2]

Roger Hutchinson, in his Sermons OF OPPRESSION, AFFLICTION, AND PATIENCE (1553) is amusingly careful to explain that when Paul blames Christians for going to law, " the fault which he affirmeth to be in suits must be referred to one party, not to the plaintiff and defendant both. . . . These words [' Why rather suffer ye not wrong ? '] are spoken to unjust and contentious suitors, and do not disprove rightful suits " [3]—an audacity of misinterpretation at which an attorney would have blenched. The England of that day, in fact, appears to have been a scene of manifold oppression as well as of litigiousness ; and a doctrine of non-resistance would not have won much assent. But Hutchinson devoutly protests that " for as much as . . . malice increaseth daily by delays, and long continuance of suits through the covetousness of lawyers ; would God the King's Majesty, by the assent of his Parliament, would make some statute that all suits should be determined and judged within the compass of a year, or of half a year if their value were under a hundred pound, upon pain of some great forfeiture to the judges before whom such matters come." [4]

---

[1] *Works*, ed. McKerrow, i, 189.   [2] *All Fools*, iv, 1.
[3] *Works of Roger Hutchinson*, Parker Soc. ed. 1842, p. 328.
[4] *Id.* p. 332.

It might have been well to set up some machinery for the discouragement of frivolous suits. Latimer in his first Sermon before King Edward VI tells of a lawsuit

betwixt two friends for a horse. The owner promised the other should have the horse if he would : the other asked the price ; he said twenty nobles (five pounds). The other would give him but four pound. The owner said he should not have him then. The other claimed the horse, because he said he should have him if he would. Thus this bargain became a Westminster matter : the lawyers got twice the value of the horse ; and when all came to all, two fools made an end of the matter.[1]

In his Second Sermon before the King, again, Latimer tells of unjust judges, who listen only to the rich litigant, and help him to oppress the poor. " I cannot go to my book, for poor folks come unto me, desiring that I will speak that their matters may be heard." [2] Purely oppressive suits were common ; but there were as many fools as knaves, all making work for the lawyers.

This mania for litigation is dramatically set forth again in the poor play, IF YOU KNOW NOT ME, YOU KNOW NOBODY, Part II—obviously, as it stands, the work of several hands and different times, but ascribed to Heywood, who doubtless had " a hand or a main finger " in it as in two hundred more. In one of the earlier scenes Gresham and Sir Thomas Ramsey, the eminent London merchants, are brought together to be reconciled over a foolish lawsuit in which they have been embroiled for six or seven years. Doctor Nowell tells

How by good friends they have been persuaded both,
Yet both but deaf to fair persuasion ;

and old Hobson jovially rates them on their passion

To beat yourselves in law six or seven year,
Make lawyers, " turneys' " clerks, and knaves to spend
Your money in a brabbling controversy,
Even like two fools.

The two litigants for a time snap at each other, revealing the animal pugnacity of the race, which turned sponta-

[1] *Sermons of Hugh Latimer*, ed. in " Everyman's Library," p. 76. [2] *Id.* p. 108.

neously to litigation when the reign of law set limits to
private warfare. Their ground of quarrel was that
Ramsey had " given earnest " for a piece of land which
Gresham, not knowing of the previous transaction,
bought and built upon ; and they are now induced to
shake hands upon the friendly arbiter's decision that
Gresham shall pay Ramsey a hundred pounds compensation, each losing the five hundred pounds he has spent
during the futile lawsuit. If it be objected that plays
are not valid evidence as to social usage or habit, it may
suffice to cite Mr. Hubert Hall's account [1] of the lawsuits
over the inheritance of " Wild Darrell " for unimpeach-
able evidence of Elizabethan manners, morals, and
practices. We there seem to find ourselves in a world
still half-savage, where law and lawlessness are in a
perpetual, breathless grapple, and where the authentic
record at once makes credible many episodes in the contemporary and later drama which at a first reading seem
grotesque exaggerations. The litigiousness and the lawlessness, the legal and the illegal frauds and violences,
are correlative.

Apart from such stress of strife, the whole Elizabethan
drama tells of a normal resort to the procedure of arrest
for debt. One of the commonest situations is that in
which a personage is either rightfully or fraudulently
" attached " or arrested ; and the invariable question,
" At whose suit ? " tells of a general familiarity with the
occurrence. People in humble life are made normally
to use technical language in regard to such mishaps. In
the play last cited, the pedlar, Tawnycoat, utters a
soliloquy which, had it occurred in a Shakespearean play,
would have been triumphantly cited by the critical tribe
of Lord Campbell as proof positive of the playwright's
" profound " acquaintance with legal procedure :

> I broke my day with him. O had that fatal hour
> Broken my heart ; and, villain that I was,

[1] *Society in Elizabethan England.*

> Never so much as writ in my excuse ;
> And he for that default hath sued my bill,
> And with an execution is come down
> To seize my household stuff, imprison me,
> And turn my wife and children out of doors.
>
> Ed. cited, p. 303.

Heywood was no lawyer, but he makes a non-legal character, still in the same play, quote in due form legal maxims that would have proved his lawyership for both Lord Campbell and Mr. Rushton. Twice over, Jack Gresham quotes one such maxim, the second time thus :

> Friend, Ployden's proverb : *the case is alter'd ;* and, by my troth, I have learn'd you a lesson ; *forbearance is no acquittance.*[1]

That phrase, " The case is alter'd," is a standing tag in Elizabethan drama, and Ben Jonson makes it the title of a play. In the second part of his KING EDWARD THE FOURTH, again, where Aire, after being saved from execution for piracy by the influence of Jane Shore, is executed for succouring her, Heywood makes the doomed man thus play on legal terms and procedure in his farewell speech :

> Jane, be content !
>
> I am as much indebted unto thee
> As unto nature : I owed thee a life
> When it was forfeit unto death by law.
> Thou begdst it of the King and gav'st it me.
> This house of flesh, wherein this soul doth dwell,
> Is thine, and thou art landlady of it,
> And this poor life a tenant but at pleasure.
> It never came to pay the rent till now,
> But hath run in arrearage all this while,
> And now for very shame comes to discharge it
> When death distrains for what is but thy due.
>
> Pearson's ed. of Works, i, 181.

Here we have the very fashion of lawyerism seen in those Sonnets of Shakespeare which are cited as proof of his " profound technical knowledge," and this in a play meant for common folk and tolerable only to them. To such phraseology they were daily accustomed. Such a

[1] *Id.* p. 332. (Cp. p. 329.)

proclivity meant, further, a habitual haunting of law courts ; and in Stratford-on-Avon, where a fortnightly court was regularly held, it is morally certain that people with any idle time on their hands would frequently seek there what must have been the most interesting entertainment regularly open to them. If such resort is still common in days of newspapers and in towns supplied with theatres, it must have been much more so in a time and in places where news-sheets were still unknown and theatres non-existent. Drayton draws a picture which generalises one that must have been familiar to many thousands of his countrymen :

Like some great learned judge, to end a weighty cause,
Well furnished with the force of arguments and laws,
And every special proof that justly may be brought ;
Now with a constant brow, a firm and settled thought,
And at the point to give the last and final doom :
The people crowding near within the pester'd room.
A slow soft murmuring moves amongst the wond'ring throng,
As though with open ears they would devour his tongue.[1]

In respect of the state of society in which this was a normal experience, it is hardly necessary to prove that Shakespeare had any special inducement in youth to take an interest in legal procedure. But, as it happened, he had. It is generally known, and the legalists might have been expected to remember, that Shakespeare's father was a man of many lawsuits. But nowhere in connection with this question, I think, has note been taken of the extent and significance of that experience in the Shakespeare household. It has been left to a clerical writer—partly bent on proving the quite arguable thesis that John Shakespeare was a Puritan recusant, partly on pressing the fantastic one that William Shakespeare was a profound Biblical student—to bring out the full force of the evidence as to the father's manifold experience of law courts. The summary is that " He was one of the most litigious of men. . . . From July, 2 Philip

---

[1] *Polyolbion*, 5th Song, ii, 29-36.

K

and Mary, to March, 37 Elizabeth, there are no less than sixty-seven entries of cases in which his name appears on one side or the other ; and *some of his actions are with his best friends*, as Adrian Quiney, Francis Herbage, Thomas Knight, and Roger Sadler ; but in 1591 there is only one entry, wherein John Shakespeare sued as plaintiff in a debt recovery action and won with costs."[1]

This noteworthy record, and many of the details on which it is based, bring out three facts of obvious importance in the biography of Shakespeare : (1) the *normality* of litigation in Stratford as in Elizabethan England in general ; (2) the abundant share of the Shakespeares in legal experience ; and (3) the possibility of error in the old inference, accepted by most of us, as to the father's impecuniosity. The fact seems to be that when John Shakespeare was distrained upon for debt and the writ was returned (1586) endorsed with the note, " quod praedictus Johannes Shakspere nihil habet unde distringere potest habet," he was not at all devoid of means, but was simply baffling the suit against him. Real property he certainly possessed at that time,[2] as did other substantial citizens who were also being proceeded against ;[3] to say nothing of the obvious consideration that he must have had household furniture. I will not attempt here to decide the problem as to whether the whole episode of John Shakespeare's finings and the disqualification consequent on his non-attendance at the Council was simply a matter of his recusancy. The *prima facie* case for that view is extremely strong ; but it calls for a more searching investigation than I have yet met with ; and I simply note that it puts in doubt the whole theory of John Shakespeare's progressive impecuniosity, which in the past I had accepted like others. Mr. Halliwell-Phillipps had indeed pointed out that when Alderman

[1] Rev. T. Carter, *Shakespeare : Puritan and Recusant*, 1897, p. 166.
[2] Work last cited, pp. 30, 93, 124, 159.   [3] *Id*. p. 165.

Shakespeare went on paying heavy fines for persistent non-attendance at the Council, it was " not an evidence of falling-off in circumstances, but rather the opposite, for it implies on the contrary the ability to pay the fines for non-attendance, for we cannot doubt that if he had not paid them some notice would have appeared in the books."[1] This, however, was not convincing ; and the theory of lack of funds was ostensibly the reasonable one. But on a review of all the data the question must be pronounced unsettled ; and among other things the theory that the boy William *had* to leave school at thirteen because of his father's pecuniary embarrassments is obviously put in doubt.

Whatever be the ultimate solution, it is at least clear that the boy Shakespeare had not less but more than the normal Elizabethan ground of interest in legal matters. It would be idle for the " anti-Stratfordians " to argue that we have no evidence of his taking any interest in his father's litigations. It might as well be said that we have no evidence of his caring about anything. Common sense warrants the belief that he heard endless talk in the home circle on legal matters ; and the very illiteracy of his father, so often stressed by the Baconians and their allies, carries the irresistible presumption that the boy was called on to read some legal documents for his parents. In view of our previous survey of the legalisms in the plays it is worth noting that the enigmatic document of agreement between John Shakespeare and Robert Webbe, entered into in 1579, makes mention of " feoffments, grants, entails, jointures, dowers, leases, wills, uses, rent charges, rent sects, arrearages of rent, recognizance, statute merchant and of the staple, obligations, judgments, executions, condemnations, issues, fines, amercements, intrusions, forfeitures, alienations without license," &c.[2] Of most of these terms John Shakespeare, with his many litigations and title-deeds, was likely enough

[1] Citation by Carter, p. 125.   [2] Carter, as cited, p. 98.

to know the meaning, whether or not he could sign his name. Between the documents and the lawsuits, his son had occasion enough to know as well as any layman of his day the common vocabulary of lawyers, which is practically all that his plays indicate him to have known. And as that very transaction about the Asbies, with which the Webbe agreement connects, dragged on long after he was a grown man, and came into the court of Chancery in 1597—" after the days of persecution were over," as Mr. Carter notes, when a recusant could go to law without fear of amercement—William Shakespeare had a personal interest in studying all the documents concerned. If Mr. Grant White and the legalists had taken such things into account, they might have found a simple solution for the occurrence of legal terms in the plays.

But Shakespeare's experience, be it repeated, was not abnormal in that litigious and court-haunting age. The public in general had the same proclivities, and the other dramatists, as we have seen, catered freely for the same appetite. The habit of court-haunting is indicated in Webster and Rowley's CURE FOR A CUCKOLD (iii, 1) :

> A judge, methinks, looks loveliest when he weeps,
> Pronouncing of death's sentence ;

and in the same scene a character sententiously puts sex attraction in a legal figure :

> Although the tenure by which land was held
> In villanage be quite extinct in England,
> Yet you have women there at this day living
> Make a number of slaves.

Latimer in the pulpit (1529) turns to homiletic account

three terms which we have common and usual amongst us, that is to say, the sessions of inquirance, the sessions of deliverance, and the execution day. Sessions of inquirance is like unto judgment ; for when sessions of inquiry is, then the judges cause twelve men to give verdict of the felon's crime, whereby he shall be judged to be indicted : sessions of deliverance is much like council : for at sessions of deliverance the judges go among themselves to council, to determine sentence against the felon ;

execution-day is to be compared with hell-fire. . . . Wherefore you may see that there are degrees in these our terms, as there be in those terms.[1]

The same habit of court-haunting is taken for granted by Sir Thomas Elyot (1531) :

And in the country, at a sessions or other assembly, if no gentyl men be thereat, the saying is that there was none but the commonalty.[2]

The habits of Henry the Eighth's day in this regard had not changed in Elizabeth's.   No matter in what country they lay their scene, the dramatists assume the universal interest in matters of law and litigation.

> I walking in the place where men's lawsuits
> Are heard and pleaded—
> > Chapman, *All Fools*, ii, 1,

is quite a natural way of beginning an account of an episode ; equally by the way is the description :

> Heard he a lawyer, ne'er so vehement pleading,
> He stood and laugh'd.
> > *Id.   Revenge of Bussy D'Ambois*, i, 1 ;

and Chapman had made a personage say, before Dickens :

> The law is such an ass.
> > *Revenge for Honour*, iii, 2.

The natural result of such a general preoccupation is that not merely the phraseology but the procedure of the law-courts everywhere obtrudes itself in literature. Even in our day, trial scenes are often the central features in melodramas, the spontaneously dramatic character of a trial giving the playwright an easy opportunity ; and as soon as the Elizabethan drama had come in touch with normal life, even on a poetic plane, it availed itself of this obvious resource.   Not only does the drama swarm with trials and trial scenes, lawsuits, advocates, judges, magistrates, scriveners, warrants, sergeants and affairs of justice, but the judicial procedure and the legal

---

[1] *Sermons*, ed. cited, pp. 9–10.
[2] *The Boke named the Governour*, ed. in same series, p. 2.

terminology are alike constantly resorted to in poetic and polemic literature.

Nashe, in one of his hilarious wrangles with Gabriel Harvey, in FOUR LETTERS CONFUTED, plunges into the trial form as naturally as any dramatist, thus :

> The Arraignment and Execution of the Third Letter.
> *To every reader favourably or indifferently affected.*
> Text, stand to the Bar. Peace there below.

After a quotation and a comment, we have :

> You would foist in *non causam pro causa.* . . . If you have any new infringement to destitute the indictment of forgery that I bring against you, so it is.
> Here enters *Argumentum a testimonio humano,* like Tamburlaine drawn in a chariot by four kings.[1]

In Greene's story, A QUIP FOR AN UPSTART COURTIER, similarly, the onlooker in the quarrel between Velvet-breeches and Cloth-breeches says to the former :

> Listen to me, and discuss the matter by law; . . . you claim all, he [Cloth-breeches] would have but his own : both plead an absolute title of residence in this country : then the course between you be trespass or disseisin of frank tenement : You, Velvet-breeches, in that you claim the first title, you shall be plaintiff and plead a trespass of disseisin done you by Cloth-breeches, so shall it be brought to a jury, and tried by a verdict of twelve or four-and-twenty.

The reply is that Velvet-breeches cannot rely on juries' justice, " for my adversary is their countryman and less chargeable : he shall have the law mitigated if a jury of hinds or peasants should be empannelled." Upon this comes the rejoinder :

> You need not doubt of that, for whom you distrust and think not indifferent, him you upon a cause manifested, challenge from your jury.
> If your law allow such large favour, quoth Velvet-breeches, I am content my title be tried by a jury, and therefore let mine adversary plead me *Nul tort nul disseisin.*[2]

---

[1] Works, ed. cited, i, 293.
[2] Works, ed. Grosart, xi, 228–9.

Later there is a literary jury-trial, and the narrator addresses the jury, first naming a knight as foreman :

> Worshipful sir, with the rest of the jury, whom we have solicited of choice honest men, whose consciences will deal uprightly in this controversy, you and the rest of your company are here upon your oath and oaths to inquire whether Cloth-breeches have done disseisin unto Velvet-breeches, yea or no, in or about London, in putting him out of frank tenement, wronging him of his right and imbellishing [weakening] his credit : if you find that Cloth-breeches hath done Velvet-breeches wrong, then let him be set in his former estate and allow him reasonable damages.[1]

Greene's story, as it happens, is a systematic plagiarism from the doggerel poem THE DEBATE BETWEEN PRIDE AND LOWLINESS, by Francis Thynne, a young attorney, probably written and privately printed, but not published, before 1570.[2] The curious thing is, however, that Greene puts the case in a more lawyerlike way than does the lawyer, who is mainly concerned to moralise, and whose point lies in the destruction of Cloth-breeches by a miscellaneous jury whose sympathies are with Velvet-breeches, the rich oppressor ; whereas Greene gives the legal victory to the man with right on his side, on legal grounds. Thynne mentions the maxim *nul tort, nul disseisin*, merely as a comment in epilogue : Greene brings it into the case. The story was long popular : evidently the public taste for legalism could be relied on by both authors and publishers. And Greene, as we have seen, freely employs legal phraseology in other tales. In this he has a phrase about " statute marchant or staple " which is not in his original ; and in the DEFENCE OF CONEY-CATCHING (Works, xi, 55), among other " legal " expressions, there is a transaction in which a borrower " promised to acknowledge a statute staple " to the borrower, " with letters of defeysance," and further " made an absolute deed of gift from wife

---

[1] *Id.* p. 293.
[2] See J. P. Collier's preface to the Shakespeare Society's reprint (1841) of Thynne's poem.

and children to this usurer of all his lordship," [worth in " rent of assise seven score pounds by the year "] " and so had the 2000 marks upon the plain forfeit of a bond." In ALCIDA, GREENE'S METAMORPHOSIS (1588), we have the dictum " Where love serveth his writ of command, there a *supersedeas* of reason is of no avail " (Works, ix, 42). If such a quantity of technical phraseology and procedure had been found in a Shakespearean play, it would have been pronounced proof positive of the saturation of the poet's mind with legal ideas through a legal training. But Greene was no more a lawyer than Nashe.

Even Spenser in the FAERIE QUEENE[1] follows the prevailing fashion :

> On a day when Cupid held his court,
> As he is wont at each Saint Valentine,

a fair cruel maid is found to have " murdred " many sighing lovers.

> Therefore a Jury was impannelled straight . . .
> Of all these crimes she there indited was.
> All which when Cupid heard, he by and by
> In great displeasure willed a Capias
> Should issue forth t' attach that scornful lass.
> The warrant straight was made, and therewithal
> A Bailiff-errant forth in post did pass,
> Whom they by name there Portamore did call,
> He which doth summon lovers to love's judgment hall.

> The damsel was attacht, and shortly brought
> Unto the bar whereas she was arraigned ;
> But she thereto nould plead, nor answer ought. . . .
> So judgment past, as is by law ordained
> In cases like, which when at last she saw . . .
> Cried mercy, to abate the extremitie of law.

Turning to the drama, we find the expedient of a trial resorted to by half the dramatists of the period. Peele makes a trial the central matter of his ARRAIGNMENT OF PARIS (1584), which precedes Marlowe. Jonson employs the expedient again and again. In THE POETASTER he

[1] B. VI. c. vii, 33–37.

puts into the form of a trial his quarrel with his rivals
and calumniators, as does his antagonist Dekker in
SATIROMASTIX. An elaborate trial scene is inserted in
VOLPONE, with " Avocatori, Notario, Commandatori,
Saffi, and other officers of justice " : and the procedure
is incomparably more court-like than that in the trial
of the case of Antonio and Shylock. In THE SILENT
WOMAN there is a long scene in which a divine and a
canonist debate at length on the law of divorce as they
might have done in a court. In THE STAPLE OF NEWS
there is a parade of characters representing legal abstrac-
tions—Mortgage, Statute, Band, Wax, with a lawyer
Picklock ; and in THE NEW INN we have, as aforesaid,[1]
a " Court of Love " scene in a room " furnished as a
tribunal," where the maid Prudence " takes her seat of
judicature " and calls for the clearing of the court and
administration of oaths. In his other plays, as we have
seen, legalisms abound : in THE MAGNETIC LADY, as we
shall see, there is far more legal " shop " and talk about
lawyers than in any three plays of Shakespeare. A play-
scene was in fact counted-on as a " draw," though Jonson
did not succeed with THE NEW INN. Chapman and
Rowley make their entire play of THE ADMIRAL OF FRANCE
a tissue of judicial investigations. An inquiry, held by
way of a trial, and corruptly swayed by an iniquitous
Chancellor, is followed by another trial, in which, the
King's Advocate prosecuting, the Chancellor is exposed
and brought to justice. One or both of the authors had
certainly watched trials, as nearly everybody in that
day did ; and there is a probability that the elaborate
harangues in this play were modelled upon printed
reports. Yet neither Chapman nor Rowley was a lawyer.
A less elaborate but still lengthy trial scene occurs in
BYRON'S TRAGEDY : the device was evidently popular
in the period ; and in Chapman's plays it must have been
the main attraction.

[1] Above, pp. 123–5.

Other playwrights show the same proclivity. In Dekker's OLD FORTUNATUS (v, 2), in the scene in which Vice and Virtue and Fortune dispute, the effect of a trial is got by a reference to the Queen in the audience :

> *Fortune.* Thou art too insolent : see, here's a court
> Of mortal judges : let's by them be tried,
> Which of us three shall most be deified.

And in IF THIS BE NOT A GOOD PLAY, THE DEVIL IS IN IT [1] we have similar extempore effects :

> *Pluto.* Sit, call a sessions : set the souls to a bar.
> 3. *Jud.* Make an Oyes ! . . .
> *Shacklesoul.* A jury of brokers impannell'd and deeply sworn, to pass on all the villains in hell.

Then follows a trial of souls of bad men—Ravaillac, Faust, &c. In A WARNING FOR FAIRE WOMEN (1599) there is a long trial scene to which, for detail, formality, and general realism, there is no parallel in Shakespeare's plays. A murderer, concerning whose case there has already been much amateur detective investigation, is tried before " the Lord Mayor, the Lord Justice, and the four Lords, and one clerk, and a Sheriff," who enter in due form. The Lord Justice calls :

> Bring forth the prisoner, and keep silence there.
> Prepare the Inditement that it may be read.

The clerk duly does so, the document being given in full, in the strict form of the day. The criminal is told in full legal detail how " with one sword, price six shillings," he accomplished his crime : and on his pleading guilty the case proceeds exactly as such a case might, the judge pronouncing a homily before passing sentence. The abettors of the crime are then brought in and indicted " jointly and severally," with the same technical precision, and searching questions are put to the guilty persons. The "inditements" stand as documents of Elizabethan criminal procedure. Had such a scene been found in a Shakespearean play, it would have been

[1] Pearson's ed. vol. iii, p, 353.

claimed by the legalists as overwhelming evidence of Shakespeare's lawyership. The play is anonymous, and is conjecturally ascribed by Fleay to Lodge, whose training was in medicine. Shakespeare's it certainly is not, though Shakespeare in MACBETH echoed some of its lines. (*See below*, Ch. ix.)

In A LOOKING GLASS FOR LONDON, Greene and Lodge insert an elaborate trial scene for the purpose of showing how justice was perverted both by advocates and judges in the interest of usurers : the trial being here presented, as it were, for its own sake.

In THE FATAL DOWRY, Massinger sets out, in " A Street before the Court of Justice," with a discussion on the arbitrary ways of law courts ; and the second scene consists in the hearing of a plea to set aside the rigour of justice in the case of a dead body seized for debt. In the second Act the debate is continued. In the fourth Act the wronged husband causes his father-in-law, an ex-judge, to try the cause of the unfaithful wife, telling the servants to set down the body of the slain seducer " before the judgment seat "; and the wife is to "stand at the bar " :

> For me, I am the accuser.

In the fifth Act, finally, the husband is himself formally tried in court for his act of vengeance ; the victim's father, a judge, being present. The whole conduct of these trials is sufficiently unlawyerlike ; but that is not the question. The point is that, like Shakespeare, the other dramatists, without legal training and without concern for strict legal form, spontaneously resorted to trials and court procedure as a dramatic method.

In THE MAID OF HONOUR, Massinger makes the heroine plead her cause before the King as before a judge :

> To do me justice,
> Exacts your present care, and I can admit
> Of no delay. If, ere my cause be heard,
> In favour of your brother you go on, sir,

> Your sceptre cannot right me.   He's the man,
> The guilty man, whom I accuse ; and you
> Stand bound in duty, as you are supreme,
> To be impartial.   Since you are a judge,
> As a delinquent look on him, and not
> As on a brother : Justice painted blind
> Infers her ministers are obliged to hear
> The cause : and truth, the judge, determine of it ;
> And not sway'd or by favour or affection,
> By a false gloss or wrested comment, alter
> The true intent or letter of the law. . . .
> I stand here mine own advocate.

Legal style and diction are lent to the scene in excess of
any need in the situation, for it takes place in a room of
the palace.   The King in judicial style says :

> Let us take our seats.
> What is your title to him ?

And the heroine answers :

> By this contract,
> Seal'd solemnly before a reverend man,
> I challenge him for my husband.
> *[Presents a paper to the King.]*

We are witnessing a drama cast in legal forms, for the
entertainment of an audience accustomed to hear law
and talk law, by a dramatist who has no more special
legal knowledge than they.   Had Lord Campbell had it
before him as a Shakespearean work he would unquestionably have professed to find in it proof of close familiarity
with legal procedure, though in point of fact, like Shakespeare's own legal scenes, it is as loose as may be in its
imitation of the real work of courts.

Middleton, in turn, makes the whole play of THE WIDOW
turn on the getting of warrants, arrests, bails, the attempt
to secure a widow in marriage by having concealed
witnesses to her verbal " contract," the attempt on her
part to escape by litigation, and her " deed of gift "
which, as she announces, " was but a deed in trust."
Middleton, we shall be told, was a barrister ; and it must
have been his professional experience that so filled his

head with legal ideas and terms that he bestows them
on the widow. But in his other plays he uses no such
machinery ; and Webster, who was a " Merchant Taylor,"
makes three of his plays—THE WHITE DEVIL, THE
DEVIL'S LAW CASE, and APPIUS AND VIRGINIA—turn
upon formal trials, besides introducing a trial scene into
THE FAMOUS HISTORY OF SIR THOMAS WYAT, which he
wrote in collaboration with Dekker. Concerning the
second of the plays named, Mr. Devecmon has remarked
that it contains " more legal expressions, some of them
highly technical, and all correctly used, than are to be
found in any single one of Shakespeare's Works." [1] Upon
my citation of this judgment [2] Mr. Greenwood protests [3]
that

the fact is that the statement as to *The Devil's Law Case* is not
only not true, but so preposterously contrary to the truth that
one can hardly believe that Mr. Devecmon had read the drama
in question.   There is, incredible as it may sound, practically
no law at all in Webster's play !   There are indeed a few legal
terms such as "livery and seisin," a "caveat," "tenements,"
"executors," thrown in here and there, and there is an absurd
travesty of a trial where each and everybody—judge, counsel,
witness, or spectator—seems to put in a word or two just as it
pleases him ; but to say that there are " more legal expressions "
in the play " (and some of them highly technical and all correctly
used) than are to be found in any single one of Shakespeare's
works," is an astounding perversion of the fact, as any reader
can see who chooses to peruse Webster's not very delicate drama.
I cannot but think that Mr. Robertson had either not read the
play, or had forgotten it when he quoted this amazing passage.

I am quite willing to stake the entire question upon
this issue. Mr. Greenwood might, I think, have taken
the trouble to collate the legal references in THE DEVIL'S
LAW CASE, and compare them with Lord Campbell's
citations from any one Shakespearean play : it would
have been more to the purpose than any amount of simple

[1] *In re Shakespeare's Legal Acquirements*, p. 8.
[2] *Did Shakespeare write ' Titus Andronicus '?* 1905, p. 54.
[3] *The Shakespeare Problem Restated*, p. 398.

asseveration, however emphatic. He would thus have learned that the " few " legal terms which he dismisses as of no account are exactly on a par with most of those cited by Campbell from Shakespeare (only more realistic), and with those cited by Grant White in a passage which he himself has quoted with approbation. Having read Webster's play thrice—which is more, I fear, than Mr. Greenwood had done by Campbell's book—I will make good his omission. The following " legal " phrases are cited as they come, Act by Act :

ACT I.   SCENE I.

Romelio.   He makes his colour
Of visiting us so often, to sell land.

Contarino.   The evidence of the piece of land
I motion'd to you for the sale.

Leonora.   To settle your estate.

ACT I.   SCENE 2.

Jolenta. Do you serve process on me ?

Rom. Keep your possession, you have the door by the ring.
That's livery and seisin in England.

Ercole. To settle her a jointure.

Jolenta. To make you a deed of gift.

Winifred. Yes, but the devil would fain put in for's share
In likeness of a separation.

Contarino. You have delivered him guiltless.

ACT. II.   SCENE 1.

Julio. Any action that is but accessory.

Crispiano. One that compounds quarrels.

Ercole. Your warrant must be mighty.

Contarino.   has a seal
From heaven to do it.

ACT II.   SCENE 3.

Ariosto. What should move you
Put forth that harsh inter'gatory ?

Romelio. The evidence of church land. . . .
A supersedeas be not su'd.

Lonora. To come to his trial, to satisfy the law.

ACT II. SCENE 4.

Capuchin. The law will strictly prosecute his life.

ACT III. SCENE 2.

Romelio. He has made a will . . . and deputed Jolenta his heir.

Romelio. If we can work him, as no doubt we shall,
To make another will, and therein assign
This gentleman his heir.

Romelio. I must put in a strong caveat.
To put in execution Barmotho pigs.
Here's your earnest.

ACT III. SCENE 3.

Romelio. You are already made, by absolute will,
Contarino's heir : now, if it can be prov'd
That you have issue by Lord Ercole,
I will make you inherit his land too. . . .
I have laid the case so radically
Not all the lawyers in [all] Christendom
Shall find any the least flaw in't. . . .
No scandal to you, since we will affirm
The precontract was so exactly done
By the same words us'd in the form of marriage,
That with a little dispensation,
A money matter, it shall be register'd
Absolute matrimony.

ACT IV. SCENE I.

A long quibbling dialogue between Ariosto, the advocate, and Sanitonella, who has been " dry-founder'd " in a pew of a law office " this four years, seldom found non-resident from my desk," and presents a brief which " cost me four nights' labour." Ariosto tears it up ; and the clerk " must make shift with the foul copy." Cantilupo, being next consulted, pronounces, " 'Tis a case shall leave a precedent to all the world " ; Sanitonella concluding, " The court will sit within this half hour ; peruse your notes ; you have very short warning."

ACT IV. SCENE 2. TRIAL.

Ercole pays an officer to get a seat in " a closet belonging to the court," where he " may hear all unseen " ; and Sanitonella warns the officers to " let in no brachygraphy-men to take notes," and, as " this cause will be long a-pleading," produces a pie which he " may pleasure some of our learned counsel with," as he has done " many a time and often when a cause " has dragged long.

The judge asks whether the parties are present ; and on Romelio saying he is ignorant of what he is to be charged with, says :

> I assure you, the proceeding
> Is most unequal then, for I perceive
> The counsel of the adverse party furnish'd
> With full instruction . . .
> Sir, we will do you
> The favour, you shall hear the accusation ;
> Which being known, we will adjourn the court
> Till a fortnight hence : you may provide your counsel.

After further dialogue, Cantilupo opens :

> May it please your lordship and the reverend court
> To give me leave to open to you a case
> So rare, so altogether void of precedent,
> That I do challenge all the spacious volumes
> Of the whole civil law to show the like.
> We are of counsel for this gentlewoman.
> We have receiv'd our fee : yet the whole course
> Of what we are to speak is quite against her.
> Yet we'll deserve our fee too.

After he has lengthily stated his case, the judge comments :

> A most strange suit this ; 'tis beyond example, &c.

and proceeds to question the parties. When a witness is asked for, Sanitonella responds, " Here, my lord, *ore tenus*," and there is a long cross-examination.

In Act v, Scene 4, we have a passage which may be instructively contrasted with Lord Campbell's illustration of Shakespeare's deep and accurate knowledge of the procedure of trial by battle :

> *Julio.* I have undertaken the challenge very foolishly.
> *Prospero.* It would be absolute conviction
> Of cowardice and perjury ; and the Dane
> May to your public shame reverse your arms,
> Or have them ignominiously fasten'd
> Under his horse-tail.

And in Scene 6 we have the actual trial by battle. The Marshal begins in due form :

> Give the appellant his summons : do the like
> To the defendant ;

the proceedings go on with ostensible technical accuracy ;
and we have the herald's cries : "*Soit la bataille, et
victoire à ceux qui ont droit !*" What would not Lord
Campbell have made of it all !

How Mr. Greenwood, in the face of all this matter,
can say that Mr. Devecmon's assertion " is an astounding
perversion of the fact," I cannot understand. He must
have written in total oblivion, or ignorance, of the matter
upon which Lord Campbell founded *his* amazing dicta.
If there is " no law at all in Webster's play," Lord Campbell has cited none from Shakespeare ; and Mr. Greenwood's handling of the matter, in view of the use he has
made of Lord Campbell's egregious treatise, calls for
somewhat serious reprehension. Evidently he had no
idea of the nature of the grounds on which Campbell
proceeds. He speaks of " a few legal terms thrown in
here and there." What did Campbell produce from
Shakespeare ? If the trial in Webster is an " absurd
travesty of a trial, where each and everybody—judge,
counsel, witness, or spectator—seems to put in a word
or two just as it pleases him," what, in the name of honest
controversy, is the trial in THE MERCHANT OF VENICE,
which Lord Campbell alleged to be " conducted according
to the strict forms of legal procedure " ? Upon Lord
Campbell's scandalous deliverances Mr. Greenwood founds
his main case. Will *he* venture to discriminate between
Shakespeare's law case and Webster's ? And if Lord
Campbell is entitled to ascribe to Shakespeare a full
knowledge of the procedure of trial by battle on the sole
ground of his use of the word " craven," and to make
this unspeakable absurdity part of his case for Shakespeare's " profound and accurate knowledge of law,"
upon what critical principle does Mr. Greenwood sweep
aside the actual trial by battle in Webster, with all its
technicalities ?

I am not concerned to go into the question of the
accuracy of Webster's or Massinger's phraseology : that

L

is neither here nor there. Even Campbell, in flat contradiction of his own claims, admitted inaccuracies in Shakespeare; and Mr. Greenwood, in turn, fatally pressed
by Mr. Devecmon, makes further admissions, forgetting
that they absolutely destroy his own case, which rested
not upon mere citation of legal matter in Shakespeare,
but upon the repeated claim that Shakespeare's law was
impeccable, never open to demurrer or writ of error, and
therefore possible only to one within the freemasonry of
the profession. It may be left to either lawyers or laymen to judge for themselves whether there is not much
more show of legal knowledge and recourse to legal
phraseology in Webster than in Shakespeare. From
twenty-three of Shakespeare's plays Lord Campbell
can cite on the average only two or three legal allusions
apiece : Webster's one play yields over thirty. I do not
for a moment pretend that they exhibit " deep " or
" accurate " knowledge : I leave these follies to the
other side, who profess to certify a playwright's lawyership on grounds that would move a policeman to derision.
The question is whether Webster's multitude of " legalisms " do not, by every principle on which Lord Campbell
proceeded in his extracts and his comments, exhibit
tenfold more preoccupation with legal matters than do
Shakespeare's, and, by mere variety of allusion, far more
" knowledge."

I have dealt thus far only with one of Webster's plays—
apart from the incidental citations I have made from him
in common with other playwrights in dealing with Lord
Campbell's proofs. But an almost equal abundance of
legal allusion is found in APPIUS AND VIRGINIA, as the
following citations show :

> Were you now
> In prison, or arraign'd before the senate
> For some suspect of treason ;
>
> (i, 1.)
>
> Virginius, we would have you thus possess'd,
> We sit not here to be prescrib'd and taught,

Nor to have any suitor give us limit
Whose power admits no curb.

(i, 3.)

Is my love mispriz'd ?

(ii, 3.)

Hadst thou a judge's place above all judges
That judge all souls, having power to sentence me.

(*Ib.*)

Your rashness we remit.

(*Ib.*)

Blind misprision.

(*Ib.*)

I'll produce
Firm proofs, notes probable, sound witnesses,
Then, having with your lictors summon'd her,
I'll bring the cause before your judgment seat,
Where upon my infallid evidence
You may pronounce the sentence on my side.

(*Ib.*)

The cause is mine ; you but the sentencer
Upon that evidence which I shall bring.
The business is, to have warrants by arrest
To answer such things at the judgment bar
As can be laid against her : ere her friends
Can be assembled, ere himself can study
Her answer, or scarce know her cause of summons,
To descant on the matter, Appius may
Examine, try, and doom Virginia.

(*Ib.*)

The most austere and upright censurer
That ever sat upon the awful bench.

(iii, 1.)

If you will needs wage eminence and state
Choose out a weaker opposite.

(*Ib.*)

First, the charge of her husband's funeral, next debts and
legacies, and lastly the reversion.

(iii, 2.)

The term-time is the mutton-monger in the whole calendar.
Do your lawyers eat any salads with their mutton ?

(iii, 2.)

Deny me justice absolutely, rather
Than feed me with delays.

(*Ib.*)

My purse is too scant to wage law with thee :
I am enforc'd be mine own advocate.

                                        (*Ib.*)

                    to let you know,
Ere you proceed in this your subtlement,
What penalty and danger you accrue
If you be found to double.

                                        (*Ib.*)

Having compounded with his creditors
For the third moiety.

                                        (*Ib.*(

Your reverence to the judge, good brother.

                                    (iv, 1.)

May it please your reverend lordships.

                                        (*Ib.*)

                    Now the question
(With favour of the bench) I will make plain
In two words only without circumstance.

                                        (*Ib.*)

Here's her deposition on her death-bed.

                                        (*Ib.*)

If that your claim be just, how happens it
That you have discontinu'd it the space
Of fourteen year ?

                                        (*Ib.*)

I shall resolve your lordship.

                                        (*Ib.*)

Where are your proofs of that ?
Here, my good lord,
With depositions likewise.

                                        (*Ib.*)

                    For your question
Of discontinuance : put case. . . .

                                        (*Ib.*)

I bend low to thy gown, but not to thee.

                                        (*Ib.*)

Let us proceed to sentence.

                                        (*Ib.*)

Over and above all this resort to forms of trial, the
habit of legal phraseology and legal allusion, as we have
seen, pervades the Elizabethan drama to an extent which
implies a general proclivity in the people. Even the
many parallels above presented to the citations of Lord

Campbell from Shakespeare give but an inadequate idea
of the extent of the practice ; and at the risk of wearying
the reader I will transcribe for him a string of the legalisms
and references to law and litigation in a single play of
Ben Jonson's—THE MAGNETIC LADY.

Compass. He is the prelate of the parish here. . . .
Makes all the matches and the marriage feasts
Within the ward ; draws all the parish wills,
Designs the legacies. . . .
For of the wardmote quest he better can
The mystery, than the Levitic law.

Lady Loadstone. He keeps off all her suitors, keeps the **portion**
Still in his hands, and will not part withal
On any terms.

[Many references to this]

Compass. Master Practice here, my lady's lawyer
Or man of law (for that is the true writing),
A man so dedicate to his profession
And the preferments go along with it. . . .
So much he loves that night-cap ! the bench-gown
With the broad gard on the back ! these shew a man
Betroth'd unto the study of our laws. . . .
He has brought your niece's portion with him, madam,
At least, the man that must receive it, here
They come negociating the affair ;
You may perceive the contract in their faces,
And read the indenture.

Sir Diaphanous. I have seen him wait at court there, with his
maniples
Of papers and petitions.

Practice. He is one
That over-rules though, by his authority
Of living there ; and cares for no man else :
Neglects the sacred letter of the law ;
And holds it all to be but a dead heap
Of civil institutions : the rest only
Of common men, and their causes, a farrago
Or a made dish in court ; a thing of nothing.

Compass. And that's your quarrel with him ! a just plea.

Lady Loadstone. Will Master Practice be of counsel against us ?

Compass. He is a lawyer and must speak for his fee,
Against his father and mother, all his kindred,

His brothers or his sisters ; no exception
Lies at the common law.   He must not alter
Nature for form, but go on in his path ;
It may be, he'll be for us. . . .
He shall at last accompt for the utmost farthing
If you can keep your hand from a discharge.

   Sir Moth. The portion left was sixteen thousand pound :
I do confess it as a just man should. . . .
Now for the profits every way arising.
                 Well sir, the contract
Is with this gentleman, ten thousand pound.
An ample portion for a younger brother . . .
He expects no more than that sum to be tender'd
And he receive it : these are the conditions.

   Practice. A direct bargain, and sale in open market.

   Sir Moth. And what I have furnish'd him withal o'the by
To appear or so, a matter of four hundred
To be deduced upon the payment. . . .
                 Draw up this
Good Master Practice, for us, and be speedy

   Practice. But here's a mighty gain, sir, you have made
Of this one stock : the principal first doubled,
In the first seven year, and that redoubled
In the next seven, beside six thousand pound,
There's threescore thousand got in fourteen year,
After the usual rate of ten in the hundred,
And the ten thousand paid . . .

   Sir Moth.   . . . 'Tis certain that a man may leave,
His wealth or to his children or to his friends ;
His wit he cannot so dispose by legacy. . . .

   Compass. He may entail a jest upon his house,
Or leave a tale to his posterity,
To be told after him.

   Practice.   . . . The reverend law lies open to repair
Your reputation.   That will give you damages !
Five thousand pound for a finger, I have known
Given in court ; and let me pack your jury.
           . . . Sir, you forget
There is a court above, of the Star Chamber
To punish routs and riots.

   Compass.   . . . There's no London jury but are led,
In evidence, as far by common fame
As they are by present disposition

. . . a man
Mark'd out for a chief justice in his cradle.

Practice. . . . I am a bencher, and now double reader

Compass. But run the words of matrimony over
My head and Mistress Pleasance's in my chamber ;
There's Captain Ironside to be a witness,
And here's a license to secure thee.—Parson
What do you stick at ?

Palate. It is afternoon, sir,
Directly against the canon of the church.

Sir Diaphanous. I saw the contract and can witness it.

Compass. Varlet, do your office.

Serjeant. I do arrest your body, Sir Moth Interest,
In the King's name, at suit of Master Compass,
And dame Plancentia his wife. The action's enter'd,
Five hundred thousand pound. . . .

Lady Loadstone.   I cannot stop
The laws, or hinder justice : I can be
Your bail, if it may be taken.

Compass.   With the captain's,
I ask no better.

Rut. Here are better men
Will give their bail.

Compass. But yours will not be taken. . . .

Serjeant. You must to prison, sir,
Unless you can find bail the creditor likes.

Compass. Bring forth your child, or I appeal you of murder.

Prac. The law is plain : if it were heard to cry,
And you produce it not, he may indict
All that conceal it, of felony and murder.

Polish. . . . Here your true niece stands, fine Mistress
      Compass,
To whom you are by bond engag'd to pay
The sixteen thousand pound, which is her portion
Due to her husband, on her marriage-day.
I speak the truth, and nothing but the truth. . . .

Ironside. You'll pay it now, Sir Moth, with interest. . . .

Sir Moth. Into what nets of cozenage am I cast
On every side ? . . . What will you bate ?

Compass. No penny the law gives.

Sir Moth. Yes, Bias's money.

Compass. What, your friend in court !
I will not rob you of him, nor the purchase.

Lady Loadstone. . . . There rests yet a gratuity from me
To be conferr'd upon this gentleman,
Who, as my nephew Compass says, was cause
First of the offence, but since of all amends.
The quarrel caused the affright, the fright brought on
The travail, which made peace ; the peace drew on
This new discovery, which endeth all
In reconcilement.

Compass. When the portion
Is tender'd, and received.

Sir Moth. Well, you must have it ;
As good at first as last.

The whole play, in fine, is the working out, without resort to courts, of a dispute in law. Plays in a similar taste will be found in Chapman, Heywood, Dekker, and Massinger, who were not lawyers, and in Middleton, who was. But, as it happens, no such play of pervading legal intrigue is to be found in Shakespeare. In no Shakesperean play, indeed, apart from the MERCHANT OF VENICE, is there to be found nearly so much reliance upon and reference to a legal interest as is to be seen in Chapman's first play, THE BLIND BEGGAR OF ALEXANDRIA, where a question about a mortgage alleged to be forfeited recurs half a dozen times, with long discussions about " statutes " and " assurances " such as Shakespeare nowhere indulges in. Where Shakespeare merely uses legal phrases, as often as not metaphorically, the other dramatists introduce actual matters of litigation.

Apart from the endless allusions to concrete litigation in Tudor literature, again, we find in the writings even of the theologians constant evidence of the legalist habit of mind. They often put religion in lawyer-fashion; knowing their readers would so relish it. Thus Bishop

Hooper, answering Bishop Gardiner on the subject of the Eucharist, writes of

the promise of God . . . of the which . . . these Sacraments be testimonies, witnesses ; as the seal annexed unto the writing is a stablishment and making good of all things contained and specified within the writing. This is used in all bargains, exchanges, purchases, and contracts.

When the matter entreated between two parties is fully concluded upon, it is confirmed with obligations sealed interchangeably, that for ever those seals may be a witness of such covenants as hath been agreed upon between the both parties. And these writings and seals maketh not the bargain, but confirmeth the bargain that is made. No man useth to give his obligation of debtor before there is some contract agreed upon between him and his creditor. No man useth to mark his neighbour's ox or horse in his mark before he be at a full price for the ox, or else were it felony and theft to rob his neighbour. Every man useth to mark his own goods, and not another man's ; so God, in the commonwealth of his church, doth not mark any man in his mark, until such time as the person that he marketh be his. There must first be had a communication between God and the man, to know how he can make any contract of friendship with his enemy, the living God.[1]

In a similar vein he handles the Ten Commandments :

Forasmuch as there can be no contract, peace, alliance, or confederacy between two persons or more, except first the persons that will contract agree within themselves upon such things as shall be contracted . . . ; also, seeing these ten commandments are nothing else but the tables or writings that contain the conditions of the peace between God and man, Gen. xix, and declareth at large how and to what the persons named in the writings are bound unto the other . . . ; it is necessary to know how God and man was made at one, that such conditions could be agreed upon and confirmed with such solemn and public evidences, as these tables be, written with the finger of God. The contents whereof bind God to aid and succour, keep and preserve, warrant and defend man from all ill, both of body and soul, and at the last to give him eternal bliss and everlasting felicity.[2]

[1] *Answer to the Bishop of Winchester*, Parker Soc. vol. p. 136.
[2] *Declaration of the Ten Commandments :* pref. " Unto the Christian Reader," 1550.

And this comes from an evangelical writer, a martyr, much prized in the generation following him.

After this we can understand how a later divine, Thomas Adams, could deliver in a sermon the " legal " passages cited from him by Mr. Judge Willis, and candidly quoted by Mr. Greenwood,[1] who can offer no better semblance of a rebuttal than the suggestion that Adams had " *probably* looked into some law books, and *perhaps* been thrown into legal company." Now, the passages cited are so technical that, had Lord Campbell found them in Shakespeare, he would have reckoned them " the best stakes in his hedge," as Hooker would say. And if it be rational to explain Adams's law by the " probably " and the " perhaps " above cited, why, in the name of reason and consistency, should not the same suggestion hold in the case of Shakespeare ?

It is idle on Mr. Greenwood's part to fall back on an appeal to the " intelligent and unprejudiced reader " to go through the plays and poems and note " the persistence, the accuracy with which he makes use of legal terms and legal allusions, in season and out of season," and all the rest of it, " and then say if he thinks these expressions, culled from the sermons of Thomas Adams, furnish anything like a parallel case to that which we have been considering." The intelligent and unprejudiced reader will reply (1) that the expressions of Adams are more technically lawyerlike than anything in Shakespeare, and (2) that parallel cases to Shakespeare's are furnished by half a dozen of the dramatists whom we have put in evidence, and whom Mr. Greenwood, like Lords Campbell and Penzance and the other lawyers, had never thought of examining—the only difference being that Jonson and Webster and Chapman show much *more* knowledge of and interest in law than does Shakespeare.

Mr. Greenwood's answer to me on the subject of THE DEVIL'S LAW CASE is a sufficient proof that he had adopted

[1] *The Shakespeare Problem Restated*, pp. 392–3.

the conclusions of Lord Campbell without studying his exposition. I will not believe, unless he makes affidavit to that effect, that he thinks the trial-scene in the MERCHANT OF VENICE is lawyerlike in comparison with that in Webster's play. His attack on that is a mere distortion of the issue. He has prodigally and blindly endorsed alike Lord Campbell and Mr. Castle and the other legalists —save where he candidly avows (p. 381) that he " cannot attach much weight to the judgment of a critic [Mr. Churton Collins] who sees the trained lawyer's hand in TITUS ANDRONICUS " on the strength of such items as " affy," " warrants," " *suum quique*," " seizeth," " fee," " purchase," and so forth. But it is just on such things as these that the case of Campbell is mostly built up. It includes even far weaker items. If such data be disallowed, nine-tenths of his book goes by the board at once.

Replying to Mr. Devecmon, Mr. Greenwood strangely protests (p. 400) against what he calls the " curious idea " that " a dramatist cannot be a lawyer unless he makes his ladies and laymen speak in the language that a trained lawyer would employ," Mr. Devecmon having shown that Shakespeare did not do so. At this line of argument I must express my astonishment. Twice over, Mr. Greenwood has in effect surrendered his case. Proceeding as he does upon Lord Campbell's deliverance, without examining the absurd evidence by which it is supported, he at a pinch throws over that evidence while still insisting upon the judge's finding. Met by Judge Willis with *more* technical legalisms than Shakespeare's in the writings of a divine of Shakespeare's day, he denies that such instances furnish " any analogy with the case of Shakespeare."

It is not (he goes on) a question of the mere use of legal phrases or maxims, such as " acknowledging a fine," " a writ *ad melius inquirendum*," " *non est inventus*," " *noverint universi*," " seised," " *volenti non fit injuria*," " tenants at will," " tenants

in capite," " bargain and sale," and the like. The question is,
whether Shakespeare, when we consider his works as a whole,
does not exhibit such a sound and accurate knowledge of law,
such a familiarity with legal life and customs, as could not
possibly have been acquired (or " picked up ") by the Stratford
player ; whether it be not the fact, as Richard Grant White
puts it, that " legal phrases flow from his pen as part of his
vocabulary, and parcel of his thought " ? *It is not to the purpose*
to compile mere lists of legal terms and expressions from the
pages of *other* Elizabethan writers, and those who do so simply
display an *ignoratio elenchi*, as the old philosophers would say. [1]

I regret to have to say that there is something worse here
than *ignoratio elenchi ;* but I will not characterise it
further than by use of the phrase of the distinguished
living statesman who pronounced certain political arguments to be samples of the " black arts of surrebuttal
and surrejoinder." Mr. Greenwood has simply sought
to change the issue while professing to argue it. It *is*
a question of " the mere use of legal phrases or maxims "
—or, still worse, of the inferences to be drawn from mere
scoffing allusions to the practices of lawyers. Campbell
did not scruple to found on *these* as proofs of an inside
familiarity with legal life. He actually cited the phrase
" crow like a craven " as proof of a technical knowledge
of the law of wager by battle. Beyond such ineptitudes
as these, he could cite *only* the use of legal phrases, apart
from a very few claims as to legal knowledge being implied
in the plots of plays. To all the ineptitudes of Campbell's
case Mr. Greenwood is committed when he founds on
the deliverances which Campbell so justified. If Mr.
Greenwood means to assert that a " sound and accurate
knowledge of law " is to be proved in the plays *apart
from* the use of legal phrases, he is talking, I must say,
even more heedlessly than Campbell, for Campbell did
at least make a parade of evidence in respect of the legal
phrases. Had Campbell found " writ *ad melius inquirendum* " in Shakespeare he would have made it the head-

---

[1] Work cited, p. 395.

stone of the corner. It is really carrying special pleading beyond the bounds of professional licence to turn round as Mr. Greenwood does, after staking his whole case on a judgment [1] *founded* on a " mere list of legal terms and expressions," and assert that lists of other men's legal terms and expressions count for nothing as against an alleged general knowledge of law in the Shakespeare plays for which he has no other evidence worth mentioning.

I am at a loss, I confess, to know finally what Mr. Greenwood does mean ; for in this very passage, disparaging mere legal phrases, he resumes the claim that " legal phrases flow from Shakespeare's pen as part of his vocabulary and parcel of his thought." Does he mean that other men's legal phrases flowed from their pens in some other way ? If so, whose ? The plain truth is that Mr. Greenwood had never looked at the legal phrases of the other Elizabethan and Jacobean dramatists. Had he done so, he would not have written his book. Indeed I cannot believe that if, instead of taking Campbell's mere dictum at second hand from Lord Penzance, he had merely gone through the Shakespeare plays *ad hoc* in the critical spirit in which he approached the Shakespeare biography, he would ever have dreamt of formulating for himself any legalist theory. Reading the trial scene in the MERCHANT OF VENICE, he would have said of that, as he quite irrelevantly says to me concerning the DEVIL'S LAW CASE, that it " contains no law at all." He dismisses with just contempt the " legal " phrases cited by Mr. Churton Collins from TITUS ANDRONICUS, and agrees with Mr. Castle that the play " seems to do everything that a lawyer would not do, and leave undone everything that he would." I am curious to know whether he would say otherwise of the MERCHANT OF VENICE, which Mr. Castle does not examine. But the phrases cited by Mr. Collins from TITUS are not a whit more

[1] Lord Penzance, be it remembered, merely quoted Campbell, making no investigation of his own.

nugatory than most of those founded upon by Campbell. Furthermore, on his unfortunate presupposition that what eminent lawyers affirm in his favour about law in Shakespeare must be true, Mr. Greenwood has committed himself to Mr. Castle's special claim about the use of " colour " in Shakespeare, which we have seen to be as worthless as Campbell's and Grant White's claim about " purchase," and Campbell's case in general.

Mr. Greenwood's respect for legal opinion vanishes, of course, when it goes against his thesis. We have seen how he treats the dicta of Mr. Devecmon. I fancy that any open-minded lawyer who has followed the discussion will give Mr. Greenwood short shrift—if I may so mix professional metaphors. In his impatience of the other lawyer's contradiction, he unwittingly falls foul of a fellow legalist, Senator Davis. From that writer Mr. Devecmon quoted the admission that " Antony in speaking of the real estate left by Cæsar to the Roman people, does not use the appropriate word ' devise.' " Upon which Mr. Greenwood retorts (p. 403) that the dramatist was not " so absurdly pedantic " as to make Antony use a correct legal expression when the " left " of North sufficed. Then he proceeds to quote " the critic " as saying that the expression " unto your heirs for ever " was unnecessary. " Really, really ! " exclaims Mr. Greenwood, " This is just a little irritating." Perhaps ; but the offence comes from Senator Davis, who affirms in general the profundity and accuracy of Shakespeare's legal knowledge, not Mr. Devecmon, who denies it ! And only thirty pages earlier (p. 374), Mr. Greenwood had cited *this very Senator Davis* as one giving weighty testimony to Shakespeare's command of a legal vocabulary in which " no legal solecisms will be found." If then the irritating phrase is, as Mr. Greenwood protests, " surely an argument fit only for the least intelligent of readers," the protest should go to the right address.

When he repugns against Mr. Devecmon's criticisms

of Shakespeare's law, Mr. Greenwood merely cuts the bough on which he sits. In an amusing footnote he quotes from my book on TITUS ANDRONICUS the phrase, " putting a few necessary caveats." " No lawyer," he comments, " would speak of ' putting a caveat.' The legal term is to ' *enter* a caveat.' " And the compiler of his index sternly clinches the matter by the entry, " Robertson, Mr. J. M., betrays his ignorance on law, 372, note." The most amusing item of all, perhaps, is that I happen to have spent four and a half years of my youthful life in a law office. But it was a Scotch office (to say nothing of the fact that I was immensely more interested in iterature than in law) ; and in Scotch law they do not, to my recollection, speak of " caveats," which word is therefore for me simple English, and not " jargon." " Enter a caveat " is a phrase well entitled to the latter label. But let Mr. Greenwood's and the indexer's judgment stand : what then becomes of Mr. Greenwood's attempted rebuttal of Mr. Devecmon ? [1] He really cannot have it both ways. If he insists that no lawyer would say " put a caveat," he has quashed his own objection to the argument that Shakespeare makes his characters talk law as no lawyer would. He does not deny that Shakespeare makes Queen Catherine " challenge " a judge, as lawyers " challenge " jurors. Then Shakespeare was no lawyer. It is idle for Mr. Greenwood to say that " challenge " was used in a general sense. What about " caveat " ? . . .

---

[1] At one point, I will offer Mr. Greenwood my humble literary support against Mr. Devecmon, my ally. Mr. Devecmon criticises Shakespeare's use of " statutes " in *Love's Labour's Lost*, i, 1. " A statute," he objects, " is an act of the legislature." It was really other things as well ! Apart from its perfectly legitimate application to the laws of a college, the word was habitually applied in Shakespeare's day to " statutes marchant " &c. *without* the defining term. I think my ally is in the wrong for once—in the course of an argument in which he is overwhelmingly in the right.

I am not concerned to follow Mr. Greenwood through the rest of the difficulties in which he has enmeshed himself. It is sufficient to repeat that he cannot without self-stultification plead that the laxities of Shakespeare's law do not prove him to have been no lawyer. The summing-up of Campbell, upon which Mr. Greenwood proceeded, was to the effect that Shakespeare *did* invariably use legal terms—that is, make his characters use them—as a trained lawyer would. It was Mr. Greenwood's citation of that and similar enormities of nonsense that enabled Mark Twain to die contented in the Baconian faith. The breakdown of Campbell's case at the first serious push tells of the levity with which it was framed. But if we allow Mr. Greenwood to recall Campbell's extravagances and restate the proposition as he will, it is annihilated for every candid student by that comparison of the Shakespeare plays with those of his contemporaries which has been made in these pages, and which neither Campbell nor Mr. Greenwood attempted.

When, then, Mr. Greenwood winds up his legal chapter by citing the passage about " common " and " several " from LOVE'S LABOUR'S LOST (ii, 1), and the similar passage from the Sonnets, and triumphantly puts the questions, " Did the provincial player, the ' Stratford rustic,' write such sonnets as those [*i.e.* the various ' legal ' sonnets] I have quoted ? Is it *his* law which appears in Venus's allusion to a common money bond, or in the various passages of LUCRECE ? Did *he* write the travesty of ' Hales *v.* Petit ' in HAMLET ? Did *he* discourse of common of pasture ' and ' severalty ' in LOVE'S LABOUR'S LOST ? Is it to *him* that we owe the thousands (!) of legal allusions scattered throughout the plays ? "—to the whole series of challenges we answer, Yes !—with the qualification that " thousands " should be " dozens." On the very previous page Mr. Greenwood had obliviously cited an allusion to a " several " in the First Part of SIR JOHN OLD-CASTLE. Was *that* play written by a lawyer ? The jesting figure about " common " and " enclosed " ground, applied to a woman, occurs twice in Dekker's HONEST WHORE (Pt. II, iv, 1). Was *that* written by a lawyer? In Bacon's APOPHTHEGMS Mr. Greenwood will find a sufficiently free jest about " common and several " ascribed to Sir Walter Raleigh. Was Raleigh a lawyer? And can Mr. Greenwood doubt that such stories were widely current in Shakespeare's day? In his own words, " I think not. *Credat Judæus* "; or let us rather say, " *Credant judices* "—Campbell and Penzance !

The other items in Mr. Greenwood's challenge are as void as this. We have seen them one and all put down on test. His final affirmation of " profusion of legal phraseology and wealth of legal knowledge," made *without* any judicial comparison of Shakespeare's plays with other men's, will not, I trust, be repeated after such a comparison has been laid before him. But I am moved to put two additional challenges, after the model of his. (1) If " Shakspere " the actor *were* a " Stratford rustic," why on earth should that rustic, of all people, be supposed to be ignorant of the rurally notorious facts about the usage of " common " and " several " ? (2) But why, on the other hand, should Shakespeare, coming to London in early manhood and living there till near his death, be singled out for rusticity any more than Bacon ? Myself born a rustic, I have some interest in the answer.

M

CHAPTER VII

THE ALLEGED CLASSICAL SCHOLARSHIP OF THE PLAYS

(I) *Lord Penzance* and *Mr. Donnelly*

ONE province of our inquiry, that constituted by the argument from "legal knowledge," has been traversed, not without tedium. Two others remain to be explored. The "legal" argument is backed up by the "classical"—the argument from the "classical scholarship" said to be revealed by the Plays ; and both are sought to be corroborated by the citation of "coincidences of thought and phrase" in the Shakespearean plays and Bacon's works. We are now to deal with the "classical" position.

The dialectical experience will be found to be curiously similar to that which we have undergone. The pervading fallacy of the legalist argument has been, in a word, that of incomplete induction. The quality of lawyership has been assigned to one playwright mainly by inference from a study of his plays alone ; when a wider survey proves that he had no special proclivity or accomplishment. Where a form of testing *has* been gone through, it has been carelessly and misleadingly applied. Substantially the same error we shall ·find made in respect of the inference that the plays of Shakespeare exhibit wide classical scholarship because they contain classical allusions and classical commonplaces. For in this case also the conclusion has been drawn without resort to the comparative method, which would reveal non-classical sources for Shakespeare's small classical knowledge.

Much of the discussion, indeed, proceeds on the assump-

tion that the commonplaces of antiquity are unique, and
incapable of being independently invented by other
peoples, whereas it is of the very nature of commonplaces
to be universal.   Such tropes as that of " a sea of
troubles," such saws as " time tries all," " your father
lost, lost his," and so forth, have been seriously cited
as ideas possible only to men who knew them by classic
quotation.   The late Professor Churton Collins, while
repeatedly conceding that such phrases are mere coincidences of ordinary reflection, claimed that the saw
" Fat paunches have lean pates " (L. L. L. i, 1) is " *undoubtedly* from the anonymous Greek proverb " to the
same effect.   It was a current English proverb, and is
found in two forms in Dekker's OLD FORTUNATUS :

> For a lean diet makes a fat wit.
> (i, 2).
>
> I am not fat.
> *Andel.*   I'll be sworn thy wit is lean.
> (ii, 2).

Even as regards less common sayings, common sense and
common experience remind us that a hundred lessons of
life are learned and briefly recorded by common folk
to-day even as they were by the ancients.   An old friend
of my own, a Scotch foreman carpenter, once remarked
to me, with regard to his function as foreman, " I can
say, ' Come on, chaps ' ; I canna say, ' Go on.' "   I
am very sure he knew nothing of the classic *Docet tolerare
labores, non jubet :* the idea was as natural to him as to
any ancient.   And in the case of a writer so obviously
given to sententious phrase as the author of the Shakespearean plays and poems, common sense might admit
the probable spontaneity of many items of every-day
reflection that happen to have been penned in antiquity.
Antithesis and alliteration, again, are natural devices in
all languages. Learned Professors—Mr. Churton Collins and
Mr. Lowell, for instance—cannot read such a line as :

> Unhouseled, disappointed, unaneled,

without suspecting reminiscence of Greek sets of terms
beginning with the privative a. Now, not only are lines
of sequences of words in " un" common in Spenser, [1]
they are common in Fairfax's translation of Tasso's
JERUSALEM DELIVERED (1600), and still more common
in Daniel's CIVIL WARS :

> Unseen, unheard, or undescried at all.
>> Fairfax, B. i, st. 65.
> Unseen, unmarked, unpitied, unrewarded.
>> *Id.* B. ii, st. 16.

Daniel has :

> Uncourted, unrespected, unobeyed.
>> B. ii, st. 52.
> Unheard and unarraigned.
>> B. iii, st. 23.
> Undaunted, unaffeared.
>> B. iii, st. 76.
> Unsupported and unbackt.
>> B. iii, st. 79.

There is no reason to infer here any reminiscence of Greek
tragedy : the device goes back to Chaucer, and might
be independently reinvented. Daniel and Fairfax were
not Greek scholars.

The main stress of the " classical " case, of course, is
laid upon direct classical allusions and upon non-pro-
verbial passages which may fairly be described as quotations. But in this connexion also the inference of
original scholarship is often quite uncritically drawn.
Even Shakespearean scholars in some cases seem to fail
to realise how much popular knowledge of classical
matters was scattered by both homilies and popular
plays in the Tudor period, apart from the publication of
translations. Some of the Interludes are notably abundant in their classical allusions. That of THE TRIAL OF
TREASURE, printed in black-letter in 1567, has references,
often discursive and explanatory, to Diogenes, Alexander,
Antisthenes, Pythagoras, Pegasus, Morpheus, Hydra;

---

[1] See refs. in *Montaigne and Shakespeare*, 2nd ed. p. 299.

Hercules, Hector, Tully, Epicurus, Crœsus (thrice), Esop, Aristippus, Prometheus, Solon, Adrastia, Circe, Dionysius, Tarquin Superbus, Heliogabalus, Helen, Thales, and Cressida, to say nothing of gods and goddesses. It contains such passages as these :

> The advice of Aristippus have in your mind
> Which willed me to seek such things as be permanent. . .
> For treasures here gotten are uncertain and vain,
> But treasures of the mind do continually remain.

> Thou never remembrest Thales his sentence,
> Who willeth men in all things to keep a measure,
> Especially in love to incertainty of treasure.

The remarkable interlude called THE FOUR ELEMENTS, with its elaborate argument to prove the roundness of the earth, its discussions of natural phenomena, its introduction of the scholastic " Nature Naturate," and its frequent allusions to " cosmography," is a notable reminder that the stage even in the time of Henry VIII could be a source of popular culture as well as of entertainment.[1]

In this fashion, people who could not read might have some acquaintance with the lore of " clerks " ; and common folk whose reading did not go beyond homiletic works could easily meet with a multitude of classical allusions, sufficiently explained. Tyndale's translation of the ENCHIRIDION MILITIS CHRISTIANI of Erasmus, printed in 1533 by Wynkyn de Worde, is a small storehouse of such lore, the many allusions of Erasmus being

[1] Dr. C. W. Wallace, after the most thorough research yet made upon the subject (*The Evolution of the English Drama up to Shakespeare :* Berlin, Reimer, 1912), confidently decides that *The Four Elements* and several of the better Interludes ascribed to Heywood were written by his predecessor Cornish. It may well be so ; but documentary evidence seems still to be lacking. Dr. Wallace holds that the best Interlude work was produced for the court ; and that this play is " evidently " by Cornish (p. 17). Yet it lacks the dramatic character which he ascribes to Cornish's work. In any case, as printed, it appears to have been intended for general performance.

marginally " glossed " by the translator with long elucida-
tions. Thus the English reader was brought into much
contact with Plato, reading, for instance, the famous
similitude of the cave, and getting accounts of Phocion,
Apelles, Crates, Alcibiades, Hesiod, and of Catullus, besides
mythic personages such as Prometheus and Pandora,
Proteus, Ajax, Achilles, Æneas, Ixion, Tantalus, Hercules
and Hydra, Ulysses and the Sirens, &c. &c. Similar
allusions must often have been made in the pulpit, though
the later Puritan school would tend to shun the scholarly
liberalism of Erasmus. In the treatise of the Minister
Northbrooke AGAINST DICING, DANCING, PLAYS AND
INTERLUDES (1577) there are scores of quotations from
both Fathers and pagan writers, with exact translations
and much elucidatory comment, embracing a wide range
of classical allusion. In the face of such a variety of
ordinary sources for matters of ordinary classical knowledge, it is a sufficiently reckless course to credit Shakespeare with scholarly knowledge on the score of the very
ordinary classical references in his plays.

Here again, orthodox writers are as deep in fallacy as
any of the Baconians. Long ago, Dr. Farmer proved
to the satisfaction of the scholars of his generation that
the author of the Plays had little classical scholarship,
and that the instances put forward by Upton, Lewis
Theobald, and others, were all reducible to English
sources. The contrary thesis, however, has been zeal-
ously revived in recent times by two strongly anti-
Baconian scholars, the late Professor Fiske and the late
Professor Churton Collins, who drew upon the previous
argumentation of Dr. Maginn and Professor Baynes.
Having elsewhere[1] discussed at length the " classical "
case put by these critics and by Mr. Greenwood, I will
first deal with it mainly as it is put by Lord Penzance,
who proceeds uncritically upon the data given him by

[1] See the author's *Montaigne and Shakespeare*, 2nd edition,
1909 ; per index.

Mr. Donnelly and upon the sweeping assertions of several " orthodox " scholars. For Lord Penzance, who could not believe that the Plays were written by the Stratford actor, it is quite certain that their author was " master of French and Italian as well as of Greek and Latin, and capable of quoting and borrowing largely from writers in all these languages," and this mainly because the assertion is made by certain " orthodox " scholars, though he attaches no weight whatever to the authority of these scholars when they contemptuously repudiate the Baconian theory. And he appears to attach equal weight, on the classical question, to the authority of Mr. Donnelly, who appears to have had no classical scholarship whatever. Yet he accepts at the same time,[1] on the authority of Mr. Halliwell-Phillipps, the statement that Shakespeare's " acquaintance with the Latin language throughout his life was of a very limited character," though Mr. Halliwell-Phillipps grounds this verdict largely if not mainly on the internal evidence of the Plays. Lord Penzance does not seem ever to have asked himself what critical method means.

The first piece of evidence offered by him to prove the classical scholarship of the author of the dramas is the familiar citation from 1 HENRY VI (i, 6) :

> Thy promises are like Adonis' gardens,
> That one day bloom'd and fruitful were the next.

It is almost needless to say that Lord Penzance does not once glance at the critical case for the attribution of the HENRY VI plays—Part I in particular—in large measure or wholly to other hands than Shakespeare's. Here he is in accord with the whole Baconian school. Mr. Greenwood, I think, is the only " anti-Stratfordian " writer who realises that a large portion of " Shakespeare " is alien matter ; that TITUS ANDRONICUS, for instance, is non-Shakespearean; and that Shakespeare merely wrought

---

[1] P. 50.

over the HENRY VI group. Lord Penzance was quite unaware, apparently, that a large number of Shakespearean critics, for over a century, have ascribed the bulk of 1 HENRY VI to Marlowe, Peele, and Greene.

But even as to the significance of the particular passage under notice he has, as usual, made no critical investigation. It suffices for him that Mr. Grant White, whose treatment of the Baconian problem he regards as utterly uncritical, made the astonishing assertion that " no mention of any such garden in the classic writings of Greece and Rome is known to scholars, as the learned Bentley first remarked."[1] Even this grossly erroneous passage Lord Penzance quotes without any first-hand investigation, for he goes on [2] to write :

A recent commentator, James D. Butler, has found out the source of this allusion, says Mr. Donnelly. He pointed out that the couplet might have been suggested by a passage in Plato's *Phædrus*, which he translated thus : " Would a husbandman (said Socrates) who is a man of sense, take the seeds which he values and wishes to be fruitful, and in sober earnest plant them in some garden of Adonis, that he may rejoice when he sees them in eight days appearing in beauty ? "

Now, the very passage here cited from the PHÆDRUS was actually produced by Mr. Grant White in 1869 in his essay on " Glossaries and Lexicons " (reprinted in his STUDIES IN SHAKESPEARE, 1885). There, improving slightly on his note to the passage in his first edition of Shakespeare—where, however, he had already fathered the negative statement on Bentley, and cited Milton's allusion—Mr. Grant White blunderingly writes :

The mention of Adonis' gardens in *Henry VI*, Pt. I, Act i, Scene 6, *gave Bentley the opportunity* of remarking that there is no authority for the existence of any such gardens, in Greek or Latin writers ; the κῆτοι Ἀδώνιδος being mere pots of earth planted with a little fennel and lettuce, which were borne by women on the feast of Adonis, in memory of the lettuce-bed where Venus laid her lover. But Spenser, writing before Shakespeare, says :

[1] Note *in loc.* in his ed. of Shakespeare.   [2] P. 60.

> But well I wote by tryale that this same
> All other pleasant places doth excell,
> And callèd is by her lost lover's name,
> The Garden of Adonis, far renown'd by fame.
>
> .   .   .   .   .
>
> Daily they grow and daily forth are sent
> Into the World.
>
>   *Faerie Queene*, Book III, Canto 6, st. 29, 36.

And the scholar-poet Milton calls Eden

> Spot more delicious than those gardens feigned
> Or of revived Adonis or renowned
> Alcinous.
>
>   *Paradise Lost*, ix; 440.

But, after all, Shakespeare, or the author of the First Part of *King Henry VI*, whoever he was, whether from knowledge or by chance, was more correct, or rather less incorrect, than Spenser or Milton.   He does not speak of the gardens of Adonis as a place, or as a spot : he only compares speedily redeemed promises to " Adonis's gardens, that one day bloomed and fruitful were the next."   So Plato says in his *Phaedrus* :

Now do you think that a sensible husbandman would take the seed that he valued, and, wishing to produce a harvest, would seriously, after the summer had begun, scatter it in the gardens of Adonis for the pleasure of seeing it spring up and look green in a week ? [1]

When all is said, however, the whole theorem remains a mare's nest.   The " gardens of Adonis " referred to in the Phædrus are just the proverbial κῆτοι 'Αδώνιδος, the baskets or pots or trays of lettuces or herbs borne by women at the feast of Adonis.   What the worshippers did was to plant seeds (or put young plants) in earth, in their trays or pots—here employing a primitive form of " sympathetic magic," now well understood by anthropologists, [2] for the promotion of all plant life.   Even as Mr. Donnelly discusses Grant White without reading him, and Lord Penzance copies Mr. Donnelly's citations without reading Mr. Grant White, Mr. Grant White in

---

[1] *Studies in Shakespeare*, 1885, pp. 296-7.

[2] *See* the classical references and the anthropological explanation in Dr. Frazer's *Adonis, Attis, Osiris*, 1906, ch. ix.

turn had cited Bentley without reading *him*. Bentley's note has no reference whatever to the play. It is to be found in his edition of Milton,[1] wherein he sets forth his theory that PARADISE LOST was (not written by Bacon! but) edited by a fraudulent and incompetent personage who committed many blunders and many forgeries. The allusion to the gardens of Adonis *or* Alcinous gives Bentley the opportunity to convict this imaginary villain at once of bad taste and bad scholarship ; and the note is a standing warning of what a scholar may come to under the spell of a fixed idea.

Our Editor [says Bentley] confesses that those gardens were feigned. Why then brought in here at all ? What *Deliciousness* can exist in a fable ? or what proportion, what compare, between Truth and Fiction ? And then for Solomon's Garden, which he makes real, not mystic, contriv'd it seems for the *sapient King's Dalliance*, our Editor might have had more Sapience than to introduce such silly and prophane Ideas. But if these exceptions do not fully detect his Forgery, what follows, certainly will. He supposes the *Garden of reviv'd Adonis* to be some magnificent and spacious Place, like that of *Alcinous* in *Homer*. There was no such Garden ever existent or even feigned. Κῆτοι 'Αδώνιδος, the Gardens of Adonis, so frequently mentioned by Greek writers, Plato, Plutarch, &c., were nothing but portable earthen Pots, with some lettuce or fennel growing in them. On his yearly Festival, every woman carried one of them for *Adonis's* worship, because Venus had once laid him in a lettuce bed. The next day they were thrown away ; for the herbs were but raised about a week before, and could not last for want of root. Hence the *Gardens of Adonis* grew to be a proverb of contempt for any fruitless, fading, perishable affair. And now is not a *Garden of Adonis*, a Pot with a few Herbs in't, a proper comparison for the Garden of Paradise ? They that can believe Milton guilty of such Ignorance, have not the opinion of his Learning, which I profess to have.

Thus Bentley, cracked but learned still. Mr. Grant White cannot have seen this note, which has no shadow of connection with the passage in I HENRY VI, and applies solely to that in Milton. So far from denying that there were references in the classics to " Gardens of Adonis,"

[1] 1732, 4to. Pp. 282-3.

Bentley gives an exact account of what those references convey, contending—rightly enough, at the height of his hallucination, save as regards an overlooked passage in Pliny—that there was no classic mention of *such* Gardens of Adonis as are described by Milton. Had Bentley known his Spenser as he knew his classics, he would have realised that Milton had simply followed his predecessor's wrong lead—unless he and Spenser had alike been misled by Pliny or some Italian poet.[1] Upon this subject there was a comprehensive brawl among the Shakespearean commentators of the eighteenth century, duly recorded in the variorum editions. The only excuse to be made for Spenser and Milton is the passage in Pliny (xix, 4) :

> Antiquitas nihil prius mirata est quàm Hesperidum *hortos* ac regum Adonidos Alcinoi,

which Bentley might justly have dismissed as a mere utterance of Roman error, cited to justify that of two English poets. Mr. Grant White, overlooking all this, and knowing nothing about the point in question, blunderingly applied Bentley's negative to the use of the phrase in I HENRY VI, where it is *not* applicable, since the lines there, as he sees later, are loosely compatible with the classic description. In the end, accordingly, he claims for the dramatist a scholarship more accurate than that of Spenser and Milton. But he is still astray. The very nature of his conclusion, raising as it does the question *how* the young Shakespeare could have acquired a wider and more exact scholarship than Milton's, might have startled him into distrust of the whole theorem of the classic scholarship of the author of the Plays. His own, clearly, was neither wide nor exact. If on the one hand he had but consulted the variorum edition, and on the other either looked up Bentley's note, or but turned to

---

[1] Warton, who does not seem to realise the nature of Spenser's error (*Observations*, ed. 1807, i. 122), mentions no Italian source, but I have some vague recollection of one.

the old Classical Dictionary of his countryman, Professor Anthon, he would have learned that " the expression Ἀδώνιδος κῆτοι became proverbial, and was applied to whatever perished previous to the period of maturity "— as is witnessed by the ADAGIA VETERUM, p. 410. The passage in 1 HENRY VI is simply a loose application of this proverbial phrase, and expressly excludes knowledge of the PHÆDRUS, where " eight days " are allowed for the growth of the plants.

Such then, on analysis, is the foundation for Lord Penzance's assertion that " William Shakespeare (if he was the author) had so far progressed in his studies by the month of March 1592, as to have *mastered the Greek language thus early ;* and that he had pushed his reading in directions not traversed by the ordinary run of classic readers." We are witnessing a game of literary blind-man's-buff. Nobody in the whole discussion, not even Bentley, turned monomaniac, has drawn a sane inference. Bentley, knowing the classical facts, cannot believe that Milton was ignorant of them. The clear fact is that both Spenser and Milton—the latter copying the former; or both following an Italian poet—were *misled* by the bare traditional phrase, and created in imagination an idea which had no conformity with its historical origin. Spenser commits his error repeatedly—in the FAERIE QUEENE, B. II, c. x, st. 71 ; in the motto to the canto before cited ; in Stanza 39 of the same canto ; and in COLIN CLOUT'S COME HOME AGAIN, l. 855. Nor was he the only Elizabethan who so erred. So ripe a scholar as Ben Jonson, probably following Spenser, has the phrase :

Remember thou art not now in Adonis' garden, but in Cynthia's presence.

Cynthia's Revels, v, 3.

Where Spenser, Jonson, and Milton fell short, it was not by dint of deep scholarship that the playwright came nearer the truth. An unquestioning acceptance of Mr. Grant White's fallacious note, and of the fallacies appended thereto by himself and the Baconians, serves as passport to the wildest generalisations concerning the scholarship of the playwright. It is all in the air. The writer of the lines in 1 HENRY VI was probably Marlowe, who was no very deep classicist, and was here merely employing a classic commonplace. But Shakespeare, much less of a classicist still, *might* very well have known it as such.

In this connection it may be well to note a cognate error on the part of Mr. Grant White, whose fundamental mistakes as to the legal and classical knowledge in the Plays have given so much countenance to the Baconian theory, which he contemned. In the same essay on " Glossaries and Lexicons," dealing with Achilles' speech in TROILUS AND CRESSIDA (iii, 3) as to the eye being unable to see itself, he quotes from Plato's FIRST ALCIBIADES this passage :

> We may take the analogy of the eye.   The eye sees not itself, but from some other thing ; for instance, a mirror.   But the eye can see itself also by reflection in another eye ; not by looking at any other part of a man, but at the eye only ;

remarking that the " similarity of thought between it and Achilles' speech . . . seems quite inexplicable, except on the supposition that Shakespeare was acquainted with what Plato wrote." Now, as Mr. Grant White ought again to have remembered, the commentators long ago pointed out, on the similar passage in JULIUS CÆSAR (i, 2), that in Sir John Davies' poem NOSCE TEIPSUM (1599), the classicism about the eye being unable to see itself is fully elaborated (Grosart's ed. i, 20, 25) :

> It is because the mind is like the eye
> > Through which it gathers knowledge by degres—
> > Whose rays reflect not, but spread outwardly :
> Not seeing itself when other things it sees.
>
> > Mine eyes, which view all objects, nigh and far,
> > Look not into this little world of mine,
> Nor see my face, wherein they fixed are.

That Shakespeare[1] had read Davies' poem, whether or not he found the idea there for the first time, is nearly certain, in view of the fact that in TROILUS AND CRESSIDA he twice uses the phrase " spirits of sense," which is thrice used in NOSCE TEIPSUM. But, further, as I have elsewhere pointed out,[2] the classicism about the eye was available to him in Cicero's TUSCULANS, which had been translated by Dolman in 1561 ; and the expatiation on this and other themes in the speeches of Achilles and Ulysses, and in the analogous passages in MEASURE FOR MEASURE (i, 1), could all have been derived by him from Davies *plus* passages in Cicero and Seneca which lay to his hand in Florio's translation of Montaigne. The late Professor Churton Collins, who independently advanced the reference to Plato's FIRST ALCIBIADES for the same purpose, has wasted his labour like Mr. Grant White, for lack of resort to the comparative method.

Returning to Lord Penzance, we find him accepting as perfectly conclusive the allegation of Charles Knight, who in turn was no classical scholar, that

the marvellous accuracy, the real and substantial learning, of the three Roman plays of Shakespeare, present the most complete evidence to our minds that they were the result of a profound study of the whole range of Roman history, including the nicer details of Roman manners, not in those days to be acquired in a compendious form, but to be brought out by diligent reading alone. [3]

Over such utterances one has a discouraging sense of the waste of time and thought set up in all fields of criticism by heedless assertion. No scholar will to-day grant a tithe of the claim made by Knight for Shakespeare in regard to Roman history, even if we put aside the consideration that JULIUS CÆSAR is probably founded on or inclusive of other men's work, of which, in the

[1] Whether or not we assume him to have written originally the whole of *Julius Cæsar*.

[2] *Montaigne and Shakespeare*, 2nd ed. pp. 95–105.

[3] *Biography of Shakespeare*, p. 61.

judgment of some of us, there are palpable remains in the extant play.[1] It is now perfectly well established that Shakespeare drew for his Roman plays mainly on North's translation of Amyot's Plutarch;[2] that where

[1] As to this problem, see Fleay's argument (*Life of Shakespeare,* p. 215) to the effect that the play is a condensation of two, a *Cæsar's Tragedy* and a *Cæsar's Revenge.* "That the present play has been greatly shortened," remarks Fleay, "is shown by the singularly large number of instances in which mute characters are on the stage; which is totally at variance with Shakespeare's usual practice. The large number of incomplete lines in every possible position, even in the middle of speeches, confirms this point." Fleay's theory has not been duly considered by later critics, though they have noted Gildon's remark that the play is rather a *Brutus* than a *Cæsar ;* and though Craik had argued (*The English of Shakespeare,* 6th ed. p. 55) that "it might almost be suspected that the complete and full-length Cæsar had been carefully reserved for another drama." The question arises : If the play be a condensation, what and whose work does it condense ? As we have no text before that of the Folio, it is impossible to say that Shakespeare has not taken up the composite performance of Dekker, Munday, Drayton, Webster, and Middleton, entitled *Cæsar's Fall* (or "The Two Shapes") mentioned in Henslowe's Diary, May 22, 29, 1602. Unless this can be excluded, the view that Drayton copied Shakespeare in the phrase about "the elements . . . so mixed" cannot be established. Professor MacCallum, in discussing the point in his *Shakespeare's Roman Plays,* takes no account of the possibilities of mixed authorship, though these are obtruded by the style of much of the play ; and though a recognition of them would suggest a solution of the anomalies in the characterisation, on which he dwells.

[2] See Professor MacCallum's *Shakespeare's Roman Plays and their Background,* 1910, Appendices, as to the possible use of Appian (of which Bynniman's translation had been published in 1578) in *Julius Cæsar,* and the very probable use of it in *Antony and Cleopatra.* For *Coriolanus* there appears to be no source save North's Plutarch. But all along Shakespeare's own creative genius vivifies and expands his material, achieving what mere "culture" could never do. As to his possible knowledge of Garnier's *Marc Antoine* or the Countess of Pembroke's translation, of Garnier's *Cléopatre* or Daniel's translation, and of Garnier's *Cornélie* or Kyd's translation, see the same work, introd. §3. That Shakespeare recalled some lines of Kyd's version of Garnier's *Cornélie* in the speech of Antony to Eros, IV, xiv, 72, was long ago suggested by Steevens (Reed's ed. of Dodsley, 1780, ii, 263).

North errs, following Amyot, Shakespeare errs, following
North ; that at no point does he supplement him ; and
that, in his ignorance or disregard of chronology, he
makes additional mistakes of his own. The blunder of
making Lartius speak of Cato (COR. I, v, 59) as a contemporary or predecessor, is one of these. The blunder
about " the napless vesture of humility " (COR. II, i, 224)
is another, made through following North, who took
Amyot's " *robbe simple* " to mean " a poor gown." The
Baconians and the critics who persist in assigning TITUS
ANDRONICUS to Shakespeare have alike failed to realise
that the writer of the " *Candidatus* " passage in that
play knew the fact that public men seeking office in Rome
wore a white toga, whereas the writer of CORIOLANUS
knew of no such usage. To ascribe to him profound and
exact knowledge of Roman history in the face of such
facts as these is but to exhibit superficiality and inaccuracy.

(2) *Mr. G. G. Greenwood*

In the whole of this discussion we have a standing
illustration of the vitiating force of a prepossession. It
was an idolatrous prepossession that set scholars like
Upton and Theobald in the eighteenth century upon
crediting Shakespeare with high scholarship. Farmer
appreciated Shakespeare as much as they did ; but his
habit of comparative scholarship and his inductive faculty
made clear to him their error. Later idolaters and
Baconians alike have visibly hated him for his pains.
" Anti-Stratfordians " like my friend Mr. G. G. Greenwood, setting out with a primary ideal of a highly " cultured " mind as being alone capable of writing " Shakespeare," clutch desperately at every semblance of classical
knowledge which the plays and poems present ; and,
fiercely intolerant of any semblance of too-ready belief
on the " Stratfordian " side, are profuse of their " certainlys " and " undoubtedlys " over the merest shadows

of evidence for their own faith. Mr. Greenwood, I see, takes me to task[1] for representing him as claiming to prove Shakespeare's familiarity with Horace on the strength of two lines of a hackneyed quotation, when in point of fact he had *in another passage* extended the two lines to four. I cheerfully allow the correction, noting afresh the absurd exiguity of the case as thus stated. Had Mr. Greenwood come to the thesis of the scholarship of the plays in the temper in which he handles what he calls the " tradition " of the authorship, he would have laughed to scorn the notion that a writer's " scholarship " is to be proved by a few scraps of translated quotation, all of the most hackneyed order. He labours to persuade us that when Shakespeare wrote " Most sure, the goddess," he must [2] have remembered, in the original, Virgil's " O dea certe ! " Well, supposing the poet had remembered the whole passage, where is the proof of " scholarship " ? Supposing that, without blenching over Mr. Greenwood's amusingly violent conjunction of Miranda's " certainly a maid " with Venus's " Virginibus Tyriis mos est," we allow that Shakespeare may well have read that and more of Virgil at school, how much nearer are we, in the name of common sense, to proving " wide familiarity with the classics," the now modified form to which Mr. Greenwood reduces his former claim of " remarkable classical attainments " ?[3] On a perfectly straightforward induction, we are not entitled even to claim that the poet had " O dea certe " in mind. Such lines as Chapman's :

Without all question, 'twas a God, the Gods are easily known,

Trans. of *Iliad*, xiii, 69 ;

[1] *The Vindicators of Shakespeare*, (*n.d.*), p. 133.

[2] " It can hardly be doubted," are his words, p. 96.

[3] " The proof " that the dramatist had " a large knowledge of Latin," he originally declared, " is so cogent that it cannot be disputed " (p. 102)—this after deriding every " certainly " and " doubtless " of the " Stratfordians." The claim is simply ridiculous ; and the assertion as to " a very fair amount of Greek " is no better.

N

> These ears and these self eyes approved
> It was a Goddess,
>
> *Id.* xxiv, 209–10 ;
>
> Straight he [Achilles] knew her [Athênê] by her eyes, so terrible they were.
>
> *Id.* i, 204 ;
>
> Whose [Aphroditê's] virtue Helen felt and knew, by her so radiant eyes,
>
> *Id.* iii, 415,

should serve to remind us that, apart from direct translations, Elizabethan *belles lettres* were steeped in classical allusion of every kind, and that no poet could miss knowing many such passages, whatever may have been his schooling. Mr. Greenwood, without going to Farmer for himself, does not scruple to cite from Mr. Churton Collins—whose judgment he elsewhere derides—the charge that Farmer is silent " on almost all the classical parallels which are really worth considering." That charge was disingenuous in the highest degree ; and Mr. Greenwood's reproduction of it without investigation is a confession of critical insolvency. Farmer dealt with all parallels of any importance that had in his day been put forward ; and Mr. Churton Collins has but advanced equally untenable parallels, of which Farmer could have disposed at a glance. The argument (of Mr. Collins) on which Mr. Greenwood relies seems to be that Shakespeare was as likely to have gone to Virgil or Ovid as " to spell out mediæval homilies and archaic Scotch." This again is mere misrepresentation on Mr. Collins's part. Stanyhurst's Virgil is not mediæval homily or archaic Scotch ; and Farmer's point was that the phrase could have *currency* in English. But the essential thing is that the passages founded on are never such as a poet would " go to " a classic for, but passages and phrases such as were in the mouths of all men who affected literature. Neither Mr. Collins nor Mr. Greenwood has made the slightest attempt to meet Farmer's point, that Taylor, the water-poet, who avowed his failure to get through the Latin accidence, and his ignorance of all languages but his own, has a far greater number of classical allusions than occur in all the Shakespeare plays.

In his determination to deny the possibility of any use of translations by an Elizabethan dramatist, Mr. Greenwood, like Mr. Collins, falls into complete misapprehension and distortion of an opponent's statement. He thus represents me as having found a cheap " solution " for the small element of classical knowledge in the LUCRECE :

Shakespeare, " having decided to write a LUCRECE as contrast to the VENUS," [1] may have " had a translation made for him " ! In this easy manner difficulties are jauntily disposed of *per saltum.*

Now, what I actually wrote was :   " It is *not impossible, indeed,*" that Shakespeare may have had a translation made for him " . . . *but that hypothesis is unnecessary.*" The " indeed," one would suppose, must have led any reader, however hasty, to note the waiving of the possible plea.   In the passage from which Mr. Greenwood quotes, I expressly proceed to indicate that, according to one testimony, there *was* a translation of the FASTI, published in 1570, and that there certainly were three " ballads," which might mean poems, or even plays, of any length. Of all this Mr. Greenwood's readers could have no notion from the kind of account he has given of my argument.

In this connection Mr. Greenwood endorses another of Mr. Collins's arguments which, upon any other issue, he would have seen to be worthless.   Whereas I had spoken of " the many manuscript translations then in currency " of Latin poetry, he cites Mr. Collins's statement that in the British Museum MSS. " there are only two versions from *classical dramatists* which can be assigned to the sixteenth century," and that " this seems proof positive that classical translations could not have *circulated on a large scale.*"   Mr. Collins's language might

---

[1] Ref. to *Montaigne and Shakespeare,* 2nd ed. p. 314.

almost have been specially chosen in order to obscure
the problem.   The reason for believing that MS. translations of Latin poetry were numerous in Shakespeare's
day are manifold ; and I confess to being astonished that
any one, even in the ardour of an *idée fixe,* should doubt
the likelihood.   The argument from the lack of *preserved*
MSS. is surprisingly uncritical.   Lady Lumley's translation of the IPHIGENEIA IN AULIS, made about 1530, might
well be preserved by her family ; but who would lay
store by a contemporary manuscript version of the FASTI
made about 1590 ?   That actual versions even of Greek
plays were not all preserved we do know.   Mr. Collins
ought to have been aware that Peele translated one of
the two IPHIGENEIAS of Euripides, and that *that* translation is not extant.   But translations from Ovid, if not
by noted poets, or if unmarked by special merit, would
be much more likely to be let go as old scribblings.

It is a question of supply and demand.   I have seen
a number of French MS. versions, made in the eighteenth
century, from the works of English deists, of which
translations were printed.   The MS. versions, which were
fair copies, may, for aught I know, have been made
either before or after those actually printed ; in those
days even printed deistical books soon became scarce
through seizures and destructions ; and fresh versions
might readily be made by enthusiastic readers for their
friends.   Of the genuine and complete TESTAMENT DE
JEAN MESLIER a good many MS. copies are known to have
been current in the eighteenth century, but not till late
in the nineteenth was one recovered for a printed edition.
The MSS. seen by me were not in the Bibliothèque
Nationale, but in a Paris bookseller's shop.   If such
MSS. translations from English into French were current
in France in the eighteenth century, why should any
one doubt that the habit of doing MS. versions of Latin
poetry, certainly common since, was common in Shakespeare's day ?   Did Mr. Greenwood, I wonder, never

do such translations in his youth ; and, if so, has he preserved them ?[1]

The question of the source of the COMEDY OF ERRORS moves Mr. Greenwood to further exclaim against all who suggest that the author of the plays ever used a translation, though he is perfectly well aware that North's Plutarch was " certainly " used for the composition of the three Roman plays.   Not content with insisting that Warner's translation of the MENÆCHMI is not to be traced anywhere in the COMEDY,[2] he protests against the natural surmise that the play is founded on the old HISTORIE OF ERROR recorded to have been played before Elizabeth " by the children of Powles " in 1576–77.   " Nothing at all," says Mr. Greenwood, " is known about this early play."   After all, we do know that there was such a play, and Mr. Greenwood should let that count for something.   He has committed himself to a theory of the authorship of the plays by a man of whom he professes to know not even the name.   Is all the latitude of hypothesis to be one way ?   But the question is otiose ; and in the interests of rational Shakespeare-criticism I will simply indicate what seems to me the reasonable view of the genesis of the early play, as to which Mr. Greenwood appears to halt oddly between two opinions.

It is really not in the least necessary to find a given original for the COMEDY.   The essential point is that it is a composite work.   Any one who will carefully scan the first two scenes will note that in the first, which has 152 blank-verse lines, the double-endings are only 2 per

---

[1] I can remember doing, in my early teens, a punctilious translation of the Life of Hannibal (then my favourite hero) from Cornelius Nepos ; and in my later teens, versions from Catullus, Horace, Boileau, &c.   Three hundred years hence, doubtless, even those humble performances might be catalogued if they should then exist.   But they certainly will not !

[2] This, of course, is no proof that Warner's version had not been used.   I may point out to Mr. Greenwood, who is so contemptuous of any " manuscript " suggestion, that the printer's

cent ; while in the second, with 103 blank-verse lines, the double-endings number 25 —over 24 per cent. I know no theory of verse evolution which would ascribe the two scenes to the same hand in the same period. But whereas Shakespeare, like the preceding poets, can broadly be seen to have *increased* his proportion of double-endings as he progressed in his art, the first scene of the COMEDY, which has only three double-endings, is much better and more pregnant in style than the shorter second scene, which has twenty-five. No such diffuse verse as that is to be found in any unquestioned work of his at the time at which he used any such large proportion of double-endings.[1] The verse of the second scene, with all its double-endings, is mostly end-stopped—a sure mark of early work. Then the second scene is not Shakespeare's, to begin with ; and the disparity of styles is to be noted throughout the play.

Two alternative inferences are open. The play may have been one of collaboration, or it may have been an adaptation by Shakespeare of a previous work. There is certainly no trace of versification in the style of 1576 : the double-endings in the second scene could hardly be dated earlier than 1591 for any author ; and the theory of collaboration is therefore the more likely one. But on either theory we are relieved of the problem of the classic " source " ; for the collaborator may have known his Plautus without resort either to Warner or to the HISTORIE OF ERROR ; and it is the collaborator (or previous writer) who begins the Plautine work of the play.

By this strictly inductive line of inference we reach a view of Shakespeare's early work which clears up other

advertisement to Warner's translation (entered in 1594) expressly states that it had been circulated for some time in MS.

[1] His share in *Richard III*, where the double-endings are so numerous, has long been in dispute. I have always held that play to be but a partial recast of other men's work—Marlowe's and Kyd's, for choice.

mystifications. For my own part, I have always insisted on a loyal acceptance of Shakespeare's own express declaration that VENUS AND ADONIS was the " first heir of his invention ";[1] and I have never been able to believe that he would have kept such a work by him for years unpublished. The only justifiable interpretation of his phrase is " the first work *planned and composed* by me." Standing to that interpretation, I have always argued that the dramatic work done by him before 1593 was but collaboration or adaptation. But I never held, as Mr. Greenwood so strangely assumes in his SHAKESPEARE PROBLEM RESTATED, that Shakespeare had done no dramatic writing before 1593. Mr. Greenwood puts the case thus : [2]

Mr. J. M. Robertson, too, roundly asserts that we must take Shakespeare strictly at his word, and believes, since *Venus* and *Adonis* was the first heir of his invention, *that all the plays were written subsequently to that date.* If so, these eleven, twelve [" the Meres list "] or more dramas must have been composed by Shakespeare, and brought upon the stage (if not also published) between 1593 and 1598. If Mr. Robertson can believe this, he has indeed great faith, which seems to be reserved for the Strat-fordian Gospel only, *Credat Judæus, non ego !*

I regret to observe that my friend, who is always so scrupulously respectful to the wildest theses of the Baconians, resorts to his " Credat Judæus " only when he is exclaiming at a " Stratfordian " thesis which he has entirely misunderstood, or at some point where his own view is demonstrably the irrational one.[3] It is his indiscriminating zeal for his own thesis of an absolutely unknown and untraceable author—in regard to whom his " faith " is truly transcendental—that has led him so hopelessly to misconceive me. Yet his own footnote to the very passage I have quoted shows him to have

[1] As to this see *Did Shakespeare write " Titus Andronicus "?* pp. 22-23.
[2] Work cited, p. 517.   [3] See above, p. 177.

had the facts in view. To the words above italicised by me he has appended the note :

> With this *alternative*, however, viz. that " Shakespeare for the best reasons would not regard as heirs of his invention plays in which he used other men's drafts or shared with others the task of composition " (*Did Shakespeare write ' Titus Andronicus ' ?* p. 29). It is suggested therefore that he had collaborators [I wrote " collaborators or draughtsmen "] for *The Two Gentlemen, Love's Labour's Lost, The Comedy of Errors,* the *Dream, Richard II,* and other early plays.

Thus Mr. Greenwood had my real opinion before him. What he oddly calls an alternative is the substantive thesis. Why then did he leave standing in the text his complete misconception of it ? Apparently a fling at " the Stratfordian Gospel " could not be foregone. If Mr. Greenwood could only get his " Stratfordian " troubles out of his head, he would, with his power to recognise the non-Shakespearean character of TITUS ANDRONICUS, soon realize that the loyal construction of " first heir of my invention " brings everything into line. The only plays commonly dated before 1598 which we have good ground for pronouncing wholly Shakespearean in style are THE MERCHANT OF VENICE and HENRY IV. With Fleay, indeed, I am willing to date the first draft of TWELFTH NIGHT as early as 1594, agreeing with him that the play was certainly revised or rewritten later. It may, in my opinion, have been the LOVE'S LABOUR'S WON of Meres' list, though it only imperfectly answers to that title. But whether we assign that title to TWELFTH NIGHT or to MUCH ADO or to ALL'S WELL, and date the first form of any one of them before 1598 ; and whether or not we give Shakespeare the whole of the TWO GENTLE-MEN[1] (I prefer to posit a foundation play by Greene), we have no difficulty about placing the plays in question between 1593 and 1598. On the other hand there can be no reasonable doubt that of the plays indicated by

---

[1] Some critics have doubted the genuineness of the entire play.

me as works of collaboration or adaptation a number were written before 1593, as were the HENRY VI group. I would only add that I see nothing of Shakespeare in TITUS, nothing in 1 HENRY VI, and next to nothing in the SHREW.

If the reader will keep in view these last propositions, he may be assisted in his scrutiny of the " classical " thesis, as put by Baconians and others. Quantitatively, the classical case, as regards direct classical allusions and quotations, points precisely to the most doubtful of all the plays published as Shakespeare's in the Folio. This alone is surely a reason for vigilant examination of the general ascription to the dramatist of a " wide knowledge of the classics." Mr. Greenwood, who is so confident about the Latin scholarship of the playwright, agrees with me in dismissing TITUS and most of the HENRY VI group ; and I do not see how he can differ from the mass of critical opinion as to the SHREW ; yet it is on these plays that the bulk of the classical case, which he supports, is founded. But it is only rarely that we need even recall this particular ground for demurrer. The Baconian case, as we have thus far examined it, and as it presents itself in the writers dealt with in the following sections, consists in imputing classical scholarship for every semblance of a classical allusion, and generally collapses on the first application of comparative tests.

(3) *Dr. R. M. Theobald* [1]

Dr. Theobald follows up Mr. Donnelly in this as in other matters, naturally making the most of what had been said by idolatrous commentators, in particular Mr. and Mrs. Cowden Clarke, of the " miraculous " quality of the classical learning shown in the plays. Taking these and other pronouncements as unchallenged, taking Leigh Hunt's verdict (that Shakespeare's poetry is if

[1] *Shakespeare Studies in Baconian Light*, ed. 1904, ch. xiii.

anything " too learned ") as one which " completely
disposes of Milton's uncritical lines," and without saying
a word of the old ESSAY ON THE LEARNING OF SHAKE-
SPEARE by Dr. Farmer, he proceeds in the customary
Baconian way to claim that Shakespeare, the actor,
cannot have had ᵗhe scholarship thus ascribed. " The
poet was assuredly no untutored child of nature, but a
scholar and a man of the world." " The unbiassed,
uncritical [sic !] reader of the poems must inevitably
conclude that the Poet *was* a learned man, and that
neither genius, nor good fellowship, nor cribs can account
for the classic element in his writings." " There can
be no doubt that if there were no controversial necessity
for maintaining that William Shakespeare was a very "
[who said *very* ?[1]] " imperfectly educated man, if it could
be proved that he . . . had had a university education
and acquired a complete mastery of the classic languages
and literature, . . . no one would hesitate to accept the
very strong indications of scholarship in the poems as
. . . entirely characteristic of such antecedents and
training."

Such are the preliminary assertions : let us come to
the proofs. After all his parade of asserted abundance
of classic learning and allusion in the plays, Dr. Theobald
dutifully proceeds to repeat,[2] after Mr. Donnelly and
the rest :

1. The argument which we have fully dealt with above
(p. 189), helplessly copied from Richard Grant White, as
to the derivation from Plato of the passage in TROILUS

[1] Mr. Greenwood, noticing in his *Vindicators of Shakespeare* my
demurrer to his assumption that the view opposed to his ascribed
ignorance and complete lack of culture to the Poet, pleasantly
observes that I " admit " I do not entertain such an idea ; but
adds : " Such an idea has been held and maintained by many "
(p. 136). What I want to know is, who were they ?

[2] For most of his references, he admits, he is " indebted either
to Stapfer or Lewis Theobald." Work cited, p. 305. I take his
selection as showing what Baconians are disposed to stand to.

about the eye not seeing itself.   On that head, no further refutation is needed.

2. Next comes the other well-worn plea from the " most profound and philosophic discussion " in HENRY V (I, ii, 180–213), " of the mutual dependence of different offices and functions in a government, which is compared to the structure of a harmonic combination in music. This idea," we are dogmatically assured, " is taken from a portion of Cicero's long lost treatise DE REPUBLICA, a fragment of which is preserved by St. Augustine." Charles Knight is of course quoted, to the effect that " the lines of Shakespeare are more deeply imbued with Platonic philosophy than the passage of Cicero," so that Shakespeare had inferribly read Plato's REPUBLIC in the original.

We have here the standing illustration of the childish position that Shakespeare had read deeply in the Greek and Latin classics, only to produce a few references to commonplaces which had for centuries been themes of didactic writing. He is assumed on the one hand to have gone to Augustine for the fragment of Cicero, though he gives no other sign of having read the DE CIVITATE DEI ; and he is held on the other hand to have read Plato's REPUBLIC, though he nowhere else seems to quote it. Knight solemnly averred that the passage " develops unquestionably the great Platonic doctrine of the Tri-unity of the three great principles in man with the idea of a State."   It is all a futile mystifi- cation. The Baconians cannot even pretend that the passage is duplicated in Bacon : they do but take for granted that, being " classic," it must be from Bacon's pen. Obviously, the passage is ultimately traceable to Augustine's quotation from Cicero ; and if Shakespeare *had* seen that in the original, his small Latin might suffice to translate it.   But it is idle to make such an assumption in regard to a passage so likely to be dilated upon by divines and moralists. Richard Grant White, whose

far-fetched parallel between Plato and the TROILUS
passage has fooled the Baconians to the top of their
bent, swung to the other extreme when he wrote[1] that
" it is more than superfluous to seek, as some have sought,
in Cicero's DE REPUBLICA the origin of this simile ; for
that book was lost to literature, and unknown, except
by name, until Angelo Mai discovered it upon a palimpsest
in the Vatican, and gave it to the world in 1822." A
professed commentator might have been supposed to
know that Lewis Theobald in his notes on his edition
cited the very passage in question from the DE CIVITATE
DEI. "Cicero," adds White, "very probably borrowed
the fancy from Plato ; but it was not Shakespeare's way
to go so far for that which lay near to hand." *This*
opinion is ignored by the Baconians. They might indeed
reply that the expressions "through high and low and
lower, put into parts, doth keep in one concent . . . like
music," do point specially to Cicero's "Sic *ex summis,
et mediis et in infimis interjectis* ordinibus, *ut sonis . . .
consensu dissimiliorum concinere ;* et quæ harmonia a
musicis . . . in civitate concordiam." But the reasonable inference is that the passage had often been applied
to politics by previous writers.

The passage cited from HENRY V is followed by the
well-known one on the polity of the bees, which Malone
long ago showed to be substantially derived from EUPHUES
AND HIS ENGLAND. But there are other clues. The
theme of "the state of man" is handled afresh in TROILUS,
which the Baconians do not cite in this connection. But
both passages suggest very distinctly reminiscences of
Elyot's BOKE OF THE GOVERNOUR, or of some discourse
or discourses which drew upon that and upon Lilly.
Elyot insists on "degree," and "higher and lower," and
he combines with his thesis the illustration of the bees'
commonwealth. The first chapter of THE GOVERNOUR

[1] *Essay on Shakespeare's Genius*, pref. to ed. of Works, vol. i,
p. ccxxv.

sets out with a pointed discrimination between " publike weale " and " commune weale," the latter term being condemned (with an obvious aim at Sir Thomas More) as suggesting " that every thinge should be to all men in commune." Elyot dwells on

the discrepance of *degrees*, whereof proceedeth ordre. . .   Moreover, take away *ordre* from all things, what should then remayne ? Certes nothynge finally, except some man would imagine eft soones *Chaos.* . . .   Where there is any lacke of ordre needes must be perpetuall conflicte ; and in thynges subiecte to Nature *nothynge of hym self only may be norisshed ;* but when he hath destroyed that wherewith he doth participate by the ordre of his creation, he himselfe of necessite must then perisshe, whereof ensueth universal dissolution. . . .

Hath not [God] set *degrees* and estates in all his glorious workes ? Fyrst in his hevenly ministres, whom . . . he hath constituted to be in divers *degrees* called hierarchies.   Beholde the four elements whereof the body of man is compacte, how they be set in their places called spheris, *higher or lower*, . . . so that in every thing is ordre, and without ordre may be nothing stable or permanent, and it may not be called ordre, except it do conteyne it in *degrees, high and base*. . .   And like as . . . the fire which is the most pure of elements . . . is deputed to the highest sphere or place. . . .

In the second chapter follows an account of the life of the bees :

lefte to man by nature, as it seemeth a perpetuall figure of *a just governance or rule*, who hath among them one principall Bee for their governeur, who excelleth all other in greatness, yet hath he no prick or stinge. . . .   The capitayne hym selfe laboureth not for his sustenance, but all the other for him ; he only seeth that if any drone or other unprofitable bee entreth into the hyve . . . that he be immediately expelled from that company. . . .

Compare Shakespeare :

While that the armed hand doth fight abroad
The advised head defends itself at home.
For government, through *high and low and lower*
Put into parts, doth keep in one concent. . . .
        Therefore doth heaven divide
The state of man in divers functions. . . .

To which is fixed, as an aim or butt,
Obedience ; for so work the honey bees,
Creatures that *by a rule in nature*, teach
The act of *order* to a peopled kingdom.
They have a king. . . .
Who, busied in his majesty surveys . . . .
Delivering o'er to executors pale
The lazy yawning drone.

Henry V. i. 2.

When that the general is not like the hive,
To whom the foragers shall all repair,
What honey is expected ? *Degree* being vizarded,
The unworthiest shows as fairly in the mask.
The heavens themselves, the planets and the centre,
Observe *degree*. . . .
And therefore is the glorious planet Sol
In noble eminence enthroned and sphered. . . .
O, when *degree* is shaked
Which is the ladder to all high designs,
Then enterprise is sick ! How should communities,
Degrees in schools, and brotherhoods in cities. . . .
But by *degree*, stand in authentic place ?
Take but *degree* away, untune that string
And hark, what discord follows ! each thing meets
In mere oppugnancy. . . .
Great Agamemnon,
This *chaos*, when *degree* is suffocate,
Follows the choking. . . .

Troilus and Cressida, i, 3.

It does not follow that Shakespeare had Elyot directly
in mind when he wrote : the general topic is obviously
likely to have been commented often between Elyot's
day and his. Long before Elyot and Lilly, Bartholomew
had discoursed imaginatively of the bees in his cyclopædia
De proprietatibus rerum ;[1] and a hundred homilists must
have handled the theme. But *some* line of connection
between Elyot and Shakespeare there surely was ; and
there is no need to make the latter resort to Augustine
for ideas so certainly current in his own tongue, whether

[1] See the extracts from Berthelet's ed. (1535) of Trevisa's
trans. in Dr. Seager's *Natural History in Shakespeare's Time*, 1896,
pp. 32–33.

written or spoken. The Baconians should be the last
people to dispute that Shakespeare had read and remembered either Elyot's treatise or others which drew from
it and from Bartholomew. Had they found any such
" echoes and correspondencies " between Shakespeare
and Bacon, they would have been glad to rest their whole
case upon them. For the rest of us it is sufficient to say
that Shakespeare certainly did thus utilise English books
and discourses ; and that, this being clear, it is worse
than idle to ascribe to him Greek and Latin erudition
to account for his knowledge of a few classical commonplaces. And still more futile, in this connection, is the
Baconian hypothesis. Dr. Theobald does not make out
one verbal coincidence between Shakespeare and Bacon
in respect of the " Platonic " passages, familiar as were
the commonplaces they set forth.

3. Dr. Theobald reproduces the parallel between
Hamlet's

> Lay her i' the earth,
> And from her fair and unpolluted flesh
> May violets spring !

and Persius'

> Non nunc e manibus istis,
> Non nunc e tumulo, fortunatâque favilla,
> Nascentur violae ?

As I have elsewhere[1] pointed out, the second and third
lines cited from Persius are quoted by Montaigne in his
essay OF GLORY, and are duly translated by Florio (1603).
As there are a number of clear echoes of Montaigne in
HAMLET, the reasonable presumption is that Shakespeare
found them there. But

4. Shakespeare speaks of " method in madness " in
HAMLET, II, ii, 207 ; M. FOR M., V, i, 63 ; and LEAR, IV,
vi, 178–9. This Dr. Theobald refers to Horace :

> Insanire paret certâ. ratione modoque,
> > > *Sat.* II, iii, 271 ;

[1] *Montaigne and Shakespeare*, 2nd ed. 1909, section on " The
Learning of Shakespeare," p. 329.

citing in this connection Bacon's "cum ratione quâ-
dam et prudentiâ insanirent " (Nov. Org. pref.), and an
extract in the Promus from Horace, Sat. II, iii, 120.
This item Shakespeare might very well have known with
" small Latin." But the first two Books of the Satires
had been twice translated in English—by Lucas Evans
in 1564, and by B. L. in 1567 ; and the whole of the
Satires, with the Art of Poetry and the Epistles, by
Thomas Drant in 1567.

5. As might have been expected, the " undiscover'd
country " lines in Hamlet are by Dr. Theobald as by
his predecessors affirmed to be " evidently taken from
Catullus " ; though Dr. Theobald does not repeat Mr.
Donnelly's exploit with the " brief candle " rendering
of *brevis lux*. I must repeat here, what I have pointed
out elsewhere, that the old commentators cited for the
line in question the phrase in Sandford's translation of
Cornelius Agrippa (*circa* 1570 : described by Steevens
as " once a book of uncommon popularity ") : " The
countrie of the dead is irremeable, that they cannot
return " ; and the parallel in Marlowe's Edward II :

> Weep not for Mortimer,
> That scorns the world, and as a *traveller*,
> Goes to *discover* countries yet unknown.

The Catullus derivation is thus one more delusion.

6. Dr. Theobald, however, undertakes to show " many
other quotations from Catullus." He cites from 2
Henry IV, I, i, 47, the phrase " devour the way," claiming to be the first to refer it to " its classic source " in
Catullus (xxxiii) :

> Quare, si sapiet, viam vorabit.

The variorum edition would have informed him that
Blackstone and Malone between them traced it to
Nemesian—

> latumque fuga consumere campum.

But it would further have referred him to Job xxxix :

" He swalloweth the ground with fierceness and rage,"
and to Ben Jonson's SEJANUS (v, 10, near end) :

> With that speed and heat of appetite
> With which they greedily devour the way
> To some great sports.

It was evidently a current trope, like Ariel's " I drink
the air."

7. Parallels between Miranda's " I am your wife "
speech (TEMPEST, III, i, 83) and Ariadne's cry in Catullus'
EPITHALAMIUM PELEI ET THETIDOS (158 *sq.*) :

> Si tibi non corda fuerant connubia nostra, &c. ;

and again between Catullus' *lenta vitis* lines (IN NUPTIAS
JULIÆ ET MANLII, 106 *sq.*) and Adriana's

> Thou art an elm, my husband, I a vine,
> > (*Comedy of Errors*, II, ii, 176 *sq.*)

are really not worth discussing.   The image is of universal
vogue, *e.g.* :

> As the Vine married unto the Elme
> With strict embraces.
> Daniel, *Complaint of Rosamond*, 1592, ll. 829–30.

And it is nearly always those universally current tropes
that are cited to prove Shakespeare's classical scholarship.

8. Of course the lines :

> What stronger breastplate than a heart untainted ?
> Thrice is he arm'd that hath his quarrel just
> > (2 *Henry VI*, III, ii, 232),

must be derived from the equally familiar lines :

> Illi robur et aes triplex
> Circa pectus erat.
> > Horace, *Carm.* I, ii , 9–10.

In vain did Malone point out that in LUST'S DOMINION,
an old play probably in part by Marlowe (*circa* 1588)
occur the lines :

> Come, Moor ; I'm arm'd with more than complete steel,
> The justice of my quarrel.

Those cited from 2 HENRY VI are almost certainly

non-Shakespearean. In any case they are *not* the equivalent of the Horatian phrase.[1]

9. Dr. Theobald naturally affirms that the allusion to Roman lachrimatories in ANTONY (I, iii, 63) is " very remarkable " for its " classic learning," " referring as it does to usages not likely to be familiar to an unlearned writer." It is as likely to have been known to English readers in Shakespeare's day as the Roman usage of burning the dead.

10. " When Aegon begins the story of his life with :

> A heavier task could not have been imposed
> Than I to speak my griefs unspeakable "
>
> *(Com. Er.* I, i, 32),

says Dr. Theobald, " the poet *must* certainly have had in his mind the well-known line of Virgil :

> Infandum, regina, jubes renovare dolorem."

And if he had, he was only referring to one of the most hackneyed lines in Latin literature, which he had paraphrased to his hand in Marlowe and Nashe's DIDO, 1594 :

> A woeful tale bids Dido to unfold,
> Whose memory, like pale Death's stormy mace,
> Beats forth my senses from this troubled breast.

But in neither case do we have a close resemblance.

11. " In the same speech," adds our Baconian, " when he says :

> For what obscured light the heavens did grant
> Did but convey unto our fearful minds
> A doubtful warrant of immediate death.

---

[1] In discussing many other passages of plays which I believe to have been only worked over, adapted, or collaborated-in by Shakespeare, I make no attempt to meet the Baconian argument by suggesting other authorship. To such a consideration Baconians seem to be impervious ; and in nearly every case they can be easily confuted even on their own lines. But as I have in some cases pointed out the non-Shakespearean character of passages stressed by them, I think it well to explain that omission to say the same thing in other cases where it would apply does not mean acceptance of the passage discussed as really Shakespearean.

the poet is reproducing Virgil's

> Praesentemque vires intentant omnia mortem."

It is not necessary to discuss such a " reproduction."

12. The allusions to " Sybil," Xantippe, and the swelling Adriatic in the SHREW (I, ii, 70), prove to Dr. Theobald that the poet's mind is " full of classic illustration " ; and we are reminded that Bacon refers to " Sybilla " [1] in his essay on DELAYS. All this is truly remarkable classical learning ! The fact that most good critics are of opinion that the SHREW was *not* by Shakespeare will naturally have no influence with Baconians.

13. The references to the " many-headed multitude " in CORIOLANUS (II, iii, 17) and to the " blunt monster with uncounted heads " in 2 HENRY IV (Induction, 18) are of course declared to be " derived from Horace— *Bellua multorum es capitum.*"   The Baconian is as usual unaware that in Elyot's GOVERNOUR (1531) occurs the remark that the Athenian democracy " moughte well be called a monstre with many heedes " (B. i, c. 2) ; and that " many-headed multitude " occurs in Sidney's ARCADIA (B. ii).   Yet he might have learned the latter fact from Bartlett's FAMILIAR QUOTATIONS.   Without going to either Elyot or Sidney, Shakespeare could have got the tag from a previous play.   It occurs in the first part of Marlowe's TAMBURLAINE (Pt. I, iv, 3)

> A monster of five hundred thousand heads ;

also in THE TROUBLESOME RAIGNE OF KING JOHN :

> The multitude, a beast of many heads,
> Hazlitt's *Shakespeare Library*, Part II, vol. i, p. 290 ;

and in Daniel's poem (1595) on THE CIVIL WARS (ii, 12) :

> This many-headed monster Multitude ;

[1] Bacon of course wrote " Sibylla."   Shakespeare in the *Merchant* (i, 2) spells " Sibilla " ; and in *Othello* (iii, 4) " Sybill." But in the non-Shakespearean *Shrew* also (i, 2) we have " Sibell " and " Zentippe " ; and in *Titus* (iv, 1) " Sibel."

to say nothing of the later plays which show it to have been a common expression. And Bacon quoted Horace too !

14. Juliet's lines :

> Thou mays't prove false : at lovers' perjuries
> *They say*, Jove laughs,

" may have been taken either from Tibullus or Ovid," says Dr. Theobald, with comparative moderation. The implication is that when Shakespeare puts a " they say " into the mouth of a girl he is writing something which he does *not* know to be a common saw, and is importing a classical quotation from his own reading. Dr. Theobald admits that " in Marlowe there is a metrical version :

> For Jove himself sits in the azure skies
> And laughs, below, at lovers' perjuries."

This he learned from one commentator, and, being convinced that Bacon wrote Marlowe, is willing to mention it. From Malone he might have learned that the phrase occurs also in GREENE'S METAMORPHOSIS. And if he had read Lilly's ENDIMION he would have noted (i, 2) :

If the gods sit unequal beholders of injuries, or laughers at lovers' deceits, then let mischief be as well forgiven in women as perjury winked at in men.

15. The same inveterate unwisdom is shown in the citation of Lewis Theobald's note to the jocular direction of Launcelot in the MERCHANT OF VENICE (II, ii, 42) : " Turn upon your right hand at the next turning, but at the next turning of all," &c. The commentator suggested that it " seemed to be copied " from Terence's ADELPHI, iv, 2. It is simply *not* copied. It is a piece of such fooling as spontaneously goes on in all countries, at all times. Those who thus strive to credit the dramatist with classical learning make him a pedantic fool, who from wide reading harvests only commonplaces and trivialities. Such was neither Shakespeare nor Bacon.

16. Proceeding on his own learning, Dr. Theobald writes that the " sentiment " of the passage :

> If our virtues
> Did not go forth of us, 'twere all alike
> As if we had them not,
>
> *M. for M.* I, i, 34,

" appears to have originated " in Horace's

> Paullum sepultæ distat inertiæ
> Celata virtus.
>
> *Od.* iv, 9.

The sentiment in question is the same as that put in the mouth of Ulysses in TROILUS (III, iii, 96 *sq.*) and it " originated " before Horace. It is substantially put by Cicero, DE AMICITIA, 19. It is developed afresh by Seneca, DE BENEFICIIS, B. v. And if Shakespeare had not met with it—as probably he did not—in the current translations of those treatises, he had it all to his hand, with a thousand other classic saws, in Florio's translation of Montaigne.[1] But it would be folly to suppose that such a maxim as *Frustra habet qui non utitur*, given in the ADAGIA of Erasmus, had not been a thousand times quoted before Shakespeare. The argument that " nothing is seen here to be made for itself . . . the noblest creatures have need of the basest, and the basest are served by the noblest," is elaborated by De Mornay in his treatise on the Truth of the Christian Religion, translated by Sidney and Golding in 1587 (ed. 1604, p. 18) ; and must have been many times employed. In this passage, be it noted, we have the argument found in HENRY V, with the phrase, " so many and so divers pieces . . . so coupled with one another, making one body, and full of so apparent *consents* of affections." The general sentiment that men are not made for themselves is a standing theme :

As learned men have remembered, saying, we be not borne solely to ourselves, but partly to the use of our Countrey, of our

---

[1] See *Montaigne and Shakespeare*, 2nd ed. pp. 95–104.

Parentes, of our Kinsfolkes, and partly of our Friendes and Neyghboures. . . .

Stafford, *Brief Conceipt of English Pollicy*, 1581, N.S.S. rep. p. 15.

How certaine it is, both by the tradition of ancient and moderne judgments avowed, that everie man is not borne for himselfe. Ford, *Honor Triumphant*, 1606, first sentence.

The same Ciceronian maxim is employed twice over by Northbrooke in his Treatise Against Dicing, Dancing, &c. (1577)—in the Epistle Dedicatory and in the text (Sh. Soc. rep. p. 57) ; with the addition of a similar saying translated from Plato, *Homines hominum causa esse generatos*. It was evidently a familiar exordium.

17. And this is the fitting comment on the set of parallels cited to Horace's *Extinctus amabitur idem* and *Virtutem incolumen odimus*. The phrase " I shall be loved when I am lack'd " (Coriolanus, IV, i, 15) is flagrantly proverbial. Such things are said everywhere by unlearned men who never read a line of Latin or even a translation of a classic. It is the very ecstasy of error that moves Dr. Theobald to write : " It is curious to note how frequently the word *lack'd* is used in the Shakespeare passages : it is the equivalent of *Extinctus*." Bacon's Promus, where the quotation is found, is a mere garner of proverbial and colloquial sayings.

18. " Catullus," says Dr. Theobald, " again turns up in the following :

> Be now as prodigal of all dear grace
> As nature was in making graces dear,
> When she did starve the general world beside,
> And prodigally gave them all to you.
>
> *L. L. L.* II, i, 9.

" In the 84th [should be 86th] Epigram, Lesbia is similarly complimented :

> Quae cum pulcherima tota est,
> Tum omnibus una omnes surripuit Veneres."

It would be hard to cite a sentiment more completely run to death in the whole world of amorous poetry.

Surrey's " Praise of his Love," developing this theme,
is the type of a hundred Elizabethan lyrics.

19. Following his namesake, Lewis, Dr. Theobald
refers the opening lines of TROILUS :

> I'll unarm again.
> Why should I war without the walls of Troy,
> That find such cruel battle here within,

to Anacreon : " 'Tis in vain I have a shield," &c.   Once
more we are dealing with a poetic commonplace.   *E.g.* :

> Why fearest thou thy outward foe,
> When thou thy selfe thy harme doste feede ?
>> *Tottel's Miscellany*, Arber's *rep.* p. 204.

It is mostly to such familiar sentiments that the Baconian
references point, making " scholarship " a mere means
of access to common metaphor.   And we have the same
thing in the deducing of Pandarus' comment on the
Trojan warriors from Homer's episode of Helen on the
walls of Troy, copied by Euripides and Statius and a
score of poets more.   Chapman's translation of the first
seven books of the ILIAD appeared in 1598.

20. Following Lewis Theobald again, our Baconian
refers Hamlet's " large discourse " (IV, iv, 36) to Homer
(ILIAD, iii, 109 ; i, 343 ; xviii, 250) ; and notes that
" the profound philosophical expression ' discourse of
reason ' " is " used by Bacon." The expression in
question, as I pointed out long ago, occurs four times
in Florio's translation of Montaigne, demonstrably read
by Shakespeare while he was writing HAMLET. It is
also found in Sidney and Golding's translation of De
Mornay on the Christian Religion (1587) ; repeatedly in
Fenton's translation of Guicciardini (1579) ; four times
in Holland's translation (1603) of one essay (" Of Moral
Virtue ") in Plutarch's MORALIA, and frequently in other
essays ; to say nothing of Hooker (1594) and earlier
writers such as Jewel and More. " Discourse " is an
absolutely normal word in Tudor literature :

> Discourse of state and government.
>> Fenton's ep. ded. to trans. of Guicciardini.

> By the light of natural discourse.
>
> > Hooker, *Eccles. Polity*, B. I, ch. xiv, § 1.

> If you desire to see me beat my breast. . . .
> Then you may urge me to that sad discourse.
>
> > Heywood, *Fair Maid of the West*, v, 1.

> The mind, which in discoursing reacheth far beyond all sensible things.
>
> > Sidney and Golding's trans. of De Mornay.
> >
> > Ed. 1604, p. 7.

> The manner of his [man's] discourse is but to proceed from kind to kind.
>
> > *Id*. p. 42.

The word occurs scores of times in Florio and Holland.

21. " The classic scholarship shown in TITUS ANDRONI-CUS is very remarkable," says Dr. Theobald. " This play is crowded with classic allusions." All scholarship seems to Dr. Theobald " very remarkable." But TITUS is not Shakespeare's work ; and the allusion to Hecuba's killing of Polymnestor (I, i, 136) is from the hand of Peele.[1] If Lewis Theobald and Steevens, who dwell on the classic knowledge exhibited in the allusion to the burial of Ajax (I, i, 379), had done their work properly, they would have noted that the very phrase " wise Laertes' son " occurs in Peele's TALE OF TROY (1589, l. 362), where the quarrel and suicide of Ajax are lengthily described.

So much for Dr. Theobald's selection of classical parallels to prove the Baconian case. " The list," he writes, " might be very easily extended ; but it is needless to do so." It would be useless : the whole " classical " case is hollow, the work of men with preconceived notions, seeking to buttress them by any semblance of proof. On the foregoing series of miscarriages there follows a final attempt to prove " classical knowledge " in the playwright from an alleged use of Latin idioms and

[1] See the point discussed in *Did Shakespeare write " Titus Andronicus " ?* pp. 226–7.

grammatical forms, as set forth in Dr. Abbott's SHAKE-
SPEREAN GRAMMAR. Such forms as "the mightiest
Julius," "without all bail," "after" = *secundum*,
"mere" = sheer, "my very friends," "your," as in

Your serpent of Egypt is bred now of your mud by the operation
of your sun ; so is your crocodile.

Antony, II, vii, 29 ;

such forms as

What with your help, *what with* the absent king ;
What with the injuries of a wanton time,

1 *Henry IV*, v, i, 49

—these and other universally used idioms of the period
are seriously cited as "classic footprints." The argument is not worth discussion. Even if such forms had
all been classic in origin—which they were not—they
had become part and parcel of common English speech,
built up as that so largely was by men schooled in Latin,
in ages when priests wrote interludes for the people, and
preachers quoted from the Vulgate. The "your" form
is put by Shakespeare in the mouths of carters and grave-
diggers, and we are asked to suppose that it stood for
familiarity with Latin.

"Verray," which comes through French *vrai* and not
by imitation of Latin usage, is already completely established in Chaucer, who uses it scores of times in BOECE
alone : "Verray tears," "a more verray thing," "thilke
selve welefulnesse" and "thilke verray welefulnesse,"
"verray blisfulnesse," "verray and parfit good," "false
goodes . . . verray goodes," "verray good," "right
verray resoun," "verray resoun," "no more verraye
thing," "verray light," &c. &c. The usage remained
fixed till Shakespeare's time. "Very" is a normal
usage in Elyot in 1530, as in "my very son Esau." "Very
God" was a standing term in the creeds ; and thus
"very," with somewhat the force of "sheer" or "absolute," was constantly used in theology. It could be
cited twenty times from one popular book : *e.g.* "very

corruption," " in very deed," " in very truth," " a very man," " verie goodness and wisdom," &c. (Sidney and Golding's trans. of De Mornay, ed. 1604, pp. 93, 97, 264, 271, 272, 273, 282, 295, 298, 329, &c. &c.). " Mere " = " pure " or " sheer " was in equally universal use, as will be shown in the next chapter. *Solvuntur tabulæ.*

Uneasily conscious that there are some notoriously awkward facts which he must face, Dr. Theobald avows :

> In writing these plays, it is probable that English translations were used *as a matter of convenience*, even though the writer *might have been* (*sic*) capable of going to the original sources. *My conviction is* that any unbiassed reader will not easily lose the impression that a poet who could so faithfully reproduce the spirit and *entourage* of classic events and persons must have studied them carefully in their most authentic setting. But when this impression does not arise, or is resisted, *I have no means of enforcing it by argument.*" [1]

Quite so. After all the confident bluster we have examined ; after all the " certainlys " and " undoubtedlys " ; after all the procession of quotations and sources in regard to which it is claimed that only one inference is open, we have the inept conclusion that the dramatist " probably " used translations " for convenience "— that Bacon, who so often wrote and so constantly quotes Latin, found it inconvenient to translate for himself. And in fine we have, *pro ratione*, the proposition : " My conviction is. . . . I have no means of enforcing it by argument." That is my case.

§ 4. *Mr. William Theobald*

In 1909 there was posthumously published, under the editorship of Dr. R. M. Theobald, THE CLASSICAL ELEMENT IN THE SHAKESPEARE PLAYS, by his cousin, the late Mr. William Theobald. In the editorial preface there is cited a particular coincidence (non-classical) of idea and phrase between Shakespeare and Bacon, with which I

[1] Work cited, pp. 308–9.

shall deal in the next chapter ; and there is advanced
an argument in regard to the " integration of a number
of small or doubtful resemblances," which will there also
be discussed on its merits. I mention it here by way of
noting that even Dr. Theobald perceived the " faint and
probably accidental " character of some of the " resemblances " alleged by his relative, concerning which he
claims, however, that they are " not entirely valueless."
As to this the reader can decide for himself when he has
perused the series of alleged classical parallels examined
hereinafter. I have gone through one entire chapter
of these, ignoring nothing. But before coming to them
it may be well to note how Mr. William Theobald in his
Introduction deals with the general question of Shakespeare's scholarship.

He begins by accepting the existence of one Shakspere
or Shaksper, for whom he accepts as properly applicable
the epithets of " poet-ape," " Johannes factotum," and
" upstart-crow," which, it is alleged, " two of his contemporaries, who knew him personally," apply to him.
The second and third epithets are those of Greene, concerning whose personal acquaintance with Shakespeare Mr.
Theobald offers no evidence whatever ; and who in any
case wrote as his enemy. The first is from Ben Jonson's
epigram, which might fitly be applied to any one of three
or four of Jonson's enemies ; which is absolutely incompatible with Jonson's express praise of Shakespeare ;
and concerning which also Mr. Theobald makes no attempt
to prove that it was directed at Shakespeare. Then the
theorist proceeds to accept the testimony of Ben Jonson
that " Shakespere " [sic] had " small Latin and less
Greek," saying nothing of the significance of the fact
that this testimony is part of a panegyric upon Shakespeare of Stratford as one of the great dramatists of all
time.

Beyond this Mr. Theobald's exposition consists in
affirming that the author of HAMLET " certainly " knew

Greek ; and in charging " unblushing dogmatism " upon Sir Sidney Lee and others who claim that, beyond rational dispute, Shakespeare of Stratford-on-Avon wrote the plays which we cherish as his. On the point of the " non-Shakespearean " character of some of them, Mr. Theobald is as uncritical as the rest of the Baconians and some of the orthodox, merely arguing that the editors of the Folio " should have known the author of the plays included therein," and that Jonson " must have known also." All the while he assumes that the plays assigned to Shakespeare were written by Bacon, to whom he has no scruple in ascribing TITUS ANDRONICUS.

In so far as he argues that " all writers are, consciously or unconsciously, indebted for ideas, facts, allusions, and, in a word, literary material, to previous writers," he is forcing an open door. The purpose of his book is to prove that Shakespeare did his borrowing largely at first hand from Greek and Latin writers ; and it is in this undertaking that Mr. Theobald fully reveals his incapacity to draw rational inferences from literary evidence. Dr. Furnivall's deliverance, that

Chaucer, George Gascoigne, Holinshed's *Chronicle*, Lyly's *Euphues*, Painter's *Palace of Pleasure*, and other collections of novels, Greene's prose tales, Montaigne's *Essays*, are the main books we trace in [Shakespeare's] works,

Mr. Theobald pronounces a " preposterous utterance." We shall see in due course the value of his opinion.

At one point Mr. Theobald's argument becomes so incoherent that it is difficult to understand how even a careless editor could pass it without comment. He accuses of gross misrepresentation an anti-Baconian writer who first remarked on the folly of the thesis that Bacon would choose as his mask " a rude unlettered fellow " ; and later observes that " the Baconians had to prove that Shakespeare was a scholar." Obviously the writer meant that they had to prove that the *play-wright* was a scholar. But after thus fiercely denouncing

a mere ellipsis, Mr. Theobald in his own person reasons
thus :

> The true reason why the writer of the plays (Bacon) did not
> care to bring too prominently forward his knowledge of the Greek
> tragedies, was probably the risk thereby incurred of jeopardising
> his cherished incognito ; as his literary stalking-horse, Shakspere,
> was too well known to be readily credited with deriving materials
> from the works of Sophocles, Æschylus, or Euripides. *Even at
> second-hand, through Seneca, the risk was too great to be encountered.*

I invite attention to this piece of reasoning. It affirms
(1) That the man Shakespeare was too well known (*i.e.*,
by implication, to be no scholar) to permit of the real
author introducing into the plays any signs of knowledge
of the Greek classical drama, or even of a dramatist so
widely read in those days as Seneca. But it is involved
in this proposition (2) that Shakespeare *could* pass among
those who knew him not only as the author of all the
poetry and eloquence in the plays, but as having scholarship enough for what scholarly touches there *are* in them.
That is to say, those who knew Shakespeare would see
no reason for doubting that he was able to write all the
plays and poems he signed—this by the admission of the
Baconian.

Be it now noted (3) that Mr. Theobald in his opening
chapter undertakes to show that the *plays* reveal not
only a " good," a " thorough," nay, even a " pedantic "
knowledge of Latin literature in general, but a knowledge
of Aristotle, Euripides, and Homer ; and (4) that in
subsequent chapters he claims to prove, still from the
plays, a knowledge not only of these writers but of Æschylus, Anacreon, Aristophanes, Athenæus, Ælian, Appian;
Plato, Theocritus, Tyrtæus, and Apollonius Rhodius,
to say nothing of such out-of-the-way Latin writers as
Alanus, Ausonius, Avienus, Fracastorius, &c. &c. Bacon,
then, could safely let his unlettered mask figure as
possessed of all that classical reading, while forced to
withhold all signs of knowledge of " Sophocles, Æschylus,
or Euripides," or even Seneca !

After this sample of his mental processes, it is perhaps superfluous to explain that when Mr. Theobald undertakes to convict Farmer of gross ignorance he merely exhibits entire failure of comprehension. Farmer remarked that Taylor, the " Water Poet," has " more scraps of Latin and allusions to antiquity than are anywhere to be met with in the writings of Shakespeare." Upon this Mr. Theobald thus explodes : " To understand the audacity of this assertion, it is sufficient to quote the authority of Taylor himself," citing the poet's avowal that he could never get beyond *possum* and *posset*. Of this fact, Farmer was not only perfectly aware : he had given the very clue which Mr. Theobald takes ! In his preface [1] he had mentioned the passage about *possum* and *posset* ; and in the text he had expressly quoted Taylor's avowal that " he never learned his Accidence, and that Latin and French were to him heathen Greek " ; going on : " *yet, by the help of Mr. Whalley's argument,* I will prove him a learned man, in spite of everything he may say to the contrary." The whole point of Farmer's argument was that an English poet avowedly ignorant—in the scholarly sense—of any language but his own could nevertheless make hundreds of classical allusions in virtue of his English reading, and could even use many scraps of Latin.

I do not accuse Mr. Theobald of gross misrepresentation : his infirmity appears to have been intellectual rather than moral. But when he proceeds to pretend that Farmer, in pointing to the English books where Shakespeare could have found his " classical " matter, in positing something harder of belief than the " classical " thesis itself, Mr. Theobald exhibits a fairly low standard of candour. He actually names French writers without mentioning that Farmer had referred to English translations of them. But he probably could not understand

---

[1] To the second edition, in which first occurs the passage above cited and denounced by Mr. Theobald.

that in pointing to the English currency of the classical items in dispute Farmer did not mean to claim that Shakespeare had necessarily read every one of those books—though he very well might—but simply to show that the knowledge in question was current for English readers without resort to Greek and Latin.   The rationale of the whole problem is hidden to a writer of Mr. Theobald's intellectual habits.

This is finally made clear by his handling of the point of the parallel, pressed by himself, between the declaration in the SHREW that " 'Tis death to any one in Mantua, To come to Padua." For this Mr. Theobald was bound to find a classic original ; and he fathers it on Aulus Gellius' story (vii, 10) of the decree of the citizens of Athens against those of Megara. In the eighteenth century, George Colman had traced a character in the SHREW to the untranslated TRINUMMUS of Plautus ; whereupon Farmer pointed out, in his ESSAY, that both the character and the part of the plot in question had been borrowed from the previous comedy of SUPPOSES, a translation by George Gascoigne from Ariosto's SUPPOSITI. Colman was convinced on this head, though he held out on others. Not so Mr. Theobald. He decides (p. 167) that " as the work of Gascoigne was published without date, Farmer's argument does not carry conviction." Farmer, I fancy, would not have been concerned to carry conviction to Mr. Theobald. But in the interest of minds more permeable to reason it may be well to mention that Gascoigne's SUPPOSES was published as having been " presented " at Gray's Inn in 1566.   It would thus have been known to actors apart from publication ; but it is known to have been published by Jeffes in 1587.

Since Farmer's day, the critical examination of the SHREW has been carried far enough to make us sure that Shakespeare had no hand in its framing, but at most touched it up and inserted some passages.   This, of course, is not a matter to be put to Baconians ; but it is one the consideration of which may save some brands from their burning. Mr. Theobald is not an investigator of historic fact, but a myth-maker. In his pages, I suppose, are to be found all the standard mares' nests of his sect. He duly enshrines the " *Honorificabilitudinitatibus.*" He has read in the *Athenæum* the sentence on it from the CATHO-LICON of Giovanni da Genova ; and then, in the true Baconian manner, he pronounces (p. 170) : " Whether Bacon was the more likely man to have had recourse to the pages of that work, or Shakespeare, I confidently leave to the common sense of my readers." Mr. Theobald is truly a precious authority on common sense. The old variorum edition could have informed him that the " word " is to be met with in Nashe's LENTEN STUFF, in a passage (WORKS, ed. McKerrow, iii, 176) which shows it to have been quite familiar in that day. We are dealing with perhaps the most impossible of all the Baconians.

None the less his entire chapter on " Classical Allusions Generally " shall be examined in detail. I hesitate to express my opinion of its general critical quality before the reader has had a full opportunity of judgment ; and thereafter he may be more moved to compassion than to censure. Let him but note that in a number of instances Mr. Theobald coincides in his claims with Dr. R. M. Theobald ; and that in these cases I refer back, or forward to the next chapter.

1. Captious (ALL'S WELL, I, iii, 193).
    See below, Ch. VIII, p. 283.

2. **Lethe'd** (" a Lethe'd dulness " : ANTONY, II, i, 27).
" Simply the Latin *Lethæus* in an English dress," says Mr. Theobald, " as when Statius uses the expression *Lethæum vimen*, a rod dipped in Lethe (or Lethe'd rod), *Thebais*, ii, 30."
There was no need to resort to Statius. " Lethe " had the current force of " oblivion." Ascham in THE

Scholemaster notes (Arber's rep. p. 75) that Plato
" doth plainelie declare that pleasure . . . doth ingender
in all those that yield up themselves to her, foure notorious
properties," the first being λήθην, " forgetfulness of all
good things learned before."   In the drama and in poetry
the word was in common use :

> I have drunk Lethe.
> > Webster, *The White Devil*, iv, 2.

> His memory to virtue and good men
> Is still carousing Lethe.
> > Id. *Appius and Virginia*, iv, 1.

> To drown the pain it did abide
> In solitary Lethe's sleepy tide.
> > Kyd, *Cornelia*, Act ii.

> Drinking of the Lethe of mine eyes,
> He is forced forget himself.
> > Daniel, *Complaint of Rosamond*, 1592.

3. **Exigent** (Antony, IV, xiv, 62).
See below, p. 310.

4. **Prosecution** (= following up : same passage).
" Used precisely as in Latin," says Mr. Theobald.   But
also precisely as in many English writers :

> Cæsar . . . also prosecuted them [his enemies] with such
> celerity and effect. . . .
> > Elyot, *The Governour*, i, 23 ; Dent's rep. p. 100.

> He with his army did prosecute after.
> > Latimer, *First Sermon before Edward VI*. Dent's rep. p. 73.

> To prosecute their purposes.
> > Ascham, *Scholemaster*, Arber's rep. p. 69.

> Our intent is not so exactlie to prosecute the purpose.
> > Puttenham, *Arte of English Poesie*, Arber's rep. p. 127.

> The King . . . prosecuted still in questioning.
> > Greene, *Penelope's Web*, 1587 : Works, v, 232.

> I will prosecute what disgrace my hatred can dictate to me.
> > Jonson, *Cynthia's Revels*, v, 2.
> Left then to prosecute her.
> > Lilly, *Love's Metamorphosis*, i, 2.

P

Whose bodies are followed in the world with lust, and prosecuted in the grave with tyranny.

Id. ib.

Prosecuting of this enterprise.   Prosecute the cause.
Sir John Oldcastle, Pt. I, iii, 1 ; v, 10.

Go prosecute the Senate's will.
A Knack to Know an Honest Man, 1596, l. 516.

One of Cæsar's captains which was sent to Rome to prosecute his suit.

North's trans. of *Life of Cæsar*.   Skeat's *Sh. Plutarch*, p. 70.

5. The Ablative Absolute :

My music playing far off, There, I will betray, &c.,
Antony, II, v, 10.

Such constructions were perfectly normal in English— the natural result of Latin culture.   Latimer has :

Those premises considered, I would have you, &c.,
Fifth Sermon before Edward VI.

Elyot has many such constructions.

6. Percussion (CORIOLANUS, I, iv, 59).

" Not an English word," says Mr. Theobald, on the score that Richardson gives only this and instances from Bacon.

The Oxford Dictionary gives instances from Phaer, REGIMENT OF LYFE, c. vii, and Holland's PLUTARCH, p. 1348.

Compare :
Salute me with thy repercussive voice.
Jonson, *Cynthia's Revels*, i, 1 (1601).

7. Progeny (= ancestry. CORIOLANUS, I, viii, 11).

" Used not in *its English sense*," says Mr. Theobald, " but as the equivalent of ancestry and of the Greek word *progenêtor*. It is occasionally used in this sense of ' ancestry ' in Latin by Cicero and Terence, but I make bold to say it would not have been so used by a man who was not a good classical scholar and aware of the authority he had for *so uncommon a use of the word*." No man who

knew anything of Tudor English could have advanced
such an assertion. The sense of " ancestry " was if anything more common than that of offspring or posterity.
The Oxford Dictionary gives instances from Wiclif,
Gower, Higden, Fabyan, and Cranmer. Add :

> They descend of famous progeny.
>> Roye, *Rede me and be nott Wrothe*, 1528.
>> Whittingham's rep. p. 101.

> His name is Person, and his progeny,
> Now tell me of what ancient pedigree ?
>> Greene, Lacena's Riddle, in *The Tritameron of Love*, 1584.

Honour'd for his parentage and progeny [said of an unmarried
youth].
>> *Id. Mirror of Modesty*, 1584 : Works, iii, 9.

Whose [Danae's] parentage and progeny [before bearing
children].
>> *Id. Tritameron of Love*, 1587 : Works, iii, 69.

I therefore dissent because the destinies have appointed my
progeny from such a peevish parent.
>> *Id. Planetomachia*, 1585 : Works, v, 40.

> My parents and progeny.
>> *Id. Menaphon :* Works, vi, 110.

> The honour of thy house and progeny.
>>> Peele, *David and Bethsabe*, ii, 2.

Neither noble progenie, succession, nor election be of such force
that. . .
>> Elyot, *The Governour*, B. ii, c. 1 ; Dent's ed. p. 117.

In a horse or good greyhound we praise that we see in them
and not the beauty or goodness of their progeny.
>>> *Id.* B. ii, c. 5, p. 130.

> Born of worshipful progeny.
>> Stubbes, *Anatomie of Abuses*, Collier's rep. p. 42.

> Wot ye not how great lord I [Pride] am,
> Of how noble progeny I came ?
>> Medwall, *Nature*, in Farmer's *Lost Tudor Plays*, p. 66.

8. Microcosm (Coriolanus, II, i, 57).

" The word ' microcosm,' " remarks Mr. Theobald,
" occurs in Bacon, Syl. Syl. Cent. x, introd., which was
not published in Shakespeare's lifetime. Also in Sir

Walter Raleigh's HISTORY OF THE WORLD (B. i, ch. 2);
but this was not published when the play was written
(the first volume being published in 1614)." Mr. Theobald does not expressly say that these were the first uses
of the word in English books apart from Shakespeare,
but unless he means that he is saying nothing. Let us
then supplement somewhat his literary information :

Microcosm, as the Oxford Dictionary notes, occurs in
Lydgate (1426), Norton (1477), Dee (1570) ; the First
Part of THE RETURN FROM PARNASSUS (1597), and Florio's
Montaigne (1604). Compare the following :

> That is to say, *Macrocosmus* and *Microcosmus*, which is to say,
> the greater world and the lesser world.
> > Gascoigne, *Viewe of Worldly Vanities :* Works, ed.
> > Cunliffe, ii, 234.

> Let us make Man ; that is, a wonderful creature, and therefore
> is called in Greek *Microcosmos*, a little world in himself.
> > Stubbes, *The Anatomie of Abuses*, 1583, Ep. Ded.

> For our English *Mikrokosmos or Phenician Dido's* hide of
> ground.
> > Nashe, *Lenten Stuffe*, 1599. Works, ed. McKerrow, iii, 186.

> No my harts, I am an absolute *Microcosmus*, a pettie world of
> myself.
> > Lilly, *Endimion*, 1591, iv, 2.

In 1603 John Davies of Hereford published a long poem
entitled MICROCOSMUS. It would thus appear that the
word was attainable without resort to consultation with
Bacon or Raleigh.

9. **Illustrous** (CYMBELINE, I, vi, 108).

" Who but a classical scholar, nay, a very pedant,
would have used the word ' illustrous ' in place of dim ? "
asks Mr. Theobald—after explicitly arguing that Bacon
dared not indicate his scholarship in the plays put out
by him under the name of Shakespeare. As it happens,
we do not know that Shakespeare ever did this. The
Folio reads " illustrious " ; and as there is no warrant for
giving to *that* word the sense of " dim," some editors

have substituted " illustrous." Rowe put " unlustrous,"
and that reading is adopted in the Globe edition. So
that " Shakespeare's " pedantry is still to prove.

The Oxford Dictionary, as it happens, does not include
the word " illustrous " at all. This is surprising, for that
word does actually appear in Shepherd's edition of Chapman's MINOR POEMS AND TRANSLATIONS, in the prose
JUSTIFICATION OF " PERSEUS AND ANDROMEDA " (1614)
p. 194, col. 2, in the phrase " their present doctrinal and
illustrous purposes." Unless Shepherd gives a false
reading, the Dictionary has fallen into a sin of omission.
The word appears again, however, with the meaning
" illustrious," in Shepherd's edition of Chapman's translation of the ILIAD, viii, 182. Here the bare scansion calls
for three syllables, though four could pass. On the
whole, the presumption is that the word had some
currency, and that Shakespeare did *not* coin it.

10. **Eager** (HAMLET, I, ii, 68).

" The word ' eager,' " Mr. Theobald informs us, " is
here used in its classical or root sense of sharp, from the
Greek ἀκίς (!), a sharp point, whence metaphorically sharp
in the sense of acid, which none but a scholar would have
so introduced. The commoner word acid is not used
in the plays. *' Posset' here is introduced, too, into the
language for the first time.*"

Such folly " striketh a man dead," as the Elizabethans
would say. Mr. Theobald is unaware that " eager " is
simply the French *aigre*, and is so used by scores of
writers between Chaucer and Shakespeare. He does
not even know that " the commoner word acid "—then
very *un*common—is found in Bacon ; or else he ignores
the point, as not serving the Baconian purpose. His
remark as to " posset " is astounding even to a reader
of the Baconians. It was an every-day word in every
English household. Heywood puts it twice in the mouths
of farmer-folk in the First Part of his EDWARD IV,

published in 1600. Ben Jonson in the preliminary matter to EVERY MAN OUT OF HIS HUMOUR (1599) has (List of Characters : Carlo Buffone) :

A slave that will swill up more sack at sitting than would make all the guard a posset.

It occurs in BLURT, MASTER-CONSTABLE (1602, iii, 3) assigned to Middleton ; and thrice in Webster and Marston's MALCONTENT, published in 1604.

A posset, the commentators explain, was " wine boiled with milk." The dialogue in THE MALCONTENT illustrates this description.

11. **Implorators** (HAMLET, I, iii, 129).

Mr. Theobald's note on this word must be cited in full, to do it justice : " The word ' implorators ' is neither Latin nor English, though it might conceivably have been formed (as *amator* is from *amare*) had the metre required it. But the metre forbids it, and Lewis Theobald was therefore justified in treating the word as a printer's error for implorers. If, however, the word ' implorators ' was the poet's own word, it clearly shows how the classical bias of his mind *was so strong as to overpower elementary requirements*, in this case of prosody." Q. E. D.

Most modern editors, recognising, *pace* Mr. Theobald, that prosody does *not* reject " implorators," retain the word. They happen to know that there was a French legal word *implorateurs*, which probably was Anglicised long before Shakespeare by the lawyers.

12. **Green Wound** (2 HENRY IV, II, i, 93).

Mr. Theobald impressively notes that Bacon in the Essay OF REVENGE speaks of a man keeping his own wounds green. " It was also," he explains, " a classical usage, as Euripides applies the term *chloros*, green or fresh, to blood " (HECUBA, 129). So that Shakespeare had appropriately put a Greek expression in the mouth of Mrs. Quickly, the better to reveal his scholarship !

This perhaps deserves to rank, even in competition with the assertion about " posset," as the last word in Baconian wool-gathering. The phrase must be about as old as English. In the MORTE DARTHUR we read how Sir Tristram " in his raging took no keep of his green wound that King Mark had given him " (B. viii, ch. 14). In Surrey's first poem in TOTTEL'S MISCELLANY (1557) is the line :

> Of mine old hurt yet feel the wound but green.

And in Sackville's COMPLAINT OF BUCKINGHAM—part of his Induction to the MIRROUR FOR MAGISTRATES (1563) —is the line :

> And feeling green the wound about his heart.
> Sackville's Works, ed. 1859, p. 135.

It may be well to add, in a world in which Baconians flourish, that the phrase was current in the Elizabethan drama :

> Lest he dismount me while my wounds are green.
> Kyd, *Soliman and Perseda*, i, 4.
> That wound yet too green.
> Chapman, *The Blind Beggar of Alexandria* (1596) i, 1.
> Wounds must be cured when they be fresh and green.
> Greene, *Alphonous King of Arragon*, iii, ed. Dyce, p. 236.
> And for your green wound . . .
> Jonson, *Every Man in his Humour*, iii, 2.
> That [comfort which green wounds receive from sovereign balm.
> Dekker, *The Honest Whore*, Part I, v, 2, near end.

13. **Absque hoc** (2 HENRY IV, V, v, 28).
See above, p. 72.

14. **Cæsar and his Fortune** (1 HENRY VI, I, ii, 138).
Mr. Theobald, in a lucid interval, admits that the phrase " is almost too familiar to quote," but proceeds to point out that " the epithet ' insulting ' applied to the ship, is used . . . in its purely Latin sense."   As to this *see below*, p. 321.

15. **Proditor** (*Id*. I, iii, 31).

This, Mr. Theobald explains, " is a Latin word and not an English one," quoting Cicero and Horace. It will be shown below, p. 337, that the word *was* in English use.

16. **Simular** (LEAR, III, ii, 54).
See below, p. 348.

17. **Virtue** (*Id*. V, iii, 104).

" Here the word ' virtue ' is used in its primary classical sense, without any reference to moral goodness : that is, trust to thy ' valour ' alone to save you."

The word in this sense was perfectly familiar, and there is absolutely no innovation in the matter. Elyot in his GOVERNOUR has the saying :

> A man is called in Latin *vir*, whereof, saith Tully, vertue is named.
>
> B. iii, c. 9. Dent's rep. p. 229 ;

and he has the phrase :

> A semblance of vertue or cunning (B. i, c. 20).

About the same date, Tyndale in his translation of the ENCHIRIDION of Erasmus has the expression :

> Christ, the virtue or strength of God ;

and in the first chapter of Sir Thomas North's translation of Plutarch's Life of Coriolanus, read by Shakespeare, we have the sentence :

> Now in those days valiantness was honoured in Rome above all other virtues : which they called *virtus*, by the name of virtue itself, as including in that general name all other special virtues besides. So that *virtus* in the Latin was as much as valiantness.
>
> Skeat's *Sh. Plutarch*, p. 2.

On the stage we have :

> And, valiant with a forced Vertue, longs
> To die the death.
>
> Hughes, *Misfortunes of Arthur*, IV, ii, 206–7.

One is moved to ask whether Mr. Theobald, at the

height of his hallucination, could suppose that the gospel phrase, " Virtue had gone out of him," and such a constantly used phrase as " the virtue of herbs," were classic mysteries for common folk ?

18, 19, 20, 21. **Epitheton, Festinately, Pernicious,** and **Sequent,** all previously put forward by Dr. Theobald, are dealt with below, in ch. viii.

22. **Laus Deo, bone intelligo** (L.L.L. V, i, 24).

" The author," declares Mr. Theobald, " must have been a fair scholar to know that there is no such word as *bone*, but only *bene*." It would be interesting to know what Mr. Theobald would regard as " small Latin." For the rest, the context is corrupt ; [1] and " bone " does *not* occur in the original, being merely an editorial guess.

23. **Perge** (L.L.L. IV, ii, 50).

" This is not a word that would be picked up in any translation," says Mr. Theobald. It might, however, have been picked up at school ! Mr. Theobald, with ripe learning, points to Seneca, THYESTES, i, 23 ; Virgil, ECLOGA, vi, 13 ; Claudian, DE BELLO GILDONICO, 201, from which it " *may* have been borrowed." Several other instances of the use of the word *may* be found in Stephanus. With all of the writers named, says Mr. Theobald, " the author of the plays was familiar." " Paper is patient," say the Germans—borrowing from the Latin.

24. **Deformed** (L.L.L. IV, ii, 50).

" Your beauty . . . hath much deformed us." The word is " here used in its classical or root sense, which does not necessarily involve the idea of ugliness as the English word does ; and its use in this place is, I consider, a clear indication of the scholarly mind of the author," says Mr. Theobald. Unluckily, the word had been used

[1] *See above,* p. 3.

in the " classical or root sense " by English authors long
before Shakespeare :

> His hair and beard deformed with blood and sweat.
> Kyd, Cornelia, Act iii.

> He shall not reform himself, but rather deform his conscience.
> Hooper, Declaration of Christ and His Office,
Parker Soc. rep. p. 29.

> To rip up all our deformities I mind not here.
> Foxe, Four Considerations, pref. to Martyrs.

> Now over and beside this deformity of life.
> Id. Exordium. Cattley's ed, i, 12.

> Joys that deform us with the lusts of sense.
> Chapman, The Gentleman Usher, iv,1.

> A . . . jester that . . . with absurd smiles will transform any
> person into deformity.
> Jonson, Every Man out of his Humour : List
of Characters ; CARLO BUFFONE.

> Where they shall see the time's deformity
> Anatomized in every nerve and sinew.
> Id. Ib. Induction.

25. **Receipt** (= receptacle : MACBETH, I, vii, 66).

" The word . . . in this sense is very classical," says
Mr. Theobald, referring to Cicero's TUSCULANS, I, xx
(should be xxii), 52, for " receptacle." The astonishing
thing is that there is no reference to Bacon, who in the
Essay OF GARDENS (No. 46) speaks of two kinds of
fountains of which one is " a faire receipt (= pool or
basin) of water." How comes it that the Baconians had
not detected such a " coincidence " ? Of course, as
Bacon's phrase shows, the word was in common use in
that sense. It was so long before. Hoccleve has :

> My . . . greedy mowth, (receite of swich outrage).
> La Male Regle de T. Hoccleve, l. 114.

Lydgate has :

> The thought, resceyt of wo and of complaynt.
> Complaynt of the Black Knight, l. 226.

Roye has :

> The prestes of Babilone . . .
>   Had an ydole called Bell.
> Outwardly made all of bras,
> And inwardly of earth it was,
>   Having a *resceyte* so devised
> That the ydole semed to devowere
> An C shepe with wine and flower
>   Daily unto it sacryfised.
>
> *Rede Me and be nott Wrothe*, 1528.

And Heywood uses the word twice for the " capacity " or
" holding power " of a theatre in his APOLOGY FOR ACTORS.
Compare his line :

> Of all the houses for a king's receipt.
>
> 2 *Edward IV* (1599), iii, 2.

26. Multitudinous—Incarnadine (II, ii, 62).

Not content with " incarnadine," Mr. Theobald announces, *more suo*, that " multitudinous " is " here used
for the first time." Enlightened from within, the Baconian dreams not of consulting the variorum edition,
where he might learn that the word is used by Dekker
in THE WONDERFUL YEAR, 1603, in the phrase, " the
multitudinous spawn." As to incarnadine, *see below*;
p. 361.

27. Way of life (MACBETH, V, iii, 22).

Some one having expressed perplexity over this phrase,
Mr. Theobald pityingly observes that it is " an example
of how the eyes of critics, commentators and editors are
sealed by the absurd assumption that the author of the
plays was a poor classical scholar." He confidently
points to " *secretum iter et fallentis semita vitæ* " in
Horace, EPIST. I, xviii, 103, as " probably the source
whence the phrase ' way of life ' was derived." The
puzzle is, how came Shakespeare to be able to speak
English at all save through Latin ?

Not for the Baconian is the old leisurely debate over
" way " and " May." Colman gave two instances to

justify Johnson's emendation, " May," that word being a common poetic figure for the period of youth, as Steevens further proved by seven more instances. But, as it happens, other poets and dramatists *did* write " way of life " for " course of life "—*e.g.* Massinger in VERY WOMAN and NEW WAY TO PAY OLD DEBTS ; and in PERICLES, i, 1, that simple form occurs, as in HENRY VIII we have " the way of our profession." And even apart from such usages, it seems sane to infer that English people could think or speak of the path or the journey of life without getting the idea from Horace.

28. Wicked Hannibal (M. FOR M. II, i, 170).

Mr. Theobald with profound learning shows that Hannibal was a name for detestableness among the Romans. He is convinced that Bacon-Shakespeare studied the classics thus to illuminate the dialogue of contemporary clowns !

And he would doubtless give the same explanation in the case of Ben Jonson :

> Your maids too know this, and yet would have me turn Hannibal, and eat my own flesh and blood.
> *Every Man in his Humour*, iii, 2.

" Hannibal " for " cannibal " was a standing tag.

29. Loss of Question (M. FOR M. II, iv, 90).

Mr. Theobald takes joy in the explanation, given so long ago as 1852, that " loss of question " stands for *casus questionis*. He does not explain why Shakespeare should translate *casus* by " loss." The passage is in all likelihood corrupt. Johnson's suggested emendation, " toss of question," flouted by Grant White, would make it clear enough.

30. Delighted spirit (M. FOR M. III, i, 122).

This old crux gives Mr. Theobald another opportunity. His cousin, Dr. Theobald, is all for " delated " : he himself prefers to read " delighted " as *de-lighted* = deprived of light, because Homer (ILIAD, xviii, 6) uses the phrase " to lose the light " as the equivalent for " to die." And yet probably Shakespeare just wrote " delighted " and *meant* " delighted " in the sense of " hitherto full of the delight of life " !   Anyhow, " de-lighted " is not classical.

31. On p. 40, whether of artistic intent or by the skill of his editor, Mr. Theobald has the oracular passage :

> In *Hamlet* Polonius says (II, ii, 105) " Perpend,"

making no comment.   On p. 48 we have a similar intimation with reference to THE MERRY WIVES, II, i, 19.   Here Mr. Theobald censures an editor for saying that " perpend " was " an affected term."   This hits Dr. R. M. Theobald, who noted that in Shakespeare " the word is used only by pedantical speakers or professional fools." " There was no affectation in its use in the time of Elizabeth," says Mr. W. Theobald, " as it was a word used in all seriousness by Bale, *Burnet*, Fox, and *Brown*."   The general proposition is quite true.   But only the Baconian can follow Mr. Theobald in proceeding to connect Shakespeare's use of it with Lucretius.   It was current English. *See below*, p. 330.

32. **Evitate** (MERRY WIVES, V, v, 215).

The word, says Mr. Theobald, " is rarely used in English, but Bacon was one of the few who adopted it," and this in " a work not published in Shakespeare's lifetime."

See below, p. 308, as to another source of vocabulary open to poor Shakespeare in this matter.

33. **Thrice-blessed** (M.N.D.; I, i, 74).

" The use of ' thrice,' as an intensitive," says the indefatigable Mr. Theobald, " was *a peculiarity of Shakespeare's style* " ; and " this is very suggestive of the Greek," and also of the Latin.   It was even such a peculiarity as the taking of salt with meat. Every dramatist of the period did it :

Thrice-happy. Thrice dreadful. Thrice mighty. Thrice noble.
Thrice royal. Thrice sacred. Thrice almighty. Thrice sacred.
> Chapman, Shepherd's vol. of *Minor Poems*, &c., pp. 4, 10, 16, 49, 128, 243, 255, 342. A dozen more instances could easily be found in the same poet.

Thrice reverend (thrice). Thrice valiant (twice). Thrice haughty. Thrice worthy. Thrice honourable.
> Peele, Dyce's vol. of Greene and Peele, pp. 365, 366, 367, 377, 380, 462, 543, 547.

Thrice-renowned.
> Kyd, *Soliman and Perseda*, i, 3.

Thrice-renowned.
> Daniel, *Cleopatra*, l. 704. (III, ii).

Thrice fortunate.
> Lilly, *Endimion*, iv, 3.

"Nothing hath made my master a fool but flat scholarship," says Epiton in the last-cited play.

34. By lifting a lost passage from p. 40 to p. 49 we realise that Mr. Theobald finds " peculiarity " in Shakespeare's use of " liberal " in HAMLET (IV, vi, 171) as well as in OTHELLO (II, i, 164 ; V, ii, 223). " In both these instances the word ' liberal ' is used in one of its classical senses, which it *never* bears in English, though the synonymous word ' free ' does." Mr. Theobald's monotony of error approaches the miraculous. " Liberal " was in Elizabethan use in all of the senses in question :

> To declare his mind in broad and liberal speeches.
> > Puttenham, *Arte of English Poesie*, Arber's rep. p. 234.

> Thus when her fair heart-binding hands had tied
> Those liberal tresses.
> > Chapman, *Ovid's Banquet of Sense*, 1595. Shepherd's ed. of *Minor Poems and Translations*, p. 31.

> Fair Phillis wore a liberal tress.
> > Chapman, *Phillis and Flora*, 1595

Committing their bitterness, and liberal invectives against all estates, to the mouths of children.

Heywood, Apology for Actors, 1612.

Their breasts liberal to the eye.

Sidney, Arcadia, B. iii, ed. 1627, p. 235.

35. Generous (OTHELLO, III, iii, 284).
See below, p. 355.

36. Infection (RICHARD II, II, i, 44).

Mr. Theobald is " certain " that we should here read " infestion," because that enables him to impute classicism, albeit " the word is itself corruptly formed from *infesto*, and is the Englished form of *infestatio . . .* shortened for the sake of the metre into infestion." Thus is scholarship demonstrated ! All the while, the actual reading is " infection." Those who stand for *infestion* = *invasion* make a tautology, the line being " Against infection *and* the hand of war."

37. Beat your breast (RICHARD III, II, ii, 3).

" The idea of ' beating the breast ' as a sign of grief is, I think "—thus Mr. Theobald—" more likely due to classical literature than to personal observation of the poet either in Warwickshire or in Middlesex." So that the Baconian is for the moment " Stratfordian." But as beating of the breast figures as an English usage in fifty Elizabethan poets and dramatists, it is not clear why Mr. Theobald should bar either Warwickshire or Middlesex.

38. Gallop apace (ROMEO AND JULIET, III, ii, 1).

" Fiery-footed steeds," Mr Theobald reminds us, " is the classical epithet for the horses of the Sun," as in Ovid and Statius. But why not also cite " bright Phœbus " and " chaste Diana " ?

39. Aristotle's Checks (SHREW, I, i, 32).

Mr. Theobald endorses the argument of some one

("the same writer"—no one being mentioned in this connection) in 1853, to the effect that "checks" must be the right reading, because any tiro might have written "ethics," "but no person except one well read in the philosophy itself would think of giving it such a designation as 'checks.'" Thus again is a man's scholarship to be demonstrated.

40. **Piece.** ("Thy mother was a piece of virtue": TEMPEST, I, ii, 56.) Mr. Theobald interprets this to mean *pars virtutis.* "It illustrates the author's habit of thinking in Latin, as when writing ' piece ' he had the Latin equivalent *pars* in his mind"—as in Horace, *partem animæ* (CARM. II, xvii, 5).

If Mr. Theobald could only have been as consummately ignorant of all English literature as he was of the pre-Shakespearean, he might have furnished us with commentaries on living writers for which the comic press would have been grateful. As it is, the foregoing will be appreciated by those who know that "piece" was a standing figure (usually laudatory) for a woman (sometimes it is applied to a man) in Elizabethan poetry and drama:

> Have won . . . a peece that hath no peere.
> > Gascoigne, *Adventures of Master F. J.,* 15 : Works, ed. Cunliffe, i, 414.

> Behold here a peerelesse piece.
> > *Id.*   *The Glass of Government :* ii, 6 (Cunliffe, ii, 41).

> A pece surely of price.
> > *Id.*   *Hemetes the Heremyte :* ii, 481.

> Make such another piece as Scudmore is.
> > *A Woman is a Weathercock* (*c.* 1606), i, 1.
> So fair a piece.
> > Spenser, Sonnet 14.
> A beautiful and brave attired piece.
> > Jonson, *Cynthia's Revels,* i, 1.

> In fine, a piece, despite of beauty, framed
> To show what Nature's lineage could afford.
> > Greene, verses in *The Tritameron of Love* (1587).
> > Dyce's Green and Pede, p. 285.

Fair Helena, that brave and peerless piece.
> Peele, *Tale of Troy*, l. 112.

Touched with the rape of this reproachful piece.
> *Id.* l. 218.

To paint the colours of that changing piece.
> *Id.* ed. 1589. Dyce's ed. p. 555, *note*.

To intimate that even the daintiest piece
And noblest-born dame should industrious be.
> Chapman, *Hero and Leander*, 5th Section : *Tale of Teras*.

The sweet Armida . . . a tender piece.
> Fairfax, tr. of Tasso's *Jerusalem*, 1600, B. iv, st. 27.

This figure of man's comfort, this rare piece.
> Chapman, *An Humorous Day's Mirth*, 1599,
> (Shepherd's ed. of Plays, p. 32).

41. Pole-clipt Vineyard (TEMPEST, IV, i, 68).

" This is a poetic reflection of Homer's description of a vineyard *surrounded by a ditch encompassed by a fence—that is, pole-clipt* (ILIAD, xviii, 564)."   Q. E. D. !

42. Scarcity (" Scarcity and want shall shun you " :

TEMPEST, IV, i, 116). " This impersonation of ' scarcity,' and her inability to remain where ' plenty ' was to be found, recalls the PLUTUS of Aristophanes. . . ." Similarly, doubtless, it was classical training that enabled the early English to propose to " drive away dull care " and " banish sorrow."

43. Sea of wax (TIMON, I, i, 47).

" This," says Mr. Theobald, " is a classical allusion to the use of wooden tablets, covered with wax, to write on—the tablet used by the poet for the praises of Timon being so large as to suggest the idea of a sea of wax." It may be so, though the interpretation has been flouted. In any case, Mr. Theobald might have learned from the commentators that the same practice existed in England as late as the end of the fourteenth century. But a non-Baconian can conceive that Shakespeare heard of the Roman practice at school.

Q

44. Remotion (TIMON, IV, iii, 338).

Remotio, Mr. Theobald informs us, " is a rare Latin word used by Cicero, and *not used by English writers before Shakespeare's time.*" For the literary facts, see the next chapter, p. 372. Dr. R. M. Theobald, who had learned from Judge Willis's " Baconian Mint " that the word *was* current before Shakespeare's time, writes a preface to his cousin's book in 1909 without any attempt to rectify his ignorant assertion.

45. Pantheon (TITUS, I, i, 240).

" This reference to the great temple of Jupiter . . . infers a considerable knowledge of Roman archæology." More knowledge, certainly, than Mr. Theobald had of Tudor literature. " The name of Lavinia, too . . . ! "

46. Palliament (TITUS, I, i, 179).

" Here we have a word, ' palliament,' wholly unknown to the English language, but derived from the Latin word *pallium*, a cloak." Mr. Theobald has for once the excuse that the commentator Steevens knew of no previous use of the word. But it was previously in print, like so many othe r words unknown to Mr. Theobald. *See above*, p. 121.

47. Candidatus (*Id. ib.*).

" Representing " for Mr. Theobald, of course, " an idea which would be familiar only to a *thoroughly* classical scholar." The word is Peele's, not Shakespeare's, who in CORIOLANUS shows that he did *not* know what *candidatus* [1] meant ; but what a truly Baconian basis for a certificate of scholarship !

48. Assubjugate (TROILUS, II, iii, 185).

" A word which could only have been coined by a classical scholar, as it is assuredly derived from no transla-

---

[1] Though its significance had been noted in Puritan controversy. Marsden's *Hist. of the Early Puritans*, ed. 1853, p. 26.

tion." Mr. Theobald's assurance on this head is truly valuable. But as we have "assubject" in Fenton's Guicciardini, and "assecured" and "assiege" (after Chaucer) often in Daniel, the non-Baconian reader must reluctantly doubt.

49. **Sacred** (TROILUS, IV, v, 132).

Steevens is responsible for Mr. Theobald's conviction that in "my sacred aunt" Shakespeare betrayed the knowledge that *theios*, "sacred," was "used as a noun for a father's brother, or uncle," and that the poet, "by a daring stretch of orthography transferred the expression in its adjectival sense from uncle to aunt." But Mr. Theobald does not mention Steevens' inference that TROILUS is not wholly by Shakespeare. The open-minded reader will want to know how a *mis*application of an alleged Greek usage proves deep scholarship.

50. **Galathe : Sagittary** (TROILUS, V, v, 14, 20).

These allusions to items *not* mentioned in Homer move Mr. Theobald to assert that " the writer was familiar with the *medieval* versions of the tale of Troy." As the old commentators pointed out, they are both derived from Lydgate and THE THREE DESTRUCTIONS OF TROY, printed by Caxton.

51. **Tears of joy** ("sorrow wept . . . for their joy waded in tears " : WINTER'S TALE, V, ii, 44).

" This idea of joy producing tears is very classical, as in the case of the Herald, who returned safe to his native Argos—AGAM. 541 ; ILIAD, vi, 482." So our profound scholar. As Shakespeare thus demonstrably could not have had the notion from personal knowledge, we must take refuge in the hypothesis that he had been electrified by previously meeting the phrase " tears of joy " in Peele's EDWARD I, i, 1.

With that theorem about " tears of joy " Mr. Theobald's first chapter appropriately ends. I have dealt with every item in it, and leave to the reader the characterization of its merits. I will not ask them to follow any such detailed examination of the follies which follow. A few samples will indicate how effectually they maintain the level reached in the opening chapter.

52. The proverb, " Smooth runs the water where the brook is deep " (2 HENRY VI, III, i, 53) is declared (p. 58) to refer " to a fable of Abstemius, which shows that there is more to be apprehended from a silent than from a noisy enemy ! " Why did not Mr. Theobald cite instead Quintus Curtius, who has : Altissima quæque flumina minimo sono labi (vii, 4, 13) ? Unhappily for our Baconian, the line he quotes as Shakespeare's belongs to the old CONTENTION.

53. The " Mouse-hunt " passage in ROMEO AND JULIET (IV, iv, 11) is alleged (p. 59) to display " a thorough acquaintance . . . with some of the nicer points of classical idiom," inasmuch as " we learn from Ælian the unsavoury sense the word bore in amatory phraseology."

54. The lines in JULIUS CÆSAR (III, i, 106)

And let us bathe our hands in Cæsar's blood
Up to the elbows, and besmear our swords

—which may be paralleled in twenty rants in previous Elizabethan plays—are gravely referred (p. 63) to the passage in the SEPTEM CONTRA THEBAM which describes the ceremonial cutting of a bull's throat, and the touching of the blood by the seven chiefs !

55. The identity of Shakespeare with Bacon is proved (p. 91) by the fact that, among other things, both held by the common error that snails voluntarily cast their shells.

56. Lady Macbeth's " fate and metaphysical aid " is declared (p. 91) to be the phrase of " a thorough scholar, versed in classical idioms," in the face of the cited fact that Marlowe previously made Faustus speak of " these

metaphysics of magicians." Of course, Bacon wrote Marlowe. It follows, then, presumably, that he wrote THE PURITAN, since there we have :

You see I know your determinations, which must come to me metaphysically, and by a supernatural intelligence.

(Act ii, Sc. 1.)

And he must previously have written Marston's SCOURGE OF VILLAINE (1599), where we have (l. 10) :

My soule—an essence metaphysicall.

57. The phrase, "lurched all swords of the garland" (CORIOLANUS, II, ii, 99), is declared (p. 108) to be "a metaphorical use of a word derived from the Latin *lurco*, to devour ; an uncommon word, *and one it is hardly credible Shaksper (sic) could ever have come across*," but which was known to Bacon, who, by implication coined "lurcheth" (Essay 45). It has been given to few, even in the Baconian camp, to flaunt such evidences of arrogant ignorance as are multiplied by Mr. Theobald. From the variorum or a school edition he might have learned that Ben Jonson in THE SILENT WOMAN has the phrase :

You have lurched your friends of the better half of the garland ;

that in Florio's Italian Dictionary, 1598, the phrase *Gioco marzo* is defined, "A maiden set, *or lurch*, at any game"; and that in Cotgrave *Bredouille* is defined "a lurch at cards, at tables"; and *Lourche* "the game called Lurche, or a Lurch in game." The vernacular phrase "left in the lurch" might indicate even to a Baconian the common use of the term. In the sense of filching or over-reaching, "to lurch" was a common Elizabethan word. In the MERRY WIVES (ii, 2) Shakespeare puts it in the mouth of Falstaff, talking to Pistol. Nashe, in CHRIST'S TEARES OVER JERUSALEM, speaks of courtesans "laughing at the punies they had lurched" (Works, ed. McKerrow, ii, 150). Lilly in ENDIMION (ii, 2) has :

Is not love a lurcher, that taketh men's stomacks away, that they cannot eate ?

and the old interlude of William Roye, REDE ME AND
BE NOTT WROTHE (1528) has the lines :

> Yea, but thorowe falce lorchers,
> And unthryfty abbey lobbers.
>
> Whittingham's rep. p. 108.

Shakespeare is fortunate in his foes !

58. **Many-headed beast.** Mr. Theobald, going halves
in this as in so many other mares' nests with his cousin,
Dr. R. M. Theobald, cites the phrase *in English* from
Buchanan's *De Jure Regni apud Scotos*, c. 27, proceeding
to explain that Buchanan copied Horace. Buchanan
actually quotes the words of Horace. Apparently this
is supposed to strengthen the claim that Shakespeare
drew the phrase hence. Mr. Theobald, like his cousin,
has not an inkling of the fact that Shakespeare could
have found the phrase in Elyot even if it were not already
current on the stage. *See above*, p. 211.

59. Falstaff's " If the rascal have not given me medicines
to make me love him, I'll be hanged," is explained to be
" an allusion to the classical belief in the efficacy of love-
potions," though in the next breath it is avowed that
such potions were traded in by witches " ancient and
modern." That is to say, the idea was known in every
English village.

60. A notable sample of the method of learned ignorance is furnished in Mr. Theobald's assertion that the
line in MUCH ADO (I, i, 226) :

> In time the savage bull doth bear the yoke,

is " paraphrased from a line of Ovid—

> In time the unbroken steers come beneath the yoke,
>
> *Ars. Amat.* 471."

In so well-known a play as THE SPANISH TRAGEDY
(ii, 1) he might have found it in English :

> In time the savage bull sustains the yoke ;

and from the commentators he might have learned that

the passage is an almost literal transcription from Watson's
HECATOMPATHIA, Sonnet 47, which in turn is adapted
from a sonnet by Serafino d'Aquila.   It was one of the
most hackneyed quotations of the age, in English.

61. Of course Mr. Theobald repeats (p. 298) the stock
Baconian argument that " the eye seeing not itself " is
from the FIRST ALCIBIADES of Plato [1] (this after positing
at the outset the view that Bacon did not dare indicate
his scholarship in works to be ascribed to Shakespeare) ;
and, following previous speculators, is sure that the " To
be " soliloquy is derived from Plato, Parmenides, and
" the Eleatic fragments."   The items in the soliloquy
have been traced to many sources, often unnecessarily
enough.   The " sea of troubles " continues to be traced
to the κακων πελαγος of Æschylus, in disregard of the
words " of troubles " and " by opposing end them,"
which point to the old story of the Celts rushing into
the sea to fight it—a story made current in English by
the translation of THE REGYSTRE OF HYSTORIES of
Ælian, published in 1576.   The simple idea of " a
sea of troubles " was a current poetical commonplace
in Shakespeare's day, as it doubtless was in that of
Æschylus.   Lewis Theobald admitted that it " grew
into a proverbial usage."   A metaphorical use of " sea "
was in fact one of the very commonest tropes in the
language. [2]   " A sea of evils," as Steevens pointed out,
is found in Morysine's translation of Ludovicus Vives'
INTRODUCTION TO WYSEDOME, 1544 ; and Malone cited
" seas of guiltless smart " from Higgins's MIRROUR FOR
MAGISTRATES (1575).   There also we find " seas of care "
(Induction, st. 5), which is repeated as " seas of never-
ceasing care " in SELIMUS, l. 1761 (1594).   We have " sea
of blood " in Fairfax's Tasso and in MUCEDORUS (1598) ;
" sea of bloody tragedy " in A KNACK TO KNOW AN
HONEST MAN (1598) ; and " seas of heinous faults " in

[1] *See above*, p. 189.   [2] *See below*, ch. ix.

Gascoigne's JOCASTA, i, 1, (1566). In Florio's Montaigne, again, we have (ESSAY OF PHYSIOGNOMY) " tide of mischief," after " arm myself to expel or wrestle against " " unpleasant conceits." In the fortieth essay, again, we have Montaigne's citation and translation of Augustine's *malam mortem non facit, nisi quod sequitur mortem*, which may be said to be the gist of the whole soliloquy. The reference to Plato is idle ; as perhaps is that to Cardan's DE CONSOLATIONE, translated by Bedingfield into English in 1576. If Socrates' Apology be a source for part of the soliloquy, it lay to Shakespeare's hand, substantially reproduced in Montaigne (iii, 12), Florio's translation of which we know him to have read, and parts of which he may well have seen, as we know others did, before it was printed.[1] The *theme* is one that must have been often discussed in Shakespeare's day as in every other ; and there is not an idea in the soliloquy that would not readily arise in such discussion.

62. And this is the best of Mr. Theobald's matter : the rest, which we have sufficiently sampled, runs to such follies as the derivation of " Time tries all " from Pindar :

Future days forsooth are the wisest witnesses.

It was a trite English saw, and is found in the interlude *Respublica*, 1553 :

Yet time trieth all, and time bringeth truth to light.

Farmer's *Lost Tudor Plays*, 1907, p. 180.

63. In an Appendix, with suicidal industry, Mr. Theobald busies himself to show, among other things, what everybody knows, that the author of the plays freely used the English Chronicles and borrowed from Lilly and Florio's Montaigne—as if " the Stratford actor " could not even read English. But in the same Appendix we are informed that the common proverb " two may keep counsel when the third's away " (TITUS, IV, ii, 144) is " borrowed from the Seventh Fable in the HITOPADESA." It was simply

[1] See *Montaigne and Shakespeare*, 2nd ed. pp. 40, 77, 161, 139.

a standing English proverb, and is to be found in Greene's
MAMILLIA (1580) : Works, ii, 30 ; and in Lilly's MOTHER
BOMBIE (1589), ii, 1. The other recondite proverb about
the man born to be hanged was a household word.

64. In one case Mr. Theobald is able to cite a distinguished critic for " an absolutely conclusive proof that the
author of the plays knew Italian." Georg Brandes had
pointed to the " prophetic fury " passage in OTHELLO,
and its derivation from the ORLANDO FURIOSO (Canto 46,
Stanza 80), adding :

> The agreement here cannot possibly be accidental. And what
> makes it still more certain that Shakespeare had the Italian text
> before him is that the words *prophetic fury*, which are the same
> in *Othello* as in the Italian, are not to be found in Harington's
> English translation, the only one then in existence. He must
> thus, whilst writing *Othello*, have been interested in *Orlando*,
> and *have had Berni's and Ariosto's poems lying on his table*.[1]

The reference to Berni has regard to the passage beginning " Who steals my purse steals trash " ; concerning
which Mr. Theobald affirms that " Grant White remarks
that this " [the opening phrase] " is taken from the
ORLANDO INNAMORATO of Berni." If Grant White said
so, he erred. There is nothing about " stealing trash "
in Berni, whose lines are cited in full by Brandes : it is
the rest of the passage that points there. But the critic's
confident conclusion that Shakespeare read Berni and
Ariosto is a notable instance of unwarranted induction.
He has overlooked (1) the question whether OTHELLO is
a first-hand play ; (2) the fact that the allusion is remote,
Ariosto naming Cassandra whereas Shakespeare does not,
but speaks of a " sybill " ; while the poet tells of a canopy
and the dramatist of a handkerchief ; (3) the endless
possibilities of translated passages of Italian poetry
coming in Shakespeare's way ; and (4) the *English* books in
which the " steals my good name " thesis is explicitly put
forth. Hunter cited from Wilson's *Rhetorique* (1553) the

[1] *William Shakespeare*, 1898, ii, 123.

suggested argument " that a slanderer is worse than any
thief, because, . . . the loss of money may be recovered ;
but the loss of a man's good name cannot be called back
again " ; and Mr. Hart in his excellent edition of OTHELLO
adds from Humphrey Gifford's POSIE OF GILLOFLOWERS
(1580 : ed. Grosart, p. 8) the sentence :

> Such as take men's purses from them undesired, passe often
> by the sentence of a cow ; and shall such as rob men of their
> good names undeserved be supposed to escape scot-free ?

To these instances may be added earlier :

> First of all it [lust] pulleth away from thee thy good fame, a
> possession far-away most precious.
>
> **Tyndale's** trans. of Erasmus' *Enchiridion*, 1533, ch. 32.

> After he [the merchant] hath put his honest reputation of good
> report that is sprung of him, his life, his soul, in a thousand
> jeopardies.
>
> *Id.* ch. 11.

> We will appear religious in such using of meats, and in hurting
> men's fame we be bold and hardy.
>
> *Id.* Pref. Epist.

But Shakespeare, if he needed a hint on such a well-worn
topic, had it much nearer home, in Ben Jonson :

> When no malicious thief
> Robs my good name, the treasure of my life.
>
> *The Poetaster*, iii, 2.

In the face of all this, it is a strain upon common sense
to be referred to Berni for the simple sentiment in question.
And it is hardly less precipitate to take it for granted
that any slight verbal parallel in OTHELLO to an Italian
classic must be an original adaptation by Shakespeare,
who took so much other Italian matter at second-hand.
The phrases " prophetic fury " and " poetic fury," be
it added, are very common in Elizabethan literature.

This summary handling of critical problems in regard
to authorship is one of the blemishes of Brandes' comprehensive book on Shakespeare.   It affects his treatment
of TITUS ANDRONICUS ; still more his handling of THE
TAMING OF THE SHREW, in regard to which he does not

even notice the doubts of many preceding critics as to Shakespeare's share. Thus he allows Gremio's description of an Italian interior (Act ii, *end*) to count in favour of the hypothesis of Shakespeare's visiting Italy ; when the hypothesis of Greene's hand in the play would dispose of the other ; to say nothing of the fact that the " Arras counterpoints " occur in the old TAMING OF A SHREW. Gremio's speech is expressly assigned by Boswell-Stone to the pre-Shakespearean hand.

With similar precipitance, Brandes has assigned the Jack Cade scenes in 2 HENRY VI to Shakespeare, here accepting the untenable theory of Shakespeare's part authorship of the old play ; and like other Shakespeareans he has played into the hands of the Baconians by uncritically adopting the thesis that " Shakespeare shows a quite unusual fondness for the use of legal expressions. He knows to a nicety the technicalities of the bar, the formulas of the bench,"[1] and all the rest of it. He has thus given with one hand while taking away with the other in his use of the demonstration that Lilly's EUPHUES and not Bruno is the source, if source be needed, for Hamlet's bitter dialogue with Ophelia.[2]

The error of such a critic as Brandes is a very different thing from the divagations of the Baconians. Mr. Theobald knew Brandes only by quotation at second-hand. It is fitting in this connection to note what Brandes says of the " ignorant and arrogant attack " of the " wretched group of *dilettanti* " who have " been bold enough, in Europe and America, to deny William Shakespeare the right to his own life-work, to give to another the honour due to his genius, and to bespatter him and his invulnerable name with an insane abuse which has re-echoed through every land."[3] And since

---

[1] Work cited, i, 109.   [2] *Id*. ii, 18–19.
[3] Work cited, ii, 413. Compare i, 104 *sq*. Brandes at the close avows that the Baconian attack was one of his two motives for writing his book.

the Baconians have also made use of Grant White, it may be well to keep under view *his* remark that " every man of common sense and even a little knowledge of the literary and dramatic history of the times of Elizabeth and James I, has the right to feel aggrieved and injured when the productions of the two greatest minds of modern times are made the occasion of a gabble of controversy, the sole foundation of which is a petty parade of fiddling, perverted verbal coincidences, which have no more real significance than the likeness of the notes of two cuckoos or of two cuckoo-clocks."[1]

We have had enough, I think, of the general Baconian argument from the alleged " classical scholarship " of the plays.   Founded on the fallacies of many orthodox Shakespeareans, it has been carried by the Messrs. Theobald to lengths which might have given pause to the most idolatrous of the orthodox.   In all stages alike, it breaks down utterly upon critical investigation.   We are left, as before, to the conclusion that Jonson knew whereof he spoke when he declared, in the midst of his splendid panegyric, that his dead friend had " small Latin and less Greek."   Those who maintain the contrary have simply ignored or been ignorant of the mass of contemporary Elizabethan literature in which the " classical " matter of the plays is scattered broadcast, and in which we can so often find the *ipsissima verba* founded on.

[1] " The Bacon-Shakespeare Craze," in *Studies in Shakespeare*, 1885, p. 153.

CHAPTER VIII

THE ARGUMENT FROM CLASSICAL SCHOLARSHIP
ii : DR. R. M. THEOBALD'S LIST OF WORDS

§ 1

AFTER giving the " examples of Latin construction " already dealt with, Dr. Theobald compiles a chapter " the object of which is to show that Shakespeare's vocabulary was in the highest degree classic, . . . that his English contains *very large augmentations from the Latin.* It shows him *constantly making linguistic experiments*, endeavouring to enrich his language by *coining new words, derived from the Latin ;* and that even ordinary English words often became plastic and elastic in his speech, carrying a larger import than their vernacular employment can account for." [1]

The claim is not Baconian in origin. So judicious a critic as Hallam suggested that Shakespeare's vocabulary showed " a greater knowledge of Latin than had commonly been ascribed to him. The phrases, unintelligible and improper, except in the sense of their primitive roots, which occur so copiously in his plays, seem to be unaccountable *on the supposition of absolute ignorance.* In the MIDSUMMER NIGHT'S DREAM these are much less frequent than in his later dramas. But here we find several instances. Thus, ' things base and vile, holding no *quantity*,' for value ; rivers that ' have overborne their *continents*,' the *continente ripa* of Horace ; ' *compact* of imagination ' ; ' something of great *constancy*,' for consistency ; ' sweet Pyramus, *translated* there ' ; ' the

---

[1] Work cited, p. 318.

law of Athens, which by no means we may *extenuate.*'
I have considerable doubts whether any of these expressions would be found in the contemporary prose of
Elizabeth's reign." [1] Hallam goes on to say that " could
authority be produced for *Latinisms so forced*, it is still
not very likely that one who did not understand their
proper meaning would have introduced them into
poetry "—a proposition which is not likely to be disputed.
Unfortunately Hallam, like so many later and less erudite
critics, had unduly trusted to his memory and general
knowledge, and has here, as we shall see, half-claimed
uniqueness for a number of Shakespearean words which
were more or less fully current before 1590. It is particularly surprising to find that Hallam hesitated over
" compact," which occurs often in Elyot's GOVERNOUR ; [2]
that he should have seen any novelty in " continents " =
bounds or banks ; and that he should have had no
recollection of the common pre-Shakespearean use of
" translate " [3] in the physical sense. Such slips by
eminent critics make for harm. Hallam's qualified
obiter dictum has been adopted, without scrutiny, by
Mr. G. G. Greenwood, as a support to the " classical "
theory ; [4] and the Baconians, mostly devoid of general
knowledge of Tudor literature, make wholesale assertions

---

[1] *Introd. to Lit. of Europe*, ed. 1872, ii, 280.

[2] *See above*, p. 205 ; and Elyot, B. i, chs. 13, 26 ; B. iii, ch. 28.

[3] See below, p. 351. *Constancy* for *consistency* is likewise
precedented. The Oxford Dictionary gives :

> A death constant and agreeable to a life honestly and godly
> led. Baret's *Alvearic*, 1580.

But the Dictionary takes " constancy," in the passage cited
by Hallam, to mean " certainty " (for which use again it cites a
precedent in 1563), not " consistency." *Extenuate* is dealt with
below in Dr. Theobald's list, No. 74, p. 312.

[4] Mr. Greenwood insists, in obvious error (p. 125), that Shakespeare's allusions to the river's " continents " is " exactly "
Horace's *continente ripa*. It is simply a normal use of the English
word. But if it *were* a reminiscence of Horace, it would count
for little.

where Hallam, possessing wide though not philologically specialised knowledge, ventured only to advance " considerable doubts." Thus we attain to the wholesale declaration above cited from Dr. Theobald. The writer who would have counted the Baconian theory insane becomes a stepping-stone thereto.

It is obvious that in Dr. Theobald's sweeping proposition there might be contained a grain of truth. If we simply rest rationally on Ben Jonson's verdict that Shakespeare had " small Latin and less Greek," we are not debarred from the assumption that what Latin he imbibed at the grammar-school had some shaping influence on his diction. A man with a genius for utterance must be supposed to reflect on the formation as well as the significance of words. Some touches of etymology must necessarily have entered into grammar-school teaching ; and questions of word-values and word-forms could hardly miss being debated at times among the company at the Mermaid, to say nothing of the greenroom. To reject such possibilities would be to revert to the miracle-mongering conception of Shakespeare which has prepared the way for the aberrations of the Baconians. It would be quite compatible with such a non-academic culture, on the basis of an ordinary middle-class schooling, that a born master of speech, such as our playwright unquestionably was, should innovate in language within certain limits ; and it would be interesting, if possible, to trace any such innovation in his work. But the tracing is obviously the task of a trained English philologist : a mere random groping, in terms of a mere general knowledge of Latin and late English literature, can yield only guesses and chimeras. Where Hallam slipped, Baconians must fall painfully.

As all English scholars are aware, all words of Latin or French derivation bore in the sixteenth century a closer relation to their source than they do now. They were then, so to speak, nearer to their roots, even as were the native words, which also have since undergone much mutation. Words which have now become specialised in narrow senses had then their larger primary significance, or something near it. " Corpse " or " corse " was still *corpus*, " body," and was commonly applied to the living body, so that " dead corse," as in HAMLET (also in Gascoigne, as often before in Sackville), was no tautology. " Success " had still much of its primary force, of " sequence " ; so that we constantly meet with such phrases as " fortunate success," " good success," and " vile success " in the poets and dramatists. " Courage " could still mean " the state of the heart," so that men could significantly speak of " good courage " and " vile courage." For a time they kept the noun " discourage." Such a phrase as " detract [=sunder] our vows " (SIR CLYOMON) was still possible to writers for the stage in Shakespeare's day ; though " detraction " was already an established term in the modern sense. " Rest " still had the force of " remain," as in " it resteth." " Painful " meant painstaking. " Presently " could still mean " now " in England, as it yet does in Scotland. " Censure " meant " judgment," not " blame " : " enormities " were still " departures from the norm," not necessarily atrocities ; and " enormous times " were times of tumult or disorder. They had the word " radicate " as well as " eradicate " ; " confer " (the " cf." of our footnote references) meant for them, as in Latin, " compare." " Edify " still meant " build " or " construct " as well as " instruct " ; " reduce " commonly or often meant " lead back " : we can see its modern sense of " subdue " coming in from the French side. " Admire " often meant simply " wonder " ; " continent "—one of Hallam's erring instances—" that which contains " ; " include " could mean " bury " ; and " prevent " had the force of " anticipate," as still in the Prayer-Book and in the daily prayers of the House of Commons. A thousand words of Latin derivation were still " unpolarised," as Dr. Holmes would say ; and many words were used in a sense in which they are now never applied, as when Latimer, thrice in a page, has the phrase " evacuate the cross of Christ," " evacuate Christ's death." [1]

The period of Elizabeth's reign was specially given to Latin formations. Some of Chaucer's constructions had missed acceptance in the illiterate period between ; but whereas Gower [2] had thought it necessary to explain that " Ire " (freely used by Chaucer) is " that in our english Wrath is hote " [=hight], the earlier preachers of the sixteenth century used " ire " frequently in the pulpit. It is noteworthy that the Authorised Bible of 1611, conservative as it is of older English, never employs the word at all. Many old words, however, were dropped for good. Where Pecock had said " overer " and " netherer," all English writers would say " superior " and " inferior." Many less common Latin formations were added to the language between More and Bacon ; but the period of early Protestant controversy was perhaps as fruitful in them as the later age of Shakespeare. They abound in the old Interludes. Preachers naturally employed both Latinic and vernacular forms, giving us such sentences as : " Our understanding and spirit is depressed with the gross lump and dungeon of the corruptible body.[3] They used " erudition " for " teaching " or " instruction," and spoke of David as " the Psalmographe " [4] : but they would use also such simple vernacular as : " Thou art pinched and nipped by the shins for thy misdoings." [5] The common folk were thus in some degree accustomed to both vocabularies.

Further, the first age of printing was bound to be a

---

[1] *Sermon of the Plough.*
[2] *Confessio Amantis*, B. ii, 19–20.
[3] Roger Hutchinson, *The Image of God*, 1550, end.
[4] *Id.* Second Sermon on the Lord's Supper, 1560.
[5] *Id.* Second Sermon of Oppression, &c.

R

period of new word-making. It was so in France. Rabelais, himself a very free-and-easy neologist, presents, in the person of the Limousin student, a type of the more extravagant word-maker, who, arising later in Elizabethan England, is satirised in its drama. Jonson,[1] Dekker, Webster,[2] and Shakespeare, alike hold him up to ridicule. In LOCRINE (*circa* 1587) it is probably Greene who makes the comic personage say to the audience : " If any of you be in love, provide ye a cup-case full of new-coined words " (i, 3). In PATIENT GRISSIL (by Dekker, Chettle, and Haughton, 1599) there is presented " one of those changeable silk gallants " who " chew between their teeth terrible words, as though they would conjure, as ' compliment ' and ' projects,' and ' fastidious,' and : capricious,' and ' misprision,' and ' the sintheresis of the soul ' and such like raise-velvet terms." This character in due course coins also " condolement," " collocution," " oblivionize," " incongruent," " delinquishment," " vapulating," " vulnerated," and other extravagances (ii, 1 ; iii, 2) ; but as the " terrible words " ascribed to him in advance mostly found acceptance, it would appear that even the fantastical neologists may have played their part in enlarging the common tongue. It was so in the case of a number of Marston's words selected by Jonson for special derision in THE POETASTER ; and many words in the old Interludes can be seen to have been rather reckless coinages.

The expansion of the language was of course not accomplished without resistance. There is extant a letter of the great scholar Sir John Cheke, stringently condemning the whole process, while in effect admitting, and indeed illustrating, its inevitableness. " I am of this opinion," he writes [3] " to his loving frind mayster Thomas Hoby,"

---

[1] *E.g.* Fastidious Brisk in *Every Man out of his Humour*, ii, 1.

[2] *E.g.* the lawyer in *The White Devil*.

[3] Letter printed at end of *The Courtier*, 1561 ; rep. in Arber's ed. of Ascham's *Scholemaster*, introd. p. 5.

that our own tung should be written clean and pure, unmixt
and unmangeled with borrowing of other tunges, wherein if we
take not heed bi tijm, ever borowing and never paying, she
shall be fain to keep her house as bankrupt.[2] For then doth our
tung naturallie and praisablie utter her meaning, when she
bouroweth no counterfeitness of other tunges to attire her self
withall, but useth plainlie her own with such shift as nature,
craft, experiens and folowing of other excellent doth lead her
unto ; and if she want at ani tijm (*as being unperfight she must*)
yet let her borow with suche bashfulnes, that it mai appeer that
if either the mould of our own tung could serve us to fascion a
woord of our own, or if the old denisoned words could content
and ease this need, we wold not boldly venture of unknowen
wordes.

It is clear that the eminent scholar had very inade-
quately considered the nature of the previous growth
of his native language, and was indeed vacillating while
he wrote. What he first forbids and then allows was
substantially what took place, before and after him,
save that his mistaken counsel about forming new
English words on old roots was put aside in favour of
formations from Latin and French, as had happened
in the past.[2]

Cheke's pupil, Roger Ascham, repugns in a like vein
at the diction of Hall's Chronicle, "where moch good
mater is quite marde with Indenture Englishe," desiring
that some one should " first change strange and inkhorne
tearmes into proper and commonlie used words." Edward
King, in his Epistle prefatory to Spenser's SHEPHEARD'S
CALENDER, writes in a similar key, complaining that his
countrymen have let slip many good old English words
and " patched up the holes with pieces and rags of other
languages, borrowing here of the French, there of the
Italian, everywhere of the Latin." All this stands for
the due revolt of the cultured " natural man " against
neology and archaism alike or in turn. So did Cæsar,
greatest of " men of the world," contemn the antiquarian

---

[1] Mem. Bacon's use of the same term in the same connection.

[2] *E.g.*, the old " spousebreaking " had long been superseded
by " adultery."

faddists of his day. So did Favorinus, with his maxim, *Vive moribus præteritis, loquere verbis præsentibus.* Neology is indeed less resistible and on the whole less open to criticism than is archaism ; and neology went on perforce. Could the scholars have recovered the whole vocabulary of Chaucer, they might have been spared much trouble. But educated England between More and Bacon read much more of Latin and translated theology than it did of Chaucer or Lydgate. In 1540 the English of 1400 was grown so strange and "northern " that Tyndale thought fit to modernise the record of the examination of the Lollard martyr William Thorpe,[1] putting it mainly into " the English that now is used in England for our southern men." Spenser, indeed, deliberately reverted to the northern speech in his SHEPHEARD'S CALENDER, and used many of its terms in the FAERIE QUEENE ; but while the lovers of poetry were mostly complaisant, Sidney and others demurred ; and the great stream of English flowed on through the new fields, receiving a multitude of rills from Latin literature and the Latin lands. Sidney could not have his way as to drama. He had it as to dialect. The readers of Puritan sermons and treatises could not be at home in Wiclif ; [2] the ordinary readers of Shakespeare and Jonson must have had hard work to construe Chaucer and Gower.

Men wont to read alike classic and post-classic Latin simply could not help Latinising if they had any turn for diction. Sir Thomas More was so fastidious about

[1] *See* the Advertisement to his Examination, in Bale's Works, Parker Soc. rep. pp. 62–63.

[2] It is a singular fact that in a sixteenth century reprint (1531) of the old *Praier and Complaynte of the Ploweman unto Christ* it is thought necessary to put " desert " in the glossary, with the equivalent "wilderness." (See rep. in *Harleian Miscellany*, ed. 1808, i, 155.) In this case, a Latin word has gone out of vogue and a Saxon one come in. Poetic instinct had taken back the more sonorous term, and it finally kept both.

the correct use of the vernacular that he took Tyndale lengthily to task, in the midst of a bitter theological controversy, for not discriminating properly between " Yes " and " Yea," " No " and " Nay " ; and in his Dialogue OF COMFORT AGAINST TRIBULACION he is evidently concerned to write simply for simple folk. But he cannot refrain from such terms as " uncogitable," " experimental," " medicinable," " prerogative," " enterpausying between," " enterparlying," " fatigacion," " recreation," and so on. He writes of " an estimacioun of the incomparable and uncogitable joye that we shall have," " the right ymaginacioun of colours," " the greate physicion God, prescribing the medicines himselfe, and correcting the faultes of theyr erronyous receyptes," " the rebellion of sensualitye " ; and so forth ; and in the page in which he translates : " And also he that overcometh shall be clothed in whyte clothes," he writes of " the very substance essentiall of all the celestiall joye," " natural possibilitie," " carnall fantasy," " fruicion of the blisse of heaven." Quoting and translating the Vulgate, he gives a lesson in new terms : " I wil give hym a whyte suffrage,[1] and in his suffrage a new name written." . . . " They used of olde in Grece (where S. John did write) to elect and chose men unto honorable rowmes, and every man's assent was called his suffrages : whiche in some place was by the voices, in some place by handes. And one kinde of those suffrages, was by certayn thinges that are in latine called *calculi*, because that in some places they used thereto round stones." [2] And throughout the treatise he translates texts from the Vulgate, first giving the original, as the divines constantly did in the pulpit.

Even Latimer helps the Latin evolution. " If I should preach in the country," he remarks in the Sermon of the Plough, " among the unlearned, I would tell what

---

[1] This word occurs repeatedly in Roye's dramatic satire *Rede me and be nott Wrothe*, 1528.　　　[2] Dialogue cited, B. iii, *c.* 26.

propitiatory, expiatory, and remissory is ; but here is a
learned auditory ; yet for them that be unlearned I will
expound it." And it was chiefly his discourses to such
audiences that were printed, to be read by thousands
in the next generation. Bale is much more Latinic in his
vocabulary, as is Hutchinson : and the whole of that
generation of Protestant churchmen, like Latimer, were
zealous for the promotion of university life. That, after
all, was one of the main factors in the cultivation of the
Latin element in English. At no time in English history
had there been so large a proportion of college-bred men
as in the age in which printing and the habit of reading
alike extended in the ratio of the general activity of the
intellectual renascence. Tyndale, writing in 1530, asks :
" Remember ye not how in our own time, of all that
taught grammar in England, not one understood the
Latin tongue ? How then came we by the Latin tongue
again ? . . . Out of the old authors." [1] Elyot, writing
about the same time, declares that " Grammers of
greke . . . now almost be innumerable ; " [2] and if that
were so, Latin must have been still more widely taught,
for the reasons which still prevail. Ascham, writing
forty years later, while complaining as did Elyot of
imperfect teaching, testifies to a much extended study of
the classics.[3] The influence and example of Cheke had
wrought effectually in that direction, and the generation
of Camden was far more widely learned than any that
preceded it. Interest in the Chronicles and interest in
theology alike promoted the resort to Latin ; and Foxe,
going about his monumental work on the martyrs in the
'fifties, felt himself withdrawn by that urgent undertaking from what he would have preferred to be doing—
writing in Latin.[4] His vocabulary, naturally, abounds

---

[1] *Answer to Sir Thomas More's Dialogue*, Parker Soc. rep. p. 55.
[2] *The Governour*, 1531, B. i, c. 10.
[3] *The Scholemaster*, Arber's rep. p. 25.
[4] Epist. Ded. to Queen Elizabeth, 2nd. ed. of *Acts and Monuments*.

in Latin formations. But so does that of John Heywood and the other scholarly writers of Interludes, who naturally were followed in this respect by the first academic writers of regular drama. Thus on all hands the scholarlike amplification of the English tongue was furthered ; so that Hooker and Bacon, writing about the close of the century, come into the use of a copious and sonorous speech, stately and almost stiff with Latinisms.

The sixteenth century, then, was in a manner Latinist even in respect of much ordinary English ; and to surmise classical knowledge on the part of every writer found to use a word in a classical as against a modern sense would obviously be mere wool-gathering. At the very outset, the " classicist " thesis commits its advocates to nonsense, even as does the " legalist." The latter involves the constant imputation to the dramatist of the folly of making his characters use a legal phraseology declared to be unintelligible to his audience ; the latter similarly presents him as putting classical neologisms in the mouths of his personages of all grades. What Bacon did not do in his books, written to be read at leisure, he is represented as doing in plays written for the stage. It is of course arguable that the very nearness of so much current English to Latin would facilitate the formation of new terms—a process which must have gone on rapidly between 1500 and 1600—and that Shakespeare was likely to participate in such an enterprise. It has to be remembered too that there survived in Shakespeare's day the pulpit practice of quoting and translating Vulgate texts and classic phrases—a usage to be noted even in such a " preacher to the people " as Latimer. Even with " small Latin " of his own, Shakespeare might thus be led to a certain amount of word-making on his own account. We may thus freely concede to Dr. Theobald ground for speculation.

But we have only to read Dr. Theobald to be warned that in this as in all other regards nothing can save us from hallucination save vigilant scrutiny upon scholarly lines. The first page of Dr. Theobald's instances of Shakespeare's " classic vocabulary " contains these four : *abruption, Academe, accite,* and *acknown.* All four, in terms of his definition, he takes to be instances either of augmentation or of expansion of the English vocabulary. A proposition of this kind one would expect to rest upon some little investigation, some research into previous and contemporary English. So far is Dr. Theobald from having made any such preparation, he had not even consulted the New English Dictionary, as regards two of the four words. Concerning " acknown " he has the egregious note that it is " probably an attempt to bring the Latin word *agnosco* into the language." Such a deliverance convicts the Baconian once for all of unfitness for his task. " Acknown " has absolutely nothing to do with *agnosco :* it is an old English formation, akin to " acknowledge " ; and the Oxford Dictionary, had he turned thither, would have furnished him with a full outline of its history. Had he read Chaucer's translation of Boethius he would have seen (B. I, prosa iv ; B. IV, pr. iv) the phrase, " that I confesse and am aknowe ; " and the glossary would have told him that it meant " I acknowledge." The word lingered long.[1] We have dropped " be acknow " and preserved " acknowledge," just as we have dropped the verbs " to custom " and " to knowledge " (=acknowledge) extant in the sixteenth century, and preserved " to accustom."

As to " accite," Dr. Theobald is in no better case. The Oxford Dictionary shows this word to have been in common and non-professional use long before Shake-

[1] Gower (also Chaucer) has the forms " am beknowe " and " wol beknowen," *Confessio Amantis,* ed. Morley, pp. 147, 57. Pocock has *aknowe* (" be aknowe us " ; " is aknowe to ") four times in his *Repressor of Overmuch Blaming of the Clergy (circa* 1455). In *Piers Plowman* we have the form " bi-knowen " (ll. 407, 1422, &c.)

speare. It had very much the legal force of " cite,"
and was spelt (and pronounced, if not always) at times
" assite." Dr. Theobald's abstention from such a facile
source of information is the more astonishing because,
in his controversy with Mr. Judge Willis, contained in the
preface to the 1904 reissue of his book, he actually implies
that he takes the earliest date given for any word *or
phrase* in the Oxford Dictionary to be the date of its
first use. This is presumably his ground for ascribing
to Shakespeare the first use of " abruption." But if
the New Dictionary was to be consulted for " abruption,"
why not for " acknown " and " accite ? "

Even to the inexpert reader, however, it is hardly
necessary to explain that the Dictionary does not profess—and, in regard to words of the sixteenth century
could not possibly pretend—to give the first instance of
use.[1] Old forms can be closely traced in the com-

[1] Mr. Harold Bayley, whose useful compilation, *The Shakespeare Symphony* (1906), might serve to explode the Baconian
delusion, albeit he speaks of it with surprising sympathy, unfortunately gives countenance to Dr. Theobald in respect that
he falls into that writer's misconception of the nature of the
testimony supplied by the *New English Dictionary*. He describes
it as recording not only the " birthday and parent, so far as known,
of every English word " (p. 208), but, by every entry, either a
" newly coined " or " newly used " word (p. 209). The latter
claim is very far astray. Myriads of the entries in the Dictionary
do but serve to trace the history or *continued use* of words, and
stand for no " new use " whatever ; and Mr. Bayley's calculation
that " we are indebted to the poet Shakespeare for enriching our
English tongue with the astonishing total of 9450 newly coined
or newly used words " is a mere midsummer night's dream. An
examination of his lists will reveal this to any reader. The great
majority of the words there cited had been in use long before
the dates given ; and in the instances noted there can be no really
new application. Let me give one illustration. Under " Ben
Jonson " we have, among other words, " expulsed, 1603." This
must refer to the phrase " the expulsed Apicata " in *Sejanus*,
v, 10. But there is no novelty here : the word has its ordinary
force, and is simply noted to show continued use. So, when Mr.
Mr. Bayley credits Shakespeare with two new uses of " except,"

paratively scanty literature before Chaucer ; and in the
case of "acknown" this is carefully done ; but as
regards Tudor English the great Dictionary gives only
illustrations, not complete historical lists. The more
need that any one going about Mr. Theobald's undertaking should do a little reading on his own account.
He might, for instance, have turned to Chaucer before
making his astounding assertion that "*perdurable* is not
really an English word at all "—implying that it was
invented by Bacon-Shakespeare. It occurs at least
ten times in Chaucer, who uses it five times in the
translation of Boethius alone, and also has " perdurably "
and " perdurabletee " several times. At least a glance at
the Chaucer glossary would seem to have been worth Dr.
Theobald's while. He, as we have seen, has not even
regularly consulted the Dictionary.

What can come of even following it, on the assumption
that its first dates for words are always cases of first use,

two of " excellent," two of " exalted," four of " exchange," four
of " exercise," six of " get," ten of " go," and twelve of " go " in
combination, as in " go before," " go off," " go round," and so on,
we are witnessing mere moonshine. At this rate, every one of
us achieves " new uses " every day.

Again, Mr. Bayley writes (p. 128) that "According to Dr.
Murray, until Massinger revived it in 1622 the word ' colon '
[the intestine] *had not been used in England since* 1541." Who,
on a moment's reflection, can possibly believe this ? Dr. Murray
would never dream of asserting it : the Dictionary merely indicates
continued use by instances in successive generations. The
whole of Mr. Bayley's theorem must simply be excised.

Even Mr. Pearsall Smith, in his charming little book on *The
English Language* (1912), goes too far in relying on first entries
in the Dictionary. Thus he gives Shakespeare " multitudinous,"
whereas Dekker used the word in 1603 ; and it is impossible to
prove that *Macbeth* is earlier than that. Mr. Smith states (p. 114)
that Shakespeare has " more new words than are found in almost
all of the English poets put together." This is an extravagant
error. Mr. Smith admits (p. 117) that Nashe, Greene and Chapman
" provide *immense* lists of words that are only used by their own
creators." Quite so. There are many more new words, surely,
in Chapman than in Shakespeare.

may be seen from a " supplementary list," compiled for
Dr. Theobald by Mr. Stronach, of fourteen " words the
first known use of which is in Shakespeare." [1] They are :
Abruption, Antic, Assubjugate, Cerements, Conflux,
Credent, Deracinate, Derogate, Dolours, Evitation, Extern
(as a noun), Festinate, Fluxive, Incony. Will it be believed that in a list thus professedly fathered on the
Oxford Dictionary the second word is a blunder ? The
Dictionary gives for " antic " two instances from
Marlowe (1590) and one from Drayton (1594), all in
senses in which Shakespeare uses the word. These
senses are but variants of the meaning of the word as
used by Spenser (F. Q. II, vii, 4) in the phrase " woven
with antickes and wild imagery " ; which again is but
a special development of " antique." Any reader with
the least judgment in word history would see at a glance
that the word *could not* be new for Shakespeare. And
while speculation might be natural as to " abruption "
and " assubjugate," which are certainly not common
forms, it is again astonishing to find any professed student
assuming that Shakespeare invented " cerements," " conflux," " credent," " deracinate," " derogate," " dolours,"
and " incony." " Deracinate " is not a classic word at
all : it is simply an adoption of the French *desraciner*,
found in Cotgrave. It has not, I believe, been traced
before Shakespeare ; but it is highly likely to have
been used. Is it remotely likely, to begin with, that
a dramatist would in serious speeches present entirely
new words on the stage ? Supposing him to invent
" conflux " and " credent," or even " deracinate," he
might indeed expect educated hearers to divine at once
his meaning ; but how could he expect comprehension of
" cerements " if the word had never been used before ?
" Credence," a word of Chaucer's, is used in Elyot's
GOVERNOUR (iii, 6) as a common term, and constantly
appears in later Tudor writers. " Credent " would

[1] *Shakespeare Studies*, p. 385.

be an easy coinage from that ; but what scholar would
believe that it was left for Shakespeare to coin ? Knowing that " dolorous " was an old word, what reader could
suppose " dolours " to be a new one about the close of
the sixteenth century ? And what sensible student
would infer that " conflux," stated to be used by Drayton
in 1612 and by Selden in 1614, was first coined by Shakespeare, merely because the Oxford Dictionary gives no
earlier instance ? Jonson has " confluctions " in the
Induction to EVERY MAN OUT OF HIS HUMOUR (1599) :
is it to be supposed that the singular was not also
current ?

In this connexion it may suffice to give a few more
illustrations.

1. " Incony " was a common Elizabethan term, of
the same force as " coney," in vulgar use. The variorum
edition mentions that it occurs in THE TWO ANGRY
WOMEN OF ABINGTON (1599), in DOCTOR DODYPOLL
(1600), in Jonson's TALE OF A TUB, in Marlowe's JEW OF
MALTA, and in BLURT, MASTER-CONSTABLE (1602).
Could any rational reader, with these facts before him,
suppose that the term was first put in currency by
LOVE'S LABOUR'S LOST ? He who will may find " coney,"
in the sense in question, four times over in RALPH
ROISTER DOISTER (*ante* 1553. Arber's rep. pp. 27, 50,
56, 87).

2. **Dolour** and **dolours** were common and familiar
English words long before Shakespeare ; and the Oxford
Dictionary of course shows as much. " Dolour," which
came in with the Normans if not earlier, occurs at least
twice in the COVENTRY MYSTERIES (Sh. Soc. ed. pp.
147, 388), which date from about 1450 ; and it remained
in constant use. It is used in the third book of the
FAERIE QUEENE (c. ii, st. 17), published in 1589; and
repeatedly in Spenser's minor poems. It also occurs
(sp. *dolor*) in the first line of Nashe's CHRISTS TEARES

OVER JERUSALEM (1593) and again in the next paragraph
(sp. *dollour*). The Oxford Dictionary cannot be supposed
to deny these facts. And the word was equally common
on the stage. It is to be found at least three times in the
archaistic rhyme-play SIR CLYOMON AND SIR CLAMYDES,
ascribed to Peele (but probably collaborated-in by Greene),
apparently first printed in 1599, but certainly written
before 1592. (Dyce's ed. of Peele and Greene, pp. 512,
527.) The word is used twice on one page. It is also
to be found thrice in Greene's MAMILLIA (1580–83), and
in at least four other places in his works (ed. Grosart,
ii, 115, 120, 243 ; iii, 83, 221 ; iv, 14 ; ix, 22). In one
place we have the phrase, "spent his doleful days in
dumps and dolors" (CARD OF FANCY, 1587 : iv, 14).
The word occurs also in Puttenham's ARTE OF ENGLISH
POESIE, 1589 (Arber's rep. p. 167). If the good Baconian
on learning this feels bound to conclude that Bacon
wrote the FAERIE QUEENE and Nashe and Puttenham's
book (some of them claim as much), and also all the
works of Greene and Peele, let him turn to Bishop Bale's
BRIEF CHRONICLE of the case of Lord Cobham (1544);
where he will soon find "dolour" (Parker Soc. rep. p.
12, &c.). Or let him peruse Bishop Hooper's DECLARA-
TION OF CHRIST AND HIS OFFICE (1547. Parker Soc.
vol. p. 60) ; or Latimer's Seventh Sermon before King
Edward, 1549 (Dent's rep. pp. 192, 193, 199) ; or the
Epistle Dedicatorie to George Gascoigne's STEEL GLAS
(1576) ; or the same writer's VIEWE OF WORLDLY
VANITIES, 1576 (Cunliffe's ed. of Works, ii, 261) ; or his
FLOWERS (*Id.* i, 55) ; or his DAN BARTHOLOMEW OF
BATHE (*Id.* i, 112) ; or Holinshed's Chronicle of Richard
III (Boswell-Stone's SH. HOLINSHED, p. 378), and he will
find it often. Or let him turn, once for all, to Sackville's
Induction to THE MIRROUR FOR MAGISTRATES where
(including the COMPLAYNT OF BUCKINGHAM) he will find
"dolour" and "dolours" five times. (Works ed. 1859,
pp. 101, 103, 104, 131, 156). He will also find several

instances of " dole " and " doleful." A perusal of the whole performance, which, dating as it does from 1563, can scarcely have been written by Bacon, may help him to realise that the English language, broadly speaking, existed before the Armada. He may chance to note, in passing, the lines (p. 133) :

> Much like a felon that, pursued by night,
> Starts at each bush, as his foe were in sight,

which will doubtless recall to him those :

> Suspicion always haunts the guilty mind :
> The thief doth fear each bush an officer.
> 3 *Henry VI*, V, vi, 12 ;

and the useful question may occur to him whether it was Shakespeare or Bacon or a third penman who thus utilised a familiar commonplace. There may thus open up for him a more profitable path of inquiry than the Baconian.

3. **Derogate** was in use long before Shakespeare.
See below, p. 303.

4. **Antics** occurs, in the secondary sense, in Stubbes's ANATOMIE OF ABUSES (1583) : " Then have they [in the train of the Lord of Misrule] their hobby-horses, dragons, and other antiques " (Collier's reprint, p. 142) ; and in Drayton and Sir John Davies in 1599 :

> Making withal some filthy antic face.
> *Idea*, Son. 31.
> Such toyes, such *antikes*, and such vanities.
> *Nosce Teipsum*, st. 32.

It is thus unnecessary to suppose that Ben Jonson, who uses the word thrice in one play (1600) :

> How antic and ridiculous soe'er.
> *Cynthia's Revels*, i, 1, end ;
> O, most antick. . . .
> *Id*. v, 2 ;
> An antic gesture. . . .
> *Id. ib.*

—had got it from Shakespeare—or Bacon. Marlowe has it twice, as aforesaid :

> And point like antics at his triple crown.
> > *Doctor Faustus*, iii, 1.
> Shall with their goat-feet dance the antic hay
> > *Id. Edward II*. i, 1.

Chapman uses it repeatedly :

> And have an antic face to laugh within.
> > Fourth Sestiad of *Hero and Leander*, 1598.
> Of all his antic shows.
> > *Id*. Sixth Sestiad.
> Off with this antic.
> > *The Widow's Tears*, v, 3.

And it occurs in A LARUM FOR LONDON (published 1599) :

> Shall as an antic in thy sight appear.
> > Simpson's rep. p. 61 ;

and twice in A WOMAN IS A WEATHERCOCK (*circa* 1606) :

> One here, one there, making such antic faces.
> I was almost frantic
> A modern knight should be so like an antic.
> > Act iv, sc. 2 (Mermaid ed. pp. 393, 398).

Of course Dr. Theobald ascribes Marlowe's plays to Bacon ; but why not also Ben Jonson's—and all the rest ?

5. **Cerements** is probably a variant of "cerecloths;" but the quartos have "ceremonies"; and in JULIUS CÆSAR (i, 1) we have "decked with ceremonies," in the sense of religious or honorary ornaments, so that the actuality of the word is uncertain.

6. **Extern** (as a noun : Sonnet 125). The word occurs only once elsewhere in Shakespeare (OTHELLO, i, 1); and there is an adjective,—on a par with "eterne" and many other common formations.

Other words in the list described as of "first known use in Shakespeare" are dealt with hereinafter, in the course of an examination of Dr. Theobald's list of words of " classic " formation of which the origin is ascribed by him to Shakespeare—that is, Bacon.

The confutation of that list as a whole has been accomplished by the late Judge Willis in a work of the most patient and assiduous research.[1] wherein the normal pre-Shakespearean currency of nearly every word cited is proved. So far as the leading Baconians are concerned, the only effect has been a determined forensic evasion by Dr. Theobald of the whole demonstration. In the preface to a reissue of his book in 1904 he does not scruple to write :

> I give [in ch. xiv] a list of words in which there is a classic sense or a classic aroma, which *could not easily arise* unless the writer was a *good* classic scholar. When Mr. Willis points to other writers who have used the same classic phraseology, that only proves that other writers besides Bacon and Shakespeare had their minds saturated with Latin. It does not prove that these words or phrases were *not* classic, and therefore *does not touch my argument in the faintest degree.* Nearly the whole of Mr. Willis's 110 pages is therefore entirely pointless and superfluous.

We here enter on a new phase of the Baconian controversy. Hitherto we have contemplated all manner of fallacy and imperfect induction : now we are faced by equivocation. Dr. Theobald had expressly undertaken to show " expansion or augmentation " of the English vocabulary in the plays of Shakespeare. The effect of Mr. Willis's book is to show that the " classic " words in question were almost all *part of the established English language in what Dr. Theobald declared to be their classic sense ;* so that the claim that that sense or aroma " could not easily arise unless the writer was a good classic scholar " is shown to be simply false. Any Englishman of Shakespeare's day, whether he knew Latin or not, necessarily used those words in the so-called " classic " sense, if he used them at all, simply because

---

[1] *The Baconian Mint : its Claims Examined.* By William Willis, One of the Masters of the Bench of the Honourable Society of the Temple. Printed by Order of the Masters. . . 1903.

they had been introduced and adopted in the past by men who *were* habituated to Latin. Dr. Theobald had clearly compiled his chapter in ignorance of the previous currency of the words : on this being exposed, he seeks to extricate himself as we have seen. The few pseudo-classic words of which Judge Willis did not trace the previous history, and to which Dr. Theobald points afresh, are mostly not words which a good Latinist would have coined. " Reverb," and " immure " as a noun, are instances in point.

Continuing his rejoinder, Dr. Theobald writes :

And even when the use of any words is represented as an unsuccessful attempt to naturalize a Latin word,—[the words given are *acknown, aggravate, evitate, immanity, ruinate,* and *simular*]—which is the only (!) kind of assertion of novelty which I make in these cases, I scarcely think there is any inaccuracy, *even if it be shown that the same attempt was made by another writer.* Indeed I admit this myself in reference to one of these words. [Which ?]

Dr. Theobald appears to be as impervious to information as to argument. " Acknown " was, as we have seen, an old English word, in no way derived from Latin. " Aggravate " was used by Shakespeare as by all other Englishmen in his day : the meaning has since partly shifted, though the old sense survives. " Evitate " was not an " attempt " on his part to innovate : the word was current ; it has since dropped, like so many others. " Immanity " was a fairly common word before Shakespeare, and was used long after him. " Ruinate " was quite common in poetry and drama. " Simular " is the one rare word in the list ; but to say that he " attempted to naturalize it " when he found it made to his hand is to trifle with the reader. The phrase, " the same attempt was *made by another writer,*" is of the same order. " Another writer " suggests a contemporary. In most cases the words in question were generations or centuries old.

In so far as Dr. Theobald's reply to Mr. Willis has

s

reference to the alleged " coincidences " between Bacon
and Shakespeare, as distinct from the " classicisms " (in
regard to most of which *no* coincidence is shown) they
will be dealt with in a later chapter. As regards the two
hundred " classical " words of which Mr. Willis has shown
the common pre-Shakespearean currency, he makes no
better attempt at rebuttal, while professing to examine
Mr. Willis's book " somewhat completely," than that
above dealt with, save in so far as he complains that
over the word " composure " Mr. Willis misrepresented
him, and cited against him a use of the word with a
meaning quite different from that which he had posited.
That might happen without any unfair intention : Dr.
Theobald should be the last person to raise questions of
candour in controversy. He further alleges that in Mr.
Willis's book he is " represented as affirming that Bacon
invented such words as Act, Fact, Consequence, Permission, Inequality, Success, Confine, and a host of such
familiar words." This is simply not true. Mr. Willis
makes no such representation. He points out that Dr.
Theobald is as ill-informed and mistaken in ascribing
to Bacon new *applications* of old words as in imputing coinages of new words and new collocations of
terms.

A word of comment should be added on Dr. Theobald's
attempt to discredit Mr. Willis's exposure of him by
charging upon his critic inadequate knowledge of the
literary ground in dispute. " The fact is," he writes,
" that whenever Mr. Willis leaves the province of Puritan
literature, in which he is an expert, and attempts
Shakespearean criticism, in which he is a novice, he is
generally pointless, and frequently mistaken." In strict
fact, Mr. Willis has not meddled with " Shakespearean
criticism " : he has effectually shown, by citations from
pre-Shakespearean and later literature, that Dr. Theobald
was completely ignorant of precisely the ground he ought
to have known. If Mr. Willis's evidence had been con-

fined, as Dr. Theobald hardly suggests, to Puritan literature; so much the more crushing was his confutation ; for if Dr. Theobald's spurious array of Baconian terms from the plays could be paralleled and stultified by selections from a single section of Tudor literature, the absurdity of the confuted thesis would only be the more clear. But, as it happens, though Mr. Willis had modestly written that he had "become familiar with only a small portion of English literature extant at the time of Bacon's birth—chiefly the writings of divines, ecclesiastical records, and correspondence," he has taken the pains to collate the collections of Richardson's and the Oxford Dictionaries, and thus does in point of fact present the results of a vastly wider range of inquiry than Dr. Theobald's. The Baconian, like most of his sect, has no pretension to acquaintance with the literature of which a knowledge was specially requisite to give him the right to hold his opinion. A tithe of the trouble taken by Mr. Willis might have cured Dr. Theobald of his delusion, and saved him from his vain task.

Judge Willis may have made incidental mistakes, like the rest of us ; but it is not on casual mistakes that he or any of us grounds the indictment of the Baconian theory as set forth by Dr. Theobald, who, broadly speaking, makes nothing but mistakes, in support of an error "gross as a mountain." It is in a manner monstrous that such a mere accumulation of blunders should have to be disposed of in detail ; but if the Baconian delusion is to be dissipated ; if credulous men of culture, with limited reading—who, as Judge Willis remarks, "seem to have no power to think for themselves"—are to be saved from the contagion of the method of ignorance, we must deal with this as we have dealt with other manipulations of the myth. After all, Dr. Theobald is on all fours with Lord Justice Campbell and all the rest of the darkeners of counsel on this theme. To the detailed examination, then, let us turn.

As THE BACONIAN MINT is not generally accessible, I will present summarily the series of words in Shakespeare which Dr. Theobald puts forward as " classically " framed and therefore Baconian, and which Judge Willis shows to have been in current use long before or about 1600 ; prefacing them, as does Mr. Willis, with an exposure of a few of the " coincidences " of phrase which Dr. Theobald cites as specially significant of Baconian authorship. Of this last order of phrases Mr. Willis took only a few samples : in a later chapter it will be dealt with more fully. I shall take leave to supplement Mr. Willis's illustrations with some borrowed from Mr. Crawford ; adding yet further instances, in a number of cases; in brackets. In regard to some words, again, I have substituted my own illustrations for those given by the first writer.[1] It is worth noting that Judge Willis wrought his demonstration in the conviction that Shakespeare *had* classical scholarship, while Mr. Crawford, who deals only incidentally with this point in his valuable essay on " The Bacon-Shakespeare Question," [2] argues to the same effect as Judge Willis in the conviction that Shakespeare was *not* classically cultured.

1. **Gross and palpable** (M. N. D., V, i, 374 ; 1 HENRY IV, II, iv, 250).

Grossly and papably offended.
Hooker, Eccles. Polity.
Gross and palpable.
Bancroft, Platform of Episcopacy, (1594),
ed. 1663, p. 187.
Gross and palpable blindness.
Trans. of Calvin's Sermons on Deuteronomy, by T. W., 1583 :
Letter to the Reader.

[1] Judge Willis's book, unfortunately, was imperfectly prepared for the press, and insufficiently corrected ; and it may be that the references, which are sometimes incomplete, are not always accurate. I have no doubt, however, that they invariably stand for real evidence. The incomplete references are mostly to citations given in the Oxford Dictionary.

[2] In *Collectanea*, Second Series, 1907.

Gross and palpable abuses.

William Fulke, *Answer to the Rhemish New Testament*, 1581.

. . . Sins, whether gross and more palpable or more secret.

Daniel Dyke, *Treatise on Repentance*, 1631, p. 161.

Gross and palpable darkness.

Arthur Dent, *The Ruine of Rome*, 1607.

[Add :

Gross and palpable faults.

Rosdell, Ep. ded. to ed. of Hooper's *Christ and His Office*, 1582.]

2. Starting holes (1 HENRY IV ; II, iv, 290).

Said by Dr. Theobald to be " another curious phrase found in both Shakespeare and Bacon." (*See below*, ch. x.) It was a standing phrase in Elizabethan speech. See it in :

The translation of Calvin's Commentary on John, 1584, p. 93 ; on Job, 1584, p. 391.

Hales' address on an Act of Parliament, Ed. VI, given in Strype's *Ecclesiastical Memorials*, iv, 361.

A letter to Thomas Cromwell, by Layton, 1535.

Mr. Crawford (*Collectanea*, ii, 136) further points to the phrase in Jonson's THE CASE IS ALTERED, and in the DISCOVERIES : *De Bonis et Malis ;* in Peele, EDWARD I (first draft : Dyce's ed. p. 415) ; and in Gascoigne's VOYAGE INTO HOLLAND, 1572.

[Add :

A fit cloud to cover their abuse, and not unlike to the starting-hole that Lucinius found. . .

Gosson, *School of Abuse*, Arber's rep. p. 41.

Peradventure some which seek for sterting holes . . . will objecte.

Elyot, *Governour*, ii, 9 (Dent's rep. p. 152).

Smoking this . . . trade out of his starting holes.

Nashe, *Christs Teares*, Works, ed. McKerrow, ii, 152.

Compare Chaucer :

I hold a mouse's herte not worth a leek
That hath but one hole for to sterte to.

Wife of Bath's Tale, 572–3.]

3. **Top** (metaph. : TEMPEST, III, i, 38, &c.).

[*See below*, ch. ix, for a number of instances of the use of this metaphor. Mr. Willis gives others, mostly from religious writings.]

4. **Sweet, sugared, honey,** as applied to words (L.L.L. V, ii, 231 ; I HENRY VI, III, iii, 18 ; &c. &c.).

Mr. Willis gives an instance of "wordes . . . well sugred and honied" from the translation of Calvin's Sermons, 1579, p. 961. I could fill pages with instances from general literature ; but it should suffice to mention that "sugar" or "sugared" or "sugaring" is thus metaphorically used six times in Sidney's ASTROPHEL AND STELLA sonnets alone ; and at least four times in the JOCASTA of Gascoigne and his friends (1566). It would probably be difficult to find an Elizabethan poet or dramatist who did *not* use it. "Honeyed" is no less hackneyed ; and "sweet," as applied to words, is one of the commonest figures in the whole range of literature, in all languages. The citation of such metaphors as special to Bacon and Shakespeare is sheer folly.

5. **Academe** (L.L.L. I, i, 13 ; IV, iii, 303, 352).

Found in *The Book of Good Manners*, 1487.
Found in Sandys' *Travels*, 1610, p. 275.

[Be it observed that the scansion of the word in LOVE'S LABOUR'S LOST is precisely what a good classical scholar would *not* do with it ; though Marston follows Shakespeare in his SCOURGE OF VILLANIE, Sat. iii.]

Academy, needless to say, is common. Judge Willis cites Caxton's CHESSE, 1474, p. 86 ; and Greene's FRIAR BACON AND FRIAR BUNGAY, Dyce's ed. p. 155.

[The lexicographers have not brought out the fact that Greene in his *four* uses of the word in FRIAR BACON, and also in his MAIDEN'S DREAM, st. 40, makes it scan Académy, as does Daniel.]

6. **Accite.** (Used by Shakespeare, jocularly, in the sense of "excite," 2 HENRY IV, II, ii, 64. Occurs in TITUS ANDRONICUS in the regular sense.)

Ascited occurs in Fish's SUPPLICATION OF BEGGARS, 1528 ; in a letter of William Barlow to Thomas Cromwell, April, 1536 ; *Accite* in Ben Jonson's UNDERWOODS (*Execration upon Vulcan*), in the phrase (" accite . . . appetite ") which may conform either to the jocular or to the serious meaning.

[Add :

> Afore that Queen I caused to be accited.
> > Wyatt's *Complaint of Love.*
> *Summer.* I asyte you in our court to appear.
> > *Impatient Poverty,* 1560, near end.]

7. **Acknown** ("be acknown" = acknowledge: OTHELLO, III, iii, 319).

(*See above,* p. 264.) Occurs in Wilson's trans. of Demosthenes, 1570, p. 98.

Aknown in Tyndale's Expos. of Matthew, 1532, Parker Soc. rep. i, 80 ; also in Message of the Council of England to Philip II, in Strype, *Eccles. Memor.,* vi, 103.

So would I not have a translator ashamed to be acknowen of his translation.

Pattenham, *Arte of English Poesie,* 1589, Arber's rep. p. 260.

Acknown is also found in Henry Smith, 1591 (no ref.) ; Ben Jonson, VOLPONE, 1605, v, 4.

[Add :

Yet are they loth to be acknowen of their skill.
> > Puttenham, as cited, p. 37.

Joseph of Arimathea and Nichodemus . . . durst not be acknowen of him [Jesus].

Tyndale, *Answer to Sir T. More,* 1531. Parker Soc. rep. iii, 38.

I do not marvel although you will not be acknowen of this marriage.

Lady Lumley's *Iphigeneya* (*c.* 1550), Malone Soc. ed. l. 750.

But ours [misfortune] of others will not be acknowen.
> > Kyd's trans. of Garnier's *Cornelia,* 1594, Act ii.]

8. **Advertising** (as used in MEASURE FOR MEASURE, V, i, 387).

Compare : To whose doctrine I did me advertise. Hawes' PASTIME OF PLEASURE, 1509, v, 1.

[Advertise = apprise is normal and common in Tudor English.]

9. **Aggravate** (= make heavier : RICHARD II, I, i, 43 ; Sonnet 146).

To aggravate their oath.

Coverdale, 1549.

Aggravate his sins.

Aggravate this tragical counsel.

Henry Smith, 1590.

Aggravation of offences.

Adams, Sermon on " The White Devil."

Aggravated their discontents.

Sandys' *Travels*, 1610.

[" To make heavier " is simply the primary and then normal meaning of the word. Compare " aggregge " in Chaucer. The very line in Shakespeare's Sonnet 146, upon which Dr. Theobald founds :

And make that pine to *aggravate* thy *store*,

is an echo from Daniel :

Then, O injurious Land, what dost thou gain
To *aggravate* thine own afflictions *store*.

Civil Wars (1595) B. ii, st. 16.

Compare :

I know my pitied love doth aggravate
Envy and wrath for these wrongs offerèd.

Id. Letter from Octavia to Marcus Antonius, st. 43.

Who, ever aggravating that which feeds
Their fears.

Id. Civil Wars. ed. 1602, i, 122.

Thereby aggravating the offence to God.

Elyot, *The Governour*, i, 19 (Dent's rep. p. 85).

Tullus, aggravating the matter.

North, tr. of *Life of Coriolanus* (*Sh. Plutarch*, p. 27).

To add more grief to aggravate my sorrow.

Daniel, *Delia* (1592) S. 54.

> But more to aggravate the heavy cares
> Of my perplexèd mind.
>> Wilmot, *Tancred and Gismunda*, 1592, v, 1.
>
> To aggravate the measure of our grief.
>> *Troublesome Raigne of King John*, Pt. I.
>> Hazlitt's Sh. Library, Pt. II, vol. i, p. 160.
>
> You did so aggravate the jest withal.
>> Jonson, *Cynthia's Revels*, ii, 1.
>
> Aggravating their offence.
>> Hooker, *Eccles. Polity*, B. I, ch. xvi, par. 1.]

10. **Antres** (= caves : Lat. *Antrum :* OTHELLO, I, iii, 140).

[? An old French word, from *antrum*. So all the commentators. But it might have come through the Italian *antro*. It could not conceivably be a new word, thus introduced in a play ; even scholars would be at a loss to associate it, on the sudden, with *antrum*. But it was certainly not common, and its meaning is not absolutely certain, though all the commentators connect it with Fr. *antre* a cave. In the Folio the spelling is *Antars ;* in the first Quarto it is *Antrees*. It is just possible that the derivation is through Chaucer's *entrée*. In BOECE (ii, pr. 2) he renders *in Jovis limine* by "in the entree, *or in the celere* [v. r. *seler*] of Jupiter." Elsewhere he translates both *adytum* and *aditum* by "entree" (ii, pr. 1 ; i, pr. 6), perhaps knowing that *adytum* primarily meant a cave, and confusing the two words.]

11. **Artificial** (= skilful, artistic, pertaining to art : M. N. D. III, ii, 203 ; TIMON, I, i, 37).

The *usual* force of the word.

> Very artificial in making of images.
>> Hakluyt's *Voyages*, 1600.
>
> A cunning and artificial graver.
>> Barnes's Works, 1541.

[Compare :

> Rhetorike, which is the science whereby is taught an artificiall form of speaking.
>> Elyot, *The Governour*, B. I, c. 13.

Artificiall speakers.

Id. ib. (P. 56 of Dent's rep.).

Artificiall science or corporal labour.

Id. ib. i, 1 ; p. 5.

Artificial tears.

Selimus, l. 449.

A very active and artificial way in driving of a prince's chariot.

Puttenham, *Arte of English Poesie*, Arber's rep. p. 313.

A garden . . . filled with fruitful trees, very orderly and artificially disposed.

Kyd, *The Householder's Philosophie*, trans. from Tasso, Works, ed. Boas, p. 241.

To entertain [deceive] one another with vain hopes and artificial practices.

Fenton's Guicciardini, 1579, p. 299.

Secret and artificial practices.

Id. p. 602.

Artificial and ceremonial magic.

Nashe, *Terrors of the Night ;* Works, ed. McKerrow, i, 367.

With all artificial magnificence adorned.   *Id.* p. 379.]

12. **Aspersion** (= dropping of fluid : TEMPEST IV, i, 18).

Aspersions of ink.   Adams, *Sermons.* i, 11.

The Oxford Dictionary cites among other instances :

By the aspersion of the blood of Jesus Christ.

Foxe's *Martyrs*, i, 497.

She did asperse the place with the waters.

Caxton, *Eneydos* (1490) xxiv, 90.

This was of course the primary meaning of the word, in English as in Latin ; the moral application is metaphorical and secondary.

13. **Cacodæmon** (RICHARD III, I, iii, 143).

The Oxford Dictionary notes that the word is given and defined, from Plato, in Bartholomew's old encyclopædia, the *De proprietatibus rerum*, of which Trevisa's translation was widely read.   It also occurs in Nashe's TERRORS OF THE NIGHT, 1593 (Works, McKerrow's ed. i, 376), and, as Mr. Willis notes, thrice in Adams's SERMONS, 1605–25.

[Add :

Maketh the image of God the image of Cacodemon.
Hooper, *Answer to the Bishop of Winchester*, 1547,
Parker Soc. rep. p. 137.

The word had thus a theological currency.]

14. **Capricious** (= goatlike : As You Like It, III,
ii, 7).

Word so defined in Carew's version of Huarte's *Examen*,
1594. [It is used with this force by T. Heywood :

What, drawers grow capricious ?
Fair Maid of the West, iii, 2 ;

by Webster :

A fine capricious, mathematically jealous coxcomb.
The White Devil, i, 1.

and repeatedly by Chapman in The Widow's Tears,
iii, 1 ; iii, 1 (capricio*ns*) ; v, 3.]

15. **Captious** (= " receptive " or " taking "—" captious and intenible sieve " ; All's Well, I, iii, 207).

So used from 1447.

Capcious, crafty in words to take one in a trap.
Palsgrave, 1530.

By captious words to make me do it.
Three Ladies of London, Hazlitt's Dodsley, vi, 293.

[Compare :

[Such captious doom [judgment] as Momus erst did use.
Higgins' add. to *Mirrour for Magistrates*, ed. 1575.
Rep. of 1810, p. 90.]

16. **Cast** (= chaste : As You Like It, III, iv, 16).

Diana . . . the cast goddess.
Lydgate, 1430.

17. **Casual, casualty** (chance, risk : Merchant, II,
ix, 29 ; Lear, IV, iii, 45 ; Pericles, V, i, 93).

The normal sense of the word in the period.

A thing hanging on such casualty.
Jacob and Esau (1555) : Hazlitt's Dodsley, ii, 221.

The Oxford Dictionary gives instances from James I
(*Kings Quair*) ; Halliwell, 1500 ; Wriothesley, 1548 ;
Fabyan, 1494 ; Wolsey, 1530 ; and Taverner, 1539.
See also CASUALITY.

18. **Circumscribed** (= limited), **Circumscription** :
TITUS, I, i, 68 ; HAMLET, I, iii, 22 ; OTHELLO, I, ii, 26.
Again, the normal meaning of the word.

Not comprehensible nor circumscribed.
> More, *Dialogue of Heresy*, 1529.

They that thronged to circumscribe him.
> Jonson, *Sejanus*, v, 10.

Circumscribed within the bounds of a certayne of studies.
> Elyot, *The Governour*, B. i, c. 14 (Dent's rep. p. 68).

[Add :

Hell hath no limits, nor is circumscribed
To one self place.
> Marlowe, *Faustus*, II, i.

Look ! a painted board [a coffin]
Circumscribes all.
> Dekker, *The Honest Whore*, iv, 1.

Not to be circumscribed in servile bounds.
> Heywood, *Rape of Lucrece*, i, 1.

The time I hope cannot be circumscribed
Within so short a limit.
> *Id.* i, 3, end.]

19. **Civil : uncivil** (in the " Latin " sense, " pertaining
to the State," also = civilised, uncivilised : RICHARD
II, III, iii, 101 ; 2 HENRY VI, III, i, 310).
Again the fundamental, and then the normal, meaning
of the terms, as still in " civil service," " civil war."
Compare :

Civil society.
> Hooker, *Eccles. Pol.* 1590, B. i, p. 10.

Civil life. Civil industry. The civility of other nations. Civil
union.
> Lewkenor's trans. of Contrareno, pp. 34, 35, 41, and pref.

Policy and civility. Civil inhabitants. Liberty and civility.
> Sandys' *Travels*, 1610 ; ed. 1637, pref. and pp. 53, 60.

[Add :

Civil service to their prince and contrie.
> Ascham, *Scholemaster*, Arber's rep. p. 135.

What's the difference twixt a Christian
And the uncivil manners of the Turk ?
> First Part of *Sir John Oldcastle*, iv, 2.

We that have been so long civil and wealthy in peace.
> King James, *Counterblast to Tobacco*, Arber's rep. p. 100.

Civil love of art.
> Chapman, *Hymnus in Noctem*.

Uncivil outrages.
> Marlowe, 1 *Tamb.* I, 1.

Laws civil. Civil law. Civil policy.
> Elyot, *The Governour*, B. i, c. 14.

Better government and civility.
Spenser, *Present State of Ireland*, Globe ed. of Works, p. 609.

Very brute and uncivill (=uncivilised).
> *Id.* p. 638.

Even the other day, since England grew to be civill.
> *Id. ib.*

Some barbarous outlaw or uncivil kern.
> Heywood, *A Woman Killed with Kindness*, v, 1.

A more civil and orderly life.
The savage and uncivil, who were before all science or civility.
The books and studies of the civiler ages.
The most civil countries and commonwealths.
The ancient and civil poets.
All manner of functions civil and martial.
> Puttenham, *Arte of English Poesie*, 1589, Arber's rep.
> pp. 22, 26, 27, 30, 31, 33.]

20. **Collect** ("collect these dangers" = *mentally*
gather together : 2 HENRY VI, III, i, 34 ; TEMPEST, I,
ii, 13).

The doctrine that may be collected thereof.
> *First Book of Discipline*, 1560.

[Add :

Whereof . . . we have collected after this manner.
> Foxe, *Acts and Monuments*, Cattley's ed. 1841, i, 96.

And all my cares by cruel Love collected.
> Spenser, *Epithalamion*, l. 267.]

21. Collection (same force : CYMBELINE, V, v, 429 ; HAMLET, IV, v, 7).

By a collection and discourse of reason.

> More's *Dialogue of Heresy.*

Your own only probable collection [of doctrine].

> Hooker, *Eccles. Pol.* ed. 1823, p. 102.

The Oxford Dictionary gives :

As by a brief collection of the whole chapter . . . shall appear
> 1579, Fulke, Heskins Parl. 35.

Most severe in fashion and collection of himself.

> Jonson, *Poetaster*, v, 1.

[Add :

Not the commandments of God but your own erroneous collections.

> Hooker, *Eccles. Pol.* pref. ch. viii, §5.

Only deduced they are out of Scripture by collection.

> *Id.* B. I, ch. xiv, §2.

All collections speak he was the soldier.

> Chapman, *The Widow's Tears*, v, 3.]

22. Comfort (legal sense, aiding or helping : LEAR, III, v, 21 ; TITUS, II, iii, 209).

See above, p. 77, as to the currency of the term in proclamations and in old English.

Neither aiding nor comforting (in an assassination).

> Grafton's *Chronicle*, 1568, ii, 74.

[Latimer has :

Thou shalt first kill the great Turks, and discomfort and thrust them down.

> *Second Sermon on the Card.*]

23. Complement (= completing, filling up : OTHELLO, I, i, 61).

For complement and execution of justice.

> Hakluyt's *Voyages*, ix, 153.

Compare *Faerie Queene*, B. III, c. v, st. 55.

[Add :

All the rare qualities humours, and complements of a gentleman.

> Jonson, *Every Man out of his Humour*, i, 1.]

24. **Composition** (= coherence, consistency : OTHELLO I, iii, 1).

Disordered composition.

Thynne's *Animadversions*, 1597.

[The Oxford Dictionary gives 26 senses of this word, putting the OTHELLO passage as a case by itself. It is really a case of the *logical* application of the term = synthesis. Bacon does *not* so use it, but it was current in the schools, in the teaching of logic, arithmetic, and mathematics. There is no *coinage* in the matter.]

25. **Composure** (= composition : ANTONY, I, iv, 22 ; TROILUS, II, iii, 251).

Demosthenes in the composure of . . . his orations.

Ben Jonson, *Cynthia's Revels*, i, 1.

[See also *Every Man out of his Humour*, ii, 1.]

The harsh composure and conveyance of the style.

R. Johnson, *Kingdom and Commonwealth*, 1603 (N.E.D.).

[Add :

Marston (THE MALCONTENT, ii, 4) has " composure " for " ingredients." Compare :

And yet even this doth the divine inspiration render vast, illustrious, and of miraculous composure.

Chapman, Ep. Ded. to trans. of *Odyssey*.

Dr. Theobald protests (pref. to 1904 ed. p. vii) that Mr. Willis's instances do not meet his case, contending that, by the testimony of the Oxford Dictionary, the word as used in TROILUS has a wider meaning than that of literary composition. It is really a mere case of using the idea of " structure " or " composition " in different applications. Obviously one sense is no more " classic" than another ; and it was the classic *derivation* of the *word* that Dr. Theobald was arguing for. The thesis of "augmentations of meaning" becomes a chimera in his hands.]

26. **Compound** (= arrange, settle; as a quarrel : JOHN, II, i, 281, &c.).

The regular force of the word. Instances needless.

27. Concent (= harmony : HENRY V, I, ii, 180).

Sing with one concent.
>> Fairfax's trans. of Tasso's *Jerusalem*, B. xviii, st. 19.

In true concent meet.
>> Drayton, *Barons' Wars*, iii, 114.

That concent . . . which doth draw things together.
>> *Id.* Eclogue vii, 177.

[Add :

> For love is a celestial harmony
> Of likely hearts composed of stars' concent.
>> Spenser, *Hymn in Honour of Beauty*.

Therefore are they called the Muses' birds, because they follow not the sound so much as the consent.
>> Lilly, *Euphues and his England*, Arber's rep. p. 262.

O sweet consent between a crowde [fiddle] and a Jewes harpe.
>> *Id. Campaspe*, ii, 1.

As in music divers strings cause a more delicate consent.
>> *Id. ib.* iii, 4.

Sung . . . with sweet concent.
>> Spenser, *Faerie Queene*, III, xii, 5.

A sweet consent, of Musick's sacred sound.
>> Gascoigne, *The Steel Glas*. Cunliffe's ed. of Works, ii, 152.

O divine Apollo, O sweet consent ! [in Apollo's song].
>> Lilly, *Mydas*, iv, 1.

My lute, though it have many strings, maketh a sweet consent.
>> *Id. Love's Metamorphosis*, iii, 1.]

28. Conduce (= educe or " be conducted," " occur " : " Within my soul there doth conduce a fight." TROILUS, V, ii, 147 ; also = lead to, promote : TROILUS, II, ii, 168). Merely variants of the fundamental meaning :

The conducing and setting forth of amity and peace.
>> Letter of Wolsey to Henry VIII, 1527.

[Compare :

That can so conduce him from the rocks on that side.
>> More, *Dialogue of Comfort*, rep. p. 213.]

29. Conduct (noun, = guidance : TROILUS, II, ii, 61).

By conduct of some star.
>> Spenser, Sonnet 34.

[Add :

Ye have also this word *Conduict*, a French word, but well allowed of us, and long since usual . . . it is applied only to the leading of a Captain.

> Puttenham, *Arte of English Poesie*, Arber's rep. p.159.

The conducted policies of wise and expert captaines.

> Elyot, *Governour*, i, 11.

And lead thy thousand horse with my condùct.

> Marlowe, 1 *Tamb*. i, 2.

To wend with him and be his conduct true.

> Spenser, *F. Q.* VI, xi, 35.

For conduct of all which.

> Chapman, tr. of *Iliad*, i, 144.]

Other instances in N. E. D.

30. **Confine** (= boundary : HAMLET, I, i, 154 : derivations in other passages).

A perfectly normal word, usually in the plural :

Princes have less confines to their wills.

> Strype, *Eccles. Mem.* iv, 370.

The countries which confine there together.

> North's Plutarch.

Also Hall's Chronicle, ii, **171** b.

[Add :

Sir, said the King, I have divers confins and neighbours.

> Elyot, *Governour*, B. i, c. 20.

He removed his camp as far from their confines as he could.

> North, *Life of Coriolanus* (Shakespeare's Plutarch, p. 29).

Leaving the confines of fair Italy.

> *Locrine*, I, i.

To which confines [of Wales] . . . we will amain.

> Peele, *Edward I*, Ed. Dyce, p. 386.

Other nations that us here confine.

> Fairfax's tr. of Tasso's *Jerusalem*, B. v, st. 50.

Is the Sophi entered our confines ?

> *Selimus*, l. 959.

Fill all the confines with fire, sword, and blood.

> *Id*. l. 1376.

To set thy feet within the Turkish confines.

> *Id*. l. 2451.

T

Those tracts divine
That are the confines of the triple world.
                    Chapman, *Eugenia*, Induc. 1. 9.
Ye are at this present in the confines and borders of Babylon.
            Philpot, Letter of 1555. Parker Soc. vol. p. 239.
Even in the confines of mine age.
                    Daniel, *Cleopatra*, 1594, l. 175.
In confines of the dead.
                                    Id. l. 331.
We durst not continue longer so near her confines.
                Hooker, *Eccles. Pol.* pref. ch. viii, §1.
The confins of Rome. . . .   The jurisdictions of confins.
                    Fenton's Guicciardini, 1579, p. 7.
We fight not, we, t'enlarge our scant confines.
                Kyd, trans. of Garnier's *Cornelia*, v, 5.
Ere this, I would have taught thee to usurp
Upon our confines.
                    The Weakest Goeth to the Wall (1600) iv, 1.
And in your confines, with his lawless train,
Daily commits uncivil outrages.
                            Marlowe, 1 *Tamb.* i, 1.]

31. **Congreeing** (HENRY V, I, ii, 180).

Dr. Theobald observes that this is " a new word,
classically *constructed* if not classically derived.   It is
probably an echo of *congredior* (*congressus*) or of *con-
geno*." (?) Mr. Willis rationally suggests that it is made
by combining " con " and " gree " = " agree " ; that is
to say, it is a pseudo-classical coinage, *not* the work of a
scholar.   But the very existence of the word is doubtful.
The Quarto of 1608 has *congrueth ;* and the earlier
editors surmised that the Folio word was a misprint for
" congruing."   Still, " congreeing " was a quite possible
coinage for one *not* restrained by scholarly usage.

32. **Congruent** (= appropriate, suitable : L. L. L. I,
ii, 14).

Not agreeable nor congruent to his Majesty.
                            Elyot, *Governour*.
Good congruity.
                    Tyndale ;   Parker Soc. ed. p. 337.

[Add :

It is therefore congruent and according that . . .

Elyot, B. i, c. 1, p. 5.

First, it is of good congruence that . . .

Id. B. i, c. 3, p. 17.

It shall not be incongruent to our matter.

Id. B. i, c. 13, p. 57.

Easy and congruent to his strength.

Id. B. i, c. 27, p. 112.

Of good reason and congruence.

Id. B. iii, c. 22.]

33. Consign (= subscribe, ratify, yield : 2 HENRY IV, V, ii, 143 ; HENRY V, V, ii, 326 ; Song in CYMBELINE, IV, ii).

The Oxford Dictionary gives :

My father hath consigned and confirmed me.

Tyndale, Works, 457.

Laying their hands upon them and consigning them with holy chrism.

Strype, Eccles. Mem. I, App. lxxxviii, 245.

So that by baptism we are initiated and consigned into the worship of one God.

Tyndale, Lord's Supper, 44.

Have all the prizes consigned into their hands

Wriothesley (1528) in Pocock, Rec. Ref. I, xii, 80.

34. Consist (= Lat. *consisto*, to take a stand, &c.— " Consist upon " : 2 HENRY IV, IV, i, 185).

Quite common. The Oxford Dictionary gives :

The English imperie consisteth on sure pillars.

Polydore Vergil, trans. circa 1534.

Parallelograms consisting upon equal bases.

Billingsley (1570) Euclid, I, xxxvi, 46.

This temple seemed to consist upon pillars of porphyry.

Segar (1602) Hon. Mil. and Civ. III, liv, §3, 197.

To think that the commonwealth consisted on his safety.

Greene, Pandosto, 1588.

35. Constringed (TROILUS AND CRESSIDA, V, ii, 173).

Constringed with a muscle.

Burton, Anatomy of Melancholy.

The Oxford Dictionary gives " constringent " from Sir C. Heydon in 1603, and "constringeth" from T. Wright in 1604. The word was clearly current before Shakespeare, though certainly rare.

36. **Contain** (= *contineo*, restrain or encompass. SHREW, Ind. I, 100 ; TROILUS, V, ii, 180, &c.). **Content** (from same root : TROILUS, I, ii, 320).

Words used in these and various other senses long before Shakespeare. *See* Oxford Dictionary, *s. v.*

37. **Continent** (same derivation) ; as in

> The rivers have o'erborne their continents.
> *Mid. Night's Dream*, II, 1, 92.

So used by Bacon : " then is the continent greater than the content." Hallam (*see above*, p. 253), cited and supported by Mr. G. Greenwood (SHAKESPEARE PROBLEM RESTATED, p. 125), pointed to Shakespeare's use of this word as an indication of "classical" knowledge. It might or might not have been a reminiscence, but it is certainly not a proof thereof. As a matter of fact, the phrase " whereof the continent exceedeth the thing contained " occurs in North's Plutarch, 1579 ; also in Field's play A WOMAN IS A WEATHERCOCK (1609), and in Adams's Sermons (1612 : preached long before that date).

[Further, the word is used in the sense of " bounds " by Marlowe :

> Afric and Europe bordering on your land,
> And continent to your dominion.
> 1 *Tamburlaine*, i, 2.

Between this sense and the normal use of continent for " that which contains," there is no room for ascribing any innovation to Shakespeare.

Compare :

> Hark how loud the Greeks laugh, who did take
> Thy fair form for a continent of parts as fair.
> Chapman, trans. of *Iliad*, iii, 43.]

38. **Contraction** (= drawing together, as in marriage : HAMLET, III, iv, 45).

The Oxford Dictionary gives :

The mutual contraction of a perpetual league.
> Hakluyt's *Voyages*, 1598, i, 180.

The city of Palma, where there is great contraction for wines.
> *Id.* II, ii, 316.

The merchants do leave their contractions and trafickes.
> Parke's trans. of Mendoza's *History of China* (1588) p. 74.

39. **Contrive** (= pass away time : TAMING OF THE SHREW, I, ii, 276).

Tarry and abide here to contrive your time.
> Painter's *Palace of Pleasure*, i, 116 *b*.

In travelling countries we three have contrived
Full many a year.
> Edwards, *Damon and Pithias*, Hazlitt's Dodsley, iv, 26.

[Compare Puttenham's title : " The Arte of English Poesie contrived into three Bookes."]

40. **Conveniences** (=agreements. OTHELLO, II, i, 234)

The Oxford Dictionary gives :

There is no convenience between Christ and Belial.
> T. Sampson, in Strype's *Eccles. Memor.* (1554) III, App. xviii, p. 52.

This kind of man created God of a marvellous convenience with all other manner of creatures.
> Sir T. More (1534), *Works*, 1274, 1.

For the conclusion of such conveniences as were drawn and articulated between the D. of Somerset and the said company.
> (1551) Strype, II, xxix, 243.

The convenience of both their ages and estates.
> Grafton's *Chronicle* (1568) ii, 772.

[Compare :

Again every sin, a remedy convenient.
> Medwall's Interlude, *Nature* (*c.* 1490), Farmer's *Lost Tudor Plays*, p. 123.

The word is constantly used with this force by Tudor writers.]

41. **Convent** (vb. from *convenit* : TWELFTH NIGHT, V, i, 391).

This again is one of the primary and common uses of the word. The Oxford Dictionary gives many instances :

> Unneth the Christians could safely convent in their own houses.
> Foxe, *Martyrs* (1563–87).

Crescentius with the people conventing against the said Gregorie.

Id.

> The king conventing his nobles and clarkes together.
> Grafton's *Chronicle*, ii, 56.

And each one to a divers sect convents.

> Warner, *Albion's England*, ix, liii.

42. **Conversation** (used of thoughts or mental life : ALL'S WELL, I, iii, 238).

As a consultation of the Concordance to the Bible would soon make clear to any one, this word in Shakespeare's day had a much wider range of meaning than it now retains. " Walk and conversation " did not mean " walk and talk." *E.g. :*

> To him that ordereth his conversation aright will I show the salvation of God. Ps. l, 23.

Compare :

> Both men and women whose conversation in old times was beautified with singular gifts of the Holy Spirit.
> Miles Coverdale's pref. to *Letters of Martyrs*.

[Add :

> In all conversation, deeds, laws, bargains, covenants, ordinances and decrees of men.
> Tyndale's *Answer to More*, Parker Soc. rep. p. 56.

> Andrew, being conversant in a city of Achaia called Patræ.
> Foxe's *Acts and Monuments*, Cattley's ed. 1841, i, 96.

> The misorder of life and conversation.

Id. i, 4.

> The life and conversation of the court of Rome.

Id. p. 6.

To lay down their old conversation.   *Id.* p. 74.

There is made conversant amonge men in authoritie a vice very ugly and monstruouse . . . this monstre is called in englysshe Detraction.

> Elyot, *The Governour*, B. iii, c. 27.

They that have their conversation in heaven under an undefiled faith.

> Bale, *The Image of Both Churches*, c. 1540, Parker Soc. rep. p. 432.

Which shall in those days live and be among men conversant.

> *Id.* Pref. to *First Exam. of Anne Askewe*, rep. p. 137.

Sithence the time that the blessed Apostles were here conversant.

> Hooker, *Eccles. Pol.* pref. iv, §1.

To be reasonable . . . through all our moral conversation.

> Pecock, *Repressor of Over Much Blaming*, Pt. iv, ch. 9 (Rolls ed. ii, 472).

To Christes Gospell your conversacyon apply.

> Bale, Interlude of *John the Baptist*, Harl. Misc. rep. 1808, i, 207.

Your conversacyon, which is in a sore decay.

> *Id.* p. 205.

He that bendeth to follow his own inclination
Must needs live a wicked and vile conversation.

> Interlude of *The Trial of Treasure*, 1567, Percy Soc. rep. p. 16.

And those that be thankful in their conversation.

> *Id.* p. 27.]

Dr. Theobald connects Shakespeare's use of " conversation " with Bacon's phrase, " a man's tossing his thoughts," concerning which Edward Fitzgerald said, " I know not from what metaphor Bacon took his ' tosseth.' " As usual, we are dealing with a common Elizabethan phrase :

The cause is debated and tossed to and fro.

> *Rhemish New Testament*, p. 89.

In tossing it often with myself to and fro.

> Edwards, *Damon and Pithias*, Hazlitt's Dodsley, iv, 65.

And while he talked, great things
Toss'd in his thought.

> Fairfax's Tasso, ed. 1624, p. 326.

[Add :

After often tossing it up and down in the mind.

Elyot, *The Governour*, B. iii, c. 24, Dent's rep. p. 277.

With much and long deliberation to be resolved and tossed in the mind.

Id. c. 28, p. 291.

Spend four or five years in tossing all the rules of grammar in common schools.

Ascham, *The Scholemaster*, Arber's rep. p. 95.

Tossing and troubling young wits (making Latin verses).

Id. p. 101.

The mind . . . occupied in turning and tossing itself many ways.

Id. p. 110.

In his breast a thousand cares he tossed.

Fairfax's Tasso, B. v, st. 92.

He left him tossing in his thought
A thousand doubts.

Id. B. vi, st. 101.

I tost my imaginations a thousand waies.

Nashe, *Pierce Penilesse ;* Works, ed. McKerrow, i, 158.

Thus my conscience being tossed in the waves of a scrupulous mind.

Henry VIII, cited in Holinshed's History.

Toss'd and tormented with the tedious thought.

Sackville, Induction to the *Mirrour for Magistrates*, st. 33.

Whose dryer brain
Is tost with troubled sights and fancies weak.

Spenser, *Faerie Queene*, B. 1, c. i, st. 42.

That troublous dream gan freshly toss his brain.

Id. ib. st. 55.

With seven years' tossing necromantic charms.

Greene, *Friar Bacon and Friar Bungay*, ed. Dyce, p. 172.

The fearful tossing, in the latest night,
Of papers full of necromatic charms.

Id. ib. p. 175.

The tempests of tossing fantasy.

Gascoigne, *Adventures of F. J.*, Cunliffe's ed. of Works, i, 421.

Tossing their light opinions to and fro.

Davies, *Nosce Teipsum*, 1599, ed. Grosart, i, 27.]

43. **Convicted, Convince** (= defeat, overcome : JOHN, III, iv, 2 ; MACBETH, I, vii, 63).

> Them to convince by force of arms.
> Preston's *Cambyses*, 1570 : Hazlitt's Dodsley, iv, 174.

Hippolita being convicted by Theseus, for her singular stoutness and courage was married to him.

> *Pilgrim Princes*, 1607.

["Convince" for "convict" was a standing usage. See the Authorised Version, Job, xxxii, 12 ; John, viii, 46 ; xvi, 8 ; Acts xviii, 28 ; 1 Cor. xiv, 24 ; Tit. i, 9 ; James, ii, 9 ; Jude, 15. Could not the Baconians consult even *this* source for Elizabethan and Jacobean English ? Of course Bacon used the word, like every one else. Convict = overcome is equally common, and convince thus = overcome. In the COVENTRY MYSTERIES we have :

> By the fruit of your [Mary's] body was convycte his [Satan's] vyolens.
> Sh. Soc. ed. p. 388.

So in the old morality play, MANKIND, *c.* 1475 (Farmer's LOST TUDOR PLAYS, pp. 18-19) :

> My father, Mercy, advised me to be of a good cheer,
> And again my enemies manly for to fight.
> I shall convict them, I hope, every one.

"Conviction," with this force, occurs in Chapman's CÆSAR AND POMPEY, v, 1.

Compare :

> Born slavish barbarism to convince.
> Chapman, Sonnets appended to trans. of Homer, 13.

> Chimera the invincible, he sent him to convince.
> *Id.* trans. of *Iliad*, vi, 182.

> Come ye to convince the mightiest conqueror ?
> Interlude of *The Trial of Treasure*, 1567, Percy Soc. rep. p. 11.

> For surely there was no great need to detect and convince the flattery of Melanthius . . .
> Holland's trans. of Plutarch's *Moralia*, Dent's selection, p. 41.

> By what different marks shall he be known and convinced . . .
> *Id.* p. 45.

When they [the Catilinarians] were convinced in open Senate.
> North, trans. of *Life of Cæsar.* Skeat's *Sh. Plutarch,* p. 48.

These backbiters and slanderers must be convinced.
> Latimer, *Third Sermon before Edward VI.* Dent's rep. p. 112.

I must stop their mouths, convince, refel, and confute.
> *Id. ib.*

Now you look finely indeed, Win ! this cap does convince.
> Jonson, *Bartholomew Fair,* i, 1.

Our Persian monarch makes his frown convince
The strongest truth.
> Daniel, *Philotas,* l. 1804.

Whose wit . . .
Secret conspiracies could well convince.
> Greene, *A Maiden's Dream,* 1591, st. 17.]

44. **Crescive** (HENRY V, I, i. 65).
" When Shakespeare was a child of three years of age," remarks Judge Willis, " Drant [trans. of Horace] was writing : ' The dragons, with proper breasts, do nurse their cresyve young.' "

45. **Crisp** (= curling or waving : TEMPEST, IV, i, 130 ; 1 HENRY IV, I, iii, 106 ; TIMON, IV, iii, 183).
Common. The Oxford Dictionary gives instances from Cooper's THESAURUS, 1565–73 ; T. Watson, 1583 ; Gerard's HERBAL, 1597 ; Higden, 1432, &c.
[Compare :

Canst drink the waters of the crispèd spring ?
> *Patient Grissel,* i, 1 ; again in iv, 2.

Thy dainty hair so curled and crispèd now.
> Drayton, *Idea,* 8.

Her hair disordered, brown, and crispèd wiry.
> Barnes, *Parthenophil and Parthenophe,* son. 13.

Young I'd have him too, and fair,
Yet a man ; with crispèd hair.
> Jonson, *Underwoods,* ix.

Crispèd Germans (" Curl'd Sicambrians," four lines later).
> *Id. Sejanus,* iii, 1.

Crispèd groves.
> *Id. The Devil is an Ass,* ii, 2.]

46. Decimation (" a tithed death " : TIMON, V, iv, 31).
It is needless to go further for this than North's
Plutarch, used by Shakespeare :

Antonius executed the decimation. For he divided his men
by ten legions, and then of them he put the tenth legion to death.

47. Defused (= confused. LEAR, I, iv, 1).
See Oxford Dictionary for many instances.
[The variorum edition gives instances from John
Maplet's A GREEN FOREST, OR A NATURAL HISTORY,
1567 ; GREENE'S FAREWELL TO FOLLY, 1591, and
Beaumont and Fletcher's PASSIONATE MAN. Add :
Greene's PLANETOMACHIA : Works, ed. Grosart, v, 126 ;
EDWARD III (sp. diffused) v, i, 126.]

48. Degenerate (implying loss of caste or status, as
in TROILUS AND CRESSIDA, II, ii, 154).
The primary and then common sense of the term.

Do degenerate from the nobleness of their stock.
Lewkenor, trans. of Cardinal Contrareno's *Republic
of Venice*, 1599, p. 111.

Degenerate from the examples of our elders.
Foxe's trans. of the Emperor's letter against
Luther, 1560.
Nothing degenerating from so worthy a father.
Camden, 1603.

[Add :
That for an evil member two or three,
Or more or less, that be degenerate,
And fallen from their office and degree.
Thynne, *Debate between Pride and Lowli-
ness (c.* 1570) Sh. Soc. rep. p. 45.]

49. Deject (adj. = *dejectus :* also verb : TROILUS, II,
ii, 49, 121).
A perfectly common usage.

Be not of a deject mind for these temptations.
Letter of the Martyr Philpot, 1555.
Christ dejected himself.
Udal, trans. of Erasmus' *Paraphrase.*

Good writers deject me too too much.

Florio's Montaigne.

[Compare :

> Is't possible that Stukly, so deject
> In England, lives in Spain in such respect.
> > *The Play of Stucley*, Simpson's rep. *Sch. of Sh.* i,
> > pp. 234–5.

Dejected [=deposed] lady.   You do forget yourself.

You are not wise, dejected [=deposed] as you are.
> *No-Body and Some-Body*, vol. last cit. pp. 303, 315.

Her authority began immediately to be dejected.
> Fenton's trans. of Guicciardini, 1579, p. 12.

> Where there is a true and perfect merit
> There can be no dejection.
> > Jonson, *The Poetaster*, 1601, v. 1.

I cannot too much diminish and deject myself.
> Chapman, pref. to trans. of *Iliad*.

Men deject.   Gold and his dejections.
> *Id.* Hymns *In Noctem* and *In Cynthiam*.]

50. **Delated,** and **delation** (? = delivering over,
accusing : HAMLET, I, ii, 36).

Judge Willis cites :

Delated to the Presbyterie.
> *Res. Kirk of Scotland*, March 7, 1575.

[The word was thus used in Scotch legal and ecclesiastical
procedure for centuries.   But, according to Steevens and
Malone (notes on OTHELLO, III, iii, 124, var. ed.) it was
not so used in England ; and the word in HAMLET is
read by most commentators as = *dilated*. (*See* No. 56,
below.)   That is the actual reading of the Folios, " delated " being found only in the Quartos.   And " delated
articles " would be a blundering use of the Roman term,
adopted in Scots law.   The word had at that date no
English legal currency in the Roman sense.   Drummond
in his CONVERSATIONS makes Ben Jonson say that " he
was delated by Sir James Murray to the King for writing
. . . against the Scots in . . . EASTWARD HO ; " but

that may be Drummond's own use of a Scots law term, though Jonson in VOLPONE (ii, 3) has :

> Yet, if I do it not, they may delate
> My slackness to my patron.

VOLPONE is dated 1605 ; and the word may have come in with King James. Dr. Theobald is oblivious of the fact that *Bacon* never uses " delate " in that sense, whereas he does use it in the sense of " conveyance " of sound and light—an extension of the force of " dilate." It is probable that if Shakespeare wrote " delated " he meant " dilated " ; and in his use of *that* word he made no " classical " innovation.]

51. **Demerits** (= MERITS : OTHELLO, I, ii, 24).
For his demerits called the good Duke of Gloucester.
Hall's Chronicle, 1548, p. 151.

[Add :
Demonstrations of prowez and valoure diverslie distributed according to the qualities and worthines of the parsons demereting the same.
Herald's document of 1568, cited by Dyce in
biog. introd. to Middleton's Works, 1840, i, p. x.]

52. **Demise** (RICHARD III, iv, 246).
Claimed by Dr. Theobald as " a legal term used once by Shakespeare and *by no other poet* "—a random assertion based, not on any study of Elizabethan poetry, but on the simple fact that the Oxford Dictionary gives no other poetic instance !

53. **Depend** (Cymbeline, IV, iii, 22 ; OTHELLO I, iii, 369).
[An unintelligible claim. All the meanings of " depend " are close to the primary. The sense in CYMBELINE is the common one of " pending."]

54. **Deprave, depravation** (= slander. TROILUS AND CRESSIDA, V, ii, 130).
Dr. Theobald actually notes this as the primary meaning. As such it was then in common use.

The word is used in this sense by Chaucer (COM-
PLEYNT OF MARS, l. 207) ; and it remained fixed.
[Compare :

> I kam nought to chide
> Ne deprave thi persone.
> > *Piers Plowman*, l. 1714.

Misjudging and depraving other men.
> More's *Dialogue of Comfort Against Tribulation*,
> 1534, Dent's rep., p. 223.

Then sought they to deprave [= defame] the translation,
notes, etc.
> Foxe, Ep. ded. to *Acts and Monuments ;* Cattley's
> ed. i, 503.

Easier to deprave all things than to amend anything.
> Stubbes, Ep. ded. to *Anatomie of Abuses*, 1583.

Even such a man as Homer wanted not his malicious depravers.
> Chapman, Ep. ded. to trans. of *Achilles' Shield*.

Homer, . . . an host of men against any depraver of any
principle he held.
> > *Id. ib.*

The worse depraving [= slandering] the better.
> *Id.* Ep. ded. to trans. of Hesiod.

Herodotus is unjustly said to praise only the Athenians, that
all Grecians else he might the more freely deprave.
> *Id.*, *A Justification of ' Perseus and Andromeda.'*

He to deprave and abuse the virtue of an herb so generally
received !
> Jonson, *Every Man in his Humour*, iii, 2.

As distant from depraving another man's merit as proclaiming
his own.
> *Id. Cynthia's Revels*, ii, 1.

To malign and deprave him.
> Pref. to Latimer's *Second Sermon before Edward VI*, 1549.

> Lewdly thou my love depravest.
> > Spenser, *Faerie Queene*, V, vii, 32.

They honoured their benefactors, we deprave and deface them.
> Hutchinson, First Sermon, *Of Oppression*, &c.
> Parker Soc. rep., p. 309.

Depravers of those that be good.
> Roye, *Rede me and be nott Wrothe*, 1528, Whitting-
> ham's rep. p. 72.

I merveyll that ye can this wise him deprave.
> Cornish or Heywood, Interlude of *The Four Elements*, Percy Soc. rep. p. 18.]

55. Derogate (adj.), **derogation** (LEAR, I, iv, 302; CYMBELINE, II, i, 48).

[Another common use of a term. Derogate is used as = derogated. The sense here is not " classical " at all. As Malone pointed out, the idea is "shrunken." Lear is speaking of a withered or shrunken body—a metaphorical application of the term. Bullokar's ENGLISH EXPOSITOR, 1616, gives for " derogate " the meaning " impair, diminish." So Hutchinson :

This endless punishment of the wicked is no derogation to God's great mercy.
> *The Image of God, or Layman's Book*, 1550, ch. xi.

Compare Tyndale (or Frith) :

Anything that should derogate, minish or hurt his [God's] glory.
> *The Supper of the Lord*, Parker Soc. rep. of Tyndale, iii, 232.

It includeth repugnance, and derogateth his glory.   *Id. ib.*

Hooper :—This ungodly opinion . . . doth derogate the mercy of God.
> *Answer to the Bishop of Winchester*, Parker Soc. rep. p. 131.

Elyot :—Whereby no law or justice should be derogate.
> *The Governour*, B. ii, 6 ; Dent's rep. p. 139.

Hooker :—We should be injurious unto virtue itself, if we did derogate from them whom their industry hath made great.
> *Eccles. Pol.* pref. ch. ii, §7.

Latimer :—What dishonour is this to God ? or what derogation is this to heaven ?
> *Sermon of the Plough.*

Doth this derogate anything from his [Christ's] death ?
> *Id. Seventh Sermon before Edward VI.* (Several times.)

Tyndale, 1533 :—Doth not derogate or minish the honour of the order.
> Trans. of Erasmus' *Enchiridion*, Methuen's rep. p. 22.]

56. Dilated (ALL'S WELL, II, i, 58 ; TROILUS, II, iii, 259).

An ordinary use of the word.

By urgent cause erected forth my grief for to dilate.
> Preston's *Cambyses* (1566) : Hazlitt's Dodsley, iv, 192.

[Add :

These and suchlike things I have dilated and expounded unto you in the pulpit.

> Latimer, *First Sermon on the Lord's Prayer*, ed. 1582.

Here I might dilate the matter.

> *Id. Seventh Sermon before Edward VI.*

Which through all the world is dilated.

> Roye, *Rede me and be nott Wrothe*, 1528, preamble.

If we would dilate, and were able to declare . . .

> More, *Dialogue of Comfort*, rep. p. 348.

Which being spread and dilated both wide and broad to the edifying of the hearers.

> Tyndale, trans. of Erasmus' *Enchiridion*, 1533. Methuen's rep. p. 61.

Were able to increase and dilate, to colour and garnish, any manner thing never so barren, simple, or homely.

> *Id.* p. 148.

I lack tyme to dylate matter here.

> J. Heywood's *Dialogue on Wit and Folly*, Percy Soc. rep. p. 11.]

57. Discoloured (K. JOHN, II, i, 305).

[Again a perfectly ordinary use. Dr. Theobald notes it in Marlowe, for him = Bacon. But it occurs also in Peele :

> Enamell'd with discoloured flowers,
>
> > *David and Bethsabe*, Sc. 1,

where the phrase has the same force as " parti-coloured flowers " in LOCRINE; ii, 1.

And it is frequent in Spenser :

> All in a kirtle of discoloured say.
>
> > *F. Q.* I, iv, 31.
>
> In garments light,
> Discoloured like to womanish disguise.
>
> > *Id.* III, x, 21.
>
> Her [Iris'] discoloured bow.
>
> > *Id.* III, xi, 47.

Also in Ben Jonson, CYNTHIA'S REVELS, V, ii, twice.]

58. Dissemble (TWELFTH NIGHT, IV, ii, 5–6).

Mr. Willis remarks that the word was in universal use long before 1590.

[Dr. Theobald seems to suppose, with Cowden Clarke, that to speak of " dissembling " by way of a material disguise is a remarkable reversion to classic usage. It was really common, notably through many stories of disguised personages. Greene has :

Dissembling yourself a shepherd.

Menaphon ; Works, vi, 144 ;

and " cloked dissimulation " occurs in REDE ME AND BE NOTT WROTHE, 1528.]

59. **Distract** : **distraction** (= dividing, breaking up. OTHELLO I, iii, 323 ; ALL'S WELL, V, iii, 34 ; ANTONY, III, vii, 42, 77).

Shunning that distraction of persons wherein Nestorius went awry.

Hooker, *Eccles. Pol.* V, 52, §4 ; 53, §2.

60. **Document** (= teaching or example : HAMLET, IV, v, 178).

[Dr. Theobald cites the special use of *documentum* = example, by Tacitus, AGRIC. ii, 3. Having consulted the Oxford Dictionary or a commentator, he avows that " the word is similarly used by Spenser," (" heavenly documents did preach," F. Q. I, x, 19,) and by Raleigh (in the phrase " stoned to death as a document to others "), but claims that " Shakespeare's use of the word corresponds more exactly to the classic sense."

This is not the fact ; but in any case Shakespeare was using the word as it had been used on the stage. In the Interlude of THE TRIAL OF TREASURE, 1567, it occurs four times :

Sapience. Truthe, indeed, and therefore, your name being Juste,
With me and my documentes must be associate.

Juste. Seeing Sapience consisteth in heavenly document,
And that heavenly document consisteth in Sapience.

Time. . . . And you shall beholde the same in this glasse
As a document both profitable and safe.

Percy Soc. rep. pp. 18, 20, 40.

U

See also Greene :

> Her [Theology's] documents are severity.
>> *Greene's Vision*, 1592 ; Works, xii, 279,

Daniel :

>> You [library and lands] the happy monuments
>> Of Charity. and Zeal . . . are documents
>> To shew what glory hath the surest hold.
>>> Dedicatory lines to *Works*, folio, 1601 ;

and Painter :

> A goodly document to men of like calling to moderate them-
> selves [the case of Appius].
>> *Palace of Pleasure*, 1566, Tom. i, Nov. 5, end.]

61. Double (" as double as " : OTHELLO, I, ii, 92).

See the New Oxford Dictionary for instances. [Compare :

>> So double was his pains, so double be his praise.
>>> Spenser, *F. Q.* II, ii, 25.

> Be he never so first in the commission of wit.
>> Jonson, *Barth. Fair*, Induction.]

62. Eminent (= physically lofty : ALL'S WELL, I, ii, 41).

The primary and normal meaning ! Compare " an
eminence."

If a person shall be excommunicate, he shall sit in a public
place and eminent.
>> *Res. Kirk of Scotland*, 1569.

Two piked rocks lift up their eminent heads.
>> Sandys' *Travels*, 1610.

The super-eminent mountain.
>>> *Id.* p. 221.

[Add :

He made . . . trees of a more eminent stature than herbs.
>> Elyot, *The Governour*, i, 1.

My lord's eminent shoulder.
>> Jonson, *Sejanus*, v, 9.

The most high and eminent part of the temple.
>> Fenton's Guicciardini, 1579, p. 4.

> Was his father of any eminent place or means ?
>> Jonson, *Cynthia's Revels*, i, 1.

Men of eminent places.
>> Chapman, *Revenge of Bussy d'Ambois*, iv, 1.]

63. **Epitheton** (L.L.L. I, ii, 14). " A word not likely to be used except by a classical scholar," says Dr. Theobald.

[It is a word that might have been used by a schoolboy who had heard it from his master ; and it might or might not be used by scholars ; because " epithet," though it occurs thrice in Shakespeare and is used by Jonson (POETASTER, iv, 1), was still in process of being naturalized. Gascoigne indeed uses it repeatedly (pref. ep. to THE POSIES, 1575 ; CERTAYNE NOTES OF INSTRUCTION ; and first ed. of THE ADVENTURES OF MASTER F. J.— Cunliffe's ed. of Works, i, 5, 465, 493) ; and King James has *Epithetis* (Scot. pl. = Epithets) in his REULIS AND CAUTELIS OF SCOTTIS POESIE, 1585 (Arber's rep. p. 64)— both probably copying a French usage. Puttenham, who had been educated abroad, and often follows French forms, has *Epithete* and *Epithet* as well as *Epitheton* (ARTE OF ENGLISH POESIE, Arber's rep. pp. 187, 188, 193, 261, 262) ; and Chapman, the scholarly, has " epethite," rhyming with light (Third Sestiad of HERO AND LEANDER ; also in verses TO THE AUTHOR OF NENNIO, 1595 ; Shepherd's ed. of MINOR POEMS, pp. 49, 71). But the Greek form was also current.]

Epitheton was certainly in English use before the writing of LOVE'S LABOUR'S LOST :

E.g. : Divers thought Theophilus to be a name appellative . . . but the *epitheton* . . . that is joined with it differeth from that opinion.
Trans. of Calvin's Harmony, 1584, p. 1.

The Oxford Dictionary gives instances from Hooper, Foxe, Holinshed, and the Douay Bible.

[Add :

Your *Epitheton* or *qualifier* . . . serves also to alter and enforce the sense.
Puttenham, Arte of English Poesie, Arber's rep. p. 193.

Which natural and proper quality [moisture] in my judgment caused the ancient poets to attribute this *Epitheton* unto Venus : *Alma, ab alendo.*
Greene, Planetomachia, 1585 : Works, v, 101.

These epithetons that Homer assigned to Ulysses.
> *Greene's Mourning Garment*, 1590 : Works, ix, 130.

The hip is not simply the red berry on the briar, unless you add this epitheton and say. . .
> F. Thynne's *Animadversions on Speight*, 1599, in Todd's *Illustrations of Gower and Chaucer*, 1810, p. 45.

With some sweet-smelling pink epitheton.
> Marston, *Satires*, iii.

This blade . . .
May very well bear a feminine Epitheton.
> Kyd, *Soliman and Perseda*, I, iii, 77.]

64. Err, errant, erring (= roving : OTHELLO, I, iii, 362 ; HAMLET, I, i, 154).

Again a perfectly common use :

Errand, vagabond, wavering persons.
> King on Jonah, 1594, p. 141.

Erring or wandering stars.
> Adams' Sermons, 1605 to 1620, i, 10.

The Oxford Dictionary gives :

An erringe pylgrym in the servyse of . . . God.
> *Lay Folks' Mass Book*, 1400.

[Add :
The erring stars.
> Chapman, Epist. ded. to trans. of Odyssey.

The erring dolphin.
> *Id. Eugenia* : Inductio.

Cynthia, lowest of the erring stars.
> Lilly, *Woman in the Moon*, v, 1, l. 2.

An " arrant rogue " was simply an " errant " or wandering rogue. Compare "most errant traitors." Bale, PROCESS AGAINST COBHAM, Works, Parker Soc. ed. p. 50. *See Extravagant*, below, No. 77.]

65. Evitate (MERCHANT, V, v, 241).

" An attempt, not successful, to introduce a new word," says Dr. Theobald, with his usual fatal confidence. It occurs in Parker's trans. of Mendoza's HISTORY OF CHINA, 1588.

66. **Exempt** (= excluded, banished : COMEDY OF ERRORS, II, ii, 173).

The Oxford Dictionary gives *inter alia* :

Exempted from Sathan, to live forever with Christ.

> T. Wilson, *Arte of Rhetorique* (1553), 39.

Exempted and banished (as it were) from the House of the Lord.

> 1563. *Homilies*, II.

He hist ; for nature now had cleane exempt All other speech.

> Golding's Ovid, *Metam.* iv, 97 (1593).

I'll exempt them [flowers] all from my smell.

> Greene, *Arcadia*, 1589.

Themselves [the Thebans] only exempted, from treaty of peace.

> North's Plutarch, *Agesilaus*.

[Compare :

A quarter not altogether exempted from witches.

> Nashe, *Terrors of the Night* ; Works, ed. McKerrow,
> i, 382.

See also the passage from BEGGARS' PETITION, under No. 177, hereinafter.]

67. **Exhaust** (" from fools exhaust [= draw out] their mercy " : TIMON, IV, iii, 118).

Innumerable sums of money, craftily exhausted out of this realm.

> Act 32 Hen. VIII, c. 29.

Charges enforced have exhaust the most part of your substance.

> Elyot, *The Governour*.

[Add :

By little and little exhaust by the negligence and folly of ignorant emperors.

> *Id.* B. iii, c. 23.

Compare our phrase " to exhaust the air " from a receiver.]

68. **Exhibition** (= maintenance : TWO GENTLEMEN, I, iii, 68).

In constant use in this sense before Shakespeare. *See*

Oxford Dictionary. Latimer uses the word in his
SERMON ON THE PLOUGH.

69. **Exigent, sb.** (1 HENRY VI, II, v, 8).
The Oxford Dictionary gives, *inter alia :*

These by degrees passed to the last exigent.
A. Day, English Secretary, 1586.

Driven her to some desperate exigent.
Dr. Doddypoll, iv, 3.

The duke seeing himself to be driven to such an exigent.
Holinshed, Chron. 1577, ii, 3.

Also Sidney's *Arcadia* (1580), B. iv, ed. 1622, p. 413.

[Add :

Now was Zelmane brought to an exigent.
Sidney, Arcadia, B. ii, ed. 1627, p. 98.]

70. **Exorcist, exorciser** (= one who *calls up* spirits :
JULIUS CÆSAR, II, i, 323 ; CYMBELINE, IV, ii, 276) ;
EXORCISM (2 HENRY VI, I, iv, 4).

I do conjure you and do exorcise you . . . that you do come
unto me.
Scot, Discoverie of Witchcraft, 1589.

This ghost of Tucca . . . was raised up by new exorcisms.
Dekker, Satiromastix.

71. **Expedient** (= expeditious : K. JOHN, II, i, 60) ;
Expedition (MACBETH, II, iii, 116, &c.).

In our ways we be expedient.
Digby Mysteries, 1485 : 1882 rep. iii, 817.

The King shall showe his good grace and favour in the expedision
thereof.
Paston Letters, 1464, No. 493.

72. **Expostulate** (= postulate, inquire, discuss : HAMLET,
II, ii, 86).

Having at large expostulated my true meaning.
A. Day, English Secretary, 1586.

The Ambassador hearing and expostulating the matter . . .
Sandys' Travels, 1610, ed. 1637, p. 86.

[Add :

> Nay, stand not to expostulate : make haste.
> *True Tragedie of Richard Duke of York*, Morley's
> ed., with *Richard III*, p. 155.
> Line varied in *First Part of the Contention*, Morley's
> ed., with *2 Henry VI*, p. 191.

Nor gave he him [Christ] any Commission to expostulate proudly of injuries.

> Nashe, *Christ's Teares over Jerusalem*, 1593, 5th par.

Gentlie expostulated their ill dealing.

> *Id. ib.* 6th par.]

73. Expulsed (= expelled : 1 HENRY VI, III, iii, 25). A *very* common word :

> Saturnus, expulsed of Jupiter his son.
> > Higden, 1432.
> Adam our first parent was expulsed from Paradise.
> > Stubbes, *Anatomie of Abuses*, ii, 49.
> Almighty God expulsed sin.
> > Fisher, *Seven Penitent Psalms*, 1505 : Works,
> > p. 115.
> Isabel Queen of Naples being expulsed the realm.
> > Strype, *Eccles. Memor.* iv, 369.
> Of whom but a woman was it 'long on
> That Adam was expulsed from Paradise ?
> > *Calisto and Melebea, circa* 1530, ll. 175–6.
> They which should honour thee shall expulse thee.
> > Henry Smith, ed. 1611, p. 186.

Sandys' *Travels*, 1610, has the word seven times. Ed. 1637, pp. 15, 36, 107, 142, 144, 145, 222.

[Add :

> They expulsed it from thence.
> > Roye, *Rede me and be nott Wrothe*, 1528, Whitting-
> > ham's rep. p. 140.
> The expulsèd Apicata.
> > Jonson, *Sejanus*, v, 10.

God found just matter and justification to expulse the inhabitants of that land.

> Hooper, *Declaration of the Ten Commandments*,
> 1550, pref.

They shall seek occasion to expulse me out of this city.
> Elyot, *The Governour*, B. ii, 12 ; Dent's rep.
> p. 173.

The apostles and disciples expulsed out of Jewry.
> Bale, *Image of Both Churches* : Works, Parker
> Soc. ed. p. 336.

Whyles those thynges be expulsed and voyded.
> Robinson's trans. of More's *Utopia* ; Dent's rep.
> p. 77.

Expulsed were we with injurious arms.
> Fairfax's trans. of Tasso's *Jerusalem*, iv, 12.]

74. **Extenuate** (= make less, take away from : M. N. D.,
I, i, 120).

Merely an application of the ordinary term to something not a fault—in which latter sense the modern use
is weakly restricted.   In the trans. of Calvin's HARMONY
OF THE GOSPELS, 1584, we have " extenuate the God-
head." Compare :

Extenuating, annulling their virtues ; aggravating their
imperfections.
> Huish on the Lord's Prayer (1623), Lect. 18, p. 11.

The Oxford Dictionary gives instances of " extenuate "
in the *physical* sense from Elyot (1533), Hakluyt's
VOYAGES (1599), Stubbes (1583), Morwyng (1559), Chester
(1601), and Holland's Pliny (1601).

[Add :

To hide or extenuate the judgment of God against sin.
> Hooper, *Declaration of Christ and his Office*, Parker
> Soc. rep. p. 92.

They . . . extenuate God's ire and displeasure against idolatry
too much.
> *Id. Answer to the Bishop of Winchester*, p. 151.]

75. **Extirp** (= extirpate, M. FOR M., III, ii, 109).
Perfectly common.

Extyrpe all heresy.
> Wm. Barlow to Henry VIII, 1533.

Extirping . . . of vyce and sin.
> Act 27 Hen. VIII, c. 28.

Extirping out all popery.
> Latimer, *Sermons on the Lord's Prayer*, vi.

[Add :
> That may extirpe or raze these tyrannies.
>> Kyd, *Cornelia*, Act iv, Sc. 2, 178.

He shall extirp and pluck away altogether.
> Latimer, *First Sermon before Edward VI*.]

76. **Extracting** (" a most extracting frenzy," TWELFTH NIGHT, V, i, 288).

[" Used in a singularly classic way," says Dr. Theobald. It is doubtful whether the word is not a misprint for *dis*tracting ! But Malone cites from the old HYSTORIE OF HAMBLET the phrase : " to try if men of great account be extract out of their wits." This is pre-Shakespearean and popular : the story must have been printed before 1608, the date of the only surviving copy, as it is demonstrably anterior to the play.]

77. **Extravagant** (HAMLET, I, i, 54).

Rogues, extravagants and stragglers.
> Stubbes, *Anatomie of Abuses*, 1583.

[Add :
> This extravagant and errant rogue.
>> Chapman, *Byron's Tragedy*, 1608, v, 1.]

The cant term " stravagant," with the force of " vagabond," appears in several old plays. The term was evidently in official use, and popularly curtailed.]

78. **Facinorous** (= wicked : ALL'S WELL, II, iii, 35).

Facinorous and vile persons.
> Strype's *Annals*, ed. 1824, vii, 133.

The Oxford Dictionary gives another instance from Hall's Chronicle, 1548.

[Compare :
> All facinorous acts that could be named.
>> Jonson, *The Silent Woman*, ii, 1.]

79. **Fact** (= act : MACBETH, III, vi, 10).

As Judge Willis remarks, " fact " in this sense is in

absolutely universal use in Tudor literature. Only one entirely ignorant of that literature could cite it as special to Shakespeare and Bacon.

80. **Fatigate** (= fatigued : CORIOLANUS, II, ii, 121).
Occurs at least six times in Elyot's GOVERNOUR !

81. **Festinate** (LEAR, III, vii, 9).
" Festination " occurs frequently : Elyot, THE IMAGE OF GOVERNANCE, 1541 ; THE DISOBEDIENT CHILD (Hazlitt's Hodsley, ii, 310 ; Chapman, Jonson, and Marston, EASTWARD HO, ii, 1.
[Painter's PALACE OF PLEASURE, T. i, Nov. 4 ; rep. 1813, p. 18 ; Interlude RESPUBLICA, 1553 : Farmer's LOST TUDOR PLAYS, p. 204.]

82. **Fine** (= the end : ALL'S WELL, IV, iv, 35 ; HAMLET, V, i, 115).
A particularly absurd instance of " innovation." The word occurs scores of times in Chaucer, who uses it six times in a single stanza of TROILUS AND CRISEYDE (v, 262).

83. **Frustrate** (ANTONY, V, i, 1 : TEMPEST, III, iii, 10)
The ordinary force of the word. Instances unnecessary.

84. **Gratulate** (TITUS ANDRONICUS, I, i, 221).
An extremely common word in Elizabethan drama. Occurs frequently in Greene and Peele and other playwrights before Shakespeare ; also in Spenser.

85. **Illustrate** (= illustrious : LOVE'S LABOUR'S LOST, IV, i, 65 ; V, i, 128).
Mr. Willis gives several instances of the infinitive *to illustrate* in the sense of = " make famous." The participle occurs in the epistle dedicatory to Chapman's trans. of the ILIAD, 1594 :

Her substance yet being too pure and illustrate to be discerned with ignorant and barbarous sense ;

also in the translation, B. iv, 74, &c. ; also in the phrase

" her illustrate brightness " in Jonson's Ode ἐνθουσιαστική. In Chester's LOVE'S MARTYR. The word is altered by Gifford in his edition to " illustrious.")

86. **Immanity** (= IMMANITAS : 1 HENRY VI, V, i, 13).
Occurs in one of the non-Shakespearean plays. Dr. Theobald, *more suo*, pronounces it " evidently an unsuccessful attempt to anglicise a Latin word." If so, the attempt was not Shakespeare's. It occurs in Dent's RUINE OF ROME, 1590, p. 112 ; and in Adams's Sermons. These writers were not likely to adopt a play-house coinage. And the word is used by Fielding in JOSEPH ANDREWS.

[*See it also* in Fleming's Continuation of Holinshed's Chronicle, 1587, iii, 1557 ; in the " Declaration of the Favourable Dealings of Her Majestie's Commissioners appointed for the Examination of Certaine Traitours," 1583 (Rep. in HARL. MISC. ed. 1808, i, 515) ; and in the play A WARNING FOR FAIRE WOMEN (1599), ii, 2. Chapman has " immane " at least twice : Postscript to trans. of Hymns of Homer, l. 5 from end ; Ep. ded. to A JUSTIFICATION OF A STRANGE ACTION OF NERO.]

The Oxford Dictionary gives instances from Foxe's MARTYRS, 1563–70, ed. 1684, iii, 649) and from North's translation of Guevara's DIALL OF PRINCES, 1557 ; and mentions that the word is used by Fotherby in 1619, and by Bentley. [Add that it occurs at least half a dozen times in Daniel's COLLECTION OF THE HISTORY OF ENGLAND (1612–18), and the scope of Dr. Theobald's erudition will be broadly gauged.]

87. **Imminent** (JULIUS CÆSAR, II, ii, 81, &c.).
Normal use of the word. *See* Oxford Dictionary. " Imminence," says Dr. Theobald, " occurs only once, and is evidently coined by the poet " (TROILUS, V, x, 13).

88. **Immures** (noun : TROILUS AND CRESSIDA, Prol. 8).
The word occurs in a prologue which has long been

held by critics to be non-Shakespearean. It is a bad coinage in any case, being framed by mere imitation from " mures."

89. **Impertinency, impertinent** (LEAR IV, vi, 178 ; MERCHANT, II, ii, 146).
The primary and at that time the ordinary meaning of the word. It is as old as Chaucer, *Prologue.*

90. **Implorator** (HAMLET, I, iii, 129).
Probably a legal usage, from the French. *See* ch. vii, above, p. 230.

91. **Imponed** (HAMLET, V, ii).
Used in State Papers, Hen. VIII, ii, 130 (1529).
[The passage shows that the word was current.]

92. **Imposed** (M. FOR M., I, iv, 40) ; **Imposition** (MERCHANT, III, iv, 32).
Absolutely normal use. *E.g. :*

Wherein, she which did impose was holy.
                    Hooker, *Eccles. Pol.* pref. ch. iii, § 15.
The imposition of this law upon himself [God].
                    Id. B. i, ch. ii, § 6.
If any law be now imposed.
                    Id. B. viii (Frag. of Sermon : ed. 1850, ii, 583).

93. **Incense** (= stir up, excite, persuade : MERRY WIVES, I, iii, 109).
[Mr. Willis gives some instances which are either not strictly relevant or later than 1600. But the word in the sense noted was common. *E.g. :*

They shall thereto [to study] be the more incensed.
                    Elyot, *Governour,* B. i, c. 14, Dent's rep. p. 68.
He being advertised and incensed by light persons about him.
                    Id., B. ii, 6, p. 139.
Secretly incensing Virginio . . . not to consent.
                    Fenton's Guicciardini, 1579, p. 9.
He knew well that Isabell . . . would use a perpetual diligence to incense her grandfather.
                    Id. ib.

Who being also secretly incensed.

Id., p. 11.

Incensed into lust and lightness.

> Patericke's trans. of Gentillet on Machiavelli, 1577,
> Ep. Ded.

Only incensed by the means of folly.

> Greene, *Debate between Folly and Love :* Works,
> iv, 218.

> The example of their light regarding,
> Vulgar looseness much incenses.
>
> > Daniel, *Tragedy of Cleopatra*, 1594, l. 1230.

Incensed his father's heart against him thus.

Id. Philotas, l. 2177 (V, ii).

> Agamemnon then
> To mortal war incenseth all his men.
>
> Chapman, Arg. to B. iv of trans. of Iliad (1598).

> Incense the people in the civil cause
> With dangerous speeches.
>
> > Jonson, *Sejanus*, iii, 1.

Elyot has the form " incende." B. i, c. 23, near end ;
B. ii, 5.]

94. Incertain (M. FOR M. III, i, 126).

[A perfectly normal Elizabethan form :

So variable and miserable is the destiny of man ; and so
incertain to every one what will be his condition in time to
come.

> Fenton's Guicciardini, 1579, p. 243 (end of lib. 4).

Not curious of incertain chances now.

> Lodge, *Wounds of Civil War*, 1594, near end.

Incertainty of treasure.

> *The Triall of Treasure*, 1567, Percy Soc. rep. p. 37.]

95. Include (" includes itself " = is included : TROILUS, I, iii, 119).

An application of the primary meaning. Compare :

The tombs are no . . . larger than fitting the included bodies.

Sandys' Travels, p. 63.

[Add :

O that I were included in my grave.

> Green, *James the Fourth*, ii, 2.

The Oxford Dictionary gives instances from Higden, Dunbar, Haward, Billingsley, Digges, and Fraunce—all before 1588.]

96. **Inclusive** (ALL'S WELL, I, iii, 232 ; RICHARD III, IV, i, 61).

[Occurs in 1515 in the modern form " from the day . . . inclusive." *See* Pitcairn's CRIMINAL TRIALS, i, 261. Also in a sixteenth-century almanack. *See* N. E. D.]

97. **Indigest** (JOHN, V, vii, 25).
In common use. *See* Oxford Dictionary for instances from Trevisa (1398), Starkey's ENGLAND (1538), and Knox's HISTORY OF THE REFORMATION IN SCOTLAND, ed. 1846, i, 333.

[Without going to these sources, Shakespeare had the word to his hand in the old TRUE TRAGEDIE OF RICHARD DUKE OF YORK (near end), and twice in Chapman's HYMNUS IN NOCTEM, 1594.]

98. **Indign** (OTHELLO, I, iii, 274).
Classic English :

Indigne and unworthy.
> Chaucer, *The Clerkes Tale*, 359.[1]

She herself was of his grace indigne.
> Spenser, *Faerie Queene*, IV, i, 30.

The most indigne and detestable thing.
> Joye, *Exposition of Daniel VI*, 1546.

[In his Addenda, Mr. Willis by oversight gives a quotation with the word *endynge* (" ending ") for indign.]

99. **Indubitate** (LOVE'S LABOUR'S LOST, IV, i, 67).
Classic English. Compare :

Eugene the fourth . . . was very and indubitate pope.
> Caxton's Chronicle, 1480.

The indubitate son of the first Clothaire.
> Fabyan's Chronicle, V, cxiii, 101.

[1] This, given in Tyrwhitt's edition, is now superseded by the reading " undigne." But it was the old printed reading.

The very indubitate heir-general to the crown of France.
Hall's Chronicles of Henry V.

100. **Inequality** (M. FOR M., V, i, 59).
The word is used only once in Shakespeare, and then obscurely. What excuse is there for ascribing here any classical peculiarity ?

101. **Infest** (TEMPEST, V, i, 246).
" The classic sense of the word," says Dr. Theobald, " is certainly implied." The classic sense is *the* sense !

102. **Infestion.** Word not in the plays. Dr. Theobald, following Farmer, conjectures that "infection " in RICHARD II (II, i, 44) is a misprint for " infestion." But there is no Latin word *infestio !* There is only the post-classical *infestatio.* The case thus collapses.

103. **Inform** (= fashion, shape : CORIOLANUS, V, iii, 70).
This again was the primary, the old, and still a usual, meaning.

To inform their judgments.
Adams' Sermons II, 43.

[Add :
Enform them well . . . sin to forsake.
Coventry Mysteries, Sh. Soc. ed. p. 41.
For to enforme and teche any other persoone a bileeve and a feith of any certain article.
Pecock, *Book of Faith*, Pt. i, ch. 2, p. 129, ed. Morison.
Infinite shapes of creatures men do find
Informed in the mud [of Nile] on which the sun hath shined.
Spenser, *F. Q.*, III, vi, 8.
To inform their mind with some method.
Hooker, *Eccles. Pol.*, B. I, ch. xvi, par. 1.
She hath him with her wordés wise
Of Cristés faith so full enformed
That they thereto ben all conformed.
Gower, *Confessio Amantis*, B. II, Morley's ed. p. 104.

Informed, reformed, and transformed from his original cynicism.

Jonson, *Cynthia's Revels*, v, 2.]

104. **Inhabitable** (= not habitable : RICHARD II, I, i, 164).

A common usage. Dr. Theobald admits that it occurs in the CATILINE (V, i, 54) of Ben Jonson, "who was classic to the point of pedantry." It would seem to follow that it is pedantically used by Shakespeare. But it occurs in Fairfax's tr. of Tasso. Compare Wiclif's Bible, Jer. ii, 6.

[Add :

Lest that thy beauty make this stately town
Inhabitable like the burning zone.
The Taming of A Shrew, 1594, Hazlitt's Sh. Lib.VI, 531.]

The Oxford Dictionary gives instances from Fish, SUPPLICATION OF BEGGARS (1529) and Stubbes (1583).

105. **Inherit, Inheritor** (RICHARD II, V, i, 85 ; ROMEO, I, ii, 30 ; TEMPEST, II, ii, 179 ; IV, i ; L. L. L., II, i, 5, &c.).

[Shakespeare uses the word in various senses—" make heir," " acquire," " possess " ; of all of which see instances in N. E. D. The " all which it [the globe] inherit " passage is *not* cited in the Dictionary as giving an unusual instance of the force of the term ; and it is clearly not specially classical. The sense of " possess," which is commonly ascribed to the word in that passage, was clearly common, as in the gospel phrase " inherit the earth " (Matt. v, 5). Tyndale translates the same passage, " possess the earth " (Exposition of Matthew, 1531). Latimer repeatedly uses the phrase " true inheritors of hell " (FIRST SERMON ON THE CARD).]

106. **Insinuation** (= thrusting in, intervention : HAMLET, V, ii, 58).

Another common usage :

Insinuate themselves in the company of flatterers
Lilly's *Euphues*, Arber's rep. p. 134.

Insinuate and wind in with their ranks and files.
> Holland's Livy, 1600, p. 1197.

A serpent he was in Paradise, winding and insinuating himself into the very bosoms of our ancestors.
> Huish on the Lord's Prayer, Lect. 18, p. 13 (1623).

Winding and insinuating themselves into our thoughts.
> *Id.* Lect. 19, p. 59.

Insinuate themselves into thy presence.
> Jonson, *Cynthia's Revels*, v, 3.

[Add :

To insinuate with my young master.
> *Id. Every Man in his Humour*, ii, 2.

Such a ready insinuation of present prattle.
> *Greene's Mourning Garment* : Works, ix, 131.

To insinuate in our secrets.
> Heywood, *The English Traveller*, i, 2.]

107. Insisture, Insisting (CORIOLANUS, III, iii, 17 ; TROILUS, I, iii, 87).

There is no point whatever in the citation of " insisting."
" Insisture " occurs once only in all the plays. It is not a " classic " coinage, having no classic original. It is further of quite uncertain meaning, and is as likely as not to be a typographical corruption.

108. Instant (" instant way " : TROILUS, III, iii, 153). Merely a variant of the common-sense " immediate." *See* N. E. D. for others, before Shakespeare.

109. Insult, Insultment (" insult on " : TITUS, III, ii, 71 ; " insult o'er," 3 HENRY VI, I, iii, 14 ; " insultment," CYMBELINE, III, v, 145).

Thus to insult over simple men.
> Lambarde, *Perambulation of Kent*, 1576, p. 174.

Because they insist so much and so proudly insult thereon.
> Hooker, *Eccles. Polity*, B. V, c. xxi, §4.

Violence and rapine insulting o'er all.
> Sandys' *Travels*, 1610, pref.

[Add :

And with a light-wing'd spirit insult o'er woe.
> Middleton, *Blurt, Master-Constable* (1602) i, 1.

X

Do not insult upon calamity.
> Daniel, *Philotas*, 1605, l. 1503.

" Insolency " is frequently used in the sense of arrogance. *E.g.* Stubbes, ANATOMIE OF ABUSES, Collier's rep. p. 59.]

110. Intend (= plan, head for, or direct : ANTONY, V, ii, 200, &c.).

One of the usual senses of the word in the period :

Eretikes there are that entenden the subversion of the Christian faith.
> In Rymer's *Fœdera*, x, 474.

Leisure to intend such business.
> Harvey's *Four Letters*, 1592, p. 13.

Iff ye entende hyddre word [hitherward].
> Paston Letters, No. 776.

[Add :

An exact parallel to the use of the word in ANTONY occurs in Hooper :

For faith intendeth and always maketh haste unto this port.
> *Declaration of Christ and his Office*, 1547, Parker Soc. rep. p. 77.

Compare :

Intend well, and God will be your adjutory.
> Interlude of *Mankind, c.* 1475, Farmer's *Lost Tudor Plays*, p. 12.

The will intendeth rather to command than obey.
> Sidney and Golding's trans. of De Mornay, 1587, ed. 1604, p. 94.

We ought not to tend or intend to any other than him.
> *Id.* p. 300.

While you intend circumstances of news.
> Jonson, *Every Man out of his Humour*, 1599, i, 1.

Look only forward to the [study of] law : intend that.
> *Id. Poetaster*, 1601, i, 1.]

111. Intentively (= attentively : OTHELLO, I, iii, 154).
" Used in this sense from 1290 downwards," remarks Judge Willis.

[Compare :
> The conningest of you
> That serveth most ententifelich and best.
> Chaucer, *Troilus and Criseyde*, i, 332.]

> That thou so longe trewely
> Hast served so ententifly.
>
> *Id. House of Fame*, 616.

Mark their life intentifely.

> Roye, *Rede me and be nott Wrothe*, 1528 : Whitting-
> ham's rep. p. 98.

Intentifly.

> Twice in Elyot's *Governour* : i, 20 ; iii, 18 ; Dent's
> rep. pp. 89, 289.

Fulgence, an ententive doctor.

> Bale, *Examination of William Thorpe*, Parker Soc.
> vol. p. 93.

Is not Chrysostom an ententive doctor ?

> *Id.* p. 113.

> With eyes intentive to bedare the sun.
>
> Peele, *David and Bethsabe*.

> Why are you so intentive to behold . . .
>
> Greene, *James the Fourth*, v, 1.

> His too intentive trust to flatterers.
>
> *Id.* ii, 2.]

112. **Intrinse, intrinsecate** (LEAR II, ii, 79 ; ANTONY,
V, ii).

" Intrinse " is a " freak " word. The Quartos read
" to intrench " ; the folio " t' intrince." " Intrinse "
is neither Latin nor English. " Intrinsecate " is pre-
Shakespearean :

> An intrinsecate matter which they understand not.
>
> Whitehorne, *Arte of Warre*, 1560, p. 409.
> Intrinsecate strokes and words.
>
> Jonson, *Cynthia's Revels*, v, 2.

Marston, girding at Jonson or another, speaks of " new-
minted epithets, such as *real* [used by himself], *intrinsecate*," *Delphic*, &c.—thus giving them further currency.
(SCOURGE OF VILLANIE, 1598.)

113. **Mere, merely** (OTHELLO, II, ii, 3 ; MACBETH,
IV, iii, 152).

The primary and common meaning of the words. *E.g.* :

> Of our certain knowledge and mere motion.
>
> Commission of Edward VI to his Council, 1552.

Mere grace : mere mercy : mere liberality : mere goodness.
> Trans. of Calvin *On Deuteronomy*, pp. 270, 322, 323.

[Add :

Bestoweth his *mercedes* of his own mere motion [*i.e.* unsolicited].
> Puttenham, *Arte of English Poesie*, Arber's rep. p. 302.

Of his own mere motion and fantasy.
> Latimer, First *Sermon on the Card*, 1529.   Dent's rep. p. 2.

> An argument to ravish and refine
> An earthly soul, and make it mere divine.
>> Chapman, *Hymnus in Cynthiam*, 1594.

Of his owne mere mocion only, without sute of fryndes.
> *The Vocacyon of John Bale*, in Harl. Misc. 1808, i, 330.

> I esteem
> Mere amity, familiar neighbourhood,
> The cousin-german unto wedded love.
>> Porter, *The Two Angry Women of Abington*, i, 1.

For meere compassion and verie ruth that pearsed his sorrowfull
hart.
> Holinshed, in Boswell Stone's *Sh. Holinshed*, p. 37.

We . . . of our especial grace, certaine knowledge, and mere
motion, did, &c.
> King's authorization, pref. to *Constitutions and
> Canons Ecclesiasticall*, 1604.

Sprung from no man, but mere divine.
> Chapman, trans. of Iliad, vi, 183.

Keep us mere English.
> Daniel, *Civil Wars*, B. v, st. 88.]

114. **Merit** (= that which is deserved : RICHARD II,
I, iii, 156).

[This meaning is implicit in the theological use of the
term, as in " the merits of Christ's passion," used thrice
in one page by Foxe, ed. Cattley, i, 72.   Hooper has " the
merits of Christ's passion," " the merits of the mass,"
" the merits of such virtues," &c. (CHRIST AND HIS OFFICE;
1547 : Parker Soc. rep. pp. 52, 55, 60). Middleton has :

My love's merit was most basely sold to him by the most false
Violetta.
> *Blurt Master-Constable*, v, 1.

Jonson has :

I shall never stand in the merit of such bounty, I fear.
> *Cynthia's Revels*, iv. 1.

Daniel has :

> Though she deserved no merit.
>
> *Cleopatra*, l. 293.
>
> To pay this thy injustice her due merit.
>
> *Id.* 1036.
>
> A lingring death with thee deserves no merit.
>
> *Id.* 1159.]

Hooker notes that " The ancient Fathers use *meriting* for *obtaining*, and in that sense they of Wittenberg have in their Confession : . . . " Good works . . . by the free kindness of God . . . merit their certain rewards " Sermon II, § 21).

115. **Modesty**, (= moderation, sobriety : HAMLET, II, ii, 461, &c.). Cited by Dr. Theobald as an illustration of " the poet's large Latinity," and " a reflection of the Baconian philosophy." It was current English, then as now :

> Whereupon the Consuls . . . went to speak unto the people . . . and used great modesty in persuading them.
>
> North, tr. of *Life of Coriolanus :*
> Skeat's Sh. Plutarch, p. 18.

They seemed to pass the bounds of modesty in abusing some men.

> Wilson's trans. of Demosthenes' third Philippic (1570).

God doth by such institutions teach the faithful modesty.

> Trans. of Calvin's *Harmony of the Evangelists*, 1584, p. 623.

[Add :

If it be cold and temperate, the style also is very modest.

> Puttenham, *Arte of Poesie*, Arber's rep. p. 161.

The meane and modest mind.   *Id. ib.*

Which modest measure of beauty.

> *Eastward Ho*, 1605, i, 1.

She humbled herself as she might with modesty.

> Greene, *Menaphon* : Works, vi, 111

Let not your words pass forth the verge of reason,
But keep within the bounds of modesty.

> Porter, *The Two Angry Women of Abington*, i, 1.

Within some bounds of modesty and subjection.

> More's *Life of Richard III*, Murray's rep. p. 194.

Whom afterward by a more modest name men called philosophers.

Sidney and Golding's trans. of De Mornay, 1587, ed. 1604, p. 9.]

116. **Obliged** (" obliged [= pledged] faith " : MER-CHANT OF VENICE, II, vi, 7). **Obligation** = a legal instrument (TROILUS, IV, v, 122 ; MERRY WIVES, I, i, 9 ; &c.)

Both old usages. Compare Wiclif (1382) :

Taak thin obligacion and sitte doon and write fifti.

Trans. of Luke xvi, 6.

[Add :

We dare not oblige us thus to be bounden to you.

Bale, Examination of William Thorpe (1382), pub. 1544, Parker Soc. rep. p. 86.

A strong bond, a firm obligation, good in law, good in law.

King Leir and his Three Daughters (1594), in Hazlitt's Sh. Library, Pt. II, vol. ii, p. 337.

The forfeit of an obligation.

Greene and Lodge, Looking-Glass for London, Sc. 3.

He hath bound and obligated his church.

Hooper, Christ and his Office, 1547. Parker Soc. rep. p. 31.

Confirmed with obligations sealed interchangeably.

Id. Answer to the Bishop of Winchester, p. 136.

Sealed me an obligation.

Lilly, Mother Bombie, v, 3.

The copy of that obligation
Where my soul's bound in heavy penalties.

Dekker, The Honest Whore, iv, 1.

As it were, obliged themselves by obligation to the devil.

Stubbes, Anatomie of Abuses, Collier's rep. p. 62.

Some tyme this world was so stedfast and stable,
That mannés word was obligacioun.

Chaucer's Balade, Lak of Stedfastnesse.

And in an obligacyon I had him bound
To paye me at a certain daye.

Impatient Poverty, 1560 ; Farmer's rep. p. 12.]

117. **Occident** (RICHARD II, III, iii, 65 ; CYMBELINE, IV, ii, 372).

As old as Chaucer, MAN OF LAWE'S TALE, l. 295.   Also in Caxton's GOLDEN LEGEND :

The sonne, moone, sterres, and planettes move from th' oryent to th' occidente.

Yet again, twice, in Cornish or Heywood's interlude, THE FOUR ELEMENTS ; Hazlitt's Dodsley, i, 18, 38. (Percy Soc. rep. pp. 16, 39.)
    [Add :

> Over all the world, from east to occident.
>> Lydate, cited in Ben Jonson's *English Grammar*.
> That brave with streams the watery occident.
>> Greene, *Orlando Furioso*, Dyce's ed. p. 103.
> What worlds in th' yet unformèd *Occident*
> May come refin'd with th' accents that are ours.
>> Daniel, *Musophilus*, ll. 961–2.]

118. **Oppugnancy** (TROILUS, I, iii, 110).
Bacon has " mainly oppugn " ; and Dr. Theobald affirms that " mere oppugnancy " and " mainly oppugn " are evidently the coinage of one mint. Oppugnancy, he asserts, " is not English at all."
" Oppugn " was current English. *See* it in Bradford's Letter of July 4, 1553 (Bickersteth, ed. of LETTERS OF MARTYRS, p. 19), and in Hooker, ECCLES. POL. B. v, Ed. 1823, ii, 10. [" Oppugnancy," by whomsoever coined, is exactly analogous to " repugnancy," found in Sidney and Golding's trans. of De Mornay (1587), ed. 1604, p. 143 and elsewhere.]

119. **Ostent, ostentation** (MERCHANT, II, ii, 205 ; MUCH ADO, IV, i, 206).
The first passage, says Dr. Theobald, " reflects Bacon's theory of behaviour." It reflects a well-worn commonplace. For the word " ostent " and the " theory " *see* Elyot, GOVERNOUR, Croft's ed., GLOSSARY. Compare :

The papists ostent their merits on earth.
                    Adams' Sermons, ii, 563.
Their ostentate charity.
                    Id. p. 57.

The Temple then shall yield a dire ostent.

Sandys' Travels.

The Oxford Dictionary gives :

Which miraculous ostent . . . was sent of God.

Foxe, Martyrs ; ed. 1684, ii, 94 ;

and adds instances from Chapman, Argument to Sestiad iv of Marlowe's Hero and Leander ; trans. of Iliad, ii, 280.

Dr. Theobald affirms that Shakespeare's use of " ostentation " (" ostentation of despised arms "); " a mourning ostentation" ; " some delightful ostentation or show ") is " exclusively classic." It is simply the primary and then normal force of the word. Compare :

In the ostentation of his lucky wit.

Adams' Sermons, i, 90–91.

[Add :

With such other false ostentations of immanitie.

Declaration as to treatment of Catholic traitors,
1583. Rep. in Harl. Misc. ed. 1808, i, 545.

Wise Jove is he hath shown
All the dire ostents of Jove.

Chapman, trans. of Iliad, v (Shepherd's ed. p. 77 b).

Can ostent or show a high gravity.

Elyot, The Governour, B. ii, 14 ; Dent's rep. p. 192.]

120. Paint, painted.

" Painted," says Dr. Theobald, " is a favourite metaphor with Shakespeare." It is ! Also with nearly every other Elizabethan writer. [*See below*, p. 419.]

121. Palliament (Titus, I, i, 182).

[The word is Peele's : Honour of the Garter, l. 92. *See* the present writer's Did Shakespeare write ' Titus Andronicus ' ? p. 64.]

122. Part (vb., Julius Cæsar, V, v, 80 ; Richard III, V, iii, 26). Party, partial, &c.

Ordinary Tudor English.

123. Perdition (= loss, not eternal : Tempest, I, ii, 30).

The original meaning. The modern is secondary. Hooker speaks of endless perdition and Raleigh of eternal perdition. " Perdition of their treasure " occurs in THE GOLDEN BOKE [of Marcus Aurelius : Bourchier's trans. of Guevara's Spanish version, 1534 and 1546], Let. ii. cited by Richardson. In the same section occurs the sentence :

> The cause gooeth to such loss and pardicion that these mischievous people are our homely and familiar enemies.

The Oxford Dictionary gives :

> Loss and perdicion of so many noble captains and strong soldiers.
> > Hall, *Chron. Henry VII* (1548) 27 *b.*

[And " my own perdition " in Gascoigne's SUPPOSES (Cunliffe's ed. of Works, i, 214) means " my own harm."]

124. **Perdurable** (HENRY V, IV, v, 7).
[Common in Chaucer. *See above*, p. 266, and compare :
> Triumphant Arks, of perdurable might.
> > Daniel, *Civil Wars*, V, 176.]

125. **Peregrinate** (put as a fantastic term : L. L. L., V, i, 14).
See under Peregrine, Peregrination, Peregrinator in N. E. D.

126. **Permission** (" of the will " : OTHELLO, I, iii, 339).
[" Clearly a reflection of the Latin word *permissus* or *permissio*, which is very frequently used by Bacon in his philosophical writings," says Dr. Theobald, who gives a page to the proposition. The passage is perfectly intelligible in itself without any such illustration : " Permission " means " letting loose," " letting go " ; and to call this " *the* Latin sense " is mere mystification.]

127. **Pernicious** (= provocative : L. L. L., IV, i, 66).
[Accepting the derivation of the word from Lat. *pernix*, Dr. Theobald describes that as " derived probably from

per and *nitor*—much struggling ; hence brisk, nimble (not to be got rid of, troublesome)," adding " *much striving* is the sense in Shakespeare " (MUCH ADO, I, i, 130). " But probably," he concludes, with an unusual misgiving, " the word is used in a sort of slang style in these passages." He refers to Horace, EPOD. ii, 42, *pernicis uxor Apuli*, concerning which his cousin, Mr. William Theobald,[1] defines *pernix* as " active." The simple solution of all this puzzling is that the common Latin words *pernix* (= *velox*), *pernicior*, *pernicitas*, and *perniciter* had given " pernicious " the secondary force of " swift," and the tertiary force of " provocative " or " inflammatory." So in Milton :

> Pernicious with one touch to fire . . .
> *Paradise Lost*, vi, 521.

This is the sense of the word in LOVE'S LABOUR'S LOST ; and this sense occurs frequently in Elizabethan literature. The term had first been made common by Catholic controversialists, who used it in the sense (moral) of " incendiary." Then it became general. *E.g.* :

> Yet their disorder in our civil streets
> May be pernicious and breed mutiny.
> *A Larum for London*, Simpson's rep. p. 46.

> Go to the Achive fleet,
> Pernicious dream [*vision*, in 1st ed.].
> Chapman, tr. of *Iliad*, ii, 8.

It is expressly used in this sense by Elyot (1533) :

> There is nothing to the strength of man's body more profitable than wyne, ne to voluptuouse appetites more pernicious.
> *Governour*, B. iii, c. 22.]

128. **Perpend** (HAMLET, II, ii, 104 ; MERRY WIVES, II, i, 119 ; &c.).

" The word [in Shakespeare] is used," says Dr. Theobald, " only by pedantical speakers or professional fools." How this supports the thesis of the dramatist's classical

---

[1] *The Classical Element in the Shakespeare Plays*, 1909, p. 42.

proclivity, he does not explain. Judge Willis justly remarks that " the word was used by grave writers before Shakespeare wrote, and in the sense in which he used it." For instances :

I desire you therefore to perpend.

Bale, Apologie, p. 17.

Let this also be perpend.

Foxe, Martyrs, sub. ann. 975.

[Add :

Herein the intent of the law is to be perpended.

Stubbes, Anatomie of Abuses, Collier's rep. p. 123.

Confer the times, perpend the history.

T. Newton " To the Reader," pref. to Higgins' add.
to the Mirrour for Magistrates, ed. 1587.

I began to perpend within myself.

Ferne, The Blazon of Gentrie, 1586, Ep. Ded.

It is finally impossible here to see what Dr. Theobald is driving at. He has not made even the semblance of a case.]

129. **Persian** (LEAR III, vi, 84).

" This," says Dr. Theobald occultly, " is not unlike the Horatian exclamation, *Persicos odi, puer, apparatus,* which Mr. Gladstone translates, " Off with Persian gear, I hate it." The commentator Steevens had previously observed, with equal profundity, that the passage alludes, " perhaps, to Clytus refusing the Persian robes offered him by Alexander." The classicists have their choice !

130. **Person** (= *persona*, part sustained : 2 HENRY IV, IV, vii, 73).

Bacon, Dr. Theobald points out, used the word in a similar sense. So did many other Elizabethan writers. Compare :

When any man is sent by a Prince, in an embassy, he must speak in such sort that men may well perceive he dissembleth not ; because he knoweth whose person he sustaineth.

Trans. of Calvin's Sermons, 1597, p. 18.

The Apostle, speaking, as it seemeth, in the person of the Christian Gentile.

Hooker, *Eccles. Pol.*

[Add :

The Patripassians and Sabellians, and after them Photinus, and of late Servetus, define a person to be a certain condition and difference of office : as when we say, Roscius sometime sustained the person of Achilles and sometime of Ulysses.

Hutchinson, *Image of God*, c. 21 ; Parker Soc. rep. p. 121.

He was contented to travell [travail] in it as in the person of a man regulated.

Fenton's Guicciardini, 1579, p. 299.

Dr. Theobald does not seem to reflect that the classic meaning of *person* is implicit in the historic description of the Christian Trinity.]

131. **Pervert** (= divert, turn aside : CYMBELINE, II, iv, 151 ; M. FOR M., IV, iii, 152, &c.).

The only uncommon usage in the passages cited is that from CYMBELINE, *pervert* = turn [anger] aside, divert. In this there is nothing more " classical " than in the various other senses of the word. The idea of " turn aside " underlies all uses of it. Compare the instances in the Oxford Dictionary from Chaucer (BOECE, B. ii, pr. 1) ; Rolls of Parlt. 1483 (vi, 240–2) ; and Nashe, " pervert foundations " (CHRIST'S TEARES, 1593). Mr. Willis cites :

But seeing they pervert all order.

Trans. of Calvin's Sermons, 1579, p. 662.

132. **Plant** (= sole of the foot : ANTONY, II, vii, 1).

There is no classic innovation here. The word was *vernacularly* used :

> Knotty legs and plants of clay
> Seek for ease or love delay.

Jonson, *Masque of Oberon.*

The variorum edition cites, further :

Grinde mustarde with vineger, and rubbe it well on the plants or soles of the feete.

T. Lupton, *Third Book of Notable Things*, bk. 1.

Even to the low plants of his feet, his form was alterèd.
Chapman, trans. of Iliad, xvi.]

[Add :
In the TENNE TRAGEDIES OF SENECA, a version which runs much to the vernacular, we have the lines :

<blockquote>Hangde was I by the Heeles
Upon a tree, my swelling plants the fruit thereof yet feeles.</blockquote>
Thebais, p. 46 a.

Again we have it in Nashe :

<blockquote>You Pilgrims, that . . . weare the plants of your feete to the likenesse of withered roots.</blockquote>
Christ's Teares over Jerusalem ; Works, ed. McKerrow, ii, 63.]

133. **Port** (ANTONY, I, iii, 45).
Dr. Theobald thinks the word here means gate. It probably does not : Sextus held the sea power. But port = gate is common old and Tudor English.

<blockquote>Dayly were issues made out of the city at divers ports.</blockquote>
Hall, Chron. Henry V.

The word occurs in this sense thrice in Fairfax's TASSO, B. xii, st. 48, 49, 51. [Also B. iii, st. 12 and 49.]

[*Port* was the word for city-gate in Edinburgh from ancient times down to the disuse of the walls.

Chapman uses the word constantly in his trans ations :

<blockquote>The Scæan ports [of Troy].</blockquote>
Trans. of Iliad (1598), iii, 280.

<blockquote>The ports and far-stretched walls [of Troy].</blockquote>
Id. iv, 64.

<blockquote>The seven-fold ported Thebes.</blockquote>
Id. iv, 433.

<blockquote>Seven-ported Thebes.</blockquote>
Trans. of Hesiod, B. i.

<blockquote>To come within the ports.</blockquote>
Iliad, vi, 77.

<blockquote>By this had Hector reached the ports of Scæa, and the towers.</blockquote>
Id. vi, 248.

<blockquote>This said, brave Hector through the ports . . . made issue.</blockquote>
Id. vii, 1.

Compare :

> Though strait the passage and the port be made.
> > Marlowe, 1 *Tamb*. ii, 1.
> Till Phœbus with his beams so bright
> From out the fiery port.
> > *Ballad of True Lovers* (before 1597), Sh. Soc. Papers,
> > 1844, vol. ii, p. 14.]

134. PORT (= bearing, status : MERCHANT, III, ii, 282).

So in Fairfax's trans. of TASSO, often.
[Add :

From Princely Port to tumble down into poor servile state.
> *Tenne Tragedies of Seneca*, 1581 ; *Thebais*, p. 53a.
> With stately bissopes a greate sorte,
> Which kepe a mervelous porte.
> > Roye, *Rede me and be nott Wrothe*, 1528.
Honourable port and majesty.
> > Elyot, *Governour*, ii, 2.
> No princely port, nor wealthy store.
> William Byrd, *Psalms, Sonnets, and Songs*, 1588.
> > Cast yourself to bear such a port
> > That, as ye be, ye may be known.
> H. Medwall, *Nature* (c. 1490). Farmer's *Lost Tudor Plays*, p. 65.
Their decayed port.
> Nashe, *Anatomie of Absurditie* : Works, ed. McKerrow, i, 33.
> > With an imperial port
> Gath'ring his spirits he rises from his seat.
> > Daniel, *Civil Wars*, B. vii, (1602) st. 67.]

135. **Portable** (MACBETH, IV, iii, 89 ; LEAR, III, vi, 115).

The Oxford Dictionary gives :

A portable ynke to be carried in the forme of a powder.
> Platt, *Jewell-House*, 1594, iii, 36.
A little portable case.
> Guillemeau's *French Chirurgeon*, 1597.

[The form "importable" = intolerable, insupportable, is common :

Be relieved and eased of many importable charges.
> Publisher's pref. to Latimer's *Second Sermon before Edward VI.*

To avoid his importable displeasure.
> Hooper, *Answer to the Bishop of Winchester*, Parker Soc. rep. p. 110.

O outrageous and importable arrogancy of man.
> Philpot, trans. of Curio's *Defence of Christ's Church* (*c.* 1550) *in Writings*, 1842, p. 356.]

136. Prefer (= bring forward, produce : SHREW, I, i, 96 ; 1 HENRY VI, III, i, 110).

Their cartel in defiance they prefer.
> Daniel, *Civil Wars.*

I . . . my vows and prayers to thee preferr'd .
> Sandys' *Travels*, 1610.

Furtherers, preferrers, and defenders on the King's behalf of the said cause.
> Foxe, *Acts and Monuments.*

[Add :

To prefer bills of accusation.
> Strype, *Mem. of Cranmer*, ed. 1848, i, 248–9.

> Her goddess, in whose fane she did prefer
> Her virgin vows.
> Chapman, Third Sestiad of *Hero and Leander*, 1598.]

137. Premised (= sent in advance : 2 HENRY VI, V, ii, 141).

In his Addenda Mr. Willis cites (from the Oxford Dictionary) Burnet's HISTORY OF THE REFORMATION, Pocock's ed. v, 173 : " Upon pain and peril premised." This is an inadequate parallel ; but the Dictionary cites from the 1540 translation of Polydore Vergil :

The King premised certain horsemen to beset all the sea coast ; and from Bishop Barlow (1609) :

There was a premission of him [Joseph] into Egypt, which prove the usage.

138. Preposterous (= " behind before " : M. N. D. III, ii, 120 ; OTHELLO, I, iii, 330).

Certainly this is the " classic " meaning of the term.

And as certainly it was commonly so used in English before Shakespeare and Bacon.

> Is not this gear preposterous, that Alexandria, where Mark . . . was bishop, should be preferred before Ephesus, where John the Evangelist taught and was bishop.
>
> Bradford to Lady Vane, 1553, in *Letters of Martyrs*, 1837, p. 313.

> Christ does not deny this to be a preposterous order, that the unlearned common people should first celebrate . . . the coming of the Messias.
>
> Trans. of Calvin's *Harmony*, 1584, p. 568.

> It is preposterous that men, being born to a better life, do wholly occupy themselves in earthly things.
>
> *Id.* p. 218.

> They deal preposterously, which busy themselves in small matters when they should rather begin at the chiefest.
>
> *Id.* p. 617.

[The word was as current, in its strict sense, in literary as in theological writing. Thus Puttenham writes :

> Ye have another manner of disordered speech, when ye . . . set that before which should be behind, et è converso. We call it in English proverb, the cart before the horse : the Greeks call it *histeron proteron* : we name it the Preposterous. . . . One describing his landing upon a strange coast, said thus preposterously : " When we had climbed the cliffs and were ashore "
>
> *Arte of English Poesie*, Arber's rep. p. 181.

> A preposterous order, to set the cart before the horse.
>
> Hooper, *Answer to the Bishop of Winchester*, Parker Soc. vol. p. 147.

The word occurs frequently in Tyndale's translation of Erasmus' ENCHIRIDION, 1533. Methuen's rep. pp. 26, 155, 169, 181, 188.]

139. **Prevent, Prevention** (= go before, anticipate : JUL. CÆS. V, i, 104).

As normal in that day as " let " for " hinder."

See the Collect at end of the Communion Service, 1547, which Dr. Theobald actually quotes. Why then did he put the word as a classicism ?

140. **Probation** (= proof : HAMLET, I, i, 54 ; OTHELLO, III, iii, 365).

The old and common use of the word, to which the sense of " trial " is secondary. It exists to this day in the technical term " probate," which is found in Hall's Chronicle, HENRY VIII, an. 17. Compare :

> Bryng forth your honest probacyons and ye shall be heard.
> > Bale's *Apologie*, fol. 92.
>
> For the more evident probation whereof.
> > Foxe's *Martyrs*, ed. 1846, p. 12.
>
> True and sufficient probation grounded upon the Scripture.
> > *Id.* iv, 287.

[Add :

> Let it be admitted for the probation of this . . .
> > Latimer, First *Sermon on the Card*, 1529.
>
> I dare saye unable he was
> Of one erroure to make probacion.
> > Roye, *Rede me and be nott Wrothe*, 1528.
>
> A more plain token and evident probation.
> > Tyndale's trans. of Erasmus' *Enchiridion*, 1533 ;
> > Methuen's rep. p. 166.
>
> By this probation and argument.
> > *Id.*, p. 272.]

141. **Proditor** (1 HENRY VI, I, iii, 31).

An established term, used in official documents. The Oxford Dictionary gives :

> In resistence of your Proditours, Rebelles, and Adversaries.
> > 1436. *Rolls of Parliament*, iv, 500–2.
>
> As manifest enemy and proditour to the Cristen State.
> > 1546. *State Papers, Henry VIII*, xi, 95.

[The word " prodition " occurs in such popular works as Henry Medwall's interlude NATURE, *circa* 1490 :

> That thou be not deceived by false prodition.
> > Farmer's *Lost Tudor Plays*, p. 48,

and Roye's REDE ME AND BE NOTT WROTHE, 1528 ; and Daniel (CIVIL WARS, B. iii, st. 78) has " proditorious wretch." A passage in Bale's BRIEF CHRONICLE concerning Lord Cobham suggests that semi-punning phrases

Y

about proditors had long been current. Bale speaks (Parker Soc. rep. p. 16) of "the general proctors, yea rather betrayers of Christ." The passage in 1 HENRY VI runs : "Thou most usurping Proditor, and not Protector." Bale's phrase seems an interpretation of "proctors, yea rather proditors," for the "yea rather" as it stands is rather pointless.[1]]

142. **Propend, Propension** (= to be inclined to : TROILUS, II, ii, 190, 132).

There is no innovation here. "Propension" is an old form of "propensity," the form which has survived. Compare :

The forwardness and propension of his mind.
King on Jonah, 1594, ed. 1611, p. 116.
Propensity of heart.
Foxe, Martyrs, sub ann. 1535.

The Oxford Dictionary give instances of *propend* from Reynold, 1545, and Sandys, 1599 ; and of *propension* (also *propensed*) from Wolsey, 1530, and Barington, 1580.

[Add :

Women propense and inclinable to holiness.
Hooper, Eccles. Pol. pref. ch. iii, §13.]

143. **Propugnation** (TROILUS, II, ii, 136).

[Mr. Willis gives no instances, but the Oxford Dictionary does : "Propugnation" in Ferne's BLAZON OF GENTRIE, 1586, ii, 62 ; and "Propugnatour" in THE MIRROUR OF SALVACIOUN, 1450, and THE COMPLAYNT OF SCOTLAND, 1549, ep. ded., p. 4.]

144. **Pudency** (CYMBELINE, II, v, 11).

Mr. Willis justly remarks that this word, of which there is no other recorded instance, is a very simple formation

---

[1] The habit of aspersive alliteration was common. Latimer has "Bishops ! nay rather Buzzards" (*First Sermon before Edward VI*) ; and he tells of much excitement in London over the phrase "Burgesses ! nay, Butterflies !" (*Sermon of the Plough*).

from " impudency." [It is not a " classic " adaptation ; there is no Latin word *pudentia*, though there is *pudens*.]

145. Questant, Questrists (ALL'S WELL, II, i, 15 ; LEAR, III, vii, 16).

Admittedly not yet traced in pre-Shakespearean writers.

But they are merely variants of old words such as quester or quaestor (*q.v.*, N. E. D.). In Pecock's REPRESSOR OF OVERMUCH BLAMING OF THE CLERGY (Roll's Ser. ii, 516, 540) we have *Questmongers* (= informers—the same thing as *quaestor*) or jurymen. *Questmen* were regularly elected annually to assist churchwardens in matters of ecclesiastical police. The " quest-house " was the chief watch-house of a parish. *See* Halliwell's and Nares' Dictionaries. There is no real " coinage " in the matter.

146. Recordation (TROILUS, V, ii, 116).

He [Xerxes] wept in recordation of their mortality.
> Rainold's *Lect. on Obadiah*, 1584. Nicholl's ed.
> 1864, p. 35.

Fair and sacred recordations.
> Holland's tr. of Plutarch's *Moralia*, 1603, p. 940.

147. Reduce (= bring back, restore : RICH. III, V, v, 35).

If the noble King Edgar had not reduced the monarchy to his pristinate estate and figure. . . . It [England] shall be reduced . . . unto a public weal excelling all other
> Elyot, *The Governour*, i, 2.

To reduce the seduced from their errors.
> Sandys' *Travels*, 1610, ed. 1637, p. 86.

[A very common usage. Compare :

To reduce not only him but also his substance to their former state of freedom and liberty.
> Rosdell's Ep. Ded. to ed. of Hooper's *Christ and His Office*, 1582.

To reduce him that erreth into the trayne of virtue.
> Elyot, *The Governour*, ii, 9.

Reduced . . . the Romans . . . to their pristinate moderation and temperance.

> *Id.* iii, 11.

Healed and reduced to his perfection.

> *Id.* iii, 26.

> Alas, I see, nothing hath hurt so sore,
> But time in time reduceth a return.
>> Surrey, first poem in *Tottel's Miscellany,* 1557, Arber's rep.

Then we shall show that he may be reduced into health.
> Philpot, trans. of Curio's *Defence of Christ's Church* (MS. *c.* 1550), 1842, p. 376.

Goeth about to reduce them into the way.

> *Id. ib.* p. 393.

How often would I have revokt, reduced, and brought you into the right way.
> Nash, *Christ's Teares over Jerusalem,* 1593. Works, ed. McKerrow, ii, 21.

Whom lyving, theyr preaching might have reduced.

> *Id. ib.* p. 26.

Let her reduce the golden age again.
> Hughes, *The Misfortunes of Arthur,* 1587, V, ii, 23.

To seek Philomela and to reduce her from banishment.
> Greene, *Philomela,* 1592. Works, xi, 193.

> When his reason had reduced
> His flying thoughts back to some certain stand.
>> Daniel, *Philotas,* 1605, ll. 235–6.]

148. Refelled (= rebutted, refuted : M. FOR M., V, i, 93). A widely current Elizabethan word.

Unless mine adversaries with true and sufficient probations . . . can . . . refel mine errors.
> Townshend ed. of Foxe's *Martyrs,* iv, 287.

Refel positions.
> Hooker's *Sermon on Justification.*

I stand not to refel absurdities.
> Henry Smith (d. 1591), *Sermon at Clement Dane's.*

[Add :

I must stop their mouths, convince, refel, and refute.
> Latimer, *Third Sermon before Edward VI.*

> Strong proofs brought out,
> Which strongly were refell'd.
>> Daniel, *Civil Wars,* B. iii, st. 13.

That which I say in company see thou refell not openly.

> T. Kendall, *Flowers of Epigrams*, 1577.   Spenser
> Soc. rep. p. 197.

The lesser [objections] then are easily refelled.

> *A Larum for London*, Simpson's rep. p. 46.

A plea so strong
As cannot be refelled.

> *Famous History of Sir Thomas Wyat*, sc. 6.

The devilishness of this new doctrine of theirs shall be refelled in my books.

> Bale, *First Examination of Anne Askewe*.   Parker
> Soc. ed. of Works, p. 171.

Paul himself doth refel such great treacheries easily.

> Philpot, trans. of Curio's *Defence of Christ's Church*
> (MS. *c.* 1550), 1842, p. 371.

Witness how clearly I can refel that paradox, or rather pseudodox.

> Jonson, *Cynthia's Revels*, ii, 1.

This argument no tyrant can refell.

> Daniel, *Philotas*, l. 2044 (2134).]

149. **Religious-ly** (= scrupulous-ly : ALL'S WELL, II, iii, 189 ; HENRY V, I, ii, 9).

Dr. Theobald refers this force of the word to the Latin *religiosus*. By limiting his quotations he keeps out of sight the fact that Shakespeare's metaphorical use of it is simply an implication of the common force of the word as " devout "=" earnest." *E.g.* :

> Religious in mine error, I adore the sun.
> *All's Well*, I, iii, 211.

A most devout coward, religious in it.

> *Twelfth Night*, III, iv, 424.

Compare :

Among the gifts of the temple which they would have regarded religiously and scrupulously.

> Udal on Matthew, c. 27.

[Add :

> Let mortals learn
> To make religion of offending heaven.
> Jonson, *Cynthia's Revels*, v, 3, near end.

I see you make religion of your word [= promise].

> *A Larum for London*, 1599, l. 24.

Loyal, religious in love's hallowed vows.
> Porter, *Two Angry Women of Abington*, ii, 1.

Do you think him honest ?
Religiously ; a true, most zealous patriot.
> Chapman, *The Admiral of France*, iii, 3.

The opinion of Faeries and elfes is very old, and yet sticketh very religiously in the minds of some.
> E. King's *Glosse* to Spenser's *Shepheard's Calender*,
> *June.*

Albe of Love I always humbly deemed
That he was such an one as thou dost say,
And so religiously to be esteemed.
> Spenser, *Colin Clout's Come Home Again*, ll. 328–30.

But we . . .
Do make religion now we rashly go
To serve that God [Cupid] that is so greatly dred.
> *Id.* l. 797.

Thy most even and religious hand,
Great Minister of Justice
> Daniel, *Certaine Epistles*, 1601–3 : To Sir T.
> Egerton, ll. 198–9.]

150. Remonstrance (substantially = demonstration : M. FOR M., V, i, 394).

This was *the* sense of the word in the period.

With strong and invincible remonstrance of sound reason.
> Hooker, *Eccles. Pol.* B. par. v, 10.

The manifest odds . . . are remonstrances more than sufficient [to show] . . .

> *Id.* par. 76.

I will remonstrate [= expound] to you.
> Jonson, *Every man out of his Humour.*

Your son shall make remonstrance of his valour.
> Barnabe Barnes, *The Devil's Charter*, i, 4.

151. Renege (from med. Lat. *renego* : LEAR, II, ii, 79). The fact that *renego* is mediæval Latin would have put any one not a Baconian on his guard. The forms " reneague " and " renay," which come from that, are common in Middle and Tudor English.

Reneyed.

> *Piers Plowman.*

Those hath he reneagued and put away from the inheritance of the promises.

> Udal on Luke 1.

In the mean season while Peter reneagueth.

> *Id.* on c. 22.

A plain renaying of Christ's faith.

> Sir T. More, *Works*, p. 179.

[Add :

Renyinge God allthough they saye naye.

> Roye, *Rede me and be nott Wrothe*, 1528.]

152. Repugn, Repugnancy, Repugnant (1 H. VI, IV, i, 94 ; TIMON, III, v, 42 ; HAMLET, II, ii, 491).

As old as Wiclif. *See* Croft's Glossary to Elyot's GOVERNOUR.

Repugnant to his will.

> Cranmer's Letter to Queen Mary, in *Letters of Martyrs*, p. 2.

His authority . . . repugneth to the crown imperial.

> *Id.* p. 3.

That discontinuance doth not repugne with the prophecy of Jacob.

> Trans. of Calvin's *Harmony*, 1584, p. 5.

Whether that which our laws do permit be repugnant to those maxims.

> Hooker, *Eccles. Pol.* B. v, par. 81.

Repugnancy or contradiction.

> *Id. ib.*

A law contrariant or repugnant to the law of nature.

> *Id. ib.*

[Add :

To withstand and repugn against the truth.

> Marg. note to trans. of Erasmus' *Enchiridion*, 1533. Methuen's rep. p. 77.

Rebel, repugne, lash out and kick.

> *The Trial of Pleasure*, 1567.   Percy Soc. rep. p. 42.

> I have suaged the old repugnance,
> And knit them together.

> Medwall's Interlude of *Nature* (*c.* 1490), Farmer's *Lost Tudor Plays*, p. 43.

Nature repugnyng.

> Elyot, *Governour*, i, 14.

To repugne again reason.

Id. iii, 25.]

153. **Repute** (TITUS, I, i, 366 ; 1 HENRY IV, V, i, 54).
Absolutely normal Tudor English.

The Church of Rome doth not repute the one oblation of
Jesus Christ . . . to be perfect.
> H. Smith (d. 1591), *God's Arrow Against Atheists*,
> ed. 1611, p. 80.

Word so used in Sandys' TRAVELS (1610), 4th ed. pp. 91,
107, 124, 145.
[Add :

Our wrong reputed weakness.
> Daniel, *Letter from Octavia to Marcus Antonius*,
> 1599, st. 15.
> Nor could she yet repute herself secure.
> Harington, trans. of *Orlando Furioso*, 1591, B. i,
> st. 33.]

154. **Retentive** (in the physical sense : TIMON, III,
iv, 81).

What words (said she) fly your retentive powers.
> Chapman, trans. of *Odyssey*, B. xix.

The Oxford Dictionary gives examples from Chaucer
(PARSON'S TALE, § 76, sent. 913 ; Holland's Pliny, II,
under *Words of Art*, &c.)
[Compare :

> Retention and ejection in her powers
> Being acts alike.
> Chapman, Third Sestiad of *Hero and Leander*.]

155. **Reverb** (LEAR, I, i, 155).
Not traced by Mr. Willis. Steevens noted the word
as perhaps of Shakespeare's own coining. However that
may be, it is obviously *not* a classicism : it is a curtail-
ment of a Latin word, such as a good scholar would not
commit.

156. **Rivage** (Fr. : Chorus to HENRY V, Act III).
Found in Pseudo-Chaucer, CHAUCER'S DREAME, l. 1105.

Also in Gower, B. viii ; in Hall ; and in Holinshed, B. iv, c. 24. Also in Spenser, FAERIE QUEENE, IV, vi, 20.

157. Ruinate (3 HENRY VI, V, i, 8).

Dr. Theobald on this word remarks that " Shakespeare often turns nouns into verbs." Judge Willis errs in denying this in general : the practice was common to the period. But he is right in denying that Shakespeare made " ruinate " in that fashion. It was a standing verb :

Till all was subverted and ruinated.
Henry Smith (d. 1591), Sermons, ed. 1613, p. 62.

The verb is found twice in the old play, THE DOWNFALL OF ROBERT EARL OF HUNTINGDON (Hazlitt's Dodsley, vol. viii, pp. 158, 184) ; in Bancroft's PLATFORM OF EPISCOPACY (1594), in Lewkenor's trans. of THE COMMONWEALTH OF VENICE (1599), &c. &c.

[Add : Spenser, FAERIE QUEENE, II, xii, 7 ; (adj. V, x, 26) ; Sonnet 56 ; Greene's SELIMUS, ll. 150, 878 ; PERYMEDES THE BLACKSMITH, 1588 : Works, vii, 45 ; FRIAR BACON, sc. 8 : ed. Dyce, p. 168 ; Kyd's trans. of Garnier's CORNELIA, Act iv ; Daniel, PHILOTAS, l. 696 ; Chapman, trans. of ILIAD, iv, 42.]

158. Sacred (" Sacred wit " : TITUS, II, i, 120).

[Dr. Theobald, following the commentators, takes this term in this place to mean " accursed." It probably did not. Peele, who probably wrote the bulk of the play, has " sacred wit " in his ARRAIGNMENT OF PARIS, IV, i, 285. But the word occurs with the " classic " significance in Massinger, EMPEROR OF THE EAST, iv, 5.]

159. Scope ($=$ *skopos*, view, or mark or aim : TIMON, I, i, 72).

Cursed Night that reft from him so goodly scope.
Spenser, *Faerie Queene*, III, iv, 52.

[Add :

So huge a scope at first him seemed best.
Id. III, ix, 46.

Shooting wide do miss the markèd scope.
> *Id. Shepheard's Calender, November.*

Ere they come unto their aymèd scope.
> *Id. F. Q.* VI, iii, 5.

To aim their counsels to the fairest scope.
> *Id. Mother Hubberd's Tale,* l. 960.

But whither am I carried all this while
Beyond my scope.
> Daniel, *Letter from Octavia to Marcus Antonius,*
> 1599, st. 51.

But since it hath no other scope to go
Nor other purpose.
> *Id. To the Angell Spirit of* . . . *Sidney,* ll. 45–46.

160. **Sect** (= a cutting : OTHELLO, I, iii, 335).

[Mr. Willis suggests that *sect* here may be a misprint for *set* (= setting), which is unlikely, though Dr. Johnson suggested that reading. The word seems to be used with the same force in the old play of KING LEIR AND HIS THREE DAUGHTERS :

> Till I have rooted out this viperous sect.
> > Hazlitt's Sh. Library, Pt. II, vol. ii, p. 376.

Gascoigne again has :

> And all good haps that ever Troylus' sect [lovers]
> Achieved yet above the luckless ground.
> > *Adventures of Master F. J.* ; Cunliffe's ed. of Works,
> > i, 426.

The term had in fact the sense of " sort," " set," or " species." Wiclif constantly applies it to the friars (TREATISE, chs. 2, 3, 4, 28, &c.), frequently in the plural, signifying " groups." Pecock speaks of " Sarrasene secte " and " Cristen sect " (BOOK OF FAITH, Pt. I, ch. 2, p. 131, ed. Morison) ; and Hooper has : " neither the one secte of people called papists, neither the other called gospellers " (ANSWER TO THE BISHOP OF WINCHESTER, Parker Soc. rep. p. 137).

Compare Spenser :

> And by the name of soldiers us protect,
> Which now is thought a civil begging sect.
> > *Mother Hubberd's Tale,* ll. 246–7 ;

and Jonson :

> But in this age a sect of writers are.
>> *The Silent Woman*, prol.]

In his Addenda Mr. Willis cites :

> As if we and they had been one sect.
>> Hazlitt's Dodsley, v, 303.

161. **Secure, Securely, Security** (= unconcerned or heedless : MERRY WIVES, II, ii, 314 ; MACBETH, III, v, 32 ; RICHARD II, II, i, 265).

Common usages. *See* Spenser, F. Q. Bk. VI, Canto v ; and Daniel, CIVIL WARS, B. i : " lived secure."

[Add : EUPHUES, Arber's rep. p. 63 ; SELIMUS, l. 367 ; A LARUM FOR LONDON (Simpson's rep. pp. 1, 43, 46, 50) ; Marlowe, trans. of Lucan, l. 135 ; Lilly, ENDIMION, ii, 1 ; WOMAN IN THE MOON, ii, 1 ; Lodge, WOUNDS OF CIVIL WAR, l. 41 ; Gascoigne, THE SPOYLE OF ANTWERP (Cunliffe's ed. of Works, ii, 594 ; Daniel, CLEOPATRA, l. 533 ; Jonson, SEJANUS, ii, 2 ; iii, 2. Dr. Theobald actually notes the use of " securely " in Prov. iii, 29, and in Ben Jonson. The citation is thus to no purpose.]

162. **Segregration** (= separation : OTHELLO, II, i, 10).

Richardson's Dictionary gives instances from Sir T. More, Feltham's RESOLVES, and Wotton; and the N. E. D. one from Philpot, 1564. Judge Willis adds :

> Segregated themselves from the Church of Rome.
>> Foxe, *Martyrs* (1560) ed. 1843, i, p. xxvi.

163. **Semblable** (adj. = similar ; sb. = resemblance : 2 HENRY IV, V, i, 72 ; HAMLET, V, ii, 24).

" Either a French word or from the Latin *similis*," says our Baconian philologist. It happens to abound in Chaucer ! " Semblable " and " semblably " are two of the commonest words in Elizabethan didactic books. They occur hundreds of times, for instance, in Elyot and in Holland's Plutarch. The passage from adjective to noun is exactly as in " equal."

164. **Sensible** (= perceptible to the senses : HAMLET, I, i, 56, &c.).

The meaning of the word in that period. *E.g.* :

Eternal damnation of sensible pain in the fire of hell.
Sir T. More, Works, p. 1281.

[Compare :

To what purpose were the senses without the sensible things ?
Sidney and Golding's trans. of De Mornay, 1587.
Ed. 1604, p. 7.

The sensible powers. The sensible wits and natural motions. The sensible powers, that is to say, the five wits. The sensible wits. Thy sensible wits. Our sensible wits.
Tyndale's trans. of Erasmus' *Enchiridion,* 1533.
Methuen's rep. pp. 89, 105, 139, 140, 141, 144.

Sensible pleasure and sensible pain.
J. Heywood, *Dialogue on Wit and Folly,* Percy
Soc. rep. p. 19.

Sensible signs. Sensible things. Sensible sacraments.
Tyndale, *Supper of the Lord* : Works, Parker Soc.
ed. iii, 265. (Thrice in a page.)]

165. **Septentrion** (3 HENRY VI, I, iv, 133).
Occurs several times in Chaucer :

Both east and west, north [slip for *south*] and septemtrioun.
The Monk's Tale, 477.

Septentrional and septentrionalis, in THE ASTROLABE ; and in BOECE (B. ii, pr. 6) " the colde sterres that highten the vii Tryones (that is to seyn . . . the partye of the north)."

166. **Simular** (LEAR, III, ii, 54).

As Christ in the Gospel . . . called them hypocrites, that is to say, simulars and painted sepulchres.
Tyndale, prol. to *Romans.*

" Simulate (= simulated) chastity " occurs in Bale, ENGLISH VOTARIES, Pt. II.

[" Dissimulers " occurs in Tyndale (*Answer* to Sir T. More. Works, Parker Soc. ed. iii, 45), who also has the verb to " simule," i, 341.]

167. Solemn (= ceremonial or stately : " solemn hunting " : TITUS, II, i, 112).

The solempne day of Pask.
> Wiclif, trans. of Luke ii. 41.

Same term in the Rhemish New Testament, 1580.

Upon ane solempne day As custom was.
> Chaucer [really Henryson], *Testament of Creseide*, ll. 112–113.

[Add :

An assembly so honourable and solemn.
> Fenton's trans. of Guicciardini, 1579, p. 6.

Affable and courteous at meals and meetings, in open assemblies more solemn and strange.
> Puttenham, *Arte of English Poesie*, Arber's rep. p. 298.

Solemne feasts. Solemn plays. Times of solemnity.
> T. Heywood, *Apology for Actors*, 1612, Sh. Soc. rep. pp. 54, 56, 60.

A solemne oration. Solemn feasts.
> Gosson, *School of Abuse*, 1579, Sh. Soc. rep. pp. 13, 15.

A day of mirth and solemn jubilee.
> Webster and Rowley, *A Cure for a Cuckold*, sc. 1.

Triumph, and solemnize a martial feast.
> Marlowe, 1 *Tamb.* iii, 3, end.]

168. Sort (= *sors*, a lot : TROILUS, I, iii, 374).]

Were it by aventure or sort or cas [= chance].
> Chaucer, *Knight's Tale*, l. 844.

[The word occurs also thrice in TROILUS AND CRESEYDE; ii, 1754 ; iii, 1047 ; iv, 116, and elsewhere in Chaucer.]

169. Speculation (phys. sense : MACBETH, iv, 95 ; TROILUS, III, iii, 109 ; HENRY V, IV, ii, 31).

Word occurs thus in Hooker, ECCLES. POL. V, and in Holland's trans. of Pliny, B. xviii, c. 28.

[Add :

When thei loken hem in the speculation or lokynge of the devyne thought.
> Chaucer, *Boece*, B. V, pr. 2.

Compare :

To be confined to the speculation of a death's head.
> Chapman, *The Widow's Tears*, iii, 1.]

170. **Stelled** ("stelléd fires" : LEAR, III, vii, 59 ;
STELL'D : LUCRECE, 1443).

[Dr. Theobald pronounces the word in LEAR to be
derived from *stella*, a star. If it were, it would be a most
unscholarlike coinage. It is really the same word as
occurs in LUCRECE ; and the derivation of that is not,
as Mr. Theobald supposes, from στέλλω, but from A. S.
stellan.]

171. **Substituted** (= placed under, in rank : 2 HENRY IV,
I, iii, 84).

And they did also substitute other which were known heads
also.
> Sir T. More, *Works*, p. 821.

[Compare :
> Have thrust out proud Octavian's substitute.
>> Day, *Humour out of Breath*, 1608, v, 2.
> Be you joint governors of this my realm :
> I do ordain you both my substitutes.
>> *The Weakest goeth to the Wall* (anon. pr. with
>> Webster), i, 1.
> So they pay their yearly tribute
> Unto his dyvlishe substitute,
>> Official or commissary.
>> Roye, *Rede me and be nott Wrothe*, 1528.
> Great Soliman, heaven's only substitute.
>> Kyd, *Soliman and Perseda*, i, 5.
> Honoured because they are the substitutes of the King.
>> Gascoigne, *Glasse of Government*, 1575, ii, 1.]

172. **Success** (= sequence, result : *e.g.* " vile success,"
OTHELLO, III, iii, 221).

Dr. Theobald gravely remarks that " Bacon also
follows the Latin." Judge Willis comments : " In the
sixteenth century every writer with whom I am acquainted uses the word *success* in the same way." This

is the fact (*see above*, p. 256) ; and Dr. Theobald's citation in this case might alone serve as the proof of his comprehensive inacquaintance with Elizabethan literature.

173. **Suspire: Suspiration** (JOHN, III, iv, 79 ; HAMLET, I, ii, 79).

Suspiring and sighing.
Sir T. More.

The long suspired Redeemer of the world.
Reliquiæ Wottonianæ, p. 269.

[Add :

> Throw forth sad throbs and grievous suspirës.
> Break, heart, with sobs and grievous suspirës.
Locrine, v, 4.

As they do that enchant the water of the font, and chafe it with many a suspire and deep-fet breath.
Hooper, *Declaration of the Ten Commandments*,
1550, Parker Soc. rep, p. 345.

And suspirable death of so brave soldiers.
Kyd, *Cornelia*, v, 287.]

174. **Tenable** (" tenable in your silence " : HAMLET, I, ii, 247).

In *this* ostensible sense (" retained ") the word is not found elsewhere ; and there is much reason to believe it a misprint. If intended, it is incongruous English. Folios 2 and 3 read *treble*. " Tenable," used of a fortress, is found in Hakluyt's VOYAGES, i, 614, and in Howell's LETTERS, B. xi, let. 4.

175. **Terms** (= limits : ALL'S WELL, II, iii, 173).

Eche chaunge hath his special end and terme [whereunto], and therefore accordynge to terme and ende hath . . .
Bishop Gardiner's *Explanation of the Presence*,fol. 109.

A perfectly normal usage.

176. **Translate** (physically remove : M. N. D., III; ii, 31).

A very common usage :

When the Romans had translated to themselves the tribute.
Trans. of Calvin's *Harmony*, 1584, p. 545.

This translation of faults from ourselves to others.

> King on Jonah, 1594, ed. 1611, p. 128.

Thither was the seat of the prince translated.

> Lewkenor's trans. of Contrareno's *Commonwealth of Venice*, 1598, p. 51.

[Add :

Thanne is thilke money precyous when it is translated into other folk.

> Chaucer, *Boece*, B. ii, pr. 5.

If kingdoms be translated for unrighteousness, they are preserved by righteousness.

> Hutchinson, *The Image of God*, Works, ed. Parker Soc. p. 71.

Whole kyngdomes . . . bee so soone translated from one manne unto another.

> More, *Dialogue of Comfort against Tribulation*, Dent's rep. p. 275.

By turning, translating, and removing these marks.

> Robinson's trans. of More's *Utopia*, Dent's rep. p. 49.

Is it [obedience] not altogether translated and exempted from your Grace unto them.

> *Beggars' Petition against Popery*, 1538, Harl. Misc. 1808, i, 221.

This . . . is all the cause of translation of your kingdom so fast into their hands.

> *Id.* p. 223.

Dreams, extraordinarily sent from [heaven to foreshew the translation of monarchies.

> Nashe, *Terrors of the Night* ; Works, ed. McKerrow, i, 362.

In the same year 1269 he [Henry III] translated with great solemnity the body of King Edward the Confessor into a new chapel.

> Stow, *Survey of London*, 1598.   Morley's rep. p. 417.

Thither hath God translated the body of Christ

> Hooper, *Declaration of Christ and his Office*, Parker Soc. rep. p. 67.

Useth no purgation nor translation of his sin.

> *Id. ib.* p. 136.

To abide perpetually to his crowne, without translatynge heeroff to any other use.

> Fortescue, *Governance of England*, 1476, ch. 11.]

177. **Umber'd** (= Shadowed; from Lat. *umbra :* HENRY V, iv, Chorus, 9).

Old English. Steevens gives the instances :

Under the umbre and shadow of King Edward.
> Caxton's pref. to *Tully on Old Age.*

Under the umbre of veryte.
> Old poem, *The Castell of Labour.*

178. **Umbrage** (= shadow or image : HAMLET, V, ii; 124).

The word is used fantastically, and certainly not classically ! It is remarkable in how many instances Dr. Theobald contrives to find in Shakespeare an expression which a classical scholar would *not* use, save facetiously.

. . . .

In an Appendix, Mr. Willis deals with more than twenty words passed over by him in the main body of his book ; and makes some additions to his former examples. Some of these I pass over here.

179. **Abruption** (TROILUS, III, ii, 69).

Dr. Theobald admits that the word " is not really English." Mr. Willis cited " dark abrupted ends " from Ford's LOVE'S SACRIFICE, III, iii ; and instances of *abrupt* and *abruptly*. But the plain fact is that the word in TROILUS is sportively used. It counts for nothing, then, for Dr. Theobald's purpose.

180. **Admiration** (= Lat. *admiratio*, wonder : HENRY VIII, V, v, 40 ; HAMLET I, ii, 192).

Quite common in the period. *E.g.* Hooker, ECCLES. POL. B. v. c. 77, sec. 13, &c. ; A MERRY KNACK TO KNOW A KNAVE : Hazlitt's Dodsley, vi, 544.

[In Shakespeare's day " I admire " often meant colloquially " I wonder." (*E.g.* Jonson, EVERY MAN IN HIS HUMOUR, i, 3 ; Chapman, THE WIDOW'S TEARS, i, 1). The ordinary reader is supposed to know the text, " when I saw her [the scarlet woman] I wondered with great admiration " (REVELATION, xvii, 6). This form could not

Z

have been used in the Authorised Version of 1611 if it were not still regular and familiar, though " admiration " had then come to bear its modern sense also. The old usage persisted down to the time of Scott (WOODSTOCK, ch. 25), and is even found in Sir William Hamilton (DISCUSSIONS, p. 14). In Shakespeare's day it was normal. Compare :

> Lordings, admire not if your cheer be this.
> > Greene, *Friar Bacon*, sc. 9 : ed. Dyce, p. 169.

> For, if thy cunning work these miracles,
> England and Europe shall admire thy fame.
> > *Id*. sc. 2 : ed. Dyce, p. 155.

> Chrysostom with admiration saith, *Miror si aliquis rectorum potest salvari* : " I marvel if any ruler can be saved."
> > Latimer, *First Sermon before Edward VI.*, Dent's ed. p. 83.

> Some judgments slave themselves to small desert
> And wondernise the birth of common wit . . .
> Perhaps such admiration wins her wit.
> > Porter, *The Two Angry Women of Abington*, iii, 2.

> And make her an example to the world,
> For after ages to admire her penance.
> *Leir and his Three Daughters*, Hazlitt's Sh. Lib. rep. p. 365.

> Yet are generally all rare things and such as breede marvell and admiration somewhat holding of the undecent.
> > Puttenham, *Arte of English Poesie*, Arber's rep. p. 294.

This last writer, under the rubric " *Paradoxon*, or the Wondrer " (p. 233), gives the word again the same force :

> Many times our Poet is caried by some occasion to report of a thing that is marvelous, and then he will seem not to speake it simply but with some signe of admiration.]

181. **Argentine** (= silvern : " Goddess Argentine " : PERICLES, V, i, 251).

Word used in Hall, CHRON. HENRY VIII, ann. 12.

The Oxford Dictionary gives instances from Holme, 1537 ; Lyte, 1578 ; and Holinshed, 1577.

182. **Determine, Determinate, Determination** (Coriolanus, III, iii, 43 ; Antony, IV, iii, 2 ; Richard II; I,
iii, 150, &c.).

Dr. Theobald finally quotes :

> My *determinate* voyage is *mere extravagancy.*
>
> *Twelfth Night,* II, i, 11,

with the comment : " In this line there are three Latin
words, *only intelligible by the help of a Latin Dictionary."*
As Mr. Willis observes, all three were common words.
" Mere " was particularly so. *See* No. 113. " Determinate " is in Chaucer, Frere's Tale, l. 161.

183. **Extravagancy.** A word formed on ordinary
lines, as *ignorancy* (Hooper, Works, Parker Soc. ed.
pp. 52, 108), *impudency, temperancy* (Hooper, p. 78), &c.

184. **Generosity** (= family pride or character;
Coriolanus, I, i, 215) ; **Generous** (M. for M, IV, vi,
14).

> Generosity prognate, and come from your atavite progenitours.
>
> Leache, Letter to Throckmorton, 1570.

[Add :

> Nobility began in thine ancestors and endeth in thee ; and the
> Generosity that they gained by virtue thou hast blotted with
> vice.
>
> Lilly, *Euphues,* Arber's rep. p. 190.
>
> Like to the eager but the generous greyhound.
>
> Jonson, *Every Man in his Humour,* i, 2.
>
> The nobilities and armes of generositie.
>
> Ferne, *The Blazon of Gentrie,* 1586, Ep. Ded.
>
> Noblenesse and generositie [of birth] hath this privilege.
>
> *Id.* p. 81.

Ferne's title-page runs :

> The Blazon of Gentrie | divided into two parts | The first
> named | The Glory of Generositie | &c.

Compare :

> Tis pity one so generously derived
> Should be deprived his best inducements thus.
>
> T. Heywood, *Rape of Lucrece,* i, 2.]

185. **Infortunate** (JOHN, II, i, 177 ; 2 HENRY VI;
IV, ix, 18).   Mr. Willis refers to Richardson's Dictionary
for early examples.   The Oxford Dictionary gives
instances from Gower, iii, 375, and Hall's CHRON.
EDWARD IV (1548), 239 *b*.

[The word occurs also in Roye's REDE ME AND BE NOTT
WROTHE, 1528 ; Sheet *c* in Whittingham's rep. of ed.
1583 ; and in Holinshed (Boswell-Stone's SHAKESPEARE'S
HOLINSHED, p. 350), where probably Shakespeare found
it.   But it is also found in J. Heywood's Interlude;
A DIALOGUE ON WIT AND FOLLY, Percy Soc. rep. p. 20 ;
and in Painter's PALACE OF PLEASURE, tom. ii, nov. 27 ;
Haslewood's rep. p. 447.

" Infortune " was also current.   *See* Boswell-Stone's
SHAKESPEARE'S HOLINSHED, p. 354.]

186. **Ingenious** (from *ingenium*, natural ability : LEAR;
IV, vi, 286 ;   HAMLET, V, i, 269).

To be captious, virtuous, ingenious.
Hazlitt's Dodsley, v, 363.

The Oxford Dictionary gives :

Ingenious wit of the French.
Hall, *Chron. Edward IV*. 231.

Ingenious — ingenuous or noble.
Hooker, *Eccles. Pol.*

[Compare :

Curtesie is a free, spontaneous and ingenious quality.
Fulbroke, cited in N. E. D.

Mine own earnest and ingenious love of him [Homer].
Chapman, pref. to trans. of *Iliad*, 1598.

Most ingenious and inimitable characters.
Id., Comm. on B. i.

He is of an ingenious and free spirit.
Jonson, *List of Characters* to *Every Man Out*, l. 1.]

187. **Lethe** (JULIUS CÆSAR; III, i, 205).
Dr. Theobald remarks that " If lethe [*sic*] represents
the Latin word *letum* or *lethum;* death, it is the solitary

instance of such usage ; but Shakespeare uses Latin so freely and inventively that there is no antecedent improbability in this interpretation of the word ; and it is more suitable to the context than the sense of Lethe as the river of oblivion, which is not crimson at all."

Neither reading is really tenable. Mr. Willis quotes the statement of Steevens that " Lethe is used by many of the old translators of novels for death." But Steevens' one instance does not prove this, since there Lethe = oblivion. " Lethe " = *lethum*, for death, would be a bad coinage, and a poor proof of scholarship. The passage is in all likelihood corrupt. The actual reading of the Folio is " Lethee." Some editors have plausibly taken it as a misprint for " death "—which in Tudor books is often spelt " dethe."

188. Office, Officious (= duty, serviceable : OTHELLO, III, iv. 113 ; TITUS, V, ii, 202).

[Dr. Theobald thoughtfully notes that " Cicero's treatise on Ethics is entitled *De Officiis* ; " but does not mention that that work was translated into English early in the sixteenth century (1533) by R. Whittington; under the title THE THREE BOKES OF TULLIUS OFFYCE. Of this the fourth edition appeared in 1553. This or another translation was issued in 1582 under the title TULLIES OFFICES IN LATIN AND ENGLISH, and again in 1591 ; Grimalde's translation, entitled MARCUS TULLIUS CICERO, THREE BOOKES OF DUTIES, appeared first in 1555, and was reprinted in 1556, 1558, and 1574. Thus no Latin classic was more widely known in Elizabethan England ; and the classic force of " office " was familiar to thousands of non-academic readers. The word in that sense is really old, occurring in Chaucer's PARLEMENT OF FOULES, l. 236. Elyot, unaware of this, wrote in 1531 that for the DE OFFICIIS " yet is no propre englisshe word to be given " (GOVERNOUR, i, 11), and suggested " dueties and maners." But Whittington's translation of 1533 would make current both the word and the meaning.

It is a normal term :

In your Majestie hath been orderly fulfilled all lawes and offices of a devout Neutrality.
Ep. Ded. to Fenton's trans. of Guicciardini, 1579 ;

and the theologians used it regularly. *E.g.* :

It is the office of a Christian to know what God can do by the word of God.
Hooper, *Answer to the Bishop of Winchester*, Parker
Soc. rep. p. 168.

The prelate, the preacher, hath many diverse offices to do.
Latimer, *Sermon of the Plough*.]

For instances of all the various meanings of the word and its derivatives, *see* the Oxford Dictionary. " Officious " in the sense of " serviceable " was common : that was in fact the usual meaning of the word :

Shew thyself officious and serviceable still.
Marriage of Wit and Science, Hazlitt's Dodsley, ii, 339.

[Add :

They make three sorts of lies, *jocosum, perniciosum, officiosum,* " jesting lies," " pernicious," and " officious " [⸗ friendly or serviceable].
Hutchinson, *The Image of God* : Works, Parker
Soc. rep. p. 51.

(Hutchinson has " office " = " duty," on p. 332.)

Assist me to make good the door with your officious tyranny.
Jonson, *Cynthia's Revels*, v, 2.

Officiously (⸗ helpfully) insinuate themselves into thy presence.
Id. v, 3.

Not altogether indutiful, though not precisely officious.
Spenser, Ep. Ded. to *Colin Clout's Come Home Again*.]

189. **Periapts** (from Gr. περίαπτον, *amulet* : 1 HENRY VI, V, iii, 2).

This is from a non-Shakespearean play. But the word is used in Reginald Scot's DISCOVERIE OF WITCHCRAFT, 1584, p. 230, &c. : Nicholson's rep. pp. 185–188.

190. **Replete** (L. L. L., V, ii, 853 ; Sonnet 113).

A *very* common word, from Chaucer onwards. *See* examples in Richardson's Dictionary, and :

I am replete with joy and felicity.
> *Calisto and Melebea*, Hazlitt's Dodsley, i, 87 ; Malone Soc. rep. 1. 945.

My heart with blasphemy and cursing is replete.
> *A Woman is a Weathercock*, Hazlitt's Dodsley, xi, 13.

[Add :

> I am the prophete called Isaye,
> Replett with Godys grett influens.
> *Coventry Mysteries :* VII, *The Prophets*, Sh. Soc. ed. p. 65.

Replete with yre.
> Roye, *Rede me and be nott Wrothe*, 1528.

Replete with mischievous vengeance.
> **Id.**

> With replete spirit went I to my bed.
> Hoccleve, *La Male Regle de T. Hoccleve*, l. 315.

> A man
> With all good so replete.
> *A Woman is a Weathercock*, i, 1.

His wordes are demure, replete with wholsom blessynges.
> Bale's Interlude, *John the Baptist*, 1538. Rep. in *Harl. Misc.*, ed. 1808, i, 209.

The earth was replete with iniquity.
> Latimer, *Last Sermon before Edward VI.*

With holy, humble and chaste thoughts replete.
> Chapman, *The Amorous Zodiac*, 1595, st. 17.

Replete with men, stored with munition.
> *Locrine*, ii, 3.

So replete with the inconstant behaviour and manifest vices of Englishmen.
> Macduff's speech in Holinshed : Boswell-Stone's *Sh. Holinshed*, p. 41.

And where repleat with virgins I erect thy temples may.
> Higgins' add. to *Mirrour for Magistrates*, 1575. Rep. of 1810, p. 79.

And every way replete with doubtful fear.
> Heywood, 1 *Edward IV*, v, 1.

Repleth by all experience.
Chester Plays : The Fall of Lucifer, Sh. Soc. rep. p. 15.
That am repleath with heavenlye grace.
Id. ib.]

191. **Seen** ("well seen " : SHREW, I, ii, 133).

Dr. Theobald gravely records that "Bacon often uses the word in this way," and, finding it also twice in Marlowe (FAUSTUS, i, 137 ; MASSACRE OF PARIS, i, 8) is the more convinced that Bacon wrote both Shakespeare and Marlowe ! It is simply a common Elizabethan idiom :

Though they be seen in Greek, Hebrew, and Latin.
Tyndale, Expos. of Matthew, 1531 ; Parker Soc.
rep. p. 13.

Sir, you seem well seen in women's causes.
The Four P's (1520) ; Hazlitt's Dodsley, i, 381.

[Add :

Fell to discourse, as one well seen in philosophy.
Greene, *Menaphon* (1589), Arber's rep., p. 58.

Those that are better seen in the tongues than I.
Tyndale, Prol. to trans. of New Testament.

Well experienced and seen in the knowledge of many countries.
Robinson's trans. of More's *Utopia*, Dent's rep.
p. 83.

This monke, monke-like, in Scriptures well seene.
Proemium of 1600 to the *Chester Plays*.

Not so well seen in the English tongue as perhaps in other languages.
E. King's Epistle pref. to Spenser's *Shepheard's
Calender*, Globe ed., p. 442.

Weening it perhaps no decorum that shepherds should be seen in matter of so deep insight.
Id. General Argument, p. 445.

He, well seen in the world, advised.
Chapman, tr. of *Iliad*, i, 251.

A man not seen in deeds of arms.
Id. B. v.

But I that am in speculation seen.
Greene, *James the Fourth*, v, 5.

He's affable, and seen in many things
> Heywood, *A Woman Killed with Kindness*, ii, 1.

Finding myself unfurnished of learning and barely seen in the arts liberal.
> Churchyard's *Spark of Friendship*, 1588, in Harl.
> Misc., 1909, ii, 111.

In sondry sciences he is sene.
> Roye, *Rede me and be nott Wrothe*, 1528 (Rep. p. 40).

Good wits seen and studied in all sciences.
> Fenton's trans. of Guicciardini, 1579, p. 2.]

.   .   .   .

There is appended to Judge Willis's "Addenda" a list of fourteen of the words founded on by Dr .Theobald, of which he has not been able to find instances before Shakespeare. They are : Incarnadine, Cadent, Candidatus, Circum-mure, Confix, Ex-sufflicate, Fracted, Intrinse, Maculate, Questant, Questrists, Sequent, Suppliance, Unseminar'd ; and he adds a further list of four " used in an unusual sense," which he has not met with in Bacon. These are :

" Factious, meaning busying oneself : active.
Name   „   Debt.
Pernicious   „   Much striving.
Plague   „   Snare."

These have now to be reckoned with.

192. **Incarnadine.** Dr. Theobald's position in regard to this word is remarkable. Mr. Willis, unable to trace it outside of Shakespeare, stated that it is the only word in the Folio " which cannot be found elsewhere, and unconnected with another word." After the publication of Mr. Willis's book, Dr. Theobald learned from Mr. Stronach, who had gone to the Oxford Dictionary, that " as an adjective it is found in Sylvester (1591)," and in a number of other writers *after* Shakespeare. Whereupon Dr. Theobald, in his preface of 1904, comments : " Yet Mr. Willis gravely informs us that it is the only word which cannot be found elsewhere." Mr.

Willis of course meant " before Shakespeare," later instances having no bearing on the problem. And now Dr. Theobald, whose own case is destroyed by the citation from Sylvester, without a word of admission or apology, assumes to exult over Mr. Willis's failure to discover the Sylvester passage, and proceeds to impute to him an assertion that no candid reader would. Finally Dr. Theobald announces : " I have no intention of discussing these words in detail " ; yet he leaves the " incarnadine " to pose as a Baconian " classical " coinage in his text.

As the commentators noted long ago, the word is simply an Anglicising of the Italian word *incarnatino*— a thing very likely to be done in that age apart from literature. As Steevens pointed out, " *carnadine* is the old term for *carnation* " :

> Grograms, satins, velvets fine,
> The rosy-colour'd carnadine.
>
> *Anything for a Quiet Life.*

There is no classical coinage in the case. At most Shakespeare may have made a verb out of an adjective.

193. **Cadent** (= falling : " cadent tears," LEAR, I, iv; 307).

Mr. Willis had forgotten to consult the Oxford Dictionary, which cites :

If the part of fortune be cadent from the Ascendant.
Lupton's *Thousand Notable Things*, 1586 (Ed. 1675, p. 201).

It appears to have been a term in astrology, like " retrograde."

194. **Candidatus** (TITUS i; 1). A Latin word, unadapted, pedantically used in a non-Shakespearean play. [By Peele : *see* the author's DID SHAKESPEARE WRITE ' TITUS ANDRONICUS ' ?]

Shakespeare *did not know* the Roman usage. *See above*, p. 192.

195. **Circummure** (MEASURE FOR MEASURE, IV, i, 28).
Likely to be a word of Greene's, who has "countermure" in EUPHUES HIS CENSURE TO PHILAUTUS : Works, vi, 218.

196. **Confixed** (MEASURE FOR MEASURE, V, i, 232).
A bad coinage, if not a corruption. It may or may not be Shakespeare's : it has not survived. Chapman has "infixed."

197. **Ex-sufflicate** (OTHELLO, III, iii, 182).
No other author has yet been cited for this word. It may stand for what it is worth ! It is certainly not "classic."

198. **Fracted** (HENRY V, II, i, 130 ; TIMON, II, i, 22).
The fact that in his *first* use of the word the dramatist puts it in the mouth of Pistol (" his heart is fracted and corroborate ") might have suggested to Dr. Theobald that it could not have been a classical neologism. Why not cite " corroborate " to the same purpose ? The serious use of " fracted " in TIMON was no innovation. The word occurs in Boorde's BREVIARY OF HEALTH (1547), § 321, cited in N. E. D. Boorde also has " fract."

199. **Intrinse.** *See above*, No. 111.

200. **Maculate : Maculation** (L. L. L. I, ii, 96 ; TRIOLUS, IV, iv, 66).
The Oxford Dictionary gives " maculated " from Higden and from Caxton's GODFREY and ENEYDOS. In the latter also occurs :

> Maculate and full of filth.

Again in Barclay's SHIP OF FOOLS (1509) we have :

> With vices maculate.
> Ed. 1570, p. 144.

Other instances occur between 1509 and 1586.
[Elyot has the verb " maculate " ; THE GOVERNOUR, B. i, c. 26. So has Henryson, TESTAMENT OF CRESSEID;

l. 81 ; so has Northbrooke, AGAINST DICING, DANCING, &c. 1577 : Sh. Soc. rep. p. 131 ; so has Marston, SATIRES, iii. *Maculation* occurs at least twice in the COVENTRY MYSTERIES (*c.* 1450) : Sh. Soc. ed. pp. 142, 193.]

201. **Questant and Questrists.** *See above*, p. 339.

It is possible that these are but variants, in all likelihood used in common speech, of the old word " questmonger," found in PIERS PLOWMAN and repeatedly used by Bale in THE FIRST EXAMINATION OF ANNE ASKEWE (Index and text : Parker Soc. rep. pp. 146, 149, 151), and by Latimer (FOURTH SERMON ON THE LORD'S PRAYER). It is applied by Bale to the members of the " wicked quest " (p. 167) or jury. But " quest " had other meanings, as in the MORTE DARTHUR and in the ordinary sense of " seeking for," and on that basis too there would be developments.

202. **Sequent** (= successive : OTHELLO, I, ii, 40 ; = a follower : L. L. L. IV, ii, 142).

The Oxford Dictionary gives :

Their words fall in, one after the other, like sequents.
                        Blount, *Horæ Subsecivæ* (1620), 49.

And scho in hand ane letter had, quhairon
Hir charge scho red, qhais tennour is sequent.
                        Rolland, *Court of Venus*, 1560, l. 810.

The word comes through the French, and is given by Cotgrave. " Sequence " is old.

203. **Suppliance.**

Found in Chapman's trans. of the ILIAD, ix.

204. **Unseminar'ed** (ANTONY, I, v, 10).

An analogue to " unschooled," in the common taste of the time. There is no such Latin word. But Nashe has " seminariz'd " (CHRISTS TEARES : Works, ii, 60).

205. **Factious** (= active : RICHARD III, I, iii, 127 ; JULIUS CÆSAR, I, iii, 118).

It is not clear why Judge Willis should have felt any difficulty in this case : the word is used in a quite obvious sense, " active *for a faction.*" In the sense of " trouble-making " we have Chapman's

> No need have we of factious Day
> To cast, in envy of thy peace,
> Her falls of discord in thy way.

Fifth Sestiad of *Hero and Leander : Epithalamion Teratos ;*

and Jonson's

> Instruct
> Others as factious to the like offence.
>
> *Sejanus,* iii, 1.

206. **Name** (As You Like It, II, v, 21 ; Comedy of Errors, III, i, 44). Alleged by Dr. Theobald to stand for *nomen* = debt.

There is nothing " classic " in the matter. " Name " in these passages does not and could not mean " debt." In the first cited, the meaning simply is that the speaker takes no note of the names, as a trader would not enter on his books names of non-debtors ; in the second there is no shadow of ground for suggesting any connection with *nomen* = a bond. Judge Willis was merely mystified.

207. **Pernicious** (L. L. L., IV, i, 66 ; Much Ado, I, i, 130).

See above, No. 127. Dr. Theobald's definition will not stand.

208. **Plague** (= snare ? Lear, I, ii, 2).

In putting down this word as a classical innovation, Dr. Theobald avows his knowledge that the Clarendon ed. connects it with the Prayer Book version of Psalm xxxviii, 17 : " And I, truly, am set in the plague," which follows Jerome's Latin, *Quia ego ad plagam paratus sum.* Yet he claims that " It is a curious passage, and cannot well be explained without going outside the vernacular sense of the word." Then what is the sense of the word in the Prayer Book ? If that were not a current phrase, how could any dramatist have ventured to use " plague " in the sense of " snare " and count on being understood ?

Again and again has Dr. Theobald thus inserted in his list words which even he, by some chance, has discovered to be current English before Shakespeare's day.

. . . .

There remain to be noted a few words in Dr. Theobald's list which Mr. Willis has overlooked.

209. Act (" act of fear " = action : HAMLET, I, ii, 205 ; HENRY V, I, ii, 188 ; OTHELLO, II, i, 229 ; III, iii, 326).

Dr. Theobald observes that this is "a sense which, though rather medieval than classic, is found in Bacon's Latin." It must be common in the Latin of a great many other men of that time ! In English, act = action is of old standing. The Oxford Dictionary cites Fabyan's Chronicle, 1494, vii, 579 ; and Drayton's

> Wise in Conceit, in Act a very sot.
> *Idea*, 860.

The phrases " in act to " and "caught in the act " are idiomatic. " Action " in Shakespeare's day was applied, among other things, to the acting of a play. *See* Webster's pref. to his WHITE DEVIL. But the alleged " classical " sense of " act " comes out clearly here :

> There is in it [the soul] a nature and abilitie of working, and as it were a mere act, whereby it liveth and giveth life.
> Sidney and Golding's trans. of De Mornay on *The Trewnesse of Christian Religion*, 1587, ed. 1604, p. 62.

Compare :

> That . . . they be induced unto the continual act.
> Elyot, *Governour*, B. iii, c. 23.
> His limbs so set
> As if they had some voluntary act,
> Without man's motion.
> Jonson, *Cynthia's Revels*, 1601, iii, 2.
> True learning's act
> And special object is . . .
> Chapman, Shepherd's ed. of *Minor Poems*, p. 158.

Preparing or going about these . . . not in present act with them.

> *Id.* Comm. on B. iii of trans. of *Iliad.*

Retention and ejection in her powers
Being acts alike.

> *Id.* Third Sestiad of *Hero and Leander*, 1598.

210. **Consequence** (HAMLET, II, i, 44; MACBETH, I, iii, 124; vii, 2).

"The classic sense," says Dr. Theobald, "gives depth, richness, and fulness to the meaning." There are many classic senses, and they are all implicit in English usage. The logical sense occurs in Chaucer's BOECE.

211. **Fortitude** (strength of a place: OTHELLO, I, iii, 222).

This is certainly not a common usage; but it is precedented in the non-Shakespearian 1 HENRY VI (II, i, 17):

> Despairing of his own arm's fortitude;

and in Eden's TREATISE OF THE NEWE INDIA (1553: Arber's rep. p. 15) where there is praise of the "fortitude and strength" of the elephant. For this there is "classic" precedent: for applying the word to a fortress there is not. But Latimer translates the vulgate *fortitudo* by "strength."

212. **Fraction** (TIMON, II, ii, 220; TROILUS, II, iii, 107; V, ii, 158).

Common: *see* the Oxford Dictionary for instances.

213. **Gentle, Gentility** (of birth: CYMBELINE, IV, ii, 39; As YOU LIKE IT, I, i, 21).

Mr. Willis might well pass over words so absolutely common as these. "Gentles" was a customary form of stage address, and variants of the word meet us everywhere, from Chaucer onwards:

> To make a blaze of gentry to the world.
>
> Nor stand so much on your gentility.
>
> > Jonson, *Every Man in his Humour*, i, 1.

Good steps to gentility too, marry.
        Jonson, *Every Man out of his Humour*, v, 1.

If thou claim gentry by pedigree, practise gentleness by thine honesty.
        Lilly, *Euphues*, Arber's rep. p. 190.
(" Gentleman " occurs six times on the next page.)

Art thou a gentle ? live with gentle friends.
        Gascoigne, *The Steele Glas*, 1576.

But we waste time on such a demonstration.

214. **Influence** (HAMLET, I, i, 118 ; TEMPEST, I, ii, 181 ; Sonnet 78).

Says Dr. Theobald : " In the exact sense required by its Latin derivation this word is used, in an astrological sense, to express the stream of power that flows from stars or planets." Quite so—only the idea goes further than stars or planets. And it was absolutely universal in Tudor times and long before. It is astonishing that even Dr. Theobald should ignore the text : " Canst thou bind the sweet influences of Pleiades ? " in the Authorised Version (Job, xxxviii, 31), which here follows the Geneva Bible of 1560. *See* the Oxford Dictionary for the history of the word. It occurs in Lydgate's " sixteen staves of metre royal " composed for a London " maying " in the reign of Henry VI :

Mightie Flora . . .
Made buddës springen, with her sweetë showres,
By the influence of the sunnëshine.
Quoted by Stow, *Survey of London*, Morley's rep. p. 124.

in the old Interlude entitled NATURE (*c.* 1490) :

There is in earth no manner thing
That is not partner of my [Nature's] influence.
        Farmer's *Lost Tudor Plays*, p. 44.

And in Francis Thynne's DEBATE BETWEEN PRIDE AND LOWLINESS (*c.* 1570) :

Where but he [the husbandman] mark the heavens' influence,
Instead of corn oft shall he gather dust.
        Shakespeare Society's rep. p. 55.

Compare the line above cited (under *Replete*) from the
COVENTRY MYSTERIES, and :

> Who addeth to the sun
> Influence and lustre.

Jonson, Poetaster, v. 1.   (Again in same scene.)

> And Jove, the Sun, and Mercury denied
> To shed their influence in his fickle brain.

Marlowe, 1 Tamb. i, 1.

Should . . . the earth be defeated of heavenly [physical] influence.

Hooker, Eccles. Pol. B. 1, ch. iii, §3 (1594).

> The starres, their influence, quantities, consents.

Histrio-Mastix, I, i, 37.

> If heavens had vowed, if stars had made decree,
> To show on me their froward influence.

Greene, Friar Bacon and Friar Bungay : Ed. Dyce, p. 171.

> What churlish influence deprives her mind ?

Lilly, Woman in the Moon, i, 1.

> I [Jupiter] will inforce my influence to the worst,
> Lest other planets blame my regiment.

Id. ib. ii, 1.

> Here, Venus, sit, and with thy influence
> Govern Pandora.

Id. ib. iii, 2.

> Now other planets' influence is done.

Id. ib. v, 1.

> Let fall a wreath of stars upon my head
> Whose influence may govern Israel.

Peele, David and Bethsabe, iii, 5.

> Which bodies lend their influence by fire.

Id. iv, 2.

> Fall stars that govern his nativity,
> And summon all the shining lamps of heaven
> To . . . shed their feeble influence in the air.

Marlowe, 2 Tamb. v, 3.

> This celestial influence
> That governeth and guides our days.

Kyd's trans. of Garnier's *Cornelia*, 1594, Chorus at
end of Act ii.

Heaven's influence was ne'er so constant yet.

Id. Act ii.

Blest be heaven, and guider of the heavens
From whose fair influence such justice flows.

Id. Spanish Tragedy, i, 2.

2 A

Yes, heavens are just, but thou art so corrupt
That in thee all their influence doth change.

Id. Soliman and Persada, ii, 1.

By theyr influens and constellacyons
They cause here corruptions and generacyons.

Cornish or Heywood, *The Four Elements*, Percy
Soc. rep. p. 8.

Of the sterris and planettes, by whose.influence
The see is compellyd to ebbe and flowe dayly.

Id. p. 11.

Celestial influence preordinate by providence divine.

Elyot, *Governour*, B. ii, 12 ; Dent's rep. p. 171.

215. Mirable (TROILUS, IV, v, 142).
The word occurs in the COVENTRY MYSTERIES (*c.* 1450) :

A ! myrable God, meche is thy myth.
Assumption of the Virgin, Sh. Soc. ed. p. 389.

which the Stratford actor may well have seen played in his youth. The N. E. D. also gives an instance from the MIROUR OF SALVACIOUN, 1450 ; and cites the forms *mirabilists* (1599) and *mirabiliaries* (1600). Bacon has *mirabilaries* (1605).

216. Mure, Mural (= Wall : 2 HENRY IV, IV, iv, 118 ; M. N. D. v, i, 209).
The Variorum ed. gives :

A long mure of ice.
D. Settle's *Last Voyage of Captain Frobisher*, 1577.

The Oxford Dictionary adds instances from Caxton, 1471 ; and Leland, 1552 ; and instances of the verb " to mure " from Maundey, 1440 ; Fabyan's Chronicle, 1494 ; and Hawes, 1503. In the sense of " to block up " again, we have instances from Barbour, 1375 ; Berners' Froissart, 1523 ; and Muleaster, 1581. Compare Spenser, F. Q. VI, xii, 34.

217. Naso.
A pun possible to any schoolboy.

218. **Plausibly** (= applausively : LUCRECE, l. 1854).
The ordinary meaning of the word in Elizabethan usage :

Every one received him plausibly, and with great submission and reverence.
> Stubbes, *Anatomie of Abuses*, 1583. Collier's rep. p. 48.

Greene uses " plausible " with this force always :

Smiling at my labours with a plausible silence.
> Ded. to *The Spanish Masquerado*, 1589 : Works, v, 241.

Would deliver up a hundred verses, though never a one plausible.
> Ded. to *Menaphon* : Works, vi, 7.

Having ended his tale with a plausible silence of both parts.
> *Euphues his Censure to Philautus* : Works, vi, 199.

Compare :

Affirming that I deserved a laurel garland, with sundry other plausible speeches not here to be rehearsed.
> Gascoigne, Ep. ded. to *The Droomme of Doomesday*, 1576.

So much the more plausible to those princes, by how much they were convenient for their service.
> Fenton's trans. of Guicciardini, 1579, p. 235.

A plausible [= laudable] and vertuous conversation.
> Puttenham, *Arte of English Poesie*, 1589, Arber's rep. p. 25.

The *dactil* is . . . most plausible of all when he is founded upon the stage.
> *Id*. p. 139.

Somewhat sour and of no plausible [= commendatory] utterance.
> *Id*. p. 153.

Old men . . . speak most gravely, wisely, assuredly, and plausibly.
> *Id*. p. 154.

A condition so happy, plausible, and well governed.
> Fenton's trans. of Guicciardini, 1579, p. 2.

The souls of such as lived implausible.
> Chapman, *Hymnus in Cynthiam*, 1594.

With the like plausible alacritie received.
> Stubbes, as cited, p. vi.

So excellent and plausible in the sight of . . .
> Painter, *Palace of Pleasure*, tom. ii, nov. 26 ; Rep. p. 395.

Think it plausible to answer me by silent gestures.
> Jonson, *The Silent Woman*, ii, 3.

219. **Remotion** (= removal : LEAR, II, iv, 115 ; TIMON, IV, iii, 345).

An old word. Lydgate has it in the sense of remoteness (CHRON. TROY, ii, xx, ed. 1555). The Oxford Dictionary further shows it in official use in the fifteenth century, and thereafter, in the sense of removal :

For the remotion of such ydelness and the preferment of labour
1449.   *Rolls of Parliament*, v, 167/1, Cp. 561/2 : 1464.
The remotion of the monks.
State Papers Henry VIII, i, 540.
Remocion of the faute.
L. Cox, *Rhetorike*, *c.* 1530 (ed. 1899, p. 22).
Negatives or Remotions.
Sidney and Golding's trans. of De Mornay.
Add :

Set in absolute remotion [= remoteness].
Chapman, *Hymnus in Cynthiam*, 1594.
I dreamt Mercy was hanged : this was my vision
And that to you three I would have recourse and remotion.
Mankind, *c.* 1475 (Farmer's *Lost Tudor Plays*, p. 29).

220. **Roscius** (3 HENRY VI, V, vi, 10 ; HAMLET, II, ii, 410).

Mr. Theobald gravely comments : "*Roscius :* equivalent to *an Actor*. A skilful personator or hypocrite is called a *Roscius*. This was a classic usage."

It was a usage made known in England at least by Camden, who spoke of Burbage as *Roscius alter*. Dr. Theobald either does or does not mean to imply that the name and its generic significance were not likely to be known to all Elizabethan actors. If he does not, his citation is the worst waste of time in his entire enterprise. If he does, it may suffice to say that tag references to Roscius abound in Elizabethan literature, dramatic and other. *E.g. :*

Stately tragedies,
Strange comic shows, such as proud Roscius
Vaunted before the Roman emperors.
Greene's *Friar Bacon*, sc. 6 ; ed. Dyce p. 163.

Not Roscius nor Aesope, those admired tragedians, that have
lived ever since before Christ was born, could ever perform more
in action than famous Ned Allen.
   Nashe, *Pierce Pennilesse's Supplication to the Divell,*
   1592. Works, ed. McKerrow.

Greene in NEVER TOO LATE, 1590, makes Roscius the
representative actor. Lodge in his DEFENCE OF STAGE
PLAYS, 1580, writes that " when Rossius was an actor,"
the " Musitian in the Theater " played before his entrance;
and again : " Surely we want not a Rossius, neither are
their great scarcity of Terence's profession " (Shakespeare Society Papers, vol. ii, 1845, p. 162). Gosson in
his SCHOOL OF ABUSE, to which Lodge's tract was a reply,
had spoken of " the cunning of Roscius himself " (Sh.
Soc. rep. p. 30). Northbrooke in his TREATISE AGAINST
DICING, DANCING, &c., (1577) makes one of his inter-
locutors tell of Roscius, of Cicero's praise of him, and of
his rewards (Sh. Soc. rep. p. 84). No theatrical
allusion could have been more familiar.

221. **Salve** (L. L. L. III, i, 71–83).
A trivial pun !

222. **Stuprum** (Lat.—TITUS, IV, i, 18).
Like *candidatus*, a Latin word, unadapted, pedantically
introduced, in a non-Shakespearean play. One might
say that this is exactly the kind of thing that Shakespeare
would *not* do. But even this would be no proof of
" scholarship." In Latimer's Third Sermon before
Edward VI we have the Vulgate quotation, *Auditur
inter vos stuprum*, with the translation.

223. **Unsisting** (" unsisting postern " : M. FOR M.,
IV, ii, 91).
Dr. Theobald comments : " Latin *sisto*, stand still :
with negative prefix ; unsisting therefore means, never
at rest,"—here following Blackstone. On any possible
interpretation, the word as it stands is an utterly un-
defensible coinage. No one knows what it means.

Johnson thought the intention might be " unfeeling,"
which is alien to the etymology. The earlier editors
substituted " unresisting," which spoiled the scansion.
Hamner tried " unresting " ; and Steevens suggested
" unlist'ning " or " unshifting." So much for the
alleged influence of classical scholarship on the dramatist's diction ! The thesis ends, as it began, in utter
futility.

.   .   .   .   .

With this item we fitly close our examination of Dr.
Theobald's compilation of two hundred and more [1]
words alleged to prove the scholarly knowledge and
practice of the writer of the plays.   I see no reason why
it should not have run to two thousand, with neither
more nor less futility : the list

> Might, ods-bobs, sir ! in judicious hands,
> Extend from here to Mesopotamy.

The patient reader who has taken the trouble to follow
the examination can pronounce for himself on the result.
Cited to prove the dramatist's classical knowledge, the
two hundred words prove only Dr. Theobald's contented
ignorance of Elizabethan English, in which his " classic "
terms were nearly all demonstrably current.   We have
seen the long array collapse down to the forlorn handful
of apparent neologisms, all trivial : —" confix," " congreeing," " ex-sufflicate," " reverb," " insisture," any or
all of which may be traced to-morrow by some more
vigilant and more industrious reader.   To impute scholarship on *that* basis is beyond the courage of even the
Baconian.

Dr. Theobald winds up his weary survey with the
pronouncement that " It is scarcely necessary to give
articulate voice to the argument arising out of *this copious
and refined Latinity*—this large and comprehensive
familarity with classic language, classic literature, classic

---

[1] Dr. Theobald's numbers go to 230. Some of his words have
been bracketed together in the foregoing survey.

history, classic antiquity. If such accomplishments could be the product of education in a remote country grammar-school of the sixteenth century, we have certainly suffered most lamentable deterioration during the last three hundred years." The summing-up is worthy of the evidence. What Dr. Theobald, in his infatuation, sees as " copious and refined Latinity," large and comprehensive knowledge of classic antiquity, consists in the use of some two hundred and twenty words already current, nearly all of them for generations if not for centuries, in English books, and likely to be heard any day from the contemporary stage or pulpit.

CHAPTER IX

COINCIDENCES OF PHRASE IN SHAKESPEARE AND BACON

§1. *The Evidential Problem*

OF the three main lines of the Baconian case—the argument from legal phraseology, that from classical allusions, and that from parallelisms of phrase—we have above reviewed the first and second. It remains to deal with the third.

To the majority of unprepared readers this is perhaps the most seductive. Men of general culture, even men of legal training, little acquainted with the literature of the Tudor and early Stuart periods apart from Shakespeare, are apt, on a mere perusal of a list of parallelisms of phrase between Shakespeare and Bacon, to grant inferences of which even a smattering of the necessary literary knowledge might show them the fallacy and the absurdity. The levity with which such readers in many cases accord their assent is one of the most significant aspects of the entire controversy. Inasmuch, however, as they are kept in countenance by a judge of such distinction as the late Lord Penzance, it seems necessary to expose their and his hallucination with an amount of argument and illustration which for an instructed reader would be supererogatory and tedious beyond measure.

Of this line of Baconian argument, Mr. Ignatius Donnelly, of cryptogrammatic fame, appears to be the most generally esteemed exponent. Dr. R. M. Theobald pronounces that Mr. Donnelly's first volume, of which two-fifths are " devoted to Parallelisms," " is the most

376

masterly and convincing statement of the Baconian case ever published." [1]

It should be mentioned in this connection that both Mr. Donnelly and Dr. Theobald have drawn upon the earlier labours of the assiduous judge Nathaniel Holmes, who, though like them unconcerned to check his presuppositions by a study of Elizabethan literature in general, did most of the pioneer work for the Baconians in collocating passages of Bacon and Shakespeare. Their recent disregard of him is probably due to the fact that he repelled in advance the inference to which they are fatally drawn, that Bacon wrote a great deal more of the Elizabethan drama than Shakespeare. " No writer of the time," he declares, " neither Ben Jonson, nor Marlowe, nor Raleigh, nor Wotton, Donne, or Herbert, whose poetry approaches nearest, perhaps, of any of that age to the Shakespearean vein, can be brought into any doubtful comparison with this author." [2] As Dr. Theobald has given Marlowe to Bacon, and others of the faith have given him a great deal more, Holmes becomes suspect of a fatal leaven of orthodoxy. That being so, we may thankfully put aside his laborious treatise, and deal with the accepted demonstrators. And first as to Mr. Donnelly.

As Mr. Donnelly is shown in the present chapter to have been grossly and ludicrously ignorant of Elizabethan literature in general, we have at the outset a measure of the knowledge in virtue of which Dr. Theobald confers his panegyric. But as Dr. Theobald is at pains to preface his own contribution to the same thesis with a discussion of the evidential force of the kinds of parallelism in question, it may be well to examine that before coming to concrete matters. Opponents of this method, says Dr. Theobald, are wont to

select *one or two weak or doubtful cases,* and smuggle in the assumption that the whole case rests upon these, and is defeated by their overthrow. Nothing can be more grossly unfair. The evidence

---

[1] *Shakespeare Studies,* ed. cited, p. 223.

[2] *The Authorship of Shakespeare,* 3rd ed. 1875, p. 305.

derived from parallels is cumulative, and in such an argument even the strongest instance may be spared, and yet the weakest may possess some value as one of the gossamer threads which contribute to the construction of a cable strong enough to resist *the most violent efforts* to break it. The argument is not like a chain which is only as strong as the weakest link : it is like a faggot, *the mass of which cannot be broken, though every single stick may be brittle ;* or like a rope, made by the accumulation of a great number of slender fibres which . . . in their combination *can resist the greatest force.* I do not think the Calculus has yet been invented [1] which will enable us to cast the sum of *an indefinite series of small arguments.* But it must be included in that branch of Inductive Logic which deals with circumstantial evidence,—and it is well known how the detective import of such evidence may be constituted by a collection of facts of which each singly would prove nothing—yet each of which lends some atom of force to the entire mass, and the resultant conclusion may be as well sustained as if it rested on direct documentary evidence ; and perhaps even better. For documents may be forged or fictitious [cryptograms, for instance ?] and can generally be disputed :—this kind of circumstantial evidence consists of incontrovertible and indestructible facts. [2]

The hollowness of this pretended rebuttal is plain at two points. To say nothing of the folly of assuming that *any* cable or faggot is unbreakable—a typical case of the logical dangers of metaphor—we have not merely *suppressio veri* but *suggestio falsi.* The opponents of the Baconian argument from parallels do not merely " select one or two weak or doubtful cases.'' They have presented hundreds of cases as to which there can be no rational doubt whatever, and of which the full presentment convicts the Baconians of entire ignorance of precisely those facts which are vital to the dispute. Mr. Donnelly claimed to make a case out of " identical expressions, metaphors, opinions, quotations, studies, errors, unusual

[1] In his preface to *The Classical Element in the Shakespeare Plays,* by his cousin Mr. William Theobald, Dr. Theobald affirms that " by the integration of a number of small or doubtful resemblances, a real, finite [*sic*] result is secured, the rules of the mathematical calculus having *strict affinity* with those of the literary one " (p. 8).

[2] *Shakespeare Studies in Baconian Light,* ed. 1904, p. 224.

words," and so on. When it is shown that the words alleged to be unusual are perfectly common for the period; and that the cited expressions, metaphors, opinions, errors, and quotations are in the same case, Mr. Donnelly's thesis is annihilated.

Upon this issue Dr. Theobald commits his second sophism. His analogy between what he calls " weak " items in a " cumulative " argument and the weakness of rods in a faggot, or fibres in a rope, is pure paralogism. Ropes and fibres are not in this connection rationally to be styled " weak " at all. Unless they are all alike rotten— in which case neither faggot nor rope can possibly be " strong "—each is valid for its own purpose to the extent to which it could be. But Mr. Donnelly's and Dr. Theobald's " weak cases " are pure nullities. They are, in their handling of them, demonstrable untruths. To present coincidences of phrase in Bacon and Shakespeare as *special* to them, when such coincidences are universal, is to bear false, howbeit ignorant, witness. Now, so far from a series of proved falsities being valid items in a " cumulative argument " in support of a general proposition, they have a rapidly progressive force in discrediting that proposition. Even Lord Penzance, I suppose, would upon challenge have admitted this.[1] Dr. Theobald sophistically claims that in a case of circumstantial evidence the charge may be made out " by a collection of *facts* each of which singly would prove nothing, yet each of which lends some atom of force to the entire mass." True ! But when a long series of the alleged facts are conclusively shown to be sheer falsehoods, each falsehood has given the jury an increasing right to suspect the remaining alleged facts. If, again, the person charged with having committed a number of peculiar and suspicious actions can show that they are one and

---

[1] Mr. Donnelly, for his own purposes, used against the editors of the Folio the maxim " False in one thing, false in all." *This* is folly ; but compare it with the argument of Dr. Theobald !

all actions daily committed in similar circumstances by all his neighbours, the case against him simply falls.

The only possible plea left open to the Baconians, after the contrary evidence has been led, as hereinafter, is to claim that *not every one* of Mr. Donnelly's borrowed hundreds of alleged parallels has been dealt with. Probably no human being will ever take the trouble of adding to my exposure of a multitude of the literary follies of Mr. Donnelly and Dr. Theobald a similar exposure of all the rest. But when it is once shown that both writers, through sheer ignorance of the literature of which some knowledge was the first requisite to their having any right to an opinion on the question, have in scores of cases asserted " peculiar " coincidence in respect of words and phrases in universal use in the Tudor period, all men save those determined to stick to the Baconian theory at any cost of violation of truth and reason will cease to give it further attention.

The reader will see that in the following confutation there has been no mere picking out of " weak or doubtful cases." Lord Penzance, acting as special pleader, has selected from the mass of Mr. Donnelly's items those which seemed to him the strongest. I have proceeded—with two or three exceptions—upon Lord Penzance's selection. Dr. Theobald, in turn, in his chapter on " Echoes and Correspondences," puts forward eighty heads. Of these I have dealt with forty seriatim, missing none : of the remainder I have selected eighteen, passing over a number that seemed too trivial for discussion.

There is another section of the argument from parallelisms, from the examination of which I am happily dispensed by the notably thorough refutation supplied in Mr. Charles Crawford's essay on " The Bacon-Shakespeare Question." [1] Mr. Crawford, while glancing usefully at the " classical " thesis, and at some of the parallelisms of Dr. Theobald, has specially devoted himself to the

[1] In *Collectanea*, Second Series. Stratford-on-Avon, 1907.

Baconian contention that the multitude of commonplaces collected by Bacon in his Promus of Formularies and Elegances, not intended for publication, were gathered for use by him in the plays.   With their fatal facility in error, the Baconians—led in this matter by Mrs. Pott—have maintained that the Promus entries are *not* reproduced in Bacon's published works, and that they *are* embodied in the Shakespearean plays.   With overwhelming force, Mr. Crawford demonstrates (1) that they are abundantly reproduced in Bacon's works ; and (2) that in a multitude of instances they and other Baconian passages are closely, sometimes exactly, paralleled in the writings of Ben Jonson.   Thus once more we see how the Baconian fallacy thrives on lack of observation and on incomplete induction.   I invite the reader who can appreciate exact learning and the vivacious use of it to turn to Mr. Crawford's contribution to the Baconian controversy.   Whether the Baconians have noted it, and whether or not they have in general proceeded from it to the conclusion that Bacon wrote Jonson, I cannot tell.

§2. *Lord Penzance and Mr. Donnelly*

That an English Judge, accustomed to the sifting of evidence, should have produced a book undertaking dispassionately to establish the Baconian case after a survey of the debate, was naturally a ground for elation in the Baconian camp.   Those readers, however, who have followed our examination of the treatise of Lord Campbell will not be unprepared to discover that another judge has undertaken to prove or pronounce upon a proposition in regard to which he had not even begun to realise the scope of the issue, and has put forth as evidence a quantity of matter of which the very citation is proof positive of vital ignorance on the part of the propounders.   It is as if the judge in his own sphere had delivered a judgment in terms of common law without knowing what common law is.   Knowing practically nothing of Elizabethan

literature outside Shakespeare and Bacon, he has staked
everything on the compilation of Mr. Donnelly, who knew,
if possible, less.

Lord Penzance, professing to present a " judicial summing-up " of the debate, has not only attempted no
comparative investigation of the parallelisms put forward
by Mr. Donnelly : he has not taken note of a single
argument adduced against the inference founded upon
them. Under the name of " summing up," the (in
literature) unlearned judge has presented the merest *ex
parte* statement ; and to examine it is to realise once for
all his lack of qualification for the inquiry he had undertaken. He could see the entire futility of Mr. Donnelly's
pretence to have found a " cipher " in the Plays : and
he evidently realised the nugatoriness of many of the
" parallels " in Mr. Donnelly's list, since he makes a
selection from which many of the most insignificant are
excluded. He does indeed say [1] that " to do justice to this
branch of our subject you should study the complete
compilation to be found in that gentleman's book " ; but
any reader who will take that trouble will find that the
passages omitted are the most worthless of all. And yet
how worthless are those actually selected ! The first two
are these :

SHAKESPEARE.	BACON.
It is very cold.	Whereby the cold becomes
It is a nipping and an *eager* air.	more *eager*.
	Natural History, § 688.
Hamlet, i, 4.	
Light *thickens*, and the crow Makes wing to the rooky wood.	For the over-moisture of the brain doth *thicken* the spirits visual.
Macbeth, iii, 2.	*Id.* § 693.

Even an *ex parte* advocate of any literary culture might
have been expected to ask, what Mr. Donnelly seems to
have been incapable of considering, whether *eager* in this
sense is not an established word in medieval and Eliza-

[1] P. 168.

bethan English. A glance into the New English Dictionary would have revealed to Lord Penzance that it is used by Chaucer (as in " egre bataile," " more myghty and more egre medicyne," &c.); by intermediate writers, and by Holland in Shakespeare's day, in both the physical and moral senses in which Shakespeare applies it. Any commentator would have informed him that it is simply the French word *aigre*, in which spelling it appears in 1531 in Elyot's BOKE OF THE GOVERNOUR, in the phrase " fierce and aigre " (B. iii, c. 9). With that force it was long a standing term in ordinary English, as in THE VOCACYON OF JOHAN BALE (1553) :

> I was sick again, so eagerly, that no man thought I should have lived.
>
> (Rep. in Harl. Misc. ed. 1808, i, 341) ;

and in Webbe's DISCOURSE OF ENGLISH POETRIE (Arber's rep. p. 32) in the phrase " very sharpe and eger," in 1586. Harington has :

> Such eger fight these warriers was betweene,

in his translation of Ariosto's ORLANDO FURIOSO, 1591, B. i, st. 62 ; and Daniel has :

> Altar of safeguard whereto affliction flies
> From the eager pursuit of severity,

in his CERTAINE EPISTLES, 1601–3 (TO SIR THOMAS EGERTON, ll. 65–66) ; and

> Men running with such eager violence,

in his MUSOPHILUS, l. 744. Greene has ." far more egar rage " (Alleyn MS. of ORLANDO FURIOSO, ed. Dyce, p. 107). As well might the word " nipping," if found in any two authors, be cited as a proof of their identity.

In the second instance, what is relied on is the analogy between the use of " thicken " on the one hand in regard to light and on the other in regard to the " spirits visual." But Bacon was using the regular terminology of the physicians of the period, which he seems to have had at his fingers' ends ; and the really significant fact is that

Shakespeare not only never uses the expression " visual spirits," but only once (ROMEO AND JULIET, iv, 1) uses the much commoner " vital spirit," and seldom even uses " spirits " in the general physiological sense, in which Bacon uses it constantly in the NATURAL HISTORY.[1] Shakespeare employs the word hundreds of times in the senses of unembodied being or ghost, energy, " good spirits," courage, &c., almost never in the sense in which Bacon applies it as many hundreds of times.

The parallel is worse than futile for the Baconian's purpose : it points the way of disillusionment to any who will follow. A simple perusal of the NATURAL HISTORY, which so few of the rank and file of the Baconians attempt, might alone open one's eyes to the vastness of the error of ascribing that book and the Plays to the same hand. It exhibits a dozen preoccupations of which the Plays show no trace ; it is packed full of observations of a kind at which they hardly ever hint ; it is inspired by a scientific bias of which they are devoid ; and in every page it presents a number of words which they do not contain. It would be quite safe to undertake to produce from Bacon many hundreds of words not found in the Plays, as will be shown in a later chapter.

As regards the coincidences, nine out of ten are as irrelevant as the first above cited. Mr. Donnelly finds evidence of common authorship in the use of expressions that must have been used in every Elizabethan pulpit. The fact that Shakespeare and Bacon speak, one of " troublers of the world's peace," the other of " troublers of the world " was for him an electrifying discovery. Devoid of knowledge of secular Elizabethan and Jacobean literature, he did not even know that " the troubler of Israel " is a phrase in the authorised translation of the Bible, which here follows the Bishops' Bible of 1560. Other Biblical allusions to " troubling Israel " gave the

---

[1] E.g. §§ 22, 23, 30, 60, 66, 75, 98, 114, 294, –6, –7, –9, 301, –3, –4, –6, 312, –13, –14, –15, –16, 354, 601, &c. &c.

expression a universal vogue, as may be seen from a number of old discourses.[1] Shakespeare and Bacon alike employed household words.

In the same way Mr. Donnelly finds evidence of common authorship in the mere use of such related words as " rough-hew " and " rough-hewn," " corrosive " and " corrosion ; " such every-day Tudor words as " quality," " fantastical ; " such common metaphors as " weeds " and " weed-out " for moral evils and their extirpation ; and the metaphorical uses of " sea," " ocean," " garment "— apart from any further coincidence of phrase. If there are three words more universally used than others by way of emphasis and metaphor in Elizabethan literature of every kind, they are " infinite," " swelling," and " sea " ; and these are among the words fastened on by Mr. Donnelly as serving to identify Bacon with Shakespeare. The commonest tags and idioms are for him pregnant with mysterious evidential force when he can find them in both authors. The simple collocation " mild and gentle " is eagerly italicised in such a case ; the idiom " the top of," which was as common in Elizabeth's day (*e.g.* " the top of judgment " or " of human desires ") as " the height of " in the same sense then and to-day, is paraded, without even one case of coincidence in the completion of the phrase. One finds it everywhere in contemporary drama and poetry :

> Are we so much below you
> That, till you have us, are the tops of nature ?
> Beaumont and Fletcher, *Wit without Money*, iii, 1.

The top of their felicity.
> Painter, *Palace of Pleasure*, tom. ii, nov. 26 :   Haslewood's rep. p. 393.

In the top of all thy pride.
> Lodge, *Wounds of Civil War*, l. 316.

We must ascend to our intention's top.
> Chapman, *Byron's Tragedy*, i, 1.

[1] *See* illustrations hereinafter, p. 430.

2 B

The top of his house.

> *Id. The Widow's Tears*, i, 1.

I that whilom was
The top of my house.

> Massinger, *The Maid of Honour*, iv, 5.

The top of woman.

> Jonson, *The Devil is an Ass*, iv, 1.

His worshipful ambition, and the top of it
The very forked top, too !

> *Id. Ib.* ii, 1.

My worshipful kinsman, and the top of our house.

> *Id. The Staple of News*, ii, 1.

The highest top of honour.

Brandon, *The Vertuous Octavia*, 1598 (Malone Soc. rep. l. 110).

The highest top of their (poets') profession.

> Sidney, *Apologie for Poetrie*, Arber's rep. p. 34.

So ignorant was Mr. Donnelly of Elizabethan literature, and so blind was he to the plainest duty in the way of research, that any word with which he was unfamiliar—and they were legion—served him at once as serious evidence when he could find it both in Bacon and in the Plays, and still more when he found it also in Florio's translation of Montaigne. Thus he notes that Shakespeare and Montaigne (*i.e.* Florio : Mr. Donnelly seems to have regarded the translation as an original English work !) " both used those strange words *gravelled* and *quintessence*," and again " that strange word *eternizing*, found both in Bacon and in Shakespeare." Blundering could no further go. The verb " eternize," in various flections, is common in Spenser, Marlowe, Greene, Peele, Nashe, Jonson, Lodge, and Drayton, to say nothing of Heywood and other later dramatists. Instances could be given by the score. " Quintessence " was a standing term in alchemy, and is found in Marlowe (1 TAMB. v. 2) ; twice in Sir John Davies (NOSCE TEIPSUM, ed. Grosart, i, 40, 43) ; often in Jonson, VOLPONE, ii, 1 ; THE POETASTER, iv, 6 (7) ; THE AL-CHEMIST, i, 1 ; EVERY MAN OUT OF HIS HUMOUR, ii, 1 ; THE DEVIL IS AN ASS, ii, 3 ; THE NEW INN, ii, 21) ; in Fairfax's translation of Tasso's JERUSALEM DELIVERED

(B. x, st. 14) ; in Greene (A QUIP FOR AN UPSTART COURTIER ; Works, ed. Grosart, xi, 217) ; in Heywood (THE FAIR MAID OF THE EXCHANGE, Pearson's Heywood, ii, 18) ; twice in one play of Chapman (ALL FOOLS, i, 1 ; v, near end) ; again in another (BUSSY D'AMBOIS, iii, 1) ; and yet again in the HYMNUS IN NOCTEM in THE SHADOW OF NIGHT, and in the epistle dedicatory to his translation of the ILIAD ; often in Lilly (MYDAS i, 1 ; GALLATHEA, ii, 3 ; ENDIMION, iv, 3 ; SAPHO AND PHAON, i, 4 ; LOVE'S METAMORPHOSIS, ii, 2) ; in King James's translation of Du Bartas' URANIE (Arber's rep. p. 25) ; at least ten times in six pamphlets by Nashe (Works, ed. McKerrow, i, 135, 194, 280, 351, 373, 381 ; ii, 10, 149, 265, 311) ; in the epistle dedicatory to WILLOBIE AND HIS AVISA (1596) ; in Marston's SATIRES, iv, l. 49 ; twice in Sidney's ASTROPHEL AND STELLA (28, 77)—everywhere, in short, in Elizabethan and early Stuart literature. We find it in theology—*e.g.* in Sidney and Golding's translation of De Mornay on the Christian Religion (1587 ; ed. 1604, p. 89). It was familiar to every playgoer. Massinger puts the word in the mouth of a cook in A NEW WAY TO PAY OLD DEBTS (ii, 2)—a realistic play ; and in that of a waiting-maid in THE FATAL DOWRY (ii, middle).

" Gravelled " is so common a vernacular word that it is astonishing to find even Mr. Donnelly surprised by it. Taylor, the Water Poet, avowing his lack of learning, tells that,

> Having got from *possum* to *posset*,
> I there was gravelled, could no further get.
> > *Taylor's Motto*, near end.

It occurs in so well known a book as Ascham's SCHOLEMASTER : " Any labor may be sone gravaled " (Arber's rep. p. 41) ; and twice in one page of Sidney and Golding's translation of De Mornay on the Christian Religion (1587) :

> This . . . graveleth Plutarke more than all the rest.
> So sore graveled in this consideration.
> > Ed. 1604, p. 286;

and again :

Utterly amazed and graveled.

Id. p. 269.

In Ford's short tract, HONOR TRIUMPHANT (1606), I find
" gravelled " in the second sentence of the epistle dedicatory, " quintessence " twice, in two successive lines of the
text (Sh. Soc. rep. p. 15) and " gravel'd " again (p. 25).
Turning to Marlowe for " quintessence," I chance upon

Gravelled the pastors of the German church.

Faustus, i, 1.

I will spare the reader further instances.

Before dealing with Mr. Donnelly's other parallels it
may be worth while to note the commonness alike of
reiteration and real copying of phrase and word in
Elizabethan letters, and the varying significance of it.
Such echoings serve at times as clues to authorship, some
writers being much given to repeating phrases and words
of their own.   When the repetition is one of non-signifi-
cant phrase, a mere trick of speech, it may be a very
useful clue—a kind of thumb-print.   But men have also
tics or mannerisms in the way of reiterating saws or
commonplaces.   On the other hand, many writers certainly echo and imitate others.   Bacon did it freely.
Has not Mr. Donnelly put to his fellow Baconians the
dilemma : " Either Francis Bacon wrote the Essays of
Montaigne, or Francis Bacon stole many of his noblest
thoughts and the whole scheme of his philosophy (!)
from Montaigne." [1]   So reasons the monomaniac.
Scholars deal with such problems rationally, without
talking of "stealing."   Mr. McKerrow, whose edition
of the Works of Nashe is a model at once of accuracy
and of erudition, points to, and abundantly illustrates
in his notes, Nashe's " habit of almost literal—but un-
acknowledged—quotation."   Nashe, in prose, indulged
only a little more freely in the common habit of the poets

[1] Cited by Mrs. Stopes, *The Bacon-Shakespeare Question
Answered,* 2nd ed. 1889, p. 218.

and dramatists of the time.   Marlowe deliberately copies
Spenser in a long and fine passage, and frequently in
shorter passages.   Greene often echoes Spenser, Marlowe,
Lilly, and himself ; Peele imitates Marlowe and Spenser
and FERREX AND PORREX, but oftener himself ; and
Shakespeare at times copies Marlowe and others.   Chapman in his first play, THE BLIND BEGGAR OF ALEXANDRIA
1596), has Marlowe's line (near end) :

> None ever loved but at first sight they loved,

which Shakespeare avowedly quotes in AS YOU LIKE IT
(iii, 5).   In his BLIND BEGGAR Chapman perceptibly
imitates Marlowe, Peele, and Greene ; and his line,

> Kings in their mercy come most near the Gods,

may be an echo of Peele.

Shakespeare at times imitates without avowal.   The
passage in 2 HENRY IV (IV, iv) about the labour of the
mind wearing its covering

> So thin that life looks through and will break out,

copies[1] Daniel's CIVIL WARS (ed. 1595 : DISSENSION.
B. iii, st. 116) :

> Wearing the wall so thin, that now the mind
> Might well look thorough, and his frailty find.

The echo is not exactly an improvement.   Nor does
Shakespeare improve, in TROILUS AND CRESSIDA (ii, 2), on
the " mighty line " of Marlowe, on

> The face that launched a thousand ships,

[1] *See* the Variorum ed. *in loc.* as to Hurd's fallacious assumption that it was Daniel who copied Shakespeare.   In several
instances Shakespeare echoes Daniel.   *See* above, ch. viii, p. 280,
No. 9 ; and compare Shakespeare's line :

> Lest the wise world should look into your moan,
> > *Sonnet 71,*

with Daniel's :

> Cannot the busy world let me alone,
>   To bear alone the burthen of my grief,
> But they must intermeddle with my moan ?
> *Letter from Octavia to Marcus Antonius,* 1599, st. 44.

which he certainly had in mind; as he may have had Sidney's sentence about

a gentle South-west wind which comes creeping over flowery fields and shadowed waters,

Arcadia, p. 2,

" if and when " he wrote, in TWELFTH NIGHT,

the sweet South [1]
That breathes upon a bank of violets,

It would certainly seem that the words of Antonio :

The world . . .
A stage where every man must play a part
And mine a sad one,

Merchant, I, i, 78–79,

reproduce Sidney's sentence :

For her, she found the world but a wearisome stage unto her, where she played a part against her will.

Arcadia, ed. 1627, p. 208.

In the Sonnets (94 and 142) Shakespeare copies two lines of the play EDWARD III :

Lilies that fester smell far worse than weeds.
That have profaned their scarlet ornaments.

Even in MACBETH, at the height of his power, he noticeably echoes passages of the second-rate WARNING FOR FAIRE WOMEN (1599). That (ii, 2) has the lines :

Oh, sable night, sit on the eye of heaven,
That it discern not this black deed of darkness.

.   .   .   .

Be thou my coverture, thick ugly night ;

which he thus twice transmutes :

Come, thick night,
And pall thee in the dunnest smoke of hell,
That my keen knife see not the wound it makes,
Nor heaven peep through the blanket of the dark.

i. 5.

Come, seeling night
Scarf up the tender eye of pitiful day.

iii, 2.

---

[1] *Sound* in the Folio. It was probably the passage in Sidney that led Pope to substitute " South." *Sound* does not " steal and give odour." But perhaps Shakespeare wrote " sough."

As the WARNING was played by his company, it is highly probable that he had acted in it, and that, as in plots, so in diction, he spontaneously evolved upon his reminiscences something more intense and masterlike.[1] So he did when at one stroke he reduced to comparative ineptitude the ambitious line of Marston,

> Yet the sanguinolent stain would extant be,

by the thunder-roll of

> The multitudinous seas incarnadine.[2]

To assume that all these " echoes and correspondencies " signify the pervading presence of one writer would be to miss fatuously the whole lesson of literary history. Whether the process be one of betterment, as when the absurdity of " sit on the eye of heaven " is partly rectified by " scarf up the eye of day," or whether it be one of more or less successful reproduction of a remembered music, it is all in the normal way of poetcraft, as Roger

---

[1] Professor MacCallum (*Shakespeare's Roman Tragedies*, 1912, p. 171) has noted further echoes from the same play in *Julius Cæsar*. The *Warning* has a passage in which a murderer speaks of having given his victim fifteen *wounds* " which will be fifteen *mouths*. . . . In every mouth there is a bloody *tongue*, which will *speak*." That idea is twice duplicated, with the words italicised, in Antony's speeches, III, i, 259 ; III, ii, 228. I cannot say that there is any improvement here, as Antony's " dumb mouths do ope their *ruby* lips to beg the voice " of *his* tongue. The double repetition of such matter in *Julius Cæsar*, I confess, strengthens my lifelong suspicion (*see* above, p. 190. that that play proceeds upon or takes up other men's work, Baconians, I suppose, will prefer the inference that Bacon wrote the *Warning for Faire Women*.

[2] I am assuming that Marston's *Insatiate Countess*, though not published till 1613, was written before *Macbeth*. See *Montaigne and Shakespeare*, pp. 125, 238 sq., 256 sq. The problem, however, is a very difficult one. Marston was certainly an imitator of Shakespeare ; but if he wrote his " sanguinolent " line to rival Shakespeare's he failed egregiously. What is clear is that the dramatists of the day discussed each other's diction. *See* Jonson's *Poetaster*, passim, and Marston's *Scourge of Villanie*, pref. prose.

Ascham noted long before Shakespeare.[1] So did Virgil imitate Homer, and Horace Pindar ; so did a hundred later poets imitate Virgil and Horace ; so did Spenser imitate Chaucer, who imitated so many ; so did Milton the translation of Du Bartas and other poems of Sylvester,[2] Spenser's FAERIE QUEENE, and the verse of the two Fletchers,[3] as well as many a passage of the classics ; so did Gray jewel his verse with a score of reminiscences ; so did Wordsworth borrow from Spenser his line about Triton's wreathed horn ;[4] so did Tennyson, in our age, reproduce alike classical and English phrases in many a poem ; and so did Poe echo Mrs. Browning, as she in her turn had echoed Coleridge and as he in turn had echoed Sir John Davies.[5] To surmise identity of hand in such cases of copying, even among contemporaries, would visibly be the height of folly. Spenser repeated thrice, with variations, his own charming trope :

> Upon her eyelids many Graces sate
> Under the shadow of her even browes.[6]

This is copied by Drayton (IDEA, 4) :

> Blest star of beauty, on whose eyelids sit
> A thousand nymph-like and enamoured Graces.

But no critic would dream of arguing that this last repetition must also be Spenser's own, whether or not he

[1] *The Scholemaster*, B. ii : *Imitation*. Macrobius, of course, had in antiquity made the matter notorious as to Homer and Virgil. Ascham notes how Virgil and Cicero repeat themselves.

[2] *See* Dunster's *Commentaries on Milton's early reading, and the Prima Stamina of his Paradise Lost*, 1800.

[3] *See* H. E. Cory's *Spenser, the School of the Fletchers, and Milton*. Univ. of California Press, 1912.

[4] Spenser, *Colin Clout's Come Home Againe*, l. 245 ; Wordsworth, Sonnet *The World is too much with us*.

[5] *See* Grosart's ed. of Davies, i, p. xcvii. A number of such echoes are noted in an old paper by the author in vol. ii, of *Criticisms*.

[6] *F. Q.* II, iii, 25. Cp. Sonnet II ; *Hymne in Honour of Beautie*, st. 5 from end ; and King's Glosse to the *Shepheards Calender : June*.

knew that the idea is derived from Musæus. Such a
conception of poetic authorship is outside of argument.
Yet it would be less absurd than to identify the author
of the Shakespeare Plays with Bacon on the score of
parallelisms of phrase such as are founded on by Mr.
Donnelly.   Far closer parallels are to be found between
the Shakespeare Plays and those of subsequent dramatists,—for instance, Webster, and Beaumont and Fletcher.
Take a handful of Webster's imitations :

> I will wear him in my heart's core.
> > *Hamlet*, III. 2.
> the secret of my prince,
> Which I will wear on the inside of my heart.
> > *Duchess of Malfy*, iii, 2.
> I'll put a girdle round about the earth.
> > *Midsummer Night's Dream*, ii, 2.
> He that can compass me and knows my drifts,
> May say he hath put a girdle 'bout the world.[1]
> > *Duchess of Malfi*, iii, 1.
> 'tis the eye of childhood
> That fears a painted devil.
> > *Macbeth*, ii, 2.
> Terrify babes, my lord, with painted devils.
> > *The White Devil* (Dyce, p. 22).
> He doth bestride the narrow world
> Like a Colossus.
> > *Julius Cæsar*, i, 2.
> The high Colossus that bestrides us all.
> > *Appius and Virginia*, iii, 1.
> Richer than all his tribe.
> > *Othello*, v, 2.
> More worth than all her tribe.
> > *Appius and Virginia*, iv, 1.
> My operant powers their functions leave to do.
> > *Hamlet*, iii, 2.
> This sight hath stiffen'd all my operant powers.
> > *Appius and Virginia*, v, 3.

[1] Mr. Harold Bayley (*The Shakespeare Symphony*, 1906, p. 259)
has pointed out that this " girdle " phrase, which occurs twice in
Bacon as a name for the Equator, is poetically used by Chapman,
Massinger, Shirley, Ford, and Beaumont and Fletcher, as well as
by Webster.

> 'Tis in my memory locked,
> And you yourself shall keep the key of it.
>
> *Hamlet*, i, 3.

You shall close it (a promise of secresy) up like a treatise of your own, and yourself shall keep the key of it.

> *Northward Ho*, i, 1.

The Chapman parallels,[1] if less numerous, are no less noteworthy :

> When sorrows come, they come not single spies,
> But in battalions.
>
> *Hamlet.*

> Afflictions
> Do fall like hailstones, one no sooner drops,
> But a whole shower does follow.
>
> Chapman, *Revenge for Honour*, ii, 1.

> Spacious in the possession of dirt.
>
> *Hamlet.*

> Rich in dirt.
>
> *All Fools*, i, 1.

> Let the frame of things disjoint, both the worlds suffer.
>
> *Macbeth.*

> The breaking of so great a thing should make
> A greater crack.   The bound of the world
> Should have shaked lions into civil streets.
>
> *Julius Cæsar.*

> Methinks the frame
> And shaken points of the whole world should crack.
>
> Chapman, *Bussy D'Ambois*, v, 1.

> Why, man, he doth bestride the narrow world
> Like a Colossus.
>
> *Julius Cæsar.*

> A Colossus
> What (? That) could so lately straddle o'er a province.
>
> *The Admiral of France*, iv, 1.

> A Colossus,
> And can stride from one province to another.
>
> *Id. ib.* ii, 1.

> Unskilful statuaries, who suppose,
> In forging a Colossus, if they make him

---

[1] Apart from echoes of phrase, compare D'Olive's account of his following (*Monsieur D'Olive*, v, end) with Falstaff's description of his ragged regiment.

Straddle enough, strut, and look big, and gape,
Their work is goodly.

Id. Bussy D'Ambois, i, 1.

Similarly the visibly Shakespearean line :

The silver livery of advised age,

in 2 HENRY VI (V, ii, 47), is echoed in one of A LARUM FOR
LONDON (Simpson's rep. p. 62) :

The silver cognisance of age,

and again in the Court Prologue to Dekker's OLD FOR-
TUNATUS :

Clothed in the livery
Of silver-handed [? headed] age.

Some of these phrases were probably current formulas ;
but it can hardly be doubted that some are real echoes ; [1]
and similar identities can be noted between Webster and
other contemporaries.   There is not the slightest ground,
however, for any mystification on this score as to plays
published by their authors, save where there may be
reason to surmise collaboration or re-casting : we are
simply dealing with conscious or unconscious imitation.
The same verdict holds good of such parallels as these
between Shakespeare and Heywood :

I must be cruel only to be kind.

Hamlet.

Blanda.   Indeed you are too cruel.
Young Lionel.   Yes, to her,
Only of purpose to be kind to thee.

The English Traveller, i, 2.

Heap Pelion upon Ossa.

Hamlet.

Heap Ossa upon Pelion.

The English Traveller, iv, 3.

Such phrases may have been current tags : Kyd has :

To bear up Peleon or Ossa.

Soliman and Perseda, i, 3 ;

---

[1] It is not impossible that Shakespeare's " Colossus " is an
echo from a previous *Cæsar* which he worked over.

or one pair may be the echo of the other. The resemblance between Hamlet's reproaches to his mother (iii, 4) and those of young Geraldine to Wincott's wife, however, suggests actual reminiscence upon Heywood's part. In any case, no competent critic will suspect identity of authorship, any more than in respect of the parallels between Shakespeare's Plays and those of Beaumont and Fletcher :

> There's such divinity doth hedge a king,
> That treason can but peep to what it would.
>
> *Hamlet.*

> But there is
> Divinity about you [the King] that strikes dead
> My rising passions.
>
> *Maid's Tragedy*, iii, 1.

[That passage in HAMLET, as I have elsewhere noted, seems to echo one in Montaigne's essay OF THE INCOMMODITY OF GREATNESS.[1] It is again echoed in the anonymous play NERO (1624) :

> The beams of royal majesty are such
> As all eyes with it are amazed and weakened,
> But it with nothing.   (v, 1.)

The poet may as well be echoing Montaigne as Shakespeare ; or he—and Shakespeare before him—may instead have followed Sidney, who before Montaigne wrote of eyes " So incredibly blinded with the over-bright shining of his royalty." [2]   Beaumont and Fletcher suggest only Shakespeare.]

> My pulse as thine doth temperately keep time.
>
> *Hamlet.*

> Alas, my lord, your pulse keeps madman's time.
>
> *Philaster*, iv, 1.

> Hast thou no medicine for a mind diseased ?
>
> *Macbeth.*

---

[1] See *Montaigne and Shakespeare*, second edition, p. 57.
[2] *Arcadia*, B. ii, ed. 1627, p. 207. Sidney wrote the bulk of the *Arcadia* in 1580-1 ; and Montaigne's third book, containing the essay *Of the Incommodity of Greatness*, appeared only in 1588. The idea, of course, goes back to Augustus.

> Nature too unkind
> That made no medicine for a troubled mind.
>
> *Philaster*, iii, 1.

> Hast thou no medicine to restore my wits
> When I have lost 'em ?
>
> *Id. ib.* near end.

The last two citations may or may not be echoes of Shakespeare : the tag, a medieval commonplace,[1] is older than MACBETH in Elizabethan drama.[2] In the SPANISH TRAGEDY (iii, 8) we have :

> Ah ! but none of them will purge the heart !
> No ! there's no medicine left for my disease.

In Ben Jonson, again, we have a passage which may tell either of conversations between himself and Shakespeare, or of recollection of Hamlet's advice to the players :

> That the glass of custom, which is comedy, is so held up to me by the poet, as I can therein view the daily examples of men's lives, and images of truth in their manners. . . .
>
> *The Magnetic Lady*, ii, 1, end.

Yet it may be that both alike had but echoed a common saw, for in the old interlude IMPATIENT POVERTY (1560) we have the line :

> It is but a mirror vice to exclude.
>
> Farmer's rep. 1909, p. 35 ;

[1] Gosson has " the surfeit of the soul is hardly cured." *School of Abuse*, Arber's rep. p. 30. And Greene has :

> But griefs of mind by salves are not appeased.
>
> *James IV.*

[2] So with another ancient saw :

> Extreme diseases
> Ask extreme remedies.
>
> Chapman, *All Fools*, v, 1.

> Diseases desperate grown
> By desperate appliance are relieved.
>
> *Hamlet*, iv, 3.

This had occurred earlier in Lilly (twice) and in Nashe.

and the " mirror " metaphor was in universal use.
Another echo almost certainly stands for reminiscence.
The lines :

> Dear Angelo, you are not every man,
> But one whom my *election* hath designed
> As the true proper object of my *soul*,
>
> *The Case is Altered*, i, 2,

cannot fail to recall Hamlet's

> Since my dear *soul* was mistress of her choice
> And could of men distinguish, her *election*
> Hath sealed thee for herself.

Similarly, the speech of Hippolito, the melancholy lover
in Dekker's HONEST WHORE (Pt. I, iv, 1), on a skull, is
almost certainly an imitation of Hamlet's musings on the
skull in the grave-digger's scene.   The lines beginning

> Perhaps this shrewd pate was mine enemy's,

with the allusion to

> His quarrels, and that common fence, his law,

tell of Shakespearean suggestion.   It was inevitable, in
fact, in an age of sentientous writing, when playwrights
moralised like everybody else, that some should echo
Shakespeare as he echoed others.[1]   But these parallels
never set up in a rational reader any perplexity.   To
every student it is clear that there is no ground, in such
cases, for surmising community of authorship.   Yet
Mr. Donnelly actually builds on the remote resemblance
between Shakespeare's

> doth *bestride* this narrow world
> Like a *Colossus*,

and Bacon's phrase, " For this *giant bestrideth the sea*,"
when we actually have the closer parallels above noted
between Shakespeare's phrase and those of Chapman and
Webster ; and, again, he brackets Shakespeare's " such

---

[1] Poets as well as dramatists echoed him. See the echoes
in Samuel Nicholson's *Acolastus*, 1600, cited in Ingleby's *Centurie
of Prayse*, i, 33.

divinity doth *hedge* a *king* " with a Baconian phrase about
" the law which is the *hedge* and fence about the liberty
of the subject," when, as we have seen, Beaumont and
Fletcher wrote of the " divinity about " the king.   If we
say on such evidence that Bacon wrote the Skakespeare
Plays, we are committed to crediting him with those of
Webster and Chapman and Beaumont and Fletcher also.
It is plain folly in any of these cases to suppose any
identity of authorship whatever.   We are simply dealing
with current tags.

A very real ground, indeed, for assigning non-Shakespearean authorship to work ascribed to Shakespeare does
arise in a number of plays, long recognised by most critics
as doubtful or as based upon older work.   Thus we can
trace the original HAMLET of Kyd here and there, in
Shakespeare's play, by such remnants of Kyd's diction as
the

I will consent, conceale,

of THE SPANISH TRAGEDY (iv, 1), found in the first quarto
(sc. xi. l. 106), and in other phrases preserved in the final
text.[1]   But the three plays of the HENRY VI group, TITUS
ANDRONICUS, and THE TAMING OF THE SHREW are the
chief cases in point, apart from the various plays printed
with his name, but not included in the Folio, and PERICLES
and HENRY VIII, now generally recognised as composite.
In regard to the HENRY VI plays and TITUS, but especially
the latter, we have such grounds for diagnosing alien
authorship as would have been held by the Baconians to
be absolutely decisive if they had related to Bacon.   The
latter play contains a round score of the most marked
verbal identities with passages in the signed works of
Peele ; and a less number of equally marked identities
with passages in the signed works of Greene.   In Peele's
work in particular, the significant passages are not mere
proverbs or commonplaces such as any writer might use,

---

[1] *See* Sarrazin's *Thomas Kyd und sein Kreis*, 1892, pp. 106–8.

but tricks and peculiarities of style and phrase which tell of one hand. The Baconians have never done anything so useful as to follow clues like these : one and all, they have heedlessly accepted the whole traditional Shakespearean canon, imputing the entire mass to Bacon. Should they chance to collate the Peelean and Greenean passages in TITUS, far from hesitating about the validity of their methods, they would in all likelihood proceed in a body to ascribe the entire performance of those poets also to Bacon.

And the imbroglio does not end there. Over and above the problem of actual repetitions of non-Shakespearean diction in the plays recognised as doubtful, we have that of the signal parallelism of style, rhythm, and idea (rather than of phrase) between the chorus-prologues to HENRY V and TROILUS AND CRESSIDA and those to Acts II and IV of Dekker's OLD FORTUNATUS and Act V of Heywood's FAIR MAID OF THE WEST. Precisely because the two " Shakespearean " prologues cited are *not* in the style of the plays to which they are attached, or of any other play of Shakespeare, we are moved to suspect the hand of either Dekker or Heywood in them, Dekker's for choice. This is the more reasonable because Dekker at times wrote for the Lord Chamberlain's Company, which was Shakespeare's.[1] We are not here concerned to do more than indicate the problem, and to note the difference between such a real ground for surmising an alien hand in choruses attached to genuine Shakespearean plays, and the visionary grounds given by Mr. Donnelly and his tribe for ascribing those plays in the lump to Bacon. He might quite as plausibly ascribe to Bacon the whole of the later Elizabethan drama.

And this, it will be remembered, several Baconians have

---

[1] In this connection it is noteworthy that Henslowe has an entry, Jan. 12, 1601–2, of a payment of 10s. to Dekker " for a prologe and a epiloge for the playe of ponesciones pillett "—*i.e.* *Pontius Pilate.*

done, even as Mr. Donnelly ascribes to Bacon Burton's ANATOMY OF MELANCHOLY and Florio's translation of Montaigne's ESSAYS—here diverging from others of the faith who ascribe to Bacon the French original, leaving Florio the credit of the translation. Lord Penzance, it should be observed, withholds these items from his readers, saying nothing of the parallels discovered by Mr. Donnelly between the ESSAYS, Bacon, and the Plays. He could not but apprehend that the obtrusion of the whole Baconian case would make more laughers than converts, and he simply suppresses the more startling details. Still, what he does present may suffice, when critically considered, to satisfy most readers that a judge's judgment on a literary issue may be worth very little.

Mr. Donnelly's remaining parallels may be classed under three heads :

A. Pseudo-Baconian citations from the essay OF DEATH posthumously published as Bacon's in the volume of REMAINES in 1648, but deliberately rejected by Dr. Rawley, who afterwards republished other things from the same volume.

That this essay is not Bacon's was the confident decision of Spedding, in which, probably, all critics now share [1] who are not of the faith of Mr. Donnelly. That writer presents a series of fourteen parallels between Shakespearean passages and this non-Baconian essay; concerning which he does not once hint that there is any doubt as to its authenticity. Lord Penzance, knowing nothing else about it than Mr. Donnelly had told him, included these fourteen illicit parallels in his selection from Mr. Donnelly. And even these parallels are worthless.

B. A number of more or less trivial parallels of phrase; common to the propaganda of the whole Baconian school; of which samples have been given above. I have

---

[1] The style is singularly like that of Sir Thomas Browne, as Spedding observed.

" paralleled " only the more plausible. Mr. Donnelly finds significant parallels in the use of such phrases as Shakespeare's " Shake patiently my great affliction off," and Bacon's " The soul having shaken off her flesh " ; " He is winding up the watch of his wit " and " To wind down the watch of their life " ; " You're a fair viol " and " this harp of a man's body " ; " fret the string " and " struck upon that string " ; " The fingers of the powers above " and " The soul shows what finger hath enforced her " ; " feast of death " and " death's banquet." Over such " parallels," and coincidences of phrase such as " infirm of purpose," " piece of nature," " base and bloody," " soft and tender," &c., which can be found by the hundred as between Bacon and any other Elizabethan writer, I do not propose to spend time. Their value may be gathered from the lists which I shall give below of instances from other writers of words specified by Mr. Donnelly as specially affected by Bacon and Shakespeare. Of more plausible parallels, however, there remain a few which may here be briefly dealt with.

1. Such proverbial phrases or moral maxims as " To thine own self be true " are hardly worth tracing. The speech of Polonius to Laertes contains half a dozen indisputable echoes of phrase from Euphues' counsel to Philautus in EUPHUES AND HIS ENGLAND.[1] The " to thine own self be true " maxim is on a par with the others ; and the Baconian claim is equally applicable to Lilly. Daniel has :

> I made myself unto myself untrue.
> *Letter from Octavia to Marcus Antonius*, 1599, st. 5 ;

and

> How that deceit is but a caviller,
> And true unto itself can never stand.
> *Musophilus*, 1603, ll. 894–5.

---

[1] Pointed out by Rushton, in *Shakespeare's Euphuism*, pp. 46, 47.

2. Any one but a Baconian would divine that Shakespeare's

Love

Must creep in service where it cannot go,

and Bacon's " Love must creep where it cannot go," are simply citations of a proverb. It is given in Hazlitt's ENGLISH PROVERBS :

Love creepeth where it cannot go,

from Rowland's TIS MERRY WHEN GOSSIPS MEET (1602). There is further an old Scotch proverb : " Kindness will creep where it canna gang." It was evidently current long before 1600. Greene in FRIAR BACON (sc. 5 : ed. Dyce, p. 161) has :

Love ought to creep as doth the dial's shade ;

and in MENAPHON (Arber's rep. p. 39) :

Love creepeth on by degrees. . . . Love . . . should enter into the eye, and by long gradations pass into the heart.

The argument from such a quotation for Bacon's authorship of Hamlet would make him author of :

What is love I will you show :
A thing that creeps and cannot go.
Heywood, *Rape of Lucrece*, 1608, ii, 1.

3. Shakespeare has " majestical roof [of heaven] fretted with golden fire," and Bacon suggests that if the deity had been of a human disposition he would have cast the stars in works and orders " like the frets in the roofs of houses." It is not impossible that one of those expressions may really have suggested the other. But if this be made an argument for Bacon's authorship of HAMLET, it entails by parity of reasoning the claim that Bacon wrote the dedication to himself of Chapman's translation of Hesiod's WORKS AND DAYS (1618), which contains the clause : " wherein your Lordship may find more honour than in the fretted roofs of the mighty." Chapman's signed dedication is emphatically in Chapman's style ; but that need not trouble Baconians.

4. Shakespeare's passage (RICHARD III, ii, 3) about men's minds " by a divine instinct " anticipating danger as

> The waters swell before a boisterous storm,

is paralleled in Bacon by a phrase comparing commotions in States to " secret swelling of the sea before a tempest." Here again Bacon might very well be reproducing what he had heard in the theatre. But all students are aware that the playwright was simply reproducing a passage of Holinshed :

> Before such great things, men's hearts of a secret instinct of nature misgive them, as the sea without wind swelleth of himself some time before a tempest.
>
> Cited in Boswell-Stone's *Shakespeare's Holinshed*, p. 353.

A similar expression occurs in Hall's Chronicle. Bacon may have echoed either the chronicles or the play ; or the phrase may have had proverbial currency.

5. The last is obviously the explanation of the metaphor of " shunning a rock," that of a parasite acting as ivy on a tree, and that of a man being " limed " like a bird, which Mr. Donnelly gravely adds to his list of parallels. He does not blench at bracketing, as from the same hand, Shakespeare's

> By that sin [ambition] fell the angels,

and Bacon's

> The desire of power in excess caused the angels to fall—

a homiletic saying which must have been uttered by thousands of men and preachers many thousands of times in that generation. The fall of Lucifer and his angels through pride is one of the outstanding episodes in both the Coventry and the Chester MYSTERIES ; in the old interlude NATURE, by Henry Medwall (*c.* 1490) it is described in the lines :

> For pride and presumption,
> Lucifer, which sometime was a glorious angel,
> For that his offence had such correction
> That both he and eke many a legion
> Of his order was cast down to hell.
>
> (Farmer's *Lost Tudor Plays*, p. 123) ;

and similar formulas could be cited from a score of books
and sermons.

6. Bacon has the figure : " High treason is not written
in ice " ; and Shakespeare has : " a figure trench'd in
ice, which . . . dissolves to water; " and " their virtues
We write in water." This for Mr. Donnelly goes to prove
identity of authorship. Then Bacon wrote also Daniel's
MUSOPHILUS (1601), where we have :

> Then where is that proud title of thy name
> Written in yce of melting vanity ?   (ll. 129–130).

7. Wolsey's lines in HENRY VIII about venturing on
a sea of glory,

> Like little wanton boys that swim on bladders,

are bracketed by Mr. Donnelly with a passage in Bacon
advising the man " that seeketh victory over himself " to
begin cautiously, " and at the first . . . practise with
helps, as swimmers do with bladders." There is no
coincidence whatever in the sentiment of the two passages,
in one of which the use of bladders in swimming is metaphorically put as the taking of a great risk, while in the
other it is put as the cautious way of going to work. The
every-day allusion to the use of bladders in swimming is
the one point the two passages have in common. But a
more serious difficulty for the Baconian is the fact that by
nearly all critics the speech of Wolsey is recognised as the
work of Fletcher, not of Shakespeare. This incidentally
raises the question as to how Bacon contrived to col-
laborate with Fletcher without endangering his " secret."
But probably the Baconian solution will be that Bacon
wrote Beaumont and Fletcher.

Others of Mr. Donnelly's phrase-parallels are dealt with
in the next chapter, as reproduced by Dr. Theobald.

C. For the rest, I have thought fit to deal in some
detail, and at some cost of time and trouble, with his
unspeakable list of citations of mere words, used metaphorically or otherwise, in the Plays and Works, held by

him to be significant of single authorship. No other part
of the Baconian propaganda, I suppose, reveals such
monumental ignorance of everything that a student of
Elizabethan literature might be expected to know. We
have seen above how Mr. Donnelly is thrilled by the discovery that both Bacon and Shakespeare use such
" strange " words as " quintessence," " eternize," and
" gravelled." But there is no limit to his faculty for
surprise. He solemnly italicises such words as *mortal, ape,
infinite, scour, fantastical ;* such metaphors as *sea, ocean,
scum, dregs, cloud, wilderness,* and so on, which lie thickly
scattered over the whole territory of Tudor literature.
The portent of Mr. Donnelly's ignorance in these matters
transcends my powers of comment. But inasmuch as
uninformed readers are found to be no less impressed by
his word-parallels than by his phrase parallels, I have put
together one-and-twenty sets of illustrations of the common use in the sixteenth century of words which Mr.
Donnelly takes to be so special to the style of Bacon-
Shakespeare as to stand for idiosyncrasies of vocabulary.
If the enlightened reader's gorge should rise at such
demonstrations as that " mortal man " was an expression
in universal use, let him remember that if I have tried
him much I have spared him more. And he is free to skip.
But it may be worth his while to realise what Baconians
are capable of putting down as " coincidences " :

  1. **Ape.**
The ape of form.
O Sleep, thou ape of death.

Shakespeare.

Custom . . . an ape of nature.

Bacon.

Compare

Blind chance, the ape of counsel and advice.
Chapman, *All Fools*. i. near end.

Make their native land the land of apes.
Id.   An Humorous Day's Mirth.
(Shepherd's ed. p. 32.

In all things his sweet ape.
>   *Id.   The Gentleman Usher*, iv, 1.

Is he [the devil] not the ambitious ape of God's majestie ?
>   Nashe, *Christ's Teares over Jerusalem :* Works, ed.
>   McKerrow, ii, 40.

The painters, being the poets' apes.
>   Lilly, *Love's Metamorphosis*, ii.

Man is God's ape, and an ape is Zany to a man . . .
So are women men's she-apes.
>   Dekker, *Seven Deadly Sins of London* ; c. 8 :
>   *Apishness*, Arber's rep. p. 36.

> They that draw shapes
> Are but God's apes.
>   *Id.   The Honest Whore*, iv, 1.

2. Axle-tree.

> The axle-tree on which heaven rides.
>   *Shakespeare.*

The axle-tree whereupon I have turned.
>   Bacon, *Letter to Essex*, 1600.

The poles and axle-trees of Heaven, upon which the conversion
is accomplished.
>   *Adv. of Learning*, B. ii.

COMPARE

> The axle-tree of Heaven.
>   Marlowe, 2 *Tamb.* i, 1.

When heaven shall cease to move on both the poles.
>   *Id.* 1, 3.

> The adverse poles of that straight line
> Which measureth the glorious frame of Heaven.
>   *Id.* iii, 4.

> The axis of the world.
>   *Id.* v, 3.

Jointly move upon one axle-tree
Whose terminus is termed the world's wide pole.
>   *Id.   Faustus*, ii, 2.

The axle-tree about which Heaven hath his motion.
>   Chapman, Ep. Ded. to trans. of *Iliad.*

And may both points of heaven's straight axle-tree
Conjoin in one, before thyself and me.
>   Chapman, *Bussy D'Ambois*, end.

>   His [night's] ebon car,
Whose axle-tree was jet enchased with stars.
>   Peele, *The Order of the Garter*, 23–4.

Fire, fire about the axle-tree of heaven.

> *Id.* *Battle of Alcazar*, v, prol.

The axel tree of Heav'n.

Heaven's axeltree.

> Davies, *Orchestra*, 1596, stt. 36, 64.

3. Bowels.

The bowels of the land.

The bowels of the battle.

The bowels of ungrateful Rome.

The bowels of the deep.

> *Shakespeare.*

The bowels of morality.

Factions erected in the bowels [of the state].

> *Bacon.*

COMPARE

A civil war . . . within the bowels of that estate.

> Sidney, *Arcadia*, B. i, ed. 1627, p. 6.

Farewell all learning which is not sprung from the bowels of the Holy Bible.

> Lilly, *Euphues : The Anatomy of Wit* (ch. on
> *Euphues and his Ephœbus*), Arber's rep. p. 156.

Thirty years together suffered she [France] her bowels to be torn out. . . .

> *Id.* c. 7, Arber's rep. p. 47.

The wealthy mines
Found in the bowels of America.

> *Locrine* (before 1595), i, 1.

Ope earth, and take thy miserable son
Into the bowels of thy cursed womb.

> Peele, *David and Bethsabe*, 1594, iii, 4.

The bowels of a freezing cloud.

> Marlowe, 1 *Tamburlaine*, iv, 2.

And rent [= rend] the bowels of the middle earth.

> Greene, " Ditty " in *Perimedes the Blacksmith*, 1588.

The silver streams
That pierce earths bowels.

> Peele, *David and Bethsabe*, i, 1.

That have . . . ript old Israel's bowels with your swords.

> *Id. ib.* Ed. Dyce, p. 482.

And rend the bowels of this mighty realm.

> *Selimus* (pub. 1594), l. 1044.

The bowels of this commonwealth.

> Foxe, *Acts and Monuments*, Cattley's ed. 1841, i, 164.

The bowels of these mysteries.

> Chapman, *Hymnus in Cynthiam*.

The bowels of the earth.

> *Id.* Ep. ded. to *Ovid's Banquet of Sense*.

The bowels of the earth.

> Stubbes, *Anatomie of Abuses*, Collier's rep. p. 28.

This church, in the bowels whereof . . .

> Hooker, *Eccles. Polity*, B. IV, ch. vi, § 1.

The bowels of the earth.

> Spenser, *Faerie Queene*, I, i, 39.

The hallowed bowels of the silver Thames.

> Jonson, *Every Man out of his Humour*, Epilogue.

Within the bowels of these elements.

> Marlowe, *Faustus*, ii, 1.

4. Cloud.

The clouds that lowered upon our houses.

How is it that the cloud still hangs on you ?

> *Shakespeare.*

This cloud hangs over the house.

The cloud of so great a rebellion hanging over his head.

The King . . . willing to leave a cloud upon him.

> *Bacon.*

COMPARE

A fit cloud to cover their abuse.

> Gosson, *School of Abuse*, (1579) Arber's rep. p. 41.

A cloud of passionate affection.

> *Essaies Politick and Morall*, by D. T. Gent, 1608, fol. 4 recto.

The misty cloud that so eclipseth fame.

> Greene, verses in *Penelope's Web*, 1587.

The cloud of mortal things.

> Chaucer, *Boece*, B. I. Prosa ii.

The cloud of ignorance.

> *Id. ib.*

Those clouds that eclipse her [virtue].

> Chapman, Ep. Ded. to trans. of Hesiod.

> This black cloud

Of swollen hostility.

> *A Larum for London*, Simpson's rep. p. 62.

With sorrow's cloud eclipsing our delights.

> Lilly, *Woman in the Moon*, i, 1.

With sullen sorrows cloud her brain.

> *Id. ib.*

Swelling clouds that overcast my brain.

> *Id. ib.*

Cloudy mists of discontent.

> *Patient Grissil*, v, 2.

Cloud of prejudice, or mist of passionate affection.

> Hooker, *Eccles. Polity*, pref. ch. vii, § 1.

5. Dregs.

Dregs of the storm.

Dregs of conscience.

> *Shakespeare.*

Dregs of this age.

> *Bacon to Queen Flizabeth.*

COMPARE

The fresh supply of earthly dregs.

> Marlowe, 2 *Tamb.* iii, 2.

The massy dregs of earth.

> *Id.* iv, 2.

I'll be paid dear even for the dregs of my wit.

> *The Return from Parnassus* (1602), sc. 3.

To pay him dear for the very dregs of his wit.

Nashe, *Four Letters Confuted* : Works, ed. McKerrow, i, 287.

The fecis and dragges of the sayd noble doctrines.

> Elyot, *The Governour*, B. i. c. 14 (Dent's rep. p. 65).

The world judges such to be . . . peasants and dregs.

> Roger Hutchinson, Parker Soc. rep. p. 302.

They who know what quality and value the men are of will think ye draw very near the dregs.

> Hooker, *Eccles. Pot.*, pref. ch. iv, § 5.

An infinite rabble of such dirty dotages and filthy dregs.

> Bale, *The Image of Both Churches*, ch. vi, § 5.

Wit hath his dregs as well as wine.

> Nashe, Ep. ded. to *Christ's Teares over Jerusalem.*

The dregs and dross of mortality.

> *Id. Christ's Teares* : Works, ed. McKerrow, ii, 41.

Dregs of men.

> Chapman, *De Guiana, Carmen Epicum.*

The very dregs of servitude.

> Heywood 1 *Edward IV* ii, 3.

Fond fancy's scum, and dregs of scattered thought.
                    Sidney, Sonnet in *English Garner*, ed. 1904, p. 135.
                        The stream
Of vulgar humour, mixt with common'st dregs.
                    Jonson, *Cynthia's Revels*, Act i, near end.

6. Fantastical.

High fantastical.
A mad fantastical trick.
A fantastical knave.
Fantastical lies.   *Shakespeare.*

A fantastical spirit.
Fantastical learning.

                                                Bacon.

COMPARE

For as well Poets as Poesie are despised . . . for commonly whoso is studious in the art or shews himself excellent in it, they call him in disdain a *phantasticall* ; and a light-headed or phantasticall man (by conversion) they call a Poet . . . ; and whatsoever device be of rare invention they term it phantasticall . . . ; and among men such as be modest and grave, and of little conversation . . . they call him in scorn a Philosopher or Poet, as much as to say as a phantasticall man, very injuriously (God wot). . . .
                    Puttenham, *Arte of English Poesie*, 1589,
                        Arber's rep. p. 34.

Fantastical fools.
        Elyot, *The Governour*, 1531, B. i, c. 1, Dent's rep. p. 4.

Fantastical apparitions.
                More, *Dialogue of Comfort*, Dent's rep. p. 220.

Fantastical dreams.
Nashe, *Anatomie of Absurditie* : Works, ed. McKerrow, i, 11.

Fantastical of her mind.
                        Lilly, *Mother Bombie*, i, 1.

Fantastical heads.
                Gosson, *School of Abuse*. Arber's rep. p. 28.

Fantastical objections and reproofs.
                Chapman, Ep. ded. to trans. of *Achilles' Shield*.

Another sort, as fantastical as the rest.
                Stubbes, *Anatomie of Abuses*, Collier's rep. p. 52.

Another sort of fantastical fools.
                                Id. p. 143.

Fantastical preachings.
> Roye, *Rede me and be nott Wrothe*, 1528.

Fantastical devices.
> Sidney and Golding's trans. of De Mornay, ed. 1604, p. 339.

Fantastical satirisme.
> Nashe, *Christ's Teares over Jerusalem*, Pref. *To the Reader*.

This phantasticall treatise.
> *Id.*   Ep. ded. to *The Unfortunate Traveller*.

Dream the most fantastical.
> Marston, *The Malcontent*, i, 1.

To be fantastical or scrupulous.
> *The Weakest goeth to the Wall*, iii, 1.

Phantastically attyred.
> Dekker, *Seven Deadly Sins*, Arber's rep. p. 35.

Phantastical apishness.
> *Id.* p. 36.

For such fantastical and fruitless jewels.
> Chapman, *An Humorous Day's Mirth* (Shepherd's ed. p. 24).

'Tis pretty fantastical.
> *Id. ib.* p. 35.

Too fantastical.
> *Id. Monsieur D'Olive*, iii, 1.

Fantastical opinions.
> Beaumont and Fletcher, *Wit without Money*, iv, 1.

A strange fantastical birth.
> *Id.   The Spanish Curate*, ii, 1.

New fantastical fevers.
> *Id. ib.*

(Twice within a dozen lines)

The papists in their fantastical religion.
> *Letters of Bishop Philpot*, 1555 ; Parker Soc. rep.
> of *Examinations and Writings*, 1842, p. 222.

The dyvel . . . by his fantastical apparitions.
> More, *Dialogue of Comfort against Tribulacion*, B. ii,
> Everyman's Lib. ed. p. 220.

A fantastical body.
> Hooper, *Declaration of Christ :* Works, Parker Soc.
> ed. p. 62 ; also p. 193, &c.

A fantastical imagination.
> *Id. ib.* p. 70.

7. **Infinite.**

> Conclusions infinite.
> Fellows of infinite tongue.
> Infinite jest.
> Nature's infinite book of secresy.
>
> *Shakespeare.*
>
> Occasions are infinite.
> Infinite honour,
> Infinite flight of birds.
>
> *Bacon.*

COMPARE

We have assembled infinites of men.
  Heywood, *The Golden Age*, 1611, Pearson's ed. of Works, iii, 36.
With infinite commands.

Id. Fair Maid of the West, iii, 5.

Infinite sorts of people.

Spenser, *Faerie Queene*, I, iv, 6.

Infinite remembrance.

Id. II, ix, 56.

Infinite riches in a little room.

Marlowe, *Jew of Malta*, i, 1..

Knowledge infinite.

Id. 1 *Tamb.* ii, 7.

As those are, so shall these be infinite.

Dekker, *Old Fortunatus*, i, 1.

> In this small compass lies
> Infinite treasure.

Id. ib. ii, 2.

That infinity of strangers.

Jonson, *The Devil is an Ass*, v, 1.

You are infinitely bound.

Id. ib. iv, 1.

They (fucuses) are infinite. 　．

Id. ib.

Country madams infinite.

Id. A Tale of a Tub, i, 4.

Infinite variety of matter of all kinds.
          Hooker, *Eccles. Polity*, B. I, ch. xiv, § 1.
The differences between them grew . . . in a manner infinite.
                Id. pref. ch. viii, § 7.

Infinite bodies and infinite movings.
  Sidney and Golding's trans. of De Mornay, ed. 1604, p. 1.

And as my duties be most infinite,
So infinite must also be my love

                        Gascoigne, *Jocasta*, i, 1.

Infinite virtues.

                        Lilly, *Endimion*, i, 1.

Infinite are my creatures.

                        Id. ii, 2.

Examples infinite.

                        Id. iii, 1.

Infinite millions of them [devils].
    Nashe, *Terrors of the Night* : Works, ed. McKerrow, i, 349.
It were an infinite thing.

                        Id. ib.

Infinite thanks (twice in a page).
            Hutchinson, First Sermon on Lord's Supper, 1560.
Infinite jeopardies.

                        Id. First Sermon of Oppression.
Sin in gathering head grows infinite.

                        Knack to Know an Honest Man, l. 757.
An infinite multitude of sheep.
            Robinson's trans. of More's *Utopia,* Dent's rep. p. 24.

Infinite controversies in the law.   *Id.* p. 44.

Infinite are my creatures.

                        Lilly, *Endimion*, I, ii.
Of ripe years and infinite virtues.

                        Id. ib.

Infinite thanks.

                        Id. v, 1.
An infinite number of books.
        Foxe, *Acts and Monuments,* Cattlay's ed. 1841, i,
            521.   (Pref. on " The Utility of this Story.")
Sects and fraternities of infinite variety.

                        Id. p. 517.

It were too long, and a thing infinite.

                        Id. text, p. 10.
An infinite number daily do perish.
            Stubbes' *Anatomie of Abuses,* Collier's rep. p. 33.
Neither can this infinite power . . . stand without infinite
great dangers.

            Jewel, *Controversy with Harding,* Parker Soc. ed. of
                Works, p. 371.
These places, and infinite other like.

                        Id. p. 378.

An infinite number of people.

> Trans. of Calvin on Ephesians, fol. 113.

An infinite number of other such.

> Holland's trans. of Plutarch's *Moralia* ; Dent's ed. p. 32.

We have infinite poets and pipers.

> Gosson, *School of Abuse*, 1579, Arber's rep. p. 27.

Pleading infinite causes before the Senate and judges.

> Elyot, *The Governour*, B. i, c. 14 (Rep. p. 67).

Reasons and examples, undoubtedly infinite.

> *Id.* i, 3, p. 15.

Infinites of dreadful enemies.

> Chapman, *Cæsar and Pompey*, i, 1

An infinite number of thousands of fighting men.

> North, *Life of Cæsar* (Skeat's Sh. Plutarch, p. 66).

Bale hath mistaken it, as he hath done infinite things in that book.

> Thynne, *Animadversions on Speight*, (1599) in Todd's
> *Illustrations of Gower and Chaucer*, 1810, p. 23.

Whereof infinite examples might be produced.

> *Id.* p. 50.

Infinite in good wits.

> Fenton's trans. of Guicciardini, 1579, p. 2.

Your Majesty's other virtues which God hath made infinite in you.

> *Id.* Ep. ded.

In footmen infinite.

> *Id.* p. 21.

Men infinite in multitudes.

> *Id. ib.*

Of infinite report for shape and virtue.

> Beaumont and Fletcher, *The Chances*, i, 1.

An infinite of ills.

> *Id. Monsieur Thomas*, iii, 1.

Of Albion's glorious isle . . . the pleasures infinite.

> Drayton's *Polyolbion*, ll. 1–2.

8. Mortal.

Mortal men.

> *Bacon.*

Mortal men (thrice).

> *Shakespeare.*

COMPARE

Mortel thinges.
> Chaucer, Trans. of Boethius, B. ii, prosa 3.

Mortel folk.
> *Id. ib.* prosa 4.

Mortel folk.
> *Id. ib.* B. iii, prosa 2.

Mortel folk.
> *Id. ib.* metrum 6.

Mortal hand.
> Daniel, *Cleopatra*, ii, 268.

Mortal man.
> *Id.* l. 1406, v, ii.

Mortal eye.
> *Id. The Queenes Arcadia*, l. 371 (II, i).

Mortal eyes.
> Sidney, *Astrophel and Stella*, 25.

Mortal men.
More, *Dialogue of Comfort*, &c. B. iii. Dent's rep. p. 354.

Mortal life.
> *Ferrex and Porrex*, i, 1.

Mortal wight.
Sackville, Induction to *The Mirrour for Magistrates*, st. 27.

Mortal men (thrice).
> Gascoigne, *Works*, ed. Cunliffe, ii, 21, 43, 261.

Mortal men.
> Peele, *Old Wives' Tale* (Morley's Peele, p. 185).

Mortal man.
> *Id.   Arraignment of Paris*, iv, 1.

Mortal men.
> Dekker, *Old Fortunatus*, v, 2.

Mortal men.
> *Id. ib.*   Epilogue (two successive pages).

Mortal mankind.
> Sidney, *Arcadia*, B. ii, 3rd sent.

One mortal man.
> Elyot, *The Governour*, B. i, c. 3.

Mortal man.
> Hooper, *Christ and His Office*, Parker Soc. rep. p. 25.

Mortal man.
> *Id.   Answer to Bishop of Winchester*, p. 169.

Mortal men (twice).
> Nashe, *Christ's Teares over Jerusalem* : Works, ed. McKerrow, ii, 23, 60.

9. **Mountain.**

A mountain of affection.

Shakespeare.

Mountains of promises.

Bacon.

COMPARE

A great mountain of tribulation.

> Sir T. More, *Dialogue of Comfort*, &c., B. i, c. 2.
> Dent's rep. p. 133.

To *promise* mountains and perform molehills.

> Greene, *Card of Fancy* : Works, iv, 106.

You *promise* mountains.

> Daniel, *Philotas*, l. 1576.

Who shall remove the mountain from my breast.

> Chapman, *Bussy D'Ambois*, v, 1.

Have plucked this mountain of disgrace upon me.

> Massinger, *The Bondman*, v, 3.

An atom
To the mountain of affliction I pull'd on me.

> *Id. The Emperor of the East*, v, 2.

Mountains of vexation.

> *Id. Believe as You List*, iv, 2.

Thy *promises*
Of many golden mountains to ensue.

> Heywood, *Edward IV*, Pt. I, Pearson's ed. of Works, i, 34.

Increased this molehill
Unto that mountain which my father left me.

> *Id. A Woman Killed with Kindness*, iii, 1.

Mountain heaps of milkwhite sacrifice.

> Marlowe, *Dido*, i, 1.

This mountain of my shame.

> *Patient Grissil*, ii, 2.

Mounts of mischief.

> Sackville, *Complaynt of Buckingham*. st. 11.

Now shall the blood of Servius fall as heavy
As a huge mountain on your tyrant heads.

> Heywood, *Rape of Lucrece*, v, 2.

10. **Ocean.**

An ocean of his tears.
An ocean of salt tears.

Shakespeare.

2 D

The ocean of philosophy.
The ocean of history.

Bacon.

COMPARE

Are not our lives with mischief's ocean bounded ?
Brandon, *The Vertuous Octavia*, l. 1821.

An ocean of my tears.
The Spanish Tragedy, ii, 5.

To what sea owe these streams their tribute, but to your lordship's ocean ?
Chapman, Epist. ded. (to Bacon) of trans. of Hesiod.

In endless ocean of expected joys.
Lilly, *Woman in the Moon*, ii, 1.

Drowned in the ocean of his love.
Field, *A Woman is a Weathercock*, iii, 3.

Within the heart's-blood-ocean.
Porter, *The Two Angry Women of Abington*, i, 1.

Broad bottomless ocean sea-full of evils.
Beggars' Petition, 1538, Harl. Misc. ed. 1808, i, 221.

Our ocean shall these petty brooks devour.
Famous History of Sir Thomas Wyat, Sc. 1.

Oceans of delight.
Sidney, *Astrophel and Stella*, 69.

Unto the boundless ocean of thy beauty.
Daniel, *Delia*, 1.

The boundless ocean of your worth.
Prologue to *The Maydes Metamorphosis*, 1600.

The ocean of new toils.
Daniel, *Civil Wars*, B. iv, st. 96.

The ocean of all-drowning Sov'raintie.
Id. B. vii, st. 12.

An unknown ocean of absolute power.
Sidney, *Arcadia*, ed. 1627, p. 206.

11. Paint.

A painted devil.

Gilded loam or painted clay.

Painted word.
Shakespeare.

But paintings.

Titular and painted head.
Bacon.

Painted observance.

> Roye, *Rede me and be nott Wrothe*, 1528.

And paint ten thousand images of loam
In gaudy silken colours.

> Dekker, *Old Fortunatus*, i, 1.

Beauty is but a painting.

> *Id. ib.*

This painted idol.

> *Id. ib.* sc. 2.

I could paint o'er my cheeks
With ruddy-coloured smiles.

> *Id. ib.*

Bid him come in and paint some comfort,
For surely there's none lives but painted comfort.

> *Spanish Tragedy*, iii, 12A.

God affects not any painted shape.

> Peele, *David and Bethsabe*, iii, 5.

Paint his countenance with his heart's distress.

> *Id. ib.* iv, 2.

Not painted yet in angels' eyes.

> *Id. ib.*

Painted flowers.

> *Id. ib.*, i 3.

Wealth and painted honours.

> Webster, *The Duchess of Malfi*, iii, 2.

When in my face the painted thoughts would outwardly
appear.

> Surrey, in *Tottel's Miscellany*, Arber's rep. p. 6.

Pish ! these are painted causes.

> Field, *A Woman is a Weathercock*, iii, 2.

The very face of woe
Painted in my beclouded stormy face.

> Sidney, *Astrophel and Stella*, 45.

My pen . . . shall paint our joy.

> *Id.* 70.

Fit words to paint the . . . face of woe.

> *Id.* 1.

So lively painted forth in all things.

> Sidney and Golding's trans. of De Mornay, *Of the Trewnes
> of the Christian Religion*, 1587, ed. 1604, p. 1.

He hath so painted out his glory.

> *Id.* p. 5.

This doctrine is not bred of man's braine, though it be painted there after some sort.

Id. p. 63.

It [the existence of God] is so many ways and so lively painted forth in all things.

Id. p. 1.

Pleasant fields . . . so painted.
F. Thynne, *The Debate between Pride and Lowliness* (*c.* 1570), Sh. Soc. rep. p. 8.

By nature painted thus.

Patient Grissil, iii, 1.

Painting speech.

Chapman, *Cæsar and Pompey*, i, 1.

Death's the best painter.

Dekker, *The Honest Whore*, iv, 1.

Rather living virtues than painted Gods.

Lilly, *Endimion*, iv, 3.

The papists, who make so much of their painted sheath.
Foxe, pref. to *Acts and Monuments*, Cattley's ed. 1841, i, 519 (prolegomena).

Others which sufficiently have painted out to the world the demeanour of these holy votaries.

Id. i, 384 (text).

This painted light.

Chapman, *Hymnus in Noctem.*

When Tellus' herbals painted were.
Id. The Amorous Contention of Philis and Flora.

Examples . . . painted before your eyes in enterludes and plays.

Stubbes, *Anatomie of Abuses*, Collier's rep. p. 140.

Every one nowadayes, almost, covet to deck and paint their bodies.

Id. p. 36.

That he be never so gallantly painted or curiously perfumed.

Id. p. 41.

12. Scour.

Scour the English hence.

Shakespeare.

The scouring of some noblemen from her Majesty's presence.

Bacon.

COMPARE

To scour the sea of the pirates.

Sidney, *Arcadia*, B. i, ed. 1867, p. 46.

Scoured and wasted the country where they went.
>Nashe, *Pasquill's Return to England.* Works, Ed. McKerrow, i, 77.

Scoured the narrow seas.
>*Id. Lenten Stuff.* Works, iii, 158.

Scouring along as if he would besiege them
With a new wall of fire.
>Heywood, *If you know not me, you know Nobody,* Pearson's Heywood, i, 340.

Sirra, go you and scour about the hill.
>*Id. The Foure Prentises of London,* Pearson, ii, 190.

Thou, Prince of Wales, and Audley, straight to sea.
Scour to Newhaven.
>*Edward III.* II, ii, 204–5.

Now merrily sail these gallant Greeks to Troy,
And scour the seas.
>Peele, *The Tale of Troy* (1589), l. 255.

We see the glistering fishes scour along.
>*Id. Honour of the Garter,* l. 41.

Scour all before them like a scavenger.
>Beaumont and Fletcher, *Monsieur Thomas,* iii, 1.

And fearless scours in danger's coasts.
>Kyd, trans. of Garnier's *Cornelia,* Act. iv, *Chorus.*

Did scour the plaines in pursuit of the foe.
>*Id.* v, l. 79.

The adverse navy sent to scour the seas.
>*Id.* l. 296.

Out of the troops that scoured the plains.
>Massinger, *The Bashful Lover,* iii, 2.

Choice troops of horse
Scour o'er the neighbour plains.
>*Id. The Duke of Milan,* iv, 1.

I scour the street,
And over-tumble every man I meet.
>Chapman, *The Gentleman Usher,* i, 1.

Five hundreth sail of warlike ships he brings,
Wherewith the frothing Ocean he scours.
>Brandon, *The Vertuous Octavia,* 1589 (Malone Soc. rep. ll. 1806–7).

Scour the marches with your Welshmen's hooks.
>Peele, *Edward I.* Ed. Dyce, p. 384.

Now scour the streets and leave not one alive
>*Selimus,* l. 1241.

Who after her as hastily gan scour.

> Spenser, *Faerie Queene*, B. I, c. ii, st. 20.

Hoisting up sails . . . we scoured and returned home.

> *Greene's Metamorphosis*, Works, ix, 85.

Leviathan that scours the seas.

> Greene and Lodge, *A Looking Glass for London*,
> Dyce's Greene and Peele, p. 135.

To send and over-scour the earth in part.

> Greene, *Friar Bacon*, sc. 15.

And so scours the squadrons orderly.

> Chapman, trans. of *Iliad*, iv, 245.

> These are they that scour

The field so bravely towards us.

> *Id*. B. V.

13. Sea.

A sea of joys. A sea of air. A sea of care. A sea of glory.
Seas of tears. Sea of blood. Sea of woes. Sea of troubles.

> *Shakespeare*.

A sea of multitude. A sea of air. Vast seas of time. A sea
of quicksilver. A sea of baser metal.

> *Bacon*.

COMPARE

The bittre sea of this lyf.

> Chaucer, *Boece*, B. I, Prose iii.

This sea of fortune.

> *Id*. B. I, Metre v.

Here they draw in a sea of matter.

> Hooker, Pref. to B. I of *Eccles. Polity*, ch. viii, § 11.

Seas of heinous faults.

> Gascoigne, *Jocasta*, 1566, i, 1.

Seas of sweet delight.

> *Id*. i, 2, Chorus.

The overwhelming seas of fortune.

> Daniel, *Cleopatra*, l. 140.

A whole sea of examples.

> Sidney, *Apologie for Poetrie*, Arber's rep. p. 59.

Seas of care.

> Higgins, *Mirrour for Magistrates*, rep. of ed. 1587,
> Author's Induction, st. 5.

One turbulent sea of fear.

> Heywood, *English Traveller*, ii, 2.

A sea of pleasure and content.

> *Id. Wise-Woman of Hodgson*, iv, 1.

You are the powerful moon of my blood's sea.

> Dekker, *Witch of Edmonton*, ii, 2.

Is he a prince ? ah no, he is a sea.

> Greene, *Selimus*, l. 190.

Yon swelling seas of never-ceasing care.

> *Id.* l. 1761.

A sea of blood.

> Fairfax, trans. of Tasso's *Gerusalemme*, x, 50.

Shed seas of blood.

> Field, *A Woman is a Weathercock*, iii, 2.

In this life's rough seas tossed.

> *Id.* Chapman's pref. verses.

A sea of sins.

> Beaumont and Fletcher, *The Maid's Tragedy*, iii, 1.

The sea of happiness that from me flows to you.

> Massinger, *The City Madam*, ii, 2.

This sea of marriage.   Call it rather
A whirlpool of afflictions.

> *Id.* ii, 3.

These two arms
Had been his sea.

> Beaumont and Fletcher, *The Scornful Lady*, iii, 1.

Against the sea of every lewd assault.

> *A Knack to know an Honest Man*, 1596, l. 705.
> Malone Soc. rep.

The sea of bloody tragedy.

> *Id.* l. 47.

To stable and strength the walls of our hearts against the great surges of this tempestuous sea.

> More's *Dialogue of Comfort against Tribulation*,
> 1534. Dent's rep. (with *Utopia*), p. 127.

A sea of blood.

> *Mucedorus* (pr. 1598), Induction, 59.

Sweet seas of golden humour.

> Chapman, *The Shadow of Night*.

That dead sea of life.

> Jonson, *Underwoods*, 88.

Seas too extreme
Your song hath stirr'd up, to be calmed so soon.

> Chapman, *A Justification of " Perseus and Andromeda,"* ad init.

Shed a sea of tears.

> Massinger, *Believe as You List*, i, 1.

Embarked myself on a rough sea of danger.

> *Id. The Emperor of the East*, iv, 1.

See how it [law] runs much like a turbulent sea.

> Chapman, *Bussy D'Ambois*, ii, 1.

Swells to her full sea.

> *Id. Byron's Conspiracy*, iv, 1.

See that maiden-sea of majesty.

> *Id. ib.*

Your mitigations add but seas to seas.

> *Id. Revenge for Honour*, iii, 1.

Calm his high-going sea.

> *Id. The Admiral of France*, v.

Oh what a second ruthless sea of woes.

> *Id. Monsieur D'Olive*, i, 1.

Our State's rough sea.

> *Id. ib.* ii, 1.

14. Sinews.

> Sinews of our plot.
>
> Sinew of our fortune.
>
> *Shakespeare.*

Intercept his [the King of Spain's], treasure, whereby we shall cut his sinews.

> *Bacon, Letter to Essex.*

Sinews and springs of industry.

> *Nov. Org.* i.

COMPARE

Lycurgus was wont to say that the laws were the sinews of a kingdom.

> Greene, *The Royal Exchange* (1589–90) : Works, ed. Grosart, vii, 234.

The sinews of his dominions.

> Greene, *Menaphon*, 2nd sent.

The sinews of war.

> Lilly, *Mydas*, i, 1.

Gold is the glue, sinews, and strength of war.

> Peele, *The Battle of Alcazar* (1594), i, 2.

> Policy,

The sinews and true strength of chivalry.

> Peele, *The Tale of Troy*, ed. 1604, l. 363.

Gold is the strength, the sinews of the world.

> Dekker, *Old Fortunatus*, i, 1.

The sinews of the imperial seat.

> Marlowe, 2 *Tamb.* iii, 1.

A King
Whose welfare is the sinews of his realm.
>Heywood, Pt. II of *Fair Maid of the West*, Pearson's
>Heywood, ii, 347.

The sinews of our war.
>Massinger, *The Bondman*, 1, 3.

The nerves and sinews of your war.
>*Id. Believe as you List*, i, 2.

Familiarity and conference,
That were the sinews of societies.
>Nashe, *Summer's Last Will and Testament* ; Works,
>ed. McKerrow, iii, 271.

Some other sinews there are from which that overplus of
strength in persuasion doth arise.
>Hooker, *Eccles. Polity*, Pref. to B. I, ch. viii, 10.

Plato named anger the sinews of the soul.
>Holland's trans. of Plutarch's *Moralia* (1603).
>Rep. in " Everyman's Lib." p. 21.

The sinews of trafficke and marchandise.
>Sidney and Golding's trans. of De Mornay, ed.
>1604, p. 102.

Blood, strength, and sinews of my happiness.
>Jonson, *Every Man out of his Humour*, i, 1.

15. Sovereign.

The Sovereign'st thing on earth.
>*Shakespeare.*

Sovereign medicines.
>*Bacon.*

COMPARE

The sovereyn cure of all mortal folk.
>Chaucer, Trans. of Boethius, B. II, Prose IV.

Sovereyn blisfulnesse.
>*Id. ib.*

Sovereyn good. [Twice.]
>*Id. ib.*

Sovereyn comfort.
>*Id.* B. III, Prose i.

Sovereyn good. [Twelve times.]
>*Id.* B. III, Prose ii.

Beauty soverayne.
>Spenser, *F. Q.*, I, vi, 12.

Sovereign bliss.

> Puttenham, *Arte of English Poesie*, Arber's rep. p. 44.

Sovereign beauty.

> *Calisto and Melebea*, l. 22.

The soveraigne bewtie that me bound.

> Surrey, in *Tottel's Miscellany*, Arber's rep. p. 24,

Beauty's sovereign power.

> Drayton, *Idea*, 50.

Sovereign balm.

> Dekker, *The Honest Whore*, v, 2.

Sovereign balm.

> Heywood, Pt. II of *King Edward IV.* (Works, ed. Pearson, i, p. 167).

Sovereign magic.

> Dekker, *Old Fortunatus*, iii, 1.

Sovereign poets.

> Chapman, *Hymnus in Noctem*, 1594.

Sovereign help.

> *Piers Plowman*, l. 317.

Sovereign for the soul.

> *Id.* l. 6026.

Sovereign book.

> *Id.* l. 6033.

Sovereign good.

> Sidney and Golding's trans. of De Mornay, ed. 1604, p. 293 ; again p. 301.

Sovereign welfare.

> *Id.* p. 296 ; twice on p. 297 ; four times on p. 299.

Sovereign balm.

> Heywood, 2 *Edward IV.*, iv, 3.

The most sovereign and precious weed.

> Jonson, *Every Man in his Humour*, iii, 2.

Sovereign light.

> Daniel, *Sonnets after Astrophel*, 3.

Sovereign grace.

> Drayton, *Idea*, son. 43.

Preparations most sovereign.

> Medwall, *Nature* (*c.* 1490), Farmer's *Lost Tudor Plays*, 1907, p. 122.

Sovereign cordial.

> *Id. ib.* p. 125.

Sovereign knowledge.

> Elyot, *The Governour*, B. i, 23.

16. Spice.

This spice of your hypocrisy.

Shakespeare.

A spice of madness.

Bacon.

COMPARE

A spyce of heryse.
> Interlude of *Calisto and Melebea, c.* 1530.
> *Obsequentia, &c.* Malone Soc. rep. l. 138.

A spice of idolatry.
> Elyot, *The Governour*, i, 19 (Dent's rep. p. 86).

A spice of justice.
> Chapman, *Bussy D'Ambois*, ii, 1.

Bites too hotly of the Puritan spice.
> *Id. ib.* iii, 1.

Retain

A spice of his first parents.
> *Id. ib.* v, near end.

A spice of the green sickness.
> Jonson, *The Magnetic Lady*, i, 1.

Any spice of rashness, folly, or self-love.
> *Id. Discoveries.*

A spice of idolatry.
> *Id. Bartholomew Fair*, i, 1.

Some spice of religion.
> Sidney and Golding's trans. of De Mornay, ed. 1604, p. 9.

A spice of the sciatica.
> Chapman, *The Widow's Tears*, ii, 2.

17. Swelling.

The swelling act.
The swelling scene.
Noble swelling spirits.

Shakespeare.

Such a swelling season.

Bacon.

COMPARE

Behold all Persia swelling in the pride of their own power.
> Lilly, *Alexander and Campaspe*, iii, 4.

Swelling phrases.
> Sidney, *Apologie for Poetrie*, Arber's rep. p. 67.

The proudest outside that most swells with things without him.
> Chapman, *The Revenge of Bussy D'Ambois*, i, 1.

Can that swell me
Beyond my just proportion ?

Massinger, *The Picture*, i, 2.

Swelling thoughts.

Lodge, *Wounds of Civil War*, l. 68.

Swelling tides.

Id. l. 1054.

Swells your spleen so high ?

Dekker, *The Honest Whore*, v, 2.

Those golden piles
Which in rich pride shall swell before thy feet.

Id. Old Fortunatus, i, 1.

As the bright moon swells in her pearlèd sphere.

Id. ib. i, 3.

Swelling thoughts.

Lilly, *Endimion*, v, 2.

Swelling pride.

Id. v, 3.

Swelling wrath.

Gascoigne, *Jocasta*, i, 1.

Swelling hate.

Id. i, 2.

Swelling pride.

Id. ii, chorus at end.

Swelling sorrows.

Id. iii, 1.

Swelling hates.

Id. Epilogue.

Swelling heart.

Peele, *Battle of Alcazar*, II, iii, 3.

Swelling pride.

A Larum for London, Simpson's rep. p. 52.

Swelled with ire.

Fairfax, trans. of Tasso, ii, 19.

Our swelling mountain.

Lilly, prol. to *Campaspe*.

Love doth not frowardly, swelleth not . . .

Tyndale's trans. of 1 Cor. xiii, 1525 and 1535.

Methinks I see his envious heart to swell.

Sackville, *Ferrex and Porrex*, i, 1.

Swelling pride.

Id. ii, 1.

Swelling breast.

Id. ii, 2, Chorus.

Swelling pride.
> Foxe, *Acts and Monuments*, ed. cit., i, 33.

Some wits are swelling and high.
> Jonson, *Discoveries : Ingeniorum discrimina*, Not. 1.

With pride so did she swell.
> Spenser, *F. Q.*, I, iv, 11.

Swelling seas.
> Lilly, *Woman in the Moon*, l. 9.

Swelling thoughts.
> Lodge, *Wounds of Civil War*, l. 68.

Their swelling veins.
> Chapman, *May-Day*, iv, 2.

Thy titles, and swelling offices.
> *Id. The Admiral of France*, i, 1.

Swelling favour.
> *Id. ib.* iv, end.

18. Tide, current.

A *tide* in the affairs of men; which *taken at the flood* . . .

We must *take the current when it serves*.
> *Shakespeare.*

. . . I set down reputation, because of the peremptory *tides and currents* it hath ; which *if they be not taken in their due time*, are seldom recovered.

The *tide* of any opportunities . . . the *periods and tides* of estates.

The *tides and currents* of received errors.
> *Bacon.*

COMPARE

The tide tarrieth no man.
> *Heywood's Proverbs.*

Tide and wind stay no man's pleasure.
> Southwell, *St. Peter's Complaint*, 1595.

What avails to strive against the tide.
> Higgins, *Mirrour for Magistrates : King Albanact*, st. 72.

Carried with full tide and wind of their wit.
> Ascham, *Scholemaster*, Arber's rep. p. 116.

The current of a man's reputation, being divided into so many rivolets, must needs grow weak.
> Dekker, Ep. Ded. to *The Seven Deadly Sins of London.*

The inconstancy of love that . . . had every minute ebbs and tides, sometimes overflowing the banks of Fortune . . . otherwhiles ebbing. . . .

> Greene, *Menaphon*, Arber's rep. p. 24.

Honest against the tide of all temptations.

> Beaumont and Fletcher, *Valentinian*, i, 1.

Borne by the hasty tide of short leisure.

> Sidney, *Arcadia*, ed. 1627, p. 208.

The current of her sway.

> Daniel, *Civil Wars*, B. v, st. 70.

And now that current with main fury ran.

> *Id.* st. 89.

Borne with the swelling current of their pride.

> *Id.* B. vi, st. 78.

19. Troubler.

The troubler of the poor world's peace.

> *Shakespeare.*

The troublers of the world.

> *Bacon.*

COMPARE

Achar, the troubler of Israel.

> 1 Chron. ii, 7.

Lest ye trouble the camp of Israel.

> Josh. vi, 18.

Art thou he that troubleth Israel.

> 1 Kings xviii, 17.

I have not troubled Israel.

> *Id.* v, 18.

That troubler of the public peace.

> Bale, *Examination and Death of Cobham*, Parker Soc. ed. of Works, p. 19.

Distroublers of holy Church.

> *Id. Examination of Thorpe*, p. 75.

Distroubled the communalty.

> *Id. ib.* p. 84.

They [friars] say that they [good clerks] distrouble the world.

> Wiclif, *Treatise against the Friars*, c. 26.

Trouble her that troubles a whole empire.

> Heywood, *Rape of Lucrece*, i, 2.

Troubleth our estate.

> Marlowe, *Massacre of Paris*, i, 3.

The troublers of the commonwealth.

> North, *Life of Cæsar* (Sh. Plutarch, p. 68).

Busied the whole State
Troubled both foes and friends.

> Jonson, *Underwoods*, 88.

Troubler of the Christen Church.

> *Vocacyon of Johan Bale*, Harl. Misc. 1808, i, 361.

20. Weed.

We'll weed them all at last.

The caterpillars of the commonwealth
Which I have sworn to weed and pluck away.

> *Shakespeare.*

A man's nature runs either to herbs or weeds : therefore . . .
water the one and destroy the other.

> *Bacon, Of Nature in Man.*

COMPARE

Weeds and briers in me.

> Dekker, *Witch of Edmonton*, iii, 2.

Thus do weeds grow up whiles no man regards them.

> Nashe, *Pierce Penilesse* (Works, i, 175).

We'll join to weed them out.

> Jonson, *Alchemist*, v, 1.

Would yield more fruit than all the idle weeds
That suck up your rain of favour.

> Massinger, *The Picture*, iv, 4.

But men themselves, instead of bearing fruits,
Grow rude and foggy, overgrown with weeds,

> Chapman, *Byron's Trajedy*, iv, 1.

The greatest worldly hopes . . . ye seek utterly to extirpate
as weeds.

> Hooker, Pref. to B. I of *Eccles. Polity*, ch. viii, 3.

I'll follow ye, and ere I die, proclaim ye,
The weeds of Italy, the dross of nature.

> Beaumont and Fletcher, *Valentinian*, iv, 4.

Weeds of superstition.

> Foxe, one of the prefaces to *Acts and Monuments*,
> Cattley's ed. 1841, i, 515.

Pluck up these weeds [rebels].

> Fairfax's tr. of Tasso's *Jerusalem*, 1600, B. iv,
> st. 16.

21. **Wilderness.**

> A wilderness of sea.
>
> A wilderness of tigers.
>
> A wilderness of monkeys.
>
> *Shakespeare.*
>
> The greatest wilderness of waters.
>
> *Bacon.*

COMPARE

A wide wilderness of waters deep.

> Spenser, *Muiopotmos*, l. 288.

The errant wilderness of a woman's face.

> Chapman, *Bussy D'Ambois*, v, 1.

Ha ! is my house turn'd
To a wilderness.

> Massinger, *The Picture*, v, 3.

I must admire thy beauty's wilderness.

> Lilly, *Woman in the Moon*, ii, 1.

A wilderness of seas.

> Heywood, *Fair Maid of the West*, iv, 4, *end.*

My heart, a wasteful wilderness forsaken.

> Barnes, *Parthenophil and Parthenophe*, Son. 99.

It is perhaps unnecessary to add that any other of the tropes cited by Mr. Donnelly as being significantly common to Bacon and Shakespeare may be similarly demonstrated to be part of the common phraseology of their age. One of his words, " shadow," is as universally used in metaphor as any of those above exampled. Any student can satisfy himself on the point by a little investigation, if he needs satisfying. But I think the matter has been above decided for every rational reader.

CHAPTER X

THE ARGUMENT FROM COINCIDENCES OF PHRASE

ii. Dr. R. M. Theobald

SO obviously unqualified was Mr. Donnelly for any inquiry involving acquaintance with Tudor and Stuart literature that one turns to any later Baconian attempt of the same kind with the hope of finding some developed caution, some concern for circumspection and research in a task in which he showed so little. And though Dr. Theobald's handling of the " classical " argument has yielded us so little sign of any such development, one still turns to his handling of " coincidences " in the hope of finding something better than the parade of ignorance presented by his predecessor. He has at least some perception of the nature of the logical issue involved ; and he has actually sought to save himself from the force of some rebuttals.

The issue is, in a word, Are there such repeated co-incidences of expression, whether in idea or in mere turn of phrase, in the Plays and in Bacon's writings, as can justify *prima facie* the hypothesis of identity of author-ship ? Both kinds of coincidence, we have seen, occur as between Shakespeare and other writers ; and there can be nothing surprising in finding some as between him and Bacon, in an age so given to the reiteration of sententious sayings, proverbs, and tropes. But is there any such tissue of coincidences of mere phrase, say, as is found in TITUS ANDRONICUS and the works of Peele ? It will be found that nothing of the kind is ever produced. Coincidences of *maxim* and *sentiment* there are, such as Mr. Crawford has produced in much larger number from

the writings of Bacon and Jonson. On the Baconian
principles, either Bacon wrote Jonson, or Jonson Bacon.
Similar occasional identities of sentiment in the Plays
and in Bacon prove nothing more than in the case of
Jonson. But of any general coincidence of *doctrine*
between the plays and Bacon's writings there is and can
be no pretence. Bacon, like so many Elizabethan writers,
repeats himself many times without misgiving ; but of
doctrines and theses which so possessed him that he was
never tired of reproducing them, there is no trace whatever in the Plays. All that the Baconians can produce
is a sorry harvest of verbal parallels, nine-tenths of which
can have no evidential significance whatever.

Those which *can* reasonably challenge attention evoke
at once the query, How did such coincidences in general
come about ? The answer is obvious. Other dramatists
who echo Shakespeare either were copying previous
writers whom he had followed, or had heard or read, or
heard quoted, Shakespeare's plays. Such echoes must
have taken place, in the ordinary course of things ; and
when we find duplications of thought in Bacon and Jonson
we similarly infer, either verbal communication—which
we know took place between them—or the reading or
hearing by one of things said or written by the other.
If the reader, rather than adopt this kind of explanation,
proceeds to surmise that Bacon wrote the works of
Jonson—and, as regards similar coincidences with other
writers, their works also—he need not further follow this
argument, which is not framed for his order of judgment.
As we reason in regard to other coincidences, so do we
reason in regard to any real coincidences between Bacon
and Shakespeare. If Jonson, Chapman, Webster, and
Beaumont and Fletcher remembered and echoed Shakespearean sayings, so might Bacon. If an occasional
identity of idea and expression be a ground for surmising
his authorship of the Shakespearean plays, equally must
it be a ground for surmising *their* authorship.

To give Dr. Theobald every advantage, I will deal
first with what he evidently regards as his very best
instance, since he puts it forth with special jubilation
in the preface to his cousin's posthumous work on THE
CLASSICAL ELEMENT IN THE SHAKESPEARE PLAYS. This
it is. Shakespeare frequently introduces the idea of
reactions and relations between the greater and the less—
the greater " hiding " or overshadowing or obscuring or
absorbing the other, as in the case of lights, griefs,
maladies, or sea and river (TWO GENTLEMEN, III, i, 353 ;
CYMBELINE, IV, ii, 244 ; LEAR, III, iv, 8 ; PERICLES, II,
iii, 41 ; MERCHANT, V, i, 89 *sq.*). In the last-cited case,
Portia remarks to Nerissa (1) that the greater glory dims
the less, as a king his substitute; who (2) in the king's
presence loses his state as does a river entering the sea.
Bacon, in turn, in one passage has :

> The greater should draw the less. So we see (1) when two
> lights meet, the greater doth darken and drown the less, and
> (2) when a smaller river runs into a greater it loseth both the
> name and the stream (*Life and Letters*, iii, 98).

Here the force of the coincidence lies mainly in the *collocation* of the two ideas. Either, singly, is quite common:

> Let that high swelling river of their fame
> Leave humble streams, that feed them yet their name.
> > Daniel, *Philotas*, 1718-19 (IV, ii).
>
> [Rivers] that have made their graves
> And buried both their names and all their gold
> Within his [Thames'] greatness to augment his waves.
> [Whereafter *he*, the Thames, is] swallowed up in ocean.
> > *Id.   Civil Wars*, 1595, B. ii, st. 7.

Noting that the collocation is exceptional—though
obviously likely—we have two hypotheses open. Either
both writers copied a previous one—as they may very
well have done—or Bacon, writing in the year 1603,
recalled some notable lines he had heard at the theatre
about 1596–98, or had read in or after 1600. What
could be more natural ? This is the obvious answer to

Dr. Theobald's challenge : " If any one can explain such a coincidence as this . . . by anything except identical authorship, I should like to know the alternative explanation and the process of reasoning by which it is reached." The process of reasoning is simply that set up by the multitude of similar coincidences in other Elizabethan writers, of which Dr. Theobald has apparently no knowledge. He is in effect denying that one author can ever copy or plagiarise from another.

A friend, he tells us, actually suggested to him that " Bacon may have heard or read the MERCHANT OF VENICE "—adding unnecessarily that " *without any conscious plagiarism*, he may have reproduced the imagery of the passage." To this Dr. Theobald replies : " I can confidently appeal to any unbiased reader whether such an explanation as this is not *infinitely more difficult to accept or even conceive* than the Baconian one of common authorship." If this asseveration has regard solely to the phrase " without any conscious plagiarism," it has some excuse ; but that qualification is as needless as it is indecisive. In the Elizabethan age, nobody troubled himself about plagiarism : all men, broadly speaking, practised it freely, though they at times charged others with similar offences. Bacon in his PROMUS positively heaped up saws, proverbs, maxims, phrases for use or comparison ; and in his writings he is perpetually quoting, with or without acknowledgment. And if Dr. Theobald means to affirm the inconceivableness or even the improbability of Bacon's hearing or reading and recollecting a passage in a finely poetic play, one can but dismiss his denial as idle. Let us but take a few of the precise coincidences between Bacon and Jonson, pointed out by Mr. Crawford :

If it be well weighed, to say that a man lieth is as much as to say that he is brave towards God, and a coward towards men. For a lie faces God, and shrinks from men.

Essay *Of Truth*.

> I like such tempers well as stand before their mistresses with fear and trembling ; and before their maker like impudent mountains.
>
> *Every Man out of his Humour*, iii, 3.

Here Bacon echoes Montaigne, and Jonson one or other.

> Reading maketh a full man.
>
> Essay *Of Studies*.

> An exactness of study, and multiplicity of reading, which maketh a full man.
>
> Jonson's *Discoveries* : iv, *Lectio*.

Here Jonson echoes Bacon, as he does in many other places in the DISCOVERIES, at much greater length ; and again in the phrase :

> Suffrages in parliament are *numbered, not weighed*,

which had been used by Bacon in 1589. In all this there is no mystery : the learned man echoes another, in some respects less learned ; and so many of the phrases in the PROMUS are found in the DISCOVERIES that one wonders whether Jonson may not have done some of the collecting for Bacon. But on the Baconian principle Bacon *wrote* the DISCOVERIES, as well as all the Jonsonian plays in which Bacon's favourite stories are used, and, by consequence, all the rest !

Rejecting *that* line of inference, we reject the other. Upon the most obvious reproduction of ideas, no inference of community of authorship is rationally to be founded where (1) the general circumstances are wholly repugnant to the hypothesis, and (2) copying was perfectly probable. Community of authorship *is* rationally to be surmised—of course it must in any case be supported by many other considerations before it can be taken as proved—where in two performances there are found a number of those small coincidences which could arise from unconscious mannerism, but which are not mere cases of universal usage. It is reasonable, for instance, to guess *prima facie* at Peele's authorship of an unsigned play *circa* 1590, which contains the phrase " sandy plains," because he used that phrase in season and out of season. But to get a step beyond a guess we should have to test for (1) general resemblances in rhythm; (2) resemblances in style and sentiment, (3) resemblances in versification. That something *might* be proved in this way is recognised by Dr. Theobald when he attempts to reply to Judge Willis's exposure, in THE BACONIAN MINT, of his most confidently cited parallels. As we have seen,[1] he attempts to confute Judge Willis by arguing that a phrase might be " curious " even if used by everybody. He goes on to deny that he cited the " curious " phrase " starting-holes " as one " coined at the Baconian Mint."

Not at all [he goes on] : on the contrary, it was not likely to be used by Bacon unless it was already intelligible by more or less frequent usage. It did not certainly belong to the highways of literary resort, and as a somewhat slangy phrase the use of it in common by Bacon and Shakespeare is worth notice ; that's all ! It is merely an application of one of the laws of speech which I have elsewhere stated (p. 470) : " No two writers help themselves in precisely the same way to the current phrases and notions that may be floating in the air at the time. Some individuality is shown even in these points of correspondence." [2]

Where then is the alleged individuality in the cases under notice ? Absolutely no hint is offered on the subject. Bacon, we are shown, uses " starting-holes " twice; but he does it just as everybody else did—else how would the phrase be so intelligible as Dr. Theobald now says it must have been ? The plain fact is that Dr. Theobald had *not* been aware of the currency of the phrase, else he would not have cited the occasional use of it by any two writers as a noteworthy " echo " or " coincidence." He does reluctantly admit that Mr. Willis proves him to have been mistaken " in the coupling of the words *gross and palpable.* But in this case," he absurdly goes on, " the Oxford Dictionary is as erring as I am "—as if the Oxford Dictionary claimed to be a

---

[1] Above p. 272.   [2] Preface to work cited, ed. 1904.

dictionary of phrases, with all instances of their use !
He is disingenuous enough to add that "the learned
judge overshoots the mark by giving in *most* of his references . . . not the coupled but the separate words,
which of course prove nothing." The learned judge, as
we have seen, actually gave *six* instances of the coupled
words : the other instances were illustrative of the vogue
of the terms. And Dr. Theobald, be it noted, had
solemnly affirmed[1] that the phrase "gross and palpable "
is "one of Bacon's many contributions to verbal currency. It was a new coin when it issued from his affluent
mint. . . . Any one using it in the early part of the
seventeenth century *would have felt almost obliged to quote
Bacon while employing it."* A more flagrant example of
the method of ignorance it would be hard to find. And
it is by the confident application of this method that Dr.
Theobald finds Bacon to have written Marlowe as well
as Shakespeare.

How it works in detail we shall see in examining Dr.
Theobald's presentment of the mass of his case—largely
compiled as it is from previous Baconian writers. The
series of "echoes and correspondencies" in his twelfth
chapter is made up indiscriminately of parallels in idea
and parallels in phrase or idiom. Lest I be accused of
unfair selection, I deal with half of them *seriatim*, abridg-
ing, of necessity, the presentment of some, but giving,
I think, the full force of the argument in every case :

1. Comments on "the danger attending too much
success in public service."

The main point is that "all immoderate success extin-
guisheth merit, and stirreth up distaste and envy "
(Bacon to Essex, Letter in Spedding's LIFE, ii, 129). The
idea is fully expressed in a speech of Ventidius, ANTONY
AND CLEOPATRA, III, i, 11 *sq.* ; and less directly in
CORIOLANUS, I, i, 267 *sq.*

As Dr. Theobald himself partly indicates, this is a

[1] Work cited, p. 264.

standing commonplace, ancient and modern. Following
Lewis Theobald, he cites Quintus Curtius, i, 1, adding :
" It is not unlikely that the poet had this passage in mind
when he was writing the drama of ANTONY AND CLEO-
PATRA." There is no more reason to suppose that the
dramatist had read Quintus Curtius than that he had
written the letter to Essex. The reflection that distinguished success elicits envy and detraction is one of the
most obvious in the whole range of human experience.
In this case Dr. Theobald can suggest *no* correspondence
of diction between Bacon and Shakespeare. On the
other hand, the idea is common in Tudor and Jacobean
literature. *E.g.* : Elyot, THE GOVERNOUR, B. iii, ch. 27 ;
OF DETRACTION ; Holland's trans. of Plutarch's MORALIA
(1603) ; OF ENVY AND HATRED. Compare :

> Envy doth aye true honour's deeds despise.
>> Peele, *Welcome to the Earl of Essex.*
> Yet in the House of Fame, and courts of Kings,
> Envy will bite, or snarl and bark at least.
>> *Id. Honour of the Garter.*

> *Cicero.* Great honours are great burdens, but on whom
> They are cast with envy, he doth bear two loads.
> His cares must still be double to his joys
> In any dignity ; where, if he err,
> He finds no pardon, and for doing well
> A most small praise.
>> Jonson, *Catiline,* III, i, 1–6.
> *Sabinus.* When men grow fast
> Honour'd and loved, there is a trick in state
> Which jealous princes never fail to use,
> How to decline that growth, with fair pretext . . .
> To shift them forth into another air
> Where they may purge and lessen, etc.
>> *Id. Sejanus,* I, i.
> [Envious great men] armed with power and Princes' jealousies,
> Will put the least conceit of discontent
> Into the greatest rank of treacheries,
> That no one action shall seem innocent . . .
> But this is still the fate of those that are
> By nature or their fortunes eminent.
> Who, either carried in conceit too far

Do work their own or others' discontent,
Or else are deemèd fit to be supprest.
Not for they are, but that they may be ill.
Daniel, *Tragedy of Philotas*, 1605, Chorus at end of Act II.

Such the rewards of great employments are.
Hate kills in peace, whom Fortune spares in war.
Id. ib. ll. 1738–39 (III, ii).

2. Bacon's amplification of the text in Proverbs : " As
dead flies do cause the best ointment to stink, so does
a little folly him that is in reputation for wisdom and
honour." This is amplified in the DE AUGMENTIS, with
express reference to the Bible text ; and variants on the
idea occur in Bacon's speech to the judges in 1617 (LIFE,
vi, 213) and his Reply to the Speaker in 1620 (LIFE, vii,
178). " It is important to remark how these *singularly
subtle and, as thus expounded, original sentiments*, are
reproduced in Shakespeare," in the rebuke of Mortimer
to Hotspur (I HENRY VI, III, i, 180 *sq.*), and in Hamlet's
" So oft it chances in particular men " speech (HAMLET,
I, iv, 17).

Here one of the most often quoted sayings of the Book
of Proverbs, familiar in every English household, is
claimed as " singularly subtle and original " in its essential
and obvious meaning ; and Bacon is credited with Shakespeare's development of the common theme, though
Bacon refers to the text and Shakespeare does not ; and
though there is *no* coincidence in their diction. As
before, we are dealing with applications of a commonplace such as must have been made thousands of times
by contemporaries.

3. In one of Bacon's MEDITATIONES SACRÆ, and in his
speech at the trial of Lord Sanquhar for murder, there
are allusions to the legendary magnanimity of the lion
towards a yielding foe ; with a quotation from Ovid,
Corpora magnanimo satis est prostrasse leonem (TRISTIA,
III, v, 33). Shakespeare has the idea in LOVE'S LABOUR'S
LOST (IV, i, 90) and in TROILUS AND CRESSIDA (V, iii, 37).

Irrelevant parallels are cited by Dr. Theobald from other plays.

As usual, we are dealing with a standing commonplace. If Dr. Theobald had read Puttenham he would know the story, probably then a household word in England, of Queen Elizabeth's answer to the knight who had been insolent to her before her accession and craved pardon when she was queen : " Do you not know that we are descended of the lion, whose nature is not to harm or prey upon the mouse, or any other such small vermin ? " [1] If he had read Greene, he would have found this instance of the saying :

> The king of beasts, that harms not yielding ones.
> *James IV*, V, iii, 24,

with the variant, in the same scene :

> I, eagle-like, disdain these little fowls,
> And look on none but those that dare resist.

If he had read EDWARD III, he would have seen the line, (IV, ii, 33 :)

> The lion scorns to touch the yielding prey.

If he had consulted Douce's ILLUSTRATIONS OF SHAKE-SPEARE he might have read that

in THE CHOISE OF CHANGE, CONTAINING THE DIVINITIE, PHILOSOPHIE, AND POETRIE, &c. (1585, 4to), a work evidently constructed on the model of the Welsh triads, we find the following passage :—" three things shew that there is a great clemencie in lions : *they will not hurt them that lie grovelling,*" &c. Bartholo-mæus [trans. by Batman, 1582, folio] says, " their mercie is known by many and oft ensamples : *for they spare them that lie on the ground.*" [2]

Perhaps this may convince even Baconians that Dr. Theobald has found a mare's nest. Inasmuch as some Shakespearean critics have ascribed EDWARD III to

---

[1] *Arte of English Poesie*, 1589, Arber's rep. p. 303.

[2] Work cited, ed. 1839, p. 190. See the passage given more at length in Seager's *Natural History in Shakespeare's Time*, 1896, p. 183.

Shakespeare; Dr. Theobald and the Baconians will doubt-less do as much—meaning Bacon. Some of them, I know, ascribe to Bacon the work of Puttenham. But they can hardly father on Bacon Bartholomew's early encyclopædia, the DE PROPRIETATIBUS RERUM, written in the thirteenth century, translated in 1397 by John of Trevisa, and printed in 1495 ; or THE CHOISE OF CHANGE, cited by Douce. And I suppose even Sir Edwin Durning-Lawrence would hardly ascribe to Bacon a poem published in 1557, with the line :

> The fierce lyon will hurt no yelden things.
> Wyatt, *To his Lady cruel over her yelden Lover* ;

to say nothing of Lilly's

> Lions spare those that couch to them.
> *Euphues and his England*, Arber's rep. p. 377.

4. Thrice over, Bacon says of Aristotle that after the Ottoman fashion he could not feel secure in his kingdom of philosophy till he had slain his brothers. Shakespeare does not say this of Aristotle ; but he makes Henry V on his accession reassure his brothers with the remark that

> Not Amurath an Amurath succeeds,
> But Harry, Harry.
> 2 *H. IV*, v, ii, 46.

Dr. Theobald regretfully admits that Bacon nowhere names Amurath ; but stands all the same for his parallel ! The historic fact[1] is that in 1596 the eldest son of Amurath III murdered *his* brethren on his accession. But there had been previous episodes of the kind. In Kyd's SOLIMAN AND PERSEDA (1592); Amurath, brother of Soliman, kills his brother Haleb, and is then killed by Soliman (i, 5) ; and in Peele's BATTLE OF ALCAZAR (1594), which begins with a dumb-show of the murder of the son, two young brothers, and the uncle of " the Moor " Muly Mahamet, the name Amurath occurs many times. Thus

[1] See note *in loc*. Variorum ed.

the practice and the name were already matters of theatrical as well as general comment. There is not the slightest ground for connecting Bacon's allusion with that in the play as to authorship.

5. Dr. Theobald repeats Mr. Donnelly's citation of the phrase " troublers of the world," noting that it is used with " much the same technical (!) meaning " by Shakespeare. As to this nugatory suggestion *see* p. 430 *supra.*

6. " In a very early State paper of Bacon's," says Dr. Theobald, " dating about the end of the year 1584; and which was not published in any form till 1651," there occur the phrases " fair enamelling of a terrible danger " and " giving him a bastinado with a little cudgel." Shakespeare speaks of a snake's " enamell'd skin," and makes other allusions to snakes as dangerous things ; he also speaks of giving " the bastinado with his tongue," adding : " our ears are cudgell'd." Dr. Theobald infers that " Bacon *had in his mind* the metallic lustre of a deadly snake " ; and that the idea of a bastinado with the tongue " kept lasting hold on his mind," inasmuch as Shakespeare twice speaks of words as strokes. Comment seems unnecessary ; but it may be noted that the whole thing happens to be a historical mare's nest. The State paper in question is not and could not have been by Bacon, who in 1584 was in no position to offer State counsel to Queen Elizabeth. It figures for historical students as *Lord Burleigh's* ADVICE TO QUEEN ELIZABETH (Harl. Misc. 2nd ed. ii, 277). Did Lord Burleigh then write Shakespeare ?

7. Bacon tells the story of " Anaxarchus, who, when questioned under torture, bit out his own tongue, and spat it in the face of the tyrant." Shakespeare, in turn, makes Bolingbroke in RICHARD II speak of doing as much, without reference to Anaxarchus or Leæna or any other precedent. Dr. Theobald incidentally reveals that the story is a classic commonplace, being related by Diogenes Lærtius, Pliny, and Valerius Maximus. He

might have added that Plutarch tells it of Zeno. But as " it is not very likely that William Shakespeare had read any of the classic authors " first named, RICHARD II must have been written by Bacon ! The actor, Dr. Theobald thinks, might have been equal to the idea " bite my tongue out," but not to the stroke of spitting it out ! As usual, Dr. Theobald is unaware that the story is told by Boethius, without name; and was made known to English readers by the translations of Chaucer, Richard (1525) and Colville (1556). As little is he aware that it is told of Zeno, after Plutarch, by Lilly (EUPHUES, Arber's rep. p. 146). If he had but read so familiar an Elizabethan work as THE SPANISH TRAGEDY, he would have been aware that the act in question is made to take place in that play. So that even the Stratfordian actor had necessarily heard of the conception !

7a. In this connection, again resorting to the fountain-head of Mr. Donnelly, Dr. Theobald notes that Bacon and Shakespeare both use " top " metaphorically for *ne plus ultra* or acme of achievement or quality. As we have seen (above, p. 385), everybody else in that day did the same. The " coincidence " is another mare's nest.

8. Bacon speaks of the basilisk and the cockatrice respectively as killing by a glance those who do not see them first. So do fifty other writers of the period : the basilisk is a standing tag of the essayists and the play-wrights. Shakespeare speaks of " the fatal balls of murdering basilisks " (H. V, V, ii, 14), with a double reference to " eye-balls and cannon-balls," and several times elsewhere speaks of basilisks and cockatrices as killing by their gaze, and puns about I and *eye*. It does not occur to Dr. Theobald to note that a dozen other authors of the time did the same thing ; and that Bacon does not. Shakespeare's pun must for him be Bacon's because Bacon " never could pass by a joke." Thus does Dr. Theobald construct his " cable."

9. Bacon has allusions to the pure fire of the stars,
fire in " the heaven," and so forth ; while Shakespeare
makes Coriolanus swear " by the fires of heaven " ; makes
Hamlet write; " doubt that the stars are fire " ; and
makes other characters speak of stars as fires. Dr.
Theobald has apparently met with no other allusions
to star-fire in Elizabethan literature. Yet they occur
in such numbers that we are driven as usual to our conclu-
clusion that he limits his reading to the authors he is
concerned to identify.

In Peele's TALE OF TROY, published in 1589, we have
(l. 28) :

> Glistening like stars of pure immortal fire.

In Spenser's HYMNE IN HONOUR OF LOVE; we find the
lines :

> Kindled at first from heaven's life-giving fire.
> Some sparks remaining of that heavenly fire.
>
>   th' immortal flame
> Of heavenly light.
> The flaming light of that celestial fire—

four instances in two pages. In the next of the " Foure
Hymnes "—AN HYMNE IN HONOUR OF BEAUTIE—
besides various metaphorical allusions to fire, we have
a stanza telling how when the soule did pass

> Down from the top of purest heavens height
> To be embodied here, it then took light
> And lively spirits from that fairest star
> Which lights the world forth from his fiery car.

Perhaps the stanza in the fourth hymn (HEAVENLY
BEAUTY) about the further heavens, beyond the visible,—

> That need no sun t' illuminate their spheres
> But their own native light far passing theirs—

may be deemed irrelevant ; but it would very well have
served Dr. Theobald's end had he found it in Shakespeare ;
as would the lines about the divine light :

> In sight of whom both Sun and Moon are dark . . .
> That all about him sheddeth glorious light . . .
> . . . that immortal light which there doth shine. . . .

and so on. The same idea appears in Sir John Davies'
ORCHESTRA (1596) :

> Next her [the Moon] the pure, subtile and cleansing Fire
> Is swiftly carried in a circle even.

In Ben Jonson's POETASTER (1601) we have :

> Ay me, that virtue, whose brave eagle's wings
> With every stroke blow stars in burning heaven . . .
>
> For thine own good, fair Goddess, do not stay.
> Who would engage [= gage] a firmament of fires
> Shining in thee, for me, a falling star ?
>
> Act iv, sc. 6.

The conclusion reached by the true Baconian I presume,
will be that Bacon wrote Peele and Spenser and Davies
and all the rest. If, however, the open-minded reader
will yet a little further extend his reading to the poetical
works of Greene, Peele, Spenser, Drayton, Sidney, and
Daniel, he will not merely begin to realise the universality
of the modes of expression supposed by Dr. Theobald
to be specialties of Bacon, but will gather some such
knowledge of Elizabethan poetic diction in general as
will make partly clear to him the fashion in which the
poetic faculty, as seen in Shakespeare, handles the
material of the scientific or knowledge-seeking faculty,
seen speculatively at work in Bacon.

It is quite likely that Hamlet's line in his quatrain to
Ophelia had reference to the debate, conducted by Bacon
and other contemporaries, as to whether the stars are
fires. He would find in Greene the contrary theory that

> The stars from earthly humours gain their light,
> Melicertes' Madrigal, in Menaphon ;

and in Marlowe's FAUSTUS he would note the question
as to whether there was a sphere of fire. He must have
heard at the Mermaid *some* mention of the scientific and
other speculations of his day. Even actors hear of such

matters ! But to trace his poetic expressions to the speculative physicist who wrote the NOVUM ORGANUM is possible only to those who believed the Baconian theory in advance.

10. By parity of reasoning, Bacon wrote Shakespeare because both speak in metaphor of the mobility of quicksilver, as everybody else did, and does now ! *E.g.* :

> As if our veins ran with quicksilver.
> > Jonson, *Cynthia's Revels*, ii, 1.

Starting from his presupposition, the Baconian consistently proceeds to assign to Bacon the works of Jonson. And so on *ad infinitum*. To Bacon also, on that principle; must be assigned the plays of Webster :

> My loose thoughts
> Scatter like quicksilver.
> > *The White Devil*, iv, 2.
> He runs as if he were ballassed with quicksilver.
> > *The Duchess of Malfi*, i, 2.

11. Bacon had noted the occult fact that poisons; and likewise " certain conditions of the mind," often " cause swelling." Shakespeare, again, has the phrase :

> You shall digest the venom of your spleen
> Though it do split you.
> > *Jul. Cæs.* IV, iii, 46,

—which Dr. Theobald thinks is meant to imply a process of swelling ; and the dramatist further speaks of " highblown pride," " high-swol'n hearts," the swelling of the ambitious ocean, persons swelling in their pride, and so on. It is most true. But as the reader may have noted above (p. 427), the other dramatists of the time, not to speak of the prose-writers, used the same figure with " damnable iteration." If Dr. Theobald had but read a little in the Elizabethan drama, beginning with FERREX AND PORREX, he would have met a score of times with such figures as :

> Methinks I see his envious heart to swell.
> > *Ferrex and Porrex*, i, 1 (1561).

When growing pride doth fill the swelling breast.

> *Id.* ii, 2, Chorus.

The heat
And furious pangs of his inflamèd head.

> *Id.* iii, 1.

My brother's heart even then repin'd
With swollen disdain against mine equal rule.

> *Id.* iv, 2.

For fight I must, or else my gall will burst.

> Lilly, *Woman in the Moon*, ii, 1.

Pandora's love, that almost burst my heart.

> *Id. ib.* v, 1.

How my heart swells at these miscreants' words.

> *Id. ib.*

O then to sift that humour from her heart.

> *Id.* i, 1.

His heart did earne against his hated foe,
And bowels so with rankling poison swelled,
That scarce the skin the strong contagion held.

> Spenser, *Muiopotmos*, ll. 254–6.

Or fraught with envy that their galls do swell.

> *Id. Colin Clout's Come Home Again*, l. 760.

That poison foul of bubbling pride doth lie
So in my swelling breast.

> Sidney, *Astrophel and Stella*, 27.

Princes, whose high spleens for empery swell.

> Dekker, *The Honest Whore*, Pt. I, ii, 3.

Why swells your spleen so high ?

> *Id.* v, 2.

That I could
Contract the soul of universal rage
Into this swelling heart, that it might be
As full of poisonous anger as a dragon's.

> Chapman, *Revenge for Honour*, iii, 1.

Thy black tongue doth swell
With venom.

> Dekker, *The Honest Whore*, Pt. II, ii, 1.

The state is full of dropsy, and swol'n big
With windy vapours.

> Heywood, *Rape of Lucrece*, i, 2.

And if he went back to Langland, he would find :

For whoso hath more than I,
Than angreth me soore,

And thus I live loveless
Like a luther dog,
That al my body bolneth [*i.e.* swelleth]
For bitter of my galle.

Piers Plowman, ll. 2705–10.

Compare finally the Elizabethan prose of Puttenham :

Men would and must needs utter their spleens in all ordinarie matters also, or else it seemed their bowels would burst.

Arte of English Poesie, Arber's rep. p. 68.

12. Bacon repeatedly uses the phrase "bleed inwardly," —either concretely or metaphorically. So does Shakespeare (2 HENRY IV, IV, iv, 58 ; TIMON, I, ii, 211).

So do many other writers—with the same bearing in metaphor—speak of the danger of inward bleeding. Mr. Crawford points at once to one of the most popular budgets of such sayings. Lilly in EUPHUES, in one handful of proverbs, has : "the wound that bleedeth inwardly is most dangerous" (Arber's rep. p. 63).

12a. In this connection Dr. Theobald cites, as "still more distinctly" applying the metaphor, Hamlet's phrase (IV, iv, 27) about "the imposthume that inward breaks " ; and Bacon in the PROMUS has a note of "The launching [= lancing] of the imposthume by him that intended murder."

These too are pre-Shakespearean commonplaces. As Mr. Bayley and Mr. Crawford point out, the chance of a blow breaking an internal imposthume, and so curing it, is dwelt upon in EUPHUES (Arber's rep. p. 330) ; and Ben Jonson, in his ENGLISH GRAMMAR, quotes from Sir John Cheke the sentence :

Sedition is an aposteam, which, when it breaketh inwardly, putteth the state in great danger of recovery ; and corrupteth the whole commonwealth with the rotten fury that it hath putrified with.

13. Bacon has the phrase "to search the wounds of the realm and not to skin them over," and repeats the idea in similar words in other places. Shakespeare

repeatedly puts the same idea (HAMLET, III, iv, 147;
M. FOR M. II, ii, 134) ; and has other phrases about
searching wounds and applying plasters (TITUS, II, iii;
262 ; AS YOU LIKE IT, II, iv, 44 ; TEMPEST, II, i, 137 ;
TWO GENTLEMEN, I, ii, 114).

All this is Elizabethan commonplace. *E.g.* :

> Such imposthumes as Phantaste is . . . .
>
>   We must lance these sores
> Or all will putrify.
>
> Jonson, *Cynthia's Revels*, v, 3.

> I never yet saw hurt so smoothly healed
> But that the scars bewrayed the former wound :
> Yea, where the salve did soonest close the skin
> The sore was oft'ner covered up than cured.
> Which festering deep and filled within, at last
> With sudden breach grew greater than at first.
>
> Hughes, *The Misfortunes of Arthur*, 1587, III, i, 109–114.

Such sayings are the common stuff of homily.

14. Shakespeare's phrases about sweet things producing sourness or loathing in digestion (M. N. D. II, ii;
137 ; RICHARD II, I, iii, 236) are paralleled in Bacon.
So are they a hundred times elsewhere :

> But O ! this sweet success,
> Pursu'd with greater harms, turned soon to sour.
>
> Hughes, *Misfortunes of Arthur*, 1587, II, i, 53–54.

> Such is the sweet of this ambitious power.
> No sooner had, than turned eftsoons to sour.
>
> *Id.* II, iv, Chorus at end.

> Must taste those sowre distates the times do bring
> Upon the fulness of a cloy'd Neglect.
>
> Daniel, *Musophilus*, 1602–3, ll. 169–170.

> Held back something from that full of sweet
> To intersowre unsure delights the more.
>
> *Id. Letter from Octavia to Marcus Antonius*, 1599,
> st. 40.

14*a*. And so with the derivative metaphor about love
and friendship turning to hate (RICHARD II, III, ii, 335 ;
R. AND J.; II; vi, 11 ; LUCRECE, 867 ; Sonnet 94).

This also was a standing commonplace :

Fortune.   Did not I change long love to sudden hate,
And then rechange their hatred into love ?

Soliman and Perseda, Act i, Induction.

So, being former foes, they waxed friends.

Spenser, *Colin Clout's Come Home Again*, l. 851.

15. Bacon and Shakespeare frequently apply the terms " sugar " and " sugared " to words and speech.

So do nine Elizabethan belletrists out of ten, and many divines to boot !   *See* above, p. 278.

15*a*. But Bacon has the phrase (PROMUS, No. i, 219) : " Sweet for speech in the morning " and the Friar in ROMEO AND JULIET (II, iii, 32) asks :

What early tongue so sweet saluteth me ?

And we are asked to recognise the utterance of a single mind !

15*b*. But, again, Bacon asserts that " sounds are sweeter as well as greater in the night than in the day " (SYL. SYL. 235) ; and Shakespeare has expressions to that effect (ROMEO AND JULIET, II, ii, 166 ; MERCHANT, V, i, 55). If Dr. Theobald found in Elizabethan literature, by any chance, an allusion to the midnight sweetness of the song of the nightingale, he would doubtless recognise the unmistakable hand of Bacon.   The greater audibility of sounds in the night is a fact that perhaps escapes frequent literary comment by reason of a notoriety extending over several millenniums.

16. " Other scientific ideas (!) which Bacon held about sound," says Dr. Theobald, " are clearly reflected in Shakespeare " :

The lower winds in a plain, except they be strong, make no noise ; but amongst the trees the noise of such winds will be perceived.

Syl. Syl. 115.

You may as well forbid the mountain pines
To wag their high tops, and to make no noise.

Merchant, IV, i, 75.

When the sweet wind did gently kiss the trees
And they did make no noise.

Id. V, i, 1.

These little coincidences are rare delights for the Baconians ; who never ask whether they might not stand for reminiscences by Bacon of phrases heard by him in plays. Unhappily they occur in other writers. "Observe," says Dr. Theobald, " how the little phrase ' make no noise ' always refers to the movement of wind in the trees." Yet there are such coincidences elsewhere :

> When the least whistling wind begins to sing,
> And gently blows her hair about her neck,
> Like to a chime of bells it soft doth ring,
> And with the pretty noise the wind doth check.
> > Chester, *Love's Martyr*, 1601. Grosart's ed. p. 10.
>
> Each noise the wind or air doth cause.
> > Harington's trans. of *Orlando Furioso* (1591), B. i, st. 34.

The use of " noise " for a musical sound is common; *E.g.* :

> The spouse of fair Eurydice,
> That did enchant the waters with his noise.
> > *Locrine*, i, 1.

17. Again, Shakespeare notes, with Bacon, that hearing is more acute by night than by day (M. N. D. III, ii, 177). This occult fact has been already commented on.

18. Shakespeare has a passage on the knots in trees that " by the conflux of meeting sap " divert the tree's growth (TROILUS, I, iii, 7) ; and Bacon has one explaining how knots in trees occur " for that the sap ascendeth unequally " (SYL. SYL. 589). Obviously the theory was a current one ; and Dr. Theobald admits that " the Shakespeare passage shows a slight variation."

19. Bacon in the PROMUS quotes the proverb : " He that pardons his enemy, the amner [almoner] shall have his goods " ; and in the DE AUGMENTIS remarks that " None of the virtues has so many crimes to answer for as clemency " (Antitheta on Cruelty ; VI, iii, No. 18) ; repeating the idea more fully in another place (VIII, ii, No. 14). Again, he writes to Buckingham : " Mercy in such a case, in a King, is true cruelty " (LIFE, vi, 46).

So Shakespeare :

Sparing justice feeds iniquity.

Lucrece, 1686.

Pardon is still the nurse of second woe.

M. for M. II, i, end.

Compare *Richard II*, V, iii, 57-99 ; *Timon*, III, v, 2 ; *Romeo*, III, i, last line.

Dr. Theobald admits that " this is not a very profound or original axiom." It is not : it was an ancient common-place, often found in Elizabethan literature :

He that for every little occasion is moved with compassion . . . is called piteous, which is a sickness of the mind, wherewith at this day the more part of men be diseased.

Elyot, *The Governour*, B. ii, c. 7. (Compare c. 9.)

For most oftentimes the omitting of correction redoubleth a trespass.

Id. B. iii, c. 21.

Wrong, wreakless [= unrevenged] sleeping,
Makes men die honourless ; one borne, another
Leaps on our shoulders. We must wreak our wrongs
So as we take not more.

Chapman, *Revenge of Bussy D'Ambois*, iii, 1.

Fathers, to spare these men, were to commit
A greater wickedness than you would revenge.

Jonson, *Catiline*, v, 6.

It had been put in currency for the stage by Hughes :

No worse a vice than lenity in kings.
Remiss indulgence soon undoes a realm.
He teacheth how to sin, that winks at sins,
And bids offend, that suffereth an offence.
The only hope of leave increaseth crimes,
And he that pardoneth one, emboldeneth all
To break the laws. Each patience fostereth wrongs. . . .
Rough rigour looks out right, and still prevailes :
Smooth mildness looks too many ways to thrive.

Attonement sield [seldom] defeats, but oft defers
Revenge : beware a reconciled foe.

The Misfortunes of Arthur, 1587, III, i, 62-74.

And we have it in Fairfax's translation of Tasso's JERUSALEM DELIVERED (1600) :

There must the rule to all disorders sink,
Where pardons more than punishments appear.

B. v, st. 39 ;

and in Daniel's CIVIL WARS :

Compassion here is cruelty, my lord,
Pity will cut our throats.

B. vi, st. 65.

But it should not have been necessary thus to illustrate the vogue of a commonplace sure to be uttered by a thousand lawyers, preachers, and laymen on every occasion of the severe repression of sedition.

20. Bacon, in his HISTORY OF HENRY VII, quotes Chancellor Morton on " the *bastard* and *barren* employment of moneys to usury," and in this connection he repeats the word " bastard" twice. Shakespeare in VENUS AND ADONIS (767) speaks of gold put to use begetting gold, using no term of disparagement ; and in the MERCHANT OF VENICE (I, iii) makes Antonio speak of Shylock taking " a *breed* for *barren* money of his friend." Citing an irrelevant passage from TWELFTH NIGHT (III; i, 54), Dr. Theobald pronounces that, " Putting all these things together, Shakespeare's opinion seems to be much the same as Bacon's." The facts are plainly otherwise. Shakespeare puts in Antonio's mouth the standing medieval censure of usury—that it was unnatural, in that it made a barren thing " breed." (Compare : " I cannot abide to have money engender," in Dekker's HONEST WHORE, Pt. II, ii, 1 ; and the exposition in Kyd's translation of Tasso's THE HOUSEHOLDER'S PHILOSOPHY ; Boas' ed. of Works, pp. 279–282.) He does not call it " bastard "—that is Bacon's word. The alleged coincidence turns directly against Dr. Theobald's thesis.

20*a*. In this connection, Dr. Theobald notes that Bacon in the late essay on Usury puts forward contradictory views on money-lending—that it " doth dull and damp all industries," but that at moderate interest lent money " will encourage and edge industrious and profitable employments." Shakespeare on the contrary makes Polonius say that "borrowing dulls the edge of husbandry." Again a sharp divergence. Dr. Theobald solves his problem by the pronouncement that "when HAMLET was written, the poet does not seem to have advanced quite so far " as he did when he wrote the essay on Usury! Thus when Shakespeare and Bacon hold contrary opinions, it is to count for nothing against the Baconian theory, which in effect professes to rest upon " echoes and correspondencies "!

21. Shakespeare, in a passage on the possibility of forecasting events from the past, speaks of the " seeds and weak beginnings " of things (2 HENRY IV, iii, 1, 80 sq.). Bacon in turn speaks of " a beginning and seed " (Works, ed. Spedding and Ellis, vii, 4) ; again of " the seminary and beginnings " of monarchies (LIFE, iii, 324) ; and yet again of " fair seeds and beginnings " (Works, vii, 47). Any critical reader noting such an extremely likely coincidence of phrase would make some scrutiny before deciding that it stood for identity of authorship. The Baconian never makes such an inquiry. Yet the phrase is obviously a natural one, *likely* to be common. Compare :

> So that they have had their *beginning* of themselves in *seede*, in flower, or in kernell.
>
> > Golding's trans. of De Mornay, on *The Trewnesse of the Christian Religion*, 1587, ed. 1604, p. 6.

22. Similarly Dr. Theobald founds on the fact that Shakespeare makes the King in ALL'S WELL (I, ii, 15) utter the million-times repeated platitude about a foreign war being an " exercise " for a nation—a sentiment which Bacon gives out in his own person more than once. Dr. Theobald appears to think that he strengthens his case by first adducing the advice of HENRY IV to his son " to buoy giddy minds with foreign quarrels " (2 HENRY IV. IV, v, 210)—a totally different proposition —and even goes the length of quoting the " somewhat

coarse " language of Parolles (ALL'S WELL; II; iii; 296).
The claim is beneath discussion. Shakespeare makes one
king employ a saying about war which had been uttered
by multitudes of men in all time about every foreign war
in history ; and Bacon does as much on his own account.
It is set forth by Daniel in his CIVIL WARS, B. v, st. 17.
The inference of identity is here outside discussion.

23. Bacon somewhere (Dr. Theobald gives no reference)
speaks of indulgence as causing weakness by " expense of
spirit " ; as does Shakespeare in Sonnet 129. In the lack
of a reference the point can hardly be discussed ; but
here again the phrase is in the common way of Elizabethan
diction :

Right sacred expense of his time.
Chapman; pref. to trans. of Iliad.
The serious expense of an exact gentleman's time.
Id. Epist. ded. to Seven Books of the Iliads, 1598.
The worthy expense of my future life.
Id. ib.
Spend their souls in sparks.
Id. Verses To M. Harriots, app. to trans. of Achilles' Shield.
Spent his vital spirit.
Spenser, Ruins of Time, l. 382.
A scholar doth disdain to spend his spirits
Upon such base employment as hand labours.
Patient Grissil (1599) v. 1.
Foolish inamorates who spend their ages, their spirits, nay
themselves, in the servile and ridiculous imployments of their
mistresses.
T. Heywood, Apology for Actors, Sh. Soc. rep. p. 54.
And speak away my spirit into air.
Jonson, Induction to Every Man out of his Humour.

24. Bacon in his speech of Undertakers (LIFE; v; 43);
speaks of " the fort of affection and the fort of reason,"
and uses " fort of reason " again in the Discourse on
Fortitude which is spoken at the Conference of Pleasure.
Shakespeare has " pales and forts of reason " (Hamlet, I;
iv, 27). Bacon again (last cit.) has " fortitude the marshal
of thought, the armour of the will " ; while Shakespeare

writes of " the marshal to my will " (M. N. D.; II, ii, 120) and " armour of the mind."

It is quite possible that Bacon had heard performances of the plays cited, and echoed them. But the metaphors and phrases in question were common. *E.g.* :

Where virtue keepeth the fort, report and suspicion may assail but never sack.

> Greene; *Pandosto* (1588), Hazlitt's Sh. Lib. iv, 42.

Yet first he cast, by treaty and by trains,
Her to persuade that stubborn fort to yield.

> Spenser, *Faerie Queene*, B. I, c. vi, st. 3.

What war so cruel, or what siege so sore
As that which strong affections do apply
Against the *fort of reason* evermore.

> *Id.* II, xi, 1.

That fort of chastity.

That impregnable fort of chastity and loyalty.

> Chapman, *The Widow's Tears*, i, 1 ; iii, 1.

Thou hast the goal, the fort [of chastity] is beaten.

> *Nero* (1624), ii, 1.

To summon resignation of life's fort.

> Chapman, *The Gentleman Usher*, iv, 1.

Most tender fortress of our woes.

> Chapman, *Hymnus in Noctem.*

I must confess I yielded up my fort.

> Heywood, 1 *Edward IV*, v, 4.

To win the Fort, how oft have I essayed,
Wherein the heart of my fair mistress lies.

> W. Percy, *Sonnets to Cælia*, 1594; Son. 10.

Under pretence of friendship, where he hath a fort, as it were, commodiously seated.

> Holland, trans. of Plutarch's *Moralia* ("To discern a Flatterer from a Friend ") Everyman Lib. selection, p. 38.

" Marshal of the will " and " armour of the mind " are equally common types of figure. The second was made current for all Europe by Boethius, of which there were three English translators. Chaucer has :

Certes I gave thee such armours that, if thou thyself ne haddest first cast them away, they shoulden han defended thee.

> B. i, pr. 2.

The idea is common in Tudor *belles lettres* :

Only to think that he was out of these meditations was sufficient armour to defend him from all other torments.

Gascoigne, *Adventures of Master F. J.* Cunliffe's ed. of Works, i, 422.

But the religious use of the metaphor, starting from such texts as " the armour of righteousness," " the whole armour of God " (2 Cor. vi, 7 ; Eph. vi, 11, 13), was absolutely universal.   *E.g.* Erasmus' ENCHIRIDION, and Latimer, *passim.*

25. Bacon says in a letter to Villiers (LIFE, v, 260) that the times require a King's attorney " to wear a gauntlet and not a glove " ; and Shakespeare has :

A scaly gauntlet now . . . *must glove* this hand.

2 *Henry IV*, i, 1, 145.

The phrase is a typical Tudor commonplace.

26. Bacon " is fond of taper-light " ; speaks of events as " lights or tapers " (LIFE, i, 132) ; and has in his PROMUS (688) the proverbial phrase : " To help the sun with lanterns "—as well as others (686, 687) about digging a well by a river, and a gold ring on a swine's snout.   All these ideas are claimed to be " clearly reproduced in Shakespeare," in the passages (1) about smoothing the ice and adding taper-light to that of the sun (JOHN, IV, ii, 9) ; (2) about adding water to the sea and bringing a faggot to burning Troy (TITUS, III, i, 68) ; (3) about adding coals to Cancer (TROILUS, II, iii, 205) ; (4) about the raven chiding blackness (*ib.* 221), and (5) about honey as a sauce to sugar (As YOU LIKE IT, III, iii, 29) ; and again in the line " She doth teach the torches to burn bright."

An extremely common type of metaphor and an extremely common form of proverb are here founded on to prove identity of authorship.   Upon that principle Bacon wrote the plays of Jonson, who has

Witness thy youth's dear sweets here spent untasted, Like a fair taper, with his own flame wasted.

Cynthia's Revels, i, 1.

and of Dekker, who wrote :

'Twere impiety then to dim her light,
Because we see such tapers seldom burn.

The Honest Whore, Pt. II, iv, 2.

Whose star-like eyes have power . . . to make night day.

Old Fortunatus, ii, 2.

The tapers of the night [*i.e.* the stars] are already lighted.

Ib. Prologue at Court.

To say nothing of :

When the taper of my heart is lighted.

Barnes, *Parthenophil and Parthenophe* (1593), Son. 24.

It was a common trope long before Bacon. *E.g.* :

A light or torch to show man his filthy and stinking nature.

Hooper, *Declaration of Christ's Office*, 1547. Parker
Soc. rep. p. 89.

As to the phrase about bringing lanterns to the sun, nobody but a Baconian would need to be told that it was in everyday use among common folk. It emerges even in theology :

Man's wisdom giveth as much light unto the word of God, as a little candle giveth unto the bright sun in the mid-day.

Hooper, *Answer to the Bishop of Winchester*, Parker
Soc. vol. p. 169.

They do shewe themselves worthie to be laughed at, as which should take upon them to enlighten the Sunne with a Candle.

Sidney and Golding's trans. of De Mornay *Of the Trewnes
of the Christian Religion*, 1587, ed. 1604, p. 1.

Compare a poet :

To light
A candle to the Sun.

Daniel, pref. poem to *The Queenes Arcadia*, 1605.

27. Bacon in one letter speaks of the solitude " which is the base-court of adversity," in which he has " often remembered " the Spanish proverb, " Love without end has no end " (LIFE, vii, 335). Shakespeare in RICHARD II puns on the " Base court, where kings grow base " ; and in CYMBELINE (IV, ii, 90) says :

I have heard you say
Love's reason's without reason.

" This," says Dr. Theobald, " is evidently a variation on the Spanish proverb." It is simply another proverb of the same very common cast, and the twofold parallel is a rope of sand.

28. Bacon has the phrases " no brewer of holy water in Court," and " no dealer in holy water " (LIFE, i, 200 ; iii, 297). " The same *very curious phrase* occurs in LEAR," says Dr. Theobald :

> O, uncle, court holy water in a dry house is better than rain out o' door. (III, ii, 10.)

For Dr. Theobald, every obsolete idiom is very curious. Yet he cites the " Clarendon note " on the passage to the effect that " Court holy water " was a phrase from the French. That is to say, it was a current tag. From the variorum edition Dr. Theobald might have learned that it is so given in Cotgrave's Dictionary, 1611, and in Florio's Italian Dictionary, 1598, under the word *Mantellizare*. The " coincidence " thus stands for absolutely nothing.

29. Bacon in a speech in Parliament said : " Let not this Parliament end like a Dutch feast, in salt meats, but like an English feast in sweet meats " (LIFE, iii, 215). Shakespeare in RICHARD II (I, iii, 67), has :

> Lo, as at English feasts, so I regreet
> The daintiest last to make the end most sweet.

On the face of it, Bacon's remark was likely to have been made a million times a year in England ! Shakespeare does not mention the Dutch usage ; but, as Dr. Theobald observes, he *might* have added another line in RICHARD II :

> (Not like Dutch feasts, that end with salted meat.)

And this is a " coincidence " !

30. Bacon writes to Villiers that in regard to his friend he is " covetous " only to take away care from him (LIFE, vi, 115). Henry V says he is

> not covetous for gold . . .
> But if it be a sin to covet honour,
> I am the most offending soul alive.
>
> *Henry V*, IV, iii, 24.

So Bacon evidently wrote Shakespeare ! By the same token he wrote Ben Jonson :

> We here protest it, and are covetous
> Posterity should know it, we are mortal.
>
> *Sejanus*, i, 2.

31. Inasmuch as Bacon writes that " Fame hath swift wings, specially that which hath black feathers " (LIFE, v, 248), and Shakespeare in Sonnet 70 has :

> The ornament of beauty is suspect;
> A crow that flies in heaven's sweetest air,

" Bacon is interpreted by Shakespeare." I spare comment.

32. Dr. Theobald claims to find " the same picture " in Bacon's reference to men's holding offices after their powers are decayed and Shakespeare's allusions to (1) a disregarded *old tale* (WINTER'S TALE, V, ii, 67 ; JOHN IV, ii, 18 ; VENUS AND ADONIS, 841). There is absolutely no coincidence or parallel whatever.

33. For once Dr. Theobald does find a parallel. In HAMLET we have the lines (I, ii, 11) :

> As 'twere with a defeated joy,
> With an auspicious and a dropping eye,
> With mirth in funeral and with dirge in marriage ;

and in THE WINTER'S TALE (V, ii, 80) :

> She hath one eye declined for the loss of her husband ; another elevated that the oracle was fulfilled ;

while Bacon speaks of Perkin Warbeck (WORKS, vi, 192) " beginning to squint one eye upon the crown and another upon the sanctuary " ; and of Walpoole in the Squire conspiracy, as " carrying a waking and a waiting eye." As this common employment of a common trope is to prove identity of authorship, let us once more note in part the extent of Bacon's production :

> Avert his [Apollo's] fervent eye,
> And turn his temperate.
>
> Chapman's trans. of *Iliad* (1598), i, 62–3.

In which time came upon the Stage a woman clothed with a white garment, on her head a pillar, double-faced, the foremost face fair and smiling, the other behind black and lowring.

> Gascoigne, *Jocasta*, Dumb Shew before Act V.

As if you stuck one eye into my breast,
And with the other took my whole dimensions.

> Jonson, *The Sad Shepherd*, iii.

They have wont to give their hands and their hearts together ; but we think it a finer grace to look asquint, our hands looking one way and our hearts another.

> Cornwallis, *Essays*, 1601.

Her face was changeable to every eye ;
One way look'd ill, another graciously.

> Chapman, Third Sestiad of *Hero and Leander*, 1598.

As if she had two souls, one for the face,
One for the heart, and that they shifted place.

> *Id. ib.*

His eyes were seats for mercy and for law,
Favour in one, and Justice in the other.

> Greene, *A Maiden's Dream*, 1591, st. 9.

34. " Shakespeare's phrase ' out of joint,' which has passed into current speech, *so that its singular and original character is forgotten*, is used more than once both in Shakespeare and Bacon." So writes Dr. Theobald. I invite the attention of rational readers to the frame of mind of a writer who, knowing practically nothing of pre-Shakespearean literature, affirms that such a phrase as " out of joint " was " original " about the year 1600.

When such a thing can be written, and pass into a second edition, it seems necessary to demonstrate the folly of the assertion. Any one noting that Hamlet uses not only the phrase " out of joint," but " disjoint and out of frame " (i, 2) ; that Macbeth says " let the frame of things disjoint " (iii, 2) ; and that " out of frame " occurs also in LOVE'S LABOUR'S LOST (iii, 1); would realise that " out of joint " and " out of frame " were equivalent phrases in ordinary use—unless indeed the Baconian should decide that Bacon invented both. As Mr. Crawford has pointed out, both are pre-Elizabethan, even in the moral sense :

> To thy correccion now haaste and hie,
> For thou hast been out of joynt al to longe.
>
> Hoccleve's Works (1415) ; Furnivall's rep. p. 14.
>
> The londe he bryngeth out of frame,
> Agaynst all goddis forbod.
>
> Roye, Rede me and be nott Wrothe, 1528.

Add :

> In this worlde that we do name
> There is none so farre out of frame.
>
> Idem.

The latter phrase, which Brandes surprisingly describes as a " curiously poetic expression " in HAMLET,[1] occurs in Latimer :

> That the King's majesty, when he cometh to age; will see a redress of these things so out of frame.
>
> First Sermon before Edward VI ; Dent's rep. p. 86.

Brandes traces it from Shakespeare to Florio's Montaigne. The idea is common in Daniel, who uses this and the figure of " joint " with a frequency which indicates the absolute normality of the metaphor.   Compare :

> How things at full do soon wex out of frame.
>
> The Civil Wars, 1595, B. i, st. 8.
>
> As if the frame of all disjoynted were.
>
> Id. B. iv, st. 10.
>
> The broken frame of this disjoynted State.
>
> A Panegyricke Congratulatory to the King, 1603, St. 41.
>
> An addition to the frame
> Of this great work, squar'd fitly to the same.
>
> Id. St. 43.
>
> Which out of judgment best accommodates
> These joynts of rule.
>
> Id. St. 44.
>
> The model of this frame.
>
> Id. St. 45.
>
> [Nothing]
> Could once disjoint the couplements whereby
> It [the frame] held together in just Symetry.
>
> Id. ib.

[1] William Shakespeare, 1898, ii, 17.

And be so clos'd as all the joynts may grow
Together firm in due proportion.

Id. St. 60.

And lay the frame of Order and Content.

Id. St. 61.

This frame of pow'r.

Id. St. 63.

And as for thee, thou huge and mighty frame,
That stands corrupted so with time's despight.

Id. Musophilus, 1602–3, ll. 379–80.

Shall, with a sound incountring shock, disjoynt
The fore-contrived frame.

Id. ib. ll. 870–1.

Such phrases as " out of course," " out of order," " out of form," " out of square," " out of rank," are of course equally common. In the literal sense, " out of joint " was in everyday-use :

When a member that was out of joynt is set in again.
Sidney and Golding's trans. of De Mornay, 1587.
Ed. 1604, p. 7.

Doubtless, Apollo's axle-tree is cracked,
Or aged Atlas' shoulder out of joint.
Marlowe and Nashe's Dido (1594), iv, 1.

Not that he had put out of joynt, or lamed
His arme, his legge, or any other part.
Harington, trans. of Orlando Furioso, 1591, i, 66.

But the metaphor too was in dramatic use :

This resolution, then, hath set his wits in joint again.
Chapman, The Widow's Tears, ii, 3.

Dr. Theobald believed that Bacon-Shakespeare invented the very phrase " household words." Such faith, but no other, can conceive either as inventing " out of joint." The idea is in Chaucer before Hoccleve :

That the linage of mankinde . . . be departed and unjoined from his welle.
Boece, B. V, pr. iii, end.

What discordable cause hath to-rent and unjoined the binding of things.
Id. B. V, Met. iii, beginning.

The phrase, in short, lies at the roots of English " dis-

2 G

course." If it had been argued that the *metaphor* was new in Bacon's day, one could have set down the claim as one more instance of ordinary Baconian assumption. But the idea that the *phrase* was then originated tells of a degree of credulous folly that excludes the very faculty of judgment.

35. After the last-noted item, the reader is not unprepared to learn that Dr. Theobald finds significance in the fact that Bacon sometimes uses the phrase " money in his purse "; that Iago says " Put money in thy purse "; and that the expression repeatedly recurs in Shakespeare. A child might realise that such phrases were likely to be in habitual use ; and a reference to Mr. Hart's edition of OTHELLO will give the reader two coeval instances :

> No arts and professions are now set-by and in request but such as bring pence into our purses.
> > Holland's tr. of Pliny, proem. to Bk. xiv.
>
> Get money ; still get money, boy, &c.
> > Jonson, *Every Man In*, ii, 3.

If we turn to a later play of Jonson's, we find three instances of the phrase in one scene :

> Has still money in his purse, and will pay all.
>
> He has ever money in his purse.
>
> Thou hast money in thy purse still.
> > *Bartholomew Fair*, ii, 1.

Nashe (WORKS, ed. McKerrow, i, 163) has the occult remark that " He that hath no money in his purse " must dine on credit—a scientific truth which may be gathered from Hoccleve in the previous century.

The Baconians will presumably argue that Jonson was lending to the Bohemians of his FAIR a coinage from the " Baconian Mint." We can but speculate as to what they make of the idea when it occurs a hundred and fifty years earlier :

> And loke ye ringewele in your purs,
> For ellys your cawse may spede the wurs.
> > *Coventry Mysteries*, c. 1450.   Sh. Soc. ed. p. 131 ;

and in the morality MANKIND, dating *circa* 1475 :

> What is in thy purse ? thou art a stout fellow.
>
> Farmer's rep. p. 22.

The simple sentiment in question was also put in rhyme
by Dame Juliana Berners or another in the fifteenth
century, in the epilogue to her treatise on Hunting, with
its refrain :

> Ever gramercy mine own purse.

It is only the plain necessity of disproving, by chapter
and verse, the most childish assumptions on the Baconian
side that can keep one in countenance in thus demonstrating that the most elementary notions existed in English
literature before the reign of James I.

36. Bacon has the phrase " If time give his Majesty
the advantage, what needeth precipitation to extreme
remedies ? " (LIFE, v, 379). " Surely," says Dr. Theobald,
" this is simply a variation of the more condensed
expression of the same maxim :

> Advantage is a better soldier than rashness."
>
> *Henry V*, III, vi, 128.

It is ; and " surely " the same thing must have been said,
in similar words, by ten thousand men in every war !
" This *almost technical* use of the word *advantage*," adds
Dr. Theobald, " as applied to time, is distinctly Baconian.
It is equally Shakespearean "—citing RICHARD III, IV,
i, 49 ; CYMBELINE, IV, i, 12 ; VENUS AND ADONIS, 129.
It is the normal force of the word in Tudor English in
Bacon's day :

> Had you come one to one, or made assault
> With reasonable advantage.
>
> Heywood, *Fair Maid of the West.* iv, 1.

> Conditions such as it liketh him to offer them which hath them
> in the narrow straits of advantage.
>
> Hooker, *Eccles. Polity*, pref. ch. ii, §4.

> He should never take her at the like advantage.
>
> Gascoigne, *Adventure of Master F. J.* Works, ed.
> Cunliffe, i, 435.

Hold our enemies still at advantage.

> Gosson, *Schoole of Abuse*, Arber's rep. p. 46.

Upon a good and a military advantage.

> Middleton, *Blurt, Master-Constable* (1602) i, 1.

Backward he bears for more advantage now.

> Daniel, *Civil Wars*, B. iii, St. 77.

Make imperfections their advantages.

> *Id.* B. iii, St. Sh.

In extremes advantage hath no time.

> Kyd, *The Spanish Tragedy*, iii, 13.

Watch you 'vantages ?

> *Id. Soliman and Perseda*, 1, 2.

At his best advantage stole away.

> *Id.* i, 3.

For if the wife her at advantage take . . .

> Higgins' add. to *Mirrour for Magistrates*, 1575.
> Rep. of 1810, p. 68.

38. " The curious expression *play prizes* occurs once in Shakespeare," says Dr. Theobald, citing TITUS, I, i, 399. And it occurs thrice in Bacon ! I know nothing more " curious " in the Elizabethan age than Dr. Theobald's untiring acclamation of its household words when he chances to find them in both Bacon and " Shakespeare," never dreaming of looking further. " Play his prize," which is found only in TITUS among the plays ascribed to Shakespeare, occurs a score of times in the plays and tales of Shakespeare's day :

Getting up and down like the usher of a fence school about to play his prize.

> Greene, *A Quip for an Upstart Courtier*, Works, xi, 221.

Why should not we, ladies, play our prizes, I pray ?

> Jonson, *Cynthia's Revels*, v, 2.

If I play not my prize.

> Massinger, *A New Way to pay Old Debts*, iv, 2.

When I do play my prizes in print.

> Nashe, *Have with you to Saffron Walden* ; Works, iii, 128.

Room, let my prize be played.

> Dekker, *The Honest Whore*, Pt. II, v, 2.

Nay, let me alone to play my master's prize.

> *Id.* Pt. I, iv, 3.

To play at the wooden rapier and dagger at the end of a maister's prize.

Id. Seven Deadly Sins, Arber's rep. p. 2.

Not so nimble at their prizes of wit.

The Witch of Edmonton, i, 2.

As may be learned from Steevens' note to the MERRY WIVES, I, i, 295, the *practice* was as familiar in the London of that day as cricket in ours. Thus illustrated, the argument attains to " curious'st," as the Elizabethans would say. As TITUS is non-Shakespearean, it would appear in this connection that Bacon wrote pretty well all the Elizabethan plays *but* Shakespeare's.

39. " Starting holes is another curious phrase," continues Dr. Theobald. " Curiouser and curiouser." *See above*, p. 277.

40. Bacon has the phrase " as we now say, putting tricks upon them." Essay OF CUNNING (1612). On this passage Dr. Abbott remarked that " The word ' now ' seems to apologize for the new-fashioned colloquial phrase, *put tricks on*." It is used by Stephano in the TEMPEST (II, ii, 62), and by the clown in ALL'S WELL, IV, v, 63. " As neither of these plays were known till 1623," comments Dr. Theobald, " there is no reason for giving the phrase an earlier date than the Essay."

We are thus asked to believe that Bacon invented in 1612 the trivial phrase " put tricks on," and introduced it with the formula " *as we now say*,"—putting it at the same time into a play, to bear out his remark ! The literary *fact* is, as Mr. Crawford points out, that Jonson uses the expression in both versions of his EVERY MAN IN HIS HUMOUR, so that it was already current in 1596. And Jonson further uses it twice in CATILINE; again in THE NEW INN, and also in BARTHOLOMEW FAIR.

.   .   .   .

I have now followed Dr. Theobald *seriatim* through forty of his eighty " Echoes and Correspondencies." The remainder I shall merely sample.

41. " Bacon more than once uses the curious verb *stage* " (*e.g.* Letter to Buckingham, LIFE, vii, 151). So Shakespeare, M. FOR M., I, i, 68, ANTHONY, V, ii, 216.

The word is a perfectly normal formation of early English and the Tudor period, like " horsed," " housed," " shipped." It is used by Stow in his SURVEY OF LONDON, 1598 :

To stay and behold the disguisings and other disports . . showed in the great hall, which was richly hanged with arras, and staged about on both sides.

Morley's rep. p. 419.

and by Hall in his Chronicle (p. 596) :

The Kyng . . . caused his great chambre at Greenwiche to be staged.

43.[1] In the light of the foregoing comparisons, there is a special piquancy in Dr. Theobald's proclamation that the phrase " gross and palpable " " is one of Bacon's many contributions to verbal currency. It was a new coin when it issued from his affluent mint." *See above*, p. 276, as to its newness.

45. An instance is actually made of the title " Narcissus, or Self-Love," in Bacon's WISDOM OF THE ANCIENTS, and the reference to Narcissus and self-love in LUCRECE, 264. Narcissus *was* " Self-Love " for all who knew anything of mythology. It never occurs to a Baconian to wonder why the plays always make the ordinary use of mythological names and tales, and never hint at those interpretations or allegorisings of them which make up the bulk of Bacon's WISDOM OF THE ANCIENTS.

48. Bacon notes the observation of " some of the ancients " that " marigolds, tulippas, pimpernel, *and indeed most flowers* do open or spread their leaves abroad when the sun shineth serene and fair ; and again (in some part) close . . . when the sky is overcast " (SYL. SYL. 493). Shakespeare refers thrice to this property *in the*

[1] I follow Dr. Theobald's numbers. His instances grow more and more futile as they proceed.

marigolds only. And we are asked to infer identity of authorship ! On this principle, Bacon wrote Greene's MENAPHON, where the relation of the marigold to the sun is the theme of a whole paragraph (Arber's rep. p. 59).

50. Shakespeare has " out of tune and harsh " (HAMLET, III, i, 166) ; and Bacon has " *duras et absonas* " (NOVUM ORGANUM, i, 28). Dr. Theobald does not say whether he thinks Bacon invented this phrase. As Mr. Crawford points out, " out of tune," in the moral sense, occurs in Roye's REDE ME AND BE NOT WROTHE (1528). It must have been an extremely common trope. In Sidney and Golding's translation of De Mornay (1587) we have

Our minde [must] bee brought from . . . jarring into right tune. Which is a token that our mind is out of tune even of its own accord, seeing that it needeth so many precepts to set it in tune agayne.

Ed. 1604, p. 282.

And in the drama :

Whose voice, if it should utter her thoughts, would make the tune of a heart out of tune.

Lilly, *Midas*, iii, 3.

52. Bacon quotes Martial to the effect " that accident is many times more subtle than foresight, and over-reacheth expectation " (LIFE, v, 276), which corresponds to Hamlet's " praised be rashness for it " speech (HAMLET, V, ii, 6).

As I have elsewhere shown (MONTAIGNE AND SHAKESPEARE, 2nd ed. p. 42 *sq*.), Shakespeare found this and much other matter lying to his hand in Florio's translation of Montaigne.

54. Dr. Theobald seriously argues that these lines in ANTONY AND CLEOPATRA (V, ii, 172) :

Or I shall show the cinders of my spirit
Through the ashes of my chance,

were not written till the issue of the folio in 1623, because Bacon wrote " the sparks of my affection . . . under the ashes of my fortune " in a letter in 1621 ! The figure was

in common use. In Sidney and Golding's translation of
De Mornay we have :

> Drawen some small sparkes of truth and wisdome of them as
> out of some little fire raked under a great heap of ashes.
>
> Pref. To the Reader.

Greene has :

> Having the sparks of honour fresh under the cinders of poverty.
>
> *Menaphon*, Arber's rep. p. 82.

The figure is as old as Chaucer :

> Looke how that fire of smale gleedes, that been almoost deede
> under ashen, wollen quike agayn when they been touched with
> brymstoon. Right so ire wol evermo quyken agayn when it is
> touched by the pride that is covered in mannes herte.
>
> *Parson's Tale : Sequitur de Ira.*
>
> Yet in our asshen olde is fyr y-reke.
>
> *Prologue to the Reeve's Tale.*

55. Bacon and Shakespeare both speak of money and
worldly goods as " trash." *Ergo— !* Fifty preachers and
playwrights had done so before them. *E.g.* :

> Therefore must I bid him provide trash, for my master is no
> friend without money.
>
> Greene, *James IV*, iii, 1.
>
> Kneel hinds to trash : me let bright Phœbus swell
> With cups full flowing from the Muses' well.
>
> Jonson, *Poetaster*, I. i. (Rendering of the Ovidian
> motto of Shakespeare's *Venus and Adonis*).

59. Bacon writes hyberbolically to the King that unless
his Majesty works a miracle " I shall still be a lame man
to do your service " if others are " put in before me."
And Shakespeare has :

> So I, made lame by fortune's dearest spite. (Son. 37.)

and again :

> Speak of my lameness and I straight will halt. (Son. 89.)

Therefore Bacon wrote the Sonnets !

61. Bacon speaks of " the wrong of time " (ADVANCE-
MENT, I, viii, 6) ; and so does Shakespeare (Sonnet 19).
It was a current trope :

Books, tractations, and monuments, which hitherto, by iniquity of time, could not be contrived.

> Foxe, Ep. Ded. to 2nd ed. of *Acts and Monuments*, 1570.

Time's despight.

> Daniel, *Musophilus*, 1603, 1. 380.

Wicked Tyme.

> Spenser, *Faerie Queene*, III, vi, 39.

Wicked Time.

> *Id. ib.* IV, ii, 33.

63 and 64. Bacon speaks of Cæsar as a stag at bay ; Antony says, " How wast thou bay'd " ; and Bacon speaks of the *Revenge* in the sea-fight as " like a stag among hounds at the bay " (LIFE, vii, 491). Again, Bacon has " Truth prints Goodness " ; and Prospero in the TEMPEST calls Caliban a slave " which any *print* of goodness will not take." I spare the reader comment and confutation.

66. Bacon and Shakespeare both use the expression " pray in aid." They well might ! As the commentator Hanmer pointed out a hundred and fifty years ago, " *Praying in aid* is a term used for a petition made in a court of justice for the calling in of help from another that hath no interest in the cause in question."

67. Bacon uses the expression " to be retrograde " (LIFE, i, 357), as does Shakespeare (HAMLET, I, ii, 114 ; ALL'S WELL, I, i, 210). An " unusual expression " Dr. Theobald calls it, as usual. It was a common term in astrology, current in general literature :

Ramp up thy genius ; be not retrograde.

> Jonson, *Poetaster*, 1601 (parodying Marston, who had used the word).

Let's be retrograde.

> *Id. Cynthia's Revels*, 1600, v. 2.

You must be retrograde.

> *Id. ib.*

Till all religion become retrograde.

> Daniel, *Civil Wars*, B. vi, st. 36.

Or in our birth the stars were retrograde.

> *The Play of Stucley*, 1605, 1. 2098.

70. Bacon and Shakespeare both use the expression "*stand in* (or *within*) *his danger*" (HISTORY OF HENRY VII; Works, vi, 36; MERCHANT OF VENICE, IV, i, 180). *Ergo*—!

This is one of the most futile of Dr. Theobald's many futile citations. The phrase, to begin with, is as old as Chaucer.

> In daunger hadde he at his ownë gyse
> The yongë girlës of the diocyse.
> *Prologue to the Canterbury Tales*, 663–4 (665–6).

The old French word meant "power, dominion"; and this is its sense in the lines:

> Narcisus was a bachelere
> That Love had caught in his daungere.
> *Romaunt of the Rose*, 1469–70.
> This world is all in his daungere.
> *Id.* 1049.

We find it in the MORTE DARTHUR:

> Then said the knight unto Arthur, thou art in my danger whether me list to save thee or slay thee.
> B. I, ch. xxi;

in Fabyan's CHRONICLE, Hen. III, ann. 38:

> How they passed out of the Kynges dannger, I finde not;

in the Interlude of CALISTO AND MELEBEA (*circa* 1530):

> Out of his daunger will I be at lyberte.
> Malone Soc. rep. l. 33;

in Tyndale's PATHWAY UNTO THE HOLY SCRIPTURE (Parker Soc. ed. p. 9):

> In sin, and in danger to death and hell;[1]

and in Bale's Interlude of JOHN THE BAPTIST (1538):

> If ye mynde therefor, of God to avoyde the daunger.
> Rep. in Harl. Misc. ed. 1808, i, 208.

It continued to be common:

> Betray his fame and safety
> To the law's danger and your father's justice.
> Chapman, *Revenge for Honour*, iii, 1.

[1] The Parker Soc. editor notes that Bishop Fisher has:— "What suppose ye that Luther would do, if he had the Pope's holiness in his danger?"

Had brought herself in danger of lawe through ignorance.
> *Brief Discourse of the Murder of Saunders*, 1573, in
> Simpson's *School of Shakespeare*, ii, 225.

Against the pride of Tarquin, from whose danger
None great in love, in counsel, or opinion,
Can be kept safe.
> Heywood, *Rape of Lucrece*, ii, 1.

Not to run
Within the danger of the Gods.
> Chapman, trans. of *Iliad*, B. vi, 161.

71. " Bacon has a trick of using the word *twenty* to express a large and indefinite number " ; and so has Shakespeare. It is most true ! And the trick was in universal use. It was ordinary in Chaucer's time :

In twenty manere coude he tripp and daunce.
> *The Miller's Tale*, l. 142.

And let me slepe, a twenty devel way.
> *Id.* l. 527.

It was normal on the stage :

Comparing it to twenty gracious things.
> Kyd, *Soliman and Perseda*, i, 2.

I open Bishop Hooper at random and find :

It is a ceremony instituted by bishops more than twenty.
> *Answer to the Bishop of Winchester* (1546) Parker
> Soc. rep. p. 176.

The expletive given in Chaucer was current in Tudor times :

Come on, in twenty devils' way.
> *Gammer Gurton's Needle*, i, 3, end.

Dr. Theobald would presumably assign to Bacon the pseudo-Shakespearean play THE PURITAN, where (i, 2) Mary says :

Where I spend one tear for a dead father, I could give twenty kisses for a live husband ;

and likewise Chapman's continuation of Marlowe's HERO AND LEANDER :

A tender twenty-coloured eye.

A light of twenty hues.
> Third Sestiad.

Freckled with twenty colours.

> Fourth Sestiad.

Wanton Air in twenty sweet forms.

> Fifth Sestiad.

But there would still remain the problem of the Interlude
of THE TRIAL OF TREASURE, printed in 1567 :

> I holde twenty pounde it is Baalam's asse.
> I holde twenty pounde the knave is lousy.
>
> > Percy Soc. rep. pp. 6, 23 ;

and of the older Interlude, NATURE (*c.* 1490) :

> It would have done me more good
> Than twenty shillings of fee.
>
> > Farmer's *Lost Tudor Plays*, p. 110 ;

and of the Interlude REPUBLICA (1553) :

> Each one, twenty and twenty score
> Of that ye most long for.
>
> > *Id.* p. 182 ;

> Any time within these years twice twenty.
>
> > *Ib.* p. 214 ;

to say nothing of Ben Jonson's

> Ere you can call twenty.
>
> > *Bartholomew Fair*, Induc. 2nd sentence.

76. Dr. Theobald turns directly to Baconian account
the fact that Shakespeare makes Ford (MERRY WIVES,
II, ii, 223) speak of " a fair house built on another man's
ground," with a legalist application, while Bacon writes
of " another man's ground " *without* that application.
(*See above*, p. 40.) Be it noted that here the lawyer
does not talk law.

78. Bacon tells the hackneyed story of the ancient
musician [often, an artist] who said to a meddling king,
" God forbid that your fortune should be so bad as to
know these things better than I " ; and Shakespeare
partially reproduces the idea in dialogue (L. L. L. V, ii,
493). The story told by Bacon had been told *ad nauseam*
by previous sixteenth century writers.

Dr. Theobald actually alleges a " correspondency "
between Bacon's advice to a traveller to frequent good

company " of the nation where he travelleth " and
Rosalind's satirical advice to Jaques to " disable all the
benefits of your own country " !

In conclusion, after justly observing that " all these "
illustrations of his " might be almost indefinitely multiplied," Dr. Theobald undertakes to show that such
every-day colloquialisms as " it is strange," " it is wonderful," " it is certain," " I am very sure," " surely,"
" out of question," " to say the truth," " questionless,"
" out of doubt," are peculiar to Bacon and Shakespeare.
" So far as my reading of Elizabethan literature goes,"
he declares, doubtless with perfect truth, " the same
phrases, habitually employed, are not to be found in any
other writer."

This thesis is perhaps the uttermost mark of Dr.
Theobald's aberration. It stands for an amount of
inattention to pre-Shakespearean English literature that
seems impossible of attainment by an educated man.
Even in reading Shakespeare, Dr. Theobald must have
seen Falstaff's phrase, " A rascally yea-forsooth knave " ;
and in reading the New Testament he must have noted
the expression " Verily." Any excursion into Elizabethan
drama would have revealed to him that " forsooth " and
" verily " are types of a number of terms of asseveration
in constant use in common talk. If he had begun his
investigation with Chaucer, he might have noted the
perpetual use of " certes," " trewely," " soothly," " for-
sothe," " certeyn," " in good sothe," " verrayment," and
so on. In verse, such terms might conceivably be line-
padding ; but in Chaucer's prose translation of Boethius
they occur to the number of at least twenty in the first
book ; and in the prose TALE OF MELIBEUS they are still
more frequent—eleven times in two paragraphs (§§ 14, 15).
The usage is continuous. In the old REVELATION OF THE
MONK OF EVESHAM, first printed about 1482, " sothly "
and " trewly " occur eight times in the three short

opening chapters. Thus in English as in other tongues the habit of emphasis, exclamation, and asseveration was established in literature as in talk long before the age of Bacon and Shakespeare. And in their day it remained normal ; one can hardly open a Tudor book without seeing a multitude of such instances as these :

And Plato verily was of this opinion . . .
> Holland's trans. of Plutarch's *Moralia* (Dent's Selection, p. 4).

And verily Aristotle used these principles and grounds.
> *Id. ib.*

And verily the poet Homer most excellently expresseth.
> *Id.* p. 5.

And yet verily it is reported also of Zeno.
> *Id.* p. 6.

> (Four instances in three successive pages.)

This verily is the chief cause that hath encouraged me . . .
> Ralph Robinson, Ep. Ded. to trans. of More's *Utopia*, Dent's rep. p. 4.

Of a surety that thing could I [not] have performed.
> *Id.* More's pref. epist. p. 7.

If you cannot remember the thing, then surely I will write.
> *Id. ib.* p. 9.

And I think verily it shall be well done.
> *Id. ib.*

Howbeit, to say the very truth, I am not yet fully determined . . .
> *Id. ib.* p. 10.

Cuthbert Tunstall, a man doubtless out of comparison.
> *Id. Utopia*, p. 13.

What by his natural wit, and what by daily exercise, surely he had few fellows.
> *Id.* pp. 12–13.

> (Seven instances in seven successive pages.)

As I suppose. As God judge me.
> Sir Thomas Elyot, " Proheme " to the *Governour*.

Wherefore undoubtedly. . . . Id. B. i, c. 2.

And I verily do suppose. *Id.* c. iv.

And yet no man will deny. *Id. ib.*

I dare affirm. . . . As I might say. . . . But verily mine intent. . . . c. 8.

And surely. . . . c. 9. And what doubt is there. . . . c. 10.

And surely. . . . c. 11. Surely if a nobleman do thus. . . . c. 11. Surely, as I have diligently marked. . . . c.12. Verily. c.12, c.13. Verily. . . . Undoubtedly. . . . To say the truth. . . . Undoubtedly. . . . As I might frankly say. . . . (The last five instances in two pages.)

Dr. Theobald's argument on this head is of a piece with Mrs. Pott's amazing attribution to Bacon of the invention of the most ordinary forms of accost in Elizabethan England. As to that see Mr. Crawford's essay on " The Bacon-Shakespeare Question."

.   .   .   .

In other chapters, going about to connect Bacon with Shakespeare by other " echoes and correspondencies," Dr. Theobald claims to find proofs of community of authorship by bringing together ideas which in his opinion are complementary. For instance (ch. x, p. 179) he notes how Bacon harps on the idea that "money is like muck, not good except it be spread," and then cites from Shakespeare (COR. II, ii, 128) the phrase, " As they were the common muck of the world." Whereon we have this gloss :—" The only comment on this which I have been able to find is a suggestion that muck is equivalent to *vilia rerum*. The poet certainly intended to suggest a good deal more than this, but the rich suggestiveness of the passage cannot be easily brought out if Bacon's use of the word is not remembered." This is of course sheer fiction : the phrase of Cominius simply means, " as if they were dirt." But supposing Shakespeare *had* meant to convey an implication about muck = manure, what ground is there for bringing in Bacon ? As Mr. Crawford has remarked, the rustic saw about muck being good only when spread abroad was already current in ballad poetry (GERNUTUS, in Percy's Reliques) and on the stage (Jonson, EVERY MAN OUT, iii, 2) ; and " muck," for " money " or " riches," was a universal figure :

Worldly muck.

Wiclif, *Against the Order of Friars*, c. 48.

To get falsely muck to Antichrist's convent.   *Id. ib.* c. 19.

Winning of stinking muck.

Id. ib. c. 26.

The people give them [the friars] more dirt than is needful or profitable.

Id. ib. c. 29.

Worldly muck.

> J. Redford, Interlude of *Wit and Science,* Farmer's *Lost Tudor Plays,* p. 138.

Our mucky money.

> Editorial pref. to Latimer's Second Sermon before King Edward, end.

The wicked muck and mammon of the world.

> Hooper, *Declaration of Christ and his Office,* Works, Parker Soc. ed. p. 43.

For glory vain, nor yet for muck.

> Bauldwin, *Treatise of Moral Philosophy,* ed. 1600, B. i, c. 19.

Shakespeare uses the Baconian simile neither in the case of money nor in that of manure.   Jonson uses the proverb about manure ; the balladist partly applies it to things moral.   Surely Dr. Theobald's proper conclusion is that Bacon wrote the ballad of GERNUTUS THE JEW, and Jonson's plays !

As to Dr. Theobald's wonder over finding in LUCRECE and elsewhere the ancient sentiment about griefs being lightened by the knowledge that they are shared, I refer the reader to Mr. Crawford's comments.   Dr. Theobald, proceeding by the method of ignorance, announces that the Latin proverb *Solamen miseris socios habuisse doloris* [or *malorum*], which is found in Marlowe's FAUSTUS, *published* in 1604, " was probably invented by the author of FAUSTUS "—that is, in Dr. Theobald's system of mythology, Bacon.   " How it came to appear in LUCRECE," he adds, " is an enigma which awaits its solution."   The enigma is of Dr. Theobald's own making. As his previous extracts show, the sentiment occurs in a whole series of the Shakespearean plays ; and if he had but had a little knowledge of previous literature, he would have known it to be an established moral commonplace. Not only is the idea expressed in Kyd's CORNELIA (ii, 226-7) in 1594, but, as Mr. Crawford notes, the Latin line occurs in Greene's MENAPHON, 1589, and in Lodge's ROSALIND, 1590 ; and the English equivalent is given in EUPHUES, 1579 (Arber's rep. p. 96). It is apparently a line of Renaissance poetry, in part contradiction of Cicero's *Levis est consolatio ex miseria aliorum* (AD. FAM., VI, iii, 4) and Seneca's *Malevoli solacii genus est turba miserorum* (DE CONSOL. AD MARC., xii, 5). But in the Senecan tragedy we have *Dulce mœrenti populus dolentum* (TROADES, 1014) ; and an old SYNOPSIS COMMUNIUM LOCORUM (1742, c. 70) gives under the head of the *Solamen miseris* phrase a series of other approximations. The line is given as a standing quotation by M. Neander, ETHICE VETUS ET SAPIENS VETERUM LATINORUM, Lipsiae, 1590, p. 411.[1] Only a Baconian could for a moment suppose that such a saying had been left for Bacon to invent. The *English* form of the saying was already a current proverb in the time of Chaucer, who reproduces it again and again :

For wel sit it, the sothe for to seyne
A woful night to han a drery fere.
                    Troilus and Criseyde, i, 2.

Men seyn, to wrecche is consolacioun
To have an-other felawe in his peyne.
                    Id. i, 102.

For unto shrewes Ioye it is and ese
To have hir felawes in peyne and disese.
                    Chanoun Yemannes Tale, 193-4.

Latimer in turn has :

It is *consolatio miserorum* : it is comfort of the wretched to have company.
        Third Sermon before Edward VI, Dent's rep. p. 116.

And Dr. Theobald finds it an " enigma " that the sentiment should occur in LUCRECE !

---

[1] See W. F. H. King's *Classical and Foreign Quotations*, 1904. Mr. King gives a substantially equivalent passage from Thucydides, vii, 75.

I will not carry the " quest " further. It has its distressing as well as its ridiculous side. These divagations of men utterly possessed by a foregone conclusion, blind to all countervailing evidence, hypnotised by a hallucination, tell of an " expense of spirit " in error that is not to be contemplated without discomfort. It is the desire to minimise the amount of such aberration in future that has sustained me, as I trust it may do some readers, through the tedium of a detailed confutation.

CHAPTER XI

PROSE STYLE IN SHAKESPEARE AND BACON

IT is perhaps unnecessary to argue, even as against Baconians, that every powerful or original writer, in any long series of writings, must betray some peculiarities of diction, phraseology, clause formation, and so on, which are as special to him as are the technical methods of any artist to his work, or the gait, accent, or intonation of each of us to himself. The Baconians actually subsume this, however vaguely, in their attempts, hereinbefore discussed, to detect Baconian phraseology in the plays. But, of course, they have attempted no deeper investigation.[1] The idea of comparing the general movement and rhythm of the abundant prose in the plays with those of Bacon's signed writings is not one which would naturally occur to critics conscious of no initial difficulty in supposing that the Plays and the Essays came from the same hand.

Let the open-minded reader, however, take the trouble to compare the way of the prose in the plays with that of the prose of Bacon, and he will realise one more vital and irreducible divergence between the two bodies of work. In the course of the inquiry he may or may not detect such differences in the *verse* movement of certain of the plays as will make clear to him why some critics deny that those plays are wholly, or it may be at all,

[1] Mr. Appleton Morgan, of New York, who had a " New Theory " of his own about the authorship of the Plays (an adaptation of Delia Bacon's, that of a group of young nobles collaborating), avowed that " experts have proved that the styles of Bacon and Shakespeare are as far apart as the poles." (Cited by Mrs. Stopes, *The Bacon-Shakespeare Question Answered*, 2nd ed. 1889, p. 187.)

the work of the author of OTHELLO and MACBETH and
LEAR and CORIOLANUS.   But this is another issue.   What
is here proposed is a comparison of the prose of the unchallenged plays with that of the undisputed work of Bacon.

The first general proposition to be put in this connection
is that Shakespeare's prose is neither so masterly nor so
variously rhythmical as his blank verse.   To put the
matter bluntly I would say, *pace* certain panegyrists,
that Shakespeare is not a great writer of prose.   Greatness
in any mode of art is imputable only to exceptional power
or exceptional variety of execution.   Shakespeare's prose,
compared with that of great prose writers, cannot be
said to exhibit either.   And if any reader, before scanning
the data, be hastily moved to dispute the thesis, let him
first bethink himself how rarely, in literary history, have
men acquired enduring fame in both orders of expression.

Dryden was in his day reputed a great poet and a good
writer of prose : in the latter regard he stands higher
to-day than in the former ; but no one would to-day
put him in the highest rank of either art.   Dante wrote
both prose and verse ; no one ever ranked him with the
great prosists.   Milton has as high a twofold fame as
any ; but criticism to-day leans more and more to the
opinion that his finest English tractate, which is practically all that men read of his large prose output is rather
" a splendid example of mistaken prose," a rhetorical
tour de force, than a triumph of prose art comparable
with his poetry.   Wordsworth and Coleridge both wrote
some excellent prose and some perfect verse : both would
to-day be admitted by almost any good critic to have
produced much more of inferior verse than of good.
Shelley's prose never won much laud, though it has fine
qualities, and some warm admirers.   Byron and Keats
wrote letters and notes which certainly exhibit plenty
of prose power ; but neither ever attempted a prose
work.   Tennyson and Browning—Tennyson in particular
—hardly attempted to write prose save by way of jottings.

In all literature we shall find but some half-dozen great or fine poets (apart from Milton, Wordsworth and Coleridge, dealt with above) whose prose notably competes in fame with their verse. They are : Goethe, Heine, Poe, Leopardi, Hugo, and Arnold ; and in not one of these cases, I think, is the poet's prose style, *as* style—matter apart—such as to win him rank as a great prose artist. Goethe's fame on that side is understood to be latterly in occultation among his countrymen. Hugo and Poe are (diversely) famous rather as writers of prose romances than as writers of prose ; Leopardi certainly lives less in his prose than in his poetry ; and even Arnold and Heine, charming prosists both—if we may so speak of Arnold, who strove with success to be something more than charming—are less eminent as prose artists than as poets.

But all this is perhaps an unnecessary if not a useless preamble to the demonstration that the prose of Shakespeare lacks the distinction, the artistic mastery, of his incomparable blank verse. His supremacy in that is unchallenged and unchallengeable. To read him beside his predecessors is to perceive a new departure in rhythmic progression. They rarely exceed the chance adventure of a single run-on line ; and it is at that stage that we see him begin, if we can be sure of seeing his handiwork in the opening scene of the COMEDY OF ERRORS, a work which he almost certainly did but elaborate or collaborate-in or re-fashion. Of verse as a continuous rhythm they had hardly a conception : they write verses rather than verse, matching unrhymed lines as they had been wont to match rhymed, and measuring lengths, at best, like men pacing a cage or a ship's deck. With Shakespeare there begins a new species of motion, differing from theirs almost as does that of the bird on the wing from its little runs of hops upon the sward. For an inorganic series of self-contained lines, we have a prolonged organic pulsation in which sense-pauses and clause-pauses can occur anywhere, the rhythm or measure becoming but as the bars in music, cognised only by the rhythmic sense. There is nothing to compare with it in previous English verse : only alongside of Shakespeare, in some of the best verse of Jonson, do we see the perception of the new possibilities beginning ; and what in Shakespeare seems to have been an effortless evolution is for Jonson visibly a matter of laborious construction. But there are compensations. As Ben notes in his DISCOVERIES : " Virgil's felicity left him in prose, as Tully's forsook him in verse." There is no such absolute cleavage in the case of either Shakespeare or Jonson, but there is a certain approximation to it.

As in ancient, so in modern literature, the possibilities of prose were discovered later than those of verse. As a purposely artistic instrument, it discernibly begins to act in English in the BOECE of Chaucer, a solitary performance no more improved upon, æsthetically speaking, than his verse, down to the Tudor age. Chaucer is in fact almost more noteworthy as a prose-writer, in respect of that performance, than as a writer of verse. As a poet he belongs to the age of simple and marked measures, which he handles with a skill that distinguishes him from his English contemporaries, but with a facility and fluency that as a rule exclude greatness of cadence. With his measures, the grand style was practically incompatible. But in his rendering of Boethius, albeit he draws on the French version to eke out his Latin,[1] he is visibly awake to the æsthetic effects of classic prose, and goes about, however experimentally, to produce in English something independently beautiful.

This judgment ostensibly conflicts with that of Ten Brink, who is quoted as saying that in the BOECE " we

---

[1] The inaccuracy of the translation, remarks a close student of Boethius, " is not that of an inexperienced Latin scholar, but rather of one who was no Latin scholar at all." H. F. Stewart, *Boethius : An Essay*, 1891, p. 226.

can see as clearly as in any work of the middle ages what a high cultivation is requisite for the production of a good prose."[1]   This is most true, as is Ten Brink's remark that the translation, " in the undeveloped state of prose composition so characteristic of that age," is " often quite unwieldy."[2]   But when Ten Brink goes on to grant that " there is no lack of warmth, and even of a certain colouring," and to quote a passage in illustration, he seems to me to have partly missed sight of the æsthetic success to which Chaucer does attain.   The passage he cites does not at all fully reveal it.   Where Chaucer was not clear as to the meaning of the original, and had to deal with complicated constructions, he naturally produces unwieldy sentences.   But at times even in following the prose, and often when he is rendering or, rather, abundantly paraphrasing the " metres "—from his version of one of which Ten Brink rightly quotes—he attains to a charm of cadence, of balanced movement, and of harmonious diction, which is in itself a new and specific enjoyment for those who read.   Richard Rolle of Hampole, his predecessor, who writes with the eager sincerity that counts for so much in good prose, never aimed at such æsthetic ends as these.   Let the lover of good prose— not necessarily identical with the lover of books and literary studies—compare with the following passages any English prose before the age of Shakespeare, and say whether they can be matched for beauty.   I modernise one or two words, and the spelling of some of the particles, in the interest of the slothful reader :

Blissful was the first age of men.   They held them apayed [3] with the meats that the true fields broughten forth.   They ne destroyed ne deceived not themselves with outrage.[4]   They were wont lightly to slake their hunger at even with acorns of oaks.   They could not mingle [5] the gift of Bacchus with the

[1] *Chaucer Studien*, p. 141, cited by Stewart, pp. 226–7.
[2] *History of English Literature*, Eng. trans. ii, 78–9.
[3] Contented.   [4] Excess.
[5] *Medle* in orig.

clear honey, nor could they mingle [1] the bright fleeces of the country of Syria with the venom of Tyre. . . . They slepen wholesome sleeps upon the grass, and dranken of the running waters, and layen under the shadows of the high pine trees. No guest or stranger carved yet the high sea with oars or ships ; nor had they yet seen new strands to leden merchandise into diverse countries. Then were the cruel clarions full hushed and full still.[2]

Here we have the successful use of the short sentence : brief pausation without haste or jolting : a quality not soon reached in prose, though it began in some such way, like verse. In the next book comes a good sample of a larger and more canorous movement :

It liketh me to show by subtle song, with slack [3] and delightable sound of strings, how that Nature, mighty, inclineth and flitteth [4] the governments of things ; and by which laws she, purveyable, keepeth the great world ; and how she, binding, restraineth all things by a bond that may not be unbound. . . . And the jangling bird that singeth on the high branches, and after is enclosed in a strait cage, although that the playing busy-ness of men giveth them honeyed drinks and large meets with sweet studies, yet natheless if thilke bird skipping out of her strait cage seeth the agreeable shadow of the woods, she defouleth [5] with her feet her shed meats, and seeketh mourning only the wood, and twittereth desiring the wood with her sweet voice.[6]

This is prose written with a new perception of the possibilities of cadence, of gracious movement without metre, of long breathing and restful fall. In yet another passage the quest for beauty is still more intent. It tells the tale of Orpheus :

The poet of Thrace, that whilom had right great sorrow for the death of his wife, after that he had maked by his weeply songs the woods moveable to run, and had maked the river to standen still, and had maked the harts and the hinds to join dreadless their sides to cruel lions, for to hearkenen his song, and had maked that the bear was not aghast of the hound which was pleased with his song, so when the most ardent love of his wife burned the entrails of his breast, not even the songs which

---

[1] *Medle* in orig. [2] B. ii, met. 5.
[3] Probably a copyist's error. [4] ? Fitteth.
[5] N.B. Not defileth. Defouleth = treadeth under foot.
[6] B. iii, met. 2.

had overcomen all things might assuage his lord. He plained
him of the heaven gods that were cruel to him. He went him to
the houses of hell, and there he tempered his blandishing songs
with resounding strings, and spake and sung in weeping all that
ever he had received and laved out of the noble wells of his
mother Calliope, the goddess. . . . Cerberus, the porter of hell
with his three heads, was caught and all abashed for the new
song. And the three goddesses, furies and vengeresses of felony,
that tormenten and aghasten the souls by annoy, woxen sorrowful
and sorry, and wepen tears for pity. Then was not the head of
Ixion tormented by the overthrowing wheel. And Tantalus,
that was destroyed by the madness [1] of long thirst, despiseth
the floods to drinken. [2]

The mere alternation of short sentences with long is
æsthetically calculated, with a sense of the repose it lends
to the whole movement. Chaucer had had vision of
what Whitman was later to call " the diviner heaven
of prose," in which freedom from rhymed metre could
mean a sweep and flow of speech that such verse could
not compass. Only an artist could have written so ;
and few were the artists who could so weave words even
in the sixteenth century. Bishop Hooper, in his DECLARA
TION OF CHRIST AND HIS OFFICE, shows some of the instinctive gift for balanced prose movement, being one
of the writers who prove that the controlled sentence
was not a discovery of the eighteenth century, but merely
a rediscovery, after an age of devotion to " voluble "
construction ; but only in Nashe, perhaps, among the
bellettrists of Shakespeare's day—Nashe, so wooden in
his verse—do we find a born writer of prose *as* prose ;
and only in his CHRIST'S TEARS OVER JERUSALEM, perhaps,
does he deliberately endeavour after a large and grave
harmony of artistic diction—in a not very sincere treatise.

In this endeavour, I repeat, Shakespeare did not share.
Master of the freest of verse-forms, he had not Chaucer's
motive to seek for beauty in prose ; but there is no reason
to suppose that his genius could there have attained
supremacy if he had sought it. Jonson's dramatic prose

---

[1] *Woodness* in orig.   [2] B. iii, met. 12.

often, and his non-dramatic prose always, is more true to the laws of prose-form, more easeful, more balanced, larger-limbed, than that of Shakespeare, yet felicitous and spontaneous.[1] True, the very purpose of writing prose for reading means a different technique : the prose of dramatic speech would miss its purpose if it ran to spacious or cadenced composition : even the crisp antitheses of Lilly defeat illusion. But Jonson's feeling for prose frequently asserts itself even in his plays, and Shakespeare in his dedications and in the " Argument " to LUCRECE shows no more concern for prose artistry, as apart from mere pointed statement, than in the prose of the plays. His faculty is first and last for verse.

And herein he differs radically from Bacon, whose scanty verse, *as* verse, is without spontaneity, but whose prose, though hardly ever written, so to speak, for prose's sake, is always magistral, long-breathed even when most expressly concise, easily spacious, effortless in its opulence. As an Elizabethan would say, it is *cothurnate*, yet it is always instinct with nervous strength. There is no æsthetic kinship or community between any of Shakespeare's prose and that of the ESSAYS, early or late, the ADVANCEMENT OF LEARNING, and the HISTORY OF HENRY SEVENTH. Let us take first a representative selection of prose passages from the plays, grave and gay, didactic and impassioned, philosophic and narrative. We shall find infinite verve and vivacity, fluency and fire ; an endless fecundity of phrase, image, and epithet ; but we shall not find a great architectonic prose.

Falstaff. Not a penny. I have been content, sir, you should lay my countenance to pawn : I have grated upon my good friends for three reprieves for you and your coach-fellow, Nym ; or else you had looked through the grate, like a geminy of baboons. I am damned in hell for swearing to gentlemen my friends you were good soldiers and tall fellows : and when

[1] " For his prose I must confess a deep and reverent partiality." J. A. Symonds, *Ben Jonson,* 1886, p. 61.

mistress Bridget lost the handle of her fan, I took't upon mine honour thou hadst it not.

Pistol. Didst thou not share ? hadst thou not fifteen pence ?

Falstaff. Reason, you rogue, reason : think'st thou I'll endanger my soul *gratis* ? At a word, hang no more about me, I am no gibbet for you :—go.—A short knife and a thong ;—to your manor of Pickt-hatch, go.—You'll not bear a letter for me, you rogue !—You stand upon your honour !—Why, thou unconfinable baseness, it is as much as I can do to keep the terms of my honour precise. I, I, I myself sometimes, leaving the fear of heaven on the left hand, and hiding mine honour in my necessity, am fain to shuffle, to hedge, and to lurch ; and yet you, rogue, will ensconce your rags, your cat-a-mountain looks, your red-lattice phrases, and your bold-beating oaths, under the shelter of your honour ! You will not do it, you ?

Merry Wives, Act II, Scene 2.

. . . .

Provost. A man that apprehends death no more dreadfully but as a drunken sleep ; careless, reckless, and fearless of what's past, present, or to come ; insensible of mortality, and desperately mortal.

Duke. He wants advice.

Provost. He will hear none ; he hath evermore had the liberty of the prison ; give him leave to escape hence, he would not : drunk many times a day, if not many days entirely drunk. We have very oft awaked him, as if to carry him to execution, and showed him a seeming warrant for it : it hath not moved him at all.

Duke. More of him anon. There is written in your brow, provost, honesty and constancy : if I read it not truly, my ancient skill beguiles me ; but in the boldness of my cunning, I will lay myself in hazard. Claudio, whom here you have warrant to execute, is no greater forfeit to the law than Angelo who hath sentenced him. To make you understand this in a manifested effect, I crave but four days' respite ; for the which you are to do me both a present and a dangerous courtesy.

Measure for Measure, Act IV, Scene 2.

. . . .

Beatrice. What should I do with him ? dress him in my apparel, and make him my waiting-gentlewoman ? He that hath a beard is more than a youth ; and he that hath no beard is less than a man : and he that is more than a youth is not for me ; and he that is less than a man I am not for him. Therefore, I will even take sixpence in earnest of the bearward, and lead his apes into hell.

Much Ado, Act II, Scene 1.

Beatrice. Not till God make men of some other metal than earth. Would it not grieve a woman to be over-mastered with a piece of valiant dust ? to make account of her life to a clod of wayward marl ? No, uncle, I'll none : Adam's sons are my brethren ; and truly I hold it a sin to match in my kindred.

Beatrice. The fault will be in the music, cousin, if you be not wooed in good time : if the prince be too important, tell him there is measure in everything, and so dance out the answer. For hear me, Hero ; wooing, wedding, and repenting, is as a Scotch jig, a measure, and a cinque-pace : the first suit is hot and hasty, like a Scotch jig, and full as fantastical ; the wedding, mannerly modest, as a measure full of state and ancientry ; and then comes repentance, and, with his bad legs, falls into the cinque-pace faster and faster, till he sink into his grave.

Id. Act. II, Scene 1.

* * *

Orlando. Why, how now, Adam ! no greater heart in thee ? Live a little ; comfort a little ; cheer thyself a little : if this uncouth forest yield anything savage, I will either be food for it, or bring it for food to thee. Thy conceit is nearer death than thy powers. For my sake, be comfortable ; hold death awhile at the arm's end : I will here be with thee presently ; and if I bring thee not something to eat I will give thee leave to die : but if thou diest before I come thou art a mocker of my labour. Well said ! thou look'st cheerly : I'll be with thee quickly.—Yet thou liest in the bleak air : come, I will bear thee to some shelter ; and thou shalt not die for lack of a dinner, if there live anything in this desert. Cheerly, good Adam !

As You Like It, Act II, Scene 6.

Rosalind. No ; I will not cast away my physic but on those that are sick. There is a man haunts the forest that abuses our young plants with carving *Rosalind* on their barks ; hangs odes upon hawthorns, and elegies on brambles ; all, forsooth, deifying the name of Rosalind : if I could meet that fancymonger I would give him some good counsel, for he seems to have the quotidian of love upon him.

Id. Act III, Scene 2.

Rosalind. A lean cheek ; which you have not : a blue eye, sunken ; which you have not : an unquestionable spirit ; which you have not : a beard neglected ; which you have not :— but I pardon you for that ; for, simply, your having in beard is a younger brother's revenue.—Then your hose should be ungartered, your bonnet unbanded, your sleeve unbuttoned, your shoe untied, and everything about you demonstrating a careless desolation. But you are no such man ; you are rather point-device in your accoutrements, as loving yourself, than seeming the lover of any other.

Id. Act III, Scene 2.

Rosalind. Yes, one ; and in this manner. He was to imagine me his love, his mistress ; and I set him every day to woo me ; at which time would I, being but a moonish youth, grieve, be effeminate, changeable, longing, and liking ; proud, fantastical, apish, shallow, inconstant, full of tears, full of smiles ; for every passion something, and for no passion truly anything, as boys and women are for the most part cattle of this colour : would now like him, now loathe him ; then entertain him, then forswear him ; now weep for him, then spit at him ; that I drave my suitor from his mad humour of love, to a living humour of madness; which was, to forswear the full stream of the world, and to live in a nook merely monastic. And thus I cured him ; and this way will I take upon me to wash your liver as clean as a sound sheep's heart, that there shall not be one spot of love in't.

Id. Act III, Scene 2.

Jaques. I have neither the scholar's melancholy, which is emulation ; nor the musician's, which is fantastical ; nor the courtier's, which is proud ; nor the soldier's, which is ambitious ; nor the lawyer's, which is politic ; nor the lady's, which is nice ; nor the lover's, which is all these ; but it is a melancholy of mine own, compounded of many simples, extracted from many objects, and, indeed, the sundry contemplation of my travels, in which my often rumination wraps me in a most humorous sadness.

Id. Act IV, Scene 1.

.   .   .   .

Fabian. She did show favour to the youth in your sight, only to exasperate you, to awaken your dormouse valour, to put fire in your heart, and brimstone in your liver. You should then have accosted her ; and with some excellent jests, fire-new from the mint, you should have banged the youth into dumbness. This was looked for at your hand, and this was baulked ; the double gilt of this opportunity you let time wash off, and you are now sailed into the north of my lady's opinion ; where you will hang like an icicle on a Dutchman's beard, unless you do redeem it by some laudable attempt, either of valour or policy.

Twelfth Night, Act III, Scene 2.

Sir Toby. Now will I not deliver his letter : for the behaviour of the young gentleman gives him out to be of good capacity and breeding ; his employment between his lord and my niece confirms no less ; therefore this letter, being so excellently ignorant, will breed no terror in the youth,—he will find it comes from a clodpole. But, sir, I will deliver his challenge by word of mouth ; set upon Aguecheek a notable report of valour ; and drive the gentleman (as I know his youth will aptly receive it) into a most hideous opinion of his rage, skill, fury, and impetuosity. This will so fright them both, that they will kill one another by the look, like cockatrices.

Id. Act III, Scene 4.

. . .

Enobarbus. Under a compelling occasion, let women die : it were pity to cast them away for nothing ; though, between them and a great cause, they should be esteemed nothing. Cleopatra, catching but the least noise of this, dies instantly ; I have seen her die twenty times upon far poorer moment : I do think there is mettle in death which commits some loving act upon her, she hath such a celerity in dying.

Antony and Cleopatra, Act I, Scene 2.

Enobarbus. Why, sir, give the gods a thankful sacrifice. When it pleases their deities to take the wife of a man from him, it shows to man the tailors of the earth ; comforting therein, that when old robes are worn out there are members to make new. If there were no more women but Fulvia, then had you indeed a cut, and the case to be lamented ; this grief is crowned with consolation ; your old smock brings forth a new petticoat :— and, indeed, the tears live in an onion that should water this sorrow.

Id. Act I, Scene 2.

. . .

Duke. The Turk with a most mighty preparation makes for Cyprus.—Othello, the fortitude of the place is best known to you : and though we have had there a substitute of most allowed sufficiency, yet opinion, a more sovereign mistress of effects, throws a more safer voice on you : you must therefore be content to slubber the gloss of your new fortunes with this more stubborn and boisterous expedition.

Othello, Act I, Scene 3.

. . .

Edmund. This is the excellent foppery of the world ! that, when we are sick in fortune, (often the surfeit of our own behaviour), we make guilty of our disasters the sun, moon, and stars : as if we were villains on necessity ; fools by heavenly compulsion ; knaves, thieves, and treachers, by spherical predominance ; drunkards, liars, and adulterers, by an enforced obedience of planetary influence ; and all that we are evil in, by a divine thrusting on. An admirable evasion of whoremaster man, to lay his goatish disposition on the charge of a star !

.   .   .   .

Gloster. These late eclipses in the sun and moon portend no good to us : though the wisdom of nature can reason it thus and thus, yet nature finds itself scourged by the sequent effects : love cools, friendship falls off, brothers divide : in cities, mutinies ; in countries, discord ; in palaces, treason ; and the bond cracked 'twixt son and father. This villain of mine comes under the prediction ; there's son against father : the king falls from bias of nature ; there's father against child. We have seen the best of our time : machinations, hollowness, treachery, and all ruinous disorders, follow us disquietly to our graves !—Find out this villain, Edmund ; it shall lose thee nothing ; do it carefully.—And the noble and true-hearted Kent banished ! his offence honesty !—'Tis strange !

King Lear, Act I, Scene 2.

.   .   .   .

Letter of Macbeth. They met me in the day of success ; and I have learned by the perfectest report, they have more in them than mortal knowledge. When I burned in desire to question them further, they made themselves air, into which they vanished. Whiles I stood rapt in the wonder of it, came missives from the king, who all-hailed me, *Thane of Cawdor* ; by which title, before, these weird sisters saluted me, and referred me to the coming on of time, with, *Hail, king that shall be !* This have I thought good to deliver thee, my dearest partner of greatness ; that thou mightest not lose the dues of rejoicing, by being ignorant of what greatness is promised thee. Lay it to thy heart, and farewell.

Macbeth, Act I, Scene 5.

.   .   .   .

Camillo. Sicilia cannot show himself over-kind to Bohemia. They were trained together in their childhoods ; and there rooted betwixt them then such an affection which cannot choose but branch now. Since their more mature dignities and royal necessities made separation of their society, their encounters; though not personal, have been royally attorneyed, with interchange of gifts, letters, loving embassies ; that they have seemed to be together, though absent ; shook hands, as over a vast ; and embraced, as it were, from the ends of opposed winds. The heavens continue their loves !

The Winter's Tale, Act I, Scene 1.

Polixenes. As thou lovest me, Camillo, wipe not out the rest of thy services, by leaving me now : the need I have of thee thine own goodness hath made ; better not to have had thee than thus to want thee. Thou, having made me businesses which none without thee can sufficiently manage, must either stay to execute them thyself, or take away with thee the very services thou hast done : which if I have not enough considered, (as too much I cannot,) to be more thankful to thee shall be my study ; and my profit therein, the heaping friendships. Of that fatal country, Sicilia, pr'ythee speak no more : whose very name punishes me with the remembrance of that penitent, as thou callest him, and reconciled king, my brother ; whose loss of his most precious queen and children are even now to be afresh lamented. Say to me, when sawest thou the prince Florizel, my son ? Kings are no less unhappy, their issue not being gracious, than they are in losing them when they have approved their virtues.

Id. Act IV, Scene 1.

1 *Gentleman.* I make a broken delivery of the business.—But the changes I perceived in the king and Camillo were very notes of admiration : they seemed almost, with staring on one another, to tear the cases of their eyes ; there was speech in their dumbness, language in their very gesture ; they looked as they had heard of a world ransomed, or one destroyed : a notable passion of wonder appeared in them : but the wisest beholder, that knew no more but seeing, could not say if the importance were joy or sorrow ; but in the extremity of the one it must needs be. Here comes a gentleman, that happily, knows more. The news, Rogero ?

Id. Act V, Scene 2.

.   .   .

Lafeu. They say, miracles are past ; and we have our philosophical persons, to make modern and familiar, things spiritual and causeless. Hence is it that we make trifles of terrors ; ensconcing ourselves into seeming knowledge, when we should submit ourselves to an unknown fear.

All's Well, Act II, Scene 3.

1 *Lord.* I, with a troop of Florentines, will suddenly surprise him ; such I will have whom I am sure he knows not from the enemy : we will bind and hoodwink him, so that he shall suppose no other but that he is carried into the leaguer of the adversaries, when we bring him to our own tents. Be but your lordship present at his examination : if he do not, for the promise of his life, and in the highest compulsion of base fear, offer to betray you, and deliver all the intelligence in his power against

you, and that with the divine forfeit of his soul upon oath, never trust my judgment in anything.

Id. Act III, Scene 6.

.   .   .   .

Falstaff. No, I'll be sworn : I make as good a use of it as many a man doth of a death's head, or a *memento mori* : I never see thy face but I think upon hell-fire, and Dives that lived in purple ; for there he is in his robes, burning, burning. If thou wert any way given to virtue, I would swear by thy face ; my oath should be, *By this fire* : but thou art altogether given over ; and wert indeed, but for the light in thy face, the son of utter darkness. When thou rannest up Gadshill in the night to catch my horse, if I did not think thou hadst been an *ignis fatuus*, or a ball of wildfire, there's no purchase in money. O, thou art a perpetual triumph, an everlasting bonfire-light ! Thou hast saved me a thousand marks in links and torches, walking with thee in the night betwixt tavern and tavern : but the sack that thou hast drunk me would have bought me lights as good cheap at the dearest chandler's in Europe. I have maintained that salamander of yours with fire, any time this two and thirty years ; Heaven reward me for it !

King Henry IV. Pt. I, Act III, Scene 3.

Falstaff. If I be not ashamed of my soldiers I am a soused gurnet. I have misused the king's press damnably. I have got, in exchange of a hundred and fifty soldiers, three hundred and odd pounds. I press me none but good householders, yeomen's sons : inquire me out contracted bachelors, such as had been asked twice on the banns ; such a commodity of warm slaves as had as lief hear the devil as a drum ; such as fear the report of a caliver worse than a struck fowl, or a hurt wild duck. I pressed me none but such toasts and butter, with hearts in their bellies no bigger than pins' heads, and they have bought out their services ; and now my whole charge consists of ancients, corporals, lieutenants, gentlemen of companies, slaves as ragged as Lazarus in the painted cloth, where the glutton's dogs licked his sores : and such as, indeed, were never soldiers ; but discarded unjust serving men, younger sons to younger brothers, revolted tapsters, and ostlers trade-fallen ; the cankers of a calm world and a long peace ; ten times more dishonourable ragged than an old-faced ancient : and such have I, to fill up the rooms of them that have bought out their services, that you would think that I had a hundred and fifty tattered prodigals, lately come from swine-keeping, from eating draff and husks. A mad fellow met me on the way, and told me I had unloaded all the gibbets, and pressed the dead bodies. No eye hath seen such scarecrows. I'll not

2 I

march through Coventry with them, that's flat.—Nay, and the villains march wide betwixt the legs, as if they had gyves on ; for indeed I had the most of them out of prison. There's but a shirt and a half in all my company ; and the half-shirt is two napkins tacked together, and thrown over the shoulders like a herald's coat without sleeves ; and the shirt, to say the truth, stolen from my host of Saint Albans, or the red-nose innkeeper of Daventry : but that's all one ; they'll find linen enough on every hedge.

Id. Act IV, Scene 2.

. . . .

1 *Citizen.* We are accounted poor citizens ; the patricians good. What authority surfeits on would relieve us. If they would yield us but the superfluity, while it were wholesome, we might guess they relieved us humanely ; but they think we are too dear the leanness that afflicts us, the object of our misery, is an inventory to particularise their abundance ; our sufferance is a gain to them.—Let us revenge this with our pikes, ere we become rakes : for the gods know, I speak this in hunger for bread, not in thirst for revenge.

Coriolanus, Act I, Scene 1.

Menenius. Our very priests must become mockers, if they shall encounter such ridiculous subjects as you are. When you speak best unto purpose, it is not worth the wagging of you beards ; and your beards deserve not so honourable a grave as to stuff a botcher's cushion, or to be entombed in an ass's pack-saddle. Yet you must be saying, Marcius is proud ; who, in a cheap estimation, is worth all your predecessors since Deucalion ; though, peradventure, some of the best of 'em were hereditary hangmen. Good den to your worships ; more of your conversation would infect my brain, being the herdsmen of the beastly plebeians : I will be bold to take my leave of you.

Id. Act II, Scene 1.

2 *Officer.* He hath deserved worthily of his country : and his ascent is not by such easy degrees as those who, having been supple and courteous to the people, bonneted, without any further deed to have them all into their estimation and report : but he hath so planted his honours in their eyes, and his actions in their hearts, that for their tongues to be silent, and not confess so much, were a kind of ingrateful injury ; to report otherwise were a malice, that, giving itself the lie, would pluck reproof and rebuke from every ear that heard it.

Id. Act II, Scene 2.

. . . .

Hamlet. I will tell you why ; so shall my anticipation prevent your discovery, and your secrecy to the king and queen moult no feather. I have of late, (but, wherefore, I know not,) lost all my mirth, forgone all custom of exercises : and, indeed, it goes so heavily with my disposition, that this goodly frame, the earth, seems to me a sterile promontory ; this most excellent canopy, the air, look you,—this brave o'erhanging firmament—this majestical roof fretted with golden fire, why, it appears no other thing to me, than a foul and pestilent congregation of vapours. What a piece of work is man ! How noble in reason ! how infinite in faculty ! in form and moving how express and admirable ! in action how like an angel ! in apprehension how like a god ! the beauty of the world ! the paragon of animals ! And yet, to me, what is this quintessence of dust ? man delights not me, nor woman neither ; though by your smiling you seem to say so.

Hamlet, Act II, Scene 2.

Hamlet. I heard thee speak me a speech once,—but it was never acted ; or, if it was, not above once ; for the play, I remember, pleased not the million ; 'twas caviare to the general : but it was (as I received it, and others, whose judgments, in such matters, cried in the top of mine,) an excellent play : well digested in the scenes ; set down with as much modesty as cunning. I remember, one said, there were no sallets in the lines, to make the matter savoury ; nor no matter in the phrase that might indite the author of affectation ; but called it an honest method, as wholesome as sweet, and by very much more handsome than fine. One chief speech in it I chiefly loved : 'twas Æneas' tale to Dido ; and thereabout of it especially, where he speaks of Priam's slaughter : if it live in your memory, begin at this line ; let me see, let me see ; . . .

Hamlet. Speak the speech, I pray you, as I pronounced it to you, trippingly on the tongue : but if you mouth it, as many of our players do, I had as lief the town-crier had spoke my lines. Nor do not saw the air too much with your hand, thus : but use all gently : for in the very torrent, tempest, and (as I may say) the whirlwind of passion, you must acquire and beget a temperance, that may give it smoothness. O, it offends me to the soul, to hear a robustious periwig-pated fellow tear a passion to tatters, to very rags, to split the ears of the groundlings ; who, for the most part, are capable of nothing but inexplicable dumb shows and noise : I could have such a fellow whipped for o'erdoing Termagant : it out-herods Herod : Pray you, avoid it.

Id. Act III, Scene 2.

Hamlet. Be not too tame neither, but let your own discretion be your tutor : suit the action to the word, the word to the action ; with this special observance, that you o'erstep not the modesty of nature ; for anything so overdone is from the purpose of playing, whose end, both at the first and now, was, and is, to hold, as 't were, the mirror up to nature ; to show virtue her own feature, scorn her own image, and the very age and body of the time his form and pressure. Now this, overdone, or come tardy off, though it make the unskilful laugh, cannot but make the judicious grieve ; the censure of the which one, must, in your allowance, o'erweigh a whole theatre of others. O, there be players, that I have seen play, and heard others praise, and that highly, not to speak it profanely, that, neither having the accent of Christians, nor the gait of Christian, Pagan, nor man, have so strutted, and bellowed, that I have thought some of Nature's journeymen had made men, and not made them well, they imitated humanity so abominably.

Id. Act III, Scene 2.

In all these extracts, serious and humorous alike, there is a similarity of movement which cannot be overlooked. All alike are vivacious, crisp, incomplex, proceeding by clear sequences of short clauses, lacking in fugal breadth. There is no indication of what prose may be made by exfoliation, no large progression, no polyphony. It is true, once more, that even if he would, the dramatist cannot often put *reading* prose in the mouths of his characters ; and that the greatest prose must always be that penned for reading. But oratory is spoken prose ; and there is no sign that Shakespeare could have made a character deliver a prose speech comparable in sonority and sweep with any of the blank-verse speeches in the plays, addressed to audiences of more than one or two. Let us take the only two pieces of non-dramatic prose which Shakespeare has left us—the dedications to his two long poems. I do not cite the " Argument " to LUCRECE, which follows usage in being bald and compressed in diction : the dedications yield the better test :

DEDICATION TO 'VENUS AND ADONIS'
To The
Right Hon. Henry Wriothesly,
Earl of Southampton, and Baron of Titchfield.

Right Honourable.

I know not how I shall offend in dedicating my unpolished lines to your Lordship, nor how the world will censure me for choosing so strong a prop to support so weak a burden : only, if your Honour seem but pleased, I account myself highly praised, and vow to take advantage of all idle hours, till I have honoured you with some graver labour.   But if the first heir of my invention prove deformed, I shall be sorry it had so noble a godfather, and never after ear so barren a land, for fear it yield me still so bad a harvest.   I leave it to your honourable survey, and your Honour to your heart's content ;   which I wish may always answer your own wish, and the world's hopeful expectation.

Your Honour's in all duty.

DEDICATION TO THE 'RAPE OF LUCRECE'
To The
Right Hon. Henry Wriothesly,
Earl of Southampton, and Baron of Titchfield.

The love I dedicate to your Lordship is without end ;   whereof this pamphlet, without beginning, is but a superfluous moiety. The warrant I have of your honourable disposition, not the worth of my untutored lines, makes it assured of acceptance. What I have done is yours, what I have to do is yours ;   being part in all I have, devoted yours.   Were my worth greater, my duty would show greater :   meantime, as it is, it is bound to your Lordship :   to whom I wish long life, still lengthened with all happiness.

Your Lordship's in all duty,

There is finally no escape from the conclusion before reached.   He who in blank verse commands so many styles, and in all is easily spacious and organically continuous—master of an ever-evolving roll of cadenced utterance of every order, from the rippling flow of Mercutio, the large discourse of Ulysses, and the eager torrential thought of Hamlet, to the noble andante of Macbeth and the thunder of Coriolanus—the master poet is in his prose style (wit and wisdom apart) an ordinary Elizabethan dramatist, rather more staccato than most of the rest.

Compare any of those quick-stepping runs of prose with the swing of the verse, going as a great bird wheeling on mighty wings. See how the movement lifts and soars when the poet touches his true instrument :

> Wouldst thou be window'd in great Rome and see
> Thy master thus, with pleached arms, bending down
> His corrigible neck ; his face subdued
> To penetrative shame ; whilst the wheeled seat
> Of fortunate Cæsar, drawn before him, branded
> His baseness that ensued ?
>
> *Antony and Cleopatra.*
>
> Whether it be
> Bestial oblivion, or some craven scruple
> Of thinking too precisely on the event,
> A thought which, quartered, hath but one part wisdom,
> And ever three parts coward, I do not know,
> Why yet I live to say, ' This thing's to do ' ;
> Sith I have cause and will and strength and means
> To do it.
>
> *Hamlet.*
>
> You common cry of curs, whose breath I hate
> As reek o' the rotten fens ; whose loves I prize
> As the dead carcases of unburied men
> That do corrupt my air, *I* banish *you,*
> And here remain with your uncertainty.
>
> *Coriolanus.*
>
> O Proserpina !
> For the flowers now, that frighted thou let'st fall
> From Dis's waggon ! Daffodils
> That come before the swallow dares, and take
> The winds of March with beauty ; violets dim,
> But sweeter than the lids of Juno's eyes
> Or Cytherea's breath.
>
> *Winter's Tale.*

The remarkable thing is that the primary movement or clause formation here is broadly the same as in the prose : it is from the same mint, so to speak. The progression is as it were linear, by short clauses, the images being added to each other without involution. There is the same " bright speed," as of a vivacious talker, with no more approach to long or large constructions than in any of the prose we have just scrutinised. A subtle physiologist might perhaps divine from either the poet's rate of breathing. Let us turn Antony's speech into prose, and, reading by the comma pauses, note its structural identity with the purposed prose of other speeches :

Wouldst thou be windowed in great Rome, and see thy master, thus, with pleached arms, bending down his corrigible neck, his face subdued to penetrative shame, whilst fortunate Cæsar's wheeled seat, drawn before him, branded his baseness following ?

What has effected the profound difference ? Obviously, the magic of rhythm, which lays a transfiguring unity upon the whole, at once creating a new æsthetic fact and force. First and last, once more, this man is a master of *metrical rhythm*, the very genius of blank verse, a fundamentally different thing from prose, whereof the rhythm goes by clause and sentence, not by metre, and wherein the relation of clauses is one of balance rather than of sequence.

Turn we now to the prose which was Bacon's instrument, as verse was Shakespeare's. Like every good prosist, Bacon can vary his tempo ; and we have from him alternately curt and stately, simple and ornate diction. But in every kind there is a pulsation, a progression, a stride that is not Shakespeare's. Let us first sample him from the ESSAYS :

Examine thy customs of diet, sleep, exercise, and the like ; and try, in anything thou shalt judge hurtful, to discontinue it by little and little ; but so as if thou dost find any inconvenience by the change thou come back to it again ; for it is hard to distinguish that which is generally held good and wholesome from that which is good particularly, and fit for thine own body. . . . As for the passions and studies of the mind : avoid envy ; anxious fears, anger fretting inwards ; subtle and knotty inquisitions ; joys and exhilarations in success ; sadness not communicated. Entertain hopes ; mirth rather than joy ; variety of delights, rather than surfeit of them ; wonder and admiration, and therefore novelties ; studies that fill the mind with splendid and illustrious objects, as histories, fables, and contemplations of nature.[1]

[1] Essay XXX, *Of Regiment of Health.*

Observe, first, the deliberation and balance of the exposition, the fore-planned arrangement of the thoughts, in contrast with the kindling process of the poet ; next the instinctive balancing of the clauses in point of rhythm ; and thirdly, the climaxing movement to a full and polyphonous closing phrase—the natural method of prose, and the exact opposite of the practice of Shakespeare, whose typical period-endings are sudden or vehement arrests of speech in mid-line, as of a horse reined back on his haunches :

> Life's but a walking shadow, a poor player
> That struts and frets his hour upon the stage
> And then is heard no more : it is a tale
> Told by an idiot, full of sound and fury,
> Signifying nothing.

> Do not, as some ungracious pastors do,
> Show me the steep and thorny way to heaven,
> Whiles, like a puff'd and reckless libertine,
> Himself the primrose path to dalliance treads,
> And recks not his own rede.

>   Rather a ditch in Egypt
> Be gentle grave unto me ! rather on Nilus' mud
> Lay me stark nak'd, and let the water-flies
> Blow me into abhorring ! rather make
> My country's high pyramides, my gibbet
> And hang me up in chains !

There are hundreds of these speech-endings in the plays ; and in the prose there is the same habit of the quick stop, which is as alien to Bacon's way of writing as it would have been to his way of walking, in court or garden. In the essay before us, the very preoccupation about health and diet is a mark of Bacon, absent from Shakespeare, who did not smoke, but never discussed tobacco even to gratify James ! And in that single extract of three sentences there are seven words and phrases never used by Shakespeare : " *little by little,*" " fretting inwards," " studies of the mind," " inquisitions," " *exhilarations,*" " contemplations " ; " novelt*ies.*" Observe the Baconian plurals, much seldomer found in Shakespeare's prose. The word "exhilaration" never occurs in the plays at all, in any flexion : "splendid," a common word with Bacon, is found only once, in the dubious 2 HENRY VI; "knotty" occurs only twice ; "discontinue" only once ; "inconvenience" only once in a homogeneous play.

Another piece of Baconian prose, from the essay preceding that just cited, will convey the same lessons :

There may be now, for martial encouragement, some degrees and orders of chivalry, which nevertheless are conferred promiscuously upon soldiers and no-soldiers ; and some remembrance perhaps upon the scutcheon ; and some hospitals for maimed soldiers ; and such-like things.   But in ancient times, the trophies erected upon the place of the victory ; the funeral laudatives and monuments for those that died in the wars ; the crowns and garlands personal ; the style of Emperor, which the great kings of the world after borrowed ; the triumphs of the generals upon their return ; the great donatives and largesses upon the disbanding of the armies, were things able to inflame all men's courages.   But of all, that of the triumph amongst the Romans, was not pageants or gaudery, but one of the wisest and noblest institutions that ever was.

Again we have a handful of words and phrases never found in the plays : " *promiscuously*," " soldiers and no-soldiers," " orders of chivalry," " hospitals " (the word " hospital " occurs only once in Shakespeare), the position of the adjective in " crowns and garlands personal," " *laudatives*," " *donatives*," " largess*es*," " *disbanding*," " courag*es*," " *gaudery* "—in the course of a dozen lines, five words and three plurals never found in the plays. This habitual use of the plural is a specialty of Bacon, not of Shakespeare ; and by small peculiarities of that kind the idiosyncrasy of a writer is much more truly to be traced than by merely occasional use of current saws and formulas. Even " institutions," common in Bacon, occurs only once in Shakespeare. And always the style of Bacon is radically different from that of the dramatist —reflective rather than impassioned, deliberate rather than eager ; calm, not quick, measured in quite another sense than is the poet's verse.

Not a single essay, I believe, will fail to yield the same order of proofs. We have dipped into Essays XXX and XXIX : let us turn to XXXI, OF SUSPICION. It opens with a series of short " sententious " sentences :

> Suspicions amongst thoughts are like bats amongst birds, they ever fly by twilight. Certainly they are to be repressed, or at the least well guarded ; for they cloud the mind ; they lose friends ; and they check with business, whereby business cannot go on currently and constantly. They dispose kings to tyranny, husbands to jealousy ; wise men to irresolution and melancholy.

Here, in three sentences, we have three non-Shakespearean words : " *repressed*," " *currently*," " *irresolution*," and the form " check with," never found in the plays ; to say nothing of the opening string of Baconian plurals. " Suspicion*s* " occurs only once in Shakespeare. In the two short essays OF REGIMENT OF HEALTH and OF SUSPICION may be found several more words never found in the plays : " excess*es*," the name Celsus, " benign," which in Shakespeare occurs only in the non-Shakespearean prologue of Gower in PERICLES (ii), " *masteries*," " buzz*es*," the phrase " of a middle temper," " stout*est*," the phrase " discern *of*," and the peculiar form " owing to " in the sense of " accruing to "— " strength of nature in youth passeth over many excesses, which are *owing to* a man till his age." (" Owing " occurs only once in Shakespeare.)

But the question of vocabulary calls for separate treatment ; and our immediate business is with prose style. If the reader be not convinced by our few selections from the Essays, let him turn to the ADVANCEMENT OF LEARNING. Here will be found a multitude of sonorous and long-breathed sentences in a style never to be found in Shakespeare's prose. The second paragraph begins with a sentence of nearly two hundred words—a paragraph in itself. The third paragraph consists of one such sentence :

Therefore did I conclude with myself that I could not make unto your Majesty a better oblation than of some treatise tending to that end ; whereof the sum will consist of these two parts : the former consisting of the excellency of learning and knowledge, and the excellency of the merit and true glory in the augmentation and propagation thereof ; the latter, what the particular acts and works are which have been embraced and undertaken for the advancement of learning, and again what defects and undervalues I find in such particular acts ; to the end that though I cannot positively or affirmatively advise your Majesty, or propound unto you framed particulars, yet I may excite your princely cogitation to visit the excellent treasure of your own mind, and thence to extract particulars for this purpose agreeable to your magnanimity and wisdom.

There is no such interwoven, periodic writing as this in the whole range of Shakespeare. One more sentence will suffice to illustrate the stately and architectonic style which is normal in Bacon, and of which the plays afford no sample :

And as for those particular seducements or indispositions of the mind for policy and government, which learning is pretended to insinuate, if it be granted that any such thing be, it must be remembered withal, that learning ministereth in every of them greater strength of medicine or remedy than it offereth cause of indisposition or infirmity.

If anywhere Bacon might be expected to approximate to the prose style of the plays, it would be in the CONFERENCE OF PLEASURE or in the HENRY VII. But there we have the same measured utterance, the same enchaining of clauses. In the former, " The Praise of Fortitude " sets out with half a dozen short and crisp " sententious " sentences ; then comes one of eighty words, marked by the Baconian enchainment of clauses. The History begins :

After that Richard, the third of that name, king in fact only, but tyrant both in title and regiment, and so commonly termed and reputed in all times since, was by the Divine Revenge, favouring the design of an exiled man, overthrown and slain at Bosworth Field, there succeeded in the kingdom by the Earl of Richmond thenceforth styled Henry the Seventh.

This is a type of the style of the book—interlocked and jointed, not merely sequent clauses, with a periodic rise and fall. And in the second sentence occurs the word " militar," *always* Bacon's form of the adjective (though sometimes spelt *militare* "), and *never* found in the plays, whether in prose or verse. There the word is *always* " militarie " or " military." Thus in the most truly significant details of style, verbal and structural alike, the prose writer is once for all marked off from the poet, even as he is in a hundred points of doctrine, certainly not always to his advantage. But as a writer, he is all the more clearly differentiated ; and as a teacher turned man of letters to fulfil a mission, he belongs to another world. Bacon, indeed, is not the supreme master of prose that Shakespeare is of blank verse. He has not the signally elastic movement of Nashe, the magical cadence of Browne, or the endless flow of Jeremy Taylor. With all his professed contempt for rhetorical artifice, too, he was capable at times, by the avowal of Spedding, of " a certain affectation and rhetorical cadence . . . agreeable to the taste of the time." [1] But this, as the same critic goes on to claim, was " so alien to his own individual taste and natural manner, that there is no single feature by which his style is more specially distinguished, wherever he speaks in his own person, whether formally or familiarly, whether in the way of narrative, argument, or oration, than the total absence of it." In short, he could fault, as Shakespeare faulted ; but he stands to the prose as Shakespeare stood to the verse of his time, as a witness for the root truth in regard to all writing, that to be great it must be sincere. And this, with his large faculty for phrase, cadence, and diction, makes him one of the great writers, inasmuch as he habitually makes style a vesture for thought, and not a decoration of it. But he was an artist in spite of himself. To dislike and reject bad rhetoric is to crave for

[1] *Letters and Life of Bacon,* i, 119.

good ; to detect false ornament is to cherish the true ;
and Bacon is spontaneously an artist in his handling of
prose. With a burden of thought such as was never
given to Nashe or Browne or Taylor, and a range of
reason far wider than that of Hooker, he far outweighs
all three as a contributor to the store of human wisdom.

And with all this it is the more wildly incredible that
he should have been the greatest master of verse as well
as the chief master of philosophic prose in his age. Monstrous as is the thesis that he, taking all *knowledge* as his
province, and tied by destiny to the vocations of law
and politics, yet secretly supplied during twenty years
of his crowded life the main stock of the new plays of a
London theatre, and penned VENUS AND ADONIS and
LUCRECE and the SONNETS—monstrous in every respect
as is that fantasy, it is hardly more incredible at bottom
than would be, for those who can realise the conditions
of artistic genius, the conception of the combination in
one man of a faculty not far short of supreme for prose
and for prose themes with a quite supreme faculty for
impassioned verse. The thesis has arisen and won vogue,
in fact, among men as little wont to consider the psychology of genius as to study the literary facts by which
any theory of authorship is to be tested. And even that
is not the end of the purely literary demonstration of the
folly of the Baconian creed.

It is not to be expected that Baconians will be moved
by the argument from prose style. All these years, they
have gone on comparing Bacon and the Plays without
detecting any difference of style or manner of sentence,
any more than they can discern the antipodal difference
of preoccupation and habit of mind. Being wholly
occupied in looking for resemblances in the trees, they
never get a view of the woods ; and having always stated
their case mainly on illusory " correspondencies,"
" echoes," and " classical " and " legal " mares' nests;
they are not likely to consent to any other kind of test.

For the hitherto perplexed but open-minded reader; however, the argument from style form will doubtless carry its due weight ; and it has here accordingly been presented, after strict examination of the three orders of Baconian argument specified.

The further argument from constant disparities in the two writers, introduced in our incidental citation of Baconian words and phrases *not* found in the plays, may possibly make some appeal even to some Baconians, seeing that it turns their own method of particular comparison against their own thesis.   To that, then, we shall devote a separate chapter, before we deal in conclusion with some of the fundamental considerations which ought to have vetoed the Baconian theory from the first.

CHAPTER XII

THE VOCABULARIES OF SHAKESPEARE AND BACON

THE range of Shakespeare's vocabulary is an old theme among his admirers ; and on the strength of some very loose statistical guessing and plainly inadequate statistical comparison he has been credited with supremacy in this as in other literary aspects. Even careful comparisons between the plays of Shakespeare and the verse, say, of Milton, the bulk of whose output is prose, could not carry the conclusions founded on the hand-to-mouth statistics in question. For a just estimate of a writer's verbal range we require, it would seem, comparison of his work with an approximately equal quantity of matter by another writer ; and it might have been expected that the Baconians would give some special attention to the respective vocabularies of the two writers they identify. Significantly enough, however, there has been almost no attempt among them to compare the general use of words in the two writers, apart from such wholly nugatory undertakings as that of Mr. Donnelly and Dr. Theobald, above discussed, to find special identities in the use of the commonest terms, phrases and figures of the period. When, seeking a rational test, we compare the vocabularies in general, we find, instead of any noticeable similarity or uncommon measure of coincidence, a much wider divergence than could well have been reckoned on. So clear is this divergence that a little careful study of this one point might open the eyes of any reasonable student to the nullity of the Baconian hypothesis.

Not only does Bacon, as we have seen, employ frequently in particular works, as the NATURAL HISTORY, a large number of special terms such as Shakespeare very rarely uses, and many which he never uses at all : the language of Bacon's philosophic and general works diverges no less signally from that of the Plays in respect of the use of a multitude of words which never occur there.

Of Bacon, unfortunately, there is no concordance : the Baconians have done nothing so useful as that. But a sufficiently fair test may be set up by taking any un-biased selection of pages from Bacon and noting the words therein which do not occur in the Shakespeare concordance. The result will perhaps be found surprising by non-Baconians as well as by the Baconians who will make the experiment. In dealing with the question of prose style I have already shown that a few passages from the Essays yield a handful of words, phrases, and plurals, which are not to be found in the Plays—the three opening sentences of one essay presenting three non-Shakespearean words, though the words in question are not at all out of the way (save as regards the crucial case of " militar," which is worth a hundred), and the phrases are more or less idiomatic. But it may be sus-pected by some that the essays and passages in question are exceptional, and have been selected for that reason. In order, therefore, to secure an indisputably fair com-parison, I have taken (1) the first two pages (in Rout-ledge's edition) of the ADVANCEMENT OF LEARNING ; (2) the last page of Book First and the first of Book Second ; (3) the last two pages of Book Second ; (4) a sequence, taken at random, of four pages in the same book ; (5) the first and the last of the ESSAYS ; (6) the first page of THE NEW ATLANTIS ; and (7) the first two and the last two pages of the HISTORY OF HENRY VII. The result is the following set of lists of mostly common Baconian words which either do not occur at all in the Plays or occur there only in the rare instances specified.

First Page of " Advancement of Learning "
(Routledge's ed. of Works, p. 42)

branching [1]	penetration (mental)	propriety (= pro-
elocution	proficience	perty = quality)
oblation [2]		tabernacle

Second Page

affirmatively	politiques	tacit
amplification	propagation [3]	triplicity
compendious	propound [4]	undervalues sb.)
extraction(s)	propriety (= pro-	universality
illumination	perty=quality [5])	veneration
oblation	signature	

Last Page of B. I. (Ed. cited, p. 74) (Short page)

barleycorn	generate	knowledges (twice)
benign	illumination	magnified
consociate	immersed	renovation
demolish(ed)	incorruptible	

First Page of B. II (Ed. cited, p. 75) (Short page)

amplitude	overcomen	transitory
benign	proficience	transmit
foresight	renovation(s)	

Second Last Full Page of B. II (Ed. cited, p. 174)

commonplace(s)	edition (=giving	liturgy
concordance(s)	out)	privatively
conservation	effectually	prolix
dispersedly	harmonies (lite-	summary (adj.) [7]
	rary) [6]	

[1] " Branching *itself*." Shakespeare only once has " branch " as a verb.

[2] Occurs in the Shakespeare plays only in a clearly non-Shakespearean part of *Pericles*.

[3] Used by Shakespeare once only, and then in another and peculiar sense, " propagation of a dower " (*M. for M.*, I, ii, 154).

[4] Shakespeare has only " propound*ed*," and that only once, in the doubtful 2 *Henry VI*. The word is very common in Bacon.

[5] Often used by Bacon in this sense. Shakespeare has the word only twice, and both times in the modern sense.

[6] Shakespeare often has " harmony " in the ordinary sense ; never in this.

[7] " The works of God summary." Shakespeare has the noun twice, in the ordinary sense, never the adjective.

Last Full Page of B. II. (p. 175)

atheism	elevation	proficience
compatible	libertine (adj.)	receded
confutation (twice)	liturgy	receding
declination(s)	occupate	retribution
deducing	preoccupate	tares
deficience	privative	unsown

Four Pages in Sequence taken at Random from B.II
(Ed. cited, p. 166)

animation	emergent	multiplicity
animosities	futility	preamble(s)
aphorisms	intelligence	propound
certificate [1]	(= mind) [2]	response(s)
contrariwise	judicially	rigorously
deficience	lawmaker (twice)	

P. 167 (short)

peregrinations [3]	reprehension
propriety (= pro-	Sabaoth
perty = quality)	vivacity

P. 168 (short)

idiom	participant	theology
libertine (adj.)	reluctation (twice)	
mystical	righteousness	

P. 169

analogy	enucleating	medium
chess	examinable	nonsignificants
contradictories	grift (= graft)	relatively
deduce(th)	imposture	surd
deficience	interdicteth [4]	ward (of a lock)
dialectic	latitude	
draughts (=writ-	(Mahomet)	
ten rules)	mediocrity [5]	

[1] Occurs in Shakespeare only in the doubtful 2 *Henry VI*.
[2] Shakespeare always uses this word in the sense of information.
[3] Shakespeare has only " peregrinate," and that only once.
[4] Shakespeare has only " interdiction," and that only once.
[5] Bacon has " golden mediocrity." So has Jonson. Shakespeare has not even " mediocrity."

First Essay (whole)

allay (= alloy) [1]
comparable
discoursing
embaseth

illumination
mummeries
poles (of truth—
    metaph.)
Phrase " at a stand."

shrunken [2]
theological

Last Essay (whole)

abstruse
accurate
arietations
astrologer
computing [3]
concurrence
conflagration
degenerating
desolated (vb.)
dispeople
enervate

exhaust (= ex-
    hausted)
generate
hemisphere
luxuriant
magnitude
(Mahomet)
martyrdom
mountainous
    (= living in the
    mountains)

over-power (sb.) [4]
philology
populate
sanguinary
schism
suit (= sequence)
sustentation
version (= direc-
    tion)
vicissitude (7 times)
voluptuous

These lists, it should be explained, mostly cover flexions of words, in the senses in which they are used by Bacon. That is to say, Shakespeare never uses " extraction " or " undervalue " (sb.) or " immerse " or " magnify " or " commonplace " or " concordance " or " declination " or " tare " or " draught " (= writing) or " recede," &c. Two of the Bacon words, " Mahomet " [5] and " confutation," do occur in 1 HENRY VI, and are here included on the confident assumption that that is a non-Shakespearean play. Its presumed authors, Marlowe, Greene, and Peele, all use the name Mahomet frequently : " Shakespeare " uses it in no other play. " Certificate " I have noted as occurring in the doubtful 2 HENRY VI. " Effectually," again, occurs in TITUS

[1] Shakespeare often has the verb " allay " : the noun only once, and then in the sense of alleviation.

[2] Shakespeare has " shrunk," never " shrunken."

[3] Shakespeare has only " computation."

[4] Shakespeare has neither the noun nor the verb.

[5] I note a proper name in this case, because its use has a moral significance.

ANDRONICUS, but in no other play ascribed to Shakespeare ; and here again the word is included on the confident assumption that the play in question is non-Shakespearean. " Benign," again, as already noted, occurs in the Plays only in Gower's prologue to Act II of PERICLES—generally admitted to be non-Shakespearean matter. In no other case in these lists does this question arise, unless it be specified. " Inferring," used by Bacon (p. 174), occurs in Shakespeare only in the doubtful 3 HENRY VI, but is not here included. " Edition " Shakespeare uses once, and once only, in the now normal sense ; in the sense in which it is used by Bacon, as above cited, he never uses it at all. " Shrunken " I include, as the fact that Shakespeare always has " shrunk " is in its degree significant.

It will be observed that the lists under notice include both common and uncommon words; terms seldom used even by Bacon, and terms often used by him and by many other writers. " Benign," for instance, is a favourite word of his. The remarkable thing is the number of quite ordinary words used by Bacon that are never found in the Plays. This appears from the lists before us, and can be further proved *ad libitum.* Thus Shakespeare never uses words so common in Bacon and in Elizabethan literature as : abstruse, accurate, animate, animation, animosity, atheist, atheism, astrology, astrologer, analogy, amplitude, alloy, allegory, architecture, benign, commonplace, conflagration, compendious, comparable, compatible, compression, chess, concurrence, condense, contrariwise, contexture, collectively, compacted,[1] delicacy, deficience, or deficiency, deduce, or deducing, disbanding, dialectic, elocution, extraction, elementary, elevation,

---

[1] Twice in one page in the *Advancement,* with "compaction." Shakespeare has "compacted" once in *Lucrece ;* never in the Plays. Of course, he often has *compact* = compacted. Both forms were current : the dramatist takes one ; the prosist the other

generate, geometrical, geometry, imposture, illumination, immerse, intelligence (= mind), knowledges, latitude, liturgy, libertine (adj. — Shakespeare has the noun), luxuriant, magnitude, martyrdom, medium, mediocrity, magnify, mystical, multiplicity, oblation, overpower, prolix, proficience or proficiency,[1] physics, physical (general sense[2]), recede, renovation, relatively, repress, resplendent, retribution, righteousness, signature, sanguinary, subdivide, similitude, tacit, tabernacle, theology, theological, transmit, transmission, transitory, version (in any sense), voluptuous, veneration, vicissitude, &c. &c. Hardly less remarkable is the number of common words that occur only once. In the first few pages of the Concordance I note :—abashed (*abash* does not occur at all), abet, abetting, abjectly, abler, abominably, abomination, abounding, abrogate, abrupt, abruptly, abstains (*abstain* does not occur), abstemious, abundantly, accessible, acclamation (pl.), accommodate, accompanying, accomplice (pl.), accomplishing, accomplishment, accrue, accumulate, accumulated,accumulation—twenty-five from " ab " to " acc." The full list, which would run to thousands, includes such words as freewill, apostles, apostle (both in doubtful plays),immortality,indisposition, magnificence (so common in Bacon), maxim, inference, syllogism, reciprocal, navigation.

Such facts raise various questions as to the alleged range of the Shakespearean vocabulary. For instance, of the 15,000 words said to be found in the Plays,[3] how

---

[1] *Proficient* occurs once in the Plays.

[2] Shakespeare has the word twice in the sense of " medicinal," never in the general sense.

[3] Max Müller, *Lectures on the Science of Language*, 6th ed. i, 309, citing—of all authorities—Renan's *Histoire des Langues Semitiques !* I cannot find the passage in my copy (2nd ed.) of Renan. Mr. G. C. Bompas (*Problem of the Shakespeare Plays*, 1902, p. iv) characteristically asserts that the " estimate " is Max Muller's own. Marsh (*Student's English Language*, 8th ed. pp. 126, 180) makes the same statement as Müller cites from Renan, giving no authority. Elze (*William Shakespeare*, Eng.

many are mere plurals and verb-flexions ? how many occur only in the doubtful or non-genuine plays ? and how many are proper names ? And how does the Shakespearean vocabulary compare with, say, that of Ben Jonson ? The question involved is, broadly, whether the vocabulary of the Plays is or is not that of a scholarly man, of very wide reading and far-gathered vocabulary, or that of a poet with immense power of poetic expression in the range of words of an ordinary cultured man.

Leaving the question of comparative range of vocabulary to fuller statistical inquiry, we may note the bearing on the Bacon-Shakespeare theory of the evidence before us. Putting aside for separate discussion the problem of the intellectual interests involved or suggested, let us ask how it could come about that the same man, repeatedly using in his non-dramatic writings such familiar terms as atheism, theology, theological, knowledges, illumination, renovation, magnify, magnitude, amplitude, deficience, proficience, tacit, transitory, signature, chess, analogy, medium, mystical, imposture, commonplace, recede; tares; deduce, mediocrity; immersed; benign, righteousness, alloy, generate, magnet; superlative—and many hundreds more, equally common—could contrive to write (as the Baconians hold) thirty-seven plays, covering a productive period of some twenty years, without once using any of them dramatically ? How should he chance to avoid, in all his play-writing, the use of two such common idioms as " at a stand " and

trans. p. 389) copies Müller *verbatim*, and cites him, Renan, and Marsh ! Mr. Grant White (*Studies in Shakespeare*, p. 300) cites the 15,000 estimate with an " it is said," avowing that it seems to him excessive. I know not who made the estimate, or whether it has ever been checked. Mrs. Cowden Clarke and Mr. Bartlett offer no estimate in their Concordances. An allowance of 8000 words for Milton has the same loose currency. Mr. Morton Luce (*Handbook to Shakespeare's Works*, 1906, p. 435) writes that " *Of course* the range of his [Shakespeare's] vocabulary is far greater than that of any other writer." No evidence is offered.

" at a stay," when these came to him quite naturally in his other writings ? How should Bacon use the terms " theory " and " theoretic " freely in his didactic works; and only " theorick " (and that only thrice) in the thirty-seven plays ? How, after writing often of " politiques " in his avowed works, should he always write " politicians " in his alleged plays, when other dramatists (e.g. Ben Jonson) used " politiques " ? Using the metaphor of " oblation " so frequently in his signed works, how could he abstain from using it once in the plays ? Or will the Baconians insist on giving him one of the worst-written scenes in PERICLES because it there occurs in the plural, and in the literal sense ? Why should he write " over-comen " and " holpen " in his prose and never in his poetry ? Why should he always use the spelling " drought " in his signed works, and " drouth " when writing dramatically ? How should it be possible to him to write of " vicissitude " seven times in one essay and never once in thirty-seven plays ? How should he chance frequently to use the word " voluptuous " in didactic writings, and never once in so many plays in which the *notion* is so often suggested ?[1] And, having a habit of speaking of " knowledges " in his books, how should he abstain from using that plural in twenty years of play-writing ?

Once more, why should he always use the spelling and scansion " militarie " or " military " in the Plays, and invariably " militar " or " militare " in the books ? How, yet again, should it come about that, while in his books he often employs the word regiment = rule, which at the time was in universal English use, in all the thirty-seven plays he uses it only once, though it is there seven times employed in the special sense which has latterly become the sole one—that of a body of soldiers ? Naming Solomon as he does, with seriousness, thirty or forty

[1] Shakespeare has " voluptuously " once, and " voluptuousness " twice ; but " voluptuous " never.

times in his signed works, how came he to name him only twice in the plays, and that with levity, in the LOVE'S LABOUR'S LOST ? Why, using the word "temporary" so constantly in his serious writing, did he use it only once in the thirty-seven plays, and then frivolously, in the phrase "a temporary meddler" ? How came he in all the Plays to use only once each such words as "erudition," "rigorously" [in a non-Shakespearean play], "totally," which he uses so often in his didactic writings ?

To put these questions is to point to the answer. Of all the coincidences of diction and phrase claimed by the Baconians, there are not half a dozen worth serious discussion ; ninety-nine out of a hundred, as we have seen, are normal uses of every-day language ; while the divergences are innumerable and overwhelming in their evidential force. The vocabularies of Shakespeare and Bacon are markedly and decisively distinct. Words frequent in one are wholly absent from the other. Of two synonyms, the first habitually uses one ; the second the other. Bacon uses a number of participles in "ate," as "occupate," "preoccupate," which are not to be found in the Plays. Whereas he uses "lawmaker" twice in one page, the Plays not only have not "lawmaker," they have not even "lawgiver." He uses such verbs as "to desolate," which Shakespeare never employs. He has the locutions "evading from," "chasing after," "conlude with myself," and many more, all unknown in the Plays. Here we are considering not the special employment of sets of terms proper to particular researches or topics, but differences in the habitual use of a common language. We are contemplating two different verbal outfits, so to speak ; two largely different selections from the store of words common to all for all purposes ; two diverging sets of preferences—in a word, the output of two differently cultured men.[1]

[1] Mr. G. C. Bompas (*The Problem of the Shakespeare Plays*, 1902, p. iv) alleges—here merely following an old statement by

Incidentally it appears that the man of special culture has, as might be expected, the larger vocabulary in a given space. None of the computators seems to have sought to estimate quantitatively Bacon's vocabulary ; and I can only give my own impression. But it is founded on the above-noted facts. In every thousand consecutive words of Bacon's text as above sampled, roughly speaking, there are from ten to thirty words not to be found in the Plays. With due allowance made for repetitions, this would soon, I think, give us over a thousand ordinary words which occur in Bacon and not in Shakespeare ; and a collation of the SYLVA SYLVARUM would greatly swell the list. In no similar set of selections of sequent words from Shakespeare, I think, will there be found any such proportion of words not to be found in Bacon, though in some single pages there may be. This, of course, is not an issue that affects our conclusion as to the non identity of the two writers. If it be found that the Plays contain as large a number of terms not to be found in Bacon as we have found *vice versa*, the inference as to non-identity will in fact be *pro tanto* strengthened. I mention my own view of the proportions by way of suggesting that the playwright was really not a man of

Mrs. Pott—that " Bacon's vocabulary is practically the same as that of the Shakespeare plays." The assertion is repeated at p. 25. I know no more flagrant instance of the levity of assertion with which the Baconian case is put. Mr. Bompas sticks at nothing. He alleges (p. 39) that " there seems scarcely a sentiment or opinion expressed in the plays which has not its counterpart in the acknowledged works of Bacon." Without blenching, he adopts the monumental nonsense put forth by Mrs. Pott as to there being only three instances before 1594 of the salutation " good morrow," " good day," etc. (Upon this particular deliration, see Mr. Crawford's " Bacon-Shakespeare Question " in his *Collectanea*.) As illustrative of Mr. Bompas's first-hand knowledge may be noted his assertion (p. 51) that Thomas Kyd " is not known to have translated from the Italian." He cannot even have looked into Professor Boas's edition of Kyd's Works. I am told, however, that he is an esteemed exponent of Baconics.

supremely large vocabulary for his time : the impression
set up by a long scrutiny of the concordance is rather one
of surprise at the large number of words familiar to
educated men which do not appear in it, and the large
number which appear only once. Multitudes of them,
of course, he must have known ; and it is fairly arguable
that for the purposes of a dramatist, the expression of
human passions and the narrative of common human
actions, there is needed a much narrower range of vocabulary than is required for the ratiocinative purposes of
such a thinker as Bacon. This granted, the resulting
critical conclusion is that the kind of æsthetic effect
produced by Shakespeare is one of the inspired use of an
ordinarily fecund writer's vocabulary, and not, as the
idolaters have assumed, one of abnormal command of
variety of terms. True, he has always an *abundant*
diction ; and in some plays, as TROILUS, he resorts so
much to literate terms as to convey an impression of
special largeness of vocabulary. But the literate diction
of TROILUS, however it is to be accounted for, is not that
of his purest poetry or his intensest feeling. His most
thrilling effects are commonly produced by the exquisite
collocation and *cadenced* flow of familiar words. Such
lines as :

> Finish, good lady, the bright day is done ;
> And we are for the dark.

> Unarm, Eros : the long day's work is done.

> Revisit'st thus the glimpses of the moon.

> Nothing of him that doth fade
> But doth suffer a sea change
> Into something rich and strange.

> The prophetic soul
> Of the wide world dreaming on things to come.

> And Beauty making beautiful old rhyme.

> Daffodils
> That come before the swallow dares, and take
> The winds of March with beauty.

Give me my robe, put on my crown : I have
Immortal longings in me : now no more
The juice of Egypt's grape shall moist this lip.

As she would take another Antony
In her strong toil of grace.

Life's but a walking shadow, a poor player,
That struts and frets his hour upon the stage
And then is heard no more.

Spirits are not finely touched
But to fine issues.

In thrilling region of thick-ribbèd ice.

We are such stuff
As dreams are made on, and our little life
Is rounded with a sleep——

these and a hundred more immortal touches of rhythmic diction are not the yields of a great vocabulary : they are the masterstrokes of a poet working in the eternal and universal stuff of human feeling and passion, distilling their quintessences by his own alchemy. To assume that they were possible only or specially to a man of learning, a "courtier," a trained lawyer, a methodically practised reasoner, is an exorbitance of misconception that remains revolting alike to the literary sense and to common sense after any amount of reflection. Sidney the courtier, Davies the lawyer and the dialectician in verse, have no such jewels as these. And if there were any general conclusion rightly to be drawn either *a priori* or *a posteriori* it would be that those starry points of song *could not* be the creation of the learned lawyer and would-be renovator of the sciences, great as was his literary gift in his own large province. Not in all literature is there a known instance of a literary prodigy that could be remotely compared with such a miracle as the production of the NOVUM ORGANUM and LEAR, the NEW ATLANTIS and TWELFTH NIGHT, ROMEO AND JULIET and the essay on LOVE, by the same man, even if we consider them solely as forms of literary output, without reference to the intellectual predilections involved. Lawyers have written on philosophy ; men of science have penned verse ; and historians have produced poetic dramas ; but where in the whole roll of human achievement is there such a confounding combination of such utterly disparate forms of gift for mere utterance as would be the writing of HAMLET and the DE AUGMENTIS, MACBETH and the NATURAL HISTORY, HENRY IV and the HISTORY OF KING HENRY THE SEVENTH by the same pen in the same period ?

Those who are not repelled by the " fierce impossibility " of such a conjuncture have thus far had set before them a number of the concrete proofs that it did not take place. But the proofs are not even yet all specified. After dealing with the claims founded on false assumptions, we have considered the rebutting evidence of style and vocabulary. It remains to consider that which is furnished by (1) a contrast of the intellectual interests obtruded by Bacon's whole work with the whole tone, aim, and content of the Plays, and (2) a notation of the circumstantial facts of the history of the Plays and the personal positions of the two men.

CHAPTER XIII

THE INTELLECTUAL INTERESTS OF
SHAKESPEARE AND BACON

IF we survey the written life's work of Bacon, we find
it broadly dividing into three main masses, of
which one intellectually if not quantitatively out-
bulks the others. As a lawyer, he did a certain
amount of purely professional writing, marked by the
customary composure and ease of his style. To a layman's eye these papers indicate plenty of legal learning ;
and indeed, whatever Coke might say, Bacon's competence
as a lawyer and a judge was never doubted among his
unprejudiced contemporaries. But Bacon, be it observed,
does not lard with law his writings on other subjects,[1] as
the Baconians make him out to have done in the Plays—
a circumstance which alone might have served to guard
careful readers against the notion that the law tags in
the Plays come from his pen.

Much more keenly was he interested in the political
problems which pressed upon the governments of Elizabeth and James ; and to these he devoted an amount of
earnest and sagacious thought which makes his political
writings still the most interesting of their kind in his
period. Only in Hooker's ECCLESIASTICAL POLITY, in
that age, is there any such union of thought and style,
insight and power of speech ; and Hooker, in the less
rational world of the church, is not more bent than Bacon
on the right guidance of contemporary life. But the

---

[1] The express claim of Mr. G. C. Bompas is that of 250 law
terms occurring in the Plays " 200 are treated with more or less
fulness *in Bacon's law tracts.*" (*The Problem of the Shakespeare
Plays*, 1902, p. 29.)

greatest of all Bacon's preoccupations is that to which he gave the bulk of his published matter—the comprehensive revision and reconstruction of scientific lore of all kinds, naturalist and humanist.

To this, his master-purpose, he directed the ADVANCEMENT OF LEARNING (expanding it from two books in English into seven in Latin), the NOVUM ORGANUM, and the series of short treatises which lead up to and anticipate that ; striving further to accumulate scientific material in the NATURAL HISTORY, the HISTORIA VENTORUM, the HISTORIA VITÆ ET MORTIS, and the HISTORIA DENSI ET RARI. The WISDOM OF THE ANCIENTS, written in Latin like the NOVUM ORGANUM, was penned to the same general end of reforming men's habits of thought ; and THE NEW ATLANTIS heads in the like direction. All are parts of a high-aiming and high-hoping propaganda, impelled by a devouring aspiration, which overrode all the engrossing preoccupations of professional and political life. His few excursions into pure *belles lettres*, apart from the ESSAYS, are but passing diversions : the CONFERENCE OF PLEASURE, the version of a few of the Psalms, tell of small predilection to pure literature for literature's sake. Of the ESSAYS and the HISTORY OF HENRY THE SEVENTH alone among his larger undertakings could it be said that they are in any large measure outside the social and philosophical purposes which mainly swayed their author ; and even these, partly written as they were with an eye to getting an audience for the other works, are so far concurrents. Wide as it is, then, the mental outlook of Bacon has one prevailing bent. Persistently he strove and hoped to lead the mind of his time in matters of natural science by better paths than those it appeared to him to be treading. Of the merits and demerits of his lead, we are not here concerned to speak : the matter in hand is the nature of his intellectual ambition. The fact stands out so clearly that no one has ever questioned it save by way of those imputations of sheer self-seeking which still to some extent darken critical counsel concerning Bacon ; and for our purpose these are irrelevant. Even if we should subscribe to the sophism that Bacon's intellectual ambition was wholly of a piece with that of a Cecil or an Essex—a purely self-regarding impulse—the fact would still emerge that his master passion was one of edification, of propaganda, of persuasion. And the full perversity of the theory which identifies him with the author of the Shakespearean plays is to be realised only when we reflect on the absolute obstacle to the overpowering preoccupation of his avowed intellectual life that would be involved in the devotion of an incalculable amount of its space and energy to the production of the dramas in question.

Unless they deny it, the Baconians must be presumed to see that Bacon throughout the mass of his avowed writings has an end in view ; that he is profoundly concerned to influence opinion. Yet they impute to him the deliberate assumption of the time-devouring task of writing dozens of stage plays, in not one of which are his intellectual purposes so much as hinted at.[1] They conceive him writing LOVE'S LABOUR'S LOST and the MIDSUMMER NIGHT'S DREAM and the COMEDY OF ERRORS and VENUS AND ADONIS and the RAPE OF LUCRECE at one end of the task, and THE TEMPEST and CYMBELINE and HENRY VIII and the WINTER'S TALE at the other, with all his life's ambition still unfulfilled ; with the sciences all in his opinion still misdirected ; with the " idols " of the tribe and the cave, the theatre and the market-place, all along in command of the general allegiance. Possessed as he was by the vision of a world to reform, both on the intellectual and on the political side, we are to conceive

---

[1] Mr. Harold Bayley, in his Baconian mood (*The Shakespeare Symphony*, 1906, p. 356), pictures Bacon as penning plays, not only the Shakespearean but others, in order to forward "the New Philosophy." Neither he nor any one else has pointed to one clear enunciation in the Plays of one of Bacon's leading ideas. Dr. Theobald's theses on that head are idle.

him bending his powers year after year to the entertainment of the audiences at the Globe Theatre.

As the Baconians cannot see the incredibility of this in the mass, it behoves us to indicate it in some detail. To give the slightest primary plausibility to their thesis on this side they must assume one of two contrary positions which they may be defied to defend. Either they must stand to the old German theorem of some profound didactic purpose that inspires all the Plays, from TITUS ANDRONICUS to PERICLES, thus crediting the dramatist with a moralising aim in writing alike the Falstaff scenes and the First Part of HENRY VI and ALL'S WELL THAT ENDS WELL—an extravagance of fable which almost competes with the Baconian theory itself—or they must make the assumption that Bacon wrote the Plays in order to get away mentally from all his didactic ideals. As the didactic ideals of his works are specific and reiterated, while any implied in the plays are simply those of normal and accepted ethics, they can have no refuge save in the second alternative. They must imagine Bacon striving to drown his scientific cares in drama as other men seek to drown pecuniary cares in drink. Whatever they may say about his doctrine of dramatic teaching in the ADVANCEMENT OF LEARNING, they can find no trace in the plays of any attempt to further the aims of that treatise. They must picture Bacon as a literary Jekyll-and-Hyde, alternately absorbed in an immense philosophic ambition and in a nerve-wearing career of theatrical craftsmanship from which every thought of Baconian propaganda was expelled.

At times, by way of proving that the same hand wrote HAMLET and the NOVUM ORGANUM, they dwell on such coincidences as Hamlet's phrase about the stars being fire and the handling of that very thesis in several of Bacon's writings. There is here a real point of coincident interest or contact ; as again in the speech of Polixenes to Perdita about the art that adds to nature being an art that nature makes.[1] Those two topics, and some others, had undoubtedly occupied, in however different degrees, the thought of both writers. But on the theory that the two were one, why have we only these few coincidences of subject-matter ? If it were worth Bacon's while to raise didactically the issue of Art *versus* Nature in THE WINTER'S TALE, why should he restrict himself to a single brief discussion of that and a bare mention of the problem about the physics of the stars in HAMLET ? Were these alike uncontrollable aberrations from the policy pursued (on the Baconian theory) throughout all the other plays, of saying nothing whatever about the main aims to which Bacon devoted the mass of his signed writing ? And was it by way of self-mortification that the publicist, who in his publications quotes and discusses Aristotle over a hundred times, makes but two jejune allusions to him in the Plays ? If so, why even these two, seeing that Plato, quoted or criticised over fifty times in Bacon's prose, is never named in the Plays at all ?

Even to a Baconian there must surely be something baffling in the contrariness which excludes from the Plays all mention of Copernicus, about whose theory Bacon was so much concerned, and whose doctrine was so interesting a topic for so many Elizabethans. To a student, the crudely conventional and ignorant references to Machiavelli in 1 and 3 HENRY VI are no matter for surprise, the passages being so plainly non-Shakespearean ; but to the Baconian, for whom all " Shakespeare " is Bacon, it must at times, one thinks, seem odd that a writer who in his prose makes so many intelligent allusions to Machiavelli should write of him so obtusely in blank verse. The playwright of the Baconians is a mere miracle

---

[1] In *Montaigne and Shakespeare*, 2nd ed. pp. 203–211, I have traced the development and vacillation of Bacon's thought on this problem, and noted its final divergence from Shakespeare's. It may well be that both writers had talked on the theme with Ben Jonson, the friend of both.

of self-renunciation. He will not allow himself a word
in promotion of his dearest scheme. In the ESSAYS and
in his State Papers concerning Ireland he is deeply concerned about "plantations" : in all the Plays the word
occurs but once, in the line :

> Had I plantation of this isle, my lord.
> *Tempest*, II, i, 143.

In his traceable literary life, Bacon stands confessed a
lover of Virgil, quoting him at least fifty times. In the
Plays, there are barely three palpable Virgilian echoes,
and these of the most hackneyed kind, made in English ;
while there are many, also in English, from Ovid, for
whom the prose-writing Bacon shows much less liking.
But passing strange above all this, on the Baconian
theory, is the fact that the essayist and propagandist who
was so concerned about atheism and theology never
mentions either word in the Plays ; that he who in so
many philosophical writings speaks of "the light of
nature" should never use the phrase in his alleged work
in drama ; and that, after devoting so many critical
pages to philosophy, he there uses the term "philosophical" only once, in pure levity !

It is all too blankly unplausible for more detailed
discussion. The Plays are, in a word, the composition of
a man not at all preoccupied with problems of scientific
reform, though in one passage he disposes unanswerably,
once for all, of an old theoretic confusion over which
Bacon wavered, seeing now clearly and now cloudily.
The author of THE TEMPEST and THE WINTER'S TALE
had indeed brooded intensely over some of the great
riddles of existence, but he was not the schemer of a "New
Instauration" of the sciences ; and as little did he aspire
to reconstruct the life of Ireland. He was in no wise
zealous either to vindicate dogmatic orthodoxy or to
persuade dogmatists to change their hearts and study
Nature with open minds : it is with a smile that he makes

Perdita propound their Polynesian principles. Echoing Montaigne, he will put in the mouth of a person in a drama a proposition flouting naturalist speculation, which Bacon would have repugned with emphasis ; yet he is pervadingly non-religious in his outlook. He was no fulminator against atheism, no zealous flatterer of King James, no striver against Aristotelian scholasticism. Despite all that has been loosely said of his observation of Nature, he was no watchful student of her processes : like Bacon, he loved flowers, but not with his botanical bias.[1] Of the Latin classics he knew little, else he must have quoted Virgil as lovingly as Bacon does : his Ovid he knew mainly from translation, partly by reminiscence from his school-days. To realise the futility of the pretence that the playwright was a good classical scholar, and therefore was Bacon, we have but to turn from the few scraps of Latin which here and there dot the Plays, —chiefly three or four which are not of his making— to the pages of the ADVANCEMENT and the ESSAYS, where, for many pages together, Latin enters into almost every other sentence, and classical allusion is omnipresent.

One of the standing theses of the Baconians, not thus far considered in our survey, is that Bacon's proclivity to drama is manifested not only by his share in the planning of the masques at Gray's Inn, but by his allusions to dramatic poetry and the theatre in the Latin version of the ADVANCEMENT OF LEARNING,[2] and at the close of the sixth book of the expanded treatise.[3] It would be difficult to cite a better proof of Bacon's aloofness from the contemporary theatre. He expressly complains that though " the stage is capable of no small influence both of discipline and corruption," " Now of corruptions of this

[1] Mr. Bayley notes (Shakespeare Symphony, p. 320) that " A knowledge and love of flowers as great as that of Bacon and Shakespeare is exhibited by the minor dramatists."

[2] De Augmentis, ii, 13.

[3] Mr. G. C. Bompas (Problem of the Shakespeare Plays, 1902, p. 22) puts this passage (vi, 4, end) " in the second book."

kind we have enough, but the discipline has in our times
been plainly neglected." The DE AUGMENTIS was
published in 1623, the very year of the publication of the
Shakespeare Folio. What then is the Baconian position
here ? That Bacon meant his sweeping dispraise to apply
only to other people's plays, he having for his part been
carrying on for twenty years the discipline which he
declared to have been " in our times plainly neglected " ?
The procedure could be fitly described only in the vernacular—as " crying stinking fish." If Bacon had taken
the pains to write seven-and-thirty plays, he must be
supposed to have intended them to be witnessed. Here
he is warning all men off. The disparagement of the
whole Elizabethan drama can mean only one thing, that
it did not at all realise Bacon's ideal of moral propaganda.
In his blame he included perforce much if not all of the
work of his sworn admirer, Ben Jonson. Would the man
who blamed that for lack of moral purpose, and who saw
nothing but lack of discipline in Dekker and Webster and
Heywood, no less than in Beaumont and Fletcher,
eulogise in the mass the Plays of Shakespeare ? Bacon,
in a word, had not the playgoing temperament. He was
all for moral and intellectual improvement, not for spontaneous life, the pell-mell of poetry and ribaldry, tragedy
and farce, that crowded the Elizabethan boards. It does
not follow that before his official advancement he had not
from time to time seen a play and carried away with him
a line or two ; but he was verily no haunter of theatres.

The passage at the end of the sixth book is equally a
confutation of the Baconian claim founded on it. Recom-
mending, in his admiration of the Jesuit methods of
pedagogy, the teaching of the art of acting in the schools;
he pronounces stage-playing (*actio theatralis*) " a thing
indeed, if practised professionally, of low repute ; but, *if
it be made a part of discipline*, . . . of excellent use."
This is not a recommendation of the theatre : it is a
recommendation to avoid it, and to promote the acting

of didactic plays in the schools under pedagogic auspices.
And there is on record even a more pronounced expression
of Bacon's substantial antipathy to the theatre of his day.
When, in 1614, the Thames watermen, led by John
Taylor, the Water-Poet, presented their petition to the
King to put a stop to the removal of the playhouses from
the south to the north side of the river, a change which;
they said, took away half their livelihood, it was referred
by James to his " Commissioners for Suits," who then
included Sir Francis Bacon. The King's Players (Shakespeare's company) put in a counter petition. But, says
Taylor,

> our extremities and cause being judiciously pondered by the
> Honourable and Worshipfull Commissioners, Sir Francis Bacon
> very worthily said that so farre forth as the Publike weale was to
> be regarded before pastimes, or a serviceable decaying multitude
> before a handful of particular men, or profit before pleasure, so
> far was our suite to be preferred before theirs.

Before any decision was come to, the Commission was
dissolved, and the matter dropped, poor Taylor being in
due course accused by his fellow watermen of taking bribes
from the players to let the suit fall.[1]

The Baconians, no doubt, are honestly ignorant of the
existence of this record ; and now that it is cited they
will probably seek to explain it away. Bacon had
declared against the cause of the very company of players
who, according to the Baconians, were acting his plays ;
disparaging their work as " pastime," even as he later
disparaged the theatre in general as devoid of the " discipline " he cared about. We shall be told, doubtless,
that he had to conceal his connection with the players—
that connection which, according to the same theorists,
was actually known all the while to Ben Jonson and many
others ! Thus does the Baconian theory proceed from
inconsequence to inconsequence.

[1] *The True Cause of the Watermen's Suit concerning Players*, in
Taylor's *Workes*, 1630, Section Second, pp. 172–3.

The rational reader, following all Bacon's pronouncements on dramatic and theatrical matters, can see that
they consist with each other, and tell of a general dis-
satisfaction with what is being done. Dramatic *Poesy* he
commended as a vehicle for moral instruction ; and
perhaps FERREX AND PORREX might have satisfied him
as a duly didactic performance. The plays he wanted to
be performed in the schools could not conceivably be
those which the Baconians declare him to have written.
In the matter of the watermen's petition he took up his
usual protectionist attitude. The watermen were losing
much of the custom by which they lived, and he was
perfectly willing to meet their wishes; on the professed
principle of putting " profit before pastime," when in
point of fact the profit in question depended solely on the
continuance of the pastime in a particular place. If
Bacon disapproved of the change, his " tool " Shakespeare and the rest of the company were flouting the
wishes of their own playwright ; and he in turn, by seeking to thwart them, was, on the Baconian hypothesis,
provoking them to reveal his secret. The rational and
natural reading of the facts yields a perfectly intelligible
situation : the Baconian theory reduces it, as usual, to
nightmare. Yet I doubt not that some Baconians will
promptly accuse their idol of gross hypocrisy in order to
maintain their theory of his authorship.

But perhaps the wildest inconsequence of all in the
Baconian case is its utter disregard of the fact, witnessed-
to alike by the precept and the practice of Bacon, that he
was latterly either so convinced of the coming " bank-
ruptcy " of the modern languages as to be moved to put
forth all his serious didactic matter in Latin, or anxious
enough for foreign appreciation to forego much of the
audience he might have secured at home by writing in his
mother tongue. The Baconians would have us believe
that the Bacon who composed even the WISDOM OF THE
ANCIENTS in Latin, rather than spend less time in putting

it forth in English, determinedly gave himself to the
writing of thousands of pages of plays in English, mostly
in verse, with a great deal of " comic relief " in prose;
much of it to be spoken by stage clowns.   And, as if this
were not enough in mass, they would have him be author
of a play (RICHARD II) the reproduction of which [1] in
1601 at the request of the fellow conspirators of Essex,
on the day before his rising, brought upon the theatre the
sharp displeasure of the Government, a..d a veto on
further performance—this at a time when Bacon was
compelled by his official position to repudiate all share in
his former patron's proceedings (as he had long done),
and was on the eve of being called upon to prosecute the
rebels, as law officer of the crown.   Do the Baconians,
one wonders, suppose that Bacon was playing fast and
loose, running with the hare and hunting with the
hounds ?   If so, they outgo his enemies in imputation
against him.

It is all of a piece with the perversity that, without
blenching, ascribes to Bacon the authorship of the Sonnets,
wherein the poet avows his " rude ignorance," as in the
dedication of the LUCRECE he had spoken of his " untutored lines " ; avows that he is one whose " name
receives a brand," so that

> Almost thence my nature is subdued
> To what it works in, like the dyer's hand ; [2]

making the actor's confession :

> It is most true, I have gone here and there,
> And made myself a motley to the view,
> Gored mine own thoughts, sold cheap what is most dear,
> Made old offences of affections new ; [3]

---

[1] Messrs. Clark and Wright in their Clarendon Press ed. of
Richard II say " it is certain that this was not Shakespeare's play."
I know not whence they derived their certainty.   Few other
scholars share it.   Had Shakespeare's company *two* plays on
Richard II ?

[2] Sonnet 111.   [3] Sonnet 110.

and telling of an unhappy love-affair of which there is no faintest trace or hint in Bacon's biography.

At every turn in the investigation, the monstrosity of the whole theorem becomes more amazing, the incredibility more mountainous. The form which it has finally taken—the proposition that Bacon, writing the Plays during a period of twenty years, chose as his literary representative a " clown " who could not even sign his name (for to this complexion the argument has come), contriving that a secret thus alleged to be necessarily known to a whole theatrical company, and inferrible by all Shakespeare's fellow dramatists, should be absolutely withheld from public or official knowledge ; and yet all the while planning endless crazy " ciphers " which would reveal not only that " secret " but a hundred others to a remote posterity in the event of that cipher being guessed at—the total allegation is a critical chimera which staggers judgment and beggars comment.

Yet it will go on being propounded, by men who make no attempt to rebut confutations, heaping farce on fallacy, facing no difficulty, ignoring mountains of disproof. Again we can foresee the form of answer which such partisans will make to the argument of this chapter. They will revert for the nonce to one of the terms of Mr. William Theobald's self-contradiction. After claiming that Bacon " reveals " himself in the plays by duplications of phrase, idea, and word, they will now argue that on the contrary he could not put his ideas in the plays because he would thereby " reveal " his identity. Returning to the " coincidences," they will again claim to stand on these as revelations. Heads, the Baconian wins ; tails, the Stratfordian loses. Two mutually exclusive principles are alternately employed to defend one proposition ; and a semblance of reasoning serves to accredit two theses which contrarily flout reason. If Bacon had reason to fear being known to be a playwright; why in the name of common sense, should he have put himself in jeopardy by adapting or writing or collaborating in thirty-seven plays in collusion with a fraudulent actor, whose secret is *alleged* to have been actually divined by his literary contemporaries, must, and in the terms of the case, have been known to his colleagues ? If Bacon desired to keep secret his authorship, why, in the name of sanity, should he sow the bulk of the plays with law phrases which, according to the Baconians, reveal the deepest legal knowledge, when, all the while, he puts no such legal seasoning in his signed works of a non-legal character ? If Bacon dared not turn his plays to any of the purposes of his life, why, in the name of Baconism, did he write them ? And if, finally, he dared not reveal himself, why *did* he supererogatorily reveal himself to contemporaries as the Baconians, most of the time, allege that he did ? To these questions there is no answer. *Stat pro ratione voluntas.*

To convince such reasoners, be it plainly said, is not even desirable. But to prevent the recruiting of the army of the deluded by minds yet capable of rational enlightenment may be possible ; and to that charitable end it may be well to indicate one more set of facts, singly sufficient to satisfy any reasonable reader, not only that the Plays were the work of a man of the theatre, an " insider " and not an outsider ; but that whatever may have been the measure of occasional collaboration in the Plays from outside, and whatever the amount of adaptation of other men's work in them, the general authorship and the source of adaptation can be vested in no other man than the actor-partner, Shakespeare.

CHAPTER XIV

EXTERNAL AND CIRCUMSTANTIAL EVIDENCE:
LIVES AND PERSONALITIES

§ 1

THE Baconian hypothesis, it is obvious, arises in a certain tendency to an *a priori* view of what was *likely* to have been the preparation, and what was *likely* to have been the way of life, of the supreme dramatist. All worship presupposes worshipful characteristics ; and in regard to literary genius, more than to any other form of human faculty, men are prone to associate other forms of excellence with those put in evidence by the writer's work. One result of this propensity, as I have elsewhere remarked, is that nearly every full biography of a great man of letters sets up disappointment. A Southey may gain from biography ; a Shakespeare cannot, simply because literary admiration has given him every possible advance on credit. We know that Boswell's Life of Johnson, delightful as it was to be to later generations, for whom Dr. Johnson was not a dictator in letters and morals, was a shock to many of his admirers in that which received it ; and that Lockhart's perfectly loyal Life of Scott, in respect of its revelations of the great man's financial and other weaknesses, actually set up speculation as to whether the son-in-law wrote with a hostile animus. Milton and Shelley and Keats and Coleridge are similarly disadvantaged for adoring readers of their verse by the publication of their lives and letters. And so it has been; for men of our idealising age, with the short and simple annals of the greatest of English dramatic poets. Men not given to the study of the psychology of genius frame for themselves an unreal conception of its conditions and bases. It is only after a cool comparative study of the lives of the masters of speech and portraiture and song— as Catullus and Poe, Tourguénief and Dostoyevsky, Villon and Burns, Goethe and Heine, Carlyle and Ruskin— that we are qualified to check our instinctive expectation by a real knowledge of probabilities.

Emerson had not done so when he wrote concerning Shakespeare that he " could not marry this man's life to his verse." He had formed an ideal of a supreme intellect, identifying genius for utterance with genius for universal judgment, a commanding power of speech with command over all environment. And Emerson's lead has been followed by those—university men and others— unable to conceive how the greatest English poet can have been a man of short schooling, who gathered what knowledge he had outside of libraries and colleges. They first grossly exaggerate his knowledge under the spell of his art, ascribing to him scholarship and legal and other acquirements which he did not possess : then they call for a man who shall square with their ideal. And so we have the " Baconian " theory and the " anti-Strat-fordian " argument. I propose now to examine the *a priori* side of these positions, testing it by the relevant considerations, as we have tested all the attempts to reinforce it by literary evidence, beginning with the more concrete.

§ 2

One of the surprises of the controversy is the readiness with which a number of men avowedly incline to accept any hypothesis of the non-Shakespearean authorship of the plays on the score of the strangeness of the actor's apparent indifference to their preservation. The assumption is that none of the quartos printed in Shakespeare's lifetime was authorised ; and that the actor's abstention from issuing a collected edition implies an indifference which in his case would be unintelligible. On the other hand, the issue of the Folio in 1623 can by such reasoners be without misgiving set down to Bacon, though the actor-partners who caused it to be published ascribe the plays to Shakespeare in the most unqualified terms, as does Ben Jonson in his prefixed poem. This ascription, declared to be deliberately false, is regarded as a trifle that puts no difficulty in the way of the Baconian theory ; while the actor's mere delay in publishing his plays, to which he had been adding up to and even after the time of his retirement (presumably in broken health), is regarded as an inexplicable phenomenon, on the assumption of his authorship.

A hundred and fifty years ago, Farmer put the rational explanation that the plays were not Shakespeare's to publish ; that they belonged to the theatre-partnership ; and that it was not to its interest to print plays which continued to draw audiences. This reasonable suggestion might very well serve to allay any reasonable wonder. But even in the eighteenth century it was urged that *all* the quarto issues could not plausibly be held to have been piratical ; and in the latest and most competent discussion of the problem, Mr. A. W. Pollard's SHAKESPEARE FOLIOS AND QUARTOS (1909), this contention is pressed to good purpose. The common-sense view of the case is that, seeing the piratical publication of plays—whether from stenographers' notes or from stolen manuscripts—was clearly a source of profit, the actors who owned plays would naturally publish them when they ceased to " draw," or when for any reason the theatres were closed. This is the reasonable explanation of the uncommonly abundant publication of plays in 1593–94, when the theatres were closed for a spell of eight months on account of the plague ; and again in 1600, when the number of the licensed theatres was reduced to two, and their performances to two per week, with a close time for Lent.

In each of the two short periods specified, the number of plays entered in the Stationers' Register rises to twenty-eight ; whereas in the eight years 1585–92 only nine plays were entered, and in the years 1596–99 (after January 1596) only nine more.[1]

Further, we find that with the single exception of LOVE'S LABOUR'S LOST, all the quartos which are found to have " good " texts, or to have been used in preparing the Folio, were duly entered in the Register before being printed ; whereas all the quartos with " bad " texts were either not entered prior to publication or entered in a suspicious fashion, and printed by a dubious printer. There thus arises the inference that the " good " quartos had been printed by authority. To this exposition Mr. Pollard adds a convincing demonstration that certain of the " 1600 " and other quartos were really reprints of 1619, and may conceivably have formed part of an intended complete issue of the plays in separate quartos. With this very interesting matter, however, we are not here concerned. It suffices for us that—whether it was he or the partnership that suggested the genuine issues of the quartos—Shakespeare is shown not to have been so indifferent to the preservation of his plays as has commonly been supposed, and was thus no such prodigy of literary unconcern as to justify any resort to a desperate search for another author, who, moreover, in the terms of the case, showed no more anxiety than he did.

Still, there can be no pretence that Shakespeare did show anxiety to have his plays properly printed. Some of the authorised quartos seem to have been printed either to suppress piracies or to prevent them. They were not supervised by Shakespeare. It is clear that he did not properly—if at all—read the proofs even of the " good " quartos ; and if one might hazard a speculation on that head, it would be that he, who so constantly outran the clock in his plot construction, and wrote with

[1] Pollard, as cited, pp. 9–10.

an ease of composition which it annoyed Ben Jonson to
hear of, was not likely to be a good proof reader if he
tried.   Further, it is well that we should make the effort
to conceive that the supreme master of dramatic objec-
tivity, whose highest gift lay precisely in his power of
projecting himself into other personalities, may not have
been much exercised to see his plays in print.   Signally
spontaneous in his first composition, he was as ready as
other men to see need for revision later ; better than any
one, he knew the weakness of the alien work he had taken
over ; and he may well have felt that a mere printing of
all the plays as they had left his hand would give him
more vexation than pleasure.   He could hardly have
foreseen that an adoring posterity would come to read
with reverence, as his, all the bombast and platitude and
bad versification by other men, which he had left in the
stage versions ; and if he could have foreseen it, he might
fitly be credited with disrelish for such uncritical worship.
On the other hand, it is surely not inconceivable that he
may have scrupled to claim, in the perpetuity of print,
over his name, the credit for a quantity of *invention* by
other men to which he may have been modest enough to
attach some importance.   On the one hand, he had the
choice of the toil of rewriting all that inferior work at a
time of failing health ; on the other hand he had the
choice of publishing all that composite work, of so much
of which he of all men best knew the poverty, with
elaborate explanations of its literary history, telling how
this scene was mainly Greene's or Marlowe's ; and that
other mainly his own rewriting of their or Peele's verse :
how in this case he had elected to rewrite an entire play
(as LEAR) and how in another (as HAMLET) he had
continuously recast, yet retained some little of, the old
material.   What should move him to either of these
burdensome courses ?   We are here facing a problem
never glimpsed by the Baconians ; but one which Mr.
Greenwood is both able and bound to face, though he has

not considered it in his book, which runs so much to the uncritical and unprofitable endorsation of Lord Campbell and the classicists.

And it is a problem constantly ignored by those who dilate on the "strangeness" of Shakespeare's unconcern. If any one accustomed to stand at that point of view will reflect that certainly in much, and probably in most, of Shakespeare's ostensible work there is old matter either worked over or simply retained, or matter actually supplied by collaborators, he will realise that for Shakespeare to publish all his Plays as his works would have been a very different thing from the undertaking to that effect by Ben Jonson. Shakespeare had in his youth been railed at by Greene, the dying playwright, for eking out his and others' handiwork ; and a friend of Greene's had later asserted openly that men who had eclipsed Greene's fame in comedy had stolen his plumes, challenging them to deny it. Supposing—as we so well may—that several of Shakespeare's comedies were recasts of Greene's originals, and recognising as we must that a number of the history-plays and tragedies were undoubtedly either revisions or recasts of other men's work, we must surely realise that for a man of moderately sensitive literary conscience—such as the great master presumably was—it was not possible to issue the plays as his own work in the fashion in which the partners did it after his death. To buy and adapt and revise and recast for the theatre was both permissible and customary ; and as a play had to have a responsible author for all purposes, he had no need to scruple over being named as the author of the acting plays in which his own work was incomparably the best, where he had done any recasting. Assuredly he wrote "for gain, not glory," in the first instance ; though genius irresistibly had the casting vote. After the two "first-fruit" poems he prepared nothing for the press, definitely electing to be a writer for the stage. To leave his composite plays to the chances of the stage and the guardianship of his partners was really as congruous a course on his part as some, have thought it incongruous.

And if we make a further effort in the way of comparative criticism we may realise that, even apart from the fact that the fathering of the plays in print would have made him permanently responsible for a quantity of matter which not only was not his but was in every way inferior to his, there is a further consideration which should at least appeal to those theorists whom I am now answering. To publish one's own plays in that day was in a manner to acknowledge that they had no very sure future on the stage.[1] A feeling of this kind might fairly have been credited, in the name of modesty, to Ben Jonson, who in 1616 published his collected plays and poems, in folio, as his " Works," and thereby incurred much derision for his vanity. No playwright had ever done it before, as indeed no other playwright well could. Jonson had doubtless to receive many owners' permissions, which he would get the more easily because so many of his plays had no abiding attraction on the boards. After all, if Shakespeare in his latter years—when the competition of new men like Beaumont and Fletcher moved him to compare with them in the matter of elaborate plot-construction, as in CYMBELINE and THE WINTER'S TALE [2]—were concerned rather to hope for continued vogue in the theatre than to fall back on the solace of sales among the reading public, it would really have been a disposition on his part sufficiently human to appeal to those who profess to find it incredible that such an author should have " left his works to chance." Publication would have meant for him not so much success as withdrawal ; and we are really not entitled to

[1] Or else to cheat the theatre, as Heywood implies that some playwrights did.

[2] Compare on this, Mr. Barrett Wendell's *William Shakespeare*, 1894.

suppose that when he retired to Stratford he thought himself played out as a dramatist.

But now, supposing this line of reasoning to be still resisted by the " anti-Stratfordians," what is to be said of the Baconian theory in the same connection ? It simply disappears. The proposition that Bacon *did* cause the Plays to be published collectively in 1623, without any supervision of the press, with all their imperfections and their alloy on their heads, in order to preserve *his* work for posterity, breaks down instantly on confrontation with the typographical facts. The Folio text, though printed from authorised quartos and from theatre manuscripts, abounds in the most baffling misprints and confusions, which no author could have passed, and which are not to be paralleled in any book of Bacon's. And, having regard to the fortuitous late inclusion of Troilus, and the omission of Pericles, it is inconceivable that the responsible author had any hand in the business. All the while, upon the very argument with which we are dealing, *Bacon* must be held to have shown just such disregard for *his* literary progeny as Shakespeare is said to have done ; for Bacon, in the terms of the theory, allowed his plays to lie uncollected or unpublished till 1623, and set himself to issue them only after his fall had given him new and utterly unexpected leisure. If it be argued that up till then he had delayed the matter for lack of leisure, it follows that but for his ruin he might never have issued them at all. Thus the argument from " strange indifference " recoils upon and destroys the Baconian case.

§ 3

But this is only the beginning of the circumstantial exposure of the insanity of the Baconian theory.

It has evidently never occurred to the Baconians to wonder why the philosopher-playwright of their fantasy so strictly bent himself, not to any philosophic plan or any exposition of his own intellectual aims, but to the simple commercial needs of a going theatre, on lines dictated by the theatrical circumstances. Even on the most conservative view, the Plays are, as we have said, largely adaptations or reconstructions of previous plays. KING JOHN and HENRY V and the HENRY VI group and RICHARD III are certainly based on previous plays ; as are HAMLET, LEAR, ROMEO AND JULIET, MEASURE FOR MEASURE, THE TAMING OF THE SHREW, and probably OTHELLO and THE MERCHANT OF VENICE. MACBETH, TROILUS, PERICLES, TIMON, and HENRY VIII, are all admittedly either reconstructions of previous plays or works of collaboration ; [1] and a similar thesis might be put as to the COMEDY OF ERRORS, LOVE'S LABOUR'S LOST, THE TWO GENTLEMEN, and ALL'S WELL. RICHARD II and JULIUS CÆSAR both raise problems of derivation. As to TITUS ANDRONICUS, apart from the Germans and a few English critics, even those who suppose Shakespeare to have had *some* hand in the play limit his share narrowly, recognising that there was certainly a previous play on the subject. All these critical data, at which the Baconians hardly ever glance, are part of the problem for real students.

Now, the facts in question go as naturally with Shakespeare's authorship as they are irreconcilable with Bacon's. The actor-partner dealt with old plays as an actor-partner would. He supplied his company on business-like lines, revising and recasting plays which had actually been found to attract the public, and making new experiments from time to time. But the Baconian theory invites us to contemplate Bacon as habitually arranging with the theatre people, during a period of twenty years, for adaptations, adjustments, revisions, expansions, and reconstructions of plays previously on the boards—nay, as collaborating from time to time with other dramatists

---

[1] In *Macbeth*, the non-Shakespearean element is small, but it is unmistakable.

—and all the while counting on having his secret kept by all concerned. I believe that any one who simply takes a little pains to realise what a state of things is thus posited will need no further persuasion to dismiss the Baconian theory—though a sufficiency of confutation on other lines has, I hope, been supplied in the foregoing chapters. And to the unknown lawyer of Mr. Greenwood's nugatory hypothesis, the " busy man " writing plays and poems during a lifetime under the name of an actor, never disclosing his identity, the concrete recognition of the situation involved is no less fatal.

Incongruities of detail as between the literary facts and their theory are acknowledged by some Baconians. Even Dr. Theobald admits that the contrast between the handling of love in the Plays and that in the Essay OF LOVE has staggered many of the faith. He proceeds to resolve it by arguing that Bacon in the different cases had different objects in view ; that the Essay is a deliberately objective and as-it-were scientific study ; whereas in the Plays love is naturally handled as the great force it is in human life ; though even there, Dr. Theobald contends, love is always "subordinate." I leave it to the reader to pronounce for himself on this precious philosopheme. Thus far I have been careful to meet every concrete Baconian argument with a concrete rebuttal ; but when it comes to the æsthetic appraisement of the total literary and psychic content of the Plays and the Works, one may, in passing, fitly meet Baconian asseveration with flat counter-claim. And I submit to the reader who has an æsthetic sense, that the kind of feeling or temperament and the kind of literary faculty underlying the Plays on the one hand and the Works on the other, are about as different as those of Burns and Hume, or those of Rabelais and Descartes. I have lived, I suppose, as much in the spiritual society of both Shakespeare and Bacon as the majority of men of letters, and I have never for a moment felt it to be otherwise than a ludicrous fantasy to conceive

of Bacon as writing either the Falstaff scenes in HENRY IV
or the love scenes in ROMEO AND JULIET. I would
suggest to any reader who claims to have an open mind,
a perusal of the scene in which Antony explodes at the
sight of Thyreus kissing Cleopatra's hand :

> Approach there ! Ah, you kite ! Now, gods and devils,
> Authority melts from me : of late, when I cried " Ho ! "
> Like boys unto a muss, kings would start forth
> And cry, " Your will ? "
> Have you no ears ? I am Antony yet !
>> *Enter* Attendants.
>> Take hence this Jack, and whip him.
> *Eno.* (*Aside.*) 'Tis better playing with a lion's whelp
> Than with an old one dying.
> *Ant.* Moon and Stars !
> Whip him !

and I would then invite him to say whether he can
conceive Bacon writing it. One can go vaguely through
some conceptual process of imagining Bacon composing
one of the " philosophical " passages in the plays, where
his thought—versification apart—could chime with the
author's ; but to associate him with the lightning flash of
fury which Shakespeare can lend to Antony or Coriolanus,
Othello or Cleopatra, is as impossible, to my thinking,
for any one who has really lived with Bacon, as to imagine
that stately personage drinking with Falstaff or breathing
out his soul to Juliet.

But all this is by the way. Baconians ostensibly either
can imagine these things or can make up their minds on
the critical problem without realising that any such things
are implied. Let purely æsthetic convictions then be
waived ; and let the theory be tested as it might be by
judges competently versed in the literary subject-matter
and morally indifferent to the issue. Let what is a thesis
in literary history be judged in the light of all historical
facts available. Let us simply try to suppose Bacon,
gifted with any order of literary faculty we may care to
ascribe to him, writing the Shakespeare plays under the

known theatrical conditions in the given period, and the
hypothesis must be relegated to outer darkness.

§ 4

Considering it all comprehensively, one realises that
what plausibility it can ever have had for ordinarily
reasonable men must have arisen, as aforesaid, from some
spontaneous difficulty in conceiving that a Stratford lad,
who left school in his early or middle teens, married before
he was out of them, and soon thereafter fared to London
to make a living as an actor and actor-partner, cannot
well have been the author of what so many men of so
many nations pronounce to be the greatest total achievement in pure literature.   Most of this difficulty, I think
we have seen, either proceeds upon or takes shape through
the common assumption or acceptance of the " orthodox "
form of the doctrine that the author of the plays was at
once a skilled lawyer and a deep classical scholar.   We
have seen, I think, how baseless are both of those
positions, whether as put by Baconians or by idolatrous
Shakespeareans.   Much of what is not thus accounted
for in the difficulty felt about the writing of the plays by
the " Stratford actor " is to be ascribed to the state of
mind set up by other idolatrous propositions to the effect
that Shakespeare was a profound naturalist, a master of
Italian literature, a deep student of medicine and biology,
a man of absolutely universal reading, and so forth.
Every one of these extravagances can be as decisively
disposed of as the " legal " and " classical " theories.
Mr. Greenwood, who is professedly not a Baconian,
unwittingly puts not merely a stumbling-block in the
way of Baconians, but a weapon in the hands of the
" Stratfordians " when, proceeding upon the QUARTERLY
REVIEW article of 1894, on " Shakespeare's Birds and
Beasts," he goes about to establish the view that the
author of the plays was no observant or studious
naturalist.   Quite so, we answer.   That was part of the

idolatrous conception of the playwright as the Superman. And the rejection of it, so far from putting any difficulty in the way of the " Stratfordian " view, gives that a new force of rationality. We are not in the least bound to suppose that Shakespeare must have been an accurate naturalist because he spent his youth at Stratford. It was no scientific observer who went from Stratford to London to start as play actor and play maker : it was a youth with a genius for the perception and the rhythmic utterance of human feeling. But, above all, it was not the would-be naturalist Bacon who versified a description of a horse from Du Bartas, and one of a bee-hive from Lilly or Elyot or Bartholomew or another !

But while thus unintentionally helping Shakespeareans to rectify their conception of Shakespeare, Mr. Greenwood is at pains to demonstrate that somehow the Plays are at once incommensurable with the potentialities of the " Stratford actor " and perfectly compatible with the training of a thorough professional lawyer. He scouts the idea that " genius " with scanty schooling could capacitate any human being to write even VENUS AND ADONIS. Agreeing with me that it is absurd to suppose that Shakespeare wrote the poem in his teens and kept it by him unpublished till 1593, he proceeds to say [1] that in his judgment " the real absurdity is in the belief that the ' Stratford rustic ' could have written such a poem at all. . . . In Shakespeare's time, and for a youth in Shakespeare's environment, it would have been a miracle of tenfold marvel. The truth is that we do not gather figs from thistles, nor can we make a silk purse out of a sow's ear. Even ' Genius ' cannot do this."

I confess to being somewhat mystified by these forcible propositions. Mr. Greenwood cannot mean that the being born and bred in a country town constituted a man an irreclaimable " rustic," a moral " thistle," an intellectual " sow's-ear," even if the town were " squalid " and the

[1] Work cited, p. 64, *note.*

man were a son of "illiterate parents," whether in the
Elizabethan era or in ours. He must mean; I take it,
that to make such a youth capable of writing the Plays
and Poems there would have been required an elaborate
education ; and that this Shakespeare did not receive.
But perplexity remains. What kind of education does
Mr. Greenwood suppose is required to qualify a genius
for writing plays and poems ? What kind or degree of
culture, for instance, does he ascribe to Sappho, to
Terence, to Catullus, to Hans Sachs, to Bunyan, to Burns,
to Keats, to Jane Austen, to Balzac ?

Being myself responsible for a thesis on " The Economics
of Genius," to the effect that genius undoubtedly requires
culture-opportunities for its evocation—that, in short,

> Haud facile emergunt quorum virtutibus obstat
> Res angusta domi—

I am not going to dispute the importance of culture to
poets. But I think Mr. Greenwood misconceives the
nature of the culture they require. It is true that, on a
general survey of literary history, what we term university
culture counts for a great deal, the great majority of our
great poets having had that or its equivalent. But the
exceptions are sufficient to warn us to reject the notion
that it is essential. Keats will rank with any poet of his
age in respect of (1) " rhythmical creation of beauty,"
and (2) sympathetic seizure of the spirit of classical
antiquity. Yet Keats certainly had small Greek ; his
sonnet ON FIRST READING CHAPMAN'S HOMER tells as
much ; and though he learned Latin enough to do in his
teens (so, at least, we are told) a prose translation of the
ÆNEID—with what accuracy or what crib help no one
now can say—he " was in childhood not attached to
books. His *penchant* was for fighting. He would fight
any one—morning, noon, and night, his brother among
the rest. It was meat and drink to him." So testifies
an admiring schoolfellow.[1] It was only in his last few

[1] Colvin's *Keats*, p. 8.

terms at school, in his fourteenth and fifteenth years, that he took earnestly to books and studies ; and at fifteen he was bound apprentice to a surgeon. At nineteen he became a medical student at Guy's ; and save for that he had no "college" education. At twenty-one he produced ENDYMION, and at twenty-three the ODE TO A NIGHTINGALE. His effective culture thus came substantially from the reading of English literature.

Now, concerning the schooling of Shakespeare we know very little ; but we do know that he was entitled to free tuition at the Stratford Grammar School ; and it would be as irrational to doubt that he had it as it would be to reject Ben Jonson's testimony that, nevertheless, he had " small Latin and less Greek," which, after all, is a very different thing from saying that he had none. On the other hand we have really no testimony that can justify us in saying that he left school " very early." Sir Sidney Lee, on the strength of Aubrey's late recital of the statement of old neighbours that " when he [Shakespeare] was a boy he exercised his father's trade," of a butcher—which was *one of* his father's trades—writes (after Halliwell-Philipps) that " probably in 1577, when he was thirteen, he was enlisted by his father in an effort to restore his decaying fortunes." For this " probably " there is no clear basis. As we have seen, the " decaying fortunes " have been inferred, not proved ; and there is a strong contrary inference. But even if we knew that at thirteen Shakespeare helped his father in the village-butcher business, we should not be entitled to say that he then left school. Boys may help their fathers and still go to school. I did, for one. Having myself, nevertheless, left school at thirteen; with small Latin and no Greek, I am not prepared to admit that such an experience excludes a boy from future culture ; but I am concerned here simply to stipulate for strict adherence to the evidence. Mr. Greenwood argues that inasmuch as he accepts the " tradition " that Shakespeare went to the

Grammar School, he is entitled to press the "tradition" that the boy left school at "an unusually early age"; but he has really no tradition to that effect to go upon. Aubrey specifies no age; and Shakespeare would be "a boy" at fifteen.

That, however, is really not the vital point. Shakespeare's *special* culture for his life's work began when he went to see the players, or, it may be, to the little customary court at Stratford;[1] and his effective culture would come to him after he had gone to London. If he went thither, as is commonly reckoned, in 1586 or 1587, he spent some six or seven years as an actor before he published VENUS AND ADONIS. Mr. Greenwood seems to take it for granted that this actor's-life meant the negation or exclusion of "culture."[2] I cannot imagine a more thoughtless view of the case, unless it be taken in terms of a conception of culture which seems to me wholly irrelevant. Discussing the VENUS, Mr. Greenwood quotes approvingly Mr. Appleton Morgan's hyperbolical account of it as "the most elegant verses which the age produced, and which for polish and care surpass his very latest works"; and adds: " Polished, indeed, and scholarly, is this extraordinary poem, and, above all, it is impressed throughout with that which we now call *Culture*. It is, in fact, imbued with the spirit of the highest culture of the age in which it was written."[3]

In support of this assertion, what data are offered? Simply these : a few borrowings from Ovid ; a borrowing of the description of the horse from Sylvester's translation —then in MS.—of Du Bartas ; and a *possible* imitation

---

[1] It may be worth while here to recall Grote's luminous exposition of the relation of the Athenian drama to the Athenian Dikasteries.

[2] At the same time he notes that even the art of acting is not to be learned in a day. Quite so. It is only the art of *playmaking* that, in the opinion of Mr. Greenwood and the Baconians alike, requires no apprenticeship !

[3] Work cited, p. 59.

of the ODE DE LA CHASSE of Etienne Jodelle, which also, in the terms of the case, may have been current in an English MS. translation. That is all ; unless we are to understand Mr. Greenwood as implying that the legal allusions in the poem belong to " the highest culture of the age." It is hardly necessary to dwell on the utter inadequacy of the evidence to the assertion. The borrowings from Ovid *are made through Golding's translation ;* [1] but even if they were not, it is merely ridiculous to describe them as standing for " the highest culture of the age." The poem shows no such range of knowledge as does Sidney's APOLOGY FOR POETRIE, to say nothing of the earlier poems of Chapman. Considered as a psychic distillation of knowledge of life, the VENUS might fairly be said to stand for *want* of " culture " in the modern and larger sense of the term. But the *kind* of culture it shows, the fluent and mellifluous use of English verse, the multiplicity of image, the superfœtation of verbal fancy, the unlimited play of description—all this was just what Shakespeare, given genius to start with, would acquire in his six or seven—or even five—years of acting.

To deny it would be to refuse recognition of the obvious fact that as an actor Shakespeare was habitually using more or less academic as well as poetic diction, speaking a language above the level of that of common talk ; inflated, doubtless, but copious, colorate, rhythmic, eloquent. Even the acting of the more literary Interludes must have meant considerable training in diction, a good vocabulary, a fair range of literary and classical association ; and the young Shakespeare had a larger range open to him than that. When not engaged in acting, he could turn to the literature of the Tudor age—the prose and verse of Elyot, More, Greene, Gascoigne, Lilly, Spenser, Sidney, Peele, Lodge, Nashe, Sackville, Latimer, and the divines ; much miscellaneous English poetry, down to

[1] See *Montaigne and Shakespeare*, 2nd ed. pp. 309–316.

Lodge's Glaucus and Scilla, the model of the Venus ;
Chaucer ; the treatises of Puttenham and Webbe on
English Poetry ; the Chronicles ; a number of Voyages ;
many translations of Latin classics and of Italian prose
and poetry ; and, from the Greek, Herodotus and
Thucydides, Hall's Iliad, three orations of Demosthenes,
a good deal of Isocrates, some of Lucian, the Axiochus,
Diodorus, Appian, Ælian, the Ethics of Aristotle, Epic-
tetus, Xenophon's Cyropædia, North's Plutarch, something of Theocritus, something of Hippocrates and Galen,
and the Æthiopic History of Heliodorus.   How much or
how little Shakespeare read in these translations no man
can say ; but there they were, in English—a great deal
more of culture material than any one can pretend to
find behind the Venus and Adonis and the Lucrece.
And when we remember that Taylor the Water-Poet, a
Thames waterman, living by his boat, avowedly devoid
of all scholarship, had read in English in Ovid, Homer,
and Virgil, Plutarch's Morals and Lives, Marcus Aurelius,
Seneca, Suetonius, and Cornelius Agrippa, as well as in
Fairfax's Tasso, Du Bartas, Montaigne, Guevara, Jose-
phus ; and in Chaucer, Sidney, Spenser, Daniel, Nashe,
Camden, Purchas, Speed, Fox, and Holinshed [1]—we are
really not entitled to doubt that the Stratford actor could
have read widely enough in English to give him all the
" culture " manifested in the Plays and Poems.   Mr.
Greenwood will not deny that the Stratford actor could
read ; and as he cannot without a *petitio principii* deny
him genius, his primary case is thus quashed and done
with.   For nothing more than genius and culture in
English, with some smattering of Latin, is needed to
account for the Plays and the Poems.

The " polish " of Venus and Adonis is just the kind of

[1] Last section of *Taylor's Motto : Et Habeo, et Careo, et Curo :*
Workes, 1630, section II, p. 57.   Taylor was then, by his own
account, in his later forties.   It is here that he tells how he never
got beyond *possum, posset.*

polish that an actor who was also a poet of genius could acquire. In all ages some actors, without university training, have spoken their own language like men of culture, acquiring facility in it from the nature of their work ; and if genius be added, there is no special problem to solve in the case of Shakespeare. The general problem of genius lies outside the issue. A supreme gift for rhythmic speech involves of necessity a spontaneous study of language ; and Shakespeare, so conceived, must have read much *belles lettres* in his own tongue, as did Burns, and as did Keats. If they with their culture could produce masterpieces in song ; why in the name of reason should not he have done so in drama ? His actorship, which Mr. Greenwood and the Baconians so strangely assume to have been a bar thereto, was part of the special culture that made him supreme. Given poetic genius, the practice of acting was the very discipline required to make him transcend the declamation of his academic pre-decessors, and reach the ring of living utterance where they had mostly vended conventional rhetoric.

In failing to see the significance of Shakespeare's experience as an actor, Mr. Greenwood seems to me to be obsessed by what I would term the university fallacy. He makes a strenuous attempt to rebut the argument of Sir Theodore Martin to the effect that the early life of Shakespeare was no more a bar to the development of his genius than was that of Dickens to his. Dickens, replies Mr. Greenwood, actually found in his early life the material upon which his adult genius worked ; but he will have it that Shakespeare's " material " was the kind of " culture " he claims to find in VENUS AND ADONIS. Denying that there is any noteworthy scholarly culture in that poem, I deny that there is any force in Mr. Greenwood's attempted rebuttal. It was not scholarly culture that went to the writing of either the comedies or the tragedies ; still less could such culture have prepared the poet to create Falstaff. But as regards the writing of

living verse and the creation of living characters, his
training as an actor was relevant culture of the most
important kind.

Classical culture prepared Ben Jonson to write SEJANUS
and CATILINE and the POETASTER and CYNTHIA'S REVELS ;
but what part had it in EVERY MAN IN HIS HUMOUR and
THE ALCHEMIST and BARTHOLOMEW FAIR ? And which
were his more successful plays ? Such culture was
possessed, in some degree, by Greene and Peele ; but was
it classical example or actual experience in play-writing
that—with quickly growing faculty—made Greene capable
of rising from ALPHONSUS KING OF ARRAGON to JAMES
THE FOURTH ? and was it the scholarship indicated in
the TALE OF TROY that went to the making of what
dramatic success was attained to by Peele ? If (a very
large *if*) it was university training, and not genius, that
made Marlowe capable of writing the blank verse of
TAMBURLAINE and FAUSTUS, does it follow that it took
more scholarly training to make the poet of MACBETH and
CORIOLANUS write blank verse far finer and greater ?
The broad culture-fact is that every one of the dramatists
above-named exhibits far more of mere classical scholarship, in the way of quotation and allusion, than does
Shakespeare, who finally writes a verse incomparably
superior to theirs. If we are to frame an *a priori* hypothesis at all, should it not be to the effect that the visibly
less learned poet vitalised his English diction and rhythms
as he did in virtue of *not* having had a regular scholarly
training, and of *having*, besides genius, a practical training
in the actual handling of the verse of the other men ?

I do not stand on such a proposition : I merely urge its
relative reasonableness. I note that whereas Spenser and
Peele and Chapman held to the vicious old usage of
falsifying final accents to make rhymes, Shakespeare,
perhaps encouraged by Greene, never once conformed to
it. He seems to have been as free of mere archaism as
he was of pedantry, though he had his own faults of

diction. The VENUS AND ADONIS is for its time an essentially *modern* piece of work ; and I do not remember that any of the contemporaries who praised its " sweetness " ever said a word about its learning. So far as we know, no one in that day ever asked, How came the Stratford actor to produce this distillation of culture ? I do not ask Mr. Greenwood to accept the " tradition " ; but I do ask him how, on his view of the impossibility of the actor's having, with his culture, written such a poem at his age, not one of the actor's contemporaries, so far as we know, ever so much as remarked that any notable culture was required to write it.[1]

Much has been made, further, of the " difficulty " of supposing a mere actor to be permitted to dedicate poems to the Earl of Southampton. There is really not a grain of good ground for suggesting any difficulty in the matter ; and the very reason assigned—the difference of status between poet and patron—destroys itself the moment it is understood. If it be held unlikely that a literature-loving nobleman in Shakespeare's day should allow a mere actor to dedicate to him, as to a friendly patron, two poems, how in the name of common sense

---

[1] Mr. G. C. Bompas (*Problem of the Shakespeare Plays*, 1902, p. 70) is responsible for the statement that " One of Shakespeare's contemporaries, the author of *Polimanteia* (1595) . . . wrote that Shakespeare was both a ' schollar ' and also a member of one or more of the ' three English universities, Cambridge, Oxford, and the Inns of Court.' " No such passage is known to the commentators. Dr. Ingleby (*Centurie of Prayse*, i, 12) cites the marginal note from *Polimanteia* which runs " All praise worthy [Lucrecia] Sweet Shakespeare," and classes the poet with " well-graced authors." In a footnote, Dr. Ingleby mentions that probably it was on the strength of this side-note that the late Rev. N. J. Halpin arrived at the rather hazardous conclusion that Shakespeare was a member of " one (or perhaps more) of the English Universities." See his *Dramatic Unities of Shakespeare*, 1849, p. 12, *note*. This appears to be the source of the hallucination of Mr. Bompas. He has been guilty of more " howlers " than any other Baconian, except perhaps Mr. Donnelly.

are we to suppose that the nobleman would let all the world go on believing that the poems *were* so dedicated if they really were not ?   The cavil is sheer absurdity.

§ 5

And, once more, if, ignoring that absurdity, we are to suppose that the publication of the VENUS and LUCRECE as his own by Shakespeare the actor was a pure fraud, what kind of solution have we offered us of the mystification ? Mr. Greenwood must have a lawyer who was a " courtier," but will not say it was Bacon, herein taking up a singularly weak position. He naturally resents being called a Baconian when he is not ; but he will not say No to the Baconians, and leaves the question open, with a mere " anti-Stratfordian " negative. When he comes to the positive Stratfordian evidence, he can offer nothing but confessedly inconclusive cavils. The testimony of Ben Jonson, a solid rock of first-hand proof, he vainly seeks to get round, as we have seen, by suggesting that Ben's prose is inconsistent with his poem prefaced to the Folio ; and that the players' preface, presumably written by Jonson, is inconsistent with the facts as to the sources of the Folio. The inconsequence of the whole argument is staggering. To what exorbitance of self-contradiction this line of reasoning leads, we have partly noted in dealing with the positions of Mark Twain ; but there are further enormities of fallacy involved.   If Jonson had spoken of the player Shakespeare to Drummond as a mere actor, or had so described him in the DISCOVERIES, there would indeed have been a rift in the lute of his evidence. But the very criticisms to which Mr. Greenwood so strangely points as somehow invalidating or countervailing the poetic tribute prefaced to the Folio are explicit avowals of the artistic productivity of the man named. Ben, in talk with Drummond, said of Shakespeare that he " wanted art, and sometimes sense," even as he said of Donne that " for not keeping of accent he deserved hanging." To the same Donne he wrote, sending his Epigrams :

> If I find but one
> Marked by thy hand, and with the better stone,
> My title's seal'd.[1]

Does Mr. Greenwood infer from this either that Jonson thought Donne a good critic but a bad poet, or that he believed some one else had written Donne's verses ?   Or is he restrained merely by the fact that Drummond cites also the praise : " He esteemed him [Donne] the first poet in the world for some things " ?   Without that praise, the testimony to Donne's authorship of poems would be just as valid ; and the very criticism passed to Drummond upon " Shakespeare " is a testimony that in Jonson's belief " Shakespeare " wrote THE WINTER'S TALE.   It is a criticism of the author, whosoever he was : Mr. Greenwood unintelligibly cites it [2] as somehow hinting a knowledge that the putative was not the real author.   In what police court would Mr. Greenwood venture to advance such an argument ?

The mystification set up over Ben Jonson's testimony is the most gratuitous thing in the whole debate.   Jonson was notoriously a man both jealous and generous, given to cavilling and quarrelling, with a high sense of his own value, and a very critical eye for other men's work. Ready to flout and contemn, to strive and blame, he was also ready to forgive and praise.   After his quarrels with Marston and Dekker, he became reconciled to both.   It is reasonably to be inferred that in the " Apologetical Dialogue " appended to THE POETASTER he alludes to Shakespeare among others of his censors in the lines :

> Only, amongst them, I am sorry for
> Some better natures by the rest so drawn,
> To run in that vile line ;

seeing that in THE RETURN FROM PARNASSUS the players tell how their fellow Shakespeare had administered to

---

[1] Epigram 96.   [2] *Shakespeare Problem*, p. 482.

Jonson "a purge." Ben for his part had in his EVERY
MAN OUT OF HIS HUMOUR jeered at Shakespeare's coat of
arms, parodying the *Non sans Droit* by the motto *Not
without Mustard ;* and had well deserved his " purge " in
other ways. But he was one who could give and take,
forgive and forget. In his lines to Donne he praises him
expressly for his freedom in criticism :

> Who shall doubt, Donne, whe'r I a poet be,
> When I dare send my Epigrams to thee ?
> That so alone canst judge, so alone dost make;
> And, in thy censures, evenly, dost take
> As free simplicity to disavow
> As thou hast best authority t' allow.

These are the very qualities that he would have claimed
for himself. That such a man, alive to the greatness,
and, by his own avowal, to the lovableness of Shakespeare,
should pen a splendid panegyric for the Folio, touching
even that with critical qualification, and should at other
times, in critical talk with Drummond and in his DIS-
COVERIES, comment on what he held to be flaws in
Shakespeare's work, is so perfectly compatible not only
with literary but with ordinary human nature that it is
astonishing that either a layman or a lawyer should
profess to find in it anything strange.

By Mr. Greenwood's tests, we should be led to believe
that in Jonson's opinion Daniel wrote none of his signed
verses save the CIVIL WARS, inasmuch as Jonson (1) told
Drummond that Daniel, who wrote that work, was no
poet, and (2) wrote of Daniel that he was a " verser," and
again of Du Bartas that " He was no poet but a verser,
because he wrote not fiction." Again, Mr. Greenwood
seems bound to deny to Marston the authorship of *his*
plays, because Jonson told Drummond that " Marston
wrote his father-in-law's preachings, and his father-in-
law his comedies." Gifford in fact offers the Baconians
an opening in advance, by his footnote with the query :
" But who was this father-in-law ? Nay, who was

Marston ? " Unfortunately, Gifford supplies particulars
in respect of which, he tells us, " I flatter myself that I
have here recovered both father and son "—as well as
father-in-law.

· Jonson's gibe at Marston, obviously, is a mere jest :
his comments on Shakespeare are one and all criticisms
of a recognised author. And if Mr. Greenwood here
raises afresh his nugatory protest that the contemporary
encomiasts of Shakespeare do not tell us " who " he was,
it suffices to answer that neither did Jonson tell Drummond " who " Donne or Daniel or Spenser or Drayton
was. It was really not customary to say " who " a
man was when you praised him by his name, for his
known works. As for the astonishing argument (1) that
the famous reference to the original form of the " Know,
Cæsar doth not wrong " passage may have meant that
" Shakespeare the player misquoted the passage on the
stage," and (2) that " surely it is of the player, not the
poet, that Jonson speaks when he says that his volubility
was such that, like Aterius, he had to be (or ought to have
been) shut up," [1] I find myself at a loss to discuss it with
gravity. Where will Mr. Greenwood stop ? The sentence
he cites is from the paragraph in the DISCOVERIES in
which Jonson tells how " the players have *often* mentioned
it as an honour to Shakespeare [' their friend '], that in
his writing (whatsoever he penned) he never blotted out a
line. My answer hath been, Would he had blotted a
thousand. Which they thought a malevolent speech."
And the very sentence ending with the allusion to
Haterius tells that Shakespeare " had an excellent
phantasy, brave notions, and gentle expressions, *wherein
he flowed with that facility* that . . ." Has Mr. Greenwood found any Apella who can credit his theory
here ?

Such a fantasy is of a piece with the desperate
suggestion of " a learned German, Dr. Konrad Meier," a

[1] Work cited, p. 481.

little hesitatingly welcomed by Mr. Greenwood in a footnote,[1] that Jonson's line :

And *though* thou hadst small Latin and less Greek,

is to be read in the sense " And *if*," or " even if," = " even had it been true that." Need it really be pointed out that while " and if " *could* have meant " and though," " and though " could *not* mean " and if " in the sense suggested ? " Though " can stand for " if " when put before a hyperbole : as in " though I speak with the tongues of men and angels " ; not before a carefully quantified proposition such as " *small* Latin and *less* Greek "—a specification if ever there were one. Mr. Greenwood, for the rest, really should have spared English readers Dr. Meier's theorem that the " would " in the following line :

From hence to honour thee I *would* not seek,

" is conditional," and that " as in every conditional sentence, the conditional word *would* points to the *unreal* alternative, which is to be taken as the opposite of the actual fact." It is from a translation in BACONIANA for October 1907 (" into which, by the way, an error seems to have crept ") that Mr. Greenwood derives this precious philological sophism. It " would " seem, then, that we must explain to Mr. Greenwood as well as to Dr. Meier and the Baconians, that " I would " is perfectly normal English for " I will " in predication. Has Mr. Greenwood never said to an audience, " I would now direct your attention . . ." ? or " Before sitting down, I would like . . ." ? Anti-Stratfordianism has made him acquainted with strange allies. Jonson's lines simply mean : " Though you had small Latin and less Greek, I would not on that account seek merely to pit you against other unlearned men, but would back you against all the classic dramatists, from Æschylus to Seneca." Mr. Greenwood is as hard pressed for pleas when he seeks to

[1] Work cited, p. 475.

get behind *that* testimony as when admitting that the
" sweet swan of Avon " line " undoubtedly . . . *to all
outward appearance* " identifies the dead dramatist " with
Shakspere of Stratford." Mr. Greenwood can find no
better shift than to echo Dr. Ingleby's wish " that Ben
had said all this in Shakespeare's lifetime." O lame and
impotent conclusion !

The cavilling about the players' statement that they
had " scarce received from him [Shakespeare] a blot in
his papers " is no better. The assertion that " we now
know that this statement is ridiculous," [1] is utterly
unwarranted. We do know that Shakespeare revised
plays after they had been for some time played : we do
not know that he sweated over his anvil in first composition as Jonson did ; and Jonson's claim, in the panegyric,
that every writer of living lines must so sweat is an
impeachment of Jonson's consistency, not of the players'
veracity, or of their common sense. Elsewhere, he
accepted their statement as true. The suggestion of
Stevenson, confidently repeated by Mr. Greenwood, that
the unblotted manuscripts, if such there were, must have
been merely fair copies, is idle. Unless Shakespeare
deliberately tricked his partners—a hypothesis which
Jonson did not advance, and which Mr. Greenwood had
better not raise—they must have known that whereof
they spoke. Neither Ben Jonson nor Stevenson was
qualified to say, nor is Mr. Greenwood entitled to reaffirm,
that the abnormal genius who wrote the plays could not
compose in verse otherwise than did Jonson and Stevenson. Jonson *did* later accept the statement of the players
as true ; and the fact that he nevertheless made his
general assertion about the indispensableness of " sweat "
proves simply that he could contradict himself on a
question of that kind as he and most men could and
can on others. But to suggest that such inconsistency
discredits his evidence as to his personal knowledge that

[1] Work cited, p. 480.

Shakespeare was a man of genius, is really as unworthy of a practical lawyer as it is of a man of letters. Either Jonson was a deliberate and unscrupulous liar or he was not. If he was, neither Mr. Greenwood nor the Baconians can make anything of his testimony, one way or the other. If he was not, his evidence overthrows and overwhelms all their cavils. *He* did not think that the plays and poems could have been written only by a professional lawyer. *He* held that Shakespeare had small Latin and less Greek, yet had no hesitation in believing that his unlearned friend wrote the plays which he declared to be " for all time." And his opinion on that head surely has as much weight as any.

§ 6

In dealing with the Baconian argument from Jonson's *Scriptorum Catalogus* in the DISCOVERIES, in which Bacon is extolled and Shakespeare is not mentioned, Mr. Greenwood candidly warns his Baconian allies that the matter will not bear their inference ; that Jonson is thinking of " wits " or orators as such, and not framing a comprehensive list. In point of fact, the list names no playwright whatever ; only one or two poets, and those of a bygone generation ; and indeed only a few writers in all.[1] Yet Mr. Greenwood goes on to argue that " still " it is " remarkable " that Shakespeare is not named. If the paragraph were meant as a " bead-roll " it would be no less strange that Spenser and Marlowe are also unnamed : the only really remarkable thing is that Jonson or any one else should ever have headed such a jotting as a " Catalogus." But Mr. Greenwood, with sorrow be it said, proceeds from this trifling cavil to endorse the truly " Baconian " argument that there is a deep significance in Jonson's use of the phrase about " insolent Greece and haughty Rome " in his eulogy of Bacon, after using it in his poem on Shakespeare.

[1] The critic cited by Mr. Greenwood, who called the *Catalogus* " a bead-roll of English writers," has something to answer for.

This particular divagation, I may note, really gives a good excuse to those critics who describe Mr. Greenwood as a Baconian, though he apparently does not perceive that he has supplied them with any pretext. He insists upon his specific denials ; but to what purpose has he dwelt upon the fact that Jonson applies one phrase of panegyric to both Bacon and Shakespeare ? Through seven pages he dwells on the " remarkable," " more remarkable," and " most remarkable " aspects of that item. He finds it " extraordinary " that Jonson, after Bacon's fall, wrote of the ruined great man's character in the highest terms, and yet has not " left us any noble eulogy *of this sort* consecrated to the memory of Shakespeare." Is not the panegyric prefixed to the Folio a noble eulogy in *its* sort ? After thus making a mystery out of nothing, he proceeds to dilate on the line :

> Thou stand'st as if some mystery thou didst,

in Jonson's Ode on Bacon's Birthday. The phrase simply means that on Bacon's birthday the " Genius of the pile " stands among the guests as might a priest celebrating a rite ; but Mr. Greenwood will have it that " the Stratfordians . . . are unable to give any plausible explanation of Jonson's meaning," as against the Baconian thesis that Jonson knew " the secret Shakespearean authorship."[1] After this, how can he complain of being reputed a Baconian ? The poem itself, after speaking of " some mystery," goes on : " Pardon, I read it in thy face." None are so blind as those who will not see aught but their own theory.[2]

All the while, the argument from Jonson's double use

[1] Is it suggested, I wonder, that Bacon was *telling* his guests that he had written the plays ? The phrase " as if some mystery thou *didst* " plainly points to a *quasi-rite* or *sacramentum*, not to a " mystery " in the modern sense.

[2] The point was made clear by Mrs. Stopes four-and-twenty years ago. Yet Mr. Lang oddly acquiesced in Mr. Greenwood's cry of " mystery."

of the phrase " insolent Greece and haughty Rome " is
simply the crowning instance of the futility of non-
comparative study over the whole field of our problem.
Jonson did but repeat himself in that case as he did in
many others.   I put to Mr. Greenwood this simple and
sufficient challenge.   Jonson in his Ode on Bacon's
Birthday speaks of the Lord Chancellor as one

> Whose even thread the fates spin round and full,
> Out of their choicest and their whitest wool—

—alas for the forecast !   In THE HUE AND CRY AFTER
CUPID the same Ben Jonson writes of

> A prince that draws
> By example more than others do by laws . . .
> That was reserved *until the Parcae spun*
> *Their whitest wool ; and then his thread begun.*

Does *this* passage suggest any misgivings to Mr. Greenwood ?   Does he find it " most remarkable of all " that
Jonson should have used the same figure in benison of
Bacon and of King James ?   And does he see fit to
suggest that Jonson had cause to think that King James
wrote Bacon ?   Will he not rather grant me that Jonson,
who uses this same figure yet another time in his APOLO-
GETICAL DIALOGUE appended to THE POETASTER—

> The Fates have not spun him the coarsest thread—

applying it to *himself*, and who in the same Dialogue as
well as in his ODE TO HIMSELF wrote of " the wolf's
black jaw and the dull ass's hoof," was simply prone to
repeat a sounding phrase upon which he " fancied
himself " ?

If not ; if Mr. Greenwood still elects to minister
platonically to the Baconians, he will do well to frame
either for them or for himself some presentable rebuttal
to the bayonet-line of challenge which faces him and
them.   The hero of the Baconians, presumably, stopped
writing plays when Shakespeare died because, even in
view of his miraculous luck in having his literary secret

thus far kept for him, he could not find another " mask."
Mr. Greenwood's occult lawyer, perhaps, was similarly
swayed. For both sets of theorists, then, Shakespeare
at least had the somewhat weighty merit of supplying
the learned and legal author with a means of vent for
his plays and poems which would otherwise have been
unattained. There is no more new " Shakespeare "
after Shakespeare's death, under any signature. And
Mr. Greenwood's lawyer is as hardly pressed as Bacon
by the demand of those who insist that an author shall
prove his reality by having his manuscripts regularly
printed. Mr. Greenwood's Man in the Paper Mask,
affirmed to be lawyer enough to make Venus talk like
one, secretly produces poems, plays, and sonnets, Bacon-
wise, over a period of twenty years ; then lays down his
pen or dies ; and either in his own despite or with no
touch of supervision from him, has his work perpetuated
in an inextricable blend with that of other men, and
flawed by a multitude of printers' blunders, at the hands
of the player-partners, who, in the view of Mr. Greenwood
and the Baconians, either lied venally or were strangely
deluded for twenty years by an impostor, their partner.

I am not going to play the panegyrist for the actor-
partners, who have it standing to their account that,
with the literary heedlessness of their age, they published
what they must have known to be a mass of largely
composite work without a hint to help posterity to discriminate. But if we deal with evidence in the common-
sense spirit in which the sane lawyer is supposed to deal
with it, we are bound to say that, under the reservation
mentioned, their general testimony far outweighs all
the cavils of the various schools of critics. They have
been harshly and heedlessly accused, even by " orthodox "
scholars, of falsely professing to print solely from true
original copies when they were supplying the printer
with printed quartos for " copy." That attack, un-
important at best, is disposed of by the argument which

proves certain quartos to have been authorised, and therefore to stand reasonably enough for the " true original copies." The alleged " difficulties " of the " Stratfordian " case are thus as dust in the balance against the insanities of the other ; which posits a nightmare of protracted conspiracy and fraud unexampled out of Bedlam.

§ 7

A number of other items in Mr. Greenwood's negative case seem to me hardly to deserve discussion. All the problems he raises as to the young Shakespeare's life at Stratford, apart from the schooling, are practically outside our problem : it matters not to the question of the authorship what were young Will's relations with Sir Thomas Lucy, or what were the precise circumstances of his marriage. Equally irrelevant to our inquiry is the pother over the portraits.[1] As to Mr. Greenwood's unhappy chapter on " The Silence of Philip Henslowe," I confess to being somewhat at a loss for comment. The chapter seems to have been written without any examination of Henslowe's Diary,[2] upon some vague inferences from remarks by Collier and Judge Stotsenburg. Mr. Greenwood argues that whereas the unknown lawyer of his fantasy would naturally not take any payments from such an *entrepreneur* as Henslowe, the actor, on the contrary, readily would ; and that accordingly the absence of the name of Shakespeare (or Shakspere or Shaksper, &c.) from Henslowe's Diary " is certainly a very remarkable phenomenon, and one . . . very difficult to reconcile with the supposition that Player Shakspere wrote plays."[3] In the name of mystery, why ? Mr. Greenwood claims

[1] Long ago Dr. Ingleby pointed out : " As to portraits, Edmund Spenser stands in precisely the same position as Shakespeare. The portraits claimed for him are hopelessly discrepant " (*Shakespeare : The Man and the Book*, Pt. I, 1877, p. 78).

[2] Mr. Lang, who has an amusing chapter in reply to Mr. Greenwood's, seems also not to have studied the Diary.

[3] Work cited, p. 360.

to solve his own enigma by the simple pronouncement that " Neither Shakspere [*i.e.* the actor] nor ' Shakespeare ' [*i.e.* Mr. Greenwood's unknown lawyer] ever wrote for Henslowe." In other words, the actor (in Mr. Greenwood's opinion) could not ; and the mysterious lawyer, who provided the plays for the actor and his partners, would not write for Henslowe. Q.E.D.

I collect myself to ask, How on earth can Mr. Greenwood know this ? That Shakespeare ever " wrote for Henslowe " I do not affirm : there are no means of determining what were the business relations between Henslowe and the Chamberlain's (Shakespeare's) company when they played in either of Henslowe's theatres. I am disposed to surmise that whatever refurbishing of old or writing of new plays Shakespeare did while his company was playing at either the Rose or the Newington Theatre, in the years 1592–96, was done " for " his company and not " for " Henslowe. But seeing that the Diary does not contain *any* entry of payment to *any* writer for playwriting before 1597,[1] when Shakespeare's company were successively at the Theater and the Curtain, and had no longer any dealings with Henslowe, the nonexistence of any note of any payment to *him* is obviously neither here nor there. The payments beginning in 1597 are noted as made " for my Lord Admirall's men," for whom Shakespeare never wrote. It is simply impossible to understand the use of such an argument as Mr. Greenwood's save on the inference that he never examined the Diary at all. He notes Collier's remark that in the years 1594–96 the Admiral's men and the Chamberlain's men were jointly or alternately using one of Henslowe's theatres ; and he exclaims accordingly. But had he

---

[1] These entries begin on Folio 43v., p. 82 of Mr. Greg's edition. Earlier in the book, which is not continuous in order of time, occur similar entries for 1599—Folio 29, p. 57. Even Collier's forgeries, it should be noted, begin only in 1597. *See* ed. cited, introd.

gone to the Diary he would have found that in those years there is no note of a payment to a playwright for either company.

As to the period from 1596 onwards, there is simply no rational ground for expecting to find any note of a payment from Henslowe to Shakespeare, seeing that Shakespeare and his company had no more dealings with that personage. In 1599 they settled at the Globe, for good. Henslowe paid the playwrights who worked for him or for the Admiral's company ; and his Diary is simply a day-book of his many receipts, loans, and payments, theatrical and other, with a few " receipts " of the other sort and some notes of agreements, &c. Obviously, Mr. Greenwood's theory disposes of itself. If an outside friend *could* solely supply Shakespeare, who catered solely for his company, then Shakespeare, a partner, *might* so supply his own company, if he had the required literary capacity. Mr. Greenwood, I trust, will not insist on begging the question throughout the discussion ! Now, that Shakespeare should go on steadily supplying his own company with plays instead of writing for Henslowe was not only natural : it was the way of advantage as against the way of disadvantage. Mr. Greenwood, presumably, does not deny that Shakespeare the actor was from about 1594 a partner in the Lord Chamberlain's (first known as Lord Strange's[1]) company of actors, who successively played at the Rose and at Newington and ran " *the* Theater " and the Globe Theatre. There is, says Mr. Fleay, " no vestige of evidence that Shakespeare ever wrote for any company but one."[2] This holds whether we think of Shakespeare the actor or of Bacon-Shakespeare or of Mr. Greenwood's unknown literary lawyer. And what could be more a matter of course

---

[1] Originally, in all likelihood, Lord Leicester's, but this is matter of inference. *See* Fleay's *Life of Shakespeare*, pp. 91–6. As to the changes in the company's name, *see* Fleay, pp. 114–5, 128.   [2] *Life of Shakespeare*, p. 115.

than that Shakespeare the actor should supply with plays the company in which he was a profit-sharing partner, instead of selling plays outright to Henslowe for a few pounds ? By the former course he enriched himself ; by the latter, he would insanely have condemned himself to the life of chronic beggary led by all the other play-wrights of the day, including even Jonson. That Mr. Greenwood should see something " very remarkable " in such a choice is quite the most remarkable thing in his remarkable tissue of error and paralogism. All his attacks upon " the Stratfordian editors " and others in this connection are a mere fiasco. They and Sir Sidney Lee, as it happens, did not say, as Mr. Greenwood alleged,[1] that Shakespeare began his dramatic career " by writing plays for Henslowe " : they said that Shakespeare's work " doubtless " began[2] at the Rose theatre, about 1592. As Mr. Greenwood does not himself believe that the plays there and then played by Shakespeare's company were Shakespearean, it is hard to see why he took to this line of argument at all. But when he exults in this connection over " a delightful specimen of Strat-fordian reasoning," and proclaims it " the more extra-ordinary—*indeed incredible*—that the old manager should have made no mention " of Shakespeare in his DIARY, his Stratfordian foes are truly avenged. It *would* have been extraordinary, " indeed incredible," if Henslowe had been found entering payments to Shakespeare for plays he did *not* write, in a period of years in which the Diary records no payments to any other playwrights for the plays they *did* write, whether " for Henslowe " or for any of the companies who used his theatres.

When Mr. Greenwood goes on to quote Judge Stotsen-burg as to Henslowe's payments for a " King Leare " and " The Tamynge of a Shrowe," he strangely abets

---

[1] Work cited, pp. 353, 354.
[2] Sir Sidney Lee's words are : " The earliest scene of Shake-speare's *pronounced* successes " (*Life*, 2nd ed. p. 37).

another gratuitous confusion. Judge Stotsenburg is quoted[1] as saying, concerning those two plays, and TITUS; and HENRY THE SIXTH, that "since these plays have *the same names* as those included in the Folio of 1623 the presumption is that they are the same plays until the contrary is shown." Mr. Greenwood is well aware that the old "Leare" was KING LEIR AND HIS THREE DAUGHTERS ; that the old TAMING OF *a* SHREW is not the TAMING OF *the* SHREW ; and that both of the old plays named are extant. As he expressly admits that TITUS and the HENRY VI plays are non-Shakespearean (save for adaptations in the latter), his entire use of Judge Stotsenburg's argument is a mere confounding of confusion. Of the same order is his use of Judge Stotsenburg's contention in regard to TROILUS AND CRESSIDA. The production of a non-Shakespearean TROILUS by Dekker and Chettle in 1599 was perfectly well known to all of us, like the rest of Henslowe's record ; and the existence of plainly non-Shakespearean matter in the Shakespearean TROILUS is an old story among the critics. But if Mr. Greenwood means to suggest—as, apparently, does Judge Stotsenburg—that what is generally accepted as Shakespearean matter in TROILUS was really written by Dekker and Chettle, I am content to leave the question to Shakespearean readers, undebated. That Dekker could have written the great speeches in TROILUS is a proposition which I cannot conceive to be advanced by any critic who has read Dekker, and who can discern the qualities of a style. As to the non-Shakespearean matter in JULIUS CÆSAR, careful analytical research is highly desirable ; but it does not seem likely to be supplied by the school of Judge Stotsenburg. It seems to me a rather lamentable thing that a critic like Mr. Greenwood, who might be doing real service to the study of Shakespeare by furthering the scientific dissection of the composite plays, should join hands with con-

[1] By Mr. Greenwood, p. 355.

fusion-mongers who merely darken counsel by ignorant inference.

It all comes of *parti pris ;* and, as Johnson said of Capell, of " acquiescence in his first thoughts." In his resolve to disparage the Stratford actor, he will not even attach rational weight to Heywood's testimony that when Jaggard in 1612 published an edition of THE PASSIONATE PILGRIM with two poems of Heywood's unwarrantably included, " the author, I know, was much offended with Mr. Jaggard that (altogether unknown to him) presumed to make so bold with his name." " Here," says Mr. Greenwood,[1] " we observe that Heywood does nothing to identify ' the author ' with the player. *He is somebody of whom Heywood speaks in very deferential terms."* And Mr. Greenwood adds that " ' the author ' *does not seem* to have raised any protest as Heywood did." What possible justification can Mr. Greenwood have for this assertion ? He appears to be bent at once on disparaging the actor and affirming the authorship of the literary lawyer ; for he argues on the one hand that had not Heywood interfered, the publisher's fraud would have been acquiesced in, and, on the other hand, that the hypothetical real author—" a courtier, for instance, holding or aspiring to high office in the state "— might have thought it expedient to hold his tongue. *Yet he implies that Heywood knew who this real author was, and that it was somebody in high station.* So the secret was known to Heywood—and to how many beside ! What concern, then, had the " courtier " shown for expediency when he had already let his secret be thus known ? The whole argument is an irreparable mess. The plain answer to all Mr. Greenwood's cavils on these heads is that he knows and can know nothing whatever as to what Shakespeare the actor spontaneously did or said when his works were pirated or other men's works were ascribed to him. These were not occasions for

[1] Work cited, p. 349.

public announcements, and no one has any right to allege that " the author," whoever he were, did not do whatever little was in his power to stop the printers.[1]

It is hardly necessary, finally, to debate Mr. Greenwood's claim to support his case from subsidiary conflicts of opinion among those whom he lumps together as " Stratfordians." He actually challenges us all, under that name, to deal with the " difficulty " of the authorship of ARDEN OF FEVERSHAM, which some Shakespeareans have assigned to Shakespeare. The historical fact is that two " Stratfordians," Mr. Fleay and Mr. Crawford, have in turn claimed, and the second demonstrated, that ARDEN is a work of Kyd. The problem is exactly the same for Mr. Greenwood as for the Stratfordians ; and to suggest that any conflict on such issues discredits the common conviction that the Stratford actor wrote the plays, is to " suborn " a sophism. As well might it be said that a conflict of views among students of Bacon as to his character and capacity is a reason for doubting his authorship of any of his signed works. There will long continue to be dispute among students of Shakespeare as to his share in some of the works assigned to him, whether canonical or apocryphal : it is the business of Shakespearean scholars to go on with those quests as do other scholars with theirs. A desire to further this legitimate mission has helped in the penning of these pages. But it is hard to see how it can be otherwise than very indirectly furthered by contributions to the great " anti-Stratfordian " enterprise of straining at gnats and swallowing camels.

§ 8

Something must be said, finally, concerning the so-called arguments founded on the facts that Shakespeare in his will left only his second-best bed to his wife, and

[1] If he had sued them, would not Mr. Greenwood have accused the Stratford actor of oppressing poor tradesmen ?

that the signature to the will is tremulous—or, as some say, "illiterate." To me personally it has always been so astonishing that reasoning men should treat such items as having a real bearing on the question of authorship, that I have some little difficulty in discussing it without raising the question of their good faith. Their positions appear to be (1) that the bequest of the second-best bed proved Shakespeare to have been on bad terms with his wife; (2) that a man capable of being on bad terms with his wife could not be a man of genius; and (3) that bad handwriting is incompatible with great literary production. It seems necessary to meet these propositions seriously.

Whether Shakespeare was or was not on bad terms with his wife I do not pretend to say. No one has any clear right to an opinion on the subject. It seems unlikely that the "myriad-minded" dramatist should put as a general proposition, on the strength of his own experience, the passage in the TEMPEST in which Prospero warns Ferdinand against anticipating the marriage rite: he must have known some strictly conventional households in which the conjugal relation was inharmonious. My own youthful surmise, on first reading the will, was that the second-best bed had been the marriage bed; and that Anne desired to have it secured to her, dwelling on her past as elderly women—and men—so often do. The most probable solution seems to be that she was either physically or mentally in a condition which made it desirable that she should not be left a control of property. But, on any conceivable view of the case, what has the bequest to do with the question of the authorship? I will not go into the cases of Jonson, Molière, Byron, Shelley, Milton, Victor Hugo, Hazlitt, Goethe, and Dickens, who were so variously infelicitous in their married lives: I will take simply that of Bacon. *He* made a will in which he devised a great deal of money that he did not possess, so that it had to be administered

by creditors, who got about seven shillings in the pound—
a circumstance that does not seem ever to have troubled
the Bacon-Shakespeareans. To that will, in which he
had made an abundant nominal provision for his " loving
wife," Bacon added a codicil, curtly declaring : " Whatsoever I have given, granted, or appointed to my wife,
in the former part of this my will, I do now, for just and
great causes, utterly revoke and make void, and leave
her to her right only." Does that codicil, one asks, in
any way affect the question of Bacon's authorship of
anything he did or did not claim to have written ? If
not, what is the difference in the case of the will of
Shakespeare ?

As the Baconian argument on this topic remains purely
ridiculous for me, while appearing to have for some people
a mysterious force, I will cite one more case of a literary
man's will, which raises the question about books, much
discussed by the Baconians. The will of the poet Samuel
Daniel is extant. It begins with the customary " committing " of body and soul to their respective destinations.
It then allots " to my sister, Susan Bowre,[1] one feather
bed, and with the furniture thereto belonging, and such
linen as I shall leave at my house at Ridge." There
follow four bequests of ten pounds each to members of
the Bowre family, and " for the disposing of all other
things " the testator's brother is left a free hand, as
executor. There is not a word about books or wife,
though Daniel is supposed to have had a wife. " When
he was married, and to whom, still remain unknown."[2]
Does all this set up any doubt as to the existence of
Samuel Daniel, his authorship of the books to which

[1] The Rev. Mr. Grosart, who prints the will, mentions that
Daniel " had no sister, so far as appears "—another " mystery,"
which I do not attempt to solve. See Grosart's ed. of Daniel's
Works, 1885, i, pp. xxv-xxvi. [In his Index, I find, Grosart
admits his oversight, and says he cannot account for it.]

[2] Grosart, as cited, p. xxiv. Jonson told Drummond that
Daniel " had no children."

he put his name, and his reading of many other books ? [1]

The question of the handwriting calls for no more elaborate treatment. The allegation that the signatures to the will, written near the death of the testator, are those of an " illiterate " person, is a sample of the way in which Baconians persuade. Mr. Greenwood does not scruple to write of " the hopeless scrawls that do duty for his signatures."[2] I know not what the palæographers say on the subject : to me, on a comparison of the Shakespeare signatures with others of the period, the assertion seems simply false. The recently discovered half-signature to the deposition of 1612 [3] is indeed very hastily and badly written—apparently with the kind of impossible pen still so commonly supplied for public use in banks and other offices. But such a signature was on any view a matter of no formal importance ; and Shakespeare could conceivably have been much bored by the Mountjoye case, and impatient to get away from it. And the Baconian attack, as it happens, had been made on the signatures already known. Now, the signatures to the deeds of 1612–13, in particular the second, seem to me those of a good and firm penman : those to the will, written within a month of death, are surely not out-of-the-way.[4] Mr. Greenwood is able to cite Sir Sidney Lee

[1] The book query arises in regard to Reginald Scot, author of *The Discoverie of Witchcraft* (1584). He must have read many books, and surely owned some, but no book is alluded to in his will. (See it in Nicholson's rep. p. xxvii.)

[2] *Shakespeare Problem*, p. 14.

[3] Art. *New Shakespeare Discoveries*, by Dr. C. W. Wallace, in *Harper's Magazine*, March 1910. This half-signature goes far to validate the similar one on the Bodleian Ovid. The abbreviated form will probably be exclaimed over by Baconians. I may note that I have seen just such a half-signature by a distinguished living statesman.

[4] I once had the idea, put by Mr. Nesbit, that the tremulousness of the signatures to the will might stand for a nervous malady, the likely cause of Shakespeare's retirement. But within a month of death, any cause might so operate.

as having pronounced, on the strength of the five signatures, that Shakespeare's handwriting was of an " illegible " type. It is rarely that Mr. Greenwood and Sir Sidney are at one : in this case I take leave to deny the assertion of both. But the whole of Mr. Greenwood's argument on the subject is obscure. He seems to imply that either to write or to sign in the old " Gothic " script as late as 1600 was to give evidence of lack of culture ; but the suggestion that men who then wrote usually in the Italic script might sign law deeds in the old script he meets by citing Sir Sidney Lee to the effect that educated Englishmen in those days wrote their letters usually in the old character and signed their names in the new Italian hand. How such a question is to be settled ; how we can know whether or not Shakespeare usually wrote in modern script, I am unable to understand. Sir Sidney Lee and Mr. Greenwood seem for once to have united in a dogmatic and unprovable assertion of the kind that Sir Sidney usually eschews and Mr. Greenwood professes to reprobate.

The common sense of the matter is that either hand could be written with facility ; that probably the actors had been taught, as Shakespeare probably was, the old English script at school ; and that he was therefore not unlikely to have written his plays for them in the said script.[1] That wills and deeds, written in old script, should be signed in old script, seems natural ;[2] but I am content to leave that an open question, knowing of no adequate research on the subject. In any case, there

---

[1] The MS. of *The Birth of Hercules* (written after 1600), of which some facsimiles are given in the Malone Society's edition, is in old script, with names in italic.

[2] Mr. Greenwood jeers vigorously (p. 14) at Dr. Garnett and Dr. Philip Gosse for this suggestion. They had used the phrase, " appropriate for business matters " ; and he asks why the old should be more appropriate for business matters than the new script. He knows that by " business matters " they meant legal matters. Will he explain why an old script is still partly retained in engrossing ?

would have been nothing out-of-the-way in Shakespeare's adherence to the old script all his life, if he did adhere to it. Spedding notes that Bacon wrote the old script in his early youth, and later adopted the new. I have seen a number of books of Shakespeare's age, in which marginal annotations are made in the old English script. The writing is often firmer, doubtless, than that of the signatures to Shakespeare's will ; to say nothing of the hasty half-signature to the deposition of 1612 ; but, as already remarked, the other signatures seem firm enough.

But what if they were otherwise ? Supposing they had been all alike tremulous, or penned with apparent difficulty, what would follow ? Anti-Stratfordians either are or are not aware (1) that many literary men and scholars have written very illegibly all their lives ; (2) that men who could once write clearly and neatly have through some nervous affection or cramp ceased to be able to do so. The whole argument from the signatures is for me so nugatory that, not knowing what its supporters have in their minds, I think it well to mention (1) that the late Mr. Andrew Lang, one of the most cultured and one of the most productive men of letters of his time, wrote (latterly, at least) one of the very worst hands ever seen ; (2) that several financial magnates of our day, in the case of whose signatures legibility would seem to be important, notoriously sign in scrawls which defy decipherment, and are recognised at the banks as a species of mark ; (3) that cramp or other nerve affections will render stiff or tremulous the hand even of a man of genius ; and (4) that when we are near death, infirmity of body is likely to occur in the case of any one of us.

Having thus put briefly all the arguments that seem to me necessary[1] to meet the Baconian case concerning

[1] *See*, however, Mr. Lang's posthumous work, and the smaller book of Canon Beeching, for other and weighty confutations of Baconian inferences of this order.

the will and the signatures, as I understand it, I will not
seek finally to disguise my conviction that those who
have advanced or been impressed by it have suffered
either intellectually or morally from the contagion of a
malady of opinion. When before was a literary man's
faculty or authorship challenged on the score of the
badness of his handwriting, or, for that matter, of his
spelling ? [1]   And when before were a man's relations with
his wife considered to have a bearing on the question of
his possession of literary genius ? The Baconians tell
us that Shakespeare did not properly educate his daughters. Did Milton, who caused his to learn the mere
alphabets of dead languages so that they might read aloud
to him without understanding ? [2] In an age in which
most women, especially in the provinces, did not learn
to write, is there anything astonishing in Shakespeare's
following of the general usage ?   And even if there were,
has the matter any more evidential bearing on the question of the authorship of the plays than has the fact of
Milton's display of repellent characteristics upon the
question whether he wrote PARADISE LOST as it stands,
or whether the poem was " edited " as Bentley maintained ?

[1] In the two letters of Bacon first printed by Dr. Grosart in
the introduction to his ed. of Sir John Davies, six separate
words are given up as "illegible," and the spelling is lax.

[2] Mr. Greenwood (p. 204) has a note on this subject, in which he
strives to show that Milton did *more* for his daughters than
Shakespeare for his. Denouncing the " pitiful " pleas of " Stratford apologists," he strives to evade the fact that Milton forced
his daughters to read to him in languages which they did not
understand. All the while, he has never faced the real issue—
the probable difference between the culture-standards of *Stratford*
in Shakespeare's day and those of *London* in Milton's. Milton
had his daughters taught to read, but not to know any language
save their own, because " one tongue was enough for a woman."
In the end he was fain to teach the youngest Latin. The others,
forced to read in languages they knew not, came to hate their
father. Mark Pattison was more severe on Milton in this connection than is Mr. Greenwood on Shakespeare. (*Milton*, pp. 147–8.)

POSTSCRIPT

Even Mr. Lang, in the act of confuting the "anti-Stratfordian" case, seems to me to make one unwarranted concession to it. On the strength of Shakespeare's four law suits to recover small debts, he pronounces him a "hard creditor." Now, it is not inconceivable that the author of the Plays may have been a hard creditor ; but it seems to me unlikely ; and the four small law suits are very inadequate proof of such a charge. It ignores (1) the far greater commonness of such litigation in that day than in ours ; and (2) the obvious possibility that Shakespeare was dealing with slippery debtors. Shakespeare, described by Jonson as of " an open and free nature," might well have to leave such matters to his attorney. John Shakespeare, as we have seen, ran many more law suits than his son ever did, some of them with his personal friends. *Moi qui parle*, I once sued a rascally debtor for a small debt, because he was brazenly bilking me ; and he succeeded, despite the court's order against him ! I cannot on that score reckon myself a hard creditor—I never sued anybody else—and I can conceive that Shakespeare, in a day of lower standards than ours, found more than one of his debtors dishonest, or otherwise exasperating. Still, the point is quite irrelevant to the question of authorship or genius—as irrelevant as is that of Bacon's laxness and indebtedness, or Scott's indefensible and unprofessional speculations, or Burns's or Musset's drinking, or Defoe's trickeries, or Heine's malice, or Tourguénief's timidity, or the aberrations of Poe, or the fanaticism of Dante, or the lying of Pope, or the scurrility of Milton, or the brutal quarrelling of Jonson, to the question of the faculty of any of these writers.

CHAPTER XV

CONCLUSION

ON a broad retrospect, the Baconian theory constitutes a singular example of what men call "the irony of fate." If there was one task upon which Bacon was more bent than on any other, it was that of goading or leading men to sound methods of induction. The "idola" of his antipathy were the heedless presuppositions and prejudices, the arbitrary persistences in "fore-deeming" which with most men did duty then, as they do now, for the spirit of inquiry and truth-seeking. He miscarried often enough in his own inductions, constructive and negative; but his great service to thought and science consisted precisely in the force and instancy of his warnings against the snares of intellectual "will-worship." And it has been left to the professed "Baconians" of to-day to supply the most flagrant instance in modern history, theology apart, of the intellectual sin which he so forcefully denounced. They have trodden his law underfoot. They have gone about their task with a more complete disregard of the first principles of inductive research than was shown by any alchemist or physicist in Bacon's age. Catching at a conventional falsism as to the legal knowledge in the Shakespeare plays, they have made it an article in their creed without an attempt to check it by a collation of other men's plays. Starting with the other conventional falsism as to the classical knowledge exhibited in the plays, they have but angrily flouted all contrary contentions in a spirit of sheer fanaticism; and, instead of checking their first data by inductive comparison,

583

have heaped a Pelion of nonsense upon an Ossa of error.

If, again, there was one thing that a *true* Baconian ought to have done before drawing an inference from random coincidences in the Plays and the Works, it was to turn to the plays and works of coeval writers, to ascertain whether the coincidences were special or general. Not one in a hundred of the professed " Baconians " has ever made the attempt ; a few read one other dramatist and decide straightway that Bacon wrote his works also ; a few read a little more widely and decide that Bacon wrote everything. We are witnessing, not a process of induction, but a process of absurdity, not easily distinguishable from monomania. But the monomaniac who affirms that Bacon wrote all the Elizabethan drama and Spenser and Montaigne and Puttenham and Burton and Nashe, and in addition did the Authorised Version of the Bible, is only persisting in extending the primary fallacy of the inference that Bacon wrote Shakespeare because similar expressions occur in the Plays and the Works. His wildest extravagance is what men quaintly call a " logical " extension of the first absurdity, said to have been embraced by John Bright.

True ; but, once more, he and they have thus merely extended that play of uncritical belief and heedless advocacy which, as Bacon saw, pervades more or less the thinking and the propaganda of most men. We have had gross nonsense from Lord Campbell ; and only rather grosser nonsense from the Baconians ; he doing his special pleading with half-professional unconcern for pure truth ; they doing theirs with all the zest of self-pleasing fanatics; as little awake as he to the laws of intellectual righteousness. And other forms of " orthodox " dogmatism have sinned about as heedlessly against the true Baconian statute. A generation ago the general body of Shakespearean scholars either violently affirmed or tacitly accepted as final the " expert " dictum that poor Peter

Cunningham's discoveries in the "Revels" papers, assigning to "Shaxberd" certain plays performed at court on certain dates, were impudent, wicked, and senseless forgeries. And now Mr. Ernest Law convincingly affirms,[1] with the highest backing from expert authority, that they are not forgeries at all. In a world in which such things happen, we cannot dismiss the Baconian heresy as a mere negligible freak of human nature.

Not that I suppose it possible to lead zealous Baconians back to common sense. A preliminary passage in Dr. Theobald's SHAKESPEARE STUDIES IN BACONIAN LIGHT (p. 2) tells how, after reading Bacon and Shakespeare "in perpetual juxtaposition for years"—that is to say; *with no corrective resort to the writings of other Elizabethans* —" the persuasion which came by a flash of perception,[2] ripened into a strong and well-grounded conviction; resting on facts and arguments, solid and secure as mathematical demonstration." Quite so. All the vital countervailing facts and arguments had been ignored, and the resulting conviction, obtained like that derived from a mathematical demonstration of the squaring of the circle, is held like an article of religious faith. Such a psychosis is not corrigible. I should as soon expect to convert a bishop to rationalism as one of Dr. Theobald's way of reasoning to the comparative method.

But something may be done to prevent the spread of such hallucination among the normally uncritical. The Baconian chimera will persist, and may even be outgone. There has recently been produced, by Professor Celestin Demblon of Brussels, a new "demonstration" that the Plays were written by Roger Manners, Earl of Rutland (1576–1613), who married the daughter of Sir Philip Sidney, and shared in the insurrection of Essex. It will be interesting to follow the relations of M. Demblon with the Baconians : no one else need intervene. Transcend-

---

[1] *Some Supposed Shakespeare Forgeries*, 1911.
[2] Word so corrected by hand in my copy of the reissue of 1904

ing their method as they have done that of common sense, M. Demblon in his opening *Vue d'ensemble* tells us the circumstances under which Lord Rutland wrote the plays, and why he wrote them, sparing us the trouble of digesting any evidence to show that he *did* write them. So far as I can gather, the whole proof is contained in the plea that he *might* have written them, chronologically speaking, if we do not date any of the plays too early. Of either external or internal evidence to show that Rutland had anything to do with the plays, or wrote anything else, M. Demblon produces not a scrap.[1] He presents us with the hero's portrait, that of a sweetly pretty young man.   For the rest, we learn that this youth

has successively depicted himself in Biron of *Love's Labour's Lost*, in Bassanio of *The Merchant of Venice*, in Romeo, in Benedict in *Much Ado About Nothing*, in Jaques of *As you Like It*, in Hamlet, in Brutus of *Julius Cæsar*, in Prospero of *The Tempest*— as did Goethe in Werther, Hermann, Faust, and Tasso ; as did Honoré de Balzac in Raphael, in Balthasar Claes, in Albert Savarus, &c.[2]

[1] M. Demblon appears to have built his entire hypothesis on the discovery that at Rutland's death his brother, acting as his executor, paid "To Mr. Shakspeare *in gold, about* my Lordes impreso, xlivs. ; To Richard Burbage for painting and making it, xlivs." An "impreso," more correctly "impresa," was a personal "device" or badge, often worn in tournaments and masques. M. Demblon asserts that the payment, as noted in the family accounts, was to "William Shakspeare." It was not : there is no prenomen. M. Demblon is evidently unaware that it has been shown (by Mrs. Stopes, in the *Athenæum*, May 16, 1908) that "Mr. Shakspeare" was probably one John Shakspeare, a fashionable bit-maker of the time, concerning whom there are many entries in the Wardrobe Accounts of Charles I, as prince and as king. Among other things he made "guilt bosses charged with the arms of England." Such an artist was very likely to be employed to do the metal work of an impresa. Mr. John Shakspeare would seem to have been a cousin of the poet, which would explain the connection with Burbage. *Et voilà tout*— for the theory of M. Demblon.

[2] *Lord Rutland est Shakespeare.*   Par Celestin Demblon.   Paris; Ferdinando, 1912.   P. 16.

The details are filled in with the same masterly sim-
plicity. Rutland was incarcerated for his rebellion from
1601 till 1603, and " exhala sa douleur dans le premier
HAMLET, écrit en 1602." Why he chose for this purpose
the old HAMLET of Kyd, and how he managed to arrange
the matter with the players while he remained in custody,
are questions that M. Demblon neither asks nor answers.
In his second chapter, the Professor informs us that
" notre étude d'ensemble," published in the GRANDE
REVUE, " a fait beaucoup de bruit, dans la presse euro-
péenne, notamment à Paris, à Rome, à Milan, à Madrid,
à Cologne, à Berlin, à Moscou, et quelque pen à Londres
et à New-York. Ce n'est qu'un commencement."[1] So
one would suppose. But when, citing some of the comments, for the most part skilfully non-committal, of his
continental critics, M. Demblon deals with that of M.
Henri Roujon, of the Académie Francaise, he dashes the
cup of promise from our lips. In the best French manner,
M. Roujon had written :—" As for the proofs, in the sense
in which the word would be understood by a magistrate,
it appears that M. Célestin Demblon reserves them for
a book which he is going to publish. He will pardon our
waiting till then to adhere to his theory." To which
M. Demblon replies : " While thanking M. Roujon for
his kindness, we permit ourselves not to be of his opinion :
with the French ex-Minister of whom we have spoken,
with M. de Pawlowski, with the scholars of England, of
Germany, and of New York who have written to us, we
believe our first chapter to be *absolutely decisive*."[2] And
there the matter rests ! " That does not signify," adds
M. Demblon, " that we have not a quantity of new proofs
to give ! Our whole book so testifies, and some more
will be found already in this chapter." The further
" proofs " are of like kind with those which M. Roujon
was unable to detect in the first chapter : that is to say,
there is not a grain of evidence in the book. Running to

[1] Work cited, p. 27.   [2] Work cited, p. 29.

559 pages, it is occupied chiefly with the thesis "Shaxper de Stratford hors cause." Incidentally M. Demblon discusses at great length many biographical and literary points, sometimes quite intelligently; but as to his grounds for asserting the authorship of Lord Rutland he is resolutely uncommunicative.

It is rather hard on the Baconians. He has calmly annexed all their case against "Shaxper"; and for the rest he simply tells them that they are mistaken about Bacon, who did not and could not write the plays. It is quite conceivable that he may convert some of them : confidence of assertion seems to be the way to get at the Baconian mind; and as he spares them all worry over parallel passages he offers them some spiritual compensation for the loss of Bacon. They are not required by him to ascribe to Rutland the whole of the Elizabethan drama, and the rest of the Baconian load. It should be noted that he provides Mr. Greenwood with his lawyer ; for Rutland had done some legal study at Gray's Inn. Whether Mr. Greenwood finds this sufficient to dispose of his difficulties, I leave to him to say.

At one or two points, M. Demblon and Mr. Greenwood are partly in agreement. They concur—or incline to do so—in making Jonson's line,

> And though thou hadst small Latin and less Greek,

and the sequel, mean : " and *if* you had small Latin and less Greek I would none the less," &c. The other obstacles presented by Jonson's testimony M. Demblon gets round very much as Mr. Greenwood does. On his own account he has, as might be expected from his *Vue d'ensemble*, the courage to allege that the reminiscences of Ovid in the VENUS and the LUCRECE " recall always the original text, *never the text of Golding.*"[1] " La verité a ses droits," is nevertheless one of M. Demblon's propositions.[2] Like Mr. Greenwood, he has assumed that those who deny

---

[1] Work cited, p. 49. [2] P. 68.

Shakespeare's possession of classical scholarship represent him as being " presque inculte "—almost devoid of education. This nobody but a Baconian ever did. " Comme s'il avait jamais existé un grand poète inculte ! " continues M. Demblon. " Comme si l'on pouvait même en concevoir un ! " It may be worth while to say a final word on that head.

If by *inculte* M. Demblon means a modern who had not read the Greek and Latin classics, he in effect destroys his own case later, for he is willing to accept Plautus as knowing no tongue but Latin, and Robert Burns, " ce charmant poète," as having " fait de bonnes études primaires et lu des livres dont il nous cite lui-même les titres."[1] This is just a trifle too puerile. No one with whom M. Demblon has to debate ever suggested that Shakespeare had not read as many books as did Burns. The whole question, once more, is as to whether the Shakespeare of the Plays needed much *classical* culture to write them. If M. Demblon means to assert this, we need not argue with him as to whether Plautus had read any Greek. On his principles a *Homer* could not have been a great poet, whether or not he could read or write. M. Demblon is at pains to remind us that Musset made " bonnes études dont il ne fait jamais étalage," and to argue that Balzac was not an ignoramus because he assigned to a deputé a fictitious department. Quite so : the question about the " sea-coast of Bohemia "—copied from Greene's tale—has really nothing to do with the case ; though that was certainly not a lapse possible to Bacon. But when we are discussing Balzac, is nothing to be said on the question whether *his* " Comédie humaine" was or could have been constructed without classical culture ? Balzac (concerning whom posterity may be presented with a new Baconian myth, on the score that the family name was really " Balssa "), was certainly no scholar. He left school at seventeen. Is it alleged

[1] Pp. 42–43.

that the smattering of classics he had at a *collège* made possible for him a work of imaginative creation such as the schooling and actor-training of Shakespeare made for him impossible ? I am content to leave the issue at that—and M. Demblon to the Baconians.

In one attitude of mind they are truly akin. Determined to deny that the " Stratford actor " can have produced the Plays, they never once balk at the notion of their being produced as a kind of recreation by any university man, however otherwise engaged. Unconcerned as they are to inquire how their exalted hero contrived to be man-of-all-work to a theatre-company, they are if possible still less moved to wonder how that manifold mass of dramaturgy was created secretly by a man of affairs, ostensibly occupied throughout his life in wholly different ways. Even Mr. Greenwood has no misgiving in suggesting that his unknown lawyer-author was a " *busy man,* whose aim it was to use the stage as a means to convey instruction to the people, and to teach them a certain measure of philosophy " ![1] All that mighty mass of poetic creation was a by-product of a busy lawyer ; and its aim—from Falstaff to Coriolanus, from Juliet to Perdita—was " to convey *instruction* to the people " ! For the Baconians, it is not even a problem that the full-handed Bacon should have added the seven-and-thirty Plays to a performance which, apart from these, ranked him with the great thinkers and workers of his time. For M. Demblon, it is not even a matter for surprise that his young Earl threw off the Plays in the intervals of travel, study, rebellion, and court life. The work of the greatest of all dramatists, it appears, could be written " standing on one foot," provided one had only been at a university !

There need, then, be no limit to the list of claimants. From Mr. Greenwood's book, as above noted, and from an Appendix to Mr. Harold Bayley's entitled THE SHAKE-

[1] *Shakespeare Problem,* p. 514.

SPEARE SYMPHONY (1906), I learn that an "able work" has been written by Judge Stotsenburg, under the heading AN IMPARTIAL STUDY OF THE SHAKESPEARE TITLE, to show, says Mr. Bayley, "that the Shakespeare Plays are not the work of one single author, but of a poetic syndicate, including among others Drayton, Dekker, Heywood, Webster, Middleton, and Porter. To this group Bacon was merely a polisher and reconstructor." This last idea is, in Judge Stotsenburg's own words, "a conclusion that forces itself upon my mind because, first, I believe that Bacon if he originated the plays would have observed the unities, and secondly, because his philosophical views and peculiarities are interwoven in some of them." I confess to having abstained from taking the trouble to read Judge Stotsenburg's book. One must draw the line somewhere. The judges have an awful record in this business : only Judge Willis has stood for critical investigation and common sense,[1] as against Lord Campbell, Lord Penzance, Judge Webb, Judge Holmes, and Judge Stotsenburg. *Ne sutor ultra crepidam :* a judge is no judge in a literary problem when he lacks either due knowledge or literary judgment. The last seems to be Judge Stotsenburg's weak point.

His "syndicate" theory appears to be a modification of that of Delia Bacon. How he can assign the great tragedies to any combination of the writers above-named, and why he does not assign all *their* works to other men, I am not concerned to inquire. If he had been able to recognise in the really alien or composite plays the hands of Peele, Greene, Marlowe, and Kyd, he would have creditably marked himself off from the Baconians ; and if he could indicate in TROILUS or TIMON or JULIUS CÆSAR the hand of any of the writers he has named (Dekker, I have suggested, wrote the Prologue to TROILUS), he would be doing some critical service. That there is something

[1] Even Judge Willis did strange things in his mock-trial of the Bacon-Shakespeare question !

of Middleton in MACBETH was argued by others before
Judge Stotsenburg. But to assign the whole of the
Shakespeare plays to a syndicate of which not one (at
least of those named by Mr. Bayley) was capable of
writing the finest Shakespearean poetry, is merely to
out-Bacon Delia and the Baconians. Mr. Greenwood
notes that the learned judge assigns the Shakespeare
Sonnets to Sir Philip Sidney ; and Mr. Greenwood does
not wince ! The learned judge, says Mr. Bayley, " has
collected a large number of parallel passages from the
writers I have dealt with ; but, curiously enough, he
notes none of those which happen to have struck me."
That would seem to mean that the learned Judge, reading
the Elizabethan dramatists, has failed to notice (as Mr.
Bayley has noticed) the multitude of tags and echoes and
coincidences which might have revealed to him how
those playwrights could have tags and sentiments in
common without community of genius.

Probably the whirligig of Time will cast up yet other
fantasies in far greater numbers than rational contributions to Shakespeare study. I do not despair of seeing
seriously advanced the theory that the Plays were written
by Queen Elizabeth, who was a good classical scholar,
and must have heard, from her law officers, a good deal
about law. Sir John Davies pronounced her the " richest
mind " of all time.[1] And if any man tell us—as we are
at times tempted to tell ourselves—that in a world in
which folly is thus forever heading this way and that,
like an uncontrollable epidemic, it is a waste of time to
reason with or against it even when it affects thousands,
we can but rest on the analogies of civic life. If we are
well employed when we strive to minimise disease in
the body politic and the body corporal, we are surely not
much less rationally employed when we seek to minimise
delusion in the life intellectual.

Perhaps we may overrate the importance of that

[1] Dedication to *Nosce Teipsum*.

on the æsthetic side. But here again we can plead the common human interest. If we be asked, Who and what was this Shakespeare, that you should spend so much time and trouble in settling exactly what he wrote ? we answer that it is all part of the eternal tribute men pay to genius, as to beauty, were it only because each is so rare. The very vogue of the Baconian delusion is to be traced to that "witchcraft of the wit," that dominion of masterly speech, which has won Shakespeare his sovereignty. In seeking to dethrone one potentate of the æsthetic life, the Baconians have not chosen a commonplace substitute. It needed a great power over men's spirits to move such a multitude even of unscientific reasoners to acclaim in Bacon a possible claimant to Shakespeare's realm. And if they have loved not wisely but too well, they have therein shown themselves members of the human family.

The trouble is that, set agoing as they were by the rebound of the idolatrous habit in regard to Shakespeare, they have developed a more extravagant idolatry in regard to Bacon. As the old Shakespeare-worshipper saw in his idol the sum of all intellectual excellence, the Baconian, carrying credulity to new extremes, proclaims a double miracle, and, giving two kingdoms to one man, quadruples every folly of his predecessor. There has never been a truly critical procedure in his whole development. Instead of correcting the faults of omission and commission in the idolatrous criticism of Shakespeare, he has wholly abandoned Shakespearean analysis, taking the entire mass of the plays without question as wholly one man's work, and fathering on Bacon a quantity of matter of which the considerate Shakespearean was long ago glad to relieve Shakespeare's credit.[1] At that level of delusion, no corrective thinking is possible. Even

[1] From such blame Mr. Greenwood is honourably exempt. His discussions of the composite and spurious plays are the soundest parts of his book.

2 P

the conceivably possible gain from a reaction against
idolatry of Shakespeare has been turned to naught by
the Baconian resort to mere vilification of the rejected
divinity.   Uncontrolled in animosity as in adoration,
the heretic will see no kind of merit in the renounced
God, seeing all things in the new.   Worshipping a man
who was fain to leave his reputation to " men's charitable
speeches," they catch at every pretext for defaming the
man of Stratford.   Refusing to accept any tradition to
his credit, as they are entitled to do, they gloat over the
tradition, caught from a village vicar of a much later
time, that the worshipped poet had died of a drinking-
bout with old friends who visited him from London.
Mr. Greenwood, standing partly outside the Baconian
fold, has the fairness to admit that this is in all likelihood a myth ; but the Baconians are not that way
inclined.

The argument appears to be that if once Shakespeare
can be proved to have misconducted himself, the case
against his authorship is strengthened.   Such a method
would make short work of the claims of Marlowe and
Greene and Peele and Jonson to *their* plays ; and it is
to be hoped that saner critical methods will in future
reign even among the " anti-Stratfordians."   In so far
as they are sincerely perplexed, with Emerson, to " marry
this man's life to his verse," and are exercised by all the
" difficulties " they find in it, they may usefully ask
themselves how they can hope to solve these by a hypothesis which, whether they insert Bacon or merely Mr.
Greenwood's unknown lawyer, involves on the bare issue
of the fact the most mountainous improbability in literary
history.   And perhaps they may no less usefully ask
themselves how, on their principles, we are to solve the
difficulty of the strange incongruity between Bacon's
precepts for the right management of personal finance
and the laxity of practice which wrought his ruin.   A
little extension of this field of inquiry may lead them to

perceive that there are " difficulties " in reducing to strict congruity the life of any man.

Whatever may be the developments on that side of the dispute, it is to be hoped that something has been done in the foregoing pages to force it out of the field of literary and philological myth-mongering upon which the " anti-Stratfordian " case has been so largely founded by all its advocates. That at least seems worth doing. On any view, in the house of science there are many mansions, and the method of science is as reasonably to be applied to any one problem as to any other. After all, it may be as humanly useful to settle " æsthetic " questions of this sort as to develop the law of projectiles, to the end of more easily and surely destroying life in war, or even as it may be to perfect the theory of " the grip " in golf.

GENERAL INDEX

596

INDEX OF WORDS DISCUSSED

A large number of words not here included, used by Bacon and not by Shakespeare, will be found in chap. xii.

607

2 Q

INDEX OF PHRASES DISCUSSED